The Impact of Investment Treaties on Contracts between Host States and Foreign Investors

Studies on the Law of Treaties

VOLUME 4

This book was accepted by the University of Freiburg Faculty of Law as a dissertation for the degree of doctorate in law.
First reviewer of the dissertation (Erstgutachter): Prof. Dr. Hanno Merkt LLM
Second reviewer of the dissertation (Zweitgutachter): Prof. Dr. iur. Dr. rer. pol. Sester
Dean of the Law Faculty: Prof. Dr. Hanno Merkt LLM
Place of Dissertation: Freiburg im Breisgau, Germany
Date of the oral examination: 20 May 2009
Year of publication: 2011

The Impact of Investment Treaties on Contracts between Host States and Foreign Investors

By

Jan Ole Voss

MARTINUS NIJHOFF PUBLISHERS

LEIDEN • BOSTON
2011

This book is printed on acid-free paper.

Library of Congress Cataloging-in-Publication Data

Voss, Jan Ole.
The impact of investment treaties on contracts between host states and foreign investors / by Jan Ole Voss.
p. cm. -- (Studies on the law of treaties, 1574-9088 ; v. 4)
Includes bibliographical references and index.
ISBN 978-90-04-19223-2 (hardback : alk. paper) 1. Investments, Foreign--Law and legislation. 2. Commercial treaties. I. Title.
K3830.V67 2011
346.07--dc22
2010044955

ISSN 1574-9088
ISBN 978 90 04 19223 2

CONTENTS

FOREWORD

It is easy to forget that much of what is taken for granted in the practice of international investment arbitration was inexistent, in relative terms, just a short while ago. Indeed, prior to the conception, development and, ultimately, signature and ratification of the International Convention for the Settlement of Investment Disputes ("the Convention") in the early to mid-1960s, the rights of investors and host States were not protected through international structures like those now in place.

Before the Convention, investors faced challenges in their ability to bring claims against and, in the event of liability, recover from host States. However, after the Convention became operational, investors found themselves in a position to file suit against host States directly in an impartial forum—in arbitration—where host States would not benefit from immunity. In addition, the Convention allowed for international law to apply to the relationship in dispute between the investor and the host State, and awards resulting from such arbitrations became directly enforceable.

These concepts (and others), while young, have become so rooted in what has become the field of international investment arbitration that one can overlook what Jan Ole Voss artfully sets forth in his dissertation. Jan Ole Voss reminds us that international investment arbitration, while a part of public international law, remains a dynamic field subject to the influences of investor/State contracts, and vice versa. Furthermore, Jan Ole Voss shows us that treaties and contracts cannot be looked at discretely, as they operate in a mutually-reinforcing relationship to provide increasing protection to international investments, benefitting both investors and host States.

In short, Jan Ole Voss makes us see that what has come to be considered commonplace in international investment arbitration should not be treated as such: the field is still evolving, and its future is where treaty and contract converge.

Erica Stein, Esq.
Hanotiau & van den Berg
Brussels, Belgium

ACKNOWLEDGMENTS

This book was accepted by the Faculty of Law of the University of Freiburg as a dissertation for the degree of doctorate in law in the spring of 2009. It was revised and updated to its current form for publication.

First and foremost, I would like to thank my supervisor, Prof. Dr. Hanno Merkt, LLM, Director of the Institute for Comparative and International Private Law at the University of Freiburg, Germany, for his patience and guidance through all phases of my work. I am equally grateful to Prof. Dr. iur. Dr. rer. pol. Peter Sester of the University of Karlsruhe in Germany for his timely review of my manuscript.

The idea for this project and the early stages of research evolved during my stay in the LLM Program of the Heidelberg Centre for Latin America in Santiago de Chile. The advice and guidance given by my Chilean professors, Francisco Orrego Vicuña and Santiago Montt, were indispensable. I am truly indebted to both.

I also gratefully acknowledge Stanimir Alexandrov, Anthony Sinclair and Rainer Grote for their valuable advice and thoughts at different stages of the thesis-writing. For reading the full manuscript and providing the foreword, I wish to thank Erica Stein.

In the final stage of my work, I would have been left high and dry without the help of Mylin Sapiera-Köbele. Very special thanks go to her not only for revising the English of my manuscript but also for all other kinds of editing work that she has done for this work.

Lastly, I cannot express enough how grateful I am to my parents, Birgit and Dieter Voss, who have always stood by me. And my wife, Olga Ruppert, did not only support me on a personal level but contributed to this work by reading and rereading my drafts and giving constructive criticism. I dedicate this book to her and our son Isaak: Nothing compares to them.

Hamburg, June 2010

LIST OF ABBREVIATIONS

AAA	American Arbitration Association
AF	Additional Facility
African J. Int'l & Comp. Law	The African Journal of International & Comparative Law
A.G.	Aktiengesellschaft
AJCL	The American Journal of Comparative Law
AJIL	The American Journal of International Law
All ER	All England Law Reports
Am. Rev. Int'l Arb.	The American Review of International Arbitration
Am. Soc'y Int'l L. Proc.	American Society of International Law—Proceedings of the Annual Meeting
Am. U. Int'l L. Rev.	The American University International Law Review
Arb. Int'l	Arbitration International
Arb. J.	The Arbitration Journal
Art./Arts.	Article/Articles
A.S.	Akciová Společnost
ASA	Association Suisse d'Arbitrage
ASEAN	Association of South East Asian Nations
Austrian Rev. Int'l & Europ. L.	The Austrian Review of International & European Law
AWD	Außenwirtschaftsdienst des Betriebs-beraters
BB	Betriebs-Berater
BerDGesVölkR	Berichte der Deutschen Gesellschaft für Völkerrecht
BGB	Bürgerliches Gesetzbuch
BIT/BITs	Bilateral Investment Treaty/Treaties
Bus. Law.	Business Lawyer

B.V.	Besloten Vennootschap
BVerfG	Bundesverfassungsgericht
BVerfGE	Entscheidungen des Bundesverfassungs-gerichts
BYIL	The British Yearbook of International Law
BYU L. Rev.	Brigham Young University Law Review
Can. Y.B. Int'l L.	The Canadian Yearbook of International Law
Cath. U. L. Rev.	Catholic University Law Review
C.D. Cal.	Central District of California
Cir.	Circuit
Ch.	Chapter/Chapters
Chin. J. Int'l L.	The Chinese Journal of International Law
CIRDI	Centre International pour le Règlement des Différends relatifs aux Investissements
CLPE	Comparative Research in Law & Political Economy
Colum. J. Transnat'l L.	Columbia Journal of Transnational Law
Cornell Int'l L.J.	The Cornell International Law Journal
Current Leg. Prob.	Current Legal Problems
D. Nev.	District of Nevada
Denv. J. Int'l L. & Pol'y	Denver Journal of International Law & Policy
DePaul L. Rev.	DePaul University Law Review
EC	European Community
ECHR	European Court of Human Rights
ECJ	European Court of Justice
ECT	The Energy Charter Treaty
EGBGB	Einführungsgesetz zum Bürgerlichen Gesetzbuch
EJIL	The European Journal of International Law
European Bus. L. Rev.	European Business Law Review
F. Supp. 2d	Federal Supplement, Second Series
F.3d	Federal Reporter, Third Series
FCN	Treaty of Friendship, Commerce and Navigation

FDI	Foreign Direct Investment
Fordham L. Rev.	Fordham Law Review
FTA	Free Trade Agreement
GATT	General Agreement on Tariffs and Trade
Gaz. du Palais	Gazette du Palais—Les cahiers de l'arbitrage
Geo. Mas. L. Rev.	George Mason Law Review
GYIL	The German Yearbook of International Law
Harv. Int'l L. J	Harvard Journal of International Law
Hast. Int'l & Comp. L. Rev.	Hastings International & Comparative Law Review
Hast. L. J.	Hastings Law Journal
HJIL	Heidelberg Journal of International Law—Zeitschrift für ausländisches öffentliches Recht und Völkerrecht
Hofstra L. & Pol'y Symp.	Hofstra Law & Policy Symposium
Hous. L. Rev.	Houston Law Review
HStR	Handbuch des Staatsrechts
ICC	International Chamber of Commerce
ICC Int'l C. Arb. Bul.	International Chamber of Commerce—The International Court of Arbitration Bulletin
ICCA	International Council for Commercial Arbitration
ICJ	International Court of Justice
ICJ Rep.	International Court of Justice—Report of Judgments, Advisory Opinions and Orders
ICSID	International Centre for Settlement of Investment Disputes
ICSID Convention	Convention on the Settlement of Investment Disputes between States and Nationals of Other States
ICSID Rep.	International Centre for Settlement of Investment Disputes Reports

ICSID Rev.-FILJ	International Centre for Settlement of Investment Disputes Review—Foreign Investment Law Journal
IISD	International Institute for Sustainable Development
ILA	International Law Association
ILC	International Law Commission
ILM	International Legal Materials
ILR	International Law Reports
Indiana L. J.	Indiana Law Journal
Ind. J. Global Legal Stud.	The Indian Journal of Global Legal Studies
Indian J. Int'l L.	The Indian Journal of International Law
Int'l Arb. L. Rev.	International Arbitration Law Review
Int'l & Comp. L. Q.	International & Comparative Law Quarterly
Int'l Law.	The International Lawyer
Int'l L. FORUM	International Law FORUM du droit international: the Journal of the International Law Association
Int' l L. & Pol.	International Law and Politics
Int'l Tax & Bus. Law.	International Tax & Business Lawyer
IMF	International Monetary Fund
Iran-USCTR	Iran-United States Claims Tribunal Reports
Italian YBIL	Italian Yearbook of International Law
ITLOS	International Tribunal of the Law of the Sea
J. Bus. L.	Journal of Business Law
JDI	Journal du Droit International
J. Energy & Nat. Resources L.	Journal of Energy & Natural Resources Law
J.Int'l Arb.	Journal of International Arbitration
JIEL	Journal of International Economic Law
J. Pub. L.	Journal of Public Law (continued by Emory Law Journal)
J. Transnat'l L. & Pol'y	Journal of Transnational Law & Policy

JWI	The Journal of World Investment
JWIT	The Journal of World Investment & Trade
JWTL	The Journal of World Trade Law
Law & Pol'y Int'l Bus.	Law and Policy in International Business
LA Lawyer	Los Angeles Lawyer
LCIA	London Court of International Arbitration
Legal Bus.	Legal Business
LDC/LDCs	Least Developed Country/Countries
Leiden J. Int'l L.	Leiden Journal of International Law
Lloyd's Rep.	Lloyd's Law Reports
LOS Convention	United Nations Convention on the Law of the Sea
LQR	The Law Quarterly Review
MAI	The Multilateral Agreement on Investment
Max Planck UNYB	Max Planck Yearbook of United Nations Law
Mealey's Int'l Arb. Rep.	Mealey's International Arbitration Report
MFN	Most favoured nation
Mich. J. Int'l L.	Michigan Journal of International Law
Mich. L. Rev.	Michigan Law Review
Mich. St. J. Int'l L.	The Michigan State Journal of International Law
MIGA	Multilateral Investment Guarantee Agency
Minn. J. Glob. Trade	Minnesota Journal of Global Trade
Minn. L. Rev.	Minnesota Law Review
MIT	Multilateral Investment Treaty
MITs	Multilateral Investment Treaties
NAFTA	North American Free Trade Association
N.C. L. Rev.	North Carolina Law Review
NIEO	New International Economic Order
Nw. J. Int'l L. & Bus.	Northwestern Journal of International Law and Business

Nw. U. L. Rev.	Northwestern University Law Review
NYBIL	The Netherlands Yearbook of International Law
NYU J. Int'l L. & Pol.	New York University Journal of International Law & Politics
NYLJ	New York Law Journal
NY L. School J. Int'l & Comp. L.	New York Law School Journal of International & Comparative Law
OECD	Organisation for Economic Cooperation and Development
Oil, Gas & Energy L. Intell.	Oil, Gas & Energy Law Intelligence
OJ	Official Journal
OLG	Oberlandesgericht (Superior Provincial Court)
OPIC	Overseas Private Investment Corporation
OSPAR Convention	The Convention for the Protection of the Marine Environment of the North-East Atlantic
PCA	Permanent Court of Arbitration
PCIJ	Permanent Court of International Justice
PCIJ Rep.	Permanent Court of International Justice—Collection of Judgments, Orders and Advisory Opinions
Penn St. Int'l L. Rev.	Penn State International Law Review
PLC	Public Limited Company
RabelsZ	Rabels Zeitschrift für ausländisches und internationales Privatrecht
RdC	Receuil des Cours
Rev. Arb.	Revue de l'Arbitrage
Rev. Belg. de Droit Int'l	Revue Belge de Droit International
RIAA	Report of International Arbitral Awards
RIW	Recht der internationalen Wirtschaft

S.A.	Sociedad Anónima; Société Anonyme
SAYIL	The South African Yearbook of International Law
S. Cal. L. Rev.	Southern California Law Review
SCC	Stockholm Chamber of Commerce
SCC-Institute	Arbitration Institute of the Stockholm Chamber of Commerce
SchiedsVZ	Zeitschrift für Schiedsverfahren—German Arbitration Journal
S.p.A.	Società per Azioni
Spec. Sess.	Special Session
Sri Lanka J. of Int'l L.	Sri Lanka Journal of International Law
Stan. J. Int'l L.	Stanford Journal of International Law
Stan. L. Rev.	The Stanford Law Review
Supp.	Supplement
SYBIL	The Singapore Yearbook of International Law
TDM	Transnational Dispute Management
Texas Int'l L. J.	Texas International Law Journal
Tul. L. Rev.	Tulane Law Review
Tul. Law J.	Tulsa Law Journal (continued by Tulsa Law Review)
U.C. Davis J.Int'l L.& Pol'y	University of California Davis Journal of International Law and Policy
UN	United Nations
UNCITRAL	United Nations Commission on International Trade Law
UNCLOS	The United Nations Convention on the Law of the Sea (1994)
UNCTAD	United Nations Conference on Trade and Development
UN Doc.	United Nations Documents
UN GAOR	United Nations General Assembly Official Records
UN GA Res.	United Nations General Assembly Resolution
U. Pa. J. Int'l Econ. L.	University of Pennsylvania Journal of International Economic Law

U. Pitt. L. Rev.	University of Pittsburgh Law Review
U. Tor. L. J.	University of Toronto Law Journal
Va. J. Int'l L.	Virginia Journal of International Law
Va. L. Rev.	Virginia Law Review
Vand. J. Transnat'l L.	Vanderbilt Journal of Transnational Law
VAT	Value added tax
WLR	The Weekly Law Reports
WTO	World Trade Organisation
YB Comm. Arb'n	Yearbook of Commercial Arbitration
ZPO	Zivilprozeßordnung

TABLE OF CASES

[1] Where no print source is cited, the decision can be assessed electronically from the following website: http://ita.law.uvic.ca (investment treaty arbitration website of the University of Victoria Faculty of Law, Victoria, Canada).

Mexican Union Railway Ltd. (Great Britain v. Mexico), (1930) 5 RIAA 115 p. 277

Mihaly International Corp. v. Socialist Democratic Republic of Sri Lanka, ICSID Case No. ARB/00/2, Award, 15 March 2002, 6 ICSID Rep. 308 p. 71

Minpeco, S.A. v. Hunt, 1989 WL 57704 (SDNY) p. 147

Mobil Oil v. Iran, (1987) 16 Iran-USCTR 3 p. 184

Mondev International Ltd. v. United States of America, ICSID Case No. ARB(AF)/99/2, Award, 11 October 2002, 6 ICSID Rep. 181 pp. 90, 200, 201, 202, 210

MOX Plant Case (Ireland v. United Kingdom), PCA, Order No. 3, Suspension of Proceedings and Merits, (2003) 42 ILM 1187 p. 325

MTD Equity Sdn. Bhd. v. Republic of Chile, ICSID Case No. ARB/01/7, Award, 25 May 2004, (2005) 44 ILM 91 p. 109, 203, 208

MTD Equity Sdn. Bhd. v. Republic of Chile, ICSID Case No. ARB/01/7, Decision on Annulment, 21 March 2007, available online: ITA, investment treaty arbitration p. 106

Nagel (William) v. Czech Republic, SCC Case 49/2002, Award, unpublished award, excerpts reproduced in: Stockholm Arbitration Report 1 (2004), 141 and available online: ITA, investment treaty arbitration pp. 123, 206

National Grid PLC v. Argentine Republic, UNCITRAL, Decision on Jurisdiction, 20 June 2006, available online: ITA, investment treaty arbitration p. 60

National Iranian Oil Co. Legal Status Case, OLG Frankfurt, (1984) 65 ILR 199 p. 178

National Iranian Oil Co. Pipeline Contracts Case, OLG Frankfurt (1984) 65 ILR 225 p. 178

National Iranian Oil Co. Revenues from Oil Sales, BVerfGE 64, 1 p. 178

Neer (US) v. United Mexican States, (1926) 4 RIAA 60 p. 202

Noble Ventures, Inc. v. Romania, ICSID Case No. ARB/01/11, Award, 12 October 2005, available online: ITA, investment treaty arbitration pp. 143, 153, 207, 233, 241, 247–250, 253, 254, 264, 266, 276

North American Dredging Company of Texas (US v. Mexico), (1926) 4 RIAA 26 pp. 277, 310–312

Norwegian Shipowners' Claims (Norway v. US), (1948) 1 RIAA 307 p. 182

Nottebohm Case (Liechtenstein v. Guatemala) (Second Phase), Judgment, [1955] ICJ Rep. 4 pp. 3, 83

PSEG Global Inc. v. Republic of Turkey, ICSID Case No. ARB/02/5, Award, 19 January 2007, available online: ITA, investment treaty arbitration pp. 199, 202, 209, 212, 216, 218

Reparations for Injuries Suffered in the Service of the United Nations Case, Advisory Opinion, [1949] ICJ Rep. 181 p. 83

Revere Copper & Brass, Inc. v. Overseas Private Inv. Corp., (1978) 56 ILR 258 p. 30

RSM Production Corp. v. Grenada, ICSID Case No. ARB/05/14, Award, 13 March 2009, available online: ITA, investment treaty claims p. 47

Rudloff Case (Interlocutory), (1903–1905) 9 RIAA 244 p. 312

Ruler of Qatar v. International Maritime Oil Co., Award, (1953) 20 ILR 534 p. 31

Saipem S.p.A v. The People's Republic of Bangladesh, ICSID Case No. ARB/05/07, Decision on Jurisdiction and Recommendation on Provisional Measures, 21 March 2007, available online: ITA, investment treaty arbitration pp. 120, 121, 126, 130, 131, 134, 152, 166, 218

Saipem S.p.A. v. The People's Republic of Bangladesh, ICSID Case No. ARB/05/07, Award, 30 June 2009, available online: ITA, investment treaty arbitration p. 142

Salini Costruttori S.p.A. v. Hashemite Kingdom of Jordan, ICSID Case No. ARB/02/13, Decision on Jurisdiction, 9 November 2004, (2005) 44 ILM 573 pp. 174, 233, 234, 237, 248, 271, 319, 329

Salini Costruttori S.p.A. v. Kingdom of Morocco, ICSID Case No. ARB/00/4, Decision on Jurisdiction, 23 July 2001, 6 ICSID Rep. 398 pp. 68, 69, 120, 124, 127, 129, 133, 139, 151, 152, 156, 170, 298, 313

Saluka Investments B.V. v. Czech Republic, UNCITRAL, Partial Award, 17 March 2006, available online: ITA, investment treaty arbitration p. 205

Sapphire International Petroleum Ltd. v. National Iranian Oil Co., Award, (1967) 35 ILR 136 pp. 30, 36, 40

Saudi Arabia v. Arabian American Oil Co., Award, (1963) 27 ILR 47 pp. 3, 32

Schroeder Music Publishing Co. Ltd. v. Macaulay, (1974) 3 All ER 616 p. 38

SD Myers, Inc. v. Canada, UNCITRAL (NAFTA), First Partial Award, 13 November 2000, 8 ICSID Rep. 3 pp. 84, 200

Sempra Energy International v. Argentine Republic, ICSID Case No. ARB/02/16, Decision on Jurisdiction, 11 May 2005, available online: ITA, investment treaty arbitration pp. 166, 241, 298

INTRODUCTION

From the Protection of Foreign Property to Global Economic Governance

Since its inception, the protection of foreign property laid at the heart of public international law. Disputes between States on account of alleged violations of a national's property rights reach back to the end of the 18th century.[1] During the following period of industrialization as well as colonization, the European empires ensured the foreign property of their nationals, and thus their own business interests, through either imperial submissions or the establishment of capitulation systems.[2] In the absence of such systems, foreign investment disputes were international disputes between home State and host State based on the system of diplomatic protection. Subsequent to the exhaustion of local remedies by the infringed individual, an espousal of the claim by the national's home State on account of denial of justice could occur. This system, which emphasized the traditional concept of governmental sovereignty, had inherent considerable flaws. The foreign investor, who had no proper right to diplomatic protection nor was entitled to compensation, remained entirely contingent upon the discretion of its national State.[3] At the same time, the equation of an individual's

---

[1] Compare the statement of the US Secretary of State Adams back in 1796:

> There is no principle of the law of nations more firmly established than that which entitles the property of strangers within the jurisdiction of another country in friendship with their own to the protection of its sovereign by all efforts in his power. This common rule of intercourse between all civilized nations has, between the United States and Spain, the further and solemn sanction of an express stipulation by treaty.

Cited in R. Dolzer, New Foundations of the Law of Expropriation of Alien Property, AJIL 75 (1981), 553, 558.

[2] See, e.g., G. van Harten, Investment Treaty Arbitration and Public Law (2007), 14 et seq., who remarked that the pressure "to establish an international regime for investor protection is thus an integral aspect of the post-colonial era." See also M. Sornarajah, The International Law on Foreign Investment (2004), 22 et seq.

[3] See, e.g., E. Borchard, The Diplomatic Protection of Citizens Abroad or the Law of International Claims (1916), 366; M. Shaw, International Law (2005), 723.

interests with community interests[4] led to a "politicization" of disputes,[5] entitled States to the use of force,[6] and thus gave rise to the notorious "gunboat diplomacy".[7] The demands which were maintained by capital-exporting States chiefly concerned an international minimum standard of treatment and the payment of full compensation for expropriation.[8] Capital-importing States, on the contrary, upheld—under the flag of the Calvo Doctrine[9] and the Drago Doctrine[10]—the concepts of national treatment and national sovereignty. After World War II, the rise of Socialist ideologies and the decolonisation gave clout to perceptions

[4] J. L. Brierly, Le Fondement du Charactère Obligatoire du Droit International, RdC 23 (1928), 468, 531 who stated: "La plus grande menace—et de beaucoup—qu'encore la paix dans le monde moderne est la tendance grandissante qu'ont les gouvernements à placer le pouvoir de l'État derrière des intérêts économiques privés de leur nationaux, et à identifier ainsi les intérêts de quelques individus puissants avec le les intérêts de tout le pays".

[5] See, e.g., H. Lauterpacht, The Subjects of the Law of Nations, LQR 63 (1947), 438, 454.

[6] See, e.g., G. Kaufmann-Kohler & B. Stucki, Foreword, in: G. Kaufmann-Kohler & B. Stucki (eds.), Investment Treaties and Arbitration, ASA Special Series No. 19 (2002), I, who, somewhat exaggeratedly but essentially correctly, gave the following example: "On July 26, 1956, President Nasser of Egypt announced the nationalization of the Suez Canal. This led in a few short months to British and French armed forces launching an attack against Egypt on October 31, 1956. Egypt answered by sinking all 40 ships that were then in the Suez Canal. Obviously, the interests at stake went beyond protection of the investments made through the Compagnie Universelle du Canal Maritime de Suez. Nonetheless, one of the reasons that led France and the UK to resort to military action was the early termination of a concession initially granted for 99 years to the Compagnie." See also W. Jenks, The Prospects of International Adjudication (1964), 514–515.

[7] Cf. R. Lillich, The Current Status of the Law of State Responsibility for Injuries to Aliens, in: R. B. Lillich (ed.), International Law of State Responsibility for Injuries to Aliens (1983), 1, 3.

[8] For the minimum standard see, inter alia, A. Roth, The Minimum Standard of International Law Applied to Aliens (1949); E. Borchard, The "Minimum Standard" of the Treatment of Aliens, Am. Soc'y Int'l L. Proc. 33 (1939), 51 et seq. The standard of compensation was reflected by the so-called "Hull-Formula". In 1938, the then US Foreign Affairs Secretary Cordell Hull claimed in a dispute with Mexico that compensation had to be "adequate, effective and prompt". See L. Henkin et al., International Law (1980), 687.

[9] The Calvo Doctrine, named after the Argentine scholar Carlos Calvo who is generally deemed to be the creator of this doctrine, is based upon the idea of equal treatment between nationals and foreigners and thus proposed that foreign investment disputes had to be resolved through national adjudication and by applying national law. See D. Shea, The Calvo Clause: A Problem of Inter-American and International Law and Diplomacy (1955), 19 et seq.; A. Freeman, Recent Aspects of the Calvo Doctrine and the Challenge to International Law, AJIL 40 (1946), 121, 132–133.

[10] Essentially, the Drago Doctrine intended to prohibit the use of force to recover debts. See A. Hershey, The Calvo and the Drago Doctrines, AJIL 1 (1907), 26, 29 et seq.

which favoured the latter perspective. Particularly, newly independent States aspired to gain greater control over their economy and resources by requiring the resolution of investment disputes under their respective judiciary.[11] This momentum found expression in the assertion of the principle of permanent sovereignty over natural resources by UN General Assembly Resolutions,[12] the proposition of the New International Economic Order,[13] and subsequent nationalisations of foreign property and re-negotiations of investment concessions.

At this time, investment disputes were brought before international adjudicative bodies only in very exceptional and constrained circumstances.[14] In a parallel effort, developed States envisaged multilateral and bilateral attempts to provide for international investment protection standards. Whereas most of the multilateral efforts were abandoned due to heavy opposition from the developing countries' side or disaccord among the proponents themselves,[15] one major achievement was the creation of the International Centre for the Settlement of Investment Disputes (ICSID) in 1965.[16] Contingent upon the fulfilment of certain conditions, foreign investors were henceforth enabled

---

[11] Van Harten, *supra* fn. 2, 17.

[12] See Resolution on Permanent Sovereignty over Natural Resources, UN GA Res. 1803 (XVII), UN GAOR, 17th Sess., Supp. No. 17, UN Doc. A/5217 (1962); Declaration of the Establishment of a New International Economic Order, UN GA Res. 3201 (S-VI), UN GAOR, 6th Spec. Sess., Supp. No. 1, UN Doc. A/9559 (1974); Charter of Economic Rights and Duties of States, UN GA Res. 3281 (XXIX), UN GAOR, 29th Sess., Supp. No. 31, UN Doc. A/9631 (1974).

[13] For a summary of the NIEO, see T. Wälde, A Requiem for the "New International Economic Order", in: G. Hafner et al. (eds.), Liber Amicorum—Professor Ignatz Seidl-Hohenveldern in Honour of his 80th Birthday (1988), 771 et seq.

[14] Formerly, they were brought under the system of diplomatic protection. See, e.g., *Oscar Chinn Case* (Belgium v. United Kingdom) PCIJ Rep. Series A/B No. 63; *Nottebohm Case* (Liechtenstein v. Guatemala) (Second Phase) [1955] ICJ Rep. 4. Later, they were brought to international commercial arbitration due to individual arbitration agreements. See *Saudi Arabia v. Arabian American Oil Co.* (1963) 27 ILR 47; *BP Exploration Co. (Lybia) v. The Government of the Libyan Arab Republic* (1979) 53 ILR 279; *Texaco Overseas Petroleum Co. (TOPCO) v. The Government of the Libyan Arab Republic* (1979) 53 ILR 389; *Libyan American Oil Corp. v. The Government of the Libyan Arabic Republic* (1982) 62 ILR 140.

[15] See P. Muchlinski, The Rise and Fall of the Multilateral Agreement on Investment: Where Now?, Int'l Law. 34 (2000), 1033 et seq.; G. Schwarzenberger, Foreign Investments and International Law (1969), 109–120.

[16] The ICSID was established under the Convention on the Settlement of Investment Disputes between States and Nationals of Other States of March 18, 1965, ILM 4 (1965), 532 et seq. As of October 2010, 155 States have signed the convention and 144 States have deposited instruments of ratification of the convention. See List of Contracting States, available at http://icsid.worldbank.org (last visited: 31 October 2010).

to settle investment disputes directly with the host State and without having to contend with diplomatic protection's disadvantages.[17] Yet, as long as consent by host States to arbitration under ICSID was not given in a generally-featured way and investors had to rely on their negotiation leverage in order to include arbitral agreements referring to international arbitration into the investment contracts which they signed with host States, not much use of the institutional framework was made.[18] This situation changed fundamentally when States began to consent to international arbitration, especially under the auspices of ICSID, by investment treaties.[19] The explosive growth of investment treaties in bilateral as well as multilateral form that followed gave birth

---

[17] See, e.g., F. Orrego Vicuña, International Dispute Settlement in an Evolving Global Society (2004), 64, stating:

> This initiative was specifically aimed at making available arbitration and conciliation procedures to foreign investors and in so doing to avoid the traditional recourse to diplomatic protection. The latter is excluded under the Convention to the extent that there is consent to arbitration and compliance with the award. The Convention thus constituted a key turning point in international dispute settlement, signalling the minimization of state intervention involved in diplomatic protection and highlighting the individual's own role in acceding such arrangements.

See also D. Sedlak, ICSID's Resurgence in International Investment Arbitration: Can the Momentum Hold?, Penn St. Int'l L. Rev. 23 (2004/2005), 147, 152–153; I. Shihata, Towards a Greater Depoliticization of Investment Disputes: The Roles of ICSID and MIGA (1993).

[18] From 1984, when the first case was brought to ICSID, until the end of 1996, ICSID had registered a total of nine cases. From 1997, when the first case which was based on a BIT was brought, to 2000, 25 further cases had been registered. At the end of 2010, there are approximately 120 cases pending. See List of Pending Cases, available at: http://icsid.worldbank.org (last visited: 31 October 2010). For a short summary of the evolution of ICSID, see C. Schreuer, Keynote Address: The Dynamic Evolution of the ICSID System, in: R. Hofmann & C. Tams (eds.), The International Convention on the Settlement of Investment Disputes (ICSID)—Taking Stock after 40 years (2007), 15 et seq.

[19] See, e.g., C. McLachlan et al. (eds.), International Investment Arbitration—Substantive Principles (2007), 1.07, stating:

> Since the potential of this form of dispute resolution was realized, the results have been dramatic. The first arbitration under a bilateral investment treaty (BIT) was registered in 1987. The growth in this form of dispute resolution in the two decades since then has been exponential, with the number of registered cases now totalling over 200. If this level of activity seems daunting enough, it is dwarfed by the scale of the underlying network of BITs, with over 2,500 such agreements having been concluded since the first such treaty in 1959. (Footnotes omitted);

A. Parra, ICSID and the Rise of Bilateral Investment Treaties: Will ICSID Be the Leading Arbitration Institution in the Early 21st Century, Am. Soc'y Int'l L. Proc. 94 (2000), 41 et seq.; S. Alexandrov, The "Baby Boom" of Treaty-Based Arbitrations and

to a new concept of investment protection and international adjudication: the so-called "investment treaty arbitration" or "investor—State arbitration".[20] The overarching purpose of this system is the creation of stable investment environments and thus the general promotion of foreign investments in order to foster economic development and human well-being.[21] Arguably, it provides the investor with procedural and substantial rights which are directly enforceable vis-à-vis the host State on the international plane and thus avoids domestic adjudication and diplomatic protection.[22] Yet, the system's hybrid character[23] and the fundamental tension between its two main actors, host States want to attract foreign investment with the least possible concession of regulatory powers; investors attempt to minimize political and commercial risks to the widest possible extent,[24] create an enormous potential for interpretative conflicts.

---

the Jurisdiction of ICSID Tribunals, JWIT 6 (2005), 387, 387–388; M. Stevens, Arbitration and Investment Disputes—Are We Heading in the Right Direction?, ICSID News, Vol. 19, No. 1, Spring, available at: http://icsid.worldbank.org (last visited: 25 March 2008).

[20] Since the consent to arbitration is not provided by a previously agreed arbitration agreement, this new method of arbitration has also been termed as "arbitration without privity". See J. Paulsson, Arbitration without Privity, ICSID Rev.-FILJ 10 (2005), 232 et seq.

[21] See, e.g., R. Dolzer & M. Stevens, Bilateral Investment Treaties (1995), 17–18; R. Dolzer, The Impact of International Investment Treaties on Domestic Administrative Law, Int' l L. & Pol. 37 (2005), 953, 954.

[22] Cf. K. Vandevelde, United States Investment Treaties: Policy and Practice (1992), 20–22; R. Jones, NAFTA Chapter 11 Investor-to-State Dispute Resolution: A Shield to Be Embraced or a Sword to Be Feared?, BYU L. Rev. (2002), 527, 529–531.

[23] See Z. Douglas, The Hybrid Foundations of Investment Treaty Arbitration, BYIL 74 (2003), 151, 152, who stated:

> The analytical challenge presented by the investment treaty regime for the arbitration of investment disputes is that it cannot be adequately rationalised either as a form of public international law or private trans-national dispute resolution. Investment treaties are international instruments between states governed by the public international law of treaties. The principal beneficiary of the investment treaty regime is most often a corporate entity established under a municipal law, while the legal interests protected by the regime are a bundle of rights in an investment arising under a different municipal law. The standards of protection are fixed by an international treaty, but liability for their breach is said to give rise to a "civil or commercial" award for enforcement purposes (footnote omitted).

[24] See P. Muchlinski, Policy Issues, in: P. Muchlinski et al. (eds.), The Oxford Handbook of International Investment Law (2008),1, 6 et seq.; K. Meesen, International Investment and Dispute Settlement, in: D. Friedmann & E. J. Mestmäcker, Conflict Resolution in International Trade (1993), 111, 111–113; R. Pritchard, The Contemporary Challenges of Economic Development, in: R. Pritchard (ed.), Economic Development, Foreign Investment and the Law (1996), 1, 3–5.

Since investment treaties are international treaties which are deemed to grant legal rights directly to private individuals, they form part of an underlying current which slowly but constantly transforms international law.[25] An evolving global society requires adjustments to traditional understandings of international law as a mere horizontal regulation of an inter-State society. The growing interdependency of human societies in the aftermath of World War II and, especially, the post—Cold War phenomenon which is usually termed as "globalization", created a necessity for governance which transcended the limits of the traditional national States.[26] This necessity was faced by States through delegation of power and function and by adherence to the resulting international regulatory schemes.[27] On account of this, the traditional concept of sovereignty of States was increasingly eroded.[28]

---

[25] See, e.g., J. Crawford, Essay 1—International Law as an Open System, in: J. Crawford (ed.), International Law as an Open System—Selected Essays (2003), 17, 19–22.

[26] See, e.g., T. Wälde, Multilateral Agreements (MITs) in the Year 2000, in: L. Leben (ed.), Souveraineté étatique et marchés internationaux à la fin du 20ème siècle, à propos de 30 ans de recherche du CREDIMI; Mélanges en l'honneur de Philippe Kahn (2000), 389, 394–395, who posited:

> The leverage, discipline and sanctioning power of global markets over national governments considered to engage in regulatory misconduct has strengthened, with a concomitant weakening of the power of all national governments (except the very large countries such as perhaps only the US) to resist the demands of global markets. As such markets can run amok, some system of global regulation is necessary. Such regulation can come from the self-regulation of the agents of the global economy, but if national governments wish to assert their own legitimacy, they need to find regulatory powers equal to the transnational reach of the global economy.

See generally E. Stein, International Integration and Democracy: No Love at First Sight, AJIL 95 (2001), 489, 489–490 declaring:

> The solutions of vital problems, such as national security, protection of basic human rights, international trade and economic development, the surge of migration, environmental protection, and cross-border criminality, has moved beyond the reach of individual states and has called for institutionalized commitment and cooperation on global and regional levels.

[27] See generally T. Franck, Delegating State Powers: The Effect of Treaty Regimes on Democracy and Sovereignty (2000). See also N. Krisch & B. Kingsbury, Introduction: Global Governance and Global Administrative Law in the International Legal Order, EJIL 17 (2006), 1 et seq.

[28] See, inter alia, K. H. Ladeur, Globalization and the Conversion of Democracy to Polycentric Networks: Can Democracy Survive the End of the Nation State?, in: K. H. Ladeur (ed.), Public Governance in the Age of Globalization (2004), 89, 110;

The subject matter of this work, the protection of foreign investment through international treaties, is a progressive element of these regulatory systems and as such may represent a new dimension of the respect for individual rights by States in the global economy. In this context, the investment treaty regime embodies the recognition of the increased role played by individuals and private corporate entities under international law. As such, it mirrors similar developments in the areas of international environmental law and international human rights.[29]

The Contracts between Host States and Foreign Investors as Instruments of Investment Protection

A significant part of the evolution of the protection of foreign property was linked to the role of contracts. Prior to the establishment of the investment treaty regime, these legal instruments, i.e., contracts between host State and foreign investor were held to provide the main protection of foreign investments. In the course of the 20th century, the countenance of these contracts underwent a remarkable transformation. At present, agreements between investor and host State, which originally were one-sided concessions that entitled Western companies to resource exploitation at low cost, are concluded for a wide array of subject matters and under different legal forms. Covered activities, for instance, range from large infrastructure projects such as construction of highways, bridges, airports and power plants; the provision of banking and TV/broadcasting services; and smaller operations such as the salvage of a ship or the start-up of an advertising business. Notwithstanding these changes, an essential aspect of the protection provided for by these contracts remains the same: since they pertain to the domestic legal system of the host country, their risk allocation is generally held to be unsatisfactory for international business requirements. The reasons for the foregoing were and are manifold. Firstly, the

E. Cárdenas, The Notion of Sovereignty Confronts a New Era, in: R. Pritchard (ed.), Economic Development, Foreign Investment and the Law (1996), 13 et seq.

[29] Cf. T. Wälde & T. Weiler, Investment Arbitration under the Energy Charter Treaty in the Light of New NAFTA Precedents: Towards a Global Code of Conduct for Economic Regulation, in: G. Kaufmann-Kohler & B. Stucki (eds.), ASA Special Series No. 19, Investment Treaties and Arbitration (2002), 159, 161. This may be contrasted with the WTO which does not provide for a privately-operated system of dispute settlement.

double role of the host State, the host country is contracting partner and sovereign legislator at the same time, generates the risk of subsequent adverse changes in national legislation negatively affecting the contractual balance.[30] Secondly, the foreigner's inexperience with the local law makes the reliance upon it uncertain.[31] Finally, the domestic judiciary may often be deemed to act favourably to or even as an instrumentality of the host State's government.[32] In sum, the mere fact of being a foreigner may entail—subjectively or objectively—disadvantages not only during an investment operation but also when it comes to the resolution of eventual disputes.[33]

Moreover, and maybe most importantly, the nature of the contract between alien and host State underlying an investment operation is construed antagonistically by its respective parties. The foreign investor emphasizes the commercial aspects of the contract and thus, based upon the principle of *pacta sunt servanda*, regards the contract as principally binding.[34] The host State, by contrast, underlines the public nature of the contract and the necessity to act in deference to the public interest.[35] Therefore, when public interests under changed circumstances so require, host States are not willing to be deterred from acting by considerations of the sanctity of existing contracts.[36] This situation led to several attempts of mainly Western legal scholars to somehow detach the contractual relationship between investor and host State from the latter's domestic law system. On the one hand, formal[37] or

[30] See H. Merkt, Investitionsschutz durch Stabilisierungsklauseln—Zur intertemporalen Rechtswahl in State Contracts (1990), 26, who declared: "Die privatrechtlichen Gestaltungsmöglichkeiten auf vertraglicher Ebene kollidieren mit den hoheitlichen Gestaltungsmöglichkeiten auf gesetzgeberischer Ebene".

[31] Note that this problem can be avoided by the investor resorting to a counsel's legal opinion.

[32] See, e.g., N. Horn, Arbitration and the Protection of Foreign Investment: Concepts and Means, in: N. Horn (ed.), Arbitrating Foreign Investment Disputes (2004), 3, 24–25.

[33] See, e.g., J. Paulsson, Denial of Justice in International Law (2005), 149, who asserted: "The foreigner's obvious handicap—his lack of citizenship- is usually compounded by vulnerabilities with respect to many types of influence: political, social, cultural". See also E. Schanze, Investitionsverträge im internationalen Wirtschaftsrecht (1986), 43 et seq.

[34] See, e.g., C. Leben, Contrat d'Etat et droit international des investissements, RdC 302 (2003), 201 et seq.

[35] See, e.g., D. Bowett, State Contracts with Aliens: Contemporary Developments on Compensation for Termination or Breach, BYIL 59 (1988), 49 et seq.

[36] See, e.g., M. Sornarajah, The Settlement of Foreign Investment Disputes (2004), 264.

[37] See, e.g., K. H. Böckstiegel, Der Staat als Vertragspartner ausländischer Privatunternehmen (1971), 377 et seq.

substantial[38] characteristics of the contracts and on the other hand, the explicit or implicit choice of law by the parties,[39] were put forward in order to justify the application of another legal system than the host State's applicable law. The failure of these attempts to conclusively substantiate the desired results[40] and the following "re-nationalization"[41] of contracts between foreign investor and host State entailed a powerful inducement for the creation of the investment treaty regime[42] in order to provide for a neutral form of dispute settlement by international arbitration.[43]

The Modern Interrelationship between Treaties and Contracts in Investment Treaty Arbitration

At present, the similar existence of both instruments—contracts and treaties—for the protection of a foreigner's investment generates the question of their relationship. Traditionally, the distinction between both instruments was straightforward: a treaty, as an agreement between two sovereign States, formed part of the international sphere; a contract, between individual and State, pertained to the domestic law sphere.[44] However, given the potential repercussion of the investment treaty regime, the continuance of this dichotomy is by no means axiomatic.[45] Essentially, the relationship between contracts and treaties or, more exactly, the relationship of investment treaty arbitration to

[38] See, e.g., P. Weil, Droit international et contrats d'Etat, in: P. Bardonnet (ed.), Mélanges offerts à Paul Reuter—le droit international: unité et diversité (1981), 549 et seq.

[39] For an overview, see, e.g., U. Kischel, State Contracts (1994), 140 et seq.; E. Paasivirta, Participation of States in International Contracts (1990), 59 et seq.

[40] Cf. Horn, *supra* fn. 32, 14.

[41] Cf. H. Merkt, *supra* fn. 30, 152 et seq.; G. Delaume, The Proper Law of State Contracts Revisited, ICSID Rev.-FILJ 12 (1997), 1, 11 et seq., who termed this phenomenon "relocalization".

[42] See M. Sornarajah, State Responsibility and Bilateral Investment Treaties, JWTL 20 (1986), 79, 98, who opined: "Given the uncertainty that has resulted, states have sought protection for their investors on a bilateral basis from the confusion that exists in the international law of investment protection".

[43] On the adequacy of international arbitration for the settlement of investor—host State disputes, see B. Cremades & J. Cairns, The Brave New World of Global Arbitration, JWI 3 (2002), 173, 175 et seq.

[44] For an antique description, see J. Bentham, An Introduction to the Principles of Morals and Legislation, (1823), 326–327.

[45] See F. Orrego Vicuña, Of Contracts and Treaties in the Global Market, Max Planck UNYB 8 (2004), 341, 341, who asserted: "What used to be a useful comparison

contracts and treaties is paramount for the function of the former. The major question which arises in this regard is whether the system created by investment treaties is a self-contained, relatively concise system which dissociates specific investment treaties from other potentially applicable norms or whether the investment treaties are open-textured instruments with a broad comprehension which cover investment-related disputes irrespective of their origin.[46] In other words, do investment treaties, in principle, cover exclusively violations of rights derived from the proper treaty or do they also cover obligations created by other legal instruments, particularly contracts between host State and investor? The answers given to this question in arbitral practice evince a methodological interstice: whereas one camp construes treaty provisions narrowly and attempts to conceptually differentiate between the international and the domestic sphere, the other camp, relying on a wider interpretation, denies the existence of a principal difference between the national and the international legal system.[47] On the one hand, several treaty-based tribunals approach problems of treaty interpretation through interaction between international norms and rules

---

between international law and a separate domestic legal framework—treaties and contracts—has now become part of a single legal structure which encompasses both contracts and treaties as well as a host of other instruments".

[46] See, e.g., Y. Shany, Contract Claims vs. Treaty Claims: Mapping Conflicts between ICSID Decisions on Multisourced Investment Claims, AJIL 99 (2005), 835, 836 et seq.; J. Crawford, Treaty and Contract in Investment Arbitration, Int'l Arb. 24 (2008), 351, 351, claiming: "No issue in the field of investment arbitration is more fundamental, or more disputed, than the distinction between treaty and contract. There is a struggle between those who believe BIT claims should be insulated from contractual claims and those who want to relate the two." (Footnote omitted); A. Sheppard et al., Editorial Note—The Relationship between Local Courts and Investment Treaty Arbitration, TDM 2 (2005), No. 4, 3, asking:

> Should arbitration tribunals be seen as instruments for the resolution of disputes exclusively relating to international law standards incorporated, in particular, in bilateral investment treaties (BITs) or should they be allowed to function more broadly as fora for the resolution of any contractual disputes connected even indirectly with the underlying investment activities?

For a discussion of this aspect with regard to obligations under the GATT 1994, see G. Verhoosel, The Use of Investor-State Arbitration under Bilateral Investment Treaties to Seek Relief for Breaches of WTO Law, JIEL 6 (2003), 493 et seq.

[47] At root, this clash is reminiscent of the traditional differences between monist and dualist approaches to international law. Given the increasing fragmentation of international law, this debate can be linked to the broader contemporary debate regarding the structure of international law. For a close examination of the theoretical underpinnings, see Y. Shany, Regulating Jurisdictional Relations between National and International Courts (2007), 107 et seq.

of domestic law. The effective relationship between contract and treaty claims and the eventual impossibility of addressing them separately are acknowledged by these tribunals, and solutions to reconcile both legal instruments are carried out on a pragmatic basis. This integrationist stance—as it is termed by Shany—"supports a flexible and open-textured reading of BITs as encompassing a broad range of rights and obligations."[48] Accordingly, treaty-based tribunals are vested with jurisdiction over a broad array of issues, including contractual matters. This compatibility of both legal instruments not only has practical advantages (the employment of parallel judicial proceedings seems to be uneconomic and superfluous)[49] but also entails a favourable treatment of the foreign investor and therefore is considered to correspond to the BIT's purpose and object.

On the other hand, a second interpretative stance is based on a philosophy which comes out to be diametrically opposed to unifying or integrating attempts. This primarily dualistic point of view generally denies the existence of a relationship between the spheres of international law and domestic law. As a consequence, tribunals that rely on this approach tend to resolve tensions between both systems through rules of exclusion that separate both legal systems. BITs are regarded as "self-contained instruments, providing a closed list of rights and obligations, and entailing discrete dispute settlement procedures whose jurisdiction remains limited to BIT claims."[50] Thereby the role which domestic law and domestic courts play in the resolution of investment disputes is remarkably enhanced and the loss of sovereignty towards international adjudication bodies is mitigated.

The resulting chasm is by no means a theoretical one but it heralds important practical consequences for an investor who has concluded a contract with the country host to its investment. For example, the following hypothetical case may be instructive: let us imagine a company which constructs energy facilities such as hydro-electric power plants. After the successful bidding procedure in a foreign country[51] for the

---

[48] Shany, *supra* fn. 46, 844.

[49] Cf. C. Schreuer, Calvo's Grandchildren: The Return of Local Remedies in Investment Arbitration, The Law and Practice of International Courts and Tribunals 4 (2005), 1, 12.

[50] Shany, *supra* fn. 46, 844.

[51] Although in most of the cases this country will be a developing country, this is by no means a requirement of the investment treaty regime which, by contrast, is based on reciprocity. See, e.g., W. Park, NAFTA Chapter 11: Capital Exporters as Host States,

construction of such a plant the company concludes a contract with the competent governmental authority. The contract is supposed to regulate all aspects of the project such as identity of the parties, performance, duration, remuneration, damages and so forth. Further, the contract contains a dispute resolution clause which refers eventual disputes for resolution to the local judiciary. Prior to this, the company's home country and the foreign country where the project should take place had concluded a bilateral investment treaty.

Subsequent to the beginning of the project, the company encounters certain difficulties. For instance, it does not receive all the licenses or permits as provided for in the contract because a further governmental sub-entity estimates the project as a threat to its development policy. Likewise, the governmental authority could fail to allocate to the company the previously agreed territory or delivered production material could be defective. As a consequence, the project gets delayed. On account of this, the government may not pay the agreed tariff or it may even alter the tariff scheme under which the remuneration was determined. The company reacts by stopping the electricity production and lodging a claim before the local courts against the governmental agency on account of breach of contract. The competent court rejects the claim and accepts the counterclaims of the governmental agency. After the company refuses to cede the power plant to the governmental agency, the government orders the army to step in and to expropriate the company because of unlawful activities.

At this point, contingent upon the effect of the treaty, the investor may be left either without any further remedy or he may be entitled to submit the dispute or parts of it to international arbitration where he could obtain an award against the host country enforceable without the interference of domestic courts. However, it is not clear which parts of the dispute constitute a breach of contract and which amount to a violation of the treaty, and prior to this, whether and how this qualification will affect the investor's remedies under the treaty. Do treaty-based tribunals have competence to sit over a dispute which is essentially contractual? What if the contractual non-performance is a treaty violation? Under what circumstances does a breach of contract amount to a

---

in: G. Kaufmann-Kohler & B. Stucki (eds.), Investment Treaties and Arbitration, ASA Special Series No. 19 (2002), 9 et seq. For a discussion on the growth of capital export by emerging markets, see K. Sauvant, New Sources of FDI: The BRICS—Outward FDI from Brazil, Russia, India and China, JWIT 6 (2005), 635 et seq.

violation of treaty? In short, the effect of the treaty on the rights derived from the contract will regularly be crucial for the investor's right to international arbitration and thus to neutral adjudication.

The questions which therefore arise in this context are manifold: What is the general effect of these treaties? How and to what extent do they provide for a protection of contractual relationships between foreign investor and host State? What requirements must a contract fulfil in order to fall within this coverage? What mechanisms are set out to remedy treaty violations and what is their relation to domestic remedies? Given the present explosive rise of investment treaty disputes and the deeply entrenched inconsistency of arbitral decisions with regard to crucial aspects concerning contracts between host State and investor, this is the adequate moment to address these topics more closely. Ultimately, since reliability and predictability are essential requirements for every legal system, the continuity of a high degree of legal uncertainty surrounding the relationship of the two essential instruments of investment protection is likely to threaten the credibility and thus the legitimacy of the whole system of international investment protection.[52]

The Research Methodology and the Structure of the Work

This work intends to examine the impact which the investment treaty system has upon contracts between foreign investors and host States. Since the major effects of the system, that is the consent to a pre-established procedural framework for the resolution of disputes and the provision of substantive protection standards, take place on the jurisdictional stage as well as on the merits stage of arbitral proceedings, both the procedure and the substance have to be taken into consideration. The prime objectives are thus the determination of the jurisdictional competence of treaty-based arbitral tribunals over claims based on breach of contract and of the substantive coverage of contract-related violations by investment treaty standards.

[52] For a discussion on the danger of inconsistent decisions, see E. Gaillard, A Black Year for ICSID, TDM 4 (2007), No. 5. For a discussion of the establishment of an appeals mechanism under ICSID, see D. Bishop, The Case for an Appellate Panel and Its Scope of Review, TDM 2 (2005), No. 2; S. Franck, The Legitimacy Crisis in Investment Treaty Arbitration: Privatizing Public International Law through Inconsistent Decisions, Fordham L. Rev. 73 (2005), 1521 et seq.

The hypothesis which is proposed is that the establishment of the investment treaty regime creates a new dimension to the contracts' legal protection under international standards which operates as additional layer of protection for an investor's contractual rights. On account of this, contractual disputes under an investment treaty may be settled, entirely or partly, before neutral international arbitral tribunals under the application of international law standards.

For this purpose, notwithstanding the uniqueness of every respective treaty, a surprising degree of similarity allows for a generalized contemplation of the provisions of the created system. Since most of the investment treaties are adopted in a "boilerplate" fashion based on a few countries' model treaties and tend to contain very similar provisions,[53] such a generalized approach is convenient and tenable.[54] Although it is true that when it comes to the resolution of a concrete case, the provisions of a specific treaty may entail a result different from those warranted in the present work, a generalized approach will nevertheless serve to produce conclusive solutions for a widespread range of possible applications.

The structure of this work seeks to roughly reflect the way in which an arbitral tribunal would proceed to address the pertinent problems. This does not hold true for Chapter 1 which determines the scope of research, i.e., the contracts between investor and host State, and explains briefly for what reasons the "internationalisation" of these contracts fails in the absence of investment treaties. Chapter 2 contemplates the general requirements and effects of the investment treaty regime and examines the coverage of contracts on the jurisdictional stage. Chapter 3 then proceeds with the principal distinction between contract claims and treaty claims. This requires an examination of the substantial coverage of contractual relationships by investment treaties. Chapter 4 is concerned with the effect of umbrella clauses which are particularly important provisions for the protective coverage of contracts. Finally, in Chapter 5, an attempt is made to clarify the jurisdictional relationships which are produced by the previously examined effects.

---

[53] Cf. T. Wälde, The "Umbrella" Clause in Investment Arbitration—A Comment on Original Intentions and Recent Cases, JWIT 6 (2005), 183, 217 et seq.

[54] Cf. McLachlan et al., *supra* fn. 19, 1.08, who contend that this phenomenon makes it "possible to speak of a common lexicon of investment treaty law".

1. CONTRACTS BETWEEN HOST STATES AND FOREIGN INVESTORS IN THE ABSENCE OF INTERNATIONAL INVESTMENT TREATIES

For decades, legal opinion on a multitude of issues surrounding contracts between host States and foreign investors such as the legal nature of these contracts and the law applicable to them has been widely inconsistent.[1] This unsatisfying situation and its reasons shall be exposed shortly in the present chapter. At the outset, however, it has to be determined what kind of contracts are the subject of this examination and which characteristics make them so difficult to deal with.

A. The Existence and Characteristics of State Contracts

I. *The Notion of State Contract and Its Legal Nature*

Contracts between host States and foreign investors usually have been termed as "state contracts".[2] This notion is defined by UNCTAD as referring to a contract made between a State or an entity of a State and

---

[1] See R. Y. Jennings, State Contracts in International Law, BYIL 37 (1961), 156, 156, who declared:

> The particular topic of State contracts impinges some of the hardest questions of international law. For it cannot be considered apart from the relationship of international law and municipal law; the relationship of public international law and private international law; the question of the subjects of international law; and the limits of domestic jurisdiction and the reserved domain. Moreover, the opinions of writers on the legal position of State contracts range from the view that the State contract is directly subject to the international law rule of pacta sunt servanda to the view that "contracts cannot be the subject of international disputes since international law contains no rules respecting their form and effect" (footnote omitted).

[2] By and large, the terminology is not consistent and is often contingent upon political or legal connotations. Whilst some authors refer exclusively to the term "state contract" when dealing with long-term foreign investment contracts, others prefer the term "Economic Development Agreement" which inherits a certain political attitude. Further use is made of terms such as "foreign investment contract", "international investment agreement", or simply "investment contract". The term most commonly used, however, remains "state contract".

a foreign national or legal person of foreign nationality.[3] This general definition involves the element of frontier crossing but disregards other aspects which are fundamental to the determination of the term "state contract". Another more detailed definition describes a state contract "as a contract made between a state or a state entity vested with monopolistic control of a sector of a state's economy and a foreign entity entering that state with the intent of establishing a long term business relationship with the state or the state entity in that economic sector".[4]

The peculiar risks that characterize state contracts and differentiate them from commercial transactions are the involvement of a sovereign power as well as the application of public law and the long duration of mutual commitments.[5] Supposedly, state contracts regulate subject matters that are essential to the public interest of the host State such as the provision of infrastructure, the promotion of economic development or the running of essential services. State contracts are not founded exclusively in private law which would lead to the sanctity of commitments and the impossibility of modifying them unilaterally. Nor are they solely grounded in the public law sphere in which the community interests are to prevail over the contractual interests of the private individual.[6] The two conceptions, whose distinction under international law is not always conclusive,[7] may clash[8] and hence, produce the instability which is inherent to state

[3] UNCTAD, International Investment Agreements Issues Paper Series, State Contracts (2004), 13.

[4] M. Sornarajah, International Commercial Arbitration—The Problem of State Contracts (1990), 3.

[5] See, e.g., A. Al Faruque, The Rationale and Instrumentalities for Stability in Long-Term State Contracts—The Context for Petroleum Contracts, JWIT 7 (2006), 85, 90, who referred exclusively to petroleum contracts. Major parts of the doctrine evolved with regard to the regulation of oil exploitation but are likewise applicable to other kinds of state contracts. See also N. Horn, Arbitration and the Protection of Foreign Investment: Concept and Means, in: N. Horn (ed.), Arbitrating Foreign Investment Disputes (2004), 3, 12 et seq. Contra C. Leben, L'Évolution de la Notion de Contrat d'État, Rev. Arb. (2003), 629, 631 et seq., who differentiated between "state contracts" and "administrative contracts".

[6] See, e.g., G. Bermann, Contracts between States and Foreign Nationals: A Reassessment, in: H. Smit *et al.* (eds.), International Contracts (1981), 183, 195 et seq. See also C. Turpin, Government Contracts (1982), 69 et seq., where the author examined government contracts under various jurisdictions. In several countries such as France and the US, the law applicable differed from those of ordinary commercial contracts.

[7] Cf. K. H. Böckstiegel, Der Staat als Vertragspartner ausländischer Privatunternehmen (1971), 48.

[8] B. Audit, Transnational Arbitration and State Contracts: Findings and Prospects (1987), 77–78.

contracts.[9] The ambiguity that surrounds these contracts arises out of the contractual partners' contrary intentions: Whilst the State retains the use of sovereign prerogatives, the foreign private person attempts to evade them.[10] In the view of the latter, the State should honour its contractual commitments. The State, in turn, acts in the public interest and deems its commitments mutable if the public interest so requires.[11]

This hybrid nature of state contracts is likewise reflected by the regular coexistence of private law and public law elements in the contracts themselves. The regulations that concern commercial aspects of the contracts such as consent of the parties, repudiation, breach, and damages, and the norms with regard to commercial contents such as, inter alia, taxes, royalties, expenditure, costs of exploration, and rate of recovery of costs are governed by private law.[12] In contrast, the subject matter of the contract that is, for instance, the statutory regulation of the contract, its grants under public law, or the legislative approval of the contract are regulated by public law.[13]

II. *Traditional and Modern Forms of State Contracts*

State contracts, as seen above, are firstly defined by the legal nature of the contractual partners and their subject matter. Further characteristic features of contracts between host States and foreign investors evolved significantly in the past decades.

1. *Traditional Forms*

The fundamental principle of traditional state contracts consisted in the foreign investor's entitlement to explore and exploit natural resources. The foreign company was granted the exclusive right to do

---

[9] See, Sornarajah, *supra* fn. 4, 3, who stated:

> Such a contract contains an inconsistency within itself. Being commercial, its commercial character requires that it have certainty and that settled expectations arising from it are honoured. Being of a public nature, its public character requires that certainty and commercial expectations are sacrificed if circumstances change in such a manner as to make the performance of the contract grossly unprofitable and hence not in the public interest.

[10] Audit, *supra* fn. 8, 120.

[11] M. Sornarajah, The Settlement of Foreign Investment Disputes (2000), 86.

[12] A. Z. El Chiati, Protection of Investment in the Context of Petroleum Agreement, RdC 204 (1987–IV), 9, 27–38 et seq.

[13] H. Cattan, The Law of Oil Concessions in the Middle East and North Africa (1967), 21; A. Fatouros, Government Guarantees to Foreign Investors (1962), 232 et seq.

so without any interference by the host country. The typical agreements of this time were the so-called concessions. Albeit developed in the petroleum sector,[14] the same kind of agreement found application in all fields of natural resources. The classic form of concessions allocated the foreign company a generally huge territory in which the exploitation of natural resources was left completely to the discretion of the company. Contractual duties to exploit within certain time-limits or to exploit in a certain manner did not exist.[15] The ownership of the exploited material accrued to the foreign corporation directly through the exploitation.[16] These contracts often had durations of up to a hundred years.[17] In addition, the foreign company assumed quasi-sovereign functions in the granted area, for example, the establishment and maintenance of an infrastructure, the construction of hospitals and schools, or the construction and administration of harbours. Plainly, the foreign company's role amounted to an internal state[18] in the area of which the host country had virtually delegated its sovereignty.[19] In return, the foreign company owed royalties to the host country which were determined absolutely or dependent upon the quantity of the resources extracted.[20]

---

[14] For a detailed discussion, see E. Smith & J. Dzienkowski, A Fifty-Year Perspective on World Petroleum Arrangements, Texas Int'l L. J. 24 (1989), 13 et seq.

[15] See, e.g., U. Kischel, State Contracts (1994), 59.

[16] For the general characteristics of these concessions, see Kischel, id., 59–61; El Chiati, *supra* fn. 12, 48; J. F. Lalive, Contrats entre États ou Entreprises Étatiques et Personnes Privées. Développements Récents, RdC 181 (1983–III), 13, 171 et seq. For a detailed description, see Cattan, *supra* fn. 13, 4 et seq.; E. Smith *et al.*, Materials on International Petroleum Transactions (1993), 297 et seq.

[17] For samples, see A. El Kosheri, Le regime juridique créé par les accords de participation dans le domaine pétrolier, RdC 147 (1975–IV) 219, 347 et seq.

[18] Kischel, *supra* fn. 15, 61.

[19] Sornarajah, *supra* fn. 11, 44; M. Herdegen, Rechtsprobleme des internationalen Konzessionswesens: insbesondere aus völkerrechtlicher Sicht, in: J. Baur & S. Hobe (ed.), Rechtsprobleme von Auslandsinvestitionen (2003), 13, 14: "Das Wesen einer Konzession liegt in der Überwälzung einer ursprünglich staatlichen Funktion auf private Investoren".

[20] According to Smith *et al.*, *supra* fn. 16, 298, the archetypical Middle Eastern concession was obtained by William D'Arcy from the Shah of Persia in 1901. For the payment of $100,000, another $100,000 in stock in his oil company, and a 16% royalty, D'Arcy was granted the exclusive oil rights to 500,000 square miles of Persia for the next 60 years. A further example of a classic concession was received by Standard Oil of California from the King of Saudi Arabia in 1933. For 50,000 pounds of gold, Standard Oil was granted oil rights for a similar territory as D'Arcy for a 66-year term. For another example, see A. Suleiman, The Oil Experience of the Middle East Emirates,

These classic forms of investment contracts reflected the allocation of power at the time and cannot be deemed to represent a contractual equilibrium.[21] Occidental companies of the time took advantage of the inexperience of underdeveloped and developing States to achieve advantageous conditions. The system of concession agreements thus furthered post-colonial dependency.[22] Nowadays the bulk of these concessions have been terminated either by renegotiation[23] or by nationalisation.[24] However, the early law on foreign investment was developed largely in the context of such agreements and the disputes arising from them.[25]

2. *Modern Forms*

With the rise of independent States and the consequent re-allocation of international power,[26] new forms of foreign investment agreements emerged. This development was fostered by increased sophistication of the host States' governments and their lawyers as well as by increased awareness of the economic importance of natural resources.[27]

J. Energy & Nat. Resources L. 6 (1988), 1, 3 et seq., in which the author refers to a case where the Ruler of Abu Dhabi and the Sultan of Muscat and Oman received three rupees per ton of oil produced. This meant that the payment equalled eight cents per barrel.

[21] Georges N. Stocking, one-time president of the American Economies Association, described them in the following words: "Never in modern times have governments granted so much to so few for so long", as quoted by El Chiati, *supra* fn. 12, 48.

[22] Modern contract language usually does not apply the notion of "concession" anymore because many developing countries reject it as a term of colonial oppression. Moreover, the Arabic translation "Imtiazat" is a synonym for the capitulation system in the Ottoman Empire. See Kischel, *supra* fn. 15, 60.

[23] Cf. Smith *et al.*, *supra* fn. 16, 304 et seq. For problematic aspects of the renegotiation of state contracts, see, e.g., S. Asante, Stability of Contractual Relations in the Transnational Investment Process, Int'l & Comp. L. Q. 28 (1979), 401 et seq.; M. Sornarajah, Supremacy of the Renegotiation Clause in International Contracts, J. Int'l Arb. 5 (1988), 97 et seq. For more recent publications, see K. P. Berger, Renegotiation and Adaption of International Investment Contracts: The Role of Contract Drafters and Arbitrators, Vand. J. Transnat'l L. 36 (2003), 1347 et seq.; A. Kolo & T. Wälde, Renegotiation and Contract Adaption in International Investment Projects, JWI 5 (2000), 21 et seq.

[24] Smith *et al.*, *supra* fn. 16, 304 et seq.

[25] Sornarajah, *supra* fn. 11, 44.

[26] See, e.g., A. Cassese, International Law (2005), 42.

[27] E. Smith, From Concessions to Service Contracts, Tul. Law J. 27 (1992), 493, 499 et seq.; P. Bernadini, Development Agreements with Host Governments, in: R. Pritchard (ed.), Economic Development, Foreign Investment and the Law (1996), 161, 164 et seq.

Especially from 1973 on, when the oil crisis had disclosed the bigger powers' dependency upon the oil exporting countries, the shift of power became evident. These types of contracts show some common features: the regulations became more diversified and specific;[28] a higher variety of economic operations became the subject matter of contractual relationships;[29] and the contractual equilibrium became more balanced.[30] Essentially, the new forms of contracts left the ownership of the natural resources and the control of the operations in the hands either of a host State or a national of the host State.[31] Furthermore, contracts, which previously had been concluded exclusively and directly with the government, increasingly were concluded with substate entities or governmental agencies.[32] Modern forms of state contracts are likely to appear in one of the following basic types.[33]

a. *Modern Concession Agreements*

The countenance of concession agreements changed considerably during the course of the last century.[34] Although the essential elements remain the same—the host State transfers the rights of exploration and exploitation of natural resources and receives a determined payment—the contractual equilibrium is much more balanced. The governmental control over the corporation's activities increased and may even take direct forms of assertion.[35] The ownership of the extracted material remains largely in the hands of the host State. The agreed time-periods are shorter, the ceded territory is smaller, and the revenues of the host State are enlarged and diversified. The traditional royalties are

---

[28] Smith, *supra* fn. 27, 499 et seq.

[29] Whilst the bulk of former agreements were concluded in the natural resources sector, new forms of contracts regulated a wide array of different economic activities which fall under the notion of investment. Therefore, the term "investment agreement" is sometimes preferred. See, e.g., E. Paasivirta, Participation of States in International Contracts and Arbitral Settlement of Disputes (1990), 19–20.

[30] Smith, *supra* fn. 27, 499: "Today, of course, few countries are willing to transfer to oil companies the virtually unfettered control over petroleum reserves which was found in early agreements"; Paasivirta, id., 21: "Unlike the traditional concessions, the new forms impose a variety of duties on companies. They regularly include obligations concerning transfer of technology, employment and training of the nationals of a host country, provisions on working conditions and the protection of the environment".

[31] Kischel, *supra* fn. 15, 64.

[32] Bernadini, *supra* fn. 27, 161.

[33] Note that this classification is not a rigid system but contracts appear in a variety of different forms merging the characteristics of the different contract types. Cf. Smith, *supra* fn. 27, 523.

[34] Sornarajah, *supra* fn. 11, 44.

[35] Z. Gao, International Petroleum Contracts ? Current Trends and New Directions (1994), 29–56.

substituted by a revenue-dependent system of taxes, production-sharing and concession fees.[36]

b. *Production Sharing Agreements*

The production sharing agreement finds its main application in the petroleum sector and thus can be regarded as the legitimate successor of the traditional concession agreements. The fundamental idea of these contracts is that the foreign company is rewarded for the exploration and exploitation performed but after the lapse of a certain time period the control is ceded completely to the host State.[37] This approach reflects the growing potential of developing countries to enforce their will to maintain permanent sovereignty over their natural resources. The procedure supposed to be undertaken in these contracts is the following: A potential oil-rich field is allocated to the foreign company. It rests with the company to explore the existing oil sources and to exploit them. The risk of exploration is with the foreign company. The right to exploit, in turn, is only conferred until the costs of exploration have been met. Subsequently, a progressively diminishing percentage of benefits is assigned to the company. Finally, after the expiry of the contractually concluded time period, the host State assumes complete control over operation and acquisition.[38]

c. *Management Agreements/Technical Assistance Agreement/Service Contracts*

This type of agreement is characterised by the missing skills of the local party to run the project after completion. Typically, the ownership is in local hands but the operational control remains with the foreign corporation.[39] The foreign company is not entitled to a concession but is a mere hired contractor. Basically, these contracts require the foreign contractor to deliver all the production to the State or state agency.

[36] Kischel, *supra* fn. 15, 64; Smith, *supra* fn. 27, 513.

[37] During this time period, the company is not the holder of the mining rights but merely acts on behalf of the holder of the mining rights, i.e., the state or the governmental agency. The contractor acquires title to its share of production not at the well-head but only at the point of export or at any other agreed point. Cf. Bernadini, *supra* fn. 27, 167.

[38] Sornarajah, *supra* fn. 11, 45; Smith *et al.*, *supra* fn. 16, 342 et seq.

[39] Sornarajah, *supra* fn. 11, 44. Furthermore, with regard to management contracts and technical assistance contracts, the scope of responsibilities is supposed to be declining since the manager's purpose is, in the end, to make himself superfluous. Cf. G. Westring, Construction and Management Contracts, in: N. Horn & C. Schmitthoff (eds.), The Transnational Law of International Commercial Transaction (1982), 175, 183–184.

The company's reimbursement may be in kind, that is with the natural resource that has been found, or simply by payment.[40] Nowadays, service contracts are not only concluded in the area of natural resources but in a wide array of economic activities ranging from mere commercial exchanges of services to construction of infrastructure or maintenance of public functions.

d. *Turnkey Contracts*

The turnkey contract regulates the manufacture of a facility by a foreign company. Usually these contracts concern large projects in areas in which the host country lacks experience. The foreign company is obliged to handle the complete construction independently until the facility is built and ready to operate.[41] Regularly, with completion of the construction a technical assistance agreement is established in order to supersede the turnkey contract. The payment may be effected through a share in the production.[42]

e. *Joint Venture Agreements*

The conclusion of joint venture agreements[43] is the most conspicuous evidence of the host State's participation.[44] In principle, the notion embraces all kinds of governmental cooperation in the investment project.[45] Essentially, two different types of joint ventures can be discerned. On the one hand, there is the contractual joint venture which resembles a partnership and is created similarly.[46] On the other hand, the cooperation may take the form of a corporate joint venture which requires the formation of a corporation with proper legal capacity and hence is consistent with the traditional Anglo-American notion of joint venture.[47] The former type is regularly used for major ventures,

[40] Bernadini, *supra* fn. 27, 167–168.

[41] Sornarajah, *supra* fn. 11, 43

[42] Bernadini, *supra* fn. 27, 168.

[43] For a discussion on joint ventures, see generally M. Sornarajah, The Law of International Joint Ventures (1992); R. Pritchard & P. Fox, The Use of Joint Ventures in FDI, in: R. Pritchard (ed.), Economic Development, Foreign Investment and the Law (1996), 175 et seq.

[44] Kischel, *supra* fn. 15, 62.

[45] El Chiati, *supra* fn. 12, 52.

[46] These contractual joint ventures are frequently called unincorporated joint ventures. In China, they are commonly termed as business cooperation contracts. See R. Pritchard & P. Fox, The Use of Joint Ventures in FDI, in: R. Pritchard (ed.), Economic Development, Foreign Investment and the Law (1996), 179.

[47] Corporate joint ventures are also termed as incorporated joint ventures or equity joint ventures. See id.

especially in the petroleum and mining industries. At present, however, the latter is the most commonly used joint venture structure.[48] Whereas in the framework of the contractual joint ventures the liability continues to be personal, in corporate joint ventures the created corporation is liable for any debts incurred during the conduct of business[49] and thereby the participants can limit their own liability[50].

These days, the joint venture agreement is the most common agreement in foreign investment transactions. It is not industry specific and may be deemed advantageous for both sides of an investment project. Host States often require this form of entry in order to obtain a certain degree of control over the undertaking. Foreign corporations similarly appreciate joint ventures for various reasons.[51] A special feature of joint ventures is that developing States generally require an explicit permission of entry through an administrative body. The granting of the permission of entry is contingent upon the fulfilment of certain conditions that may vary among host States.[52] Thereby, the administrative body that is in charge of granting the permission becomes a "silent" third party to the contract. It exerts a supervisory role and may, if the investment undertaken does not correspond to the host State's expectations, interfere with the project's continuation.[53]

f. *Licensing and Transfer of Technology Agreements*

This type of agreement regulates the transfer of technology into the host country by way of permissions granted by holders of protected rights for their exploitation. Although these contracts are regularly mere ancillary agreements, they may also exist independently.[54]

---

[48] Id., 180.

[49] Sornarajah, *supra* fn. 11, 35.

[50] Pritchard & Fox, *supra* fn. 46, 180.

[51] See Sornarajah, *supra* fn. 11, 32. According to the author, these reasons are the following: Joint ventures are a means of diversifying risk. Further, they enable the pooling of capital resources as well as complementary technology. Finally, having a local partner who is conversant with the local market habits, the distribution system, and the political circumstances may redound to the foreign investor's advantage.

[52] For example, in China, the investment legislation requires the parties to make a feasibility study.

[53] According to Sornarajah, *supra* fn. 11, 37, this element of governmental participation indicates that the joint venture agreement is not an ordinary commercial contract even when it is concluded between private parties.

[54] For a discussion on licensing contracts, see generally D. Pfaff, International Licensing Contracts, Transfer of Technology and Transnational Law, in: N. Horn & C. Schmitthoff (eds.), The Transnational Law of International Commercial Transaction (1982), 199 et seq.

g. *Build, Operate and Transfer Agreements (BOT Agreements)*
In the framework of large infrastructure projects such as the building of highways, dams, ports, mass transit systems, water supply systems, or power generation plants, this new type of agreement comes into play. The underlying idea resembles modern concession agreements. In principle, the foreign corporation is charged with the financial risk of the construction. After completion, the corporation is granted the right to operate and maintain the facility during a certain time period. Thereby the corporation shall be enabled to recover its investments and operating expenses as well as a reasonable rate of return. Subsequent to this period the facility is turned over to the public entity.[55] The fixed time period may be very long, even up to 50 years. These agreements combine the elements of both turnkey and management agreements. The conclusion of such agreements is said to be complicated and thus only a few have been applied in developing countries.[56]

III. *Conclusion*

Four basic trends can be discerned when one observes the general development of the employment of state contracts throughout the past decades. On the one hand, new types of agreements emerged the contents of which reach a more balanced trade-off between the interests of the foreign investor and those of the host State. In this area chiefly the host States could gain ground on account of their improved experience and the increase in competition among investing corporations. The main feature of this development may be the regulation of the extracted material's ownership which nowadays usually rests with the host State or through joint ventures with a national of the host State and the maintenance of operational control by governmental entities.[57] At the same time the diversification of possible investment regulations has grown steadily. The old type of concession agreement had to give way to different kinds of more specific contracts which enable both parties to find forms that correspond to the respective expectations. Moreover, the signatory partners of state contracts have changed.

---

[55] See Herdegen, *supra* fn. 19, 15.

[56] Cf. Bernadini, *supra* fn. 27, 168. Exceptions are countries which adopted special legislation to implement such agreements such as, for instance, the Philippines, with Republic Act No. 6957 of 1990 and Republic Act No. 7718 of 1993.

[57] Sornarajah, *supra* fn. 11, 57.

Whereas the old concession agreements often were concluded directly with the State and through the participation of high State officials, modern investment contracts regularly are concluded with state-owned entities.[58] Finally, state contracts are not only used to regulate natural resource extraction anymore but concern a growing field of economic activities.

B. The Theories of Internationalisation

I. *Introduction*

Due to a variety of factors which are inextricably linked to state contracts such as the principal dissent about the nature of these contracts, the double role of the host State,[59] and the purported inadequacy of the host state's domestic law system and judiciary, foreign investors wanted to settle disputes arising from state contracts at a forum different from the host State's local courts and under a law different from the host State's law.[60] On account of this, the concept of an "internationalisation" of these contracts came into play. The underlying idea behind all theories of "internationalisation"[61] of state contracts is that the law applicable to these contracts is not only the municipal law of the host State but may also be—even exclusively—some kind of external legal system, be it international law, transnational law, a-national law, or simply "general principles of law recognized by civilized nations". The purpose

---

[58] See, e.g., Horn, *supra* fn. 5, 12; S. Perera, State Responsibility—Ascertaining the Liability of States in Foreign Investment Disputes, JWIT 6 (2005), 499, 500 et seq.

[59] This refers to the host State's role as a sovereign and as a party to the contract. See, e.g., D. Bowett, State Contracts with Aliens: Contemporary Developments on Compensation for Termination or Breach, BYIL 59 (1988), 49, 49: "The State party, since it can modify its own law, has the power to ensure that its actions vis-à-vis the contract are lawful under its own law. Therefore the alien claimant will seek to show that the proper law is not the law of the State party but rather some other law which lies outside that State's control".

[60] Cf. H. Merkt, Investitionsschutz durch Stabilisierungsklauseln—Zur intertemporalen Rechtswahl in State Contracts (1990), 25–29; Kischel, *supra* fn. 15, 67–70.

[61] The term "internationalisation" of contracts is generally attributed to F. A. Mann who used the phrase in various articles. See F. A. Mann, Studies in International Law (1973), chapters III–VII. The term "internationalisation" within this sense may signify the wholesale embedding of contracts in international law or the application of a non-national law system as the proper law of contracts. By contrast, it does not refer to the establishment of jurisdiction of an international arbitral tribunal. See C. Amerasinghe, Local Remedies in International Law (2004), 110–111.

behind this idea is to remove the contractual relationship from the host State's jurisdiction and thus from its influence upon it.

This "internationalisation" of state contracts is said to lie at the heart of foreign investment protection through international arbitration.[62] The competence of international arbitral tribunals to sit over a dispute which purportedly is an essentially domestic dispute, was only conceivable when the pertinent contract was somehow related to the international order.[63] During the last decades, a myriad of different theories and approaches has been published concerning on the one hand, support and substantiation[64] of this idea and decided opposition[65] on the other hand. Similarly, the practice of arbitral tribunals has been inconsistent.[66] A detailed description of the debate and its ramifications as well as an examination of the pertinent arbitral practice have been provided in several studies[67] and shall not be repeated in the present work.

---

[62] See, e.g., Sornarajah, *supra* fn. 11, 223.

[63] See, e.g., M. Sornarajah, Power and Justice in Foreign Investment Arbitration, J. Int'l Arb. 14 (1997), 103, 107 et seq.

[64] See, e.g., Jennings, *supra* fn. 1, 156 et seq.; R. Lillich, The Law Governing Disputes under Economic Development Agreements: Reexamining the Concept of "Internationalization", in: R. Lillich & C. Brower (eds.), International Arbitration in the 21st Century (1994), 61 et seq.; Leben, *supra* fn. 5, 629 et seq.; C. Leben, Contrat d'Etat et droit international des investissements, RdC 302 (2003), 201 et seq.; C. Leben, Retour sur la notion de contrat d'Etat et sur le droit applicable à celui-ci, in: E. Decaux, L'évolution du droit international (1998), 247 et seq.; I. Seidl-Hohenveldern, The Theory of Quasi-International and Partly International Agreements, Rev. Belg. De Droit Int'l 11 (1975), 567 et seq.; I. Seidl-Hohenveldern, International Economic Law (1992), 48; A. Giardina, State Contracts: National versus International Law? Italian YBIL (1980/1981), 147 et seq.; C. Greenwood, State Contracts in International Law in the Libyan Oil Arbitrations, BYIL 53 (1982), 27 et seq.; R. Bishop, International Arbitration of Petroleum Disputes: The Development of a Lex Petrolea, in: A. van den Berg (ed.), YB Comm. Arb'n 23 (1998), 1131, 1146 et seq.

[65] See, e.g., D. Bowett, *supra* fn. 59, 49 et seq.; D. Bowett, Claims between States and Private Entities: The Twilight Zone of International Law, Cath. U. L. Rev. 35 (1986), 929 et seq.; G. Delaume, The Proper Law of State Contracts Revisited, ICSID Rev.-FILJ 12 (1997), 1 et seq.; G. Delaume, State Contracts and Transnational Arbitration, AJIL 75 (1981), 784 et seq.; G. Delaume, The Proper Law of State Contracts and the Lex Mercatoria: A Reappraisal, ICSID Rev.-FILJ 3 (1988), 79 et seq.; A. A. Fatouros, International Law and the Internationalized Contract, AJIL 74 (1980), 134 et seq.; H. A. Grigera Naón, Choice-of-Law Problems in International Commercial Arbitration (1992), 113 et seq.; M. Sornarajah, The Myth of International Contract, JWTL 15 (1981), 187 et seq.; Sornarajah, *supra* fn. 63, 103 et seq.

[66] For a summary of the different approaches, see, e.g., P. Bernadini, The Law Applied by International Arbitrators to State Contracts, in: R. Briner (ed.), Law of International Business and Dispute Settlement in the 21st Century—Liber Amicorum Karl-Heinz Böckstiegel (2001), 51 et seq.

[67] In Germany see, e.g., Merkt, *supra* fn. 60, 115 et seq.; Böckstiegel, *supra* fn. 7, 105 et seq.; Kischel, *supra* fn. 15; R. Velten, Die Anwendbarkeit des Völkerrechts auf State

Neither does this work contend to contribute a further solution to this seemingly never-ending debate. Conversely, in the present section it will briefly demonstrated that the "internationalisation" of state contracts remains doubtful in the absence of international investment treaties. This is chiefly due to three reasons: firstly, because of the increasing reluctance towards these "internationalisation" tenets by arbitral tribunals;[68] secondly, due to the growing strong opposition in the writings of scholars from developing countries;[69] and finally, by reason of the widespread establishment of sophisticated legal systems in developing countries.[70]

Contracts in der internationalen Schiedsgerichtsbarkeit (1987); J. Stoll, Vereinbarungen zwischen Staat und ausländischem Investor (1982); E. Schanze, Investitionsverträge im internationalen Wirtschaftsrecht (1986), 95 et seq.; M. Hiefner, Völkerrechtliche Grenzen hinsichtlich der Vertragsfreiheit bei Verträgen zwischen Staaten und ausländischen Privatpersonen (1984); G. Jaenicke, Consequences of a Breach of an Investment Agreement Governed by International Law, by General Principles of Law, or by Domestic Law of the Host State, in: D. Dicke (ed.), Foreign Investment in the Present and a New International Economic Order, (1987), 177 et seq. In other countries, see, e.g., Audit, *supra* fn. 8; Bernadini, *supra* fn. 66, 51 et seq.; J. Kuusi, The Host State and the Transnational Corporations (1979); J. P. Regli, Contrats d'Etat et arbitrage entre Etats et personnes privées (1983); P. Weil, Problèmes relatifs aux contrats passés entre un Etat et un particulier, RdC 128 (1969-III), 96 et seq.; J. Verhoefen, Contrats entre Etats et ressortissants d'autres Etats, in: Centre Charles de Vischer (ed.), Le contrat économique international—Stabilité et evolution (1975), 115 et seq.; Paasivirta, *supra* fn. 29; P. Leboulanger, Les contrats entre Etats et enterprises étrangères (1985); V. C. Igbokwe, Developing Countries and the Law Applicable to International Arbitration of Oil Investment Disputes: Has the Last Word Been Said?, J. Int'l Arb. 14 (1997), 99 et seq.; Lalive, *supra* fn. 16, 13 et seq.

[68] See *In the Matter of an Arbitration between the Government of the State of Kuwait and the American Independent Oil Co. (Aminoil)* (1982) 21 ILM 976 (hereinafter, *Aminoil*), where the arbitral tribunal completely ignored the "internationalization" theories. For a summary of the case, see M. Hunter & A. Sinclair, Aminoil Revisited: Reflections on a Story of Changing Circumstances; N. Horn (ed.), International Investment Law and Arbitration: Leading Cases from the ICSID, NAFTA, Bilateral Treaties and Customary International Law (2005), 347 et seq.

[69] See, e.g., Sornarajah, *supra* fn. 11, 223 et seq.; Sornarajah, *supra* fn. 63, 103 et seq.; M. Sornarajah, The Climate of International Arbitration, J. Int'l Arb. 8 (1991), 47 et seq.; M. Sornarajah, Power and Justice: Third World Resistance in International Law, SYBIL 10 (2006), 19 et seq.; A. El Kosheri & T. Riad, The Law Governing a New Generation of Petroleum Agreements: Changes in the Arbitration Process, ICSID Rev.-FILJ 2 (1986), 257 et seq.; L. Atsegbua, International Arbitration of Oil Investment Disputes: The Severability Doctrine and Applicable Law Issues Revisited, African J. Int'l & Comp. Law 5 (1993), 634 et seq.; A. F. M. Maniruzzaman, State Contracts and Arbitral Choice-of-Law Process, J. Int'l Arb. 15 (1998), 65 et seq.; A. F. M. Maniruzzaman, State Contracts in Contemporary International Law: Monist versus Dualist Controversies, EJIL 12 (2001), 309 et seq.; N. Nassar, Internationalization of State Contracts: ICSID, the Last Citadel, J. Int'l Arb. 14 (1997), 183 et seq.

[70] See the examples cited in Sornarajah, *supra* fn. 11, 239. See also Delaume, *supra* fn. 65, 9–10.

The concept which all theories of internationalisation are arguing against has been formulated by the PCIJ as follows: "Tout contrat qui n'est pas un contrat entre Etats en tant que sujets du droit international a son fondement dans une loi nationale."[71]

This statement reflected the traditional view about the subject: a contract between a foreign investor and a State is governed by some municipal law, most likely the law of the State where it is performed.[72] Hence, every question of contractual performance was in principle one of internal law. Public international law exclusively came into play when there is an occurrence of additional circumstances such as denial of justice.[73]

The different ways which were perceived to substantiate an application of international law can be divided into two main approaches by means of the substantiation of the internationalisation effected.[74] Whilst several theories contended a direct internationalisation of state contracts without the application of private international law (see B.II below), others tended to take the traditional way of private international law (see B.III below). In the final analysis, the results of both approaches are the same: in general the domestic law of the host State does not find application either as the law of conflict or as the proper law of the contract.

---

[71] *Case concerning the Payment of Various Serbian Loans Issued in France (France v. Serbia)*, PCIJ Rep. Series A No. 20, 41. The court continued:

> La question de savoir quelle est cette loi fait l'objet de la partie du droit qu'aujourd'hui on désigne le plus souvent sous le nom de droit international privé ou de théorie du conflit des lois. Les règles en peuvent être établies par des conventions internationales ou des coutumes, et dans ce dernier cas avoir le caractère d'un vrai droit international, régissant les rapports entre Etats. Mais, à part de cela, il y a lieu de considérer que les dites règles font partie du droit interne.

It is interesting to note that the court itself did not apply conflict rules of any particular system of national law.

[72] See also Report of the Committee of the League of Nations Studying Loan Contracts, League of Nations Publications, Economic & Financial (1939), Doc. C145 M93 1939 II.A, 21 et seq.

[73] See, e.g., C. Amerasinghe, State Breaches of Contracts with Aliens and International Law, AJIL 58 (1964), 881, 912 et seq.

[74] For this classification, see Merkt, *supra* fn. 60, 117 et seq.; Kischel, *supra* fn. 15, 79. These categories have been termed as "direct" and "indirect internationalization", "voie directe" and "voie indirecte", or "echte" and "unechte Vertragsinternationalisierung".

II. *Direct Internationalisation*

Direct internationalisation is not contingent upon the application of municipal or international systems of private international law. The contract is tied directly—without the interference of any legal system—to an external system of law.[75] Thereby, the state contract is removed from the domestic law of the host State and, as a corollary, from the host State's eventual undue influence upon it. The dogma of the municipal law's applicability is thus circumvented completely. Instead of the host State's domestic law, the application of a variety of systems of law has been proposed in legal doctrine.

1. *State Contracts as International Law/Per Se Application*

If state contracts were similar to international treaties, these contracts would constitute international law and international law would undoubtedly be applicable to them. Based on this idea, some authors—against settled opinion[76]—tried to equate or at least to converge specific agreements between States and multinational companies with international treaties. Böckstiegel, for instance, proposed to recognize the international status of such "restrained international contract" under certain circumstances.[77] Weil[78] and others[79] contemplated the creation of a "droit international des contrats" which would be directly applicable

---

[75] Cf. Merkt, *supra* fn. 60, 121.

[76] S. Schwebel, International Arbitration: Three Salient Problems (1987), 108: "A contract between a State and an alien is not an instrument of international law; it does not give rise to obligations under the law of treaties. On this, there is no dispute".

[77] Böckstiegel, *supra* fn. 7, 368, 378 et seq. Accordingly, the conditions are the following: Firstly, the contract must be concluded with a governmental entity that is empowered to conclude international treaties. Secondly, the contract's content must regulate the State's behaviour with regard to specific governmental prerogatives. By the conclusion of such an agreement, the host State implicitly recognizes the company as a subject which has the legal capacity to conclude internationally binding agreements. This restrained legal personality is deduced from the State's own original capacity and is only valid for the specific contract and with regard to the recognizing State. This particular contract binds the host State internationally and in case of a contractual breach through the application of governmental prerogatives, the host State transgresses international law. For a variation of this approach, see P. Fischer, Die internationale Konzession (1974), 159 et seq.

[78] P. Weil, Droit International et Contrats d'Etat, in: P. Bardonnet (ed.), Mélanges offerts à Paul Reuter—le Droit International: Unité et Diversité (1981), 549, 568 et seq.

[79] Among the recent ones, see Lillich, *supra* fn. 64, 107–110. See also Lalive, *supra* fn. 16, 234–235.

to a certain category of international contracts. These tenets were, to a certain extent, picked up by arbitral tribunals in some cases. In *Sapphire v. NIOC*, the sole arbitrator held that the quasi-international character of the contract at issue required detachment from a particular legal system.[80] Likewise, in *TOPCO*[81] and *Revere*[82] the character of the contract was taken as justification for the direct application of international law. At present, however, these approaches are hardly tenable anymore since they are in conflict with essential principles of international law[83] and would lead to barely viable results[84].

2. *Genuine Legal Orders*

A variety of different concepts was developed to foster the view that a genuine legal order was the proper law of these contracts. Led by Verdross, several authors rejected the state contracts' submission to either municipal law or international law on account of their characterisation as "quasi-international".[85] According to this tenet the concurring will of the parties would create an independent legal order—the *lex contractus*—which is the contract itself. The need to link the contract with any legal system was dismissed.[86] Thereby, the positivist contention of grounding a contractual relationship in a pre-existing external legal system was disregarded and the autonomy of the parties' will was given overwhelming importance.[87] In a subsequent

[80] *Sapphire International Petroleum Ltd. v. National Iranian Oil Co.* (1967) 35 ILR 136, 173 (hereinafter, *Sapphire v. NIOC*).

[81] *Texaco Overseas Petroleum Co. v. Government of the Libyan Arab Republic* (1979) 53 ILR 389 (hereinafter, *TOPCO v. Libya*).

[82] *In the Matter of Revere Copper and Brass, Inc.* (1980) 56 ILR 258.

[83] See Kischel, *supra* fn. 15, 262 et seq., who contends that the essential problem is that the missing legal capacity of non-state actors cannot be overcome by unilateral recognition.

[84] See, e.g., Amerasinghe, *supra* fn. 61, 129: "If the contract…is placed in the international legal system, it follows that both parties have a right to invoke international law.… Not only would a breach of contract by the state party to the contract be a violation of international law, but a breach of contract by the alien party to the contract must also amount to a violation of international law".

[85] See, e.g., A. Verdross, Die Sicherung von ausländischen Privatrechten aus Abkommen zur wirtschaftlichen Entwicklung mit Schiedsklauseln, HJIL 18 (1957/1958), 635 et seq.; M. Bourquin, Arbitration and Economic Development Agreements, Bus. Law. 15 (1959/1960), 860 et seq.; H. Kipp, Verträge zwischen staatlichen und nichtstaatlichen Partnern, BerDGesVölkR 5 (1964), 133 et seq.

[86] Verdross, *supra* fn. 96, 640.

[87] A. F. M. Maniruzzaman, Choice of Law in International Contracts—Some Fundamental Conflict of Law Issues, J. Int'l Arb. 16 (1999), 141, 146–147 et seq.

refinement Verdross contended that the binding force of the *lex contractus* derived from the principle of *pacta sunt servanda* and all the other general principles of law concerning the conclusion and validity of contracts.[88]

Others authors though they assert partly differing approaches held that an autonomous transnational or a-national legal order should govern the legal relations that are not encompassed in the traditional legal systems.[89] The contractual relationship between host State and foreign investor was regarded as pertaining to such realm where neither public international law nor municipal law would be applicable.[90] The same underlying idea is inherent in the proposition of the application of the *lex mercatoria*.[91]

Finally, several arbitral tribunals applied as proper law of the contract "general principles of law recognized by civilized nations." In *Abu Dhabi*[92] this application found its justification in the lack of an existing adequate law.[93] The same reasoning was brought forward in the *Ruler of Qatar*.[94] In the legal literature this doctrine is chiefly linked to a paper by Lord McNair.[95] Therein, he argues that rights and obligations could not exist in a legal vacuum but had to be embedded in a particular legal order.[96] Since international law was inapplicable in the case of state contracts, the internationalised

---

[88] A. Verdross, Quasi-International Agreements and International Economic Transactions, Yearbook of World Affairs 18 (1964), 230, 234–235 et seq.

[89] See, e.g., H. W. Rengeling, Privatvölkerrechtliche Verträge (1971); K. G. Borchers, Verträge von Staaten mit ausländischen Privatpersonen (1966), 56 et seq.; K. Zemanek, Über das dualistische Denken in der Völkerrechtswissenschaft, in: A. von der Heydte (ed.), Völkerrecht und rechtliches Weltbild (1960), 321 et seq.; P. Jessup, Transnational Law (1956); C. F. Amerasinghe, State Responsibility for Injuries to Aliens (1967), 118–119; Lalive, *supra* fn. 16, id.

[90] See, e.g., Fatouros, *supra* fn. 13, 283–284.

[91] See, e.g., B. Goldmann, The Applicable Law: General Principles of Law—The *Lex Mercatoria*, in: J. Lew (ed.), Contemporary Problems in International Arbitration (1986), 113 et seq.; O. Lando, The Lex Mercatoria in International Commercial Arbitration, Int'l & Comp. L. Q. 34 (1985), 747 et seq.

[92] *Petroleum Development Ltd. v. Sheikh of Abu Dhabi* (1951) 18 ILR 144.

[93] Id., 149.

[94] *Ruler of Qatar v. International Maritime Oil Co.* (1953) 20 ILR 534.

[95] A. McNair, The General Principles of Law Recognized by Civilized Nations, BYIL 33 (1957), 1 et seq. However, McNair subjects the application of general principles to further conditions: firstly, the parties must not have specified the law applicable to the contract, and secondly, the host State's legal system must not be adequate for the resolution of the dispute. At present, both conditions would argue against an application of general principles in the majority of cases.

[96] Id., 7.

contract would be subject to the "general principles of law recognized by civilized nation."[97]

In the absence of a choice of law by the parties, none of the mentioned concepts finds support anymore. Their principal flaw is that contracts are incapable of existing in a legal vacuum.[98] Yet, a contractual relationship, in order to create legally binding obligations, has to be governed by a specific legal order.[99] A further corollary of the missing legal "anchorage" in a specific national law system is the problematic enforceability. A contractual agreement which is not "anchored" in any specific national law leads to delocalised arbitration[100] which, in turn, produces "floating" arbitral awards.[101] Such an arbitral award which is not linked to a national legal system generally is not enforceable.[102]

---

[97] Id., 10. See also K. Zweigert, Verträge zwischen staatlichen und nichtstaatlichen Partnern, BerDGesVölkR 5 (1964), 194, 198 et seq., who believes that "allgemeine Rechtsgrundsätze" are the most convenient body of law to govern an internationalised contract which must not be part of international public law.

[98] See *Saudi Arabia v. Arabian American Oil Co.* (1963) 27 ILR 47, 117: "It is obvious that no contract can exist in vacuo, i.e. without being based on a legal system. The conclusion of a contract is not left to the unfettered discretion of the Parties. It is necessarily related to some positive law which gives legal effects to the ...manifestations of intent made by the parties".

[99] Cf. G. Radbruch, Rechtsphilosophie (1950), 245–246.

[100] See generally J. Paulsson, Arbitration Unbound: An Award Detached from the Law of the Country of Origin, Int'l & Comp. L. Q. 30 (1981), 358 et seq.; J. Paulsson, Delocalisation of International Commercial Arbitration: When and Why It Matters, Int'l & Comp. L. Q. 32 (1983), 53 et seq. The original purpose of delocalised arbitration is to circumvent mandatory rules on the seat of arbitration. A prerequisite is thus a contractual agreement without linkage to national law.

[101] See F. A. Mann, England Rejects "Delocalised" Contracts and Arbitration, Int'l & Comp. L. Q. 33 (1984), 193, 197–198 et seq., who refers to the following statement by Lord Justice in *Bank Mellat v. Helleniki Techniki S.A.*, [1983] 3 WLR 783, 789: "Despite suggestions to the contrary by some learned writers under other systems, our jurisprudence does not recognise the concept of arbitral procedures floating in the transnational firmament, unconnected with any municipal system of law." See also W. Park, The Lex Loci Arbitri and International Commercial Arbitration, Int'l & Comp. L. Q. 32 (1983), 21 et seq.

[102] The situation is different when an international agreement which secures the enforcement of the award is applicable. However, according to article 1 of the Convention on the Recognition and Enforcement of Foreign Arbitral Awards (1958), the enforcement of such awards is, to a large extent, contingent upon the discretion of the State where enforcement is sought. See D. Di Pietro & M. Platte, Enforcement of International Arbitration Awards—The New York Convention of 1958 (2001), 179 et seq. In Germany, the admissibility and the enforceability of an award which is not linked to a national legal system is doubtful. For further references on this aspect, see W. Voit, Ausländische Schiedssprüche, in: H. J. Musielak (ed.), Kommentar zur Zivilprozessordnung (2007), § 1061(4).

In the final analysis, the application of a non-national legal order would thus generate non-enforceable awards and therefore miss the purpose of dispute settlement.[103]

3. *Customary International Law and Incorporation of International Law*

During the course of the 20th century, it was very controversial whether and under what circumstances a breach of a state contract would amount to a violation of customary international law.[104] In the past, two extreme positions in this regard had been warranted.[105] At present, it is relatively well acknowledged that certain breaches of a state contract may constitute a violation of international law.[106] Ultimately, this is a corollary of the international law principle that the characterization of an act as internationally wrongful is not affected by the internal law's characterization of the same act. However, this does not mean that an arbitral tribunal would be entitled to apply international law in any dispute arising out of a state contract but only that the national's home State may eventually be entitled to diplomatic protection on account of breach of contract and contingent upon the exhaustion of local remedies.[107]

In contrast, the application of international law to state contracts is indeed guaranteed in case of international law's incorporation in the host State's domestic law.[108] For instance, the tribunals in the case of

---

[103] According to Stoll, *supra* fn. 67, 48, when law is seen as a "Normerzwingungssystem", the lack enforcement mechanisms is the main reason for the non-existence of a proper system of law. See also Maniruzzaman, *supra* fn. 87, 147.

[104] For a summary of this controversy, see Schwebel, *supra* fn. 76, 108 et seq.; S. Schwebel, On Whether the Breach by a State of a Contract with an Alien Is a Breach of International Law, in: S. Schwebel (ed.), Justice in International Law (1994), 425 et seq.

[105] For an overview, see, e.g., L. Cavaré, La Protection des Droits Contractuels Reconnus par les Etats a des Etrangers à l'Exception des Emprunts (1956), 27 et seq.; O. Schachter, International Law in Theory and Practice, RdC 178 (1982-V), 13, 309 et seq.

[106] See, e.g., Schwebel, *supra* fn. 104, 431–432: "That is to say, the breach of such a contract by a State in ordinary commercial intercourse is not, in the predominant view, a violation of international law, but the use of sovereign authority over a State, contrary to the expectations of the parties, to abrogate or violate a contract with an alien, is a violation of international law"; C. Amerasinghe, *supra* fn. 73, 912–913.

[107] See Amerasinghe, *supra* fn. 84, 138.

[108] On this aspect of the application of international law and the variety of modalities of implementation, see, e.g., M. Herdegen, Völkerrecht (2007), 152–153; M. Shaw, International Law (2005), 128 et seq.; Cassese, *supra* fn. 26, 220 et seq.

Aminoil[109] and in the case of *SPP v. Egypt*[110] applied international law principles because they were incorporated in the national law systems. The result of this application was that domestic law was the contract's proper law insofar as it did not contravene international law.[111] Although these rulings have found vehement criticism[112] it is difficult to argue against such an application of international law. It must be clear nevertheless, that this application is entirely contingent upon the adoption of international law by the respective domestic law system.[113]

III. *Indirect Internationalisation*

The indirect internationalisation of state contracts proceeds by means of the application of private international law in order to determine the substantive law applicable to the contract.[114] In principle, this approach is in accordance with the traditional understanding of international contracts as it has been exposed in the *Serbian Loans* Case.[115] However, as can be seen in the following, legal doctrine developed means within

---

[109] *Aminoil, supra* fn. 68, para. 145.

[110] *SPP (Middle East) Ltd. v. Egypt*, ICC Arbitration No. YD/AS No. 3494, 11 March 1983, 3 ICSID Rep. 46, (1983) 22 ILM 752 (hereinafter, *SPP v. Egypt*), para. 49.

[111] Id.: "[W]e find that reference to Egyptian law must be construed so as to include such principles of international law as may be applicable and that national laws of Egypt can be relied upon only in as much as they do not contravene said principles".

[112] See, e.g., Bowett, *supra* fn. 59, 53; Maniruzzaman, *supra* fn. 69, 319; Nassar, *supra* fn. 69, 190 et seq.

[113] Consequently, the application of the international law principles as incorporated in domestic law may, at any time, be hindered by the host State through amendments of its law.

[114] On the different types of law applicable to a dispute subject to arbitration, see G. Born, International Commercial Arbitration in the United States, Commentary and Materials (1994), 98, 99–100 et seq. Accordingly, four different types have to be distinguished: (i) the law governing the substantive dispute or the law applicable to the substance; for contracts, this law is usually called the "proper law" of a contract; (ii) the law governing the arbitration agreement; (iii) the conflict of law rules applicable to each; and (iv) the law applicable to the proceedings. Paulsson, *supra* fn. 100, 367, distinguishes between (i) the law governing the contract; (ii) the rules of conflict of law; and (iii) the procedural rules. The so-called indirect internationalisation concerns the choice of the contract's proper law.

[115] Thereby, at least in the case of the application of the host State's conflict of law rules, the host State's influence on the contract is not excluded completely. Through amendments to the regulations of private international law or its *ordre publique* in particular, the contractual situation is contingent upon the host State's internal legal system. Ultimately, this is the main difference between indirect and direct internationalisation. Cf. Merkt, *supra* fn. 60, 131; Böckstiegel, *supra* fn. 7, 101 et seq. See also Sornarajah, *supra* fn. 11, 255, who, on account of this, terms this way of "internationalizing" a contract as "more sophisticated" than the direct application of a non-national system of law.

the framework of indirect internationalisation by which the contract likewise is removed completely from the State's domestic law system. Conceptually, the theories of indirect internationalisation are based on the unlimited application of the principle of party autonomy. The parties to the contract, so the argument goes, would have chosen—explicitly or implicitly—a system of law different from the host State's which in the absence of a choice would apply as the system of law most closely linked to the contract.[116] Yet, not only the unlimited application by arbitral tribunals but also the origins and consequences of this principle raise serious doubts in the context of state contracts.

1. *The Origin of the Principle of Party Autonomy*

The right to choose the law applicable to a state contract must be rooted in a system of private international law. Yet, the question of which legal order shall provide for the rules of private international law applicable to disputes concerning state contracts before international arbitral tribunals is not answered consistently by legal scholars and arbitral practice. At its root, the problem concerns the long-lasting debate about the legal nature of arbitration.[117] A traditional view asserts that in order to be binding upon the parties an arbitral award, similar to a domestic court's decision, has to be tied to a determined national law. Accordingly, the national law in force at the seat of arbitration not only gives the arbitrator his authority[118] but also gives validity to the entire arbitration process.[119] This jurisdictional view leads to the localisation of the whole arbitration process[120] and to the domestication[121] of the choice-of-law process. Thus, the determination of the substantive law applicable to the contract would have to be undertaken according to the private international law of the *lex fori*,[122] that is, the rules of conflicts of law of the State where the arbitration

[116] Paasivirta, *supra* fn. 29, 77.

[117] See A. Redfern & M. Hunter, Law and Practice of International Commercial Arbitration (2004), paras. 1-01, 2-27; P. Schlosser, Das Recht der internationalen privaten Schiedsgerichtsbarkeit (1989), 28 et seq.

[118] See, e.g., S. Jarvin, The Sources and Limits of the Arbitrator's Powers, in: J. Lew (ed.), Contemporary Problems in International Arbitration (1986), 50, 61 et seq.

[119] See, e.g., Maniruzzaman, *supra* fn. 69, 68.

[120] See, e.g., F. A. Mann, State Contracts and International Arbitration, BYIL 42 (1967), 1, 36–37 et seq.

[121] See, e.g., Grigera Naón, *supra* fn. 65, 144 et seq.

[122] The conflict of laws rules of the State which is the seat of the arbitration may also be called *lex loci arbitri* or *lex arbitri*, the former being the more exact notion.

takes place.[123] This approach was followed, for instance, by the arbitral tribunals in *Alsing*[124] and *BP v. Libya*.[125]

Several other approaches dismiss such a rigid obligation and support a certain loosening of the arbitration's linkage to the territorial jurisdiction of the State.[126] This proclivity towards delocalisation finds its explication in contractual and autonomous concepts of arbitration. For the contractual approach to the nature of arbitration the parties' agreement serves as the foundation upon which the arbitral process stands. The authority of the arbitrator is not derived from the State's sovereignty but from the mere agreement between the parties. Hence, the arbitral process and the arbitral award are not subject to the control of the State's courts.[127] Accordingly, international arbitration is independent and autonomous from any national legal system and serves exclusively to fulfil the parties' legitimate expectations of the proceedings.[128] Hence, the end—speed and flexibility of proceedings—would justify the means which is the removal of arbitration from any governmental interference.[129]

As a result of delocalisation, international arbitral tribunals would have no proper national forum and therefore no *lex fori* of their own. This lack, in turn, would allow the development of general principles of private international law (this means principles which are not formally based on a national law system) which may be applied by international arbitral tribunals in order to determine the proper law of the contract. In particular one principle thereby became the hallmark of international arbitration: the principle of party autonomy. Arbitral tribunals relied in several cases on such general principle of party autonomy and thus provided the parties with unfettered freedom to choose the substantive law applicable to the contract.[130] However, delocalisation has

---

[123] See, e.g., Mann, *supra* fn. 120, 167 et seq.; Mann, *supra* fn. 120, 4.

[124] *Alsing Trading Co. Ltd. v. The Greek State* (1956) 23 ILR 633.

[125] *BP Exploration Co. (Libya) Ltd. v. Libyan Arab Republic* (1979) 53 ILR 297 (hereinafter, *BP v. Libya*).

[126] See generally, J. Gentinetta, Befreiung der internationalen Handelsschiedsgerichtsbarkeit von der "nationalen Umklammerung"?, AWD (1969), 46 et seq.

[127] Cf. J. Paulsson, The Extent of Independence of International Arbitration from the Law of the Situs, in: J. Lew (ed.), Contemporary Problems in International Arbitration (1986), 141, 141–142.

[128] Id.

[129] Maniruzzaman, *supra* fn. 69, 70.

[130] See, e.g., *TOPCO v. Arab Republic*, *supra* fn. 81, 432–433; *Sapphire v. NIOC*, *supra* fn. 80, 171 et seq., where the arbitrator applied the parties' implied choice of law on account of "the elements of the case" or "good faith" and "good will".

been criticized for several reasons.[131] The main contention concerns the enforceability of arbitral awards rendered without prior linkage to any national legal order. Similar to the "contrat sans loi" these arbitral awards cannot make any recourse to the enforcement mechanisms of a domestic legal order and thus, in the case of refusal to comply, remain without consequences.[132] In the final analysis, without the opportunity to enforce the award, the purpose of arbitration is rendered nugatory in itself.[133] Therefore, the question of nationalised or delocalised arbitration is not so much a theoretical one but rather a practical one which concerns the proper aim of dispute settlement. Given these practical considerations the arbitrators' reliance upon party autonomy derived from general principles of private international law remains questionable.[134] In contrast, the reliance upon the private international law of the *lex fori* is in accordance with traditional approaches to international contracts and in most of the cases, would likewise bring forth the principle of party autonomy.[135]

2. *The Restrictions to the Principle of Party Autonomy*

The principle of party autonomy is the cornerstone of the state contracts' indirect internationalisation.[136] Only when the parties are deemed free to choose the law applicable to the substance of their contract may the choice of a non-state law system detach the contract from domestic jurisdiction. Therefore, the determination of whether and to what extent the principle of party autonomy finds application as regards contracts between host State and foreign investor are decisive.

a. *The Content and General Limitations of the Principle of Party Autonomy*

The doctrine of party autonomy lays down that, in principle, the parties to an international commercial contract are free to choose the

---

[131] See, e.g., H. Smit, A-National Arbitration, Tul. L. Rev. 63 (1988/1989), 629, 629–633.

[132] Park, *supra* fn. 101, 21; Stoll, *supra* fn. 67, 84.

[133] Cf. Kischel, *supra* fn. 15, 273.

[134] See Sornarajah, *supra* fn. 11, 241: "The idea of an existence of a universal system of private international law itself is a logical impossibility in that all systems of private international law are in effect national systems".

[135] In this case, however, the implementation of the principle of party autonomy would be subject to the limitations set out by the respective legislation. As a consequence, in most countries, the principle is not as unfettered as under international law.

[136] Sornarajah, *supra* fn. 11, 224, 227.

law or the legal rules applicable to the contract themselves.[137] The idea is that international business people should be enabled to fashion the contract according to their specific expectations. In essence, the principle of party autonomy is part of the freedom of contract.[138] Party autonomy, on the one hand, is an expression of the parties' need for freedom in international transactions where parties are not only competitors for commodities but also for the legal system they may offer.[139] On the other hand, it provides certainty in contractual relations. In the absence of a choice-of-law clause, the law applicable to the contract may be unknown until a court has spoken. Party autonomy expressed by choice of law makes the contractual relationship foreseeable.[140] The doctrine has found entry into several international conventions,[141] resolutions of international institutes,[142] rules of international arbitration,[143] and as a result of developments within the various national systems of conflict of laws, it is said to be independently recognised by the different legal systems of the world.[144]

Nevertheless, it can barely be contested that the application of the principle of party autonomy requires restriction in certain realms.[145] In domestic law systems, party autonomy is regularly restrained in a variety of ways, inter alia, in order to protect the weaker bargaining power[146] or the weaker overall position of one party.[147] In international undertakings the sovereignty of States requires that a State's mandatory provisions and its public policies be complied with by those who enter the

---

[137] Redfern & Hunter, *supra* fn. 117, para. 2–34.

[138] See, e.g., *The Bremen v. Zapata Off-Shore Co.*, 407 U.S. 1, 11 (1972).

[139] O. Lando, The Conflict of Laws of Contract—General Principles, RdC 189 (1984–VI), 225, 285 et seq.

[140] Id., 284.

[141] The Rome Convention on the Law Applicable to Contractual Obligations (1980), reprinted in OJ 1980 L266/1.

[142] Institut de Droit International, Arbitration between States, State Enterprises, or State Entities, and Foreign Enterprises, Session of Santiago de Compostela, 12 September 1989, Eighteenth Commission (Article 6); Institut de Droit International, La loi du contrat dans les accords entre un Etat et une personne privée étrangère, Session of Athens, 11 September 1979, Twenty-first Commission. The two resolutions are available at: www.idi-iil.org (last visited: 5 March 2010).

[143] UNCITRAL, Arbitration Rules, art. 33.1; ICC Arbitration Rules, art. 17.1.

[144] Redfern & Hunter, *supra* fn. 117, para. 2–35.

[145] For a discussion against restrictions on party autonomy in international commerce, see G. Borchers, The Internationalization of Contractual Conflicts of Law, Vand. J. Transnat'l L. 28 (1995), 421, 438 et seq.

[146] See, e.g., *Schroeder Music Publishing Co. Ltd. v. Macaulay* (1974) 3 All ER 616.

[147] See, e.g., J. Kropholler, Internationales Privatrecht (2001), 290.

respective State.[148] Finally, rules of private international law suggest that a reasonable basis for the choice of law must exist. In some way the chosen law needs to be connected to the contract. The choice of a legal system which stands aloof to the contract may invalidate the choice itself.[149]

b. *The Participation of the State as a Sovereign*

The question which arises when a sovereign State is a party to an international contract and matters of sovereignty are involved is whether the principle of party autonomy has to be restricted concerning the parties' right to choice-of-law in such a way that solely the law of the host State is applicable to the contract.[150] A majority of authors rejects such a restriction for state contracts and substantiates the parties' right to choice-of-law with the international character of the contract.[151] However, considerable arguments argue in favour of a certain restriction. Firstly, the typical feature of state contracts is their susceptibility to be altered unilaterally by an act of sovereignty. Hence, these cases concern the legitimacy of sovereign acts and therefore pertain to the realm of public law. According to prevailing doctrine public law disputes cannot be settled by courts other than those of the concerned State itself.[152] Thus, at least a strict distinction between the conduct of a State acting *iure gestionis* and acting *iure imperi* would have to be undertaken. Secondly, the principle of freedom of contract and, as corollary to it, the principle of party autonomy are outcomes of the laissez-faire mentality of the 19th century. The role of modern welfare States

[148] M. Blessing, Mandatory Rules of Law versus Party Autonomy in International Arbitration, J. Int'l Arb. 14 (1997), 23 et seq.; P. McConnaughay, Reviving the "Public Law Taboo" in International Conflict of Laws, Stan. J. Int'l L. 35 (2001), 255, 310 et seq.

[149] In the US, see The Restatement of the Law Second (Conflict of Laws) (1971), § 187; Section 1–105 of the Uniform Commercial Code (UCC). In Europe, see D. Lasok & P. Stone, Conflict of Laws in the European Community (1987), 35; C. Croff, The Applicable Law in an International Commercial Arbitration: Is It Still a Conflict of Laws Problem, Int'l Law. 16 (1982), 613, 616 et seq.

[150] Cf. H. Grigera Naón, The Evolution of International Commercial Arbitration, in: J. Bröhmer (ed.), Internationale Gemeinschaft und Menschenrechte: Festschrift für Georg Ress zum 70. Geburtstag (2005), 103, 104: "What is actually at stake…is the social function of international commercial arbitration, and once defined, if its fulfillment is better assured through largely unlimited and self-regulatory party autonomy or, instead, by introducing external limitations to such autonomy, and under certain circumstances, by excluding it".

[151] See, e.g., El Chiati, *supra* fn. 12, 43.

[152] Stoll, *supra* fn. 67, fn. 262.

cannot be compared to States' activities at this time. States nowadays have the legal obligation to act in the public interest. This interest has to be taken into account when contracts are concluded with foreign entities.[153] Finally, the principle of party autonomy presupposes the existence of equality between the contracting parties. The equality between a State and a foreign enterprise is only conceivable when a State is acting *iure gestionis*, i.e., when it is acting on a par with the private individual. The unrestrained principle of party autonomy therefore finds sole application in purely commercial matters when the State and the foreign enterprise confront each other as equals.[154]

Beside these specific arguments which argue in favour of a choice-of-law restriction when the State acting as a sovereign is involved, the abovementioned general limitations may find application likewise.[155] Sornarajah argues that in the case of state contracts the only valid choice of law could be the internal law of the host State. The only alien element in a state contract is the foreign nationality of the investor who entered voluntarily into the State and thereby subjected itself to the host State's legislation.[156] Moreover, nearly all developing countries have established elaborate foreign investment laws which regularly contain mandatory provisions of law.[157] These laws, in some cases, explicitly prohibit the choice of a law other than the local law.[158]

Nevertheless, it is still the predominant view that the principle of party autonomy governs the choice of law in international contracts between state entities and foreign investors.[159] Further, arbitral practice relies on this principle to determine the law applicable to contracts between host State and foreign investor.[160] In the final analysis, one

---

[153] Sornarajah, *supra* fn. 11, 241. Contra Böckstiegel, *supra* fn. 7, 91.
[154] Sornarajah, id., 238.
[155] See *supra* 35.
[156] Sornarajah, *supra* fn. 11, 239.
[157] See, e.g., Delaume, *supra* fn. 65, 9–10.
[158] See, e.g., 1961 Venezuelan Constitution, art. 127. For further references, see Sornarajah, *supra* fn. 4, 29 et seq.
[159] Cf. Redfern & Hunter, *supra* fn. 117, paras. 2–34 et seq. Note that generally, a differentiation between the application of the principle to commercial arbitration and investment arbitration is not made.
[160] See, for instance, the three famous Libyan nationalization cases in which the respective tribunals had to rule on exactly the same choice of law clauses and reached completely different results, namely, *BP v. Libya, supra* fn. 125, 327 et seq.; *Libyan American Oil Co. (LIAMCO) v. The Government of the Libyan Arab Republic* (1982) 62 ILR 140, 173 et seq.; *TOPCO v. Libya, supra* fn. 81, 431 et seq. See also the case of *Sapphire v. NIOC, supra* fn. 80, 171 et seq., in which the tribunal held that the parties had made an implicit choice.

cannot but be in concordance with the comparativist Hessel Yntema who, in 1952, stated the following: "Whether the parties to a legal transaction may choose the law by which it is governed and, if so, under what limitations, is a question on which…wide agreement in the judicial decisions contrasts with sharp contrariety in theoretical opinion".[161]

3. *Express Choice of Law by the Parties to the Dispute*

If the principle of party autonomy is applicable, the parties to a state contract have the right to select the law applicable to the contract. The questions which immediately follow this statement concern the range of legal systems or legal orders from which the parties may have the right to choose. Should the system be a specific legal system of a particular State or is the choice of certain parts of a system or even of legal principles that do not amount to a system proper conceivable? Is public international law a body of law which may find application to a contract between a State and a foreign enterprise?

a. *The Choice of a Genuine or Non-National Legal Order*

The choice of a genuine or non-national legal order[162] bears some difficulties. The critic chiefly points towards the existence of two major flaws which are inherent to a third legal order's choice as the applicable law to a state contract: the vagueness of the law's content and the legal uncertainty of the awards' enforceability.[163] As stated above, the same aspects make a direct governance of state contracts by such a body of rules unlikely. Further, the contention has been made that the parties' choice-of-law must refer to a defined legal system and cannot be made by choosing a body of rules or principles which in itself does not have the quality of an autonomous system of law.[164] This point of view is usually based on the dismissal of the delocalisation of arbitration and thus requires that arbitration has to be linked to a national jurisdiction. Accordingly, an arbitrator may solely apply a *lex mercatoria* or general principles of law as substantive law to the dispute when he is not tied to

---

[161] H. Yntema, "Autonomy" in Choice of Law, AJCL 1 (1952), 341, 341.

[162] This can be the *lex mercatoria*, transnational law, a-national law, general principles of law, or other bodies of law. Perhaps, the term non-national law system best describes the detachment of the rules from any specific national body of law.

[163] See, e.g., K. Highet, The Enigma of the Lex Mercatoria, Tul. L. Rev. 63 (1989), 613, 623–624; G. Delaume, Comparative Analysis as a Basis of Law in State Contracts: The Myth of the Lex Mercatoria, in: Tul. L. Rev. 63 (1989), 575, 577, 610.

[164] Mann, *supra* fn. 101, 197; Mann, *supra* fn. 120, 6; Mann, *supra* fn. 123, 563; Highet, *supra* fn. 163, 620; Park, *supra* fn. 101, 25.

a national law.[165] As a consequence, the legitimacy of the choice of a genuine legal order would be contingent upon the legitimacy of delocalised arbitration.

Yet, it is doubtful whether the latter assertion is still tenable. It is correct to say that the enforceability of arbitral awards remains dependent on their attachment to State power[166] which, of course, is subject to regulation by international agreements.[167] Based on this concept, the choice of a third legal order may be valid when the national legal order which governs the contract provides for such a choice or the particular State is bound by a convention that foresees such a choice. In this case, the link of arbitration to a legal system which gives the proceedings their validity and secures the enforceability of awards is maintained. The point is not whether such a body of rules may be the exclusive[168] legal system of a contract but whether it can be chosen as the applicable law to the substance of the contract. In sum, the choice of a genuine legal order may not be criticised from the vantage point of private international law when the national legal system which is at the root of the arbitration and of the dispute accepts such a choice. Hence, the question of whether such a body of rules may be chosen by the parties is not contingent upon the legitimacy of delocalised arbitration. When the choice of an autonomous legal system can be made in the framework of a national legal system, the delocalisation of the arbitral proceeding is not necessary in order to obtain the application of such a body of rules.[169]

The indispensable prerequisite is thus the existence of provisions of national law systems or international conventions which entitle the parties to an arbitral proceeding to select the law applicable to

---

[165] Cf. Highet, *supra* fn. 163, 619.

[166] See C. Brower, The Privatization of Rules of Decision in International Commercial Arbitration, in: R. Briner (ed.), Law of International Business and Dispute Settlement in the 21st Century—Liber Amicorum Karl-Heinz Böckstiegel (2001), 111, 112.

[167] See Smit, *supra* fn. 131, 641. Above all, mention has to be made of the ICSID Convention and the United Nations Convention on the Recognition and Enforcement of Foreign Arbitral Awards (1958).

[168] Highet, *supra* fn. 163, 613.

[169] See P. McConnaughay, The Risks and Virtues of Lawlessness: A "Second Look" at International Commercial Arbitration, Nw. U. L. Rev. 93 (1998/1999), 453, 466: "Both sides of this debate emerged somewhat victorious when nations began to legislate the delocalization of international arbitrations occurring on their soil: the proponents of delocalization achieved their substantive goal while the territorialists made their procedural point".

their dispute from a wider range of options. The point has been made that the term "rules of law" used in choice-of-law provisions relates precisely to such an option.[170] This term is used, for instance, in article 28(1) of the UNCITRAL Model Law on International Commercial Arbitration[171] and in article 42(1) of the ICSID Convention and has been adopted by several countries in their respective arbitration laws.[172] Thereby, a broad notion of party autonomy has been favoured. The parties shall not be restrained on the election of a specific national legal order but may be free to choose from several sources. This includes the opportunity for the parties to agree on rules of law that have been elaborated on by an international forum but have not yet been incorporated into any national legal system.[173] The purpose of such an entitlement is to satisfy the parties' strive for neutral regulations which heighten the potential to be part of an impartial and fair international proceeding.[174] Nonetheless, the application of such rules remains doubtful. As for the *lex mercatoria* commentators are completely split about its legal contents and its legitimacy.[175] In contrast, the application of the UNIDROIT

[170] K. P. Berger, The German Arbitration Law of 1998—First Experiences, in: R. Briner (ed.), Law of International Business and Dispute Settlement in the 21st Century—Liber Amicorum Karl-Heinz Böckstiegel (2001), 31, 40.

[171] The first sentence of art. 28(1) of the UNCITRAL Model Law on International Commercial Arbitration (1985) reads as follows: "(1) The arbitral tribunal shall decide the dispute in accordance with such *rules of law* as are chosen by the parties as applicable to the substance" (emphasis added).

[172] See, e.g., France: Code of Civil Procedure, art. 1496 (amended 1991); Germany: ZPO § 1051 I,II (amended 1997); Italy: Code of Civil Procedure, art. 834(1) (amended 1994); Netherlands: Dutch Code of Civil Procedure, art. 1054(2) (amended 1986); Switzerland: Private International Law Act 1987, art. 187(1). Art. 46(1)(b) of the UK Arbitration Act 1996 contains the wording "if the parties so agree, in accordance with such other considerations as are agreed by them" which is regarded to have a similar effect. For a recent examination of this point, see G. Rühl, Party Autonomy in the Private International Law of Contracts: Transatlantic Convergence and Economic Efficiency, CLPE Research Paper 4/2007, Vol. 3 No. 1 (2007), available at: http://ssrn.com (last visited: 4 March 2010), 1, 20 et seq., who concludes that it seems that "in both the United States and Europe the view that parties should be allowed to choose a non-state body of law is gaining ground".

[173] See Explanatory Note by the UNCITRAL Secretariat on the UNCITRAL Model Law on International Commercial Arbitration which, however, is not an official commentary on the Model Law but serves informational purposes only. The commentary is available at: www.uncitral.org (last visited: 8 March, 2010).

[174] See, e.g., Brower, *supra* fn. 166, 111.

[175] For a comprehensive compilation of both stances, see T. Carbonneau (ed.), Lex Mercatoria and Arbitration (1998).

Principles can hardly be said to fail because of the absence of concrete contents.[176]

On the contrary, for national legal systems which did not adopt a regulation using similar terms or is not bound by international conventions that provide for such a choice, the possibility to choose the application of rules not generated by a national legal system is not obvious. In this case, recourse would have to be made to the theories of delocalised arbitration that detach the arbitral process from the law of the State where the arbitration takes place. This is not the place to discuss the legitimacy and efficiency of arbitration's delocalisation. It seems, however, that legal doctrine still has not overcome the obstacles generated by such an approach, chiefly the enforcement of the awards and of interim measures.[177]

b. *The Choice of Public International Law*

The legitimacy to choose public international law as the proper law of a contract between a State being an original subject of international law and a natural or juridical person which does not hold full-fledged international legal capacity has been denied by several authors. Such dismissal, on the one hand, is based on the presumed existence of international law's negative intention to govern such relations. This intention is supposed to be inherent in a legal system which was devised to govern exclusively the relations between States.[178] This point of view is confronted by Mann who asserts that the nature of private international law allows the application of legal systems of which the assignee is not a legal subject.[179] However, as Kischel rightly points out, the correct solution to the problem does not exclusively concern the legal capacity of the assignee but the nature of the assignment by private international law. If the individual were entitled by the assignment to conclude internationally binding agreements and thereby to create international law, the lack of its capacity to do so would be unduly circumvented and the assignment under private international law would

[176] For a discussion, see P. Mankowski, Überlegungen zur sach- und interessengerechten Rechtswahl für Verträge des internationalen Wirtschaftsverkehrs, RIW 2003, 2, 11 et seq.

[177] Paulsson, *supra* fn. 100, 375–376.

[178] See, e.g., Stoll, *supra* fn. 67, 89, who spoke of the so-called "negativer Geltungswille des Völkerrechts".

[179] A. F. Mann, Die Verträge der Völkerrechtssubjekte und die Parteiautonomie, in: Juristische Fakultät der Universität Freiburg (Schweiz) (ed.), Ius Et Lex—Festgabe zum 70. Geburtstag von Max Gutzwiller (1959), 465, 481 et seq.

create new legal capacities.[180] Suffice it to say that such effect is not foreseen by private international law. Its application entails merely the application of a further legal order but does not lead to a new status within this order.[181] Hence, rules of private international law do not contradict public international law's application to state contracts. Neither does the individual's missing capacity to conclude international agreements. The argument that the choice of international law is not valid because it would entail the State's international responsibility irrespective of the private party's lack of legal capacity[182] similarly does not hit the mark. The application of international law to state contracts solely means that the contractual duties are determined according to international law. However, the stipulations thereby do not become part of international law and do not generate proper obligations under international law. Hence, a contract under international law is not norm-generating ("normerzeugend") but only norm-subordinated ("normunterworfen") whereas an international treaty is both norm-generating and norm-subordinated.[183] As a consequence, neither international law itself nor private international law opposes the legitimacy of the application of international law to state contracts.

On the contrary, the inadequacy of international law to govern relations between States and individuals is exhorted continuously.[184] The application of the principle of *pacta sunt servanda* to contracts, by analogy or by virtue of the universal character of the principle, is not deemed to produce well-balanced solutions in the concrete case but rather lead to arbitrariness and unpredictable results.[185] Furthermore, the *rebus sic stantibus* principle which constitutes an accepted exception to the principle of *pacta sunt servanda* would entitle the host State to the contract's termination under certain circumstances.[186] The undifferentiated application of the *pacta sunt servanda* principle would overlook the lack of equality between States and foreign corporations which

[180] Kischel, *supra* fn. 15, 290–292.

[181] Id., 292.

[182] See, e.g., S. Toope, Mixed International Arbitration (1990), 77 et seq., with further references; Grigera Naón, *supra* fn. 65, 134.

[183] Kischel, *supra* fn. 15, 292, provides a convincing discussion.

[184] See, e.g., Stoll, *supra* fn. 67, 79, where the author upholds a combination of both approaches; Sornarajah, *supra* fn. 11, 259; Z. Douglas, The Hybrid Foundations of Investment Treaty Arbitration, BYIL 74 (2003), 151, 198.

[185] Contra Lillich, *supra* fn. 64, 107 et seq.

[186] Sornarajah, *supra* fn. 11, 262.

is a pre-eminent condition for the legitimacy of the former.[187] Finally, it has been pointed out that to a broad extent, investment disputes are concerned with property-related matters of domestic law. Since international law by definition does not regulate such property-related questions under domestic law systems, an application of international law would indispensably lead to a *renvoi* to domestic law.[188] This point of view is rejected by other commentators who contend that international law indeed contains sufficiently elaborated rules for contracts. In particular, the increasing case law provide for appropriate norms to resolve contract issues.[189]

Notwithstanding this dispute, the legitimacy of a choice-of-law cannot be measured by the suitability of the choice but is exclusively a question of its lawfulness.[190] Even if the choice of international law as applicable law represented a "leap into the unknown" and entailed improper solutions, this would not produce the unlawfulness of the choice and thereby its illegitimacy. When the choice of international law is lawful under the legal system that provides the state contract and the arbitral process with validity, its vagueness has no effect to the contrary. Plainly, the choice of international law would not be a very determinative choice but a legitimate one nevertheless.

Maybe on account of this, the mere choice of international law is seldom used by host States and foreign investors. Notably, among the state contracts which are publicly available[191] there exist only very few which refer exclusively to international law. In a case cited by Leben, he thought that most probably, the participation of three States (Russia, Kazakhstan, and Oman) prevented agreement on one internal law and thus international law was chosen.[192] More often, however, the parties

[187] Sornarajah, id.; Stoll, *supra* fn. 67, 88–90.

[188] Douglas, *supra* fn. 184, id., 198.

[189] See, e.g., Lillich, *supra* fn. 64, 108.

[190] The lawfulness, however, is dependent upon the conflict of laws rules of the respective *lex loci arbitri*. In Germany, for instance, the legitimacy of the choice of public international law as the law applicable to the substance of a contract is still very controversial. See D. Martiny, Art. 27 EGBGB, in: Münchener Kommentar zum BGB (2006), art. 27, para. 41.

[191] Usually, enterprises and States do not publish the contents of their contracts. For a collection of concession contracts, see E. Fischer & T. Wälde, A Collection of International Concessions and Related Instruments, vol. 7 (1988).

[192] "The contract shall be governed by general international legal principles, including the principle that agreements of the parties shall be observed (pacta sunt servanda)", as cited by Leben, *supra* fn. 64, 270.

to a state contract will choose international law only in combination with domestic law.[193]

In sum, the choice of public international law as the applicable law to a state contract is possible insofar as the governing legal system allows such a choice. However, the vagueness of international law in regulating contractual relations between States and private individuals hitherto seems to have prevented parties to a state contract from making such choice.

c. *The Choice of the Host State's Internal Law*

The majority of state contracts in the world include a choice-of-law clause that declares the host State's internal law as the applicable law to the contract.[194] The application of the host State's private international law as the law which designates the proper law and the host State's municipal law as the proper law of the contract finds further support in some fundamental aspects of foreign direct investment. Most importantly, the investment physically exists in the territory of the host State. Moreover, the territory of the host State is likely to be the place of the contract's performance. Finally, it is the investor that enters into the realm of the host State. By entering into this realm, one might presume, the foreign investor must accept the conditions which are set up by the

[193] See Leben, *supra* fn. 64, 289–290, who differentiates four different groups: (i) a combination of internal law and principles of international law; (ii) a combination of internal law and principles of international law including decisions of international tribunals; (iii) application of international law only when internal law is in contradiction to the former; and (iv) gap filling application of international law. For a recent case see e.g., *Duke Energy Electroquil Partners & Electroquil S.A. v. Republic of Ecuador*, ICSID Case No. ARB/04/19, Award, 18 August 2008, paras. 194 et seq.

[194] It is interesting to note that the opinion of authors is inconsistent even with regard to this objective statement. On the one hand, see R. Kreindler, The Law Applicable to International Investment Disputes, in: N. Horn (ed.), Arbitrating Foreign Investment Disputes (2004), 401, 403 et seq., who contends that the choice of the host State's internal law is seldom. On the other hand, see Leben, *supra* fn. 5, 637; Leben, *supra* fn. 64, 266, Paasivirta, *supra* fn. 29, 57, who contend that the law of the host State is the most common choice in state contracts. Ultimately, the choice of law in state contracts is the reflection of the negotiation power of the parties. In international loan contracts, for instance, the parties regularly agree on the application of the system of law which is favoured by the lender. The higher the competition among interested corporations and the more powerful the host country, the more likely is the choice of the host State's municipal law as governing law and the submission of disputes to the jurisdiction of the courts of the host State. For a loan contract which refers disputes to the host State's courts, see, e.g., Contract between the Central Bank of Chile and Exxon Minerals Chile Inc., reprinted in Fischer & Wälde, *supra* fn. 191, 390 et seq. For a recent case see *RSM Production Corporation v. Grenada*, ICSID Case No. ARB/05/14, Award, 13 March 2009, paras. 12 et seq.

host State.[195] Hence, it can be asserted that the contract has the closest link to the host State's municipal law and would thus be applicable in the absence of a choice of law by the parties.[196]

4. *Implied Choice*

In several cases the arbitrators were confronted with the absence of a choice-of-law clause in the contract.[197] The intention of the parties or the circumstances surrounding the negotiation process did not result in a choice of applicable law by the parties. Often, the arbitral tribunals concerned reached the conclusion that international public law or some kind of international legal order was applicable to the contract nevertheless.[198] This result was usually inferred from the existence of certain types of clauses such as stabilisation clauses and international arbitration clauses in the contract which were deemed to embody the parties' implicit choice to apply a system of law different from national law or even a "negative choice" excluding the host country's domestic legal system.[199] At present, the effect of such clauses to internationalise state contracts is generally denied.

This especially holds true for stabilisation clauses. These clauses, which had their heydays in the 1970s and 1980s, essentially obligated the host State not to amend the legal regime that existed at the time of the contract.[200] In arbitral practice and legal writings the clause was held to evince the parties' intention to subject the contract to international law. However, not only this effect[201] but also the legitimacy of such a restriction to sovereignty[202] was heavily criticized. Nowadays,

---

[195] Sornarajah, *supra* fn. 11, 233.

[196] Sornarajah, id., 237; J. Cherian, Investment Contracts and Arbitration (1975), 22. See also F. A. Mann, Further Studies in International Law (1990), 266, where the author contends that the search of the proper law has to be carried out according to the ordinary rules but that the status of the State party "is a circumstance of great impact".

[197] See, e.g., *Benvenuti et Bonfant v. People's Republic of the Congo*, ICSID Case No. ARB/77/2, Award, 8 August 1980, 1 ICSID Rep. 330; *SPP v. Egypt*, *supra* fn. 110.

[198] Cf. Sornarajah, *supra* fn. 63, 107 et seq.

[199] See El-Kosheri & Riad, *supra* fn. 69, 275.

[200] For an instructive examination of the effect of stabilisation clauses, see Merkt, *supra* fn. 60. For a recent examination, see M. Coale, Stabilization Clauses in International Petroleum Transactions, Denv. J. Int'l L. & Pol'y 30 (2002), 217 et seq.

[201] For a detailed examination, see Merkt, *supra* fn. 60, 124 et seq.

[202] See Sornarajah, *supra* fn. 11, 255:

> That there could be a restriction on domestic legislative activity of a state by a treaty concluded between states is well recognised in international law. But, it has never been recognised that such sovereignty could be surrendered to a foreign

the clause only seldom finds entry into a contract and its effects are deemed to be comparatively remote.[203] In any event, the opinion that such clauses would justify a wholesale application of international law is barely tenable anymore.[204]

Further, the referral of a dispute to international arbitration was deemed to trigger the internationalisation of a contract. Accordingly, such an arbitration clause implied that the parties to the contract intended to set up a self-regulating normative framework the application of which would entail a circumvention of the State's discretionary powers.[205] As a consequence, the inclusion of such a clause was regarded as an indicator of the parties' implied choice of a system of law which is not the national order of the host State but international law.[206] The function of an arbitral clause, however, is to express the consent of the parties to arbitrate and to establish an obligation to arbitrate. Moreover, the arbitral agreement is the basic source of the powers of the arbitral tribunal.[207] In short, it affects jurisdiction and not choice of law.[208] Furthermore, the acceptance of an implied choice of law would

---

> private entity, which had voluntarily entered the territory of the state in search of profits. It takes an ordinary temerity to suggest that such a surrender of sovereignty is even a possibility (footnote omitted).

[203] See, e.g., A. Al Faruque, Validity and Efficacy of Stabilisation Clauses—Legal Protection vs. Functional Value, J. Int'l Arb. 23 (2006), 317, 334:

> While it is possible to conclude that stabilisation clauses stricto sensu are legally valid contractual undertakings, in practice, their efficacy can be severely eroded, since the state may exercise its inalienable sovereign power to enact such legislation as it deems appropriate in the public interest…the protective value of a stabilisation clause lies not in barring the state from exercising legislative power for immanent public interest, but in the fact that the presence may ensure compensation for any breach, and may result in a higher amount of compensation if the action of the state in question is not founded on good faith or is discriminatory.

[204] For the effect on the applicable law of stabilisation agreements in recent cases, see *Aguaytia Energy LLC v. Republic of Peru*, ICSID Case No. ARB/06/13, Award, 11 December 2008, paras. 71 et seq.; *Duke Energy International Peru Investmets No. 1, Ltd. v. Republic of Peru*, ICSID Case No. ARB/03/28, Award, 18 August 2008, paras. 157 et seq. Further see T. Wälde & G. Ndi, Stabilizing International Investment Commitments: International Law versus Contract Interpretation, Tex. Int'l L. J. 31 (1996), 215, 241: "This goal [of internationalization] can be achieved primarily, and perhaps exclusively, through the medium of a choice-of-law provision which places the relationship under the aegis of international law as the governing law of the agreement".

[205] See, e.g., M. Sornarajah, The International Law on Foreign Investment (2004), 413 et seq.

[206] *TOPCO v. Libya*, *supra* fn. 81, 431 et seq.

[207] See generally, Redfern & Hunter, *supra* fn. 117, para. 1–08.

[208] Cf. Bowett, *supra* fn. 59, 52; Delaume, *supra* fn. 65, 6.

undermine the choice-of-law system of institutional arbitral rules which require the parties' positive actions to justify an assumption of choice of law.[209] It is true that submission of a dispute to international arbitration will entail international law's application when the arbitral rules to which the dispute has been submitted provide for its application in the absence of a choice of law.[210] Yet, this effect is not an implied choice of the parties but a consequence of the respective arbitral rules.

IV. *Conclusion*

It has been demonstrated that a direct internationalisation which transfers a contract between a foreign investor and a host State into the international sphere is not conclusive. The application of a non-state law system to such a contract by the parties' express choice of law is contingent upon the lawfulness of this choice under the respective *lex fori* and the unrestricted validity of the principle of party autonomy. The fulfilment of both conditions would have to be examined in each case. However, even in this case the host State's domestic law remains applicable to a certain extent: on the one hand, international law or an a-national law would have to resort to a *renvoi* to domestic law in order to determine certain property-related questions; on the other hand, the application of the private international law does not avoid the application of the host State's mandatory laws. Yet, taking into account that the choice of law in state contracts usually refers to the host State's domestic law and that it is this law which has the closest relation to the contract, it has to be concluded that in the absence of international investment treaties, a foreign investor will have to rely on the host State's domestic law in order to remedy contractual breaches. For eventual violations of international law, the investor's fate is still dependent upon the willingness of its home State to espouse a claim of diplomatic protection. The following chapters will examine whether and to what extent this situation is altered by the establishment of an investment treaty regime.

[209] C. Schreuer, The ICSID Convention—A Commentary (2001), 424–425; Delaume, *supra* fn. 65, 798–799.

[210] See, for instance, the second sentence of art. 42(1) of the ICSID Convention.

2. THE REGIME ESTABLISHED BY INVESTMENT TREATIES

A. Stocktaking: The Worldwide Network of Bilateral and Multilateral Investment Treaties

I. *The Evolution of the Investment Treaty Network*

Investment treaties are often seen as successors to the FCN the conclusion of which were driven by developed countries throughout the 19th and the first half of the 20th centuries.[1] These FCN were chiefly aimed at the facilitation of trade and the regulation of foreign investment and protection of foreign property.[2] After the establishment of the GATT, these instruments lost importance and the goal of investment protection entailed the bilateral conclusion of investment treaties.[3] The succeeding creation of a worldwide network of investment treaties can be categorized into three different periods taking into account the nature of the treaties signed and the signatory States. The first wave of treaty conclusions commenced at the end of the 1950s and concerned treaties which exclusively provided for State—State arbitration.[4] The signatory States were mainly European States and developing countries in Asia and Africa. The second wave of treaty conclusion set in at the end of the

---

[1] See, e.g., T. Shenkin, Trade-Related Investment Measures in Bilateral Investment Treaties and the GATT: Moving toward a Multilateral Investment Treaty, U. Pitt. L. Rev. 55 (1994), 541, 570 et seq.

[2] See H. Walker, Modern Treaties of Friendship, Commerce and Navigation, Minn. L. Rev. 42 (1958), 805, 822 et seq., who contends that the protection of foreign property was the main purpose of the treaties. Contra K. Vandevelde, The BIT Program: A Fifteen-Year Appraisal in the Development and Expansion of Bilateral Investment Treaties, Am. Soc'y Int'l L. Proc. 86 (1992), 532, 533: "The early FCNs were dedicated largely to the establishment of trade relations between the countries, although they did have some minor property-protection provisions". However, the FNC did not provide for a dispute settlement forum or a dispute settlement procedure. On account of this, the granted rights lacked enforceability.

[3] See, e.g., Vandevelde, *supra* fn. 2, 534; J. Salacuse, BIT by BIT: The Growth of Bilateral Investment Treaties and Their Impact on Foreign Investment in Developing Countries, Int'l Law. 24 (1990), 655, 656–657; S. Gudgeon, United States Bilateral Investment Treaties: Comment on Their Origin, Purpose and General Treatment Standard, Int'l Tax & Bus. L. 4 (1986), 105 et seq.

[4] The term "State—State arbitration" refers to an arbitral proceeding which is not open to private individuals but grants rights to commence arbitration against the host State exclusively to the respective home State of the foreign investor.

so-called New International Economic Order in the 1980s. More countries such as China and several countries from the Easter European communist bloc joined the investment treaty system. In addition, the concluded treaties evinced a higher degree of diversification. In addition to the traditional treaties, new types of treaties included direct investor—host State arbitration[5] for disputes concerning the amount of compensation due to expropriation or even for all kinds of disputes. Finally, from the 1990s onward, the third wave consisted of an explosive growth of treaties and the almost unanimous acceptance of modern types of investment treaties which provided for direct investor—host State arbitration for all or at least, a wide range of disputes.[6] Besides the fall of communism, this unprecedented growth was mainly due to the fact that not only developed States entered into treaties with developing countries but also that developing countries among themselves opted for the negotiation of proper treaty programmes.[7]

II. *The Reasons for the Emergence of Investment Treaties*

The reasons why States conclude investment protection treaties have often been discussed.[8] On the capital-exporting countries' side the point is clear: the protection of their own nationals' property. Investment treaties should overcome the flaws of diplomatic protection and thus stabilize and foster foreign investments.[9] On the capital-importing

---

[5] The terms "direct investor—host State arbitration" or "investor—host State arbitration" refer to arbitral proceedings between a private individual, i.e., the foreign investor, and a State which hosts the investor's investment. Traditionally, arbitrations between an individual and a State have been called "mixed arbitrations".

[6] For a more detailed description of the evolution, see R. Dolzer & M. Stevens, Bilateral Investment Treaties (1995), 10–11; Salacuse, *supra* fn. 3, 656 et seq.; J. Salacuse & N. Sullivan, Do BITs Really Work?: An Evaluation of Bilateral Investment Treaties and Their Grand Bargain, Harv. Int'l L. J. 46 (2005), 67, 71 et seq.

[7] See J. Salacuse, *supra* fn. 3, 658–659; Dolzer & Stevens, *supra* note 6, 8–10. See also K. Vandevelde, U.S. Bilateral Investment Treaties: The Second Wave, Mich. J. Int'l L. 14 (1993), 621, 653 et seq., who holds that the entry into BIT negotiations by the US was a signal of support for political events.

[8] For a summary, see A. Guzman et al., Competing for Capital: The Diffusion of Bilateral Investment Treaties 1960–2000, 2005 American Law & Economics Association Annual Meeting, Working Paper, 1, 165 et seq., available at: http//papers.ssrn.com (last visited: 30 October 2010).

[9] See, e.g., Salacuse & Sullivan, *supra* fn. 6, 79 et seq.; K. Vandevelde, United States Investment Treaties: Policy and Practice (1992), 20–22; K. Vandevelde, Investment Liberalization and Economic Development: The Role of Bilateral Investment Treaties, Colum. J. Transnat'l L. 36 (1998), 501, 506 et seq.

countries' side, by contrast, the discussion remains unsettled. The arguments brought forward range from a prisoner's dilemma[10] over coercive theories[11] to trade-off aspects which claim that developing countries were simply of the opinion that they would somehow gain by concluding these treaties[12] or that they even did not know what they were doing.[13]

Notwithstanding continuous doubts concerning economic aspects, investment treaties appear to be favourable to capital-importing countries in at least three regards: Firstly, even if remotely, the existence of BITs may be expected to contribute to attracting FDI by effectively reducing related risks.[14] Secondly, the legal system the creation of which is required by BITs is a cornerstone of political stability and the rule of law and investment treaties may thus contribute not only to economic growth but also to the political development of a country.[15] Finally, the

---

[10] A. Guzman, Why LDCs Sign Treaties That Hurt Them: Explaining the Popularity of Bilateral Investment Treaties, Va. J. Int'l L. 38 (1997/1998), 639, 670: "If other LDCs have not signed such treaties, a country that does sign one will gain an important advantage, and if other countries have already signed BITs, a country that signs one will eliminate the advantage those other countries had in the competition for foreign investment."

[11] Guzman et al., *supra* fn. 8, 31: "Though we do not believe the pursuit of or entry into BITs is explicitly stipulated in formal loan conditions, there may be more subtle pressures on a state in balance-of-payments difficulties to use these treaties to attract foreign capital".

[12] R. Dolzer, New Foundations of the Law of Expropriation of Alien Property, AJIL 75 (1981), 553, 567 et seq. Ultimately, this argumentation is based on the assumption of a direct link between foreign direct investment and economic growth. However, this assumption is not as clear as expected either. See K. Vandevelde, The Economics of Bilateral Investment Treaties, Harv. Int'l L. J. 41 (2000), 469, 498 et seq.

[13] Supposedly, in some cases, a bilateral investment treaty was signed merely because a formal agreement had to be signed on the occasion of a state visit. At that time, the effects of bilateral investment treaties were apparently largely underestimated by developing countries' representatives.

[14] See, e.g., Salacuse & Sullivan, *supra* fn. 6, 111 et seq.; G. Wegen & M. Raible, Unterschätzt die deutsche Wirtschaft die Wirksamkeit des völkerrechtlichen Investitionsschutzes?, SchiedsVZ 2006, 225, 235–236. It is very likely that this effect will increase given the investors' growing awareness of the potential security which is provided by the treaty system.

[15] A. Reinisch, The Future of Investment Arbitration, in: C. Binder et al. (eds.), International Investment Law for the 21st Century (2009), 894, 902; M. Reisman & R. Sloane, Indirect Expropriation and Its Valuation in the BIT Generation, BYIL 74 (2003), 115, 117 et seq.:

> Hence, in a BIT regime the host state must do far more than open its door to foreign investment and refrain from overt expropriation. It must establish and maintain an appropriate legal, administrative, and regulatory framework, the legal environment that modern investment theory has come to recognize as a *conditio sine qua non* of the success of private enterprise.

increase in active participation in the investment treaty system by developing countries assures that outward investment stemming from these countries finds equal protection.[16]

III. *The Present Existence of a Worldwide Network of Investment Treaties*

At present, more than 2700 bilateral investment treaties have been signed[17] and roughly 75% of signed treaties have entered in force.[18] Moreover, several multilateral investment agreements such as the ECT[19] or the Framework Agreement on the ASEAN Investment Area[20] have been concluded and entered into force. Finally, the treaties of the worldwide network of bilateral free trade agreements and regional trade promotion agreements, such as and most importantly, the NAFTA, contain chapters on investment protection which mirror the provisions of bilateral investment treaties.[21] Taken altogether, this network embraces more than 5400 legal instruments on investment protection.[22]

---

[16] See, Reinisch, id., 901–902.

[17] By the end of 2008, the total number of signed BITs amounted to 2767. See UNCTAD, Recent Developments in International Investment Agreements (2008–June 2009), IIA Monitor No. 3 (2009), 2, available at: www.unctad.org (last visited: 8 March 2010). The country which concluded the highest number of treaties is Germany. For an overview of all German treaties signed and entered into force, see Bundesministerium für Wirtschaft und Technologie, Übersicht über die bilateralen Investitionsförderungs- und -schutzverträge (IFV) der Bundesrepublik Deutschland, 28 March 2008, available at: www.bmwi.de (last visited: 8 March 2010).

[18] UNCTAD, The Entry into Force of Bilateral Investment Treaties (BITs), IIA Monitor No. 3 (2006), 2, available at: www.unctad.org (last visited: 8 March 2010).

[19] The Energy Charter Treaty was signed in December 1994 and entered into legal force in April 1998. To date, the treaty has been signed or acceded to by 51 States plus the European Communities. See About the Charter, available at: www.encharter.org (last visited: 5 April 2010).

[20] See Framework Agreement on the ASEAN Investment Area (1998), Protocol on Dispute Settlement Mechanism, Manila, 20 November 1996 available at: www.aseansec.org (last visited: 15 April 2010); ASEAN Protocol on Enhanced Dispute Settlement Mechanism, Vientiane, 29 November 2004, available at: www.aseansec.org (last visited: 15 April 2010). It is worthy to note that the agreement and the protocols provide for the creation of a proper dispute settlement mechanism.

[21] Chapter 11 of the North American Free Trade Agreement, 17 December 1992 (1993) 32 ILM 289.

[22] See, UNCTAD, International Investment Rule-Making: Stocktaking, Challenges and the Way forward, UNCTAD Series on International Investment Policies for Development (2008), 15, available at: www.unctad.org (last visited: 8 March 2010). This estimation takes into account the number of existing free trade agreements with chapters on investment protection. To the author's knowledge, no exact number of

A survey of the most recent developments in the investment treaty network shows some remarkable patterns. First, the continuing conclusion of BITs in 2009 demonstrates that the global economic and financial crisis did not have a negative effect on the system.[23] And although the last years saw a decline in the total number of treaties concluded compared to the explosive growth rate in the years between 1995 and 2005, the growth is still considerable and robust.[24] Second, the increased role played by developing countries in concluding BITs has gained momentum. Nowadays, a substantial percentage of all BITs concluded has been between developing countries. This trend is fostered by the fact that in recent years, outward investment originating from emerging economies increased. At present, there are three developing countries (China, Egypt, and the Republic of Korea) among the top 10 signatories of BITs worldwide.[25] Finally, a trend towards the renegotiation of existing treaties can be discerned. Several States are undertaking revisions of their treaty programme in order to clarify treaty provisions, reassess the balancing of public and private interests, or include modern protection standards.[26]

IV. *The Creation of Customary International Law through Investment Treaties*

Further, short mention has to be made of the question whether the obligations under BITs and MITs bear also upon non-contracting States. In the 1980s, some authors endorsed the point of view that the content of several substantive provisions of investment treaties contributed to the creation of customary international law in such a way that in the end the investment treaty standard itself became part of customary international law.[27] Chiefly, the so-called "Hull formula"[28]

presently existing effective instruments of investment protection exists. The Compendium on International Investment Instruments by UNCTAD is probably the most exhaustive compilation of investment treaties. The compendium is searchable online by keywords, countries, categories and dates and is available at: www.unctad.org (last visited: 15 April 2010).

[23] See, UNCTAD, *supra* fn. 17, id.

[24] See, UNCTAD, *supra* fn. 22, 23.

[25] See, id., 35–38. Accordingly, by end 2007, more than 690 BITs had been concluded among developing countries, constituting about 27 % of all BITs.

[26] Id., 25.

[27] F. A. Mann, British Treaties for the Promotion and Protection of Investments, BYIL 52 (1981), 241, 249 et seq.

[28] For the "Hull formula" see *supra* Introduction, fn. 8.

whereby the compensation for expropriation has to be "prompt, adequate and effective" was held to be revived by investment treaties. As reasons for this creation, mention was made of the large number of treaties and their broad scope as well as the proof of the standard's acceptance represented by the consent given to the treaties by States which formerly objected to the validity of the standard.[29]

The argumentation of the concept's detractors has not been altered throughout the last two decades.[30] The inclusion of a similar standard of protection in some bilateral investment treaties does not meet the conditions necessary for the creation of customary international law. Even if all treaties contained the same clause, which is by no means the case, this would not suffice to affirm the creation of customary international law. It is undisputed in international law doctrine that in order for customary rules to ripen into customary international law, two elements are required: state practice and *opinio iuris*, that is, the general consideration of the rule as obligatory.[31] Since none of both elements can be deemed to be fulfilled by investment treaties, they do not constitute customary international law. The treaties' protective standards do not bind non-contracting parties and solely the investors of the respective contracting parties may enjoy the protection

---

[29] Mann, *supra* fn. 27, 249 et seq. More recently, see M. Byers, Custom, Power and the Power of Rules: International Relations and Customary International Law (1999), 59, where the author contends that investment treaties may have generated the return of the "Hull formula"; S. Schwebel, The Influence of Bilateral Investment Treaties on Customary International Law, Am. Soc'y Int'l L. Proc. 98 (2004), 27, 27:

> Customary international law governing the treatment of foreign investment has been reshaped to embody the principles of law found in more than two thousand concordant bilateral investment treaties. With the conclusion of such a cascade of parallel treaties, the international community has vaulted over the traditional divide between capital-exporting ad capital-importing states and fashioned an essentially unified law of foreign investment.

[30] For the 1980s period, see O. Schachter, Compensation for Expropriation, 78 AJIL (1984), 121 et seq.; M. Sornarajah, State Responsibility and Bilateral Investment Treaties, 20 JWTI (1986), 79 et seq. For the 1990s period, see M. Sornarajah, The International Law on Foreign Investment (1994), 357 et seq.; B. Kishoiyian, The Utility of Bilateral Investment Treaties in the Formulation of Customary International Law, 14 Nw. J. Int'l L. & Bus. (1994), 327 et seq. More recently, see A. Al Faruque, Creating Customary International Law through Bilateral Investment Treaties: A Critical Appraisal, 44 Indian J. Int'l L. (2004), 292 et seq.; B. Görs, Internationales Investitionsrecht (2004), 180–181; S. Hindelang, Bilateral Investment Treaties, Custom and a Healthy Investment Climate, JWIT 5 (2004), 789 et seq.

[31] See, e.g., A. Cassese, International Law (2005), 156 et seq.

provided for. Hence, investment protection treaties remain *lex specialis inter partes*.[32]

B. The Consent to Investment Arbitration in Investment Treaties

I. *Three Methods of Establishing Consent in International Investment Arbitration*

The consent of both parties to settle a dispute through arbitration is the cornerstone of all kinds of arbitration. Hence, every arbitral proceeding is contingent upon the consensus of the parties to arbitrate.[33] This requirement can be inferred from the consensual character of dispute resolution by arbitral means.[34]

The most common way to give consent to arbitration is by direct agreement between the concerned parties.[35] This can be done by a singular arbitration agreement or through the inclusion of a consent clause in the respective contract. This does not mean that the consent to arbitration needs to be recorded in a single instrument. If the investor's application is accepted subsequently by the host State's competent authority, a valid arbitration agreement is concluded.[36] In any event, the consent by direct agreement reflects the traditional patterns of

[32] Cf. P. Muchlinski, Multinational Enterprises and the Law (1995), 639; Görs, *supra* fn. 30, 181.

[33] A. Redfern & M. Hunter, Law and Practice of International Commercial Arbitration (2004), para. 5–30.

[34] See, e.g., Redfern & Hunter, id., para. 1–13; S. Jarvin, The Sources and Limits of the Arbitrator's Powers, in: J. Lew (ed.), Contemporary Problems in International Arbitration (1986), 50, 50.

[35] This was not different in the framework of ICSID. Cf. A. El-Kosheri, Contractual Claims and Treaty Claims within the ICSID Arbitration System, in: B. Cremades & J. Lew (eds.), Parallel State and Arbitral Procedures in International Arbitration (2005), 43–71. See, for instance, the following cases in which the parties' consent to ICSID arbitration was based on direct agreement between the parties: *Société Ouest Africaine des Bétons Industriels (SOABI) v. Senegal*, ICSID Case No. ARB/82/1, Decision on Jurisdiction, 1 August 1984, 2 ICSID Rep. 165 (hereinafter, *SOABI v. Senegal*); *Maritime International Nominees Establishment (MINE) v. Republic of Guinea*, ICSID Case No. ARB/84/4, Award, 6 January 1988, Y.B. Comm. Arb'n 14 (1989), 82; *Amco Asia Corp. v. Republic of Indonesia*, ICSID Case No. ARB/81/1, Award, 20 November 1984, 1 ICSID Rep. 413.

[36] See, e.g., *Amco Asia Corp. v. Republic of Indonesia*, ICSID Case No. ARB/81/1, Decision on Jurisdiction, 25 September 1983, 1 ICSID Rep. 389, para. 25.

arbitration whereby pride is given to the consensual character of arbitration. This basic framework of consent to arbitration is altered by two new forms of consent which enable the investor to commence arbitral proceedings unilaterally and without prior agreement.[37]

The first departure from the traditional concept of arbitration is embodied in the host State's general offer to arbitrate laid down in its legislation. In *SPP v. Egypt*,[38] the investor's right to commence arbitration based on the host State's unilateral offer contained in a host State's investment promotion law[39] was recognized for the first time. Whilst at the outset such an interpretation of investment legislation was opposed by several States,[40] this opportunity has been widely recognized in the meantime.[41] The appropriateness of drawing the consents from several instruments was never seriously challenged.[42] However, the exact formulation required to base jurisdiction on national investment law provisions remains questionable. A mere reference to investment

---

[37] See J. Paulsson, Arbitration without Privity, ICSID Rev.-FILJ 10 (1995) 232, 265–266; A. El-Kosheri, ICSID Arbitration and Developing Countries, ICSID Rev.-FILJ 8 (1993), 104, 106 et seq.; M. I. M. Aboul-Enein, Arbitration of Foreign Investment Disputes: Responses to the New Challenges and Changing Circumstances, in: A. van den Berg (ed.), New Horizons in International Commercial Arbitration and Beyond, ICCA International Arbitration Congress, Beijng 2004 (2005), 181, 186–187.

[38] *Southern Pacific Properties (Middle East) Ltd. v. Arab Republic of Egypt*, ICSID Case No. ARB/84/3, Decision on Jurisdiction, 14 April 1988, 3 ICSID Rep. 131.

[39] The English text of article 8 of Egypt Law No. 43/1974 published by Egypt's General Authority for Investment and Free Zones reads as follows:

> Investment disputes in respect of the implementation of the provisions of this Law shall be settled in a manner to be agreed upon with the investor, or within the framework of the agreements in force between the Arab Republic of Egypt and the investor's home country, or within the framework of the Convention for the Settlement of Investment Disputes between the State and the nationals of other countries to which Egypt has adhered by virtue of Law No. 90 of 1971, where it (i.e., the Convention) applies.

See id., para. 71.

[40] The contentions of Egypt that the terms "within the framework" and "where it applies" implied the need for separate consent to ICSID arbitration and that the simple reference to the convention was not sufficient to create compulsory arbitral jurisdiction were rejected by the tribunal.

[41] Cf. *Tradex Hellas S.A. v. Republic of Albania*, ICSID Case No. ARB/94/2, Decision on Jurisdiction, 24 December 1996, ICSID Rev.-FILJ 14 (1999), 161, 186 (hereinafter, *Tradex v. Albania*). Although this case was only the second case in which an arbitral tribunal presided over the question, the tribunal held this interpretation as established.

[42] C. Schreuer, The ICSID Convention—A Commentary (2001), 194; Dolzer & Stevens, *supra* fn. 6, 131.

arbitration in national legislation can hardly amount to consent to jurisdiction.[43]

The operational mode of consent to arbitration given by national legislation differs in various instances from the classic conclusion of an arbitration agreement. The respective provision works as a general offer by the State to arbitration which requires acceptance by the investor.[44] Hence, the consent to arbitration by the State is given for a wide range of future grievances and may be made effective unilaterally through a request for arbitration by the foreign investor.[45] Yet, it is worthy to note that the consent given through domestic legislation may, of course, be withdrawn at any time through an amendment or repeal of the domestic law.[46]

Subsequent to the acceptance of investment legislation as a host country's consent to investment arbitration, the next step consisted in the consideration of the increasing number of investment treaties. In general, States that conclude such a treaty tend to include a provision according to which a dispute may be submitted to international arbitration. In *Asian Agricultural Products Ltd. v. Republic of Sri Lanka*,[47] the claimant, a Hong Kong company, invoked for the first time the

---

[43] C. Schreuer, Consent to Arbitration, TDM 2 (2005), No. 5, 1, 3 et seq. See also the following survey: T. Pate, The Past, Present and Future of the Arbitral Clause in Foreign Investment Legislation: In Pursuit of "The Balance", available at: www.desolapate.com (last visited: 15 April 2010). The author carried out an assessment of several national investment laws of developing and emerging market economies and posited a three-fold classification: (i) laws that contain a unilateral and express consent to ICSID or ICC arbitration; (ii) laws that contain in addition a number of other means of dispute resolution and allow the foreign investor the option of selecting; (iii) laws that do not contain offers to submit disputes to arbitration but merely establish that the host State would be willing to enter into an agreement with a foreign investor by which it could be established that if a dispute were to arise, then the parties could resort to arbitration.

[44] Schreuer, *supra* fn. 39, 5.

[45] For examples of investment laws, see A. Parra, The Scope of New Investment Laws and International Instruments, in: R. Pritchard (ed.), Economic Development, Foreign Investment and the Law (1996), 27, 31 et seq.; A. Parra, Provisions on the Settlement of Investment Disputes in Modern Investment Laws, Bilateral Investment Treaties and Multilateral Instruments on Investment, ICSID Rev.-FILJ 12 (1997), 287, 314 et seq.

[46] Schreuer, *supra* fn. 42, 210.

[47] *Asian Agricultural Products Ltd. v. Republic of Sri Lanka*, ICSID Case No. ARB/87/3, Final Award, 27 June 1990, 4 ICSID Rep. 250 (hereinafter, *AAPL v. Sri Lanka*). Since Hong Kong was still a UK protectorate at that time, the scope of the BIT also covered Hong Kong companies.

dispute resolution clause of the UK—Sri Lanka BIT[48] which expressed the State's consent to ICSID arbitration.[49] This invocation was not challenged by Sri Lanka, and the arbitral proceedings took place based on the host State's consent given through the BIT.[50] At present, the majority of investment arbitration cases are based on consent established through investment treaties. Given the clear wording of dispute resolution clauses in BITs and the interpretation thereupon developed in legal doctrine[51] and arbitral practice,[52] the validity of a consent to arbitration expressed through a BIT can barely be doubted.[53]

---

[48] Article 8(1) of the UK—Sri Lanka BIT reads as follows:

> "Each contracting Party hereby consents to submit to the International Centre for the Settlement of Investment Disputes ... for settlement by conciliation or arbitration under the Convention on the Settlement of Investment Disputes between States and Nationals of Other States opened for signature at Washington on 18 March 1965 any legal dispute arising between that Contracting Party and national or company of the other Contracting Party concerning an investment of the latter in the territory of the former.

[49] *AAPL v. Sri Lanka*, *supra* fn. 47, para. 2.

[50] For further discussions of this decision, see C. Amerasinghe, The Prawn Farm (AAPL) Arbitration, Sri Lanka J. of Int'l L. 4 (1992), 155 et seq.; N. Ziadé, Some Recent Decisions in ICSID Cases, ICSID Rev.-FILJ 6 (1991), 514 et seq.

[51] See, e.g., A. Broches, Bilateral Investment Protection Treaties and Arbitration of Investment Disputes, in: J. Schultsz (ed.), The Art of Arbitration, Essays on International Arbitration, Liber Amicorum Pieter Sanders (1982), 63, 67 et seq.; M. I. Khalil, Treatment of Foreign Investment in Bilateral Treaties, ICSID Rev.-FILJ 7 (1992), 339 et seq.; C. Lamm & A. C. Smutny, The Implementation of ICSID Arbitration Agreements, ICSID Rev.-FILJ 11 (1996), 64, 85 et seq.; A. Parra, ICSID and New Trends in International Dispute Settlement, News from ICSID 10 (1993), 7, 8 et seq.; Schreuer, *supra* fn. 42, 210. For more recent discussions, see M. Winkler, Arbitration without Privity and Russian Oil: The Yukos Case before the Houston Court, U. Pa. J. Int'l Econ. L. 27 (2006), 115, 132 et seq.

[52] See, e.g., *American Manufacturing & Trading, Inc. (AMT) v. Republic of Zaire*, ICISD Case No. ARB/93/1, Award, 21 February 1997, 5 ICSID Rep. 11, paras. 5.17–5.23; *Generation Ukraine, Inc. v. Ukraine*, ICSID Case No. ARB/00/9, Final Award, 16 September 2003, 10 ICSID Rep. 240, paras. 12.2–12.3 (hereinafter, *Generation Ukraine v. Ukraine*); *Tokio Tokéles v. Ukraine*, ICSID Case No. ARB/02/18, Decision on Jurisdiction, 29 April 2004, 11 ICSID Rep. 313, paras. 94–100 (hereinafter, *Tokio v. Ukraine*); *Camuzzi International S.A. v. The Argentine Republic*, ICSID Case No. ARB/03/7, Decision on Jurisdiction, 11 May 2005, para. 140; *El Paso Energy International Co. v. The Argentine Republic*, ICSID Case No. ARB/03/15, Decision on Jurisdiction, 27 April 2006, paras. 35–37; *National Grid Plc v. The Argentine Republic*, UNCITRAL, Decision on Jurisdiction, 20 June 2006, para. 49.

[53] Contra M. Sornarajah, *supra* fn. 30, 267, who is more reluctant in the new edition, M. Sornarajah, The International Law on Foreign Investment (2004), 252: "Whether or not the assumption of such jurisdiction is proper, there is little doubt that many precedents have been established for the assumption of such jurisdiction in several awards" (footnote omitted).

The same kind of regulation, i.e., consent to submit disputes to ICSID can nowadays be found in the majority of BITs[54] and also in the most important MITs.[55]

Similar to the consent given through national legislation, the dispute resolution clause operates as a standing offer of the contracting States to arbitration to investors who are nationals of the other contracting party. The arbitration agreement is completed through the acceptance of that offer by an eligible investor.[56] In arbitral practice it is firmly established that an investor can accept a host State's offer of investment arbitration contained in a BIT by instituting the respectively offered arbitral proceedings.[57] Hence, the arbitral proceedings may be commenced unilaterally by a private individual.[58] This mechanism of concluding arbitration agreements has been termed by Paulsson as "arbitration without privity."[59] And indeed, the approach grants innumerable present and future investors the right to arbitrate a wide range of grievances arising from the actions of a large number of public authorities whether or not any specific agreement to arbitrate has been concluded with the particular complainant.[60] Thereby, it is "dramatically different from anything previously known in the international sphere"[61] and entailed an unprecedented expansion of international investment arbitration.[62] Unlike the offer given through national legislation, a State may not withdraw or alter its consent given in a treaty

[54] Cf. Schreuer, *supra* fn. 42, 211. For provisions in recent Model BITs, see, for instance, article 27(1)(a) of the Canada 2004 Model BIT or article 24(3)(a) of the 2004 US Model BIT.

[55] Article 1122(2)(a) of the NAFTA; article 26(4)(a)(1) of the ECT.

[56] Schreuer, *supra* fn. 42, 218–221; Schreuer, *supra* fn. 43, 7.

[57] See, e.g., *SGS Société Générale de Surveillance S.A. v. Republic of the Philippines*, ICSID Case No. ARB/02/6, Decision on Jurisdiction, 29 January 2004, 8 ICSID Rep. 518, paras. 30–31 (hereinafter, *SGS v. Philippines*); *Impregilo S.p.A. v. Islamic Republic of Pakistan*, ICSID Case No. ARB/03/3, Decision on Jurisdiction, 22 April 2005, para. 108 (hereinafter, *Impregilo v. Pakistan*); *Generation Ukraine v. Ukraine*, *supra* fn. 52, paras. 94–100.

[58] See G. Delaume, Consent to ICSID Arbitration, in: J. J. Norton et al. (eds.), The Changing World of International Law in the Twenty-First Century (1998), 155, 166 et seq.

[59] Paulsson, *supra* fn. 37, 232, 240. In the context of the distinction between private and public law, van Harten doubts whether the investor's consent perfects an agreement which equals a private arbitration agreement. See G. van Harten, The Public-Private Distinction in the International Arbitration of Individual Claims against the State, Int'l & Comp. L. Q. 56 (2007), 371, 380–381.

[60] Paulsson, *supra* fn. 37, 233.

[61] Id., 256.

[62] Aboul-Enein, *supra* fn. 37, 185–187.

unless there is a basis for termination under the law of treaties[63] and the investor is thus granted an even more reliable basis than in the case of the former.[64]

II. *Range of Choices*

As shown above, the range of possible choices in bilateral and multilateral treaties concerning the international arbitral institution before which the dispute shall be settled is diverse. Whilst some treaties refer solely to a single arbitration institution, others refer to several institutional or ad hoc proceedings. In the following part, a short presentation on the characteristic features of the most important arbitral institutions is undertaken.

1. *International Centre for the Settlement of Investment Disputes (ICSID)*

The option of ICSID arbitration entails some specific features which distinguish it from commercial arbitral institutions or ad hoc proceedings.[65] Since the ICSID Convention is an international treaty which sets out certain requirements, a dispute may be referred to ICSID arbitration only when the State party to the dispute and the State of the private disputing party are States which have ratified the ICSID Convention and the character of the dispute fulfils the requirements laid down therein.[66] The ICSID Convention detaches the arbitral proceedings

---

[63] Schreuer, *supra* fn. 43, 8.

[64] For further problems of investor—State arbitration such as the admission of amicus curiae, transparency, publicity, and confidentiality of arbitral proceedings see, e.g., H. Grigera Naón, The Settlement of Arbitral Disputes between States and Private Parties, JWI 1 (2000), 59 et seq.

[65] For the development of ICSID arbitrations, see generally C. Schreuer, Keynote Address: The Dynamic Evolution of the ICSID System, in: R. Hofmann & C. Tams (eds.), The International Convention on the Settlement of Investment Disputes (ICSID)—Taking Stock after 40 years (2007), 15 et seq.; T. Lörcher, ICSID-Schiedsgerichtsbarkeit, SchiedsVZ 2005, 11 et seq. For an overview of arbitral decisions rendered under the auspices of ICSID, see, e.g., R. Happ, Rechtsprechung der ICSID Schiedsgerichte 2005–2007, SchiedsVZ 2008, 19 et seq.; R. Happ, Aktuelle Rechtsprechung der ICSID-Schiedsgerichte, SchiedsVZ 2005, 21 et seq.; R. Happ & N. Rubins, Awards and Decisions of ICSID Tribunals in 2004, GYIL 47 (2004), 878 et seq.; R. Happ & N. Rubins, Awards and Decisions of ICSID Tribunals in 2005, GYIL 48 (2005), 581 et seq.

[66] See G. Delaume, How to Draft an ICSID Arbitration Clause, ICSID Rev.-FILJ 7 (1992), 168, 169 et seq.; Schreuer, *supra* fn. 42, 141; Lamm & Smutny, *supra* fn. 51, 66.

wholesale from any national legal system. On account of this, the awards rendered under ICSID arbitration inherit a twofold stability: Firstly, they are not subject to any means of recourse before national courts of ICSID Member countries.[67] The exclusive option to set aside an ICSID award is the annulment proceeding laid down in the Convention itself.[68] Secondly, ICSID awards are not subject to *exequatur* proceedings and thus an effective enforcement is guaranteed.[69] However, with regard to matters of sovereign State immunity and enforcement, the laws of the forum where enforcement is sought come into play. The non-enforcement of ICSID awards may constitute a violation of the ICSID Convention and thereby cause an international responsibility of the non-enforcing State different from the responsibility for breach of the investment treaty obligation.[70]

2. *ICSID Additional Facility*

Under the Additional Facility, the resolution of disputes under the auspices of ICSID is available even when not all of the jurisdictional requirements of the ICSID Convention are fulfilled.[71] For instance, although Mexico has not ratified the ICSID Convention, NAFTA disputes involving Mexico may be brought before an ICSID tribunal.[72] The same holds true for other requirements such as the characterization of the transaction underlying the dispute as investment.[73] In any

[67] See article 53(1) of the ICSID Convention: "The award … shall not be subject to any appeal or to any other remedy except those provided for in this Convention."

[68] See article 52 of the ICSID Convention. On annulment of ICSID awards, see generally C. Schreuer, Three Generations of ICSID Annulment Proceedings, in: E. Gaillard (ed.), Annulment of ICSID Awards (2003), 17 et seq.; D. D. Caron, Reputation and Reality in the ICSID Annulment Process: Understanding the Distinction between Annulment and Appeal, ICSID Rev.-FILJ 7 (1992), 21 et seq.

[69] See article 54(1) of the ICSID Convention. On the enforcement of ICSID awards, see G. Canè, The Enforcement of ICSID Awards: Revolutionary or Ineffective?, Am. Rev. Int'l Arb. 15 (2004), 439 et seq.; E. Baldwin et al., Limits to Enforcement of ICSID Awards, J. Int'l Arb. 23 (2006), 1 et seq. On the particularly thorny case of Argentina, see C. Goodman, Uncharted Waters: Financial Crisis and Enforcement of ICSID Awards in Argentina, U. Pa. J. Int'l Econ. L. 28 (2007), 449 et seq.

[70] See *infra* 87 et seq.

[71] See article 2 of the ICSID Additional Facility Rules.

[72] Several disputes involving Mexico as claimant and as respondent have been resolved by ICSID tribunals.

[73] See article 2(b) of the ICSID Additional Facility Rules. See also A. Broches, Selected Essays: World Bank, ICSID, and Other Subjects of Public and Private International Law (1995), 249, 250 et seq.

event, the required approval by the ICSID Secretary-General ensures that ordinary commercial transactions are not submitted.[74]

3. *International Chamber of Commerce (ICC)*

The ICC is a private non-profit-making international organisation created in 1919. Its main goal is the furthering of an open global economy in order to bolster global prosperity and peace among nations.[75] The new ICC arbitration rules which were adopted in 1998 maintain the basic patterns inherent in the ICC arbitration system since its inception in 1923, namely, the central role of the Court and the flexibility of the system.[76] The Court as an autonomous arbitration body carries out the administration and supervision of arbitrations taking place under the ICC Rules. Thereby, it shall be guaranteed that the proceedings and the awards are as neutral and impartial as possible. Within the framework set out by the ICC Rules of Arbitration, the freedom of the parties to create the arbitral proceedings according to their demands remains considerably. Special features of ICC arbitration are: Firstly, a document, the Terms of Reference, is issued previous to the trial pinpointing the essential claims and issues in dispute. Secondly, the basis for the determination of costs is the amount disputed in the particular proceeding. Both patterns help to increase the predictability and effectiveness of the system. The enforcement of awards rendered under the ICC Arbitration Rules is subject to the regulations of the New York Convention. It is worthy to note that States parties to an investment treaty allowing the choice of ICC arbitration are perfectly able to derogate from the ICC provisions. For instance, derogating stipulations that limit the powers of arbitral panels to grant injunctive relief or interim measures, clauses providing for third party participation, or provisions providing for consolidation of arbitral proceedings may alter the ICC system in the specific case.[77]

---

[74] See article 4(1) of the ICSID Additional Facility Rules.

[75] See Preamble of the ICC Constitution, available at: www.iccwbo.org (last visited: 16 April 2010).

[76] For a summary of the settlement of investment disputes under the framework of the ICC, see H. Grigera Naón, The Settlement of Investment Disputes between States and Private Parties—An Overview from the Perspective of the ICC, JWI 1 (2003), 59 et seq.

[77] Id., 96.

4. *UNCITRAL/AAA/LCIA/SCC Institute*

The UNCITRAL Arbitration Rules is the most common option of ad hoc arbitration provided for in investment treaties.[78] In principle, ad hoc arbitration rules exclusively offer the basic rules to carry out an arbitral proceeding. The arbitration is not supervised by a specialized institution, nor is any institutional framework imposed on the parties to the dispute. The UNCITRAL Arbitration Rules may be modified or complemented by an investment treaty.[79]

The AAA and the LCIA[80] are mainly regional arbitral institutions, focussing on the North American and European areas, respectively. The SCC is an arbitral institution which is regularly used for disputes involving Eastern European countries or Russia.[81]

III. *The Treaty's Dispute Resolution Clause*

Due to the paramount role of consent in arbitration, a dispute arising out of an investment contract may only be submitted to international arbitration when the pertinent treaty's dispute resolution clause by which the host State lays down its consent to arbitrate covers such disputes. On this account, an examination of the effect of these clauses is indispensable in order to assess the impact of investment treaties on contracts between host States and investors.

1. *The Scope of the Host State's Consent*

A classification of the different jurisdictional clauses in bilateral and multilateral investment treaties can be made by means of their scopes. Although there is huge variety of provisions,[82] by and large, investment

---

[78] Id., 83.

[79] See generally G. Sacerdoti, Arbitration of Investment Disputes under UNCITRAL Rules and the Choice of Applicable Law, in: S. Charnovitz et al. (eds.), Law in the Service of Human Dignity (2005), 276, 286 et seq. See also K. Lionnet, Die UNCITRAL-Schiedsgerichtsordnung aus der Sicht der Parteien, BB 27 (1993), BB-Beilage No. 17, 9 et seq.

[80] See, e.g., M. Blessing, Die LCIA Rules—aus der Sicht des Praktikers, SchiedsVZ 2003, 198 et seq.

[81] See, e.g., K. Hóber & A. Foerster, Die neue Schiedsordnung 2007 des Schiedsgerichtsinstituts der Stockholmer Handelskammer, SchiedsVZ 2007, 207 et seq.

[82] For an overview, see Broches, *supra* fn. 51, 67 et seq.; G. Burdeau, Nouvelles perspectives pour l'arbitrage dans le contentieux économique intéressant les états, Rev.

treaties may be divided into two groups depending upon the degree of access which is granted by the respective dispute resolution clause.

a. *Unqualified Access to International Arbitration*

One group of investment agreements contains a very broadly phrased jurisdictional clause. These stipulations provide for the submission to international arbitration of "any" or "all disputes" "concerning" or "in relation to" an investment within the sense of the treaty.[83] Investment treaties which do not specifically mention the term "consent" but entitle the investor to a similar right to immediately commence international arbitration[84] are held to have the same effect.[85] The access to international arbitration is not subject to further requirements such as a certain type of dispute or the fulfilment of procedural or other requirements. As far as treaty violations, that means violations of the substantive standards of the treaty itself, are concerned, the access granted to international arbitration can indeed be qualified as "very wide" and "unqualified".[86] However, as will be seen later, the precise scope of such broadly phrased provision is by no means certain and particularly the question of whether claims which are based on breach of a contract between host State and foreign investor are covered is rather uncertain.[87]

b. *Qualified Access to International Arbitration*

In a second group of agreements, the granting of access to international arbitration is contingent upon certain conditions. This may concern the type of dispute or, more exactly, the type of governmental activity through which the investor feels aggrieved. For example, the right to international arbitration may be narrowed to the aspect of

---

Arb. 1995, 3, 12 et seq.; Parra, *supra* fn. 45, 322 et seq.; P. Peters, Dispute Settlement Arrangements, NYBIL 22 (1991), 91, 120 et seq.

[83] See, for instance, article 8 of the Sweden 2002 Model BIT:

> (1) Any dispute concerning an investment between an investor of one Contracting Party and the other Contracting Party shall, if possible, be settled amicably. (2) If any such dispute cannot be settled...each Contracting Party hereby consents to the submission of the dispute, at the investor's choice, for resolution by international arbitration.

[84] See, for instance, article 11(2) of the Germany Model BIT (No. 201): "(2) If the divergency cannot be settled within six months of the date...it shall, at the request of the national or company of the other Contracting Party, be submitted for arbitration".

[85] Schreuer, *supra* fn. 42, 213.

[86] Paulsson, *supra* fn. 37, 237.

[87] See *infra* 68 et seq.

compensation for expropriation.[88] In the same vein, the access to international arbitration may be subjected to different kinds of procedural requirements.[89] For example, mention can be made of the requirement to use domestic remedies for a certain period of time.[90] Further, the consent itself may not have been given under the treaty, but the treaty merely provides for the obligation to do so.[91] Finally, some provisions foresee the contingency of international arbitration upon a future agreement between the host State and the foreign investor. Thus, the consent to international arbitration has to be included in this agreement.[92] In any of these cases, the existence of consent to international arbitration bears further inquiry. Yet generally, very restrictive types of provisions can only be found in treaties of an older vintage. The major part of modern investment treaties, in turn, contains broadly phrased dispute resolution clauses.[93]

---

[88] See, for example, article 10(1) of the China—Hungary BIT: "Any dispute between either Contracting State and the investor of the other Contracting State concerning the amount of compensation for expropriation may be submitted to an arbitral tribunal."

[89] Such as, for instance, the resort to local remedies, the exhaustion of local remedies, the fulfilment of a so-called "cooling off" periods, the requirement to use local remedies for a certain time and so forth. Note that it is controversial whether the local remedies rule is a procedural requirement or whether it operates as part of substantive law. On this controversy, see U. Kriebaum, Local Remedies and the Standard for the Protection of Foreign Investment, in: C. Binder et al. (eds.), International Investment Law for the 21st Century (2009), 417, 420 et seq.

[90] See article 10(a) of the Germany—Argentina BIT:

> (a) at request of one of the parties to the dispute if no decision on the merits of the claim has been rendered after the expiration of a period of eighteen months from the date on which the court proceedings referred to in para. 2 of this Article have been initiated, or if such decision has been rendered, but the dispute between the parties persists.

However, the meaning and validity of such clauses is not uncontroversial. See, e.g., C. Schreuer, Calvo's Grandchildren: The Return of Local Remedies in Investment Arbitration, in: The Law and Practice of International Courts and Tribunals (2005), 1, 3 et seq.

[91] See, for instance, article 10 of the Netherlands—Pakistan BIT (1988): "The Contracting Party in the territory of which a national of the other Contracting Party makes or intends to make an investment, shall assent to any demand on the part of such national to submit, for arbitration or conciliation...any dispute that may arise in connection with the investment".

[92] See, for instance, article 6 of the Sweden—Yugoslavia BIT (1978): "In the event of a dispute arising between a national or a company of one Contracting State and the other Contracting State in connection with an investment...it shall upon the agreement by both parties to the dispute be submitted for arbitration to the International Centre for Settlement of Investment Disputes".

[93] Recent treaties appear to phrase these clauses more specifically. This may be a consequence of the ongoing disputes concerning the scope of broadly phrased dispute resolution clauses. See, for instance, article 22 of the Canada Model BIT 2004.

2. *The Scope of a Broadly Phrased Dispute Resolution Clause*

The exact scope of broadly phrased dispute resolution clauses is very controversial. Particularly, it is questionable whether contractual contents are covered.[94] The contention has been made that such clauses which provide an option for international arbitration for "any" or "all" disputes with "respect to", "relating to" or "concerning" investments entail the jurisdiction of international arbitral tribunals for all kinds of contractual breaches, including those which do not amount to a violation of the particular treaty.[95] In principle, there is no theoretical reason why mere contractual claims should not be submitted to an international tribunal pursuant to a treaty. No rule of international law prevents States from agreeing on treaties that allow such submissions.[96] However, the question is whether States intended to do so by including broadly phrased dispute resolution clauses. The arbitral practice is inconsistent in this regard and rendered contradictory interpretations of similar provisions.

a. *Arbitral Practice*

By and large, the interpretations issued by arbitral tribunals regarding the effect of broadly phrased dispute resolution clauses to contractual contents evince two different approaches: a broad approach which, in principle, favours the inclusion of claims based on contractual violations and a narrow one which rejects such inclusion, at least when generated through dispute resolution clauses.

A similar approach has been taken by the tribunals in *Salini v. Morocco*,[97] *Consortium R.F.C.C. v. Morocco*,[98] and *Impreglio v. Pakistan*[99]. In principle, all three decisions opted for the coverage of contractual violations through the treaties' broadly phrased dispute resolution clauses. The two cases against Morocco concerned identically phrased

---

[94] The same holds true for provisions granting qualified access which contain similar references to "all disputes with regard to investments" or similar phrases.

[95] For the conceptual distinction between contract claims and treaty claims, see *infra* 160 et seq.

[96] See A. Sinclair, Bridging the Contract/Treaty Divide, in: C. Binder et al. (eds.), International Investment Law for the 21st Century (2009), 92, 94–95.

[97] *Salini Costruttori S.p.A. v. The Kingdom of Morocco*, ICSID Case No. ARB/00/4, Decision on Jurisdiction, 23 July 2001, 6 ICSID Rep. 398, para. 59 (hereinafter, *Salini v. Morocco*).

[98] *Consortium R.F.C.C. v. Kingdom of Morocco*, ICSID Case No. ARB/00/6, Decision of Jurisdiction, 16 July 2001, para. 67 (hereinafter, *RFCC v. Morocco*).

[99] *Impregilo v. Pakistan*, *supra* fn. 57, paras. 198, 211.

treaty provisions. In their scarce substantiation, the tribunals relied exclusively on the general terms[100] of the clauses in order to affirm an inclusion of all kinds of contractual breaches. Accordingly, the clause's exemplary enumeration of specific situations which were distinct from a contract's violation "cannot exclude a claim based in contract from the scope of application of this article."[101] However, the tribunals stated an important exception: the scope of the treaty's dispute resolution clause is limited to contracts that have been concluded directly with the State. An extension of the jurisdictional offer to breaches of a contract to which an entity other than the respective State was a named party could not be sustained for the following reason:

> In the case where the State has organised a sector of activity through a distinct legal entity, be it a State entity, it does not necessarily follow that the State has accepted *a priori* that the jurisdiction offer contained in Article 8 should bind it with respect to contractual breaches committed by this entity.[102]

The same argument has been brought forward by the tribunal in *Impregilo v. Pakistan*.[103] As a consequence, an examination of the status of the entity that is party to the contract has to be undertaken by the tribunal. The *Impregilo* tribunal found that the entity concerned is an autonomous corporation distinct from Pakistan and therefore denied its jurisdiction over contractual claims.[104] In *Salini v. Morocco*, the tribunal came to the non-application of article 8 of the BIT although it found before that the contracting entity, the Société Nationale des Autoroutes du Maroc (ADM) was a state entity acting in the name of the Kingdom of Morocco.[105] According to the tribunal, the reason was the legal personality of ADM which was formally distinct from the State.[106] Ultimately, this concerns the question of the scope of consent

---

[100] Article 8 of the Italy—Morocco BIT offers the option of choosing the forum with respect to: "All disputes or differences, including disputes related to the amount of compensation due in the event of expropriation, nationalization, or similar measures, between a Contracting Party and an investor of the other Contracting Party concerning an investment of the said investor on the territory of the first Contracting Party". Article 9(1) of the Italy—Pakistan BIT offers the same option to "any disputes arising between a Contracting Party and the investors of the other".

[101] *Salini v. Morocco*, *supra* fn. 97, para. 59.

[102] Id., para. 61.

[103] *Impregilo v. Pakistan*, *supra* fn. 57, para. 211.

[104] Id., para. 216.

[105] *Salini v. Morocco*, *supra* fn. 97, paras. 35, 60, 61.

[106] Id., para. 60.

given through the treaty.[107] For the controversy at hand, the relevant conclusion is that these tribunals sustain the inclusion of contractual claims through a broadly phrased dispute resolution clause. Through the limitation on the State's direct participation this effect, however, is narrowed considerably.

An exhaustive examination of the dispute resolution clause's effect has also been rendered by the tribunal in *SGS v. Philippines*.[108] In this case, the dispute arose out of a contract concerning pre-shipment inspections which SGS had concluded directly with the Government of the Philippines. In its decision, the tribunal similarly applied a broad approach to the interpretation of the dispute resolution clause. Accordingly, a differentiation had to be made between two questions: first, the interpretation of the general phrase "disputes with respect to investments" in BITs and second, the admissibility of contract claims when there is an exclusive jurisdiction clause in the contract. This distinction derives from the tribunal's concern that "the general provisions of BITs should not, unless clearly expressed to do so, override specific and exclusive dispute settlement arrangements made in the contract itself."[109]

In the first place, the tribunal gave an interpretation of the wording of article VIII(2) of the Switzerland—Philippines BIT.[110] In a prima facie approach, it contemplated the general nature of the provision and the breadth of the term "disputes with respect to investment" ("différents relatifs à des investissements" in the French text). Accordingly, the term could not be construed as limiting the choice of forum to

---

[107] For an examination of this subject matter under the investment treaty regime, see *infra* 155 et seq.

[108] *SGS v. Philippines*, *supra* fn. 57.

[109] Id., para. 134. This aspect is discussed in chapter 5.

[110] Article VIII of the Switzerland—Philippines BIT reads as follows:
Settlement of Disputes between a Contracting Party and an Investor of the other Contracting Party—1. For the purpose of solving *disputes with respect to investments* between a Contracting Party and an investor of the other Contracting Party and without prejudice to Article IX of this Agreement (Disputes between the Contracting Parties), consultations will take place between the parties concerned. 2. If these consultations do not result in a solution within six months from the date of request for consultations, the investor may submit *the dispute* either to the national jurisdiction of the Contracting Party in whose territory the investment has been made or to international arbitration. In the latter event the investor has the choice between (a) the International Centre for the Settlement of Investment Disputes (ICSID) (emphasis added).

claims of a specific legal classification. The provision thus, prima facie, was held to encompass disputes arising from contracts such as the agreement between SGS and the Philippines in the present case.[111]

This prima facie conclusion was fostered through several further considerations:[112] Firstly, all the forums which can be chosen under article VIII(2) (i.e., the national courts of the host State, ICSID panels, and UNCITRAL ad hoc tribunals) were competent to apply the host State's national law and thus its law of contract. Secondly, the further dispute resolution clause of the BIT that regulated the dispute resolution between States explicitly limited the scope of disputes which can be submitted to those which concerned a violation of the treaty.[113] Such explicit limitation had also been established in NAFTA's chapter 11, and thus it would be clear that the drafters could have included an express limitation if they wished to do so. Further reasons for a broad interpretation of the clause were seen to be the purpose of the BIT to promote and protect foreign investments as well as the prevention of parallel proceedings in order to entail an efficient resolution of investment disputes. Finally, the very nature of investment would be linked to contracts. Usually, investments are entered into by means of contracts or other agreements with the host State and the private investor. In the view of several ICSID tribunals an investment does not even exist before the contract has been signed or at least approved.[114] Consequently, "disputes with relation to investments" was held to naturally include contractual disputes.

The same broad approach was adopted by the annulment committee in *Vivendi* two years before the *SGS—Philippines* decision.[115] Albeit in a different context—there were no contract claims involved in *Vivendi*—the committee likewise relied on the broad wording and a comparison to other dispute resolution clauses where the scope of application is limited explicitly to affirm the coverage of violations that do not

---

[111] *SGS v. Philippines*, *supra* fn. 57, para. 131.

[112] Cf. id., para. 132(a)–(e).

[113] Article IX of the Switzerland—Philippines BIT covers "[d]isputes regarding the interpretation or application of the provisions *of this agreement*" (emphasis added).

[114] See *Mihaly International Corporation v. Socialist Democratic Republic of Sri Lanka*, ICSID Case No. ARB/00/2, Award, 15 March 2002, 6 ICSID Rep. 308, paras. 48, 51 (hereinafter, *Mihaly v. Sri Lanka*), where the conclusion of a binding contract is deemed to be coextensive with the entry into an investment.

[115] *Compañia de Aguas del Aconquija, S.A. v. The Argentine Republic*, ICSID Case No. ARB/97/3, Decision on Annulment, 3 July 2002, 6 ICSID Rep. 327 (hereinafter, *Vivendi Annulment*).

amount to a violation of the treaty itself but merely relate to an investment under the BIT.[116]

The opposite point of view dismisses the coverage of disputes which are based primarily on breach of contract. In *SGS v. Pakistan*, the tribunal had to sit over a similarly phrased provision as the tribunal in the first *SGS* case.[117] In the tribunal's view, the provision could not be regarded as providing a sufficient basis to vest an international tribunal with jurisdiction over purely contractual claims. Although it admitted that the phrase "disputes with respect to investments", in principle, was able to encompass disputes grounded on treaty violations as well as disputes arising from contract violations, the tribunal upheld that this is not enough to cover purely contractual claims.

> That phrase, however, while descriptive of the factual subject matter of the disputes, does not relate to the basis of the claims, or the cause of action asserted in the claims. In other words, from that description alone, without more, we believe that no implication necessarily arises that both BIT and purely contract claims are intended to be covered by the Contracting Parties in Article 9.[118]

A similarly narrow approach was applied by the tribunal in *LESI-Dipenta v. Algeria*.[119] Accordingly, the consent given by the State to international arbitration through a treaty's dispute resolution clause could not be interpreted in a way that entailed the inclusion of any violation under the BITs coverage. In fact, the consent given by the

---

[116] Id., para. 55.

[117] Article 9, which is the dispute resolution clause of the Swiss—Pakistan BIT, reads as follows:

> Disputes between a Contracting Party and an investor of the other Contracting Party—(1) For the purpose of solving *disputes with respect to investments* between a Contracting Party and an investor of the other Contracting Party and without prejudice to Article 10 of this Agreement (Disputes between Contracting Parties), consultations will take place between the parties concerned. (2) If these consultations do not result in a solution within twelve months and if the investor concerned gives a written consent, *the dispute* shall be submitted to the arbitration of the International Centre for Settlement of Investment Disputes, instituted by the Convention of Washington of March 18, 1965, for the settlement of disputes regarding investments between States and nationals of other States (Emphasis added).

[118] *SGS Société Générale de Surveillance v. Islamic Republic of Pakistan*, ICSID Case No. ARB 01/13, Decision on Jurisdiction, 6 August 2003, 8 ICSID Rep. 383, (2003) 42 ILM 1290, para. 161 (hereinafter, *SGS v. Pakistan*).

[119] *Consorzio Groupement L.E.S.I.-Dipenta v. People's Democratic Republic of Algeria*, Award, 10 January 2005 (hereinafter, *LESI-Dipenta v. Algeria*).

contracting parties is solely valid to the extent of the substantive provisions of the particular BIT. The Italy—Algeria BIT[120] prescribed certain conditions for a treaty violation which would not necessarily be inherent in any violation of contract.[121]

b. *Discussion of the Contradicting Approaches*

The interpretation of a clause in an international treaty always has to be carried out taking into account the rules laid down in article 31 of the Vienna Convention on the Law of Treaties, and hence, the wording of a clause is one of the major elements that determines the particular clause's meaning.[122] The broadly phrased jurisdictional clauses in investment treaties include terms like "any" or "all disputes" arising between a contracting party and the investor of the other contracting party "with respect to", "relating to", or "concerning" investments. At first glance, such terms seem to encompass treaty claims as well as contract claims since no differentiation is made between the two. A differentiation of the legal grounds for a claim can hardly be inferred from such a general, unspecific wording.[123]

However, jurisdictional clauses in investment treaties vary in scope. On the one hand, there are clauses which expressly refer to contractual claims such as article 24 of the US 2004 Model BIT. Accordingly, a claim can be brought for the breach of an "investment agreement."[124]

---

[120] The tribunal in this instance referred to article 4 of the BIT which reads as follows:

> Les investissements effectués par des nationaux ou des personnes morales de l'un des Etats contractant, bénéficient de la protection sur le territoire de l'autre Etat contractant, d'une protection et d'une sécurité constantes, pleines et entières, excluant toute mesure injustifiée ou discriminatoire qui pourrait entraver, en droit ou en fait, leur gestion, leur entretien, leur utilisation, leur jouissance, leur transformation ou leur liquidation sous réserves des mesures nécessaires au maintien de l'ordre public.

[121] *LESI-Dipenta v. Algeria*, *supra* fn. 119, para. 25.

[122] See article 31 of the Vienna Convention on the Law of Treaties (1969): "1. A treaty shall be interpreted in good faith in accordance with the ordinary meaning to be given to the terms of the treaty in their context and in the light of object and purpose."

[123] Cf. S. Alexandrov, Breaches of Contract and Breaches of Treaty—The Jurisdiction of Treaty-Based Arbitration Tribunals to Decide Breach of Contract Claims in SGS v. Pakistan and SGS v. Philippines, JWIT 5 (2004), 555, 573 et seq.; Sinclair, *supra* fn. 96, 102. See also *SGS v. Pakistan*, *supra* fn. 118, para. 161.

[124] The definition of the term "investment agreement" is quite restrictive in this model BIT and thus, does not encompass all contracts which can be regarded as an investment according to the broad notion of investment used in the treaty.

This explicit reference enables the investor to bring its claim before an international arbitral tribunal for the alleged violation of rights which are not per se covered by the substantive standards of the treaty.[125] On the other hand, certain clauses (often, the dispute resolution clauses for State-to-State proceedings[126] but also less frequently, State—investor clauses like article 8(1) of the UK Model BIT[127] or article 26(1) of the ECT)[128] expressly restrict the scope of a tribunal's jurisdiction to disputes which concern "this agreement."[129] In this case, the contracting parties underline that they are not willing to entitle the investor to bring claims based on other legal instruments than the respective treaty.

The distinction which can be drawn between the wording of broad State—investor jurisdictional clauses and restrained State—State jurisdictional clause has often been regarded as the main argument for an unlimited scope of the former.[130] The restrictive scope of the latter clauses, so the *e-contrario* argument goes, implies that when there is no such restriction an unlimited application was the intention of the parties.[131] This conclusion is by no means convincing. On the contrary, the existence of clauses which make explicit referral to contractual

---

[125] J. Griebel, Die Einbeziehung von "contract claims" in internationale Investitionsstreitigkeiten über Streitbeilegungsklauseln in Investitionsschutzabkommen, SchiedsVZ 2006, 305, 309 et seq.

[126] See, for instance, article 37(1) of the US 2004 Model BIT: "[A]ny dispute concerning the interpretation or application of this treaty".

[127] Article 8 of this Model BIT reads as follows:

> Settlement of Disputes between an Investor and a Host State—(1) Disputes between a national or a company of one Contracting Party and the other Contracting Party concerning *an obligation of the latter under this Agreement* in relation to an investment of the former which have not been amicably settled shall..., be submitted to international arbitration if the national or company concerned so wishes (emphasis added).

[128] Article 26(1) of the ECT reads as follows: "Disputes between a Contracting Party and an Investor of another Contracting Party relating to an Investment of the latter in the Area of the former, which concern an alleged *breach of an obligation of the former under Part III* shall, if possible, be settled amicably" (emphasis added).

[129] See E. Gaillard, Investment Treaty Arbitration and Jurisdiction over Contract Claims—The SGS Cases Considered, in: T. Weiler (ed.), International Investment Law and Arbitration: Leading Cases from the ICSID, NAFTA, Bilateral Treaties and Customary International Law (2005), 325, 331 et seq.

[130] See, e.g., *SGS v. Philippines*, *supra* fn. 57, para. 132.

[131] J. Gill et al., Contractual Claims and Bilateral Investment Treaties—A Comparative Review of the SGS Cases, J. Int'l Arb. 21 (2004), 397 et seq. (412). See also, SGS v. Philippines, *supra* fn. 57, para. 132 (e).

contents[132] renders the argument nugatory as likewise, it could be asserted that the existence of the latter shows the parties' intention not to extend the scope to contracts except if such extension is manifested unequivocally.[133]

In any event, the particularity of investment treaty arbitration has to be taken into account when interpreting clauses of investment treaties. The consent to arbitration given by States to investment treaty arbitration may entail a considerable diminution of governmental authority.[134] It may thus be reasonable to require an explicit consent of the States. That is not to say that sovereignty-restricting stipulations have to be construed restrictively as is done by applying the principle *in dubio mitius*,[135] but one may require the States to phrase their consents more specifically. As Gaillard puts it, conferral to international arbitration shall be made through specific language[136] and not based on a term as general as "all disputes with respect to investments".[137]

As a further means of interpretation, the examination of the systematic context of the clause may be convenient to clarify its scope.[138] In this respect, Griebel carried out a comparison of the construction of broadly phrased arbitration clauses in international commercial arbitration and asked whether the generally broad interpretation of the clause in this realm may likewise be suited for investment arbitration.[139] Similar to bilateral or multilateral treaties, international commercial contracts contain broadly phrased arbitration clauses and therein refer to "any" or "all disputes" "arising out of" or "relating to" the respective contract to international arbitration.[140] The referral in the particular

---

[132] See, for instance, article 24(1)(a) of the US 2004 Model BIT.

[133] Griebel, *supra* fn. 125, 310.

[134] Cf. Sornarajah, *supra* fn. 53, 207.

[135] On this principle, see A. Verdross & B. Simma, Universelles Völkerrecht (1984), 493.

[136] As example, mention is made of article 24(1)(a)(i)(C) of the 2004 US Model BIT that grants the option of international arbitration specifically in case of an investment agreement's breach. The scope of "investment agreement", however, is limited through its definition in article 1.

[137] E. Gaillard, Treaty-Based Jursidiction: Broad Dispute Resolution Clauses, NYLJ 2005, October 6, 1, 3.

[138] See article 31(1) of the Vienna Convention on the Law of Treaties (1969).

[139] Griebel, *supra* fn. 125, 310–311.

[140] Compare the model clauses of the different arbitral institutions: (i) AAA: "Any controversy or claim arising out of or relating to this contract, or the breach thereof, shall be settled by arbitration administered by the American Arbitration Association", available at: www.adr.org (last visited: 14 April 2010); (ii) ICC: "All disputes arising out

contract corresponds to the linkage to a specific investment prescribed in investment treaties. The interpretation of such clauses in commercial arbitration proceedings[141] and by domestic courts[142] sitting over arbitrability issues has been generally broad. Accordingly, the kind of language used in these stipulations is "the broadest language the parties could reasonably use."[143] Moreover, any doubts concerning the scope of arbitrability typically are resolved in favour of arbitration.[144] On account of this, broad arbitration clauses in international commercial arbitration are constructed to include non-contractual or tort claims. This reflects the severability of arbitration clauses from the underlying contract. According to the doctrine of severability, an arbitral clause is not contingent upon the continuity of the contract in which it has been included.[145] Hence, the arbitral clause by no means can be regarded as referring exclusively to substantial standards of the contract.

It remains questionable whether the doctrine of severability and, as its corollary, the broad interpretation of jurisdictional clauses, can be transferred to the system of investment treaty arbitration.[146] Several conspicuous features of investment treaty arbitration which distinguish it from mere commercial arbitration argue against such a convergence

---

of or in connection with the present contract shall be finally settled under the Rules of Arbitration of the International Chamber of Commerce", available at: www.iccwbo.org (last visited: 14 April 2010); (iii) LCIA: "Any dispute arising out of or in connection with this contract, including any question regarding its existence, validity or termination, shall be referred to and finally resolved by arbitration under the LCIA Rules, which Rules are deemed to be incorporated by reference into this clause", available at: www.lcia-arbitration.com (last visited: 14 April 2010).

[141] See, e.g., Redfern & Hunter, *supra* fn. 33, para. 3–38.

[142] See, e.g., *Germaine Music v. Universal Songs of Polygram & Broadcast Music, Inc.*, 275 Supp. 2d 1288, para 1297 (D.Nev. 2003).

[143] *Collins & Aikman Prods. Co. v. Building Sys. Inc.*, 58 F.3d 16, 18 (2nd Cir. 1995); *Fleet Tire Serv. of North Little Rock v. Oliver Rubber Co.*, 118 F.3d 619, 621 (8th Cir. 1997).

[144] Cf. M. Geibelson & B. Conn, Clause and Effect—Parties Agreeing to Standard Arbitration Clauses May Unwittingly Alter Their Rights, LA Lawyer 29 (2006), 35, 35 et seq. On critics, see S. Brekoulakis, The Notion of Superiority of Arbitration Agreements over Jurisdiction Agreements: Time to Abandon It?, J. Int'l Arb. 24 (2007), 341 et seq.

[145] See, e.g., S. Schwebel, Some Aspects of International Law in Arbitration between States and Aliens, in: S. Schwebel (ed.), Justice in International Law (1994), 197, 199: "Far from the termination or even nullification of a contract which contains an arbitration clause entailing the end of the obligation to arbitrate disputes arising under that contract, the rule is the opposite: the obligation to arbitrate survives, not least to determine the validity and consequences of the termination or nullification."

[146] Griebel, *supra* fn. 125, 310.

of both systems. Firstly, unlike commercial arbitration, investment arbitration involves regulatory disputes and thus directly impinges upon the host State's sovereign rights.[147] By creating reciprocal obligations, both State parties to an investment treaty abandon certain parts of their absolute sovereignty.[148] This undisputed fact entails several patterns which show that a State and a private individual do not confront each other as equals[149] as is the case in mere commercial relations but as asymmetrical entities with only one being an original subject of international law.[150] International investment treaties are classic international treaties and thus are part of general international law or create a special sub-system of international law.[151] Secondly, the particular legal positions in investment disputes based on investment treaties have not been negotiated by the foreign investor with the State but between the home State of the investor and the host State. The States thereby lay down explicitly the extent to which they are willing to be bound on the international plane.[152] This constellation by no means resembles international commercial arbitration where the parties' legal positions are mainly created by a contract between an investor and the host State or an entity of the host State.[153] Finally, the responsibility which is created through the system of investment treaties is a special kind of state responsibility under international law which cannot be compared to civil liability under international commercial

---

[147] See, e.g., van Harten, *supra* fn. 59, 374–375.

[148] Sornarajah, *supra* fn. 53, 207–208.

[149] Cf. N. Horn, Arbitration and the Protection of Foreign Investment: Concept and Means, in: N. Horn (ed.), Arbitrating Foreign Investment Disputes (2004), 3, 7.

[150] For the further elements of the assymetrical host State—foreign investor relationship, see K. Meesen, International Investment and Dispute Settlement, in: D. Friedmann & E. J. Mestmäcker, Conflict Resolution in International Trade (1993), 111, 113, where the author states the following:

> Dispute Settlement has to cope with the asymmetry of the relationship, which is an asymmetry of power. The monopoly of physical power on the state side is contrasted by worldwide mobility on the business end. It is also an asymmetry of decision-making processes. Since the investor's management is accountable only to the shareholder, it has the capacity to make quick and determined financial decisions, whereas the state partner, though having at its disposal all legislative, executive, and judicial functions, usually moves at a slow, bureaucratic pace.

[151] Sornarajah, *supra* fn. 53, 206; M. Shaw, International Law (2003), 747–749.

[152] Sornarajah, *supra* fn. 53, 208.

[153] This means that in international commercial arbitration, regularly, there is no treaty involved which confers additional rights to the parties.

arbitration.[154] Hence, one may conclude that the investor's protective standard and its right to bring claims directly on the international plane are inextricably linked to the underlying treaty. As a consequence, the abstraction of the jurisdictional clause from the underlying treaty and an interpretation of the clause independently from the substantive standards of the treaty are not tenable. A transferral of the interpretative standards of such clauses in international commercial disputes has to be rejected.[155]

The interpretation of an investment treaty's jurisdictional clause has to bear in mind the further provisions of the treaty. In the context at issue, this has a twofold consequence: Firstly, one has to take into account the existence or non-existence of so-called "umbrella clauses." These clauses have a paramount importance in the extension of the treaty coverage to contractual violations.[156] One may wonder why the inclusion of such clauses is heavily negotiated during the negotiation phase of investment treaties when the same result is reached through the inclusion of a standard dispute resolution clause.[157] Secondly, it seems to be common that the protective standards of investment treaties are created through the substantive provisions of the treaties. Hence, an investment dispute in the sense of the treaty arises when a standard thus created is violated.[158] On the other hand, one may ask whether jurisdictional clauses in investment treaties have a double function and could be regarded as contributing to the substantive standards of a treaty.

The direct conferral of rights upon an individual on the international plane is still the exception rather than the rule.[159] Especially in the economic sector, investment treaties may be regarded as legal instruments with the unique characteristic of granting rights to an

---

[154] See *infra* 84 et seq.

[155] The severability of the arbitration clause is laid down in the UNCITRAL Rules as well as in the ICC Rules. However, both provisions refer to "contracts" of which the clause is part. It can thus be held that the application of this rule is dispensed with in investment arbitrations based on consent by investment treaties.

[156] However, the precise effect of such clauses is not very clear. For a detailed examination, see chapter 4.

[157] See also Griebel, *supra* fn. 125, 311.

[158] Cf. Sornarajah, *supra* fn. 53, 315; E. Gaillard, Centre International pour le Règlement des Différends relatifs aux Investissements (CIRDI)—Chronique des sentences arbitrales, JDI 133 (2006), 219, 306 et seq.

[159] See, e.g., P. Daillier & A. Pellet, Droit International Public (1995), 618.

individual which are directly enforceable on the international plane.[160] Therefore, this grant of rights has to be regarded as taking place solely within the limits circumscribed by the particular treaty.[161] The question which arises within the context of jurisdictional clauses is whether the purpose of such a clause in investment treaties is to create substantive legal rights.

Conceptually, the structure of an international investment agreement consists of different parts: a preamble in which the general purpose of the agreement is laid down, substantive provisions which create a body of legal rights, and jurisdictional provisions which prescribe the manner in which arising disputes have to be settled.[162] The classic function of a dispute resolution clause pertains to the last category. In other words, it establishes the mechanisms necessary to settle a dispute arising out of the violation of one or several substantive provisions of the treaty.[163] This is certainly not an ancillary function but is an essential feature for the determination of the agreement's nature as a whole. As Guzman indicates, through the inclusion of a dispute resolution clause both parties to an agreement show their willingness to be bound by the regulations of the treaty.[164] Hence, they demonstrate their intention to create hard law which may be enforceable by either party instead of concluding a loose agreement the contents of which are malleable declarations of intent. The inclusion of mandatory dispute resolution provisions does not occur frequently in international treaty negotiations. By contrast, the inclusion of such clauses in investment treaties has become very common.[165]

The fact that such clauses are a regular feature of investment treaties evinces their special character as binding international instruments.[166]

---

[160] Cf. Z. Douglas, The Hybrid Foundations of Investment Treaty Arbitration, BYIL 74 (2003), 151, 181 et seq.; Paulsson, *supra* fn. 37, 232 et seq.; F. Orrego Vicuña, International Dispute Settlement in an Evolving Global Society (2004), 64 et seq.

[161] *LESI-Dipenta v. Algeria*, *supra* fn. 119, paras. 84–85.

[162] Cf. Parra, *supra* fn. 45, 288.

[163] Peters, *supra* fn. 82, 111; Dolzer & Stevens, *supra* fn. 6, 119.

[164] A. Guzman, The Design of International Agreements, EJIL 16 (2005), 579, 580, 584 et seq. On the compulsory character of these provisions, see Peters, *supra* fn. 82, 103.

[165] Cf. Vandevelde, *supra* fn. 7, 655 et seq.; Schreuer, *supra* fn. 42, 211; Peters, *supra* fn. 82, 120 et seq.; Parra, *supra* fn. 45, 322 et seq.

[166] Guzman, *supra* fn. 164, 595–596. See also Parra, *supra* fn. 45, 357, who remarks that this pattern shows "a great change for the many countries that had in previous years insisted on the exclusive jurisdiction of local judicial and administrative tribunals for the resolution of disputes between the State and foreign investors".

The paramount function of jurisdictional clauses in investment treaties is thus to open up and guarantee mandatory dispute resolution for the disputes arising out of a violation of the substantive standards provided for by the treaty. As Gaillard puts it:

> Absent specific language to the contrary, it may seem odd to interpret a treaty as creating a jurisdictional basis for a treaty-based tribunal in cases where it is not called upon to rule on alleged violations of that treaty. There is always the danger in divorcing the jurisdictional provisions from the substantive terms of the same treaty in that this may suggest that the treaty-based tribunal has jurisdiction but is invited to rule on a vacuum.[167]

Indeed, it seems to be sound that the jurisdiction of an arbitral tribunal created due to the consent given under a specific treaty, in principle, encompasses exclusively violations of that same treaty. It is solely when a contractual violation is similarly deemed to be a violation of the respective treaty that it may be regarded as covered by the tribunal's jurisdiction. The purpose of a dispute resolution clause is to consent to arbitration and thus to confer jurisdiction. By contrast, it is not to create new substantive obligations.

Finally, is has been contended that the extension of the competence of international tribunals to contract claims through broadly phrased dispute resolution clauses is supported by reason of practicability. Accordingly, the resolution of all claims arising from an investment dispute before one single forum is the preferable solution.[168] Admittedly, the problems of how competing jurisdictions may be channelled or how the generation of overlapping jurisdictions may even be avoided call for a solution given the spread of international tribunals and the legal remedies available to an investor.[169] However, the desire to avoid such situations and the undisputed practicability of a single tribunal's competence cannot substitute the lack of the States' consent. Likewise, the preference for a certain result cannot supplant an interpretative analysis of the provision at hand. Reasons of practicability

---

[167] Gaillard, *supra* fn. 129, 336; Gaillard, *supra* fn. 137, 3.

[168] C. Schreuer, Investment Treaty Arbitration and Jurisdiction over Contract Claims—The Vivendi I Case Considered, in: T. Weiler (ed.), International Investment Law and Arbitration: Leading Cases from the ICSID, NAFTA, Bilateral Treaties and Customary International Law (2005), 281, 299 et seq.

[169] For a more detailed examination of this problem, see chapter 5.

are not capable of extending the scope of application further than conceded by the intentions of the States parties to the treaty.

c. *Conclusion*

It goes without saying that treaty tribunals have jurisdiction to sit over contractual disputes in case the treaty's dispute resolution clause specifically mentions such disputes. Nonetheless, it remains questionable whether this holds true also for non-specific dispute resolution clauses. There seems to be some evidence that this is not the case. In particular, the specific consequences of a State's consent to arbitration and the principal differences between treaty-based investment arbitration and commercial arbitration argue for a principal confinement of the jurisdiction of treaty-based tribunals to treaty violations. Further, the function and purpose of dispute resolution clauses indicate that precise wording is required to include mere contractual claims. However, the breadth of the wording of treaty provisions that refer "any" or "all" disputes gives leeway for broader interpretations. Therefore, it remains to be seen whether tribunals will accept their jurisdiction on the grounds of such broadly phrased clauses.

C. The Legal Effects of the International Investment Treaty Regime

The legal effects of the investment treaty regime are essential for a determination of its impact upon contractual relationships. Especially, three aspects are very important in the so-called "internationalization" of investment contracts. These aspects are: (i) the direct conferral of rights upon the foreign investor, (ii) the consequences of a treaty breach, and (iii) the application of international law.

I. *Conferral of Rights upon the Private Individual*

In the context of the legal effects which international investment agreements are supposed to have, the question of the nature of the conferred rights is an essential one. Above all, it determines the role which the foreign investor is supposed to play in investment treaty arbitration. If States were the sole entities that were endowed with rights by international investment treaties, a foreign investor, being a mere beneficiary of the treaty, would ultimately depend on its home State's discretion and a politicized process for the recovery of damages that occurred to its assets.[170] An example is the state practice of entering into lump sum agreements in order to obtain compensation for a legal wrong committed by another State. Such an agreement is likely to preclude an investor from obtaining full compensation.[171] In turn, if the rights were conferred directly upon the private individual, the latter would be entitled to exercise its rights independent from any interference by its home State and thus avoid the uncertainties of diplomatic protection.[172] Further, the contention has been made that if only States parties were holders of substantive rights under investment treaties, these rights could be overridden by countermeasures.[173] Yet, the most important aspect as regards the impact of treaties on contracts appears to be the problem of whether a foreign investor may waive international treaty protection through contract stipulations such as a Calvo Clause.[174] Hence, the theoretical dispute over the nature of investment treaty rights may have very practical implications for the protection of contracts under the investment treaty system. In legal doctrine and arbitral practice, both approaches find their supporters.

1. *The "Derivative" Model*

According to the "derivative" model, the investment treaty regime entails a protection which is consistent with the traditional features of diplomatic protection under customary international law. At the heart of diplomatic protection is the idea that rights and obligations under international law exist exclusively between sovereign States.[175] The classic formula of this tenet was issued by the Permanent Court of

---

[170] As mentioned above, the depoliticization of investment disputes was one of the most important objectives of the establishment of investment protection treaties.

[171] See D. Bederman, Interim Report on "Lump Sum Agreements and Diplomatic Protection", in: ILA, Committee on Diplomatic Protection of Persons and Property, New Delhi Conference (2002), Second Report, 3, 4 et seq.

[172] Most importantly, these are the following: (i) the investor has no proper right to compensation; (ii) the investor depends entirely on the discretion of its home State; and (iii) the involvement of the home State politicizes the dispute.

[173] See *Archer Daniels Midland Co. v. Mexico*, ICSID Case No. ARB (AF)/04/5, Award, 21 November 2007 (hereinafter, *ADM v. Mexico*), paras. 161 et seq.

[174] On this aspect, see *infra* 310 et seq.

[175] Throughout the history of national States, this was the predominant view under public international law. See, e.g. *Barcelona Traction, Light and Power Co. Case* (Belgium v. Spain) (Second Phase) [1970] ICJ Rep. 3.

International Justice in the *Mavrommatis Palestine Concession Case* in 1924:

> It is an elementary principle of international law that a State is entitled to protect its subjects, when injured by acts contrary to international law committed by another State, from whom they have been unable to obtain satisfaction through the ordinary channels. By taking up the case of one of its subjects and by resorting to diplomatic action or international judicial proceedings on his behalf, a State is in reality asserting its own rights—its right to ensure, in the person of its subjects, respect for the rules of international law.[176]

Subsequently, this formula was applied in some other cases before the PCIJ,[177] and by several other international tribunals[178] including the ICJ[179]. In recent decades, however, the point has been made repeatedly that the fiction that an injury to the national is an injury to the State itself is not tenable anymore.[180] Nonetheless, a definitive renunciation of the rule by international law cannot be discerned.[181] In fact, its continued validity has been asserted on some occasions.[182] Transferred to the international regime of investment protection this approach entails that the substantive protection standards contained in investment treaties are owed to the contracting States. The investor, by referring the dispute to an international arbitral tribunal, does not exercise its own right but merely steps into the shoes of its national States. The

---

[176] See, e.g., *Mavrommatis Palestine Concessions Case* (Greece v. United Kingdom), PCIJ Rep. Series A No. 2, 12.

[177] See, e.g., *Panevezys-Saldutiskis Railway Case* (Estonia v. Lithuania), PCIJ Rep. Series A/B No. 76; *Case concerning the Payment of Various Serbian Loans Issued in France* (France v. Yugoslavia), PCIJ Rep. Series A No. 20; *Case concerning the Factory at Chorzów* (Germany v. Poland), PCIJ Rep. Series A No. 17 (hereinafter, *Chorzów Factory*).

[178] For further references, see C. Amerasinghe, Local Remedies in International Law (2004), 45 et seq.

[179] See, e.g., *Reparations for Injuries Suffered in the Service of the United Nations Case* (Advisory Opinion) [1949] ICJ Rep. 181; *Nottebohm Case* (Liechtenstein v. Guatemala) (Second Phase) [1995] ICJ Rep. 4.

[180] See, e.g., F. García-Amador, State Responsibility: Some New Problems, RdC 94 (1958-II), 365, 413 et seq.; D. O'Connell, International Law (1970), 1030; Orrego Vicuña, *supra* fn. 160, 31–33.

[181] The ILC Draft on Diplomatic Protection leaves open the question whether the State exercising diplomatic protection does so in its own right or that of its national or both. See ILC, Draft Articles on Diplomatic Protection with Commentaries (2006), 26; available at: http://untreaty.un.org (last visited: 25 March 2008).

[182] ILC, First Report on Diplomatic Protection by the Special Rapporteur Mr. John R. Dugard (52nd session of the ILC (2000)), UN Doc A/CN.4/506, paras. 10–32.

procedural right to do so has been delegated to the investor by its national State.[183] This result would be a logical extension of the concept that there are no other subjects of international law than States.

This point of view has been upheld by some authors mostly before the repercussions of the rise of the worldwide network of investment treaties set in.[184] More recently, this opinion has been put forward by respondent States when challenging awards[185] and also by some international arbitral tribunals.[186] In the *Loewen* case, the tribunal's understanding of the investor's cause of action was as follows:

> There is no warrant for transferring rules derived from private law into a field of international law where claimants are permitted for convenience to enforce what are in origin the rights of Party States.[187]

As a consequence, the tribunal applied rules of customary international law[188] the appropriateness of which for the investment treaty system seem doubtful.[189] In other words, the "derivative" theory sees the system of international investment protection under international investment treaties as an institutionalisation and reinforcement of the law on diplomatic protection. Hence, the substantive treaty rights are owed directly to the investor's home State and the foreign investor itself acts merely as an intermediary.[190]

---

183 *ADM v. Mexico*, *supra* fn. 173, paras. 171 et seq.

184 A. Asouzu, International Commercial Arbitration and African States (2001), 359–360; Broches, *supra* fn. 51, 68; C. Chinkin, Third Parties in International Law (1993), 14; F. A. Mann, *supra* fn. 27, 248–249; M. Sornarajah, *supra* fn. 30, 266–267.

185 See, e.g., Amended Memorandum of Fact and Law of the Applicant, *The Attorney General of Canada v. SD Myers, Inc.*, Court File No. T-225-01, para. 67, available at: www.international.gc.ca (last visited: 14 April 2010). This memorandum concerned Canada's challenge of the NAFTA award in *SD Myers, Inc. v. Canada*, UNCITRAL (NAFTA), First Partial Award, 13 November 2000, 8 ICSID Rep. 3.

186 *Loewen Group, Inc. v. United States of America*, ICSID Case No. ARB(AF)/98/3, Award, 26 June 2003, 7 ICSID Rep. 421 (hereinafter, *Loewen v. US*). For a more recent case, see *ADM v. Mexico*, *supra* fn. 173, paras. 168 et seq. It is noteworthy that the decision in *ADM v. Mexico* is accompanied by a concurring opinion in which the tribunal's finding in this regard is dismissed. See Concurring Opinion of Arthur W. Rovine—Issues of Independent Investor Rights, Diplomatic Protection and Countermeasures (hereinafter, ADM Concurring Opinion).

187 *Loewen v. US*, *supra* fn. 186, para. 233.

188 The tribunal applied the rule of customary international law requiring continuous nationality from the date of the events giving rise to the claim up to the date of the award. Cf. id., para. 237.

189 Cf. F. Orrego Vicuña, Changing Approaches to the Nationality of Claims in the Context of Diplomatic Protection and International Dispute Settlement, ICSID Rev.-FILJ 15 (2000), 340 et seq.

190 ADM v. Mexico, *supra* fn. 173, para. 177.

2. *The "Direct" Theory*

In contrast, the "direct" approach to the endowment of rights generated by international investment treaties endorses the creation of a direct legal relationship between the host State and the foreign investor.[191] Accordingly, the substantive rights provided for in the treaties are conferred directly upon the private individual.[192] Consequently, the latter's request for arbitration is an exercise of its own rights. This point of view finds support in the emergence of the individual as a subject of international law.[193] The fact that individuals can be subject of obligations and holder of rights outside a national legal system has become widely acknowledged.[194] The creation of international rights for individuals and private entities has been unanimously recognized in the field of human rights.[195] Recently, the International Court of Justice decided in the *LaGrand* case[196] and in the *Avena* case[197] that such conferral may also be envisaged when the specific right in question is not classified as a human right.[198] Some authors uphold a direct conferral of rights upon

[191] Recent commentators increasingly opt for this approach. See, e.g., J. Robbins, The Emergence of Positive Obligations in Bilateral Investment Treaties, U. Miami Int'l & Comp. L. Rev. 13 (2005/2006), 403 et seq.; Douglas, *supra* fn. 160, 184; C. MacLachlan et al., International Investment Arbitration: Substantive Principles (2007), 60 et seq. See also the recent holding of a NAFTA tribunal in *Corn Products International, Inc. v. Mexico*, ICSID Case No. ARB(AF)/05/2, Decision on Responsibility, 15 January 2008 (hereinafter: *CPI v. Mexico*), paras. 161 et seq.

[192] Other authors propose two different approaches to the direct theory. Either both obligations—the substantive and the procedural—are owed towards the investor or only the procedural right to submit disputes to international arbitration is a right of the investor. See Douglas, *supra* fn. 160, 184; Z. Douglas, The International Law of Investment Claims (2009), 32 et seq.; J. van Haersholte-van Hof & A. K. Hoffmann, The Relationship between International Tribunals and Domestic Courts, in: P. Muchlinski et al. (eds.), The Oxford Handbook of International Investment Law (2008), 962, 1003–1004.

[193] For a summary of this development, see, e.g., Cassese, *supra* fn. 31, 134–150; F. Orrego Vicuña, Individuals and Non-State Entities before International Courts and Tribunals, Max Planck UNYB 5 (2001), 53 et seq.

[194] P. Guggenheim, Traité de droit international public (1953), 210 et seq.; H. Lauterpacht, International Law and Human Rights (1950), 61; I. Brownlie, Principles of International Public Law (2003), 529 et seq.; H. Kelsen, General Theory of Law and State (1949), 343 et seq.

[195] In particular, see The European Convention on Human Rights (1950); The Inter-American Convention on Human Rights (1969).

[196] *LaGrand Case* (Germany v. United States of America) [2001] ICJ Rep. 466 (hereinafter, *LaGrand Case*), paras. 76–77.

[197] *Case concerning Avena and Other Mexican Nationals* (Mexico v. United States of America) [2004] ICJ Rep. 128, para. 40.

[198] See also O. Spiermann, The *LaGrand* Case and the Individual as a Subject of International Law, Zeitschrift für öffentliches Recht 2003, 197 et seq.

the investor precisely because of the investment treaty system's proximity to the human rights regime.[199] This parallelism can be justified since an investment treaty gives "unidentified individuals a right of recourse against a State in order to give effect to the latter's undertakings, pursuant to an international treaty, to accord a certain treatment to private persons".[200] The main reason why the majority of authors back the interpretation that the rights are conferred directly upon the investor is the direct access of the foreign investor to an arbitral tribunal.[201] This enables the aggrieved investor to enforce its rights on the international level without having to rely upon its national State. In other words, the true complainant is allowed to face the true defendant.[202] The ability to enforcement of one's own right is often regarded as an essential prerequisite for the creation of a proper legal capacity.[203] Hence, the foreign investor can be seen in this context to have a restrained international legal personality.[204] Within this concept, the system of diplomatic protection is decreased to a system with a mere residual function. This effect of investment treaties, indeed, would mark an impressive renunciation of the traditional means of protecting private interests on the international plane.[205] In fact, the opportunity given to avoid the pitfalls and inadequacies of diplomatic protection is regarded as one of the major progresses achieved through the new system.[206] Hence,

---

[199] T. Wälde & T. Weiler, Investment Arbitration under the Energy Charter Treaty in the Light of New NAFTA Precedents: Towards a Global Code of Conduct for Economic Regulation, in: G. Kaufmann-Kohler & B. Stucki (eds.), ASA Special Series No. 19, Investment Treaties and Arbitration (2002), 159, 160–161. Contra *ADM v. Mexico*, *supra* fn. 173, para. 171.

[200] Burdeau, *supra* fn. 82, 16: "[I]l s'agit dans l'un et l'autre cas d'ouvrir à des particuliers non identifies à l'avance un droit de recours direct contre un Etat en vue de sanctionner le respect de l'engagement pris par ce dernier dans un traité international d'accorder un certain traitement à des personnes privées".

[201] Orrego Vicuña, *supra* fn. 193, 60 et seq.; Paulsson, *supra* fn. 37, 233; Zedalis, Claims by Individuals in International Economic Law: NAFTA Developments, Am. Rev. Int'l Arb. 7 (1996) 115, 117 et seq.; Burdeau, *supra* fn. 66, 16.

[202] Paulsson, *supra* fn. 33, 256.

[203] See, e.g., C. Eustathiades, Les sujets du droit international et la responsabilité internationale, RdC 84 (1953-III), 397, 412 et seq.; C. A. Nørgaard, The Position of the Individual in International Law (1962), 32 et seq.; M. Sørensen, Principes de droit international public, RdC 101 (1960-III), 1, 127 et seq.

[204] Broches, *supra* fn. 73, 457.

[205] Paulsson, *supra* fn. 37, 256.

[206] J. Kokott, Interim Report on "The Role of Diplomatic Protection in the Field of the Protection of Foreign Investment", in: ILA, Committee on Diplomatic Protection of Persons and Property, New Delhi Conference, Second Report (2002), 27 et seq.

understood in this sense, the system of international investment protection through international investment treaties does not imply the reinforcement or institutionalisation of the system of diplomatic protection but rather a reflection of its decline.[207]

3. *Examination of the Contradicting Approaches*

In principle, none of both approaches is unattainable under the legal theory of international law. States are perfectly able to delegate their procedural right and thus, to entitle a private person to bring a diplomatic protection claim on their behalf.[208] Likewise, there is no reason why they should not have the competence to create directly enforceable rights for individuals.[209] In the final analysis, the effect of a treaty is contingent upon the intention of the parties to it.[210] An interpretation of international treaties has to be carried out in consistence with the principles laid down in articles 31 and 32 of the Vienna Convention on the Law of Treaties. It is noteworthy that the object and purpose of investment treaties do not serve as interpretative aid in this case because the general objective of encouragement of direct foreign investment is too broad to further the identification of the actual holder of the rights.[211] Further, since the existence of *travaux préparatoires* is very scarce, the main focus has to be laid upon the arbitral practice in the application of the treaties and upon the wording of treaty provisions.[212]

a. *Wording of the Substantive Provisions*

As mentioned before, the capability of an individual to be a holder of rights in some areas of international law has been acknowledged. This result has also been inferred from the specific wording of treaty stipulations. According to the ICJ, for instance, the formulation of article 36(I)(b) of the Vienna Convention on Consular Relations where

---

[207] J. P. Laviec, Protection et promotion des investissements—étude de droit international économique (1985), 5; ADM Concurring Opinion, *supra* fn. 186, para. 30.

[208] Douglas, *supra* fn. 160, 168.

[209] For an old case, see *Jurisdiction of the Danzig Courts* (Advisory Opinion), PCIJ Rep. Series B No. 15, 17–19. For a more recent discussion, see J. Crawford, The ILC's Articles on Responsibility of States for Internationally Wrongful Acts: A Retrospect, AJIL 96 (2002) 874, 888 et seq.

[210] O'Connell, *supra* fn. 180, 111.

[211] Douglas, *supra* fn. 160, 167.

[212] Id., 167–168.

it is stated that the prison authorities "shall inform the person concerned without delay of his rights under this subparagraph" suggests that the particular individual has the same rights under article 36(1) as the State party to the treaty, in this case, Germany.[213] The substantive provisions of BITs usually do not contain such directly phrased referrals to an investor's right. They are mainly phrased as enjoining obligations upon the respective host State and not as conferring a right directly upon the investor. In these stipulations, phrases like "[i]nvestors...shall be accorded treatment no less favourable",[214] "[e]ach Party shall accord to investors of the other Party treatment no less favourable",[215] "[i]nvestors...shall enjoy"[216], or "[e]ach Contracting State shall guarantee to investors" are utilized frequently. More straightforward formulations are the exception and not the rule.[217] Thus, these formulations ultimately do not clarifiy the parties' intent. Further, the ambiguity of the language used contributes to the uncertainty surrounding the rights' nature.[218]

b. *Direct Access to International Dispute Settlement*

In investment treaties, the foreign investor is generally given the opportunity to submit an investment dispute arising out of its investment to international arbitration. As mentioned above, this access has been given either in a qualified or an unqualified way. Yet, without giving too much weight to the specific formulation, the general effect of these clauses is almost unanimously discerned as a standing offer of the host State to submit investment disputes to arbitration.[219] The individual may accept this offer at any time and thus, has a continuing right to commence international arbitration proceedings.[220] This right of the investor is a strong indicator of the investor's direct endowment with substantive rights since the availability of direct dispute settlement

---

[213] *LaGrand Case*, *supra* fn. 196, paras. 89, 125.

[214] See, e.g., article 2(3) of the Belgium—Indonesia BIT (1970).

[215] See, e.g., article 4(1) 2004 US Model BIT.

[216] See, e.g., article 4(3) of the 1991 Germany Model BIT.

[217] See, e.g., article 5(3) of the Austria Model BIT: "An investor of a Contracting Party which claims to be affected by expropriation by the other Contracting Party shall have the right ...".

[218] See, e.g., the recent contradictory holdings in two NAFTA cases. Both tribunals refer to the language used in section A of chapter 11 of the NAFTA to substantiate their conflictive points of view. See *CPI v. Mexico*, *supra* fn. 191, para. 169; *ADM v. Mexico*, *supra* fn. 173, paras. 172 et seq.

[219] See *supra* fn. 56.

[220] Contra Sornarajah, *supra* fn. 30, 267.

mechanisms entitles the investor itself to ensure the effective implementation and enforcement of the host State's obligations under the treaty.[221] Yet, a conceptual understanding which differentiates between the procedural right to submit disputes to arbitration and substantive rights that provide for the treatment of investors is also feasible. Accordingly, the substantive rights remain on the inter-State level and merely the procedural right is granted directly to the investor.[222] As a consequence, the investor is not able to waive the substantive treaty rights but only the procedural right to commence arbitration.

c. *Comparison with the Systemic Features of Diplomatic Protection*

If the nature of the investment treaty protection were similar to or a part of the traditional system of diplomatic protection, then naturally, the principal features of diplomatic protection would have to be similar to the main characteristics of investment treaty protection. Thus, a comparison of the features of both systems would serve the determination of the latter's nature. A detailed example of such a comparison has been presented by Douglas.[223] It has been found out that the systemic features of diplomatic protection and investment treaty protection differ to such an extent that their affiliation to the same system and thus, the assumption that investors are bringing derivative claims on behalf of their own national State are hardly tenable.[224] The first and most important area where congruency does not exist concerns the functional control over the claim. Whilst in diplomatic protection the home State of an aggrieved individual has full discretion whether to take up the claim at all,[225] in investment treaty protection it is the investor itself who may decide whether and how to prosecute its claim. Thereby the investor is under no obligation to consult with or to inform its national State. On account of this, one may conclude that the national State does not retain any interest in the arbitration against another State. Even in the case where the investor's national State shows interest in the proceedings, it cannot exert any control over the claim.[226] This

[221] See ADM Concurring Opinion, *supra* fn. 186, para. 47: "A right to a remedy is a substantive right. Legal redress for the wrong committed is a substantive right."

[222] Apparently, this construction has been put forward by supporters of both theories. See *ADM v. Mexico*, *supra* fn. 186, paras. 168 et seq. (derivative model); Douglas, *supra* fn. 160, 184 (direct model).

[223] Douglas, *supra* fn. 160, 169–181; Douglas, *supra* fn. 192, 11 et seq.

[224] Id., 181–184.

[225] See, for instance, Orrego Vicuña, *supra* fn. 160, 32.

[226] Douglas, *supra* fn. 160, 169–170.

has been demonstrated by the fact that the commencement of proceedings could be undertaken against the express will of the investor's home State.[227] Further, Douglas states that contrary to the importance which is assigned to the nationality of claims rule in diplomatic protection, "the investment treaty regime is not overly concerned with the task of channelling the various interests of private entities arising from unlawful conduct attributable to a State into a single rubric of nationality with a single claimant State representing the affected interests."[228] In other words, the investment treaty regime established a much more flexible understanding of the nationality of claims rule. Arbitral practice, however, shows that this aspect is mainly due to the broadening of the covered investment's definition.[229] Therefore, one can hardly contend that it constitutes an intrinsic element of investment treaty protection.[230] The increased flexibility is rather due to specific formulations in the pertinent treaties. Moreover, a certain kind of flexibility similarly invades the system of diplomatic protection.[231] Hence, it is at least doubtful to what extent the increased flexibility of the nationality of claims rule by itself may serve to substantiate the distinction between investment treaty protection and the system of diplomatic protection.

Another aspect through which the distinction between diplomatic protection and investment treaty protection could become obvious concerns the applicable procedural law. If investment treaty arbitration were essentially an arbitral proceeding between two sovereign States, the latter would have to be governed by public international law. The

---

[227] See, e.g., Submission of the United States of America, 30 June 2003, concerning the case of *GAMI Investments Inc. v United States of Mexico*, UNCITRAL (NAFTA), Final Award, 15 November 2004, (2005) 44 ILM 545; Second Submission of Canada pursuant to NAFTA Art. 1128, 6 July 2001, concerning the case of *Mondev International Ltd. v United States of America*, ICSID Case No. ARB(AF)/99/2, Award, 11 October 2002, 6 ICSID Rep. 181.

[228] Douglas, *supra* fn. 160, 175.

[229] See the references in C. Schreuer, Shareholder Protection in International Investment Law, in: P. Dupuy et al. (eds.), Common Values in International Law: Essays in Honour of Christian Tomuschat (2006), 601, 606 et seq.

[230] This is so even if Khalaf Masa'deh points out that the lack of diplomatic protection for shareholders caused by the Barcelona Traction Doctrine was an important additional reason for the creation of the now existing network of BITs. Cf. A. Khalaf Masa'deh, International Rules for Investment and Investors: Light at the End of the Tunnel?, European Bus. L. Rev. 11 (2000) 157, 161 et seq.

[231] See, e.g., Amerasinghe, *supra* fn. 178, 52 et seq.

non-interference of municipal law in an arbitral proceeding or any other judicial proceeding between States is prescribed by the principle of equal sovereignty of States and the immunity from the jurisdiction of national courts which derives from this sovereignty.[232] In contrast, investment treaty arbitrations are governed by the *lex loci arbitri*, that is, the law of the seat of arbitration. Consequently, the municipal courts at the seat of arbitration can sit in judgement in respect of a challenge to the validity of the treaty's tribunal award. Such a situation would not be legitimate if the investor's claim were made on behalf of its national State.[233] However, the application of municipal procedural law does not apply to cases governed by the ICSID Convention.[234] Hence, one can argue that ICSID is not an exception that proves the rule, but ICSID is the rule and the other types of arbitration are the exception.

The next matter discussed by Douglas is the exhaustion of the local remedies rule.[235] As a concession to the sovereign independence of the host State, the rule was and is of central importance in the system of diplomatic protection.[236] By contrast, in the overwhelming part of investment treaties the requirement of exhaustion of local remedies is dispensed with as a procedural precondition for the presentation of claims to an international arbitral tribunal. Thereby, according to Douglas, the contracting States show their lack of legal interest in investment treaty claims.[237] Whilst it is true that the rule of exhaustion of local remedies has been largely dispensed with in the context of investment arbitration,[238] the conclusion drawn by Douglas does not

[232] See, e.g., Shaw, *supra* fn. 151, 622; Brownlie, *supra* fn. 194, 483–484.

[233] Douglas, *supra* fn. 160, 177–178; van Haersolte-van Hof & Hoffmann, *supra* fn. 192, 998.

[234] Article 44 of the ICSID Convention sets out that arbitration proceedings under the ICSID shall be governed by the Convention itself and its Arbitration Rules. Article 53(1) of the ICSID Convention states: "The award shall be binding on the parties and shall not be subject to any appeal or to any other remedy except those provided for in this Convention. Each party shall abide by and comply with the terms of the award except to the extent that enforcement shall have been stayed pursuant to the relevant provisions of this Convention".

[235] Id., 178–179.

[236] See, e.g., Shaw, *supra* fn. 151, 730–732; Brownlie, *supra* fn. 194, 472–473.

[237] Douglas, *supra* fn. 160, 179. See also van Haersolte-van Hof & Hoffmann, *supra* fn. 192, 1000–1001.

[238] See, e.g., Schreuer, *supra* fn. 42, 388–389. For treaty violations, see also Sornarajah, *supra* fn. 53, 255.

seem to be conclusive. The entitlement of a State's nationals to the right to avoid adjudication by local courts was pursued by developed States throughout several decades.[239] One of the chief purposes of the international investment protection regime is precisely this avoidance.[240] Hence, it is unlikely that the contracting States did not maintain the rule because of their lack of interest in investment claims. The abdication of the rule rather indicates the prevailing negotiating strength of developed countries. This argument is reinforced by the observation that developing countries, indeed, venture to reintroduce certain elements of the rule into the system of investor—State arbitration.[241] The fact that the absence of this rule is one of the main features of investment treaties, however, unequivocally marks their difference from the system of diplomatic protection.

Finally, the assessment of damages in both systems indicates the heightened concentration upon the investor as claimant by the investment treaty system.[242] Whilst in a diplomatic protection claim, several considerations may come into play in order to calculate the reparation due to the State which do not necessarily relate to the damage that occurred to the investor,[243] an investment treaty claim is assessed exclusively by taking into account the economic interests of the investor. The eventual prejudice to the home State, in turn, is by no means considered.[244]

---

239 See *supra* 22 et seq.

240 See, e.g., E. Lauterpacht, International Law and Private Foreign Investment, Ind. J. Global Legal Stud. 4 (1996/1997), 259 et seq.

241 See C. Schreuer, Calvo's Grandchildren: The Return of Local Remedies in Investment Arbitration, The Law and Practice of International Courts and Tribunals 4 (2005), 1 et seq.

242 Douglas, *supra* fn. 160, 180.

243 See, for example, the position of the PCIJ in *Chorzów Factory*, *supra* fn. 177, 28:

> The reparation due by one State to another does not however change its character by reason of the fact that it takes the form of an indemnity for the calculation of which the damage suffered by a private person is taken as a measure. The rules of law governing the reparation are the rules of international law in force between the two States concerned, and not the law governing relations between the State which has committed a wrongful act and the individual who has suffered the damage. Rights or interests of an individual the violation of which rights causes damage are always in a different plane to rights belonging to a State, which rights may also be infringed by the same act. The damage suffered by an individual is never therefore identical in kind with that which will be suffered by a State; it can only afford a convenient scale for the calculation of the reparation due to the State.

244 Douglas, *supra* fn. 160, 180.

In sum, the comparison of the central features of investment treaty protection and the system of diplomatic protection shows that the existence of considerable differences between both systems can be discerned. These differences, even if they are not as fundamental as Douglas contends,[245] represent at least a substantial indication of the proper nature of the system of investment treaty protection.

d. *Waiver of Diplomatic Protection*

It is submitted that during the arbitration process and in case the host State abides by the arbitral award, the national State of the investor is under the obligation not to exercise its right of diplomatic protection.[246] A provision which clearly expresses such an obligation can be found in article 27(1)[247] of the ICSID Convention.[248] In the NAFTA, the same result is reached through a combination of stipulations. Article 1135(1) and (2) of the NAFTA prescribe that the award be binding upon the parties. In case of non-compliance, article 1135(6) entails the home State's right to require the setting up of a panel which is entitled to establish, at inter-State level, the State's failure to comply with the arbitral award and the violation of the agreement.[249] The same conclusion can be drawn from the options afforded by article 26 ECT.[250] In the case of investment treaty arbitration, the submission to ICSID thus renders the exclusion of diplomatic protection in investment treaties superfluous. Nevertheless, in several BITs,[251] an express exclusion

245 Id., 182.

246 Schreuer, *supra* fn. 42, 402.

247 Article 27(1) of the ICSID Convention reads as follows:

> No Contracting State shall give diplomatic protection, or bring an international claim, in respect of a dispute which one of its nationals and another Contracting State shall have consented to submit or shall have submitted to arbitration under this Convention, unless such other Contracting State shall have failed to abide by and comply with the award rendered in such dispute.

248 A. Giardina, The International Centre for the Settlement of Investment Disputes between States and Nationals of other States, in: P. Šarčevič (ed.), Essays of International Commercial Arbitration (1989), 214, 214 et seq.; Schreuer, *supra* fn. 42, 397 et seq.

249 A. Giardina, International Investment Arbitration: Recent Developments as to the Applicable Law and Unilateral Recourse, The Law and Practice of International Courts and Tribunals 5 (2006), 29, 33.

250 Id.

251 See, for example, article 9(3) of the Germany—Philippines BIT: "Neither Contracting State shall pursue through diplomatic channels any matter referred to arbitration until the proceedings have terminated and a Contracting State has failed to abide by or comply with the award rendered by the International Centre for Settlement of Investment Disputes".

of diplomatic protection is provided for.[252] Traditionally, the consequence of a valid waiver under international law is the complete deprivation of the particular right waived.[253] Some authors contend that this waiver of the right to exercise diplomatic protection indicates the States' will to rule out its application in the context of foreign investment protection.[254] In this area, the system of diplomatic protection shall be replaced by an alternative dispute resolution system. Thereby, the system of diplomatic protection is restricted to a means of last resort.[255]

e. *Difference between State—State Proceedings and Diplomatic Protection*

In nearly all investment treaties two dispute-resolution procedures are envisaged: on the one hand, an investor—State proceeding and on the other hand, a State—State proceeding. The latter enables the contracting parties to submit disputes concerning the interpretation or application of the provisions of the pertinent treaty to international arbitration.[256] In a certain way, this procedure resembles diplomatic protection.[257] The compliance with awards issued in investor—State proceedings may be insured by an additional procedure in which the State exercises its own rights under the treaty. Nevertheless, the State—State procedure differs from diplomatic protection. The home State is limited to the right to submit the case to the arbitration body and is obliged to abide by the award. This very limited set of options cannot be equated with the means which the home State would be entitled to undertake by exercising diplomatic protection under customary international law.[258] Thus, exclusion of diplomatic protection is similarly prescribed in both arbitral proceedings of an investment treaty. However, the State—State proceeding shows that the substantive rights of such a treaty are not conferred solely upon the individual but also upon the contracting States.

---

252 See the references by Peters, *supra* fn. 82, 145–146.
253 See F. Pfluger, Die einseitigen Rechtsgeschäfte im Völkerrecht (1936), 271.
254 See, e.g., Schreuer, *supra* fn. 42, 399.
255 Schreuer, id., 1085; Kokott, *supra* fn. 206, 25.
256 See, for instance, article 10(1) of the 1991 Germany Model BIT.
257 Kokott, *supra* fn. 206, 24.
258 Id., 25.

f. *Conclusion*

From the above considerations, it can be concluded that it remains unclear whether and if so, to what extent investment treaties confer substantive rights on investors. Neither the usual wording of regularly-framed substantive treaty provisions nor the general purpose of investment treaties argue for a determined interpretation concerning the legal nature of the substantive rights conferred. Since the endowment of natural persons with substantive rights is still an exception under international law, a more precise language could be required. On the other hand, several features of the system installed by investment treaties signal a renunciation of the traditional system of diplomatic protection and thus argue in favour of the creation of substantive investor rights. Compared to diplomatic protection, the treaty system has evolved proper patterns such as the abandonment of the local remedies requirement or the assessment of damages on account of investor interests. Moreover, the participation in the treaty system regularly entails a waiver of diplomatic protection. The strongest argument in favour of such an endowment remains the investor's right to direct access to international dispute settlement. The majority of investment treaties contain provisions that provide for such an option. However, the right to submit disputes to international arbitration may be regarded as being a mere procedural right and not a substantive right. It appears that this concept has been put forward by both theoretical understandings of the nature of investment treaty rights.

II. *Consequences of a Treaty Breach: State Responsibility and the Investment Treaty Regime*

The next question which has to be examined refers to the general system of state responsibility under international law. Given the progressive character of the investment treaty regime, it is questionable whether it pertains to the general system or whether it constitutes a special regime of state responsibility. In case of the latter, the degree of self-contingency of the sub-system must be examined. This is particularly interesting with regard to two aspects: On the one hand, this may clarify the consequences which the breach of an investment treaty entails. On the other hand, it will determine how far general secondary rules of international law concerning state responsibility may remain applicable under the investment treaty system.

1. *The General System of State Responsibility and Sub-Systems of State Responsibility*

a. *Consequences of Breach under the General System of State Responsibility*

The general system of responsibility of States under international law is reflected authoritatively[259] by the ILC Draft Articles on Responsibility of States for Internationally Wrongful Acts (hereafter, ILC Articles).[260] The ILC Articles, according to the respective ILC's commentaries, are intended to set out a system of secondary rules on how to deal with the commission of an internationally wrongful act as such. Neither the content of primary rules nor the responsibility of non-state entities under international law is contemplated.[261]

The consequences of the commission of an internationally wrongful act by a State under these general rules of state responsibility are mainly threefold: Firstly, the State that acted wrongfully internationally is enjoined with the obligation to cease that act, guarantee non-repetition, and make full reparation.[262] Secondly, the corresponding rights accrue to the injured State.[263] Finally, in certain cases of breach, third States are granted new rights and are enjoined with new obligations.[264]

Thus, by and large, the secondary rules laid down by the ILC Articles exclusively concern traditional inter-State relationships. The consequences of a State's violation of obligations owed to entities other than States, especially to natural persons, have been treated with some reluctance by the Commission. In fact, only a very few provisions of the ILC Articles allude to the availability of a State—individual relationship.[265] In article 33(2) of the ILC Articles, which contains the only explicit referral to individuals, the Commission provides that the second part

---

[259] More specifically, see Crawford, *supra* fn. 209, 889–890.

[260] ILC, Responsibility of State for Internationally Wrongful Acts (2001), adopted by the Commission at its fifty-third session in 2001. Reproduced in Official Records of the General Assembly, Fifty-Sixth Session, Supplement No. 10 (A/56/10).

[261] J. Crawford, The International Law Commission's Articles on State Responsibility. Introduction, Text and Commentaries (2002), 75–76.

[262] Article 28 et seq. of the ILC Articles.

[263] Article 42 et seq. of the ILC Articles.

[264] Articles 41 and 48 of the ILC Articles.

[265] In addition to the two cited articles, see the commentaries to article 28 which state that Part Two "does not apply to obligations of reparation to the extent that these arise towards or are invoked by a person or entity other than a State". See, Crawford, *supra* fn. 261, 193–194.

is "without prejudice to any right, arising from the international responsibility of a State, which may accrue directly to any person or entity other than a State." Further, article 55 of the ILC Articles mandates the residual character of the general rules.[266] On account of this scarcity, the ILC Articles have been termed as "out-of-date" right after its adoption.[267] It nevertheless acknowledges the existence and the validity of the regimes that set up secondary rules for the consequences of a breach of an international obligation owed towards natural persons.

b. *Sub-Systems of State Responsibility*

At present, the existence of special systems of state responsibility under international law is no longer disputed.[268] Yet, the effect they have on the application of general international law, indeed, is somewhat opaque. Are they merely *lex specialis* to general international law and the latter thus becomes applicable as soon as a special regulation does not exist or do they represent self-contained legal regimes in which the application of rules of international law amounts to a justifiable exception.[269] Effectively, the diametrically opposed concepts of the international legal order lead to different results. On the one hand, the universal approach, which perceives international law as a unified and hierarchical system, opines that the application of general rules is regularly presumed and the creation of a special system which supersedes these norms requires proof from the parties. On the other hand, the vantage point which regards international law as a fragmented legal order, i.e., as an aggregate of different regimes without any pre-defined hierarchy, posits that the different legal regimes are, in principle, complete and only in exceptional cases do they require resort to rules outside the regime.

---

[266] Article 55 of the ILC Articles reads as follows: "Lex specialis—These articles do not apply where and to the extent that the conditions for the existence of an internationally wrongful act or the content or implementation of the international responsibility of a State are governed by special rules of international law".

[267] See E. Weiss, Invoking State Responsibility in the Twenty-First Century, AJIL 96 (2002), 798, 816: "But by largely ignoring the growing and significant international practice in which individuals and non-state entities are invoking state responsibility, the Commission produced articles that, however noteworthy, are to some extent out-of-date at their inception".

[268] For former discussions, see B. Simma, Self-Contained Regimes, NYBIL 16 (1985), 112 et seq.

[269] For a general discussion on this conflict, see, e.g., J. Pauwelyn, Conflict of Norms in Public International Law: How WTO Law Relates to Other Rules of International Law (2003); W. H. Wilting, Vertragskonkurrenz im Völkerrecht (1996).

However, as Simma and Pulkowski aptly explain, the fallback on general international law serves a useful purpose after the exhaustion of the rules and procedures of the special regime. In fact, it allows a strengthening of the special sub-systems through the ultimate recurrence to means of enforcement which only general international law can provide.[270] As example, mention can be made of special systems such as the WTO or the EC.[271] Both have attained a degree of completeness which makes them literally independent from general international law. Yet, even in those well-developed systems, continuous non-compliance may make the reliance upon general rules of international law necessary.[272] Thus, it can be summarized that no special regime—as self-contained as it may be—may avoid entirely the applicability of general international law.

2. *The Investment Treaty Regime as a Sub-System*

a. *The Differences between the Investment Treaty System and the General System*

There are several reasons why it appears appropriate to regard the investment treaty system as a sub-system of the general international law of state responsibility. In the first place, and arguably most importantly, the rights granted by the treaty system are endowed, at least in part, directly on the foreign investor.[273] More exactly, nearly all investment treaties envisage a twofold system. Whereas disputes concerning the substantive provisions of a treaty are handled between investor and host State, disputes that concern general aspects of application, interpretation of the treaty, and non-compliance with the treaty are left to the States parties to the treaty.[274] The two relationships which are

---

[270] B. Simma & D. Pulkowski, Of Planets and the Universe: Self-Contained Regimes in International Law, in: EJIL 17 (2006), 483, 507–511. Indeed, somewhat hypothetically, the authors contend that "the policy question is whether primary rules contained in special subsystems 'deserve' the additional 'bite' that enforcement through countermeasures can deliver".

[271] There are, indeed, a bulk of further sub-systems such as the Algier Accords, several human rights systems, especially the ECHR, environmental systems, and so forth.

[272] Simma & Pulkowski, *supra* fn. 270, 516 et seq.

[273] See *supra* 81 et seq.

[274] See, for instance, article 48 of the 2004 Canada Model BIT, article 37 of the 2004 US Model BIT, article 10 of the Germany—Mexico BIT, and article 9 of the UK—Nigeria BIT (1991).

created appear to differ from the general system of state responsibility: the former results in a direct relationship between investor and host State which is not envisaged at all by the general system; the latter submits the State to a comparatively strict regime.[275]

Further, two important features of the general system do not seem to be compatible with the investor—State relationship created by the investment treaty regime. Firstly, the consequences of a breach of a substantive obligation under an investment treaty do not match the State—State relationship discussed *infra*. The obligation to cease the violation and to provide reparation for the injury is owed to the investor. The corresponding rights are thus not bestowed upon the investor's home State but upon the investor itself.[276] This feature of the investment treaty regime is underpinned by the fact that awards rendered by treaty-based tribunals are not binding upon the parties to the treaty but upon the parties to the disputes, i.e., upon the host State and the foreign investor.[277] Secondly, the general rules for the invocation of state responsibility have not been applied under the investment treaty regime. Under the ILC Articles,[278] the rules on the nationality of claims and the exhaustion of local remedies are essential conditions for the invocation of a State's responsibility.[279] By contrast, under the investment treaty regime, the rule on the exhaustion of local

[275] Generally, States are bound to comply with the respective award. For a more flexible approach, see article 48(9) of the 2004 Canada Model BIT: "The Parties shall, within 60 days of the decision of a panel, reach agreement on how to resolve their dispute. Such agreement shall normally implement the decision of the panel".

[276] See Douglas, *supra* fn. 160, 191: "The status of the investor's new right, and the corresponding liability of the host State, is not equivalent to the new rights and obligations which come into existence upon a breach of an international obligation within a bilateral relationship between states".

[277] Article 1136(1) of the NAFTA is very clear in this regard and states the following: "An award made by a Tribunal shall have no binding force except between the disputing parties and in respect of the particular case". It is worthy to note that the contracting States are referred to as "The Parties" in the NAFTA text. Article 53(1) of the ICSID Convention reads: "(1) The award shall be binding on the parties and shall not be subject to any appeal or to any other remedy except those provided for in this Convention". The term used for the contracting States in this convention is plainly "Contracting States".

[278] Article 44 of the ILC Articles provides: "Admissibility of Claims—The responsibility of a State may not be invoked if: (1) the claim is not brought in accordance with any applicable rule relating to the nationality of claims; (2) the claim is one to which the rule of exhaustion of local remedies applies and any available and effective local remedy has not been exhausted".

[279] Crawford, *supra* fn. 261, 264.

remedies has been done away with entirely.[280] Furthermore, the second requirement—the rules on the nationality of claims—has been modified considerably under the influence of investment treaty regimes.[281] Ultimately, it has to be mentioned that even the ILC explicitly refers to investment treaties as a special regime of state responsibility.[282] Consequently, the investment treaty regime appears to be a sub-system of state responsibility under international law.

b. *Relationship to General Rules of State Responsibility*

Yet, this statement, in and of itself, does not permit a conclusion with regard to the question whether the general rules of state responsibility may at some time be applicable within the framework of the investor—host State relationship under investment treaties. As mentioned above, the degree of self-contingency and thus the necessity to rely upon general rules of international law may vary between the different legal subsystems. As for the investment treaty regime, the contention has been made that the system stands entirely outside of the general system of state responsibility.[283] This would be proven by the silence of the ILC Articles toward the investment treaty system and the secondary obligations owed to non-state actors in general.[284] Douglas further alleges that the non-adherence to the general system of state responsibility by the investment treaty regime would be proven by the fact that the tribunals accepted the distraction from the rule of exhaustion of local remedies although the treaties were silent on this subject. If the investment treaty system were part of the general system, so the

---

[280] See, e.g., C. Dominicé, La clause CIRDI dans les traités bilateraux suisses de protection des investissements, in: W. Haller et al. (eds), Im Dienst an der Gemeinschaft, Festschrift für Dietrich Schindler zum 65. Geburtstag (1989), 457, 472 et seq.; Paulsson, *supra* fn. 37, 239–240. For jurisprudence of treaty-based tribunals, see, e.g., *SGS v. Pakistan*, *supra* fn. 118, para. 151; *Compañia de Aguas del Aconquija, S.A. v. The Argentine Republic*, ICSID Case No. ARB/97/3, Award, 21 November 2000, 5 ICSID Rep. 299 (hereinafter, *Vivendi Award*), para. 81; *Vivendi Annulment*, *supra* fn. 115, para. 52.

[281] See generally Orrego Vicuña, *supra* fn. 189, 340 et seq. For investment treaty arbitration, see A. Sinclair, The Substance of Nationality Requirements in Investment Treaty Arbitration, ICSID Rev.-FILJ 20 (2005), 357 et seq.

[282] Crawford, *supra* fn. 261, 210.

[283] Douglas, *supra* fn. 160, 189.

[284] Douglas, *supra* fn. 160, 187–189. The author contemplates that parts two and three of the articles were not applicable and that "[a]n uncritical transplantation of secondary rules that govern, inter alia, the consequences of a diplomatic protection claim between two state parties is inappropriate".

argument goes, an explicit waiver would have been required since the implication of a waiver of the local remedies rule was not conceivable under international law.[285] However, one of the principal purposes of investment treaties is the disposal of the local remedies rule.[286] Thus, it can hardly be argued that silence of a treaty on this matter would require the implication of a waiver when the essential *raison d'être* of this treaty is precisely to do away with this principle.[287]

Other commentators seem to regard the problem merely as one relating to the scope of application of the ILC Articles. On the one hand, this serves to question the applicability of general rules to investor—State relationships claiming that they address exclusively responsibility as between States.[288] According to Hobér, on the other hand, there are several reasons which argue for the wholesale application of the ILC Articles and thus the general system of state responsibility in investment treaty arbitrations.[289] Firstly, article 1 of the ILC Articles covered all international obligations, not only those owed to other States but also those owed to other entities including individuals. Secondly, this universal application would be confirmed by article 2 of the ILC Articles which did not specify the term "international obligation of the State" the breach of which leads to state responsibility. Thirdly, a similar rationale, i.e., the broad scope of the obligations covered, can be inferred from article 12 of the ILC Articles. Finally, strict applicability in a formalistic sense cannot be required since the ILC Articles are merely draft articles and not a conventional treaty.[290]

The last statement is certainly correct, yet, it somehow fails to consider the essential aspects of the subject matter at hand. The ILC Articles are a reflection of customary international law. Investment treaties, in turn, do not merely lay down customary international law

---

[285] Id., 192, where the author refers to the *ELSI Case* in which the ICJ held that important principles of customary international law could not "be held to have been tacitly dispensed with". See *Elettronica Sicula S.p.A. (ELSI)* (United States v. Italy) [1989] ICJ Rep. 14, para. 42.

[286] See, e.g., J. Paulsson, Denial of Justice (2005), 102–103; G. van Harten, Investment Treaty Arbitration and Public Law (2007), 110 et seq.

[287] Contra Amerasinghe, *supra* fn. 178, 253.

[288] This point of view is contradicted expressly by the ILC in its commentaries on the ILC Articles. Nonetheless, it is true that the ILC Articles are primarily intended to govern inter-state relationships.

[289] K. Hobér, State Responsibility and Investment Arbitration, in: C. Ribeiro (ed.), Investment Arbitration and the Energy Charter Treaty (2006), 261, 265 et seq.

[290] Id., 265.

but progressively develop international law on state responsibility. Thus the question is not whether the ILC Articles find application but to what extent the investment treaty system is autonomous so that it does not require the application of the general rules. Given the methodological approach exposed above, legal sub-systems fall back on general international law when its applicable rules are exhausted. This cannot be different when the special regime does not regulate a certain subject matter at all. Thus, whereas some rules of general state responsibility which do not suit to an investor—State relationship such as the legal consequences of an internationally wrongful act are superseded, others such as the rules on attribution of conduct to States remain intact. In sum, an application of general rules of state responsibility under the investment treaty system is subsidiary. A treaty-based arbitral tribunal, for example, will not require the exhaustion of local remedies, since this principle has been done away with by the investment treaty regime. By contrast, if the treaty does not contain a regulation, for instance, on attribution of conduct, the general rules of international law will have to be applied.

3. *Special Consequences under the Investment Treaty Regime*

As for the rules concerning the consequences of a breach of an international obligation under the investment treaty regime, generally, a two-step system is envisaged. The first step consists of the creation of a new legal relationship between investor and host State. Since the infringement of substantive obligations can be invoked directly by the investor, the host State is enjoined to cease the violation and make reparation for the damages and the investor is granted the corresponding rights. The system thus created is a system of "special-liability" under international law directed towards monetary compensation directly payable to the investor. In *Siemens v. Argentina*, for instance, the tribunal ruled that Argentina had to pay compensation amounting to approximately $220 million, deliver the contract performance bond, and pay interests at the rate of 2.66%.[291] In general, however, the amounts rendered

---

[291] *Siemens A.G. v. The Argentine Republic*, ICSID Case No. ARB/02/8, Award, 6 February 2007 (hereinafter, *Siemens v. Argentina*), para. 403. For the exact calculation of the compensation, see id., paras. 348 et seq. Originally, Siemens claimed US$283,859,710 as the book value of its investment, US$124,541,000 on account of *lucrum cessans*, and additional damages such as subcontractors' damages amounting to approximately US$55,000,000.

by the tribunals are significantly less than the amount claimed. In a significant number of disputes, the decisions on jurisdiction rendered by the tribunals serve primarily to enhance the standing for further business negotiations.[292]

The second step comes only into play in case of non-compliance with a final award. In such an event, which admittedly occurs very rarely under investment treaties,[293] the investor—host State relationship turns into a home State—host State relationship.[294] In fact, the breach of obligations in this case does not concern the infringement of the substantive obligations owed towards the investor but the obligation to abide by the enforcement system set out by the treaty and owed additionally to the investor's home State. If the non-compliance equally persists under this second step, the general system would re-emerge due to the fallback on the customary international law of state responsibility. In this case, the whole range of measures under international law including countermeasures may be employed by the home State. Yet, the investment treaty system was set up precisely to avoid such results.

III. *The Application of International Law in International Arbitration over Contracts between Host States and Foreign Investors*

1. *General*

The application of international law to the substance of foreign investor—host State disputes has always been regarded as one of the essential elements of the "internationalisation" of the investor—host State relationship.[295] The dependency of the investor's fate upon the host State's arbitrary alternations of its domestic legal system can only be avoided by applying international law. In this context, in the absence of international investment treaties, the application of international

[292] On account of this, many disputes do not reach the merits stage but get settled after the issuance of a decision on jurisdiction.

[293] This is certainly due to the fact that ICSID awards are regarded as final and self-executing and are thus excluded from the influence of national courts. See, e.g., Baldwin et al., *supra* fn. 69, 22, where the authors state that up to date, no court has refused to enforce an ICSID award.

[294] See, for instance, article 64 of the ICSID: "Any dispute arising between Contracting States concerning the interpretation or application of this Convention … shall be referred to the International Court of Justice by the application of any party to such dispute, unless the States concerned agree to another method of settlement".

[295] See *supra* 29 et seq.

law was and remains controversial to such an extent that would dissuade investors from relying thereupon. By contrast, the conclusion of investment treaties and the establishment of the ICSID Convention are supposed to have poured oil on troubled waters.[296]

The investment treaty regime necessarily sets up a direct or, at least, an indirect choice of international law as applicable to the substance of disputes. Thereby, the application of international law becomes an inherent pattern in investment treaty disputes.[297] Insofar as they are covered, this application, of course, extends to contractual relationships between foreign investor and host State. In this regard, however, a further element complicates the situation. As explained above, investment contracts often order the application of domestic law.[298] It is thus necessary to examine whether this choice somehow alters the law applicable to investment disputes. Prior to this examination, it is apposite to shortly examine the system introduced by investment treaties concerning the direct and indirect choice of international law.

2. *Application of International Law due to Direct Choice by Treaty*

a. *The Source of the Choice of Law Rule*

The right to choose the law applicable to an investment dispute cannot be self-evident in a dispute between a State and a private person but must be conferred upon the parties by legal rules that somehow are linked to a body of national law.[299] In principle, the right to choice of law in international investment arbitration may be drawn from several sources.[300] Yet, in investment treaty disputes, virtually all choices of law rely on two sources of the choice of law rule: either the treaty itself or the arbitral rules under the auspices of which the treaty-based arbitration takes place.

---

[296] P. Bernadini, The Law Applied by International Arbitrators to State Contracts, in: R. Briner (ed.), Law of International Business and Dispute Settlement in the 21st Century—Liber Amicorum Karl-Heinz Böckstiegel (2001), 51, 64 et seq.

[297] See generally C. Schreuer, The Relevance of Public International Law in International Commercial Arbitration: Investment Disputes, available at: www.univie.ac.at (last visited: 12 April 2010), 1 et seq.

[298] See *supra* 47 et seq.

[299] See, e.g., J. Kropholler, Internationales Privatrecht (2001), 288.

[300] These sources may be (i) the investment treaty itself; (ii) national investment legislation; (iii) the investment contract; (iv) the arbitral rules; (v) the *lex loci arbitri*; and (vi) general public international law. See also Douglas, *supra* fn. 160, 194.

b. *The Direct Choice by Treaty*

Several investment treaties contain provisions which constitute a direct choice of law. The particular choice is, of course, contingent upon the specific wording of the relevant provision. Whereas the two most important multilateral treaties and several BITs contain clear choices of international law and of its applicable provisions,[301] the majority of BITs which contain a choice of law lay down a combination of international law and domestic law.[302] These combinations frequently encompass four elements: (i) the host State's law, (ii) the relevant investment treaty itself, (iii) any contractual undertaking relating to the investment, and (iv) general international law.[303] The choice of law effectuated by such treaty provisions is thus without any doubts very broad. This very broad range of applicable laws makes it even questionable whether one may speak of the parties' choice of the law applicable at all. Indeed, the choice in these cases is so wide that one may hardly see any rules of law that the tribunal may not apply.[304] Arbitral tribunals that were confronted with similar provisions tried to consider all elements of this "broad framework of the applicable law."[305] The tribunal in *Antoine Goetz v. Burundi*[306] appears to be the sole tribunal that carried out a profound analysis of a provision on applicable law in a BIT.[307]

---

[301] Article 1131 of the NAFTA reads as follows: "Governing Law—1. A Tribunal established under this Section shall decide the issues in dispute in accordance with this Agreement and applicable rules of international law." Article 26(6) of the ECT states: "(6) A tribunal established under paragraph (4) shall decide the issues in dispute in accordance with this Treaty and applicable rules and principles of international law." See also article 30 of the US 2004 Model BIT: "[T]he tribunal shall decide the issues in dispute in accordance with this Treaty and applicable rules of international law"; Article 16 of the Austria Model BIT, UNCTAD Compendium, vol. VII (2002), 256.

[302] Only a minority of BITs refer exclusively to international law. See, for instance, article 8(5) of the Ethiopia—Sudan BIT (2000). Similarly, only a minority of agreements refer solely to domestic law. For an example of a combined choice, see article 9(3) of the Bulgaria—Thailand BIT (2003).

[303] See, inter alia, article 7(4) of the South Africa Model BIT, UNCTAD Compendium, vol. VIII (2002), 277; article 9(4) of the Benin Model BIT, UNCTAD Compendium, vol. IX (2002), 284.

[304] Schreuer, *supra* fn. 297, 20.

[305] *Fedax N.V. v. Venezuela*, ICSID Case No. ARB/96/3, Award, 9 March 1998, (1998) 37 ILM 1378, para. 30 (hereinafter, *Fedax v. Venezuela*). The tribunal applied the ICSID Convention, the investment treaty, the Venezuelan Commercial Code, and the Venezuelan Law on Public Credit.

[306] *Antoine Goetz v. The Republic of Burundi*, ICSID Case No. ARB/95/3, Award, 10 February 1999 (hereinafter, *Goetz v. Burundi*).

[307] Article 8(5) of the Belgium—Luxembourg Economic Union—Burundi BIT reads as follows:

The four categories of the clause were regrouped by the Tribunal into national law and international law.[308] The application of both groups was substantiated as follows:

> Que le Tribunal doive faire application du droit burundais ne saurait faire de doute, puisque aussi bien ce dernier est cité en tout premier lieu par la disposition pertinente de la Convention belgo-burundaise d'investissement. Quant au droit international, son application s'impose pour une double raison. D'abord, parce que...le droit burundais paraît incorporer el droit international et le rendre ainsi directement applicable.... Ensuite, parce que la République du Burundi est tenue par les obligations internationales qu'elle a librement assumées en vertu de la Convention de protection des investissements...."[309]

Hence, in addition to international law, be it the provisions of the treaty itself or be it general principles of international law, arbitral tribunals have to apply the domestic law of the host State when such a wide choice has been made.[310]

In any event, the choice in investment treaties at the outset is a mere choice of the contracting States and not of the parties to the particular dispute. Yet, when treaties contain provisions on applicable law, the investor, by consenting to the State's standing arbitration offer, accepts the choice-of-law thus made between the two or several States parties to the agreement. The treaty's provision on applicable law thereby becomes part of the arbitration agreement[311] and can be

---

L'organisme d'arbitrage statue sur base: - du droit national de la partie contractante partie au litige, sur le territoire de laquelle l'investissement est situé, y compris les règles relatives aux conflits de lois; - des dispositions de la présente Covention; des termes de l'engagement particulier qui serait intervenu au sujet de l'investissement; - des règles et principes de droit international généralement admis.

[308] *Goetz v. Burundi, supra* fn. 306, para. 96.

[309] Id., para. 98.

[310] See also *Emilio Agustín Maffezini v. Kingdom of Spain*, ICSID Case No. ARB/97/7, Award, 13 November 2000, paras. 68, 82, 89, 90 (hereinafter, *Maffezini v. Spain*), where the tribunal applied international law, Spanish legislation, an EC directive, and the investment treaty; *MTD Equity Sdn. Bhd. v. Republic of Chile*, ICSID Case No. ARB/01/7, Decision on Annulment, 21 March 2007, paras. 59 et seq.; *Eastern Sugar B.V. v. The Czech Republic*, UNCITRAL Arbitration, SCC No. 088/2004, Partial Award, 27 March 2007 (hereinafter, *Eastern Sugar v. Czech Republic*), paras. 195–197.

[311] C. Schreuer, Failure to Apply the Governing Law in International Investment Arbitration, Austrian Rev. Int'l & Europ. L. 7 (2002), 147, 151 et seq.; Schreuer, *supra* fn. 297, 10.

regarded as the choice of law undertaken by the parties to the particular dispute.[312]

3. *Indirect Choice of International Law by Treaties*

The question whether, in the absence of an express choice of the parties in a treaty, an implicit choice can be deduced from the relationship of the parties and the circumstances surrounding the dispute is controversial.[313] Notwithstanding this, investment treaties contain two further elements which regularly introduce international law's application.

a. *Framework of Arbitral Rules*

The right to submit disputes to international arbitration opens up new opportunities to select international law and in some cases, even entails a prescription of international law's application. The arbitral institutions to which parties to an investment treaty dispute may refer the settlement of their dispute do not set out substantive rules for the relationship between host State and foreign investor. They merely provide for a procedural framework which may give a certain degree of guidance to the parties and the arbitrators.[314] Primarily, the applicable substantive law may be determined by the choice of the parties to the dispute.[315] In the absence of such a choice, however, the tribunal concerned is granted considerable freedom to choose the applicable law.[316]

---

312 See Parra, *supra* fn. 45, 332; Peters, *supra* fn. 82, 147–148; I. Shihata & A. Parra, The Experience of the International Centre for Settlement of Investment Disputes, ICSID Rev.-FILJ 14 (1999), 299, 336 et seq.; Schreuer, *supra* fn. 42, 433. See also *Siemens v. Argentina*, *supra* fn. 291, para. 76.

313 See, e.g., Schreuer, *supra* fn. 42, 573 et seq.; Giardina, *supra* fn. 248, 217; I. Shihata & A. Parra, Applicable Substantive Law in Disputes between States and Private Foreign Parties: The Case of Arbitration under the ICSID Convention, ICSID Rev.-FILJ 9 (1994), 183, 190 et seq.

314 See, e.g., UNCITRAL Model Law on International Commercial Arbitration (1985).

315 See, e.g., article 28(1) of the UNCITRAL Model Law on International Commercial Arbitration (1985); article 17(1) of the ICC Rules of Arbitration (1998).

316 Article 17 of the ICC Arbitration Rules (1998) reads as follows: "Applicable Rules of Law (1) The parties shall be free to agree upon the rules of law to be applied by the Arbitral Tribunal to the merits of the dispute. In the absence of any such agreement, the Arbitral Tribunal shall apply the rules of law which it determines to be appropriate." Article 33 of the UNCITRAL Arbitration Rules (1976) states the following: "1. The arbitral tribunal shall apply the law designated by the parties as applicable to the substance of the dispute. Failing such designation by the parties, the arbitral tribunal shall apply the law determined by the conflict of law rules which it considers applicable".

This discretion has regularly been used to apply international law[317] and in the case of investment treaty disputes, even requires its application. In the ICSID framework, the wording of the second sentence of article 42(1) of the Convention has triggered a fierce debate on the importance of international law.[318] Notwithstanding the theoretical inconsistency of the question concerning international law's application in this regard, ICSID tribunals have shown a considerable degree of consistency in doing so.[319]

b. *Investment Treaties as International Law*

An investment treaty in and of itself constitutes international law. The substantive standards which are set out by an investment treaty such as, for instance, the obligation to accord fair and equitable treatment, not to impair investments by discriminatory measures, not to expropriate property without paying an effective and appropriate compensation, or to provide full security and protection[320] constitute international law standards with which the conduct of the host State has to be in conformity. As a corollary, the mere application of a treaty's substantive standards leads to the application of international law. It is thus the nature of the treaties themselves which makes international law so relevant to the resolution of investment treaty disputes.[321] In the words of Weil: "The very fact that certain rights and obligations of the host State and the foreign investor are set out in an international treaty confers an international character on those rights and obligations."[322]

---

[317] See *supra* 48 et seq.

[318] Whereas some authors prefer a more prominent role for international law, others argue that international law has a mere supplemental function. For a summary of this debate and a description of the different points of view, see E. Gaillard & Y. Banifatemi, The Meaning of "and" in Article 42(1), Second Sentence, of the Washington Convention: The Role of International Law in the ICSID Choice of Law Process, ICSID Rev.-FILJ 18 (2003), 375 et seq.

[319] Moreover, arbitral tribunals held that ultimately, international law was the controlling law. See, e.g., *Compania del Desarollo de Santa Elena, S.A. v. Costa Rica*, ICSID Case No. ARB/96/1, Award, 17 February 2000, ICSID Rev.-FILJ 15 (2000), 169, para. 64.

[320] These are the protective standards which are present in virtually all modern investment treaties.

[321] Cf. A. Broches, The Convention on the Settlement of Investment Disputes between States and Nationals of Other States, RdC 136 (1972-II), 331, 392; R. Kreindler, The Law Applicable to International Investment Disputes, in: N. Horn (ed.), Arbitrating Foreign Investment Disputes (2004), 401, 405–406; G. Sacerdoti, Investment Arbitration: Under ICSID and UNCITRAL Rules: Prerequisites, Applicable Law, Review of Awards, ICSID Rev.-FILJ 19 (2004), 1, 25.

[322] P. Weil, The State, the Foreign Investor, and International Law: The No Longer Stormy Relationship of a Ménage À Trois, ICSID Rev.-FILJ 15 (2000), 401, 411.

This has not been sufficiently appreciated by some tribunals. In *AAPL v. Sri Lanka*, for example, the tribunal held that the submissions of both parties evinced their mutual agreement on the investment treaty's rules as the primary source of applicable rules.[323] Since the mere application of the treaty's provisions in a dispute based on treaty violations cannot be disputed, this was not necessary. As pointed out by Spiermann, "[t]o the extent that the host state has undertaken treaty obligations relevant to the dispute, it can be taken for granted that they will be applied directly by an arbitral tribunal, in addition to the overlapping international law for the protection of aliens and the implications derived from the principle *pacta sunt servanda*"[324].

More recently, the ad hoc committee in *Vivendi v. Argentina* recognized this principle albeit in a different context.[325] Hence, to a certain extent, inasmuch as the treaty standards itself are concerned, the law applicable to investment disputes, by definition, has to be international law. This approach has been followed by several tribunals in more recent decisions.[326]

In sum, the contention that no conclusions as to applicable law may be drawn from the fact that the dispute has been submitted to international arbitration[327] is not tenable under the investment treaty regime. Inasmuch as treaty violations are concerned, the submission of a dispute to international arbitration based on this treaty requires the application of international law. In other words, a choice of international law

---

323 *AAPL v. Sri Lanka*, *supra* fn. 47, para. 20.

324 O. Spiermann, Applicable Law, in: P. Muchlinski et al. (eds.), The Oxford Handbook of International Investment Law (2008), 89, 108.

325 *Vivendi Annulment*, *supra* fn. 115, para. 96:

> In accordance with this general principle … [according to which, an international law's characterization of a State's act as wrongful is not affected by the act's characterization as lawful by internal law], whether there has been a breach of the BIT and whether there has been a breach of contract are different questions. Each of these claims will be determined by reference to its own proper or applicable law—in the case of the BIT, by international law.

326 See, e.g., *Waste Management, Inc. v. United Mexican States*, ICSID Case No. ARB(AF)/00/3, Award, 30 April 2004, (2004) 43 ILM 881, para. 73; *MTD Equity Sdn. Bhd. v. Republic of Chile*, ICSID Case No. ARB/01/7, Award, 25 May 2004, (2005) 44 ILM 91, para. 87: "At this point, the Tribunal will limit itself to note that, for purposes of Article 42 (1) of the Convention, the parties have agreed to this arbitration under the BIT. This instrument being a treaty, the agreement to arbitrate under the BIT requires the Tribunal to apply international law".

327 See Schreuer, *supra* fn. 42, 425. By contrast, this statement is certainly true in the absence of an applicable investment treaty.

as the law applicable is certainly made when consent to arbitration is given through an investment treaty. This holds true irrespective of the arbitral framework chosen by the foreign investor.

4. *The Role of Domestic Law*

What remains to be examined is the role of domestic law under this regime and the relationship between domestic law and international law. It is particularly material to examine whether some kind of hierarchy exists between both systems of law under the investment treaty regime. This question further becomes relevant when a contractual choice of law clause stipulates domestic law as the law applicable to disputes arising out of the investment contract.

a. *Necessity of the Application of Domestic Law*

Notwithstanding the above described importance of international law in investment treaty disputes, the correct functioning of the system is likewise based on the application of domestic law. This is clear when domestic law, as in *Goetz v. Burundi* or *Maffezini v. Spain*, has been chosen by the parties. However, even in absence of a choice, domestic law regularly retains an essential role. The foregoing is the result of the legal nature of investment disputes.[328] The determination of the existence and extent of an investment is often closely related to preliminary questions concerning domestic law.[329] For instance, the conclusion of a contract, the effective granting of a license, and the nature of rights with regard to tangible property are questions which are primarily regulated by domestic law. International law, by contrast, does not deal with those property-related questions. An examination, for instance, of the question whether the sale of a certain territory was made in compliance with local real estate laws, by definition, cannot be made

---

[328] Douglas, *supra* fn. 160, 195:

> It is important to emphasize that the substantive law governing investment disputes is necessarily a hybrid of international and municipal law due to the private or commercial interests at the heart of the jurisdiction. This may be contrasted with state/state disputes arising out of the interpretation or application of the investment treaty which are governed purely by international law.

[329] Cf. C. Schreuer, International and Domestic Law in Investment Disputes—The Case of ICSID, Austrian Rev. Int'l & Europ. L. 1 (1996), 89, 89: "Investment relationships typically involve domestic law as well as international law. The host State's domestic law regulates a multitude of technical questions such as admission, licensing, labour relations, tax, foreign exchange and real estate".

through international law. As a corollary, international law must resort to *renvoi* to domestic law for those issues.[330] It is only subsequent to the recognition of a right under the municipal law of the host State that the respective investment treaty may be relied upon. Of course, this does not mean that the foreign investor is entirely dependent upon the host State's regulations. As a last resort, the conduct of the host State towards the foreign investor is subject to assessment against the international minimum standard under customary international law.[331]

An example of the proper application of *renvoi* to municipal law even when the BIT does not refer to domestic law is the case of *EnCana v. Ecuador*.[332] In this case, the tribunal had to examine whether the non-payment of a VAT-refund was an infringement of the relevant investment treaty. After the confirmation that a right to VAT-refund would fall within the notion of investment under the treaty, the tribunal had to examine whether such a right did exist. Although the investment treaty made no reference to the host State's law, the tribunal held that the question of the existence of the right to a VAT-refund had to be resolved by application of Ecuador's taxation law.[333]

b. *The Relationship between Domestic Law and International Law*

The conjoint applicability of domestic law and international law immediately entails the question of the relationship between the two. For a long time, the question concerning this relationship in investment disputes has been regarded as the most complex aspect of the area of the law applicable.[334] The corresponding controversy was led mainly by the interpretation of the second sentence of article 42(1) of the ICSID Convention and the question of the proper function of international law in the absence of its choice. The prevailing view among arbitral tribunals and legal commentators was that international law served

---

330 Douglas, *supra* fn. 160, 198; S. Montt, State Liability in Investment Treaty Arbitration (2009), 325.

331 See, e.g., E. Borchard, The Diplomatic Protection of Citizens Abroad or the Law of International Claims (1916), 178.

332 *EnCana Corp. v. Republic of Ecuador*, LCIA Case No. UN3481, UNCITRAL, Award, 3 February 2006.

333 Id., para. 184: "Unlike many BITs there is no express reference to the law of the host State. However for there to have been an expropriation of an investment ... the rights affected must exist under the law which creates them, in this case, the law of Ecuador".

334 Schreuer, *supra* fn. 329, 112.

a mere supplemental and corrective function towards domestic law.[335] This means that an ICSID tribunal was authorized "to apply rules of international law only to fill up lacunae in the applicable domestic law and to ensure precedence to international law norms where the rules of the domestic law [were] in collision with such norms".[336] The reason for this rather restricted function[337] of international law was, presumably, that consent to the ICSID Convention would otherwise be hardly achievable.[338] Be that as it may, arbitral practice, endorsed by legal doctrine which favoured a more prominent role for international law,[339] began to shift its approach from a restricted doctrinaire function to a more pragmatic way of application. Whereas the doctrine of supplementary and corrective function had intended to set up a rigid relationship between both systems, the pragmatic approach signified that tribunals had to apply the system of law which was suitable for the relevant question.[340] Hence, pride is given to an increased degree of

---

[335] See, e.g., O. Chukwumerije, International Law and Article 42 of the ICSID Convention, J. Int'l Arb. 14 (1997), 79, 100–101; G. Elombi, ICSID Awards and the Denial of Host State Laws, J. Int'l Arb. 11 (1994), 61, 66–68; P. Feuerle, International Arbitration and the Choice of Law under Article 42 of the Convention on the Settlement of Investment Disputes, Yale Studies in World Public Order 4 (1977/1978), 89, 118–119; M. Hirsch, The Arbitration Mechanism of the International Centre for the Settlement of Investment Disputes (1993), 140–141; G. Jaenicke, The Prospects for International Arbitration: Disputes between States and Private Enterprises, in: A. Soons (ed.), International Arbitration: Past and the Prospects (1990), 155, 159 et seq.; P. Kahn, The Law Applicable to Foreign Investments: The Contribution of the World Bank on the Settlement of Investment Disputes, Indiana L. J. 44 (1968), 1, 27–29.

[336] *Amco Asia Corp. v. Republic of Indonesia*, ICSID Case No. ARB/81/1, Decision on Annulment, 16 May 1986, 1 ICSID Rep. 509, para. 20.

[337] It is, of course, arguable to what extent a corrective function may be seen as restrictive. Ultimately, the corrective function is nothing more than a confirmation that it is international law which governs decisively. Cf. *Amco Asia Corp. v. Republic of Indonesia*, Resubmitted Case: Award, 5 June 1990, 1 ICSID Rep. 569, para. 40, where the second tribunal in the *Amco* case stated the following: "[W]here there are applicable host-state laws, they must be checked against international law, which will prevail in the case of conflict. Thus international law is fully applicable and to classify its role as 'only' 'supplemental and corrective' seems a distinction without difference".

[338] In any event, municipal law was regarded to be the primarily governing law of the relationship between the investor and the host State. See Schreuer, *supra* fn. 42, 598.

[339] See Gaillard & Banifatemi, *supra* fn. 318, 403 et seq. Contra M. Reisman, The Regime for *Lacunae* in the ICSID Choice of Law Provision and the Question of Its Threshold, ICSID Rev.-FILJ 15 (2000), 362, 380.

[340] See *CMS Gas Transmission Company v. The Argentine Republic*, ICSID Case No. ARB/01/8, Award, 12 May 2005, (2005) 44 ILM 1205, para. 116: "More recently, however, a more pragmatic and less doctrinaire approach has emerged, allowing for the

discretion of the arbitral tribunal in the choice of the applicable law without restricting international law to a "supplemental and corrective" function. In *CMS v. Argentina*, for instance, the tribunal, faced with the question of the law applicable to the merits, held that there was such a close interaction between "the legislation and the regulations governing the gas privatization, the License and international law, as embodied in both the Treaty and in customary international law" that these rules were "inseparable" and would be applied by the tribunal "to the extent justified". This more prominent role of international law is inextricably linked to the investment treaty regime upon which the consent in majority of international investment arbitrations is based.[341]

Hence, both systems of law may find application when convenient in the respective area. This approach upholds the allocation of prevalence upon international law in the case of collision: despite the necessity of applying domestic law and the conjoint application of both systems, it is clear that international law must prevail in case of conflicting provisions of both systems.[342] This holds true irrespective of the role which the particular host State's constitution provides for

---

application of both domestic and international law if the specific facts of the disputes so justifies".

[341] The reason for this link is that, as mentioned above, the treaties entail an automatic application of international law. By contrast, a more restricted role of international law is tenable when the arbitral proceedings do not rely on consent given by treaty but on consent given by direct agreement between the parties, which is seldom the case in recent times.

[342] See, e.g., *M.C.I. Power Group L.C. v. Ecuador*, ICSID Case No. ARB/03/6, Award, 31 July 2007, para. 218 (hereinafter, *MCI Power v. Ecuador*):

> In the event of possible contradictions between the rules of Ecuadorian law and the BIT and other applicable rules of general international law, the Tribunal will decide on their compatibility, bearing in mind the contents and purpose of those rules in light of the precedence that international rules take over the domestic legislation of a State.

In *Eastern Sugar v. Czech Republic*, *supra* fn. 310, para. 197, the tribunal appears to even exclude the application of conflicting provisions: "[T]he Arbitral Tribunal should consider … how non conflicting provisions of Czech law might be relevant". See also T. Wälde, Investment Arbitration under the Energy Charter Treaty: From Dispute Settlement to Treaty Implementation, Arb. Int'l 12 (1996), 429, 433: "The Treaty, however, has primacy over national law when national law would be used to undermine the effectiveness of the Treaty's investment obligations, for example retroactive negation of the legal character of a contract/concession in order to escape the Treaty's obligations."; Kreindler, *supra* fn. 321, 413.

international treaties.[343] Any other result would be in conflict with the fundamental principle of international law according to which the international wrongfulness of an act is not affected by domestic law.[344]

c. *The Contractual Choice of Domestic Law*

As explained above in Chapter 1, many host States attempt to include the choice of their domestic law as the proper law of the contract in investment agreements that are concluded with foreign investors. This choice has been, based on the assumption of principal party autonomy or on restrictions of law of conflicts provisions, precisely the main reason why the application of international law to such contracts has to be dismissed in the absence of international investment treaties.[345] Therefore, the question arises whether this situation is different under the impact of investment treaties. Under the investment treaty regime, the prevalent application of international law has become an essential element of the investor—host State relationship. Insofar as treaty violations are concerned, the pertinent treaty itself will require the application of international law. This holds true irrespective of whether the particular dispute arose out of a contract or not and whether the contract stipulates a different regime or not. Further, even when the treaty itself orders the applicability of the rules of law as set out in the

---

[343] In *Enron Corp. v. Argentine Republic*, ICSID Case No. ARB/01/3, Award, 22 May 2007, para. 208, for instance, the tribunal stated the following:

> It must be noted also that the very legal system of the Argentine Republic … provides for a prominent role of treaties under both Articles 27 and 31 of the Constitution. Treaties are constitutionally recognized among the sources considered "the supreme law of the Nation". It follows that in case of conflict between a treaty rule and an inconsistent rule of domestic law, the former will prevail. This is not just the consequence of the Constitution so providing, *but also* the solution dictated by Article 27 of the Vienna Convention on the Law of Treaties in that a State "may not invoke the provisions of its internal law as justification for its failure to perform a treaty" (emphasis added).

[344] Cf. article 3 of the ILC Draft Articles, *supra* fn. 260: "The characterization of an act of a State as internationally wrongful is governed by international law. Such characterization is not affected by the characterization of the same act as lawful by internal law". Giardina, *supra* fn. 249, 32–34 substantiates this with two reasons: (i) the home State's waiver of exertion of diplomatic protection and (ii) the binding force of the award upon the contracting States.

[345] Contra Spiermann, *supra* fn. 324, 28: "While treaty claims are naturally decided on the basis of the treaty and international law, contract claims are not solely decided on by reference to the contract and national law. This is a consequence of applicable law having been internationalised in the 20th century, ensuring general principles of law, or public international law, a role".

contract,[346] the ultimate dominance of international law cannot be disputed. Thus, a contractual choice of domestic law cannot be regarded as a valid choice of law for treaty disputes.[347]

By contrast, this scheme is altered entirely when treaty-based arbitral tribunals are vested with jurisdiction over claims which are not based on treaty violations.[348] In this case, the substantive treaty standards are not involved in the resolution of the dispute. In other words, the conduct of the host State in these cases is not tested against the international law set out by the treaty.[349] As a corollary, international law finds no per se application. This means that when a contract contains a choice of the host State's domestic law, this system of law is exclusively applicable when State conduct which does not amount to a violation of the treaty is assessed. The precise elements of this distinction and the sole case involving such a jurisdiction over non-treaty claims will be further analyzed in Chapters 3 and 4.

D. The Notion of "Investment" and Contracts between Foreign Investor and Host State

The magnitude of the protective regime which is established by international investment treaties for contracts between host States and foreign investors depends first of all on the scope of application of the treaties. Generally, the scope can be determined through an interpretation of the treaty provisions defining "investments", "nationals",

---

[346] See, e.g., article 30(2)(a) of the US 2004 Model BIT:

> [When respondent is alleged to have infringed an investment agreement], the tribunal shall apply: (a) the rules of law specified in the pertinent investment authorization or investment agreement, or as the disputing parties may otherwise agree; (b) if the rules of law have not been specified or otherwise agreed: (i) the law of the respondent, including its rules on the conflict of laws; and (ii) such rules of international law as may be applicable (footnote omitted).

[347] See, e.g., *MCI Power v. Ecuador, supra* fn. 342, paras. 215, 217.

[348] According to some legal commentators and arbitral tribunals, this is the case when the treaty contains a broadly phrased jurisdictional clause. According to the point of view warranted in this work, the only way such a jurisdiction may be envisaged is on account of an umbrella clause. See the further analysis in chapter 4 and the consequences thereof in chapter 5.

[349] The minimum standard of international law, of course, still finds application. Further, an application of international law in such a case is available inasmuch as the host State's law eventually incorporates international law.

"companies", and "territory" of the Contracting Parties.[350] For the purpose of the present work, the main focus will be laid on the notion of "investment" provided for in investment treaties and on the extent to which contracts between a foreign investor and the host State may thereby be included in the agreement's protective standards. The notion of "investment" is, *per definitionem*, of crucial importance to the magnitude of the investment treaty regime. On the one hand, "[i]t may be tempting for a defendant State to argue, as a basis for an objection to jurisdiction, that either there was no investment whatever or no investment under the definition of the BIT or under the particular contract."[351] On the other hand, an excessively wide definition put forward by the investor would trigger a State's undue loss of control over assets in its territory.[352] Hence, legal certainty as to what can be considered as an "investment" pursuant to the pertinent treaty is in the interest of the host State as well as the investor's.[353] A contract between a foreign investor and a host State is only protected by an investment treaty if it falls under its notion of investment. Yet, what requirements must be fulfilled by a contract in order to be assessed as an investment within this sense? Can every contract between a foreign company and a State be regarded as an "investment" or does the term "investment" require a special quality of the subject matter? For instance, is a contract for the construction of a highway an investment? What about long-term contracts for the sale of goods or service contracts such as the provision of customs services?

I. *The Specific Regulations concerning Contracts*

The extent to which contracts and contractual contents are covered by investment agreements is, first of all, a question of the scope of

[350] See Salacuse, *supra* fn. 3, 664; Dolzer & Stevens, *supra* fn. 6, 19–20.

[351] Cf. P. Lalive, Some Objections to Jurisdiction in Investor-State Arbitration, in: A. van den Berg (ed.), International Commercial Arbitration: Important Contemporary Questions, ICCA Congress Series No. 11 (2003), 376, 384.

[352] T. H. Cheng, Power, Authority and International Investment Law, Am. U. Int'l L. Rev. 20 (2004), 465, 472.

[353] See also J. Karl, Aktuelle Probleme des Investitions- und Enteignungsschutzes am Beispiel des Internationalen Konzessionsvertrages, in: J. Baur & S. Hobe (eds.), Rechtsprobleme von Auslandsinvestitionen: Konzessionen, Vertragsanpassung, Vergabeverfahren (2003), 37, 44, who states the following: "Ohne eine klare Definition steht das gesamte Gebäude des internationalen Investitionsschutzes aber auf einem wackligen Fundament."

application of the particular agreement.[354] In order to enjoy the protective standards of an investment treaty, the legal position of an investor must fall into its scope of application. Hence, the definition of investment is of crucial importance to the question whether and to what extent contracts between the investor and the host State are protected by international investment treaties. In other words, the threshold of investment laid down in investment treaties is the essential hurdle which has to be cleared by the investor in order to reap the benefits of investment treaty protection. Notwithstanding the generally broad approach of investment treaties, parties to a particular treaty are free to include or exclude contractual contents. In addition to the definition of investment, further elements of treaty drafting may be decisive for the question whether contractual contents are included. Treaties may be drafted containing express exclusions of contracts between foreign investor and host State from their coverage. Moreover, treaties may be annexed with negative or positive listings of matters protected. Concerning the inclusion of contracts between investors and host States, three categories of protection can be discerned.[355]

1. *Exclusion of Contractual Contents*

In order to exclude the protection of contracts between a foreign investor and the host State from the scope of the particular treaty's application, the negotiating States have two options: they can expressly exclude such contracts from the scope of the treaty or they can refrain from referring to breaches of contractual obligations as protected assets in the definition of investment.[356] Examples of such an approach can be barely found among the recent investment arbitration cases.

---

[354] It is clear that the contract itself is a mere legal document and thereby, not an asset or an investment. However, the legal rights which parties are granted and the obligations with which parties are enjoined by the contract may be regarded as an investment. The question therefore, always has to be whether the content of the contract, i.e., the rights and obligations provided for in the contract can be classified as investment. Cf. *Petrobart Ltd. v. The Kyrgyz Republic*, SCC Institute (Energy Charter Treaty), Arbitration No. 126/2003, 29 March 2005, 71 (hereinafter, *Petrobart v. Kyrgyz Republic*).

[355] This refers exclusively to the definition of investment in an investment treaty. The consequences entailed through the inclusion of a broad dispute resolution clause or an "umbrella clause" are addressed in other sections.

[356] UNCTAD, Series on International Investment Agreements, State Contracts (2004), 46.

However, some treaties of older vintage contained rather narrow notions of "investment".[357] Nonetheless, in times of economic globalization and globalized competition among capital-importing States, a complete exclusion of contractual contents from investment treaty protection appears to be a very seldom occurrence.

2. *Limited Protection of Contractual Contents*

The specific protection of certain types of contracts between an investor and a host State can be achieved through several means. In a positive listing, the types of state contracts that are covered by the agreement can be listed. A negative listing can open the door for protection of the type of contracts not included in the listing. Further, the definition of investment in the treaty can make specific reference to certain conditions or exceptions.[358]

As an example of a treaty providing limited protection of contractual contents, mention can be made of a string of very recent treaties.[359] The precursor of these recent versions was the 2004 US Model BIT. This Model Treaty contains a concept of investment that argues against the coverage of commercial transactions.[360] As a consequence, the contention that by the referring to "investment agreements", all contracts between foreign investors and the host State, including mere commercial transactions, are covered appears untenable.[361] The precise and narrow definition of "investment agreements" contradicts such

---

[357] See, for instance, the definitions cited by C. Amerasinghe, The Jurisdiction of the International Centre for the Settlement of Investment Disputes, Indian J. Int'l L. 19 (1979), 166, 178–180.

[358] UNCTAD, *supra* fn. 356, 47.

[359] Several investment chapters of recently concluded FTA's require investment to have the abovementioned specific features. See, e.g., fn. 15-1 of the US—Singapore FTA: "Where an asset lacks the characteristics of an investment, that asset is not an investment regardless of the form it may take. The characteristics of an investment include the commitment of capital, the expectation of gain or profit, or the assumption of risk".

[360] The term "investment" is defined as "every asset ... that has the characteristics of an investment, including such characteristics as the commitment of capital or other resources, the expectation of gain or profit, or the assumption of risk". Secondly, it is stated that "claims to payment that are immediately due and result from the sale of goods or services, are less likely to have such characteristics". See also the definition of "investment" in the Canada 2004 Model BIT.

[361] Contra A. Crivellaro, Consolidation of Arbitral and Court Proceedings in Investment Disputes, in: The Law and Practice of International Courts and Tribunals 4 (2005), 371, 409 et seq.

a statement. Finally, the express coverage of "turnkey, construction, management, production, concession, revenue-sharing, and other similar contracts" acknowledges the protection of so-called new forms of investment. Thus, the purported restriction has a very limited magnitude. In fact, it only excludes simple sales and similar commercial transactions. The same result should normally be reached by arbitral tribunals through appropriate interpretation of the term "investment". Hence, rather than providing for a limited protection of contractual contents, these recent treaties intend to give a more concrete definition of contracts that can be considered as "investment". Thus, a truly limited protection of contractual contents, similar to their wholesale exclusion, can be found only in very few treaties.[362]

3. *Full Protection of Contractual Contents*

A full protection of contractual contents can be reached chiefly through an unlimited and unconditional definition of investment that includes any contractual obligation owed to an investor by the host country.[363] Given the domination of very broad definitions of investment in modern investment treaties,[364] there are several examples that provide a broad definition of contracts covered. In most of the cases, the underlying treaties pertain to the category of "illustrative list" treaties.[365] The tribunals confronted with the question of whether the respective economic activity constituted an "investment" within the sense of the treaty usually proceed by confirming, firstly, that the respective contract or the activity provided for by the contract falls under the broad general definitions such as "any kind of asset",[366]

[362] Generally, limitations on the scope of investment are not made expressly with regard to state contracts but concern the underlying transactions. See, e.g., UNCTAD, Bilateral Investment Treaties 1995–2006: Trends in Investment Rulemaking (2007), 11 et seq.

[363] UNCTAD, *supra* fn. 356, 48.

[364] See Dolzer & Stevens, *supra* fn. 6, 26.

[365] Rubins proposes three categories of investment treaties depending on the different approaches used by them to define the notion of investment: "illustrative list" treaties, "exhaustive list" treaties, and "hybrid list" treaties. The "illustrative list" treaties contain a very broad general definition of investment which is accompanied by a non exhaustive list illustrating the subject matter scope. See, N. Rubins, The Notion of "Investment" in International Investment Arbitration, in: N. Horn (ed.), Arbitrating Foreign Investment Disputes (2005), 283, 292–295.

[366] See *SGS v. Pakistan*, *supra* fn. 118, para. 134.

"any kind of property",[367] or just "assets"[368]. Secondly, the tribunals examine whether this is also the case for one or several of the illustrative, non-exhaustive categories. Thereby, several formulations were deemed to cover contracts or contractual contents. In *Salini v. Morocco*, the formulations "rights to any contractual benefit having an economic value" and "any right of an economic nature conferred by law or by contract" were considered sufficient to encompass the rights created by the construction contract at issue.[369] In *SGS v. Pakistan*, the right granted by the contract to the company to carry out pre-shipment inspection services was held to fall under the categories "claims to money or to any performance having economic value" and "concessions under public law, including...all other rights given by law, by contract or by decision of the authority in accordance with law".[370] In *Saipem v. Bangladesh*, the respondent had argued that the rights resulting from an ICC award concerned with a contractual dispute would not fall within the investment notion of the pertinent investment treaty.[371] The tribunal held in this regard that:

> [T]he rights embodied in the ICC Award were not created by the Award, but arise out of the Contract. ... It can thus be left open whether the Award itself qualifies as an investment, since the contract rights which

---

[367] See *Saipem S.p.A v. The People's Republic of Bangladesh*, ICSID Case No. ARB/05/07, Decision on Jurisdiction and Recommendation on Provisional Measures, 21 March 2007, para. 122 (hereinafter, *Saipem v. Bangladesh*).

[368] *Bayindir Insaat Turizm Ticaret Ve Sanayi S.A. v. Islamic Republic of Pakistan*, ICSID Case No. ARB/03/29, Decision on Jurisdiction, 14 November 2005, para. 121 (hereinafter, *Bayindir v. Pakistan*).

[369] *Salini v. Morocco, supra* fn. 97, para. 45. See also *Azurix Corp. v. Argentine Republic*, ICSID Case No. ARB/01/12, Decision on Jurisdiction, 8 December 2003, (2004) 43 ILM 262, para. 62: "[A] concession contract, such as that entered by ABA with the Province qualifies as an investment for the purposes of the BIT given the wide meaning conferred upon this term in the BIT that includes 'any right conferred by law or contract'."

[370] *SGS v. Pakistan, supra* fn. 118, paras. 134–135. See also *RFCC v. Morocco, supra* fn. 98, para. 52 et seq.

[371] Article 1(1) of the Italy—Bangladesh BIT (1990), reads as follows:

> The term "investment" shall be construed to mean any kind of property invested before or after the entry into force of this Agreement .... Without limiting the generality of the foregoing, the term "investment" comprises ... c) *credit for sums of money* and any right for pledges or services having an economic value connected with investments[,] ... e) *any right of a financial nature accruing by law or by contract* and any license, concession or franchise issued in accordance with current provisions governing the exercise of business activities (emphasis added).

> are crystallized by the Award constitute an investment within Article 1 (1)(c) of the BIT.[372]

In continuation, the tribunal held it unnecessary to decide whether an arbitration agreement contained in the contract constituted a right within the sense of article 1(1)(e) of the BIT.[373] In the arbitration of *Petrobart v. Kyrgyz Republic*, which took place before the SCC Institute, the tribunal had to decide whether a contract about the supply and transfer of ownership of 200,000 tons of gas condensate over a period of one year on a monthly basis could be considered as "investment" pursuant to article 1(6) of the ECT.[374] The tribunal took two categories into consideration: firstly, "claims to money and claims to performance pursuant to contract having an economic value and associated with an investment", and secondly, "any right conferred by law or by virtue of any licences and permits granted pursuant to law to undertake any Economic Activity in the Energy Sector."[375] As for the former, the tribunal held that the ambiguities concerning the importance of the phrase "associated with an investment" entailed a logical problem of circularity. As for the latter, it is not entirely clear whether it refers to both categories of claims. Correctly, the tribunal points out that a definition of "investment" is not available when one of the phrases by which investment is to be defined contains the term "investment" itself. The tribunal then turned to the second alternative and affirmed that "a right conferred by contract to undertake an economic activity concerning the sale of gas condensate" fell under article 1(6)(f) of the ECT and was thus an investment according to the ECT.[376] This decision certainly stands aloof of general interpretation of investment definitions in investment treaties. The tribunal gave a mere literal interpretation of article 1(6)(f) and did not take into account any traditional views

---

372 *Saipem v. Bangladesh*, *supra* fn. 367, para. 127.

373 Id., para. 128.

374 *Petrobart v. Kyrgyz Republic*, *supra* fn. 354.

375 In this regard, the tribunal noticed the following definition in article 1(5) of the ECT:

> "Economic Activity in the Energy Sector" means an economic activity concerning the exploration, extraction, refining, production, storage, land transport, transmission, distribution, trade, marketing, or sale of Energy Materials and Products except those included in Annex NI, or concerning the distribution of heat to multiple premises.

376 *Petrobart v. Kyrgyz Republic*, *supra* fn. 354, 72.

concerning the distinction between sales and investment. Even given the breadth of the concept of investment in modern investment treaties compared to the first generation of treaties, such an interpretation can be considered as too broad.

The evolution of investment treaties in this regard is well illustrated in *Jan de Nul v. Egypt.*[377] In this case, the tribunal had to determine the existence of investment pursuant to two treaties between the Belgo-Luxembourg Economic Union and Egypt: one dating from 1977[378] and the other from 2002[379]. The contract at issue concerned dredging work at the Suez Canal. Whilst the tribunal had no doubts that the activities performed under the contract fall within the phrase "contribution in... services", the determination with regard to the 1977 treaty was not that clear. It was particularly questionable whether the dredging of the Suez Canal related to "communications" within the meaning of article III(1) of the 1977 BIT.[380] Finally, the tribunal decided that the dredging was, indeed, an enterprise in the field of communications and thus both investment treaties were applicable.[381]

Thus, it becomes apparent that a wide range of different types of contracts generally falls within the notion of "investment" in investment treaties. However, it cannot be doubted that there are limits to this applicability. These limits are overstepped, for instance, in case of pre-contractual expenditures or mere options to purchase shares.[382]

---

377 *Jan de Nul N.V. v. Arab Republic of Egypt*, ICSID Case No. ARB/04/13, Decision on Jurisdiction, 16 June 2006, paras. 97 et seq. (hereinafter, *Jan de Nul v. Egypt*).

378 Article III(1) of the 1977 BIT contained the following definition of investment: "The term 'investments' shall comprise every direct or indirect contribution of the capital and any other kind of assets, invested or reinvested in enterprises in the field of agriculture, industry, mining forestry, communications, and tourism".

379 The 2002 BIT is a typical "illustrative list" treaty and thus contains the general wide definition "any kind of assets and any direct or indirect contribution in cash, in kind or in services", followed by a non-exhaustive list of typical categories.

380 Article III(1) read as follows: "1. The term 'investment' shall comprise every direct or indirect contribution of capital or any other kind of assets invested or reinvested in enterprises in the field of agriculture, industry, mining, forestry, communications and tourism".

381 The tribunal relied on several dictionaries in order to determine the ordinary meaning of "communication". It cited, inter alia, the following definition from the Websters New Collegiate Dictionary (1973): "a system (as of telephones) for communicating; a system of routes for moving troops, supplies, and vehicles". See, Jan de Nul v. Egypt, *supra* fn. 377, para. 101.

382 See *PSEG Global Inc. v. Republic of Turkey*, ICSID Case No. ARB/02/5, Decision on Jurisdiction, 4 June 2004, para. 189. In this case, the US company PSEG had concluded a contract with the Government of Turkey for the construction, operation,

A further example is the case of *Nagel v. Czech Republic.* In 2002, a tribunal under the auspices of the SCC Institute had to decide whether a cooperation agreement between a British businessman and an enterprise wholly owned by the Czech Republic amounted to an investment or not.[383] The alleged investor had filed a claim contending that the refusal to award him a license to establish, own and operate a GSM cellular phone network in a public tender constituted a violation of the BIT between the UK and the Czech Republic. The cooperation agreement concerned the creation of a consortium with the aim of obtaining such a licence. The tribunal refused to consider the agreement as an "investment" within the meaning of the BIT. For the tribunal it was clear that only a right which had a financial value could be considered as an investment.[384] The cooperation agreement, by contrast, neither guaranteed that the licence would be obtained nor obliged the parties to make specific financial contributions to their project. Hence, the tribunal considered that the agreement was only of a preparatory nature and did not create any rights which had a financial value.[385]

Furthermore, it has to be noted that mere commercial transactions were held on some occasions as falling outside the scope of investment treaties even if broadly phrased. In *Joy Mining v. Egypt,* for example, the tribunal stated that a bank guarantee related to a sales contract did not fall within the terms "claims to money or to any performance having a financial value" or "pledge". Although literally, such a claim could be regarded as having a financial value, it could not

and transfer of a power station. The subsequent claim at the ICSID for breach of the US—Turkey BIT was not only brought by PSEG alone but conjointly with NACC, a company which held an option to purchase shares in the local project company. Whilst the tribunal upheld PSEG's claim, it rejected the claim of NACC.

[383] *William Nagel v. Czech Republic,* SCC Case 49/2002, Award. The award was not published and the date of the award is not available. For available information, see IISD News Bulletin, October 8, 2003, available at: www.iisd.org (last visited: 16 April 2010). In addition, see the excerpts from the award reproduced in Stockholm Arbitration Report 2004:1 (hereinafter, Nagel Excerpts), available under: www.sccinstitute.com (last visited: 16 April 2010). See also I. Szász, Some Disputable Issues in Investment Treaty Arbitration and in Contractual Arbitration of Foreign Investment Disputes, in: A. van den Berg (ed.), New Horizons in International Commercial Arbitration and Beyond, ICCA International Arbitration Congress, Beijing 2004 (2005), 192, 195–196 et seq.

[384] See Nagel Excerpts, *supra* fn. 476, 157.

[385] Id., 164.

"amount to recharacterizing as an investment dispute a dispute which in essence concerns a contingent liability."[386] Thus, the decision by the tribunal in *Joy Mining v. Egypt* claimed that an essential differentiation between investment and commercial transactions had to be made in determining "investment" pursuant to investment treaties.

II. *Contracts and Contractual Contents as "Investment" under the ICSID Convention*

The parties' definition of investment is only the first step in determining the coverage of contracts in investment treaties. Under the ICSID Convention at least, it has been submitted that further characteristics have to be fulfilled.[387] Arguably, these requirements are not jurisdictional conditions in a strict technical sense but may be handled with some discretion.[388] This test has generally been referred to as the Salini test. In *Salini v. Morocco*, the tribunal tested the following requirements in order to determine its jurisdiction: contributions, a certain duration of the performance of the contract, participation in the risks of the transaction, and the contribution to the economic development of the host State.[389] In the following, it shall be examined which benchmark has been laid down by arbitral practice for the coverage of contracts between a foreign investor and a host State and whether such benchmark is justified given the original purpose of the convention and of the States consenting to arbitration under it.

It is true that in several cases, the contract over which the subsequent dispute took place was a mere part of an overall project that

---

[386] See *Joy Mining Machinery Ltd. v. Arab Republic of Egypt*, ICSID Case No. ARB/03/11, Award on Jurisdiction, 6 August 2004, ICSID Rev.-FILJ 19 (2004), paras. 46–47 (hereinafter, *Joy Mining v. Egypt*).

[387] For probably the most authoritative stance on this subject matter, see Schreuer, *supra* fn. 42, 140 et seq.

[388] For an exhaustive description of this problem and the two opposing stances, see the decision in *Malaysian Historical Salvadors SDN, BHD v. The Government of Malaysia*, ICSID Case No. ARB/05/10, Award on Jurisdiction, 17 May 2007, paras. 69–106 (hereinafter, *Salvadors v. Malaysia*). This decision was subsequently annulled. See *Malaysian Historical Salvadors SDN, BHD v. The Government of Malaysia*, ICSID Case No. ARB/05/10, Decision on the Application for Annulment, 16 April 2009 (hereinafter, Salvadors Annulment). The annulment decision is accompanied by Judge Mohamed Shahabuddeen's dissenting opinion on the notion of investment in article 25(1) of the ICSID Convention. See also W. Ben Hamida, Two Nebulous ICSID Features: The Notion of Investment and the Scope of Annulment Control, J. Int'l Arb. 24 (2007), 287, 288 et seq.

[389] See *Salini v. Morocco*, *supra* fn. 97, para. 52.

included other contractual arrangements like general understanding agreements, profit-sharing agreements, establishment conventions, joint-venture contracts for the operation of the built plant, management contracts, technical assistance contracts and so forth.[390] In the case of such a conglomerate of contractual relations, the acceptance of an investor—host State relationship and thereby, the distinction from a mere sale, is facilitated.[391] Besides, in most of the cases, the disputes arose not only from one contract but from the whole cooperation.[392] The classification of the activities as investment in these cases is perspicuous and is not to be disputed. Yet, in several cases, the operation was based exclusively on one contract the characterisation of which was disputed heavily by the parties to it. Under these circumstances, arbitral tribunals relied on the five typical characteristics of investment in order to decide whether the contract fell within their competence.

1. *Substantial Contributions*

In the first place, it is submitted that investment pursuant to the ICSID Convention requires that the activity at issue makes a contribution to the host State.[393] This can be in the form of a financial or technical contribution.[394] The requirement of a substantial contribution refers to the debates of the drafters concerning a minimum amount of the claim or of the entire project.[395] Rubins alleges that this is the most malleable criterium. Given the high degree of heterogeneity of the world's States

390 See, e.g., *Klöckner Industrie-Anlagen GmbH v. United Republic of Cameroon*, ICSID Case No. ARB/81/2, (1999) 114 ILR 157; *SOABI v. Senegal*, *supra* fn. 35, id.

391 F. Yala, The Notion of "Investment" in ICSID Case Law: A Drifting Jurisdictional Requirement?: Some Un-Conventional Thoughts on Salini, SGS and Mihaly, J. Int'l Arb. 22 (2005), 105, 107 et seq.

392 See, e.g., *Benvenuti et Bonfant v. People's Republic of the Congo*, ICSID Case No. ARB/77/2, Award, 8 August 1980, 1 ICSID Rep. 330.

393 Schreuer, *supra* fn. 42, 140.

394 The former aspect concerns the question whether a transfer of capital or, in other words, an injection of capital into the host State actually has to occur. This question is controversial irrespective of the fact whether the investment is based on a contract or not. As Vandevelde correctly points out, the core problem concerns not so much the transfer of capital but rather the control over it. See K. Vandevelde, The Economics of Bilateral Investment Treaties, Harv. Int'l L. J. 41 (2000), 469, 476: "Indeed, foreign direct investment may not involve movement of capital at all, but only a shift in control, as acquisition of control could be wholly financed within the host state."

395 Schreuer, *supra* fn. 42, 123. Particularly, it was discussed whether claims of less than US$100,000 should be excluded. Other comments concerned the total value of the investment and not the claim as determinative.

and companies, it is hardly conceivable how this feature could establish any objective boundaries. For example, an expense of EUR 100.000 would amount to a major commitment for a small start-up company whereas it would be a negligible expense for a bigger company or even a worldwide player. The same reasoning is valid for States: an insignificant amount for, say, Canada could signify a major influx for countries like El Salvador or Estonia.[396]

As regards the former category, i.e., financial contributions, some tribunals did not mention the necessity of such a contribution at all[397] or were satisfied with little evidence of it.[398] Other tribunals held that the requirement of financial contributions was met by the company's undertaking in the particular case. For instance, in *Bayindir v. Pakistan* the provision of bank guarantees by Bayindir equivalent to the amount of the mobilisation advance payable to the State entity and the amount that Bayindir allegedly incurred in bank commission charges in excess of $ 11 million met the particular tribunal's requisitions.[399] In *Saipem v. Bangladesh*, Bangladesh contended that Saipem "was [never] a net creditor vis-à-vis Petrobangla [i.e., the State entity enjoined with the task to conduct the construction] in respect of the Pipeline Contract having actually put its own money into the project."[400] The tribunal asserted that an actual injection of capital into the host country generally was not required. An exception thereto is when the host State had imposed such a requirement beforehand. In the case at issue, Bangladesh had not introduced a similar requirement. The tribunal held this to be a question of origin of funds and consequently ruled that the origin of the funds was irrelevant.[401] Similarly, it was held in some instances that this was the case unless the investment treaty or the

[396] Rubins, *supra* fn. 365, 298.

[397] G. Destanne de Bernis & M. Byé, Relations Économique Internationales (1977), 994. See also D. Hanink, The International Economy: A Geographical Perspective (1994), 234.

[398] See, e.g., *Yaung Chi OO Trading PTE Ltd. v. Government of the Union of Myanmar*, ASEAN I.D. Case No. ARB/01/1, Award, 31 March 2003, (2003) 42 ILM 540, para. 45, where the tribunal held that there was a substantial contribution "although there may have been unresolved questions regarding the full extent and form of these contributions".

[399] *Bayindir v. Pakistan, supra* fn. 368, paras. 119–120.

[400] *Saipem v. Bangladesh, supra* fn. 367, para. 103.

[401] Id., paras. 106–107: "However, in the absence of such a requirement [in an invesment treaty], investments made by foreign investors from local funds or from loans raised in the host State are treated in the same manner as investments funded with imported capital".

investment legislation prescribed differently.[402] The purpose of the convention to settle international disputes requires that, at least, the investor is of a different origin than the respondent State.[403] Whether the same holds true for the financial contribution is not relevant.[404] In a similar vein, the tribunal in *LESI-Dipenta v. Algeria* upheld that an actual influx was not necessary for the element of financial contribution. In its point of view, even expenditures for the preparation of the investment made in the national country of the investor could justify the assumption of a financial contribution.[405]

As for technical contributions, the question may arise whether the ordinary execution of a particular project as foreseen in the contract suffices to meet the standard for the contribution requirement. It is in this sense that the argumentation put forward by the tribunal in *Salini v. Morocco* is to be understood. The contract at issue included the provision of necessary equipment and qualified personnel, the setting up of an appropriate production tool, and so forth. In the tribunal's view, the regular accomplishment by Salini of these contractual obligations could qualify as a technical contribution regardless of whether the equipment and the profit were repatriated subsequently to the construction and whether nationals of the host State were introduced to technological knowledge.[406] According to some authors, this assertion is by no means justified. The qualification of an activity as investment would require an efficient transfer of technology or know-how. Hence, technical contribution, inter alia, presupposes technical assistance, training programmes benefiting host State employees, and permanent consultation with the local authorities in charge of operational aspects of the project.[407] Otherwise, the contribution would not lead to

---

[402] See *Tradex v. Albania, supra* fn. 41, paras. 108–110; *Eudoro Armando Olguín v. Republic of Paraguay*, ICSID Case No. ARB/98/5, Award, 26 July 2001, para. 66; *Tokio v. Ukraine, supra* fn. 52, para. 74. The last case was special since, for the first time under the ICSID, it opposed a State and a corporation which was incorporated in another country but the owners of which were nationals of the respondent State.

[403] See *Tokio v. Ukraine, supra* fn. 52, Dissenting Opinion of Prof. P. Weil, para. 5. In any event, this is a question of "nationality" of the investor and not one of "investment" under the convention.

[404] Id.

[405] *LESI-Dipenta v. Algeria, supra* fn. 119, section 2.2, para. 14.

[406] *Salini v. Morocco, supra* fn. 97, para. 53.

[407] M. Salem, Les contrats d'assistance technique, in: P. Judet et al. (eds.), Transfert de Technologie et Développement (1977), 467, 480 et seq.; K. V. S. K. Nathan, Submissions to the International Centre for Settlement of Investment Disputes in Breach of the Convention, J.Int'l Arb. 12 (1995), 27, 44 et seq.

enhanced development of the host State but rather to "dependence through engineering services."[408] Arbitral tribunals did not pay much attention to such demands. In *Bayindir v. Pakistan*, the tribunal merely stated that Bayindir's allegations to having trained 63 engineers and having provided significant equipment and personnel cannot be disputed and thus, that a sufficient contribution took place.[409] In *RFCC v. Morocco*, the tribunal was satisfied with the transfer to Morocco of funds, equipment, personnel, and know-how amounting to MAD 316.938.686,06.[410] Further, the tribunal mentioned the registration of a subsidiary in Casablanca.[411] In *Jan de Nul v. Egypt*, the mobilization of two heavy ships and the related compensation represented a clear indication for the tribunal that the claimant's technical contribution was substantial.[412] The tribunal in *LESI-Dipenta v. Algeria* even stated that any kind of contribution would be valid inasmuch as it had an economic value.[413] Whilst the last decision is questionable as regards the substantiality of a contribution, the general approach of the tribunals is correct. The element of a "substantial contribution" does not refer to the economic development of the host State. It would thus be exaggerated to require the foreign investor to provide long-lasting technical contributions. The adequate fulfilment of the contract must be sufficient if the contract foresees a substantial contribution at all.

2. *Duration*

The duration of the investment is the next feature which is applied in order to determine whether an activity is within the notion of investment of article 25(1) under the ICSID Convention.[414] By this element,

---

[408] Destanne de Bernis & Byé, *supra* fn. 397, 994. See also Yala, *supra* fn. 391, 111, who asks: "When a bricklayer comes to your home, builds a wall, and you pay him for his work, do you consider that he has made 'a contribution' to your benefit—that he has invested in your garden, your kitchen or your living room?" Whereas the author's answer to his rhetoric question seems clear, in fact it is not. Termed differently: when the bricklayer works one year and builds your home and subsequently you fire him and do not pay him anything—in such a case, one would indeed say that he has made a contribution to your benefit.

[409] *Bayindir v. Pakistan*, *supra* fn. 368, paras. 115–116.

[410] This sum amounts to approximately €27,600,000.

[411] *RFCC v. Morocco*, *supra* fn. 98, para. 61.

[412] *Jan de Nul v. Egypt*, *supra* fn. 377, para. 92.

[413] *LESI-Dipenta v. Algeria*, *supra* fn. 119, section 2.2, para. 14.

[414] E. Gaillard, Centre International pour le Règlement des Différends relatives aux Investissements (CIRDI)—Chronique des sentences arbitrales, JDI 126 (1999),

simple commercial transactions, especially one-time sales or purchases of goods, are supposed to be excluded from the ICSID's jurisdiction. Moreover, short-term financial commitments such as short-term credits would normally not be regarded as investment. This element evinces the host State's need and desire for a long-lasting relationship on which it can rely in order to foster growth of the domestic economy. By contrast, short-term capital flows which might be germane to withdrawal at anytime are held to be sources of monetary and economic instability.[415] Be that as it may, it is true that the fixation of a minimum duration is more than difficult. The first draft of the convention contained a minimum of five years.[416] In ICSID arbitrations, the duration of three years has been deemed to be sufficient.[417] However, even a shorter period by all means may be subsumed under the requirement of "certain duration". Given the diversity of existing economic activities, it is furthermore questionable at what time a project advents and under what circumstances it has to be regarded as having elapsed.

Consequently, the importance of the element of a contract's duration is far from clear. Whereas the tribunal in *Bayindir v. Pakistan* contends that the element of duration is the paramount factor which distinguishes between investment in the sense of the ICSID Convention and that of ordinary commercial transactions,[418] it remains doubtful whether the sheer length of time can serve to qualify a contractual undertaking as an investment. According to such argumentation, thousands of internationally concluded long-term contracts between States and private entities could be regarded as investment. In legal doctrine, the approximate minimum duration of a contract to meet the objective requirement of investment is not specified but only excludes short-term transactions.[419] The problem with regard to the duration,

---

273, 292–293; Rubins, *supra* fn. 365, 297; Schreuer, *supra* fn. 42, 140. But see US Senate, 89th Congress, 2d Session, Executive Report No. 2, 15: "[I]t is entirely clear from [the] negotiating history that the term 'investment' in article 25(1) of the convention does not exclude from its scope an investment simply because it is a short-term investment".

415 Rubins, *supra* fn. 365, 297.

416 The definition included in the first draft read as follows: "(i) 'investment' means any contribution of money or other assets of economic value for an indefinite period or, if the period be defined, for not less than five years". Reprinted in Schreuer, *supra* fn. 42, 122.

417 See, e.g., *Salini v. Morocco*, *supra* fn. 97, para. 54.

418 *Bayindir v. Pakistan*, *supra* fn. 368, para. 132.

419 Cf. Rubins, *supra* fn. 365, 297.

however, is not so much the duration itself but rather which time span is to be evaluated.

Arbitral practice does not provide for a more certain yardstick for the assessment of the duration requirement either. In *RFCC v. Morocco*, the tribunal took into account the duration foreseen in the contract plus a subsequent time extension.[420] The arbitrator in *Malaysian Salvadors v. Malaysia* correctly pointed out that the contingency of duration upon the actual performance of the foreign investor introduces a considerable degree of fortuity in the determination of this element.[421] In *Jan de Nul v. Egypt*, the aspect of the contract's duration was one of the main objections to ICSID jurisdiction by Egypt. The contract between the Belgian companies and Egypt started on 29 July 1992 and the delivery of the works took place in June 1994. On account of this, Egypt pointed out that the duration of the contract was "a little less than two years." The claimants argued that in the construction industry an investment started from pre-qualification, i.e., from the moment the investor starts spending money and preparing the offer and deciding whether to pre-qualify or not. Accordingly, the span of time in the case lasted from the "pre-tender or tender stage" which was initiated in March 1991 until autumn 1994, "when the two ships went back to Europe".[422] The tribunal's resolution of the problem was given in a single sentence: "The Tribunal agrees with the Claimants that the duration of the operation was sufficient for it to qualify as an investment within the meaning of Article 25 of the ICSID Convention, even starting from the execution of the Contract on 29 July 1992."[423]

Another aspect of the duration element was challenged by the respondent in *Saipem v. Bangladesh* where the period during which Saipem had actually performed its contractual obligations was less than one year.[424] The tribunal rejected this objection on the ground that Bangladesh had not put forward any particular reason why the actual duration of the work should be considered or pointed to any authority supporting that position. In the view of the tribunal, the time of the

---

420 *RFCC v. Morocco, supra* fn. 98, para. 62. The originally fixed time period of 20 months was subsequently prolonged so that it exceeded two years.

421 *Salvadors v. Malaysia, supra* fn. 388, para. 110. On account of this, the sole arbitrator appears to rely exclusively upon the contract's nature. This, however, does not lead to a higher degree of legal certainty but further widens his discretion.

422 *Jan de Nul v. Egypt, supra* fn. 377, para. 94.

423 Id., para. 95.

424 *Saipem v. Bangladesh, supra* fn. 367, para. 101.

project during which the works were interrupted or suspended,[425] which in this case lasted for a whole year, entailed an even higher risk than those incurred while the works were being performed.[426]

In sum, one can draw the conclusion that the requirement of certain duration of the investment is, to a wide extent, subject to the particular tribunal's discretion. This is not due to the non-existence of a minimal time span but to the incertitude concerning the concrete point in time for its assessment. None of the tribunals actually attempts to clarify the specific content of the requirement or to render more clearly the limits to which a tribunal is subjected in determining the essential constituents of the time period. This conclusion is worrisome as the requirement of duration is the most clear-cut of the requisitions laid down by legal doctrine. However, when one includes in the assessment the preparation period of an enterprise during the pre-tender stage, the door is opened to complete volatility of the results achievable.

3. *Risk-Assumption/Return of Gains or Profit*

A further element required for an investment is the investor's risk assumption. Effectively, when the risk is placed primarily or entirely upon the host State (for example, a service agreement where substantial prior payment is requested), the project cannot be considered an investment.[427] This means that the risk involved in the activity must justify the investor's right to protection through the investment treaty system.[428] In other words, there must be a certain degree of risk taken in the performance of the contract. As the extent of the term "risk" already indicates, the questions what kind of risk the investor has to assume and which types of risk are deemed appropriate to consider an activity as investment is a matter of some controversy. Several authors assert that the distinction between price and profits is the decisive factor that distinguishes investment and sale.[429] Whereas the seller obtains its remuneration from the delivery of a good or service, the characteristics of an investor are that its profits are generated by the

---

[425] It is worthy to note that the parties entered into the contract on 14 February 1990. On 14 June 1992, the pipeline was taken over by Petrobangla.

[426] *Saipem v. Bangladesh*, *supra* fn. 367, para. 102.

[427] Schreuer, *supra* fn. 42, 140.

[428] Rubins, *supra* fn. 365, 298.

[429] See, e.g., Yala, *supra* fn. 391, 113.

subsequent exploitation of the delivered or constructed good. In this sense, risk means that the activity at issue involves a certain regularity of profit and return.[430] The uncertainty which thereby arises for the investor as well as for the host country shows the commitment of the investor and represents the required risk.[431] Hence, the main focus has to be put on the type of remuneration laid down for the company.[432]

Yet, it has been submitted that the risk criterion was often misunderstood by arbitral tribunals.[433] In *Fedax v. Venezuela*, for instance, the tribunal held that the very existence of a dispute as to the payment of the principal and interest would evidence the risk that the holder had taken.[434] This statement, indeed, mixes up different spheres of risk.[435] The risk-criterion for an "investment" must transcend the mere commercial risk which is inherent in every economic transaction and, of course, also go beyond the legal risk of non-performance.[436]

---

[430] This criterion has not been mentioned by some commentators and arbitral tribunals. See, e.g., S. Manciaux, Investissements étrangers et arbitrage entre États et ressortissants d'autres États (2004), 63. However, other commentators see it as an indispensable aspect of any true investment. See, e.g., CME Czech Republic B.V. v. The Czech Republic, UNCITRAL, Partial Award, 13 September 2001, 9 ICSID Rep. 121, Separate Opinion of Ian Brownlie on the Issues at the Quantum Phase of CME v. Czech Republic, para. 34.

[431] See, e.g., C. Oman, Les Nouvelles Formes D'Investissement dans les Industries des Pays en voie de Développement (1989), 11.

[432] See, e.g., D. Carreau & P. Juillard, Droit international économique (2005), para. 1117:

> [L]es opérations de vente de bien d'équipment pourront, selon le cas, constituer ou ne pas constituer des opérations d'investissements. Elles ne sont pas constitutives d'un investissement dès lors que la rémuneration de l'investisseur est parfaite par le seul paiment du prix de vente, même si ce prix n'est pas déterminé, mais déterminable, et même si son paiement n'est pas instantané, mais échélonné. Elles seront constitutives d'un investissement si la rémunération de l'investisseur consiste, pour partie, en le paiment d'un prix, et pour partie, en le versement de montants calculés d'après les résultats financiers de l'exploitation.

[433] Manciaux, *supra* fn. 430, 74–75.

[434] *Fedax N.V. v. The Republic of* Venezuela, ICSID Case No. ARB/96/3, Decision on Jurisdiction, 11 July 1997, 5 ICSID Rep. 183, para. 40.

[435] Manciaux, *supra* fn. 430, 75, where the author states the following:

> Le tribunal a en effet confondu ici le risque économico-politique (de non-rentabilité du projet entrepris) avec le risque 'juridique' d'inéxecution de ses obligations par l'un des cocontractants, ce dernier critère conduisant à qualifier d'investissement toute relation juridique puisqu'existe toujours le risque d'inéxecution des obligations souscrites.

[436] See also Gaillard, *supra* fn. 414, 293.

Nonetheless, the arbitral practice concerned with contracts between investor and host State applies a somewhat more generous standard. The tribunal in *Jan de Nul* confined itself to declaring that the operation of the contract is of great magnitude and complexity and thus involves the sharing of operational risks. Likewise, the tribunal in *LESI-Dipenta* refused to apply a strict benchmark. In its view, every kind of contract that has inherent risks is susceptible of being covered by the ICSID Convention. As a reason for this broad approach, the tribunal put forward the purpose of the convention which is to offer the company that desires to invest in a foreign country a "particular guarantee of jurisdiction". The contract at issue, however, does not come under scrutiny. In contrast, the tribunal seemed satisfied with the claimant's assertion that some of the intrinsic risks of the contract have eventuated.[437]

Other tribunals carried out a more detailed examination of the element of risk assumption. The *Salini v. Morocco* tribunal enumerated several aspects that flow from the nature of the contract at issue which make its consideration as investment likely. These are, inter alia, risks that arise due to the fact that Morocco is a sovereign State which permits it to prematurely end the contract or whose modifications of law could increase the cost of labour, any accident, or damage caused to property during performance of the works; risks relating to problems of co-ordination possibly arising from the simultaneous performance of other projects; and risks related to the absence of any compensation in case of increase or decrease in volume of the workload not exceeding 20% of the total contract price.[438] As for the importance of the remuneration, the tribunal added that the lack of a link to the exploitation of the completed work is not relevant but that the impossibility to establish a price in advance with certainty reflects the risk for the claimant.[439] In its objections to jurisdiction of the tribunal in *Bayindir v. Pakistan*, Pakistan observed that the risk assumed by Bayindir was minimal by reason of the fact that it had received a substantial mobilisation advance which it was to retain until the end of the contracts.[440] The tribunal did not accept this contention. In its view, the inherent risk in long-term contracts argues against the presumption of

---

437 *LESI-Dipenta v. Algeria*, *supra* fn. 119, section 2.2, para.14.
438 *Salini v. Morocco*, *supra* fn. 97, para. 55.
439 Id., para. 56.
440 *Bayindir v. Pakistan*, *supra* fn. 368, para. 118.

the existence of a minimal risk. Moreover and quite more convincingly, the tribunal took a closer look at the contract which laid down a defect liability period of one year and a maintenance period of four years against payment. According to the tribunal, these elements created a significant risk on behalf of Bayindir.[441] In *Saipem v. Bangladesh*, the tribunal pointed out two factors which indicate the claimant's risk assumption. Firstly, the necessity to renegotiate the completion date and the stopping of the works in 1991 are evidences of the risk of long-term contracts. Secondly, the contractual mechanism providing for retention money created an obvious risk for Saipem.

If it is true that arbitral tribunals evince a certain kind of "liberalism in the implementation of the objective criteria",[442] this applies especially to the characteristic of risk assumption. In this regard, the tribunals concerned relied repeatedly upon risks which pertain to all kinds of contracts and do not serve to distinguish investment contracts and commercial transactions. Particularly, reliance upon the economic risk of loss and profit which is inherent in every economic transaction obviously does not serve any determinative purpose.[443]

4. *Significant Contribution to Economic Development*

The final feature is the significance of the operation in the host State's development. This element can be distinguished from those previously mentioned for two reasons: Firstly, this criterion does not apply to investments in general but is a requirement specifically introduced by the preamble of the ICSID Convention. Secondly, this feature entails a change of perspective. Whilst the former elements concern the investor's participation, the contribution to the host State's economy exclusively takes into account the State's motivation in accepting and protecting the transaction.[444] It has been suggested that, on account of this, the host State's viewpoint of the operation should have a dominant importance in the definition of investment. When a State is willing to accept this definition because it deems the project favourable to its economic development, then even transactions which normally

[441] Id., para. 136.
[442] Yala, *supra* fn. 391, 114.
[443] Cf. *Salvadors v. Malaysia*, *supra* fn. 388, para. 106, where the tribunal stated the following: "The Claimant has not provided any convincing reasons why the risks assumed under the Contract were anything other than normal commercial risks".
[444] Rubins, *supra* fn. 365, 299.

would not be investments could be regarded as such.[445] As the breadth of the term "economic development of the host State" indicates, an objective determination appears barely possible.[446] What does contribution to the economic development of a country mean? And what makes a contribution significant?[447] What kind of industrial project finally furthers economic development, which one does not? What level of furtherance has to be achieved? To what extent is the specific situation of the particular country to be taken into account? What has to be examined: the intention of the company or the objective suitability of the planned undertaking? The prolonged debate over international development aid and the string of theories which developed throughout decades[448] indicate that these questions can hardly be solved by an arbitral tribunal in determining whether a project can be considered as an investment. Consequently, the attention that has been paid by arbitral tribunals to the requirement can be said to be fairly remote. When tribunals posed the question of a contribution to economic development at all,[449] the arbitrators affirmed the project's suitability straightforward. As substantiation served issues such as the public interest in a highway,[450] declarations of the importance of the road infrastructure for the development of the country,[451] or the fact

---

[445] G. Delaume, Convention on the Settlement of Investment Disputes between States and Nationals of Other States, Int'l Law. 1 (1966), 64, 70.

[446] See the questions posed by Manciaux, *supra* fn. 430, 71: "Quel indicateur utiliser? Quelle période de référence retenir? Et que va-t-on décider si une opération économique se révèle bénéfique pour le développement d'un État pendant un certain laps de temps et néfaste par la suite?"

[447] Furthermore, arbitral practice is inconsistent on the question whether the contribution must be "substantial" at all. See, on the one hand, *Ceskoslovenska Obchodni Banka, AS (CSOB) v. Slovak Republic*, ICSID Case No. ARB/97/4, Decision of the Tribunal on Objections to Jurisdiction, 24 May 1999, 5 ICSID Rep. 330, para. 76 (hereinafter, *CSOB v. Slovakia*), where the tribunal required that a loan has to substantially contribute to a State's economic development in order to be classified as investment. On the other hand, see *Patrick Mitchell v. The Democratic Republic of Congo*, ICSID Case No. ARB/99/7, Decision on the Application for Annulment of the Award, 1 November 2006, para. 33, where the ad hoc committee stated that it "suffices for the operation to contribute in one way or another to the economic development of the host State".

[448] See generally T. Moran, Harnessing Foreign Direct Investment for Development: Policies for Developed and Developing Countries (2006).

[449] The tribunal in *LESI-Dipenta v. Algeria* asserted that the requirement is superfluous because the other conditions indicate the existence of a contribution to economic development. See *LESI-Dipenta v. Algeria*, *supra* fn. 119, section 2.2, para. 13.

[450] *Salini v. Morocco*, *supra* fn. 97, para. 57.

[451] *Bayindir v. Pakistan*, *supra* fn. 368, para. 137.

that the operation of the Suez Canal—to which the project was supposed to contribute—is of paramount significance to Egypt's economy and development[452].

In *Malaysian Salvadors v. Malaysia*, the importance of this element, in contrast, was paramount.[453] The dispute in this case arose out of a salvage contract concerning the location and salvage of the "DIANA", a British vessel tank that sank off the coast of Malacca in 1817.[454] After having determined the legal nature of the "requirements" laid down by the ICSID Convention, the sole arbitrator undertook an exhaustive examination of the characteristics of investment focussing especially on the element of contribution to the host State's economic development. He held that any contract would make some economic contribution to the place of its performance and that, therefore, a differentiation had to be made between simple commercial benefits and significant contribution to the host State's economy. In order to make this differentiation, the arbitrator relied exclusively on a casuistic approach. Since the operations involved in all the other ICSID cases in which there was a "contribution to the host State's economic development" concerned lasting infrastructure improvements, the tribunal dismissed the fulfilment of this element. The provision of employment, the largely cultural and historical benefits of the project, or its eventual positive repercussions on tourism cannot alter this assessment.[455] Thus, the lasting character of an operation and the lasting, non-speculative benefit which it brings to the economy of the host State have to be regarded as the decisive criteria. Accordingly, the sole arbitrator denied the existence of investment on account of objective requirements set out by the ICSID Convention and without paying attention to the investment definition under the treaty at hand.[456]

---

[452] *Jan de Nul v. Egypt*, *supra* fn. 377, para. 92.

[453] See *Salvadors v. Malaysia*, *supra* fn. 388, paras. 112, 124. Accordingly, this was the case because all the other characteristics only appeared to be satisfied superficially. The decision of the tribunal was subsequently annulled. See Salvadors Annulment, *supra* fn. 388.

[454] *Salvadors v. Malaysia*, *supra* fn. 388, para. 7.

[455] *Salvadors v. Malaysia*, *supra* fn. 388, paras. 125–145.

[456] The Annulment Committee held that the tribunal exceeded its powers by failing to exercise the jurisdiction with which it was endowed for three reasons: (i) it altogether failed to take account of and apply the BIT; (ii) it elevated the criteria of the Salini test to jurisdictional conditions; (iii) it failed to take account of the preparatory work of the ICSID Convention. See Salvadors Annulment, *supra* fn. 388, para. 80.

5. *Investment Treaties as* Lex Specialis

The decision on jurisdiction in *Malaysian Salvadors v. Malaysia* evoked strong criticisms with regard to the nature of the above-discussed elements of the notion of investment under article 25(1) of the ICSID Convention and the legitimacy of the Salini test.[457] Accordingly, the prime source for the determination of investment must not be the ICSID Convention but the investment treaty that provides the consent for arbitration. This is because the ICSID Convention does not contain a definition of the term investment and thus, left substantial discretion to the Contracting States in determining the notion of investment which has been exercised by drafting investment treaties.[458] Beyond the distinction between investment and sale transactions, the ICSID Convention does not impose outer limits on the Contracting States whereby certain activities or assets could not be defined as investment.[459] The arbitral practice under the Salini test—if regarded as a fixed and inflexible test—would risk arbitrary exclusions and contradict individual agreements.[460] In *Biwater Gauff v. Tanzania*, the claimant argued that the particular project was a "loss leader", i.e., an inevitably unprofitable venture designed only to further other interests of the investor. Therefore, it would not meet the criteria of risk and substantial commitment. The tribunal denied the existence of objective requirements derived from the ICSID Convention and held "that a more flexible and pragmatic approach to the meaning of 'investment' is appropriate, which takes into account the features identified in Salini, but along with all the circumstances of the case, including the nature of the instrument containing the relevant consent to ICSID".[461] Hence, the Contracting States to an investment treaty are almost entirely free to define investment and the magnitude of the contracts' protection may differ depending on the particular treaty.

---

457 See Y. Andreeva, Salvaging or Sinking the Investment? *MHS v. Malaysia* Revisited, The Law and Practice of International Courts and Tribunals 7 (2008), 161 et seq.; *Biwater Gauff (Tanzania) Ltd. v. United Republic of Tanzania*, ICSID Case No. ARB/05/22, Award, 24 July 2008, paras. 310 et seq. (hereinafter, *Biwater Gauff v. Tanzania*); Salvadors Annulment, *supra* fn. 388, paras. 56 et seq.

458 Andreeva, id., 169.

459 *Salvadors Annulment, supra* fn. 388, para. 69.

460 *Biwater Gauff v. Tanzania, supra* fn. 457, para. 314.

461 Id.

III. *Conclusion*

Majority of modern investment treaties set out broad definitions of the concept of investment. Contracts between foreign investors and host States were generally held to fall within formulations such as "any kind of asset", "any kind of property", "claims to money or to any performance having economic value" or the like. It remains questionable to what extent the parties' freedom is circumscribed by objective requirements of investment. In particular, the influence of the ICSID Convention on this subject matter has become doubtful. Subsequent to the annulment decision in *Malaysian Salvadors v. Malaysia*, it will be hard to argue for an objective limitation introduced by the ICSID Convention. Even if the Salini test is upheld, three aspects have to be recalled: Firstly, the terms which circumscribe the characteristics are broad and malleable. Secondly, these characteristics are not rigid jurisdictional requirements. And thirdly, as nearly all tribunals emphasize,[462] they are interdependent and thus, have to be assessed in their entirety.[463] Therefore, the Salini test can hardly be seen as more than a mere practical tool for differentiation. In sum, the parties to an investment treaty principally remain free to determine what kind of contracts they deem to be an investment. A clear exclusion of contracts going beyond the the distinction between investment and simple sale contracts and like transient commercial transactions is not discernible.

E. Investment Treaties and Sub-State Entities as Parties to Contracts

When a foreign investor concludes a contract not directly with the host State, i.e., its government, but with a further entity of the host State such as a territorial sub-entity, an administrative agency, a state enterprise, or a government-owned enterprise, the question becomes whether and under what circumstances can the State be held liable under the investment treaty for the conduct of the entity concerned.

[462] Id., para, 72.

[463] It may well be that this leads to a "drifting" notion of investment. See, e.g., Yala, *supra* fn. 391, 105. However, since economy and economic circumstances are also "drifting", it would be strange if the notion of investment remains the same.

Since foreign investors increasingly deal with such an entity instead of directly with the government, this question has become highly relevant to the extent of the protection of contracts between a host State and a foreign investor provided for by the investment treaty regime.

I. *Sub-State Entities as Contractual Partner under General International Law*

1. *General Aspects*

The proclivity towards privatization appears to be the crucial current by which economic activity of States during the last three decades may be characterized.[464] Since the beginning of the 1980s and increasingly after the collapse of communism and the Soviet Union,[465] economic activities which were formerly carried out by States or public institutions were allowed to be organized by the private sector. Thereby, States significantly reduced their direct participation in vital sectors of the economy.[466] At the same time, States increased and diversified their indirect participation in economic activities.[467] On account of this, foreign investors increasingly have to deal with entities which do not directly represent the host State. Nevertheless, it is not unusual that a State retains some kind of control over the economically active entity.

---

[464] See, e.g., M. Adil Khan, Introduction: Reinventing Public Enterprises, in: UN, Department of Economic and Social Affairs (ed.), Public Enterprises: Unresolved Challenges and New Opportunities (2007), 3, 3–4 et seq.

[465] On the transformation of the socialist economy through privatization in Eastern Europe, see B. Grahovac, Privatization in Former Socalist States (2001), xiii: "In addition to embracing a market economy and abandoning government-planned and -arranged economies, the most significant aspect of these changes has been the legal reassertion of pluralism in ownership".

[466] See, e.g., Khan, *supra* fn. 464, 13. However, this does not mean that public enterprises would have lost a major presence in many national economies. This can be assessed by their GDP shares, e.g., France (32.9%), Germany (21.1%), or by source of government revenue, e.g., China (7%), Egypt (12%), Algeria (60%), Syria (24%).

[467] See, for instance, the comments of the tribunal in *Salini v. Morocco*, *supra* fn. 97, para. 35:

> In order to perform its obligations, and at the same time take into account the sometimes diverging interests that the private economy protects, the State uses a varied spectrum of modes of organisation, among which are in particular semi-public companies, similar to ADM [the Moroccan company with which the Italian claimants signed the construction contract], a company mostly held by the State which, considering the size of its participation (over 80%), directs and manages it.

This may be due to ownership, political mechanisms of influence, or other traditionally grown ties which are not always clearly conceivable from a vantage point which is not acquainted with the local circumstances.[468] In short, a private foreign investor will often be obliged to conclude contracts with entities which are legally separate from the host State but which nevertheless are somehow related to it. In such a case, it is questionable and crucial to the purpose of the present work to what extent a liability of the host State under the investment treaty regime is available. In other words, at stake is whether the "corporate veil" between the host State and state enterprises can be lifted.[469]

2. *Attribution of Conduct to the State*

The question at issue—the responsibility of a State under international law by account of the conduct of one of its sub-divisions or a state-owned or controlled company—is essentially one of attribution of conduct to a State. A State may only be held responsible for acts and omissions which are attributable to it. Whilst theoretically, the conduct of all natural persons and juridical persons somehow linked to the State can be attributed to the State, a more restrictive approach has been taken under international law. On account of this, only conduct of organs of the State or of others who acted under the instigation of a public authority, i.e., as agents of the State, are attributed to the State.[470] Thereby, the responsibility of States is limited and the autonomy of persons acting on their own account is acknowledged.[471] In 2001, at its fifty-third session, the ILC adopted its final version of the Articles on

---

[468] This is one of the disadvantages Paulsson refers to in describing the inequality a foreigner is subjected to. See J. Paulsson, Denial of Justice (2005), 149.

[469] Cf. K. H. Böckstiegel, General Introduction to Investment Treaty Arbitration, in: G. Kaufmann-Kohler & B. Stucki (ed.), Investment Treaties and Arbitration, ASA Special Series No. 19 (2002), 1, 6.

[470] See, e.g., I. Brownlie, System of the Law of Nations: State Responsibility, vol. I (1983), 132–166; D. D. Caron, The Basis of Responsibility: Attribution and Other Trans-Substantive Rules of State Responsibility, in: R. Lillich & D. Magraw (ed.), The Iran-United States Claims Tribunal: Its Contribution to the Law of State Responsibility (1998), 109 et seq.; L. Condorelli, L'imputation à l'Etat d'un fait internationalement illicite: solutions classique et nouvelles tendences, RdC 189 (1984-VI), 9, 171 et seq.; M. Diez de Velasco Vallejo, Instituciones de Derecho Internacional Público, (2005), 801 et seq.

[471] Crawford, *supra* fn. 261, 91.

Responsibility of States for Internationally Wrongful Acts (ILC Articles).[472] Through the ILC Articles, the ILC chiefly intended to codify the customary international law on international state responsibility.[473] Especially since its adoption the text has to be regarded as authoritative statement in this regard.[474] According to the ILC Articles, a general distinction concerning the attribution of conduct to the State can be drawn between the conduct of state organs and non-state organs.[475]

As a general rule, a State is responsible for any conduct of its organs.[476] This holds true irrespective of whether an executive, a legislative, or a judicial organ is acting or whether any territorial or further subdivision of the State is acting. This rule has been recognized in article 4 of the ILC Articles.[477] Essentially, it is a reflection of the principle that a State must not circumvent its international responsibility on account of its internal organisation.[478] Since any and all conduct of State organs, that is, sovereign and mere commercial conduct, can thus be attributed to the State,[479] the differentiation between state organs and non-state organs is of major importance. Hence, the question arises which entity is a state organ? It is clear that the government itself, government ministries, and agencies regardless of their governmental level are state organs within this sense.[480] Further, legislative organs as well as courts and other adjudicative bodies may straightforwardly be regarded as

---

[472] See ILC Articles, *supra* fn. 260.

[473] Cassese, *supra* fn. 31, 244.

[474] More specifically, see J. Crawford, *supra* fn. 209, 889–890.

[475] Cf. Crawford, *supra* fn. 261, 92.

[476] See, e.g., Cassese, *supra* fn. 31, 246; Brownlie, *supra* fn. 470, 132.

[477] Article 4 of the ILC Articles reads as follows:

Conduct of organs of State—1. The Conduct of any State organ shall be considered an act of that State under international law, whether the organ exercises legislative, executive, judicial or any other functions, whatever position it holds in the organization of the State, and whatever its character as an organ of the central government or of a territorial unit of the State. 2. An organ includes any person or entity which has that status in accordance with the internal law of the State.

[478] Crawford, *supra* fn. 261, 98.

[479] Id., 96.

[480] See, e.g., *Metalclad Corp. v. United Mexican States*, ICSID Case No. ARB(AF)/97/1, Award, 30 August 2000, ICSID Rev.-FILJ 16 (2001), 168, para. 73; *Loewen v. US*, *supra* fn. 186, para. 148.

state organs.[481] In the words of the ILC, "[t]he reference to 'State organs' covers all the individual or collective entities which make up the organization of the State and act on its behalf".[482] However, in an inconceivable amount of situations ranging from specially created state agencies to state-owned enterprises, this differentiation may pose hard questions. For this determination, article 4(2) of the ILC Articles refers explicitly to the State's internal law. This *renvoi* by international law to internal law does not exclude the application of international law criteria,[483] but it merely makes clear that no further difficulties arise in case of the entity's characterization as an organ by internal law.[484] When such characterisation is not laid down under internal law, several other factors such as the State's participation in funding the entity's activities, the entity's performance of public functions, or the control by the State of the entity's activities may be utilized in order to determine whether the entity is a state organ within the meaning of international law.[485] In *Wintershall v. Qatar*,[486] for example, the Qatar General Petroleum Corporation, a corporation wholly owned by Qatar but legally separate from it, was held to be an agent of the Government of Qatar because of the involvement of government officials in the board of directors.[487] In any event, mere ownership of an enterprise does not lead to the conclusion that an enterprise is a state organ.[488] By contrast,

---

[481] This reflects customary international law. See, e.g., Shaw, *supra* fn. 151, 701; Brownlie, *supra* fn. 194, 432 et seq.; *Saipem S.p.A. v. The People's Republic of Bangladesh*, ICSID Case No. ARB/05/07, Award, 30 June 2009, paras. 188 et seq.

[482] Crawford, *supra* fn. 261, 96: "It is irrelevant for the purposes of attribution that the conduct of a State organ may be classified as 'commercial' or as 'acta iure gestionis.'"

[483] On account of this, the criticisms by Manciaux, *supra* fn. 430, 576–577, are superfluous.

[484] Crawford, *supra* fn. 261, 98.

[485] A. C. Smutny, State Responsibility and Attribution—When Is a State Responsible for the Acts of State Enterprises? Emilio Agustín Maffezini v. The Kingdom of Spain, in: T. Weiler (ed.), International Investment Law and Arbitration: Leading Cases from the ICSID, NAFTA, Bilateral Treaties and Customary International Law (2005), 17, 35 et seq.

[486] *Wintershall A.G., et al. v. Government of Qatar*, Partial Award on Liability of 5 February 1988 (1989) 28 ILM 795.

[487] Accordingly, the most striking facts supporting the identity of QGPC and the Government were that "[t]he Board of Directors of QGPC is appointed by the Emir and consists of 7 to 11 members, the majority of whom are officials of the Department of Petroleum Affairs of the Government. They can be removed by the Emir at will. The Minister of Finance and Petroleum is the Chairman of the Board."

[488] Smutney, *supra* fn. 485, 36.

it is safe to say that the autonomous or private nature of an entity generally indicates that it is not a state organ. In such a case, attribution to the State is by no means excluded. It is, however, far more uncertain under which circumstances an attribution can take place.

In sum, if an entity is an organ of the State, the situation is relatively clear: any conduct by this entity can be attributed to the State for the purpose of establishing the State's international responsibility. This cannot be altered by a contractual provision to the contrary included in a contract between a foreign investor and such a state-organ. The findings of the ICSID tribunal in *Vivendi v. Argentina* was not clear in this regard.[489] Consequently, the relevant part of the tribunal's decision was subsequently annulled by the Annulment Committee's decision.[490]

A further limitation to state responsibility with regard to agreements with state organs and the attribution of conduct to the host State is apparently generated by article 25(3) of the ICSID Convention.[491] In *Cable Television of Nevis v. The Federation of St. Christopher & Nevis*, the state entity, the Nevis Island Administration, with which the private company had concluded an agreement concerning the construction of a cable television system, was held to be a "constituent Subdivision or Agency" of the State. On account of this, the tribunal declined its jurisdiction and seemingly alleged that the conduct of such an entity was not imputable either. This interpretation of article 25(3) is not correct. This provision does not restrict the attribution of conduct of sub-state entities but is intended to allow them to be parties in ICSID proceedings in their own right.[492]

---

[489] The tribunal ruled that because of the interdependence of contractual and treaty violations, an attribution of the conduct of an Argentine province to the central Argentine government would only be available if the contractual remedies were exhausted. See *Vivendi Award*, *supra* fn. 280, para. 18. For an explanation of the apparent limitation of state responsibility, see S. M. Perera, State Responsibility—Ascertaining the Liability of States in Foreign Investment Disputes, JWIT 6 (2005), 495, 510 et seq. The author seemingly is not aware of the Annulment Decision. For a correct description, see C. Larsen, ICSID Jurisdiction: The Relationship of Contracting States to Sub-State Entities, in: N. Horn (ed.), Arbitrating Foreign Investment Disputes (2004), 353, 364–370.

[490] For a more detailed examination of the corollaries of this case, see *infra* 163 et seq.

[491] Article 25(3) of the ICSID Convention reads as follows: "Consent by a constituent subdivision or agency of a Contracting State shall require the approval of that State unless that State notifies the Centre that no such approval is required."

[492] See Schreuer, *supra* fn. 42, 335; Larsen, *supra* fn. 489, 337. See also *Noble Ventures, Inc. v. Romania*, ICSID Case No. ARB/01/11, Award, 12 October 2005, para. 68 (hereinafter, *Noble Ventures v. Romania*).

The attribution of conduct of non-state organs, i.e., every person or entity which is not an organ of the State in the aforementioned sense, appears to be more complex. As a general principle, the conduct of private persons or entities is not attributable to the State under international law.[493] This principle, however, can only be legitimate inasmuch as the respective State is not enabled to circumvent its international obligations. At what point such an illegitimate control by the State over private entities is given and which criteria may be applied in order to determine illegitimate control is not answered consistently in international law.

Several authors advocate the importance of the degree of actual control which is exercised by a State over an entity. Accordingly, a State's effective control over a company entails the legitimacy of attributing the company's conduct to the State. Hence, a contract which is concluded with such an entity has to be regarded as a contract with the State itself.[494] Effective control within this sense is given, for instance, when the company is assigned as governmental entity in the contract itself or when the contract does not become effective until ratification or ministerial signing.[495] Albeit mere reliance upon control, in principle, could lead to a wide responsibility of States, the demand of those strict requirements for the determination of control restrains State responsibility considerably.

Böckstiegel who extensively researched the subject proposes the identification of a separate legal entity as pertaining to the State and thus the attribution of its conduct to the State in four cases.[496] In the present context particularly two of these propositions become pertinent. This is, on the one hand, the reliance upon the exertion of

---

[493] Crawford, *supra* fn. 261, 91.

[494] U. Kischel, State Contracts (1992), 47; J. Verhoeven, Contrats entre Etats et Ressortissants d'autres Etats, in: Centre Charles de Vischer (ed.), Le contrat économique international—Stabilité et évolution (1975), 115, 119; J. Chalmers, Attribution Issues in State Responsibility, Remarks by Jane Chalmers, State Responsibility for Acts of Parastatals Organized in Corporate Form, Am. Soc'y Int'l L. Proc. 84 (1990), 60, 61 et seq.; Perera, *supra* fn. 489, 513.

[495] Kischel, id., 47–48.

[496] For the so-called "internationale Identifizierung", see K. H. Böckstiegel, Der Staat als Vertragspartner ausländischer Privatunternehmen (1971), 47–75. The four cases are the following: (i) State alike appearance authorized by the State (Durchgriff kraft Vertrauensschutz); (ii) performance of governmental tasks (Durchgriff kraft Funktionsausübung), (iii) circumvention of international obligations (Durchgriff kraft völkerrechtlicher Verantwortlichkeit), and (iv) attribution of certain acts of the legislation and the administration (Durchgriff kraft Einflusssphäre).

governmental functions by the entity, i.e., when the entity exercises acts of *jure imperii* character[497] and, on the other hand, the prevention of a State's circumvention of its international obligations by acting through entities endowed with separate legal identity. As for the former, Böckstiegel alludes to the general difficulties in differentiating between governmental and non-governmental conduct.[498] He nevertheless maintains the criterion and points out that exclusive reliance upon domestic law for determination matters would be contrary to the purpose of attribution.[499] Other authors contradict such marginalisation of domestic law and allege that it is the State's own perspective of its acts as public or commercial which would serve best for differentiation matters.[500] However, like the abovementioned determination of state organs, the sole reliance upon internal law is not tenable. The rule that a State must not elude its international obligations through the creation of separate legal entities finds its basis in the well-known principle that the invocation of national law may not justify an international wrong.[501] As the separateness regularly derives from domestic law, the invocation of the separateness in order to justify an international wrong is illegitimate.[502]

The attribution of conduct of non-state organs to States is considered in articles 5 and 8[503] of the ILC Articles. Article 5 states the following:

> The conduct of a person or entity which is not an organ of the State under article 4 but which is empowered by the law of that State to exercise elements of the governmental authority shall be considered an act of the State under international law, provided the person or entity is acting in that capacity in the particular instance.

---

497 See also I. Seidl-Hohenveldern, Corporations in and under International Law (1987), 58–59.

498 Id., 64–65. See also C. Schreuer, State Immunity: Some Recent Developments (1988), 24 et seq.

499 Seidl-Hohenveldern, *supra* fn. 497, 61–62.

500 See, e.g., B. Smith, State Responsibility and the Marine Environment: The Rules of Decision (1988), 30.

501 See article 46 of the Vienna Convention on the Law of Treaties (1969).

502 Böckstiegel, *supra* fn. 496, 69. Böckstiegel mentions, for example, the obligation of Germany not to deliver gasmasks to Israel during the Arab—Israeli war in 1967. This obligation extended similarly to state enterprises.

503 Article 8 of the ILC Articles reads as follows: "Conduct directed or controlled by a State—The conduct of a person or group of persons shall be considered an act of a State under international law if the person or group of persons is in fact acting on the instruction of, or under the direction or control of, that State carrying out the conduct".

This provision submits the attribution of a private company's conduct to States to a quite strict regime. The entity at issue must be empowered by the law of the State to exercise functions of a public character normally exercised by State organs, and the particular conduct of the entity must relate to the exercise of the governmental authority concerned.[504] The crucial element is thus the exertion of governmental authority. Only the involvement of certain elements of governmental authority may justify the attribution of a private entity's conduct to the State. As examples in this regard, the ILC mentions private airlines which were granted immigration control powers or private security firms that act as prison guards. Private or commercial activity of such entities must not be attributed to the State.[505]

Unlike the approach that focuses primarily on control, this formulation excludes the importance of governmental control over the enterprise.[506] According to the ILC Commentary, certain criteria such as the classification of an entity as private or public under a given legal system, the existence of a greater or lesser participation by the State in its capital, the ownership of its assets by the State or the fact that it is not subject to executive control are not pertinent.[507] This estimation is not altered by the application of article 8. The term "under the control of" in article 8 is not understood in a wider sense of influence but has to be construed in light of article 5. Hence, the entity cannot be deemed to act under the control of the State unless it exercises governmental authority.[508] The conduct of separate entities which do not exercise governmental authority thus cannot be attributed to the State regardless of the level of control which the State is actually exerting.

This point of view is consistent with traditional doctrine[509] and several decisions of international tribunals. The Iran—US Claims Tribunal

---

[504] Crawford, *supra* fn. 261, 100.

[505] Id., 100–101.

[506] According to Perera, this creates confusion as to the situation of state-owned enterprises which do not exercise governmental authority. In his point of view, ownership obviously creates an indication of liability. Otherwise, the major part of state-owned enterprises would not be covered. See Perera, *supra* fn. 489, 513–514.

[507] Crawford, *supra* fn. 261, 100.

[508] Id., 112–113. For an example of conduct of a private person by which the national State was not bound, see *Tradex v. Albania*, *supra* fn. 41, para. 182. In this case, a civil servant signed an admission agreement expressly "on behalf of" the state-owned enterprise. The tribunal held that the admission did not bind the State because it could not be expected that this act represented the Albanian State.

[509] Cf. G. A. Christenson, The Doctrine of Attribution in State Responsibility, in: R. Lillich (ed.), International Law of State Responsibility for Injuries to Aliens (1983), 321, 332–333 et seq.

ruled several times that the mere establishment of a separate legal entity by a State does not entail the State's responsibility for the entity's conduct.[510] The ICJ acknowledged that the principle in municipal law was to uphold the legal separateness of corporate entities and deemed this principle adequate for the international plane.[511] The corporate veil should only be lifted exceptionally under special circumstances in order "to prevent the misuse of the privileges of legal personality, as in certain cases of fraud or malfeasance, to protect third persons such as a creditor or purchaser, or to prevent the evasion of legal requirements or of obligations."[512] An even more pronounced reluctance to overcome the separate legal personality was shown by domestic tribunals.[513] In *Baneco*, the US Supreme Court ruled that form was more important than function and refused to acknowledge the legal unity of the Cuban Government and the strictly controlled Cuban official bank for foreign trade financing.[514] The issue whether a particular entity can be regarded as a state entity also appeared during the late 1970s in relation to the question whether a state enterprise can invoke the force majeure clause in a contract when the force majeure is based on an action of the controlling State.[515] The enterprise, in order to be discharged from its obligations under a contract, inter alia, must be a legal entity distinct from that of the State.[516] Thereupon, the House of Lords ruled that a separate legal identity under domestic law is sufficient to justify legal separateness.[517] Although the minister concerned could tell

---

[510] See, e.g., *Otis Elevator Co. v. Islamic Republic of Iran*, (1987) 14 Iran-USCTR 283; *Eastman Kodak Co. v. Islamic Republic of Iran*, (1987) 17 Iran-USCTR 153; *Foremost Tehran v. Islamic Republic of Iran*, (1986) 10 Iran-USCTR 228.

[511] See, e.g., *Barcelona Traction*, *supra* fn. 175, paras. 56–58.

[512] Id., para. 56.

[513] See, e.g., *Letelier v. Republic of Chile*, 471 U.S. 1125 (1985); *Hercaire International Inc. v. Argentina*, 821 F.2d 559 (11th Cir. 1987); *Minpeco, S.A. v. Hunt*, 1989 WL 57704 (SDNY). However, the purpose of obstructing the piercing of the corporate veil in commercial law, the preservation of limited shareholder liability, considerably differs from attribution matters under international law. For a recent analysis, see S. B. Presser, The Bogalusa Explosion, "Single Business Enterprise", "Alter Ego", and Other Errors: Academics, Economics, Democracy, and Shareholder Limited Liability: Back Towards a Unitary "Abuse" Theory of Piercing the Corporate Veil, Nw. U. L. Rev. 100 (2006), 405 et seq.

[514] *First National City Bank v. Banco Para El Comercio Exterior De Cuba*, 462 U.S. 611 (1983).

[515] For a summary, see C. Scott Maravilla, The Ability of a State-Owned Enterprise to Declare Force Majeure Based upon Actions of the State, The Journal of International and Comparative Law at Chicago-Kent 2 (2002), 82 et seq.

[516] On force majeure, see generally Shaw, *supra* fn. 151, 710–711.

[517] *Czarnikow Ltd. v. Centrala Handlu Zagranicznego* ("Rolimpex") 1978 Lloyd's Rep. 305 (1978).

the enterprise "what to do and how to do it", the company's ability to independently make decisions regarding its commercial transactions, demonstrated by the facts that it was managed on the basis of economic accountability and that it was expected to make profit, assured the court to rule against the existence of a connection between the enterprise and the State.[518]

In sum, the principle that legal separateness on the domestic level has to be respected on the international plane is still valid. Seemingly, the sovereignty of States requires such a conclusion which, finally, leads to a somewhat restrained attribution.[519] However, this principle is restrained by the exception of exertion of governmental exercise by the separate entity. In this case, the state entity can be deemed to be linked sufficiently to the State. In this respect, it is important to underline the role of internal law. The legal separateness almost uniquely derives from domestic law. However, the subsequent scrutiny whether to treat both entities as separate cannot be made by relying solely on internal law as this would lead to an unequal application of general rules of international law.

II. *Investment Treaty Arbitration and Attribution of Conduct of Sub-State Entities*

Investment treaties regularly contain jurisdictional clauses that restrain their applicability to disputes between an "investor of a Contracting State" and a "Contracting State". The same is laid down in article 25(1) of the ICSID Convention. Thereby, it is ensured that arbitral tribunals endowed with jurisdiction solely sit over cases that confront a private entity and a State.[520] As a corollary, a treaty-based arbitral tribunal will be confronted regularly with the question of whether the foreign investor concluded the investment contract with the State or one of its entities or whether the contractual partner of the investor is

[518] Id., p. 310.

[519] Weiss, *supra* fn. 267, 816.

[520] See, e.g., A. Broches, The Convention on the Settlement of Investment Disputes: Some Observations on Jurisdiction, Colum. J. Transnat'l L. 5 (1966), 263, 265; Schreuer, *supra* fn. 42, 82; Orrego Vicuña, *supra* fn. 160, 65. The relevant part of article 25(1) of the ICSID Convention reads as follows: "The jurisdiction of the Centre shall extend to any legal dispute arising directly out of an investment, between a Contracting State ... and a national of another Contracting State, which the parties to the dispute consent in writing to submit to the Centre".

a private entity as well. When the contract has been concluded with an entity which is not the State itself, the entity's conduct must be attributed to the State in order to fulfil the jurisdictional requirements of the pertinent treaty or the ICSID Convention. The practice of arbitral tribunals distinguishes between conduct that amounts to a treaty violation and breaches of contract that do not amount to such a violation.[521]

1. *Attribution of Conduct under International Law*

In *Maffezini v. Spain*,[522] the tribunal had to determine whether the conduct of the Sociedad para el Desarollo Industrial de Galicia (SODIGA) could be attributed to the Kingdom of Spain and thus the requirements *ratione personae* set up by article 25(1) of the ICSID Convention would be met.[523] At the outset, the tribunal laid down the methodological frame for the attribution of entities to a State.[524] Accordingly, the tribunal had to answer two questions: "first, whether or not SODIGA is a state entity for the purpose of determining the jurisdiction of the Centre and the competence of the Tribunal, and second, whether the actions and omissions complained by the Claimant are imputable to the State."[525]

The jurisdictional examination itself, according the tribunal, had to be carried out in two steps: Firstly, the structure of the entity has to be evaluated. The ownership of the entity by the State, the indirect or direct control by the State, or the entity's purpose to carry out governmental functions give rise to the rebuttable presumption that the entity is a State entity.[526] Secondly, the function of the entity has to be

---

[521] On the distinction between treaty claims and contract claims, see *infra* 160 et seq.

[522] *Emilio Agustín Maffezini v. Kingdom of Spain*, ICSID Case No. ARB/97/7, Decision on Jurisdiction, 25 January 2000, 5 ICSID Rep. 387 (hereinafter, *Maffezini Jurisdiction*); *Maffezini v. Spain*, *supra* fn. 310. The dispute in this case did not arise out of a contract between investor and host State. Notwithstanding this, the exhaustive examination of attribution matters by the tribunal makes it relevant for the present purpose. The essential question whether the company was an organ of the State would have to be treated similarly in case of a state contract.

[523] On account of this, the tribunal did not refer to the BIT underlying the dispute but examined the question exclusively with regard to the jurisdictional requirements of the ICSID Convention.

[524] The tribunal referred to Brownlie, *supra* fn. 470, 132.

[525] *Maffezini Jurisdiction*, *supra* fn. 522, para. 75.

[526] Id., para. 77.

examined. The tribunal mentions that "a mixed economy company or government-owned corporation should not be disqualified as a 'national of another Contracting State' (i.e., as claimant) unless it is acting as an agent for the government or is discharging an essentially governmental function"[527] This permits the tribunal to evaluate the reverse situation: a mixed economy or state-owned corporation can only be considered as pertaining to the "Contracting State" when it discharges essentially governmental functions delegated to it by the State.[528] The tribunal concluded that the fulfilment of both requirements—structural and functional—were not mandatory but merely served as an indicator for the finding of a State action.[529]

The following presents the detailed examination of SODIGA's structure and function made by the tribunal. SODIGA was created by a decree issued by the Ministry of Industry which authorized a national state agency to establish SODIGA. In December 1990, the government owned over 88% of SODIGA's capital.[530] The purpose of SODIGA's establishment was to create an entity that carried out governmental functions. SODIGA was intended to promote regional industrial development in the Region of Galicia.[531] Its functions were, inter alia, the undertaking of studies for the introduction of new industries, seeking and soliciting such new industries, investing in new enterprises, processing of loan applications with official sources of financing, providing guarantees for such loans, and providing technical assistance.[532] Hence, the tribunal concluded that SODIGA, which met both requirements discussed above, prima facie was a state entity acting on behalf of Spain.[533] This allowed the tribunal to accept jurisdiction.

On the merits, the tribunal then turned to the specific actions of SODIGA which were claimed to be violating the treaty. The crucial distinction in this regard was whether SODIGA had acted *jure iimperi*. Ultimately, several actions of SODIGA were held to be an exertion of

---

[527] The tribunal referred to Broches, *supra* fn. 321, 355.

[528] *Maffezini Jurisdiction*, *supra* fn. 522, paras. 80–81. The tribunal also cited *CSOB v. Slovakia*, *supra* fn. 447, para. 250, where the tribunal held that the state ownership of the shares of the corporate entity did not suffice to exclude the claimant's characterisation as "national of a Contracting State" when the entity's function is "essentially commercial rather than governmental in nature".

[529] Id., para. 81.

[530] Id., para. 83.

[531] Id., para. 85

[532] Id., para. 86.

[533] Id., para. 89.

sovereign authority. Firstly, behaviour relating to a transfer of funds from Mr Maffezini's bank account initiated by SODIGA was regarded as involving public elements. Secondly, the fact that SODIGA was charged with the implementation of governmental policies entitled it to perform several functions normally not open to ordinary commercial companies such as, for instance, the right to manage the payments and finances of EAMSA[534] and to intervene on its behalf before the Spanish authorities without being paid for its services. Thirdly, the tribunal saw an evidence of governmental function in the manner in which the private banks conducted themselves with regard to SODIGA.[535] Finally, the fact that the transfer amounted to an investment increase decided by SODIGA and not by Mr Maffezini was considered as an exercise of governmental authority.[536]

The same approach as regards the jurisdictional stage was applied by the tribunal in *Salini v. Morocco*[537] in determining its jurisdiction *ratione personae*. Whilst Morocco contended that ADM, a limited liability company with which Salini had concluded a construction contract relating to the construction of a highway joining Rabat to Fès, was a private legal entity with its own assets,[538] the facts taken into account by the tribunal pointed in the other direction. The Kingdom of Morocco, through the medium of the Treasury and various public entities, held at least 89% of the shares of ADM. This majority stake enabled the Moroccan State to appoint the board of directors which had widespread powers to control and manage ADM. The membership of several government officials in the board of directors was seen as persuasive evidence of such powers by the tribunal.[539] The functional test did not alter this estimation. The objective of ADM was to accomplish tasks that were under state control, namely, the building, managing, and operating of highways and communication routes of a large dimension.[540] Thus, the fact that ADM was distinguishable from the

---

534 Emilio A. Maffezini S.A. (EAMSA), i.e., the corporation which was established and invested in by Emilio Maffezini. EAMSA was incorporated under the laws of Spain.

535 *Maffezini Jurisdiction, supra* fn. 522, para. 78.

536 Id., para. 79.

537 *Salini v. Morocco, supra* fn. 97, paras. 28–35. A decision on the merits stage was not rendered since the parties settled the dispute after the decision on jurisdiction.

538 Id., para. 28.

539 Id., para. 32.

540 Id., para. 33.

State solely on account of its legal personality cannot prevent the conclusion that for ICSID jurisdictional purposes the corporation was regarded as a "State company".[541] Since ADM was not held to be a state organ, the tribunal correctly upheld its jurisdiction for conduct which could amount to a treaty violation and rejected its jurisdiction over mere breaches of contract.[542]

In several recent jurisdictional decisions, ICSID tribunals evinced a somewhat abbreviated approach to attribution matters in the jurisdictional stage.[543] Accordingly, a closer examination of the respective entity's nature at this stage of the proceedings is only required in exceptional cases.[544] As example for exceptional cases, mention is made to cases in which it is manifest that the entity involved has no link whatsoever with the State or in which the respondent relies heavily upon the absence of such a link.[545] In ordinary cases in which some link between State and entity obviously exists and the respondent's allegations do not require further inquiry, the question whether a particular conduct can be attributed to the State must be answered in the merits stage. In *Jan de Nul v. Egypt*, for instance, the fact that SCA[546] was a public agency apparently sufficed to confirm the existence of such a link. For jurisdictional purposes, the tribunal plainly accepted the claimant's allegations.[547] Further, these tribunals referred explicitly to the

[541] Id., para. 35.

[542] Contra R. E. Vinuesa, Jurisdictional Objections to ICSID Arbitration under Bilateral Investment Treaties, in: J. Bröhmer (ed.), Internationale Gemeinschaft und Menschenrechte: Festschrift für Georg Ress zum 70. Geburtstag am 21. Januar 2005 (2005), 331, 337: "[T]he distinction of responsibility attributed to the State as different from responsibility attributed to a State entity is a misleading Tribunal's construction with no legal foundation".

[543] See, e.g., *Jan de Nul v. Egypt*, *supra* fn. 377, paras. 83–89; *Saipem v. Bangladesh*, *supra* fn. 367, paras. 144 et seq; *LESI-Dipenta v. Algeria*, *supra* fn. 119, para. 19.

[544] *Jan de Nul v. Egypt*, *supra* fn. 377, para. 85.

[545] In this regard, the tribunals refer to *Salini v. Morocco*, *supra* fn. 97.

[546] The SCA was a public agency which organized the whole transaction, i.e., the tender and the implementation of the contract.

[547] See *Jan de Nul v. Egypt*, *supra* fn. 377, para. 88, where the tribunal cited the relevant passage of the claimant's statement:

> Looking at the law which established SCA, if you have been constituted by law and your governance, presidency and the board are appointed not only by the government, but the President of the Republic himself, and replaced by this decision, and the law gives you the power to issue decrees for administrative delegation, which includes admitting or excluding passages, applying fines, applying charges, this should be an organ, this is a body which speaks and acts in the name of the State.

articles 4, 5 and 8 of the ILC Articles and upheld that during the merits stage they would adhere to these rules. In sum, this approach determines during the jurisdictional stage only whether the entity involved has any link whatsoever with the State.

As an example of a decision in the merits stage, mention can be made of *Noble Ventures v. Romania*.[548] In this case it was questionable whether the conduct of the Romanian "State Ownership Fund" (SOF) could be attributed to the State. The tribunal, applying customary international law laid down in the ILC Articles, found that, even under domestic law, no legal separation between SOF and the Romanian State was conceivable. In fact, the Romanian Privatization Law explicitly empowered SOF to act as a governmental agency in managing the whole legal relationship with investors.[549] SOF was thus deemed to be an organ of the State, and therefore, the distinction between *acta iure gestionis* and *acta iure imperii* became immaterial.[550]

In its decision on the merits, the tribunal in *Jan de Nul v. Egypt* gives a further example of the ILC Articles' application.[551] The tribunal denied the attribution of SCA's conduct to Egypt. In its view, SCA was not a state organ since structurally under Egyptian law, it was not part of the Egyptian State (article 4 of the ILC Articles).[552] Neither did SCA exercise the governmental authority with which it was empowered (article 5 of the ILC Articles).[553] Finally, the tribunal found no instruction of SCA by the Egyptian State to exist (article 8 of the ILC Articles).[554]

The contention has been made that the application of a functional and structural test is superfluous since the only relevant element of attribution is the exertion of sovereign authority with regard to the specifically incriminated behaviour.[555] Allegedly, this is confirmed by the

---

[548] *Noble Ventures v. Romania*, *supra* fn. 492, paras. 68–80.

[549] Id., para. 79.

[550] Moreover, the tribunal appears to draw doubts upon the distinction of commercial acts and sovereign acts in general. See id., para. 82. According to the customary rules of international law as laid down in the ILC Articles, the distinction is significant when the respective entity is not an organ of the State.

[551] *Jan de Nul N.V. v. Arab Republic of Egypt*, ICSID Case No. ARB/04/13, Award, 6 November 2008, paras. 155 et seq.

[552] Id., para. 162.

[553] Id., para. 171.

[554] Id., para. 173.

[555] Cf. Manciaux, *supra* fn. 430, 578–579, where the author states that: "le recour aux critères structurels et fonctionels est tout simplement inutile dans un tel cas; seule l'application du critère du caractère comportement en cause s'imposait dans cette affaire".

decision in *Maffezini v. Spain* in which, ultimately, only the examination of the specific conduct's nature was decisive. This may be true insofar as the fulfilment of jurisdictional requirements is concerned.[556] However, as far as the attribution of specific conduct is concerned, the decisive distinction is the one between state organs and non-state organs. For instance, if a formally separated agency of a State, say, an agency for the privatization of the State's energy sector, is regarded as a state organ under international law, the whole of the entity's conduct can be attributed to the State. By contrast, if the agency is viewed as a non-state organ, only the conduct by which it exerts public powers would be attributable to the State.[557] In this context, a functional and structural test contributes to an exact determination. Yet, this would require the tribunals' awareness of the principal distinction in the first place.[558]

In sum, insofar as the conduct at question is deemed to amount to a treaty violation, the attribution of conduct of entities to States under investment treaties is made pursuant to customary international law as laid down in the ILC Articles. Whereas this entails a broad attribution for conduct of state organs, the conduct of non-state organs is covered by a strict regime which confines the protective extent of investment treaties considerably.

---

[556] In cases in which the "link" between the entity and the host State is not so clear, the test may also serve to underpin a jurisdictional decision. In *Maffezini v. Spain* where it was not obviously conceivable that the particular entity had a link with the Spanish State, the test may well be regarded as having served a useful purpose. In any event, the test must not be regarded as a mandatory requirement for jurisdictional purposes.

[557] It is difficult to differentiate clearly between state organs and non-state organs which exercise governmental authority. The ILC gives the following guidelines: i) state organs: "state organs" is to be understood in the most general sense, i.e., "it extends to organs of government of whatever kind of classification, exercising whatever function, and at whatever level in the hierarchy"; ii) non-state organs that exercise governmental authority: "they may include public corporations, semi-public entities, public agencies of various kinds and even, in special cases, private companies". See Crawford, *supra* fn. 261, 95, 100. On state organs, see also Brownlie, *supra* fn. 470, 135 et seq.

[558] In *Maffezini v. Spain*, an explicit distinction between state organs and non-state organs was not made. The tribunal examined exclusively whether the entity was a "state entity". This characterisation of the entity as "State entity", however, did not entail a wholesale attribution. It must thus be assumed that "State entity" within this sense and "State organs" pursuant to the ILC Articles are not similar. For criticism on the textual confusion of the tribunal in *Maffezini v. Spain*, see also Smutny, *supra* fn. 485, 45.

2. *Determination of the Parties to a Contractual Dispute*

With regard to claims that are based on breach of contract, arbitral tribunals applied a different concept to determine their jurisdiction.[559] In *Impregilo v. Pakistan*[560], an Italian company had concluded two contracts with the Pakistan Water and Power Development Agency (WAPDA) concerning the construction of hydroelectric power facilities. In order to determine its jurisdiction over contractual claims, the tribunal addressed the scope of the jurisdictional clause of the underlying BIT which stated that "any disputes arising between a Contracting Party and the investors of the other" may be submitted to arbitration.[561] The tribunal's reasoning went as follows: The contracts out of which the dispute arose were concluded with WAPDA and not with the State of Pakistan. In contrast to Pakistan, WAPDA is not a party to the BIT. The scope of article 9 only covers breaches of a contract to which the State as party to the BIT is itself a party.[562] The relationship between WAPDA and Pakistan was thus decisive for the tribunal's jurisdiction. Unlike the tribunals exposed *supra*, the *Impregilo* tribunal assessed the status of WAPDA by relying exclusively on Pakistan law under which WAPDA was endowed with proper legal capacity.[563] It turned out that both the structure and the function of WAPDA tended to be government-related. The members of its board of directors were appointed by the government and the government retained the right to remove the chairman and any member for various reasons.[564] The function of WAPDA was to prepare a comprehensive plan for the development and utilization of water and power resources in Pakistan. Subsequent to the government's approval, WAPDA may take action for the implementation of the plan.[565] The government's liability to the creditors of WAPDA is limited to the extent of the grant made by the government and the loans passed by WAPDA with the sanction of the government.[566]

[559] A treaty-based tribunal arguably has jurisdiction over mere contractual claims when either the treaty contains an umbrella clause or a broadly phrased dispute resolution clause.

[560] *Impregilo v. Pakistan, supra* fn. 57.

[561] See article 9 of the Italy—Pakistan BIT.

[562] *Impregilo v. Pakistan, supra* fn. 57, paras. 198, 211, 214.

[563] Id., para. 200.

[564] Id., paras. 201–202.

[565] Id., paras. 204–205.

[566] Id., para. 207.

The tribunal summed up that the Government of Pakistan exercised a strict control on WAPDA. However, due to its strict reliance upon internal law, the tribunal's view was that WAPDA is an autonomous body, legally and financially distinct from Pakistan.[567]

The tribunal in *Impregilo* substantiated its decision as follows:

> Much of Impregilo's argument on this issue rested upon international law principles of state responsibility and attribution. However, a clear distinction exists between the responsibility of a State for the conduct of an entity that violates international law (e.g. a breach of a Treaty), and the responsibility of a State for the conduct of an entity that breaches a municipal law contract (i.e. Impregilo's Contract Claims).[568]

In other words, when the breach of contract does not amount to a treaty violation, the question of whether a State may be held responsible for the conduct of an entity that breaches an investment contract with a foreign investor is not governed by the rules of attribution under international law but by normal contractual principles.[569] This rationale likewise was applied by the tribunal in *Salini v. Morocco* concerning the jurisdiction over Salini's contract claims.[570] Hence, the determination of the parties to a contractual dispute and consequently, the jurisdiction ratione personae follows the contractual principles as laid down in the host State's domestic law. In case the host State's laws determine the particular entity as distinct from the State, this distinction has to be acknowledged by arbitral tribunals that sit over contractual disputes. Thereby, as Sinclair notes, "States are free to participate in an investment, alongside a foreign investor, through a separate legal entity and to enjoy the benefits of the corporate form".[571]

III. *Special Regimes of Attribution of Particular Investment Treaties*

Yet, the application of the customary rules of attribution as laid down in the ILC Articles may be altered by special agreement between the parties and thereby a progressive and more comprehensive scheme may be established. In the following two examples of such a modification are shown.

---

[567] Id., para. 209.
[568] *Impregilo v. Pakistan, supra* fn. 57, para. 210.
[569] See also Sinclair, *supra* fn. 96, 103.
[570] *Salini v. Morocco, supra* fn. 97, paras. 30 et seq., 59 et seq.
[571] Sinclair, *supra* fn. 96, 103.

1. *Articles 22 and 23 of the ECT*

Articles 22[572] and 23 of the ECT may be deemed to be the most progressive provisions of international law in the field of state responsibility. Although they do not provide for direct, treaty-based litigation between the two concerned entities, i.e., the foreign investor and the state enterprise,[573] they expand the breadth of host State responsibility by placing the obligation to ensure compliance with ECT substantive rules by its public service and other enterprises directly on the Member States.[574]

Whereas article 23 appears to merely confirm international customary law, the meaning and function of article 22 of the ECT present progressive development. In fact, it is contended to establish a State's strict liability for conduct of its state enterprises. Noteworthy in this respect are the different levels of obligation[575] by which the strictness of articles 22(1) and (3) seems to be confirmed.[576] Hereby, the ECT is supposed to avoid the flaws of state enterprise attribution. Instead of introducing a further means of attribution of conduct which does not fall into the categories of the international customary law on state responsibility, the ECT makes the contracting States directly liable for the

---

[572] Article 22 of the ECT reads as follows:

State and Privileged Enterprises—(1) Each Contracting Party shall ensure that any state enterprise which it maintains or establishes shall conduct its activities in relation to the sale or provision of goods and services in its Area in a manner consistent with the Contracting Party's obligations under Part III of this Treaty. (2) No Contracting Party shall encourage or require such a state enterprise to conduct its activities in its Area in a manner inconsistent with the Contracting Party's obligations under other provisions of this Treaty. (3) Each Contracting Party shall ensure that if it establishes or maintains an entity and entrusts the entity with regulatory, administrative or other governmental authority, such entity shall exercise that authority in a manner consistent with the Contracting Party's obligations under this Treaty. (4) No Contracting Party shall encourage or require any entity to which it grants exclusive or special privileges to conduct its activities in its Area in a manner inconsistent with the Contracting Party's obligations under this Treaty. (5) For the purpose of this Article, "entity" includes any enterprise, agency or other organization within its Area.

[573] Such a system of direct horizontal effect of substantive principles exists only within the framework of the EC.

[574] See T. Wälde, In the Arbitration under Art. 26 Energy Charter Treaty (ECT), Nykomb v. The Republic of Latvia—Legal Opinion, TDM 2 (2005), No. 5, 1, 58 et seq.

[575] Compare the different wordings "shall ensure" and "shall encourage or require".

[576] T. Wälde & P. Wouters, State Responsibility and the Energy Charter Treaty: The Rules regarding State Enterprises, Entities, and Subnational Authorities, Hofstra L. & Pol'y Symp. 2 (1997), 117, 129.

actions of their respective enterprises and entities.[577] However, the precise content of article 22 remains unclear. In the first ECT arbitral award, the issue emerged whether the State was responsible for the double-tariff agreement between the investor's domestic subsidiary and a state electricity monopoly. Nykomb Synergetics, a private enterprise, put forward the argument that article 22 was an attribution norm which provided for a guarantee by the State of compliance by a state enterprise with the part III obligations under the ECT.[578] Accordingly, article 22 was "clarificatory" of and "progressively developing" international law. The tribunal, however, avoided ruling on this issue and merely applied international customary law in order to attribute the particular conduct to the State.[579]

2. *Article 2(2) of the 2004 US Model BIT*

A range of more recent investment treaties provide for a special regime of attribution. Article 2(2) of the 2004 US Model BIT, for instance,[580] reads as follows: "2. A Party's obligation under Section A shall apply: (a) to a state enterprise or other person when it exercises any regulatory, administrative, or other governmental authority delegated to it by that Party; and (b) to the political subdivisions of that Party."

The term "state enterprise" is defined as "an enterprise owned, or controlled through ownership interest, by a Party". Hence, whilst article 2(2)(b) does not more than to repeat customary international law, article 2(2)(a) clarifies the treatment of "state enterprises"as defined therein. This approach has been termed as "globalised" by one commentator since it purportedly provided for state responsibility for a wide range of sub-state entities.[581] Yet, given the requirement of exertion of public authority for state enterprises, there is no real progression conceivable compared to the rules of customary international law.

---

[577] Id., 128; R. Happ, Dispute Settlement under the Energy Charter Treaty, GYIL 45 (2002), 331, 354. For a discussion of whether article 22 of the ECT constitutes "new" primary obligations or refers to chapter III obligations which entails the applicability of article 26 of the ECT, see Wälde & Weiler, *supra* fn. 199, 159, 181.

[578] Part III, i.e., articles 10 to 17, of the ECT contains the substantive standards of investment protection.

[579] See T. Wälde & K. Hóber, The First Energy Charter Treaty Arbitral Award, J. Int'l Arb. 22 (2005), 83, 91–92.

[580] See also article 2 of the 1999 France Model BIT.

[581] Manciaux, *supra* fn. 430, 571.

IV. *Conclusion*

Since investment treaties usually do not contain special rules of attribution, the tribunals have to rely on the general rules of attribution as laid down in the ILC Articles. Due to the rigidity of these provisions, the attribution of the conduct of non-state entities such as state-owned enterprises or public agencies separate from the State itself is contingent upon their respective exertion of public power. Since it is questionable whether this still corresponds to the economic realities in which States act indirectly in a multitude of ways, it can be endorsed that treaty drafters attempt to lay down more comprehensive treaty regimes. In the absence of such a special regime, a foreign investor is well advised to deal with official state organs in order to enjoy investment treaty protection.

3. THE SUBSTANTIVE COVERAGE OF CONTRACTS BETWEEN HOST STATES AND FOREIGN INVESTORS THROUGH INVESTMENT TREATY STANDARDS

A. The Distinction between Treaty Claims and Contract Claims

The conclusion of investment treaties by States creates, in addition to state contracts, a second legal instrument for the protection of foreign investment. As a corollary to the co-existence of contracts and treaties, the question of the relationship between both elements of investment protection becomes relevant. Principally, a host State's unlawful conduct may entitle a foreign investor to lodge claims grounded on both legal sources.

I. *Conceptual Distinction*

At first sight, the distinction between claims based on an investment agreement between a private investor and a State or a state entity and claims based on an investment treaty, i.e., an international treaty concluded between two or several States seems to be an obvious and clear-cut one.[1] But a second glance at the criteria for distinguishing the two claims reveals the possible complications of the undertaking.

Five legal criteria can be put forward to distinguish the two types of claims.[2] The first criterion refers to the source of the right or the cause of the claim. The basis of a treaty claim is a right established and defined in an investment treaty while a contract claim is based on the contract. This criterion is supposedly the only one that does not allow

[1] Cf. B. Cremades & D. Cairns, The Brave New World of Global Arbitration, JWI 3 (2002), 173, 192 et seq.

[2] The five criteria were proposed in B. Cremades & J. Cairns, Contract and Treaty Claims and Choice of Forum in Foreign Investment Disputes, in: N. Horn (ed.), Arbitrating Foreign Investment Disputes (2004), 325, 327–332 et seq. They are also referred to in G. Tawil, The Distinction between Contract Claims and Treaty Claims: An Overview, Presentation Delivered at ICCA Congress 2006 Montreal, formerly available at: www.iccamontreal2006.org (on file with the author), 2.

any overlap between the two categories. By definition, a treaty claim cannot be based on a contract and vice-versa. The second criterion posits that a distinction can be made by reason of the right's content. Whilst treaty rights established by BITs are of a generic nature and defined by international law, the contents of contractual rights usually are connected to the specific investment and find their definition in the domestic law of the host State. The possibility of overlap in this category is relatively high. Several rights, for instance the right to compensation subsequent to expropriation, may be granted through treaty as well as through contract. The impact of an "umbrella clause" could even lead to the situation that the whole of the contractual obligations becomes part of the treaty's coverage.[3] The third criterion is made up of the parties to the claim. As mentioned before, investment treaties are concluded between two or more States, and the parties to a treaty claim therefore are the investor, which is a national of the other State party to the treaty, and the host State itself. By contrast, the parties to a contract claim are the parties to the contract. Whereas the investor is the same, the State party may often be a federal or regional unit or some other entity of the host State. Identity of the parties to the claims occurs when the contract is entered into by the foreign investor directly with the host State. A further aspect of distinction between the two instruments is the applicable law. Adjudication of treaty claims generally deals with the provisions of the BIT itself, the domestic law of the host State and the general principles of international law. The contract claim, in contrast, generally is subject to the domestic law of the host State. Finally, the liability of the host State comes into play in order to distinguish the two claims. Whereas under the treaty claim the responsibility of the host State takes place on the international plane, contractual responsibility will result in the State's responsibility under the rules of its domestic laws. Again, the possible application of an "umbrella clause" may blur such a distinction completely. Moreover, the tenet according to which contractual violations can amount under certain circumstances to treaty claims does not support the effectiveness of this last criterion.

[3] For a detailed examination of the effect of so-called "umbrella clauses" and their impact on the distinction between contract claims and treaty claims, see chapter 4.

II. *Relevance of the Distinctions*

The distinctions between treaty claims and contract claims in international investment arbitration have become a highly debated subject.[4] Since the distinctions are paramount for the relationship of local courts and international arbitral tribunals,[5] their practical consequences are highly relevant for a foreign investor. When the breach of contract is deemed to be a violation of the treaty, the investor will enjoy the whole protective regime created through the respective investment treaty. In contrast, the classification of its claim as pertaining to the contractual sphere will, at least in the absence of an "umbrella clause",[6] confine the investor to the application of contractual devices. In this case, a dispute regularly has to be brought before the domestic courts of the host State exposing the investor to the well-known disadvantages a foreigner is likely to experience.[7] It is thus no exaggeration to assert that the actual debate on the distinction between contract claims and treaty claims is somewhat the reflection of the whole history of investment protection. Whilst investors and capital-exporting countries were always eager to detach investment disputes from domestic systems and to "internationalise" them, capital-importing countries pursued the contrary, presumably under the assumption of national treatment.[8] The recent rise of investment treaties adopts this antagonism and transforms it into the question whether a breach of contract amounts to a treaty violation or not.

---

[4] Cf. J. Crawford, Treaty and Contract in Investment Arbitration, Int'l Arb. 24 (2008), 351, 351: "No issue in the field of investment arbitration is more fundamental, or more disputed, than the distinction between treaty and contracts." For further discussions, see the contributions of Bernardo Cremades, Nigel Blackaby, Phillippe Sands, and Alejandro Escobar on the Occasion of the Third Public Conference of the Investment Treaty Forum at the British Institute of International and Comparative Law, 10 September 2004, reproduced in: A. Sheppard et al., Editorial Note—The Relationship between Local Courts and Investment Treaty Arbitration, TDM 2 (2005), No. 04. Cremades, for instance, states the following: "[W]e come to the conclusion that the main issue is the distinction, if it happens to exist, between contract claims and treaty claims." For a short overview, see G. Zeiler, Treaty v. Contract: Which Panel?, TDM 4 (2007), No. 05.

[5] In principle, a treaty claim can be brought before an international arbitral tribunal as laid down in the investment treaty. A contract claim, by contrast, is not governed by a treaty but by the respective contract. Contract claims thus regularly have to be lodged before the contractually agreed domestic forum. For a more detailed exposition, see *infra* chapter 5.

[6] See *infra* chapter 4.

[7] See *supra* 5 et seq.

[8] See, e.g., M. McDougal et al., Human Rights and World Public Order (1980), 749.

III. *The Evolution of Arbitral Case Law*

1. *The Authoritative Annulment Decision in* Vivendi—*Analytical Separation and the Principle of Coincidence*

In arbitral practice, the interplay between treaties and contracts gave rise to some confusion. In *Wena v. Egypt*, the tribunal underlined the fundamental separation between the two types of disputes.[9] Egypt contended that the claim, which arose out of several "lease agreements" between Wena and a state agency concerning the operation of hotels in Luxor, was not based on a treaty violation but on "a succession of disputes arising out of a series of private relations."[10] In other words, the respondent's argument was that various contract claims were gathered in order to construct a treaty violation and that this was not permissible. The tribunal rejected this argumentation stating that a claim against Egypt independently of the contractual disputes may be discernable.[11]

By far the most influential case with regard to the question of the distinction between treaty claims and contract claims was the so-called *Vivendi* case.[12] The adjudication of this case foreshadowed how confusing the interplay between treaty claims and contract claims can become. The dispute was closely linked to the performance of a concession contract that was signed between Compañia de Aguas del Aconquija, S. A., an Argentine affiliate of the French company Compagnie Générale des Eaux with the Argentine province of Tucumán.[13] The contract governed

---

[9] *Wena Hotels Ltd. v. Arab Republic of Egypt*, ICSID Case No. ARB/98/4, Summary Minutes of the Session of the Tribunal Held in Paris on May 25, 1999, 25 May 1999, (2002) 41 ILM 881 (hereinafter, *Wena Jurisdiction*).

[10] Id., 890.

[11] *Wena Hotels Ltd. v. Arab Republic of Egypt*, ICSID Case No. ARB/98/4, Award, 8 December 2000, (2002) 41 ILM 896, paras. 80 et seq. (hereinafter, *Wena v. Egypt*), where the tribunal stated the following:

> Even if Egypt did not instigate or participate in the seizure of the two hotels, as Wena claims, there is sufficient evidence to find tat [sic] Egypt was aware of EHC's [the state agency with which Wena had concluded the lease agreements] intentions and took no actions to prevent the seizures or to immediately restore Wena's control over the hotels.

[12] *Compañia de Aguas del Aconquija, S.A. v. The Argentine Republic*, ICSID Case No. ARB/97/3, Award, 21 November 2000 (hereinafter, *Vivendi Award*); *Compañia de Aguas del Aconquija, S. A. & Vivendi Universal (formerly Compagnie Générale des Eaux) v. The Argentine Republic*, ICSID Case No. ARB/97/3, Decision on Annulment, 3 July 2002 (hereinafter, *Vivendi-Annulment*). For a summary of both decisions, see C. Schreuer, Investment Treaty Arbitration and Jurisdiction over Contract Claims—The *Vivendi I* Case Considered, in: T. Weiler (ed.), International Investment Law and Arbitration (2005), 281, 281–288; B. Cremades, Clarifying the Relationship between Contract and Treaty Claims in Investor-State Arbitrations, Bus. L. Int'l 2003, 207 et seq.

[13] *Vivendi Award*, *supra* fn. 12, para. 24.

the privatisation of Tucumán's water and sewage facilities.[14] The distinction between claims based on the BIT and claims based on the contract served the tribunal in affirming its jurisdiction.[15] In the merits stage, however, the tribunal declined the possibility of maintaining this differentiation. Accordingly, the linkage between the actions of the Province of Tucumán and the performance or non-performance of the parties under the contract was so close that the tribunal was not able to decide over the treaty claims without an exact examination of the contractual performances. The tribunal stated that:

> [B]ecause of the crucial connection in this case between the terms of the Concession Contract and these alleged violations of the BIT, the Argentine Republic cannot be held liable unless and until Claimants have...asserted their rights in proceedings before the contentious courts of Tucumán and have been denied their rights, either procedurally of substantively.[16]

Further the tribunal made clear that:

> "[I]t is not possible for this Tribunal to determine which actions of the Province were taken in exercise of its sovereign authority and which in exercise of its right as a part to the Concession Contract.... [A] detailed interpretation and application of the Concession Contract [is] a task left by the parties to that contract to the exclusive jurisdiction of the administrative court of Tucumán."[17]

In other words, the tribunal held that the determination of the treaty claim required an assessment of the parties' conduct under the contract.[18] The contract, in turn, referred contractual disputes to the courts of Tucumán. On account of this, the tribunal dismissed the claims involving an eventual breach of contract. Vivendi's request for annulment of the tribunal's award led to the partial annulment of the decision. The ad hoc committee found that the tribunal was in excess of its

---

[14] Id., para. 25.

[15] Id., para. 53: "As formulated, these claims against the Argentine Republic are not subject to the jurisdiction of the contentious administrative tribunals of Tucumán, if only because, *ex hypothesi*, those claims are not based on the Concession Contract but allege a cause of action under the BIT".

[16] Id., para. 78.

[17] Id., para. 79. Article 16.4 of the Concession Contract states the following: "For purposes of interpretation and application of this Contract the parties submit themselves to the exclusive jurisdiction of the Contentious Administrative Tribunals of Tucumán".

[18] Cf. B. Cremades, Litigating Annulment Proceedings—The Vivendi Matter: Contract and Treaty Claims, in: E. Gaillard (ed.), Annulment of ICSID Awards (2004), 87, 92–93.

powers[19] by failing to exercise a jurisdiction which it possessed.[20] Thereby, the committee introduced a fundamental point of view concerning the relationship between contract claims and treaty claims. The committee stated:

> [W]hether there has been a breach of the BIT and whether there has been a breach of contract are different questions. Each of these claims will be determined by reference to its own proper applicable law-in the case of the BIT, by international law; in the case of the Concession Contract, by the proper law of the contract, in other words, the law of Tucumán.[21]

Accordingly, what the tribunal did not bear in mind in its decision is that: "[I]t is one thing to exercise contractual jurisdiction and another to take into account the terms of a contract in determining whether there has been a breach of a distinct standard of international law."[22]

Hence, the tribunal erred in dismissing its entitlement to rule on the treaty claim by reason of the treaty claim's closeness to a breach of contract. Accordingly, the same set of facts can trigger claims which are grounded on violations of the treaty and claims which are grounded on a breach of contract. The determination of each violation has to be made independently of the other. For instance, an unlawful termination of a contract by a host State may entitle the investor to claim under the treaty, irrespective of whether the same right arises under the contract. This concept is in line with the general principle of international law whereby the international wrongfulness of a State's act is not affected by its characterization as lawful or not under internal law.[23] As Gaillard put it: "[The Committee's rationale is] based solely on the distinction between the separate causes of action based on the contract, taken in isolation, and on the treaty, even where it encapsulates in turn a violation based on the contract."[24]

---

[19] See article 52(1)(b) of the ICSID Convention. On the general evolution of ICSID annulment decisions, see C. Schreuer, Three Generations of ICSID Annulment Proceedings, in: E. Gaillard (ed.), Annulment of ICSID Awards (2004), 17 et seq.

[20] *Vivendi Annulment, supra* fn. 12, para. 86.

[21] Id., para. 96.

[22] Id., para. 105.

[23] See article 3 of the ILC Draft Articles on Responsibility of States for Internationally Wrongful Acts (2001): "The characterization of an act of a State as internationally wrongful is governed by international law. Such characterization is not affected by the characterization of the same act as lawful by internal law".

[24] E. Gaillard, Vivendi and Bilateral Investment Treaty Arbitration, 68 NYLJ 264 (2003), 1, 3. See also Cremades, *supra* fn. 12, 210.

On account of this, the existence of three conceptually different types of claims can be regarded as being conclusive: (a) mere contractual claims which do not amount to a violation of a treaty; (b) pure treaty claims which are not necessarily linked to a breach of contract or another domestic illegality; and (c) treaty claims that are based on breach of contract.[25] As a corollary hereof, a similar set of facts may give rise to a contract claim and also, separately, to a treaty claim.[26] Both disputes, however, pertain to separate categories.[27] This concept has been termed as the principle of possible coincidence of treaty claims and contract claims.[28] It has been followed by almost all subsequent decisions of arbitral tribunals[29] and the principle is thus correctly regarded as "well-established".[30]

---

[25] Cf. Tawil, *supra* fn. 2, 6.

[26] *Impregilo S.p.A. v. Islamic Republic of Pakistan*, Case No. ARB/03/3, Decision on Jurisdiction, 22 April 2005, para. 258 (hereinafter, *Impregilo v. Pakistan*): "Hence, ..., the fact that a breach may give rise to a contract claim does not mean that it cannot also—and separately- give rise to a treaty claim. Even if the two perfectly coincide, they remain analytically distinct, and necessarily require different enquiries". *Siemens A.G. v. The Argentine Republic*, ICISD Case No. ARB/02/8, Award, 6 February 2007, para. 267 (hereinafter, *Siemens v. Argentina*): "The fact that the Contract is subject to Argentine law does not mean that it cannot be expropriated from the perspective of public international law and under the Treaty. The two issues are unrelated".

[27] See S. Alexandrov, The *Vivendi* Annulment Decision and the Lessons for the Future ICSID Arbitrations—The Applicant's Perspective, in: E. Gaillard (ed.), Annulment of ICSID Awards (2004), 97, 114.

[28] *Bayindir Insaat Turizm Ticaret Ve Sanayi A.S. v. Islamic Republic of Pakistan*, ICSID Case No. ARB/03/29, Decision on Jurisdiction, 14 November 2005, para. 262 (hereinafter, *Bayindir v. Pakistan*). On this decision, see also L. Martinez & D. Bray, The Interplay of Contract Claims and Treaty Claims: Bayindir v. Pakistan, TDM 3 (2006), No. 03.

[29] See, e.g., *Aguas del Tunari S.A. v. Bolivia*, ICSID Case No. ARB/02/3, Decision on Jurisdiction, 21 October 2005, ICSID Rev.-FILJ 20 (2005), 450, para. 114; *Azurix Corp. v. Argentine Republic*, ICSID Case No. ARB/01/12, Decision on Jurisdiction, 8 December 2003, para. 81 (hereinafter, *Azurix v. Argentina*); *AES Corp. v. Argentine Republic*, ICSID Case No. ARB/01/17, Decision on Jurisdiction, 26 April 2005, para. 94; *CMS Gas Transmission Co. v. Argentina*, ICSID Case No. ARB/01/8, Decision on Jurisdiction, 17 July 2003, paras. 72 et seq.; *Camuzzi International S.A. v. Argentine Republic*, ICSID Case No. ARB/03/7, Decision on Jurisdiction, 10 June 2005, paras. 61 et seq.; *Eureko B.V. v. Republic of Poland*, Ad Hoc Arbitration under the Agreement between the Kingdom of the Netherlands and the Republic of Poland on Encouragement and Reciprocal Protection of Investment, Partial Award, 19 August 2005, para. 112 (hereinafter, *Eureko v. Poland*); *PSEG Global Inc. v. Republic of Turkey*, ICSID Case No. ARB/02/5, Decision on Jurisdiction, 4 June 2004, para. 158; *Saipem S.p.A. v. The People's Republic of Bangladesh*, ICSID Case No. ARB/05/07, Decision on Jurisdiction and Recommendation on Provisional Measures, 21 March 2007, para. 141; *Sempra Energy International v. Argentine Republic*, ICSID Case No. ARB/02/16, Decision on Jurisdiction, 11 May 2005, para. 95.

[30] *Bayindir v. Pakistan*, *supra* fn. 28, para. 148.

2. *The Prima Facie Approach for Jurisdictional Purposes*

In investment treaty arbitration, the distinction between contract claims and treaty claims naturally plays an important role in the jurisdictional phase of arbitral proceedings. The objection that a treaty-based arbitral tribunal has no competence to hear the claims at issue because they are mere contract claims is often put forward by respondent States.[31] As a consequence of the voluntary nature of arbitration, arbitral tribunals are only entitled to determine disputes that the parties have agreed that it should sit over.[32] Since the tribunals are established by a treaty, i.e., the necessary consent to arbitration is given through the treaty, the claims which they are competent to hear, *per definitionem*, seem to be confined to violations of the treaty.[33] If, so the argument goes, the claims are based exclusively on a breach of an investment contract or in other words, when the treaty claims are, in truth, contract claims, the contractual dispute resolution mechanism prevails and a treaty-based arbitral tribunal lacks jurisdiction. As a corollary, an arbitral tribunal deciding upon its jurisdiction has to undertake a characterisation of the claims brought before it.[34] The question which thus arises is whether for jurisdictional purposes, an arbitral tribunal has to rely on the claimant's allegations or whether it can inquire into the claim. In short, who decides whether a claim is a treaty or a contract claim during the jurisdictional phase, the arbitral tribunal or the claimant through its submission?

a. *Competence/Competence of International Arbitral Tribunals*

It is an established principle of international law that international courts and tribunals which sit over disputes between private individuals and States have the competence to decide upon their own

---

[31] See, e.g., id., para. 139:

> It is Pakistan's "primary submission" that "Bayindir's (treaty) claims, however skilfully repackaged, are inextricably bound up with the Contract" and that "the only rights which Bayindir claims have been violated are rights which it asserts are derived from the contract". In other words, regardless of how they have been formulated in this arbitration, Bayindir's Treaty Claims "are in reality contract claims … and thus beyond the scope of this tribunal's jurisdiction" (references omitted).

[32] A. Redfern & M. Hunter, Law and Practice of International Commercial Arbitration (2004), para. 5-30.

[33] See *supra* 68 et seq.

[34] Schreuer, *supra* fn. 12, 314.

jurisdiction.[35] The same holds true for arbitral tribunals in international commercial disputes.[36] This so-called principle of competence/competence is laid down in a string of national legislation[37] and international arbitration rules[38]. The principle is not altered by the fact that the arbitrator's decision may eventually be subject to review by courts of the country where enforcement of the award is sought.[39] On account of this principle, one may assume that, generally, the discretion of an arbitral tribunal to inquire into a claim on the jurisdictional phase is broad.[40] Nonetheless, it has not always been clear to what extent such an inquiry is legitimate.

b. *Determination of Jurisdiction*

The ICJ evinced two different approaches to the determination of its jurisdiction. In *Ambatielos*,[41] the court had to deal with a claim brought by the Greek Government against the United Kingdom concerning the rights of a Greek ship owner. With regard to its jurisdiction, the court relied foremost on the plausibility of the Greek application.[42]

---

[35] See, e.g., S. Schwebel, Some Aspects of International Law in Arbitration between States and Aliens, in: S. Schwebel (ed.), Justice in International Law (1994), 196, 197–199.

[36] Redfern & Hunter, *supra* fn. 32, para. 5–39. For an examination of recent developments, see F. González de Cossío, The Compétence-Compétence Principle, Revisited, J. Int'l Arb. 24 (2007), 231 et seq.

[37] See, e.g., article 41(1) of the ICSID Convention: "The Tribunal shall be the judge of its own competence".

[38] See, e.g., article 6.2 of the ICC Arbitration Rules; article 21(1) of the UNCITRAL Arbitration Rules, GA Resolution 31/98; article 16(1) of the UNCITRAL Model Law on International Commercial Arbitration, which reads as follows: "The arbitral tribunal may rule on its own jurisdiction, including any objections with respect to the existence or validity of the arbitration agreement".

[39] Schwebel, *supra* fn. 35, 199. Moreover, in the ICSID framework, which is the most frequently used institution for treaty arbitrations, an award is not subject to domestic review procedures. See article 54(1) of the ICSID Convention.

[40] In any event, in commercial arbitration, this decision on jurisdiction is subject to review by domestic courts.

[41] *Ambatielos* (Greece v. UK) (Merits) [1953] ICJ Rep. 10.

[42] Id., 18. The court stated the following:

> In order to decide, in these proceedings, that the Hellenic Government's claim on behalf of Mr. Ambatielos is "based on" the Treaty of 1886 within the meaning of the Declaration of 1926, it is not necessary for the Court to find and indeed the Court is without jurisdiction to do so—that the Hellenic Government's interpretation is the correct one. The Court must determine, however, whether the arguments advanced by the Hellenic Government in respect of the treaty provisions on which the *Ambatielos* claim is said to be based, are of a sufficiently plausible character to warrant a conclusion that the claim is based on the Treaty. It is not enough for the claimant Government to establish a remote connection between the facts of the claim and the Treaty of 1886.

This subjective approach, however, was not applied in more recent cases.[43] Instead of merely referring to the plausibility of the claimant's pleading, the court also examined objective criteria. In *Legality of Use of Force*, for instance, the court stated:

> [T]he Court cannot limit itself to noting that one of the Parties maintains that the Convention applies, while the other denies it; [I]t must ascertain whether the breaches of the Convention alleged by Yugoslavia are capable of falling within the provisions of the instrument.[44]

A similar approach was applied by one of the early ICSID tribunals the jurisdiction of which was not treaty-based. In order to examine the fulfilment of the requirements of the ICSID Convention, the tribunal in *Amco v. Indonesia* had to determine the nature of the claims.[45] Whilst the claimant contended that it was deprived of its investment by the Indonesian Government, the respondent sustained that the dispute was a mere lease dispute and as such, did not fall into the competence of an ICSID tribunal. The tribunal described its duty as follows:

> In other words, the Tribunal must not attempt at this stage to examine the claim itself in any detail, but the Tribunal must only be satisfied that *prima facie* the claim, as stated by the Claimants when initiating this arbitration, is within the jurisdictional mandate of ICSID arbitration, and consequently of this Tribunal.[46]

On account of this prima facie condition, the examination needed to take into account objective criteria. It can thus be contended that the non- or pre-investment treaty practice of international adjudicatory bodies concerning the determination of submitted claims for jurisdictional purposes relied on objective criteria. The acceptance of the claimant's allegations based on their mere plausibility in relation to the violation of an international treaty has not been maintained by international courts and tribunals.

A revision of the pertinent jurisprudence of investment treaty arbitrations reveals a certain degree of difference between the approaches

---

43 See *Case concerning Oil Platforms* (Islamic Republic of Iran v. United States of America) [1996] ICJ Rep. 810, paras. 16–17; *Case concerning Legality of Use of Force* (Yugoslavia v. Italy) [1999] ICJ Rep. 490, para. 25.

44 *Case concerning Legality of Use of Force* (Yugoslavia v. Italy), id.

45 *Amco Asia Corp. v. Republic of Indonesia*, ICSID Case No. ARB/81/1, Decision on Jurisdiction, 25 September 1983, 1 ICSID Rep. 377.

46 Id., para. 38.

of the tribunals. According to Schreuer, the different approaches chosen by arbitral tribunals can be categorized as two distinct stances: whereas one point of view relies exclusively upon the claimant's pleadings, another current already at the stage of jurisdiction looks behind the claim as presented by the claimant.[47] This difference recalls the distinction between the two abovementioned approaches advanced by the ICJ.

Effectively, some tribunals give overwhelming importance to the claimant's submission in determining their jurisdiction. As examples, mention can be made of the unannulled part of the first award of the *Vivendi*[48] case in which the tribunal argued as follows:

> As formulated, these claims against the Argentine Republic are not subject to the jurisdiction of the contentious administrative tribunals of Tucúman, if only because, *ex hypothesi*, those claims are not based on the Concession Contract but allege a cause of action under the BIT.[49]

The ad hoc committee sitting over the annulment of the decision seemingly assented to this approach.[50] The tribunals in *Salini v. Morocco*[51] and *Azurix v. Argentina*[52] maintained this school of thought which endorses an exclusive adherence to the claimant's submission. By this means, the claimant's contention that its claims are based on an investment treaty rather than on a contract, in and of itself, suffices to trigger the competence of treaty-based arbitral tribunals. Such an approach, if applied consequently, would even be more subjective than the ICJ's holding in *Ambatielos* as the plausibility of the claimant's arguments does not appear to become examined. In fact, such an approach would open the door to abuse by unsatisfied investors and would thus entail the implementation of superfluous proceedings. The tribunals in *SGS v. Pakistan*,[53] *Enron v. Argentina*,[54] and

---

[47] Schreuer, *supra* fn. 12, 315.
[48] *Vivendi Award*, *supra* fn. 12.
[49] Id., para. 53.
[50] *Vivendi Annulment*, *supra* fn. 12, paras. 72 et seq.
[51] *Salini Costrituttori S.p.A. v. The Kingdom of Morocco*, ICSID Case No. ARB/00/4, Decision on Jurisdiction, 23 July 2001, para. 64.
[52] *Azurix v. Argentina*, *supra* fn. 29, para. 76.
[53] *SGS Société Générale de Surveillance S.A. v. Islamic Republic of Pakistan*, ICSID Case No. ARB/01/13, Decision on Jurisdiction, 6 August 2003, ICSID Rev.-FILJ 18 (2003), 301; (2003) 42 ILM 1290, para. 145 (hereinafter, *SGS v. Pakistan*).
[54] *Enron Corp. v. Argentine Republic*, ICSID Case No. ARB/01/3, Decision on Jurisdiction, 14 January 2004, para. 67.

Siemens v. Argentina[55] also upheld their competence based on the position put forward by the claimant. However, their approach is more objective and attempts to find an improved balance by examining prima facie whether the alleged conduct may entail treaty violations. This reasoning is consistent with the holdings of the ICJ and strongly resembles the decision of the *Amco v. Indonesia* tribunal.

A handful of tribunals took a further step and examined not only whether the assertions put forward by the claimants were plausible but also gave a definitive interpretation of the substantive standards invoked.[56] This purported anticipation of examinations that pertain to the merits stage reflected the tribunals' needs to dismiss clear cases of non-violation of treaty standards. In *SGS v. Philippines*, for instance, the tribunal had to deal with a dispute which was essentially about the determination of an amount of money owed under a contract.[57] In particular, the claimant had invoked the violation of the fair and equitable treatment standard as well as the expropriation standard. As for the latter, the tribunal pointed out that, taking into account the material presented by the claimant, no conduct of the respondent could be regarded as being tantamount to an expropriation and thus rejected its jurisdiction concerning such a claim. As for the violation of the fair and equitable treatment standard, the tribunal admitted that the position is "less clear-cut" and consequently affirmed its jurisdiction.[58] In *Occidental v. Ecuador*, the tribunal held that a refusal to refund value added tax could not be considered as amounting to direct or indirect expropriation.[59] In *Joy Mining v. Egypt*, the central issue was the non-existence of investment within the meaning of article 25(1) of the ICSID Convention. The tribunal, however, added that a contingent

---

[55] *Siemens A.G. v. Argentine Republic*, ICSID Case No. ARB/02/8, Decision on Jurisdiction, 3 August 2004, (2005) 44 ILM 138, para. 180 (hereinafter, *Siemens Jurisdiction*).

[56] See *Société Générale de Surveillance S.A. v. Republic of the Philippines*, ICSID Case No. ARB/02/6, Decision on Jurisdiction, 29 January 2004 (hereinafter, *SGS v. Philippines*); *Occidental Exploration & Production Co. v. The Republic of Ecuador*, LCIA Case No. UN 3467, UNCITRAL, Final Award, 1 July 2004, [2005] 2 Lloyd's Rep. 707 (hereinafter, *OEPC v. Ecuador*); *Joy Mining Machinery Ltd. v. The Arab Republic of Egypt*, Award on Jurisdiction, 6 August 2004 (hereinafter, *Joy Mining v. Egypt*); *Bayindir v. Pakistan*, *supra* fn. 28.

[57] *SGS v. Philippines*, *supra* fn. 56, para. 159.

[58] Id., paras. 160–163.

[59] *OEPC v. Ecuador*, *supra* fn. 56, paras. 80, 89.

liability could not be expropriated and thus, "in this case not even the *prima facie* test would be met."[60] Albeit it referred to the prima facie test, the tribunal contradicted the rule of strict adherence to the test.[61] Accordingly, the specific circumstances of each case must be taken into consideration and in case of complete divergence about the meaning of the dispute in the light of the contract and the treaty, the tribunal has to include the respondent's view in its deliberations.[62] In *Bayindir v. Pakistan*, the tribunal basically affirmed the validity of the prima facie test. Its subsequent examination of the invoked treaty provisions and the purported facts, by contrast, appear closer to the point of view expressed in *Joy Mining* than to the prima facie test as handled in several other decisions.

In the final analysis, the difference between both approaches which were applied by treaty-based arbitral tribunals by no means appears to be unbridgeable.[63] Particularly, the tribunals which dismissed certain claims subsequent to a closer scrutiny of their content do not seem to be a whole new school of thought but rather represent the consequent application of the prima facie test to situations that are unlikely to constitute a treaty violation. Furthermore, the majority of arbitral tribunals that were based upon investment treaties followed a prima facie approach.[64] Thereby, the tribunals clarified that the starting point must be the claimant's application. However, the characterization put forward by the claimant cannot remain as the unique element of determination. Rather, a tribunal has to consider whether the facts as alleged by the claimant, if established, are capable of coming within those provisions of the BIT which have been invoked.[65] In any event,

[60] *Joy Mining v. Egypt, supra* fn. 56, para. 78.

[61] Cf. N. Gallus, Joy Mining v. Egypt: No Joy for British Mining Equipment Company at the ICSID, TDM 4 (2004), No. 04, 1, 2 et seq.

[62] *Joy Mining v. Egypt, supra* fn. 56, para. 30.

[63] It is interesting to note that on 10 April 2006 the amendments to the ICSID Arbitration Rules came into effect and established the opportunity for an expedited procedure for making preliminary objections. See rule 41(5) of the ICSID Arbitration Rules.

[64] In addition to the cases already mentioned, see, e.g., *Emilio Agustín Maffezini v. Kingdom of Spain*, ICSID Case No. ARB/97/7, Decision on Jurisdiction, 25 January 2000, ICSID Rev.-FILJ 16 (2001), 212 et seq., para. 69; *Methanex Corp. v. United States of America*, UNCITRAL, Preliminary Award on Jurisdiction and Admissibility, 23 July 2001, 7 ICSID Rep. 208, paras. 117–118; *United Parcel Service of America Inc. v. Government of Canada*, UNCITRAL, Award on Jurisdiction, 22 November 2002, 7 ICSID Rep. 285, para. 33; *Wena Jurisdiction, supra* fn. 9, 891.

[65] See, e.g., *Impregilo v. Pakistan, supra* fn. 26, para. 254.

the decision can only be provisional as the ultimate examination of the claims' nature belongs to the merits stage. Thus a tribunal has to find a determination of a claim's character without prejudging its nature.[66] In the final analysis, a balance that ensures that, on the one hand, tribunals are not flooded with claims which have no chance of success and thereby would entail the waste of time and resources, and on the other hand, the claimant is able to present its arguments to support its claim which, in essence, derives from its right to due process, has to be struck.[67]

IV. *The Fundamental Differences between Contract Claims and Treaty Claims*

The final decision of whether a breach of contract amounts to a violation of treaty cannot be made on an abstract basis but will rather depend on the specific protection standards of the relevant treaty and on the specific circumstances of the respective case. Nevertheless, before examining the typical protection standards of investment treaties more closely, some general observations on the conditions of a treaty violation shall be made.

1. *The Nature of Investment Treaties and the Consequent Distinction between International Commercial Arbitration and Investment Arbitration*

A contract between a State and an alien is not an international treaty and must not be equated with it.[68] Therefore, a breach of contract and a violation of treaty are conceptually and substantively different. Whereas treaties enjoin a State with international obligations, contracts may merely entail responsibility on the domestic level.[69] This difference is the substrate for the traditional classification of conduct of States as commercial and governmental. The classic tenet goes: a violation of an international treaty, i.e., rules of international law, by a State may only

[66] Tawil, *supra* fn. 2, 10.
[67] Cf. *Impregilo v. Pakistan*, *supra* fn. 26, para. 254. For cases under the auspices of the ICSID, the ICSID secretary is supposed to reject a case in which a lack of jurisdiction is manifest. This screening power, however, is limited and relies primarily on the information submitted by the claimant. See article 36(3) of the ICSID Convention.
[68] See *supra* 22 et seq.
[69] Id.

be perpetrated when the State is acting in its governmental capacity.[70] Breaches of contract committed as an ordinary commercial partner equivalent to the conduct of every other participant in commercial transactions, in contrast, are not susceptible of amounting to a violation of an international treaty and thus, of entailing the State's international responsibility.[71]

In principle, this concept is maintained under the regime of international investment treaties.[72] For instance, in *Salini v. Jordan*, the tribunal asserted that:

> Only the State, in the exercise of its sovereign authority, and not as a Contracting Party, has assumed obligations under the bilateral agreement. ...In other words, an investment protection treaty cannot be used to compensate an investor deceived by the financial results of the operation undertaken, unless he proves that his deception was a consequence of the behaviour of the receiving State acting in breach of the obligations which it had assumed under the treaty.[73]

Since international investment treaties are international treaties within the conventional sense, a breach of an investment contract is not per se a violation of an investment treaty.[74] Consequently, arbitral tribunals applied the so-called *puissance publique* test in order to determine the nature of the violation.[75] Nonetheless, this practice is increasingly subject to criticism. This is not only due to the constant difficulties which the differentiation between commercial and governmental conduct

---

[70] See, e.g., C. de Visscher, Théories et Réalités en Droit International Public (1970), 311; C. Amerasinghe, State Responsibility for Injuries to Aliens (1967), 42; E. Borchard, The Diplomatic Protection of Citizens Abroad or the Law of International Claims (1916), 177 et seq.

[71] See, e.g., J. Crawford, The International Law Commission's Articles on State Responsibility—Introduction, Texts and Commentaries (2002), 96.

[72] Cf. R. Happ & N. Rubins, Awards and Decisions of ICSID Tribunals in 2004, GYIL 47 (2004), 878, 921 et seq.

[73] *Salini Constrituttori S.p.A. v. Hashemite Kingdom of Jordan*, ICSID Case No. ARB/02/13, Decision on Jurisdiction, 29 November 2004, para. 155 (hereinafter, *Salini v. Jordan*).

[74] See *supra* 22 et seq.

[75] *Waste Management, Inc. v. United Mexican States*, ICSID Case No. ARB(AF)/00/3, Final Award, 30 April 2004, (2004) 43 ILM 967, paras. 172–174 (hereinafter, *Waste Management v. Mexico*); *Joy Mining v. Egypt*, *supra* fn. 56, para. 72; *Salini v. Jordan*, *supra* fn. 73, paras. 154–155; *Impregilo v. Pakistan*, *supra* fn. 26, para. 266; *Siemens Jurisdiction*, *supra* fn. 55, paras. 253–260; *Bayindir v. Pakistan*, *supra* fn. 28, paras. 180–184.

entails[76] but also and perhaps, more importantly, to the nexus between both legal instruments. Orrego Vicuña contends that treaties and contracts which previously allowed a useful comparison between international law and separate domestic legal systems have become part of a single legal structure.[77] In the view of Alexandrov, the *Vivendi* commission's statement that "whether particular conduct involves a breach of a treaty is not determined by asking whether the conduct purportedly involves an exercise of contractual rights" even evinces a renunciation from the classic distinction between "sovereign acts" and "commercial acts".[78] However, the commission likewise stated that "[a] treaty cause of action is not the same as a contractual cause of action; it requires a clear showing of conduct which is in the circumstances contrary to the relevant treaty standard." In any event, the main purpose of international investment treaties is not to settle mere commercial disputes. This has been put forward repeatedly by authors who stressed the differences between commercial arbitration and investment arbitration.[79] Since the principal feature of investment treaties is that they provide for the host State's consent to investment arbitration,[80] the characteristics of treaty arbitrations correspond to the purpose of investment treaties.

Several authors underline the fundamental differences between the two types of arbitration.[81] These concern the origin, the nature, and the

[76] Cf. C. Schreuer, State Immunity: Some Recent Developments (1988), 24 et seq.

[77] F. Orrego Vicuña, Of Contracts and Treaties in the Global Market, Max Planck UNYB 8 (2004), 341, 341.

[78] Alexandrov, *supra* fn. 27, 115.

[79] See, e.g., T. Wälde, The "Umbrella" Clause in Investment Arbitration—A Comment on Original Intentions and Recent Cases, JWIT 6 (2005), 183, 185; Z. Douglas, The Hybrid Foundations of Investment Treaty Arbitration, BYIL 74 (2003), 151, 153; N. Horn, Arbitration and the Protection of Foreign Investment: Concept and Means, in: N. Horn (ed.), Arbitrating Foreign Investment Disputes (2004), 3, 7 et seq.

[80] See *supra* 65 et seq.

[81] See, e.g., Cremades & Cairns, *supra* fn. 1, 193–194; *International Thunderbird Gaming Corp. v. Mexico*, UNCITRAL (NAFTA), Arbitral Award, 26 January 2006, Separate Opinion in the Arbitration under Chapter XI of the NAFTA and UNCITRAL Arbitration Rules: Thunderbird v. Mexico, paras. 4, 12 (hereinafter, *Thunderbird v. Mexico*, Separate Opinion); S. Franck, The Nature and Enforcement of Investor Rights under Investment Treaties: Do Investment Treaties Have a Bright Future, U.C. Davis J. Int'l L. & Pol'y 12 (2005), 47, 70–79; G. van Harten, Investment Treaty Arbitration and Public Law (2007), 59 et seq.; G. van Harten, The Public-Private Distinction in the International Arbitration of Individual Claims against the State, Int'l & Comp. L. Q. 56 (2007), 371, 373–377.

purpose of both mechanisms. International commercial arbitration is a private consensual method of dispute resolution.[82] It serves the resolution of disputes between parties who are presumed to be on equal footing.[83] Its principal purpose of creation is the provision of a neutral forum which ensured efficient dispute resolution, decreased the burden on judicial resources, and honoured the parties' freedom of contract.[84] Commercial arbitral tribunals do not have to take into account the eventual weakness or inferiority of one party and they barely face abuse of governmental powers. International investment arbitration, on the other hand, is a matter of public law and a form of public law adjudication.[85] It is not based upon the parties' consent given by contract but on a system of public international law treaties. The purpose of its creation was to detach the dispute resolution process from political and diplomatic means and thereby to depoliticize it.[86] The underlying aim of investment arbitration is the promotion of foreign investment. Treaty-based arbitral tribunals thus do not simply have to resolve a dispute between two equals but have to take into consideration various further factors such as public interests of the host country,[87] the eventual weakness of one party,[88] or the overarching principle of investment

[82] Redfern & Hunter, *supra* fn. 32, para. 1–01.

[83] See, e.g., *Thunderbird v. Mexico*, Separate Opinion, *supra* fn. 81, para. 4.

[84] Redfern & Hunter, *supra* fn. 32, para. 1–42.

[85] G. van Harten, The Public-Private Distinction, *supra* fn. 81, 380–381. Van Harten tries to prove this by an examination of the States' consent and the state act that triggers the dispute which is brought before investment arbitration. He assumes that when both pertain to public law fields, the public law nature of the dispute and the dispute resolution mechanism become clear.

[86] See *supra* introduction, 2 et seq. See also G. Alvarez & W. Park, The New Face of Investment Arbitration: NAFTA Chapter 11, Yale J. Int'l L. 28 (2003), 365, 366–367; Franck, *supra* fn. 81, 72; S. Franck, The Legitimacy Crisis in Investment Arbitration: Privatizing Public International Law through Inconsistent Decisions, Fordham L. Rev. 72 (2005), 1521, 1536–1538.

[87] See generally, N. Blackaby, Public Interest and Investment Treaty Arbitration, in: G. Kaufmann-Kohler & B. Stucki (eds.), Investment Treaties and Arbitration, ASA Special Series No. 19 (2002), 145, 147–148, who states that the public interest in investment treaty arbitration derives from its effects of "depoliticising the dispute, reducing investment risk and thereby increasing cross-border investment".

[88] Wälde claims that the weaker party naturally is the investor being foreigner and facing a State with regulatory power as opponent. See *Thunderbird v. Mexico*, Separate Opinion, *supra* fn. 81, para. 12. Sornarajah, by contrast, contends that the State is the weaker party. See M. Sornarajah, The International Law on Foreign Investment (2004), 207–208. Ultimately, this question depends on the vantage point. Given the economic power of transnational enterprises, they can be regarded as more powerful than many smaller States. However, if one takes into account the nature of States as sovereign powers, the tide may turn.

promotion. Among others, the host State may have a specific interest in the measure that is challenged or an interest in the appropriate interaction between federal, state, and local governmental authorities.[89] The system was not created to make arbitration more efficient but to avoid a situation in which the party the conduct of which is under scrutiny would be not only a party but also regulator, legislator, and adjudicator.[90] Essentially, investment-treaty based arbitration is directed against the abuse of governmental power. The investor is to be protected against undue interference by the host State based on its regulatory, administrative, or other governmental power.[91] Thereby, investment arbitration is a novel form of restricting the regulatory power of States through international law. It therefore has been referred to as an emerging global administrative law.[92] In sum, the features of investment treaty arbitration compared to those of international commercial arbitration seem to endorse the traditional distinction between sovereign conduct and commercial behaviour of States and state entities.

2. *The Distinction between Commercial and Governmental Conduct*

In public international law, the distinction between acts *iure imperii* and *iure gestionis* chiefly serves to determine the sovereign immunity of a State.[93] According to the restrictive approach to sovereign immunity, which nowadays is recognized almost universally,[94] the doctrine of state immunity does not apply to the activity of States in the commercial field.[95] The necessary distinction was formerly carried out by focussing predominantly on the nature of the transaction at issue.[96]

---

[89] B. Legum, Trends and Challenges in Investor—State Arbitration, Arb. Int'l 19 (2003), 143, 144–145.

[90] S. Franck, Foreign Direct Investment, Investment Treaty Arbitration and the Rule of Law, Global Business and Development Law Journal 19 (2007), 337, 372 et seq. The purpose of enhancing neutrality, however, is a matter for both systems of arbitration.

[91] See, e.g., Horn, *supra* fn. 79, 7; J. Salacuse, BIT by BIT: The Growth of Bilateral Investment Treaties and Their Impact on Foreign Investment in Developing Countries, Int'l Law. 24 (1990), 655, 659.

[92] Cf. G. van Harten & M. Louhglin, Investment Treaty Arbitration as a Species of Global Administrative Law, EJIL 17 (2006), 121 et seq.; S. Montt, State Liability in Investment Treaty Arbitration (2009), 12 et seq.

[93] K. Doehring, Völkerrecht (1999), 280.

[94] See, e.g., § 1605(a)(2) of the US Foreign Immunity Act 1976; European Convention on State Immunity (1972); article 10 of the ILC Draft Articles on Jurisdictional Immunities of States and their Properties (1991).

[95] See, e.g., M. Shaw, International Law (2005), 628–630.

[96] From the characterisation of the contract's nature, tribunals derived the nature of its breach or repudiation.

More recently, Schreuer proposed a string of criteria which may be useful in making the distinction.[97] In any event, the development of case law evinced a general difficulty in determining borderline cases. For instance, natural resource related activities by a State, which would include contracting with foreign investors in this area, were held to be commercial by European courts[98] and sovereign by US courts[99].

Be that as it may, in the present context, the purpose of the classification is different. By consenting to treaty-based arbitration, States are regarded to have entirely waived their immunity,[100] and the question of state immunity is thus not relevant. In the context of investment treaties, the distinction between governmental and commercial conduct serves to differentiate between a breach of contract and a violation of treaty and thus to determine the international responsibility of the State. This different purpose alters the attitude of the parties considerably. Whereas States traditionally had a generous understanding of which activities pertain to *iure imperii* actions and which would be covered by their immunity before the courts of another State, in investment treaty arbitration the reverse situation is the order of the day. States espouse an argumentation which relies on a wide content of their *iure gestionis* acts. The private party, on the other hand, which formerly was interested in a narrow interpretation of sovereignty, regularly adopts the point of view that the relevant conduct was governmental.[101] Therefore, it is doubtful whether the traditional tenets of state immunity analysis for the distinction of commercial and governmental conduct are transmissible to investment treaty protection.

---

[97] Schreuer, *supra* fn. 76, 42–43. Schreuer mentions, inter alia, the following aspects: i) does the state entity involved regularly engage in commercial acts; ii) is the entire setting of the contacts between claimant and State typically commercial; iii) did the State use sovereign prerogatives; and iv) were the legal forms and methods employed in the transaction purely commercial.

[98] OLG Frankfurt, *National Iranian Oil Co. Legal Status Case* (1984) 65 ILR 199; OLG Frankfurt, *National Iranian Oil Co. Pipeline Contracts Case* (1984) 65 ILR 439; BVerfG, *National Iranian Oil Co. Revenues from Oil Sales*, BVerfGE 64, 1.

[99] *International Association of Machinists and Aerospace Workers v. OPEC*, 477 F. Supp.553 (C.D. Cal. 1979), (1982) 63 ILR 284; *In re Sedco*, 543 F.Supp. 561 (S.D. Tex. 1982).

[100] See, e.g., G. Delaume, Sovereign Immunity and Transnational Arbitration, in: J. Lew (ed.), Contemporary Problems of International Arbitration (1986), 313, 314–315. See also U. Kischel, State Contracts (1994), 209 et seq.

[101] Cf. *Siemens Jurisdiction*, *supra* fn. 55, para. 247.

B. The Substantive Protection Standards of Investment Treaties and Their Coverage of State Contracts

The substantive protection standards of investment treaties comprise, on the one hand, a handful of positive treatment standards which require that the host State act in a certain manner towards the foreign investor and, on the other hand, the negative protection against expropriation without due compensation. The former standards have been classified by Görs into preferential, specific, relative, and absolute standards.[102] The preferential treatment standard, that is, the enjoinment of performance requirements or performance incentives such as local content, export performance, domestic sale,[103] and the specific treatment standard which describe free movement of persons and capital under specific circumstances[104] do not entail or set up specific consequences for breach of a state contract. The relative standards, which encompass "most favoured nation treatment" and "national treatment" and thus, express the general obligation of non-discrimination and the absolute standards, namely, the "fair and equitable treatment standard" and the obligation to provide for "full protection and security" may render certain types of breach of contract as violations of an investment treaty. Combined with the expropriation standard which, under international law, constituted the paramount protection standard for alien property, these standards cover to a certain extent the content of state contracts and thereby subject them to the treaty regime outlined in Chapter 2. In this section, the actual coverage of contracts by each of the substantive standards is examined. In this regard, the non-expropriation standard and the fair and equitable treatment standard are of primary importance.

I. *Expropriation*

1. *Expropriation under Customary International Law*

The protection of alien property against expropriation or nationalisation by the host State is one of the core legal issues of international investment protection.[105] In principle, States are allowed under

[102] B. Görs, Internationales Investitionsrecht (2004), 200–211.

[103] In this realm, an overlap may occur between investment treaty protection and trade liberalisation through the TRIMS Convention in the framework of the WTO.

[104] See also IMF, Article VI Section 3 of the Founding Treaty, July 1944.

[105] See, e.g., E. Lauterpacht, International Law and Private Foreign Investment, Ind. J. Global Legal Stud. 4 (1996/1997), 259, 263.

international law to exercise takings[106] of alien property.[107] Likewise, it is not controverted that the lawfulness of such an expropriation is subject to certain conditions. Generally, three conditions are said to be required so that an expropriation is lawful under public international law: (i) the taking must serve a public purpose, (ii) it must be non-discriminatory, and (iii) it must be accompanied by compensation.[108] As the breadth of the terms already indicates, States hold a considerable degree of discretion with regard to foreign property lying within their jurisdiction. Among the three conditions, the last, the payment of compensation, has been the subject of heavy disputes under international law for a long time.[109]

At present, it is acknowledged that an expropriation may not only be undertaken directly through formal transfer of title or outright physical seizure but also through measures which indirectly expropriate the property or which have a similar effect to expropriation or nationalisation.[110] This shift from a formal to a consequential determination of expropriation has become characteristic of the bulk of modern expropriation cases.[111] Thereby, it gets increasingly difficult to distinguish an expropriation or a measure tantamount to an expropriation from a legitimate regulative act of the State.[112] Similarly questionable is whether the sole effect of the measure needs to be expropriatory or whether the

---

[106] In addition to "taking" and "expropriation", the terms "dispossession", "wealth deprivation", "deprivation", or "privation" are similarly used. See OECD, "Indirect Expropriation" and the "Right to Regulate" in International Investment Law, Working Papers on International Investment, No. 2004/4 (2004), 3. The term "nationalisation" describes the complete taking of a single or all branches of production in the host country. See A. Verdross & B. Simma, Universelles Völkerrecht (1984), 812.

[107] Shaw, *supra* fn. 95, 738.

[108] Id., 740 et seq.; A. Cassese, International Law (2005), 523–524; Verdross & Simma, *supra* fn. 106, 805 et seq.

[109] See Lauterpacht, *supra* fn. 105, 263.

[110] See generally G. Aldrich, What Constitutes a Compensable Taking of Property?: The Decisions of the Iran-United States Claims Tribunal, AJIL 88 (1994), 585 et seq.; G. C. Christie, What Constitutes a Taking of Property under International Law?, BYIL 38 (1962), 307 et seq.; B. Weston, "Constructive Takings" under International Law: A Modest Foray into the Problem of "Creeping Expropriation", Va. J. Int'l L. 16 (1975/1976), 103 et seq.

[111] Cf. J. Paulsson & Z. Douglas, Indirect Expropriation in Investment Treaty Arbitrations, in: N. Horn (ed.), Arbitrating Foreign Investment Disputes (2004), 145, 151; M. Reisman & R. Sloane, Indirect Expropriation and Its Valuation in the BIT Generation, BYIL 74 (2003), 115, 118.

[112] See, e.g., K. Yannaca-Small, Indirect Expropriation and the Rights of the Governments to Regulate Criteria to Articulate the Difference, in: C. Ribeiro (ed.), Investment Arbitration and the Energy Charter Treaty (2006), 159 et seq.

State's expropriatory intent must be discernable.[113] The tension which arises between the need to protect the rights and expectations of the foreign investor and the necessity not to unduly restrict the State's regulative authority is often difficult to resolve.[114] At stake is, ultimately, who between the society as a whole represented by the State or the owner of the affected property is going to pay the economic cost of responding to the public interest.[115]

2. *Expropriation of Contracts under Customary International Law*

The specific context of the protection of contracts or contractual rights against expropriation under international law embraces two aspects. In the first place, a contractual relationship or the rights deriving from a contract between the host State and a foreign investor must be an appropriate subject of an expropriation. If this can be affirmed, the second question is under what circumstances can the existence of a contract's expropriation be sustained under international law. In other words, what kind of conduct by the State or what sort of violation is required to constitute an expropriation?

As for the former question, international law by no means can be regarded as pure inter-state law anymore, and the assertion that private rights principally may be protected under international law thus needs no further substantiation.[116] As a matter of logic, the existence of property is a prerequisite for an expropriation, and thus, the notion of property under international law has to be examined. More exactly, the question becomes whether contracts or contractual rights constitute property within the meaning of property under international law. Naturally, tangible property, movable or immovable, may be the subject of expropriation.[117] In this regard, international law does not differ

---

[113] See, e.g., R. Dolzer & F. Bloch, Indirect Expropriation: Conceptual Realignments?, Int'l L. FORUM 5 (2003), 155, 158–163.

[114] See I. Brownlie, Principles of Public International Law (2003), 509; R. Dolzer, Indirect Expropriation of Alien Property, ICSID Rev.-FILJ 1 (1986), 41 et seq.; S. Subedi, The Challenge of Reconciling the Competing Principles within the Law of Foreign Investment with Special Reference to the Recent Trend in the Interpretation of the Term "Expropriation", Int'l Law. 40 (2006), 121, 121.

[115] R. Higgins, The Taking of Property by the State: Recent Developments in International Law, RdC 176 (1982–III), 259, 276–277.

[116] See, e.g., Brownlie, *supra* fn. 114, 529 et seq.

[117] See, e.g., J. H. Herz, Expropriation of Foreign Property, AJIL 35 (1941), 244, 244–245.

from the majority of domestic legal systems. By contrast, whether the same holds true for intangible property and as a part thereof, for contracts and contractual rights, is not so clear.

In earlier decisions, the PCA and the PCIJ affirmed that contractual rights may be susceptible of expropriation under international law. In *Norwegian Shipowners' Claims*, the PCA ruled that the US "intended to take and have taken" the contracts which were the property of the Norwegian owners.[118] In *Certain German Interests*, the expropriation of a nitrate plant owned by a German company was likewise regarded as an indirect expropriation of a third party which held the contractual rights to operate the plant.[119] In both cases, however, the contracts at issue were contracts between private parties and did not involve the State as a contracting party. The situation may be a different when the State is not only involved as regulating authority but also as a party to the contract itself.

It is widely contended that international law does not provide for an acknowledged definition of the term property[120] as it is common to most if not all[121] systems of municipal law. Rather, the specific content of property under international law has to be determined through a scrutiny of the sources of international law. Several authors[122] and international tribunals asserted that contracts or contractual rights derived from a contract between a foreign investor and a State may be nationalized or expropriated. The differences in extent and argumentation amongst them, however, vary considerably. One school of thought

[118] *Norwegian Shipowners' Claims* (Norway v. US) (1948) 1 RIAA 307, 334.

[119] *Certain German Interests in Polish Upper Silesia* (Germany v. Poland), PCIJ Rep. Series A No. 7, 44.

[120] S. A. Benton, The Protection of Property Rights in Commercial Treaties of the United States, HJIL 25 (1965), 50, 50 et seq., who referred to the famous dispute between the US and Mexico during which Hull formulated his position as to the payment of "prompt, adequate and effective" compensation; K. H. Böckstiegel, Die allgemeinen Grundsätze des Völkerrechts über Eigentumsentziehung (1963), 22; G. White, Nationalisation of Foreign Property (1961), 48.

[121] According to Jeremy Bentham: "Property and law are born together. Before the laws there was no property: take away the laws, all property ceases", as cited in G. Schwarzenberger, The Protection of British Property Abroad, Current Leg. Prob. 5 (1952), 295, 295.

[122] See, e.g., M. Banz, Völkerrechtlicher Eigentumsschutz durch Investitionsschutzabkommen (1987), 136–137; Böckstiegel, *supra* fn. 120, 24; H. Kelsen, Théorie Générale du Droit International Public, Problèmes Choisis, RdC 42 (1932–IV), 117, 259 et seq.; I. Seidl-Hohenveldern, Völkerrecht (2000), 310; W. Veith & K. H. Böckstiegel, Der Schutz von ausländischem Vermögen im Völkerrecht (1962), 112 et seq.

espoused an unconditional coverage of state contracts by international law. As early as 1927, the United States—Mexican Claims Commission had ruled in *George W. Cook v. Mexico* that an outright refusal to pay a postal money order could be regarded as a measure tantamount to expropriation of the value of the order.[123] Relying thereon the American—Turkish Claims Settlement Commission in *Singer Sewing Machine Co. v. The Republic of Turkey* held that the failure of a government to pay money due under a contract for commodities may be seen as a confiscation of the purchase price, or alternatively, of the commodities or the property rights in the contract.[124] In several instances,[125] Nielsen upheld that if a government agreed to pay money for commodities and failed to make payment, the purchase price had been confiscated.[126] In any event, the scholars and tribunals that sustained this very broad understanding of "property" remained a minority.

A more restrictive approach was advocated by a far greater number of authors and adjudicative bodies. Based on the above exposed tenet according to which a State may only violate an international treaty when acting in its governmental capacity, a classification of the State's actions was introduced. The crucial element of this distinction was whether the State acted pursuant to its governmental powers or not. Consequently, when a State, acting in its sovereign capacity, breached or repudiated the contract, the breach of contract amounted to an expropriation under international law. By contrast, mere commercial conduct of a State by which a breach of contract is effectuated does not per se amount to an expropriation.[127] In international adjudication, the tribunal in *Shufeldt Claim*[128] was one of the first to apply this principle. In *Jalapa Railroad*, the United States—Mexican Claims Commission stated:

---

[123] *George W. Cook v. Mexico*, Opinion, 3 June 1927, AJIL 22 (1928), 189, 191 et seq.

[124] The tribunal referred to F. K. Nielsen (ed.), The American-Turkish Claims Settlement Commission under the Agreement of December 24, 1923, and Supplemental Agreements between the United States and Turkey (1937), 491, where the decision of *Singer Sewing Machine Co. v. The Republic of Turkey* is summarized. Cf. *Waste Management v. Mexico*, *supra* fn. 75, para. 169.

[125] See *International Fisheries Company* (US v. Mexico) (1931) 4 RIAA 691, 715.

[126] It is noteworthy that Kurt Nielsen also acted as commissioner in the *Singer Sewing* case.

[127] See, e.g., S. Schwebel, International Arbitration: Three Salient Problems (1987), 108.

[128] *Shufeldt Claim* (US v. Guatemala) (1930) 2 RIAA 1079, 1097.

> In the circumstances, the issue for determination is whether the breach of contract alleged to have resulted from the nullification of clause twelfth of the contract was an ordinary one involving no international responsibility or whether the said breach was effected arbitrarily by means of a governmental power illegal under international law.[129]

In the case at issue, the commission held that the legislative decree by which the Government of the State of Veracruz had nullified the contractual payment clause was a breach of international law.[130] Several decisions of the Iran—US Claims Tribunal[131] further entrenched this practice in international law.[132] Moreover, it became constant practice that not only breach of contract through exertion of governmental authority triggered international law responsibility but also that a discriminatory breach of contract generated a violation of international law.[133]

On the other hand, some authors who researched the subject profoundly came to a contrary conclusion. Dolzer carried out an exhaustive analysis of the sources of international law in order to determine the general constituents of the term "property" under international law.[134] The fact that an overwhelming number of authors endorses that "property" under international law encompasses contractual claims does not seem conclusive to him.[135] Rather, as he pointed out, a closer look at state practice raises doubts as to the correctness of the general assertions. Particularly, he referred to the Hickenlooper Amendment and the 1961 Harvard Draft Convention on the

---

[129] *Jalapa Railroad & Power Co.* (U.S. v. Mexico), reprinted in M. Whiteman (ed.), Digest of International Law, vol. 8 (1976), 908–909.

[130] Id.

[131] See, e.g., *Phillips Petroleum Co. v. Iran*, (1989) 21 Iran-USCTR 79, 106; *Starrett Housing Corp. v. Iran*, (1987) 16 Iran-USCTR 112, 230; *Mobil Oil v. Iran*, (1987) 16 Iran-USCTR 3, 10. See also A. Mouri, The International Law of Expropriation as Reflected in the Work of the Iran-U.S. Claims Tribunal (1994), 39 et seq.

[132] See also Restatement (Third) of the Foreign Relations Law of the United States Section 712 (1987) (hereafter, the "Restatement") where state responsibility under international law is laid down for injuries resulting from: "(2) a repudiation or breach by the state of a contract with a national of another state (a) where the repudiation or breach is (i) discriminatory; or (ii) motivated by non-commercial considerations, and compensatory damages are not paid".

[133] A. F. M. Maniruzzaman, Expropriation of Alien Property and the Principle of Non-Discrimination in International Law of Foreign Investment: An Overview, J. Transnat'l L. & Pol'y 8 (1998), 57, 67–68.

[134] See R. Dolzer, Eigentum, Enteignung und Entschädigung im geltenden Völkerrecht (1985), 153.

[135] Id., 171 et seq.

International Responsibility of States for Injuries to Aliens (hereafter, Harvard Convention).[136] The property notion within the Hickenlooper Amendment, which regulates the domestic consequences of an expropriation in a foreign country, was construed by courts as not including contracts.[137] The Harvard Convention by Sohn and Baxter treats contracts to which the central government and an alien are parties as separate from property.[138] According to both authors, the point of view whereby concessions and contracts, similar to property, may be taken against the payment of compensation would foster the view that a debtor has the option of performing his contract or paying the compensation. Compliance with contracts, however, was not a matter of expediency but a legal obligation which must not be equated with the widely acknowledged right of a State to expropriate property within its jurisdiction.[139] A violation of the contract through an "arbitrary" action of the State is deemed to be internationally wrongful regardless of whether contracts are seen as part of property or not. "Arbitrariness" within this sense is further circumscribed by four sub-paragraphs which leave considerable leeway for interpretation.[140] The succeeding explanatory note, however, gives an interpretation which seemingly comes close to the governmental—commercial distinction applied by majority in the literature.[141]

---

[136] Id.

[137] In fact, American case law is inconsistent on this question. Cf. the description of several contrary judgments by P. Coharis, U.S. Courts and the International Law of Expropriation: Toward a New Model for Breach of Contract, S. Cal. L. Rev. 80 (2006), 1, 7 et seq.

[138] See articles 10 and 12 of the draft, reproduced in: L. Sohn & R. Baxter, Responsibility of States for Injuries to the Economic Interests of Aliens: II. Draft Convention on the International Responsibility of States for Injuries to Aliens, AJIL 55 (1961), 548, 553, 566–567.

[139] Id., 567–568.

[140] Accordingly, for the determination of "arbitrariness", it is relevant to consider whether the action constitutes

> (a) a clear and discriminatory departure from the proper law of the contract or concession as that law existed at the time of the alleged violation; (b) a clear and discriminatory departure from the law of the State which is a party to the contract or concession as that law existed at the time of the making of the contract or concession, if that law is the proper law of the contract or concession; (c) an unreasonable departure from the principles recognized by the principal legal systems of the world as applicable to governmental contracts or concessions of the same nature or category; or (d) a violation by the State of a treaty.

[141] Sohn & Baxter, *supra* fn. 138, 569–572.

An analysis of several international judicial decisions on the character of property under international law has been undertaken by Friedman.[142] In his view, nothing in positive law restricts the meaning of the term "property", and hence, it has to be taken in its broadest possible sense, including tangible property and incorporeal rights. Nevertheless, an exception is made in relation to public service concessions and contracts concluded between a State and a foreign national. Both categories (which, under the present understanding pertain to the notion "state contract") are subject to special regimes. Accordingly, breaches of concession agreements are not considered expropriations but "mere contractual violations."[143] The same is valid for others contracts concluded between a host State and a foreign individual. Accordingly, international law would not contain appropriate rules to deal with them, and the distinction between the concepts of denial of justice and expropriation requires the exclusion of contractual contents from the coverage of the latter.[144] Therefore, recourse had to be taken to the domestic remedies available. More recently, authors from developing countries increasingly argue against the coverage of these contracts by the customary international law standard of expropriation.[145]

In the final analysis, the question at issue concerns the same aspect as the debate surrounding international law's applicability to state contracts.[146] Whether a breach of contract by a host State may be susceptible of being classified as an expropriation under international law and whether international law is applicable to a contract are ultimately two sides of the same coin. What matters in the end is the question, in the words of Jennings, of "how far does a sovereign State which enters into a contract with an alien become subject thereby to obligations of public international law."[147] As has been exposed above in Chapter 1, this question remains unsettled under international law in the absence of

---

[142] S. Friedman, Expropriation in International Law (1953), 145 et seq.

[143] Id., 152.

[144] Id., 156.

[145] See, e.g., M. Sornarajah, The Pursuit of Nationalized Property (1986), 81 et seq.; M. Sornarajah, The Settlement of Foreign Investment Disputes (2000), 267:

> Rights in property are acquired by the *lex situs* and contractual rights are conferred by the proper law. It has to be demonstrated that international law prevents changes being made to the *lex situs* or the proper law of the contract, except in the situation where treaties between states exist creating an obligation not to make the changes (footnote omitted).

[146] See *supra* 25 et seq.

[147] R. Jennings, State Contracts in International Law, BYIL 37 (1961), 156, 156.

a special treaty regime, and it is not advisable for investors to rely exclusively on customary international law for the "internationalisation" of their contractual relationship with a State.

3. *Expropriation of Contracts under the Regime of Investment Treaties*

The conclusion of a bilateral or multilateral investment treaty creates a special regime of protection thereby superseding the rules of customary international law. The treaty establishes obligations under international law for the contracting States directly enforceable by the foreign investor.[148] The question thus becomes: to what extent does the non-expropriation standard under investment treaties cover state contracts.

a. *Coverage of State Contracts*

The coverage of state contracts by a treaty's protective expropriation standard is principally contingent upon the fulfilment of two conditions. First, the treaty's scope must extend to contractual relationships between a foreign investor and the host State. This is a matter of the definition of "investment" concluded by the respective contracting States.[149] Second, the particular treaty must contain an expropriation provision.

As for the first condition, it is worthy to note that investment protection treaties do not rely on the traditional notion of property but on the notion of investment.[150] Dolzer assumes that this was originally due to the avoidance of the narrow construction of "property" traditionally adopted in continental law doctrine.[151] Nowadays, in any event, the usage of a broadly defined notion of investment assures an extraordinary breadth of the treaties' coverage. As explained above, the specific coverage of a contract is ultimately contingent upon the concrete terms used in the respective treaty.[152] Although there is no generalised notion

---

[148] See *supra* 98 et seq.

[149] See, e.g., *Consortium R.F.C.C. v. Kingdom of Morocco*, ICSID Case No. ARB/00/6, Award, 22 December 2003, ICSID Rev.-FILJ 20 (2005), 391, para. 60 (hereinafter, *RFCC v. Morocco*).

[150] Cf. C. U. Kriebaum & C. Schreuer, The Concept of Property in Human Rights Law and International Investment Law, in: S. Breitenmoser (ed.), Human Rights, Democracy and the Rule of Law—Liber Amicorum Luzius Wildhaber (2007), 734, 735.

[151] Dolzer, *supra* fn. 134, 156.

[152] See *supra* 115 et seq.

of investment, it can be contended that the typical modern investment protection treaty regularly extends its protective coverage to contracts concluded between the host State and a foreign investor.[153]

Virtually all investment treaties, whether bilateral or multilateral, contain a provision providing for protection against expropriation. In general, referral is made to all three types of conceivable expropriation. Article 1110(1) of NAFTA, for instance, states the following:

> Article 1110: Expropriation and Compensation
> 1. No Party may directly or indirectly nationalize or expropriate an investment of an investor of another Party in its territory or take a measure tantamount to nationalization or expropriation of such an investment ("expropriation"), except:
> (a) for a public purpose;
> (b) on a non-discriminatory basis;
> (c) in accordance with due process of law and Article 1105(1); and
> (d) on payment of compensation in accordance with paragraphs 2 through 6.

Similar or even more comprehensive formulations are used in the overwhelming majority of modern investment treaties.[154] As a consequence, one has to conclude that state contracts, insofar as they fall within the investment notion of the pertinent treaty, are covered by investment treaties and thereby protected against expropriation. Conceptually, the treaties accord the same legal treatment to direct expropriations, indirect expropriations, and measures tantamount to expropriation.[155] This means that not only the repudiation of a contract with a foreign investor or its gross violation may lead to an international wrong as the single constituent of a direct expropriation or an indirect expropriation[156] but also that a breach of contract may be one of several constituents of an indirect expropriation or a measure tantamount to expropriation.[157]

---

[153] Id.

[154] See, e.g., article 13(1) ECT; article 7 of the Australia—Argentina BIT (1995); article 4 of the Austria—China BIT (1986); article 4(2) of the Germany—Bulgaria BIT (1986); article 5 of the UK—Venezuela BIT (1995); article 3 of the US—Senegal BIT (1990).

[155] R. Dolzer & M. Stevens, Bilateral Investment Treaties (1995), 99.

[156] For the distinction between a direct and an indirect expropriation of contractual rights, see the claimant's allegations in *Sempra Energy International v. Argentine Republic*, ICSID Case No. ARB/02/16, Award, 28 September 2007, paras. 273–274 (hereinafter, *Sempra v. Argentina*).

[157] Cf. Reisman & Sloane, *supra* fn. 111, 118–119.

b. *Distinction between Breach of Contract and Expropriation*
The coverage of state contracts in principle, however, does not clarify when a breach of contract is a mere breach of contract and when it amounts to an expropriation under the treaty. The notion of expropriation under the investment treaty system was not created *ex nihilo* but is based upon the expropriation standard of customary international law. Therefore, notwithstanding the uncertainty surrounding customary international law in this regard, a certain gravity of the contractual non-performance may also be required under this system in order to distinguish a mere breach of contract and an expropriation. In this context, commentators on expropriation under investment treaties refer unanimously to the above exposed distinction between the exertion of governmental powers and the private performance of contracts.[158] Several arbitral tribunals ruled upon this question.

In *Waste Management*,[159] the tribunal undertook an exhaustive examination of the problem whether a persistent failure to observe contractual duties could be tantamount to an expropriation.[160] The dispute arose out of a concession agreement for the provision of waste disposal services between the Mexican City of Acapulco and Acaverde, a Mexican company wholly owned by the US enterprise Waste Management, Inc. The claimant asserted that the permanent failure by Acapulco City to pay the amounts due under the contract amounted to a violation of article 1110 NAFTA. At the outset, the tribunal introduced the distinction between an expropriation of the enterprise as a whole and an expropriation of contractual rights. It dismissed the contention that contractual non-performance such as the failure by the Mexican State to provide land or the non-payment of monthly due fees could amount to an expropriation of the enterprise as a whole.[161] The tribunal then addressed the expropriation of contractual rights. Thereby, it took into consideration that the protection provided by

[158] A. Reinisch, Expropriation, TDM 2 (2005), No. 05, 12: "The guiding principle in locating an expropriation appears to be whether a state has acted in its sovereign capacity, exercising its governmental or public power or authority."; C. Schreuer, The Concept of Expropriation under the ECT and Other Investment Protection Treaties, in: C. Ribeiro (ed.), Investment Arbitration and the Energy Charter Treaty (2006), 108, 140: "The most important criterion for distinguishing between the simple breach of contract and the expropriation of contract rights is whether the State acts in its commercial role as a party to the contract or in its sovereign capacity" (footnote omitted).

[159] *Waste Management v. Mexico*, *supra* fn. 75.

[160] Id., paras. 141–178.

[161] Id., paras. 159, 160.

article 1110 NAFTA extended to intangible property interests and that the Claims Settlement commissions involving the US and Mexico had opted for a broad interpretation of the term "expropriation" on two occasions.[162] The *Waste Management* tribunal pointed out that such a broad construction would eliminate the distinction between breach of contract and breach of treaty which, in its view, is essential.[163] Therefore, the tribunal admitted three different categories of situations where a State's contractual non-performance might amount to expropriation: (1) the termination of an enterprise or its functioning by decree or executive act; (2) contractual rights may be affected by virtue of an acknowledged taking; (3) cases exist where the only right affected is incorporeal. Accordingly, the claim of mere contractual non-performance pertains to the last group of cases and, unless accompanied by other elements, cannot be equated with a taking of property. The tribunal held that these elements were the exertion of governmental authority or denial of justice.[164] In the framework of NAFTA, the same conclusion has been reached in *Azinian v. Mexico*.[165]

The tribunal in *SGS v. Philippines* had to deal with the question whether the non-payment of contractual debts by the Philippines could be regarded as conduct amounting to expropriation under the Swiss—Philippines BIT.

> In the Tribunal's view, on the material presented by the Claimant no case of expropriation has been raised. Whatever debt the Philippines may owe to SGS still exists; whatever right to interest for late payment SGS had it still has. There has been no law or decree enacted by the Philippines attempting to expropriate or annul the debt, nor any action tantamount to an expropriation. The Tribunal is assured that the limitation period for proceedings to recover the debt before the Philippine courts under Article

---

[162] Id., paras. 167–169.

[163] Id., para. 171.

[164] Id., paras. 172–174.

[165] *Robert Azinian v. The United Mexican States*, ICSID Case No. ARB(AF)/97/2, Award, 1 November 1999, 5 ICSID Rep. 269, para. 87:

> The problem is that the Claimant's fundamental complaint is that they are the victims of a breach of the Concession Contract. NAFTA does not, however, allow investors to seek international arbitration for mere contractual breaches. Indeed, NAFTA cannot possibly be read to create such a regime, which would have elevated a multitude of ordinary transactions with public authorities into potential international disputes. The Claimants simply could not prevail merely by persuading the Arbitral Tribunal that the Ayuntamiento of Naucalpan breached the Concession Contract.

> 12 has not expired. A mere refusal to pay a debt is not an expropriation of property, at least where remedies exist in respect of such a refusal. A fortiori a refusal to pay is not an expropriation where there is an unresolved dispute as to the amount payable.

In *RFCC v. Morocco*,[166] an Italian consortium had entered into a contract with the Moroccan company Société Nationale des Autoroutes du Maroc (ADM) for the construction of a highway. By reason of several construction delays and a delayed handover of the site, ADM imposed a contractual penalty for late performance and retained a performance bond. The tribunal had to decide whether these actions by ADM amounted to an expropriation. The tribunal stated: "Pour qu'il y ait droit à compensation if faut que la personne de l'exproprié prouve qu'il a été l'objet de mesures prises par l'Etat agissant non comme contractant mais comme autorité publique."[167]

The tribunal examined whether the conduct of ADM could be regarded as measures within this sense. It held that the dispute concerned exclusively the interpretation of certain contractual stipulations and the question of who did not perform adequately its contractual obligations. The imposition of a contractual penalty and the retention of a performance bond are the exercise of contractual rights and do not require the exertion of governmental prerogatives.[168] Hence, neither of the two actions could be qualified as a violation of the expropriation standard under the relevant investment treaty.[169]

The same conclusion was reached by the tribunal in *Impregilo v. Pakistan*.[170] It distinguished between the State's interference with a contract and its performance of a contract. When the State acts as contracting party, it "performs" the contract and thereby cannot be deemed to violate the expropriation standard unless it exercises specific functions of sovereign authority. The classification of "interference" and "performance" can thus be equated with the distinction between governmental and non-governmental acts.

A further case in which an arbitral tribunal had to deal thoroughly with the question of whether a contractual termination could amount

---

[166] *RFCC v. Morocco*, *supra* fn. 149.

[167] Id., para. 65.

[168] Id., paras. 85–87.

[169] The decision on annulment to which the decision has been subjected was issued on 18 January 2006 but is not publicly available.

[170] *Impregilo v. Pakistan*, *supra* fn. 26, paras. 272–281.

to expropriation was *Bayindir v. Pakistan*.[171] Whilst Pakistan contended that its conduct constituted a mere contractual termination, Bayindir asserted that its contractual rights had been expropriated. The tribunal made clear that it was willing to adhere to customary constructions of the expropriation standard whereby expropriation might extend to contractual rights and did not require a technically regulatory act but might be generated by a State's simple interference in the investor's rights. Likewise, it stressed the importance of the exercise of sovereign power for the distinction between treaty violations and contract breaches. The measures at issue, however, namely the expulsion from the construction site enforced by the Pakistan Army and an encashment of bank guarantees were much more conclusive actions than in the former cases. Consequently, the tribunal held that the ruling out of sufficient State involvement was not tenable at the jurisdictional stage and that the question of expropriation, therefore, was one for the merits.[172]

In sum, arbitral tribunals which ruled upon expropriation provisions of investment treaties acknowledged unanimously that a contract may be expropriated. In turn, the determination whether an expropriation effectively has occurred is done by having recourse to the general yardstick set up through the distinction between *ius imperii* and *ius gestionis* under international law. It is only in the case of the former that a violation of the treaty standard of expropriation may be envisaged.[173]

c. *Findings of an Expropriation of State Contract*

Still, the distinction between commercial and governmental interference with a state contract is hardly the only criterion for the determination of an expropriation but has to be coupled with other factors so that the conduct of a host State at a certain point may be deemed to be expropriatory. Generally, a direct expropriation requires a "transferral of property rights to a beneficiary" and an indirect expropriation requires a "substantial loss of control or value".[174] At what point the

[171] *Bayindir v. Pakistan*, *supra* fn. 28, paras. 253–263.

[172] For the decision on the merits, see Bayindir Insaat Turizm Ticart Ve Sanayi A.S. v. Islamic Republic of Pakistan, ICSID Case No. ARB/03/29, Award, 27 August 2009, paras. 447 et seq. (hereinafter: *Bayindir Award*).

[173] *Siemens v. Argentina*, *supra* fn. 26; *Biwater Gauff (Tanzania) Ltd. v. United Republic of Tanzania*, ICSID Case No. ARB/05/22, Award, 24 July 2008, paras. 491–493 (hereinafter, *Biwater Gauff v. Tanzania*).

[174] See, e.g., UNCTAD, International Investment Agreements Issues Paper Series, Taking of Property (2000), 47.

respective conditions are fulfilled by breaches of state contracts can hardly be determined on an abstract basis but will depend on the circumstances of the particular case.

As hypothetical examples, Reisman and Sloane mention the privatization of a state-owned enterprise where the host State fails to establish the promised regulatory apparatus or where the regime enacted proves inadequate or a license required for the engagement in certain activities is not granted albeit it was previously authorized by contract.[175] In the same vein, cases in which the host State subsequently revoked a contractually granted permit, refused to grant contractually agreed permits, or disregarded the contractually acquired right to purchase shares of a state-owned company have been regarded as an expropriation of contractual rights.[176] Although no investment treaty was involved, mention can be made of the case *Benvenuti et Bonfant v. People's Republic of the Congo* as another example.[177] An Italian company and the Government of Congo entered into an agreement to establish a local company to manufacture plastic bottles for mineral water. Subsequently, the Congolese government, inter alia, failed to implement the agreed upon preferential tax regime, pay all its share capital obligations, adopt protectionist measures limiting the import of mineral water, and neglected to call regular meetings of the board. Whereas none of the facts could substantiate an expropriation in itself, the tribunal held that the cumulative effect of the government's acts and omissions de facto expropriated the Italian company's shares in the local company.[178] Hence, breaches of contractual obligations are thus, undoubtedly, strong indicators of an indirect expropriation.

---

[175] Reisman & Sloane, *supra* fn. 111, 131.

[176] For an unpublished award of the Stockholm Chamber of Commerce, see K. Hobér, Investment Arbitration in Eastern Europe: Recent Cases on Expropriation, Am. Rev. Int'l Arb. 14 (2003), 377, 400–406. In this case, the parties, an American oil company and a state-owned company of one of the former republics of the Soviet Union, had concluded a contract for the development of an oil field. Subsequent to a change in government, the land use permit originally granted to the company was revoked by resolution. The tribunal held the repercussions of this revocation to be tantamount to expropriation. See also *Técnicas Medioambientales Tecmed, S.A. v. United Mexican States*, ICSID Case No. ARB(AF)/00/2, Award, 29 May 2003, (2004) 43 ILM 133 (hereinafter, *Tecmed v. Mexico*); *Metalclad Corp. v. United Mexican States*, ICSID Case No. ARB(AF)/97/1, Award, 30 August 2000, ICSID Rev.-FILJ 16 (2001), 168 (hereinafter, *Metalclad v. Mexico*).

[177] *Benvenuti et Bonfant v. People's Republic of the Congo*, ICSID Case No. ARB/77/2, Award, 8 August 1980, 1 ICSID Rep. 330.

[178] Id., 350 et seq.

The abrogation of the contractually agreed remuneration system of an operation has been assessed contrarily. In the same dispute between Argentina and Ponderosa Assets, an OPIC[179] tribunal affirmed an expropriation[180] whereas an ICSID tribunal rejected such a finding.[181] The dispute between Ponderosa and Argentina, like the majority of investment treaty claims filed against Argentina, arose out of the Emergency Laws enacted between 2000 and 2002.

In order to determine whether Ponderosa's claim under the OPIC Insurance Contract was valid, OPIC had to examine whether an expropriation of Ponderosa's assets or rights had taken place.[182] OPIC stated that the license granted by Argentina had contractual character as "an exclusive license is an agreement that gives the licensee the exclusive right to perform the licensed act and that prohibits the licensor from granting the right to other parties."[183] Under the license, a certain tariff scheme was guaranteed which was central to the deal since 80% of the revenues flowed from tariffs. The Emergency Law nullified these provisions and consequently, in the view of OPIC, constituted a repudiation or abrogation of the Argentine entity's obligations under the license. In addition, the contractual repudiation was motivated by non-commercial reasons as Argentina acted for public policy reasons, specifically to curb the risk of inflation and devaluation and to control the flight of foreign exchange from Argentina. Hence, the contract's repudiation was regarded as an expropriation under international law irrespective of whether the conduct was discriminatory.[184] According to the ICSID tribunal sitting over the same case, a measure tantamount to expropriation may be seen in actions such as the investor's deprivation of the control of the investment, the management of the day-to-day operations of the company, arrest and detention of company officials

---

[179] The Overseas Private Investment Corporation is a governmental agency which provides political risk insurance in order to encourage US investment abroad. For further information, see www.opic.gov. In Germany, such insurance is provided by PwC Deutsche Revision AG and Euler Hermes Kreditversicherungs AG which are mandated by the Federal Republic of Germany to do so.

[180] Cf. OECD, Investor-to-State Dispute Settlement in Infrastructure Projects, Working Papers on International Investment, Number 2006/2 (2006), 16.

[181] *Enron Cooperation and Ponderosa Assets, L.P. v. Argentine Republic*, ICSID Case No. ARB/01/, Award, 22 May 2007, para. 246 (hereinafter, *Enron v. Argentina*).

[182] The OPIC Contract covered the equity investment against the risks of inconvertibility, expropriation, and political violence.

[183] OPIC, Memorandum of Determinations, Expropriation Claim of Ponderosa Assets, L.P.—Argentina, Contract of Insurance No. D733, 7.

[184] Id., 8–9.

or employees, supervision of the work of officials, interfering in the administration, impeding the distribution of dividends, interfering in the appointment of officials and managers, or depriving the company of its property or control totally or in part. Since nothing of this sort had happened in the case at issue, the tribunal denied the existence of an indirect expropriation.[185] In the quite similar case of *Sempra v. Argentina*, the claimant's case was that Argentina had directly and indirectly expropriated its contractual rights under a gas distribution license by repudiating those rights through the Emergency Law. The tribunal rejected both allegations holding that since the claimant was still the rightful owner of the companies, no direct expropriation had occurred, and since no substantial deprivation of rights had taken place, there was also no indirect expropriation.[186]

An expropriation by a termination of contract was confirmed in *Siemens v. Argentina*.[187] In this case, the dispute arose out of a contract between Siemens IT Services S.A., an Argentine company wholly owned by Siemens, and Argentina concerning the provision of an integral service for the implementation of an immigration control, personal identification, and electoral information system. The halt of the system's operation only one day after its inception was explained by Argentina through the absence of a required authorization and failures of performance. Subsequent to renegotiation attempts, the contract was terminated by a decree based upon the Economic-Financial Emergency Law 2000 which empowered the President to rescind public sector contracts.[188] Siemens claimed that defaults on contractual performance by Argentina such as the failure to meet budget allocations, provision of human resources, obligations to adopt statutory and executive measures necessary to carry out the replacement of the existing identification system, and to pay compensation after the termination of the contract amounted to expropriation.[189] Argentina opposed this claim mainly putting forward the arguments that the claims of Siemens were merely contractual and that it had not acted under its *ius imperii* powers.[190]

---

185 *Enron v. Argentina*, *supra* fn. 181, para. 246.
186 *Sempra v. Argentina*, *supra* fn. 156, paras. 279–285.
187 *Siemens v. Argentina*, *supra* fn. 26, para. 253.
188 Id., paras. 81–97.
189 Id., para. 218.
190 Id., paras. 221–222.

In order to distinguish treaty and contract claims, the tribunal relied on the above exposed differentiation between governmental and commercial conduct. It then went on to examine the measures which it deemed susceptible of constituting an exertion of governmental authority. Contrary to the Argentine submission, the tribunal held that various actions of Argentina met this requirement. Foremost of these is the termination of the contract through the issuance of a decree which was not based on contractual non-performance but on fiscal emergency. In addition, although the decree required the payment of compensation, such was not paid. The interference in the contractual relationship by requiring changes in the economic equation was justified by referral to the rights of Argentina as a State under administrative law to request such changes. Further, Argentina's effort to excuse itself from contractual obligations such as by citing the duty to enter into agreements with the provinces, relying upon its political structure, indicates the governmental involvement of the Argentine State. Finally, the permanent suspension of the project maintained by the subsequent introduction of an authorization requirement was seen as a governmental act.[191]

d. *Conclusion*

In principle, a contract may be the object of an expropriation. However, this does not mean that there is a violation of the expropriation standard for every breach of contract. By contrast, the nature of a State's conduct serves as the criterion for the decisive differentiation: if a State acted in its commercial role, no violation of the expropriation standard can be envisaged. In turn, when a State breached a contract by exercising governmental authority, a violation of the investment treaty is possible[192] contingent upon the fulfilment of further conditions such as the transfer of property rights to a beneficiary for direct expropriations or a substantial deprivation for indirect expropriations.[193] Yet, the

---

[191] Id., paras. 254–260.

[192] See Reinisch, *supra* fn. 158, 12; Schreuer, *supra* fn. 158, 140; T. Wälde & K. Hobér, The First Energy Charter Treaty Arbitral Award, J. Int'l Arb. 22 (2005), 83, 98; T. Wälde, *supra* fn. 79, 196:

> On the other hand, where the contract itself, and in particular the alleged breach and pertinent dispute, involves the State not, in traditional language, as the "fisc" but rather as the sovereign State, with its regulatory, administrative and political power in operation, this is considered as pertinent for the application of international disciplines.

[193] See, for instance, the very recent decisions in *Sempra v. Argentina*, *supra* fn. 156, paras. 279–285 and *Biwater Gauff v. Tanzania*, *supra* fn. 173, paras. 451 et seq.

diversity of the relevant circumstances in expropriation cases makes it difficult to determine general standards other than the principal distinction between commercial and governmental conduct. Whereas the non-performance by a host State of requirements which are essential for the implementation of the contract such as the grant of permits or licenses as well as conduct that causes the termination of the contract appears to be deemed expropriatory, the amendment of the contractually agreed remuneration scheme is not. In sum, treaty-based arbitral tribunals base their assessment of the treaties' non-expropriation standard on traditional concepts of customary international law and a difference as to the extent of the protective coverage is thus barely conceivable.

II. *The Fair and Equitable Treatment Standard*

The fair and equitable treatment standard increasingly turns out to be the most important protective standard under international investment treaties. The vague obligation of States to assure "fair and equitable treatment" to foreign investments extends the treaties' coverage considerably. Despite its frequent application the interpretative limits of the standard are barely conceivable.[194] In the present context, the standard has to be examined with respect to its coverage of commitments set out through a state contract.

1. *General Considerations*

a. *Origins of the Standard*

In 1948, the International Trade Organisation elaborated its Havana Charter and therein referred to "just and equitable treatment" which

---

[194] On account of this, the breadth of the claimants' reliance upon the standard is considerable. See, e.g., id., para. 290:

> The Claimant has argued that … the Respondent has in various ways breached the standard of fair and equitable treatment established under Article II(2)(a) of the Treaty, including by failing to act in good faith, frustrating the Claimant's legitimate expectations, unreasonably interfering with the investor's property rights, violating and repudiating assurances and representations offered to attract foreign investment, altering the legal and business environment upon which the Claimant had relied in making the investment, failing to provide a stable and predictable legal environment, and abusing its rights.

should be accorded to foreign investments.[195] From then on the obligation to provide foreign investment with "equitable" or "fair and equitable" treatment was included in several legal instruments.[196] After the standard's inclusion in several of the "modern"[197] bilateral US FCN treaties,[198] the concept was introduced in the two most important drafts on investment protection, the Abs-Shawcross Draft Convention[199] and the 1967 OECD Draft Convention on the Protection of Foreign Property.[200] Both drafts considerably influenced the negotiations and conclusion of BITs.[201] Hence, from its inception on, the fair and equitable treatment standard became an inherent part of the attempt to create a bilateral investment protection system.

Today, the standard is contained in nearly every BIT[202] and appears to be the core standard of international investment protection. The concept not only found its way in the two most important multilateral agreements—the NAFTA[203] and the ECT[204]—but is also mentioned in multilateral efforts to improve investment protection and promote

---

Further, it is submitted that, contrary to the ordinary understanding of investment treaties which contends that these treaties only set out obligations for States, the standard could enjoin the investor with an obligation to reasonably operate its investment. See P. Muchlinski, "Caveat Investor"?—The Relevance of the Conduct of the Investor under the Fair and Equitable Treatment Standard, Int'l & Comp. L. Q. 55 (2006), 527 et seq.

[195] Article 11(2) of the 1948 Havana Charter for an International Trade Organisation, available at: www.worldtradelaw.net (last visited: 12 April 2010).

[196] For a summary, see OECD, Fair and Equitable Treatment Standard in International Investment Law, Working Papers on International Investment, Number 2004/3 (2004), 3–7.

[197] The modern FCN treaties pertain to a second wave of such kind of treaties. See K. Vandevelde, The Bilateral Treaty Program of the United States, Cornell Int'l L. J. 21 (1988), 201, 206 et seq.

[198] See, e.g., article V of the US—Ireland Treaty on Friendship, Commerce, and Navigation, 21 January 1950, which states the following: "Each Party shall at all times accord equitable treatment to the capital of nationals and companies of the other Party".

[199] 1959 Draft Convention on Investments Abroad, reprinted in UNCTAD, International Investment Instruments: A Compendium, vol. V (2000), 395.

[200] Reprinted in UNCTAD, International Investment Instruments: A Compendium, vol. II (1996), 113. Article 1(a) of the draft stated the following: "Treatment of Foreign Property: Each Party shall at all times ensure fair and equitable treatment to the property of the nationals of the other Parties."

[201] Cf. A. Sinclair, The Origins of the Umbrella Clause in the International Law of Investment Protection, Arb. Int'l 20 (2004), 411, 421 et seq.

[202] However, exceptions are treaties concluded by certain Asian countries such as Pakistan, Saudi Arabia, and Singapore. Cf. OECD, *supra* fn. 196, 5.

[203] Article 1105 of the NAFTA.

[204] Article 10(1), first sentence of the ECT.

foreign investment such as the MIGA Convention,[205] the World Bank Guidelines on Treatment of FDI,[206] and the MAI.[207]

Unlike what its frequent appearance may suggest, the nature and the content of the standard remain unclear, and the debate thereupon is by no means settled. First and foremost, it is not clear whether the standard may be equated with the international minimum standard or whether it is a non-contingent treaty standard. Further, the content's ramifications are manifold and uncertain.

b. *Fair and Equitable Treatment and the International Minimum Standard*

As explained by Kreindler,[208] the enquiry on the clause's nature is approached from three sides: firstly, the concept whereby the standard pertains to customary international law and equals the international minimum standard of treatment of aliens. Secondly, the standard may be a broader international law standard deriving from several sources of international law such as treaties and general principles.[209] Finally, the standard is regarded as an autonomous concept based on the specific context of investment treaties and without any bond to customary international law.[210] Apparently, these distinct approaches

---

205 Article 12(d)(iv) of the MIGA Convention reads as follows: "In guaranteeing an investment, the Agency shall satisfy itself as to: … (iv) the investment conditions in the host country, including the availability of fair and equitable treatment and legal protection for the investment".

206 Article III(2) of the guidelines state that "[e]ach State will extend to investments established in its territory by nationals of any other State fair and equitable treatment according to the standards recommended in these Guidelines".

207 Article 1.1, chapter 4 of the OECD, The Multilateral Agreement on Investment Draft Consolidated Text (1998), available at: www1.oecd.org (last visited: 12 April 2010).

208 R. Kreindler, Fair and Equitable Treatment—A Comparative International Law Approach, TDM 3 (2006), No. 3, 2. See also OECD, *supra* fn. 196, 8 et seq. Formerly, authors tended to contemplate only two alternatives: the customary law approach whereby the standard equates the international minimum standard and the so-called "plain meaning" approach which corresponds to the autonomous, non-contingent concept. See, e.g., Dolzer & Stevens, *supra* fn. 155, 58–60; S. Vasciannie, The Fair and Equitable Treatment Standard in International Investment Law and Practice, BYIL 70 (1999), 99, 102–104.

209 See, e.g., *Sempra v. Argentina*, *supra* fn. 156, para. 296: "Customary international law, treaties of friendship, commerce and navigation, and more recently bilateral investment treaties, have all contributed to this development".

210 See, e.g., *PSEG Global Inc. v. Republic of Turkey*, ICSID Case No. ARB/02/5, Award, 19 January 2007, para. 239 (hereinafter, *PSEG v. Turkey*): "This role has resulted in the concept of fair and equitable treatment acquiring a standing on its own, separate and distinct from that of other standards, albeit many times closely related to them".

would ultimately lead to different extents of the investor protection provided for by the standard.

Several scholars posit that the concept of fair and equitable treatment is a part of or even similar to the minimum standard,[211] and within the framework of NAFTA, it nowadays constitutes the prevailing doctrine.[212] This standard is supposed to provide for a relatively low level of investor protection. Due to the pronouncement of the NAFTA Free Trade Commission in 2001 that the standard does not provide for a higher level of protection for alien treatment than the customary international minimum standard,[213] the hitherto heterogeneous jurisprudence[214] of NAFTA tribunals became more uniform.[215] Outside of NAFTA, the picture remains heterogeneous. Several authors uphold the non-contingent and additive nature of the standard.[216] Whilst some treaty-based tribunals followed the NAFTA approach, others adhered to non-contingent approaches which seemingly provided for additional protection. The latter tend to take into account increasingly the specific wordings of the respective stipulations. As a consequence, the provisions of the standard in recent investment and free trade agreements are enacted with more specificity. Article 10.4 of the US—Chile FTA, for instance, evinces the parties' restrained understanding of the clause.[217]

---

[211] See, e.g., P. Gann, The US Bilateral Investment Treaty Program, Stan. J. Int'l L. 21 (1985), 373, 389; R. Paterson, Canadian Investment Promotion and Protection Treaties, Can. Y.B. Int'l L. 29 (1991), 373, 379.

[212] Dolzer & Stevens, *supra* fn. 155, 60.

[213] NAFTA Free Trade Commission, Statement on NAFTA Article 1105 and the Availability of Arbitration Document, 31 July 2001, available at: www.naftaclaims.com (last visited: 26 March 2010).

[214] See, e.g., *Metalclad v. Mexico*, *supra* fn. 176, paras. 74–101; *SD Myers, Inc. v. Canada*, UNCITRAL (NAFTA), First Partial Award, 13 November 2000, 8 ICSID Rep. 3, paras. 258–269; *Pope & Talbot Inc. v. The Government of Canada*, UNCITRAL (NAFTA), Award on Merits, 10 April 2001, 7 ICSID Rep. 102 paras. 105–118.

[215] See, e.g., *Pope & Talbot Inc. v. The Government of Canada*, UNCITRAL (NAFTA), Award on Damages, 31 May 2002, 7 ICSID Rep. 148, paras. 8–66; *Mondev International Ltd. v. United States of America*, ICSID Case No. ARB(AF)/99/2, Final Award, 11 October 2002, 6 ICSID Rep. 181, paras. 119–125 (hereinafter, *Mondev v. US*).

[216] See, e.g., B. Choudhury, Evolution or Devolution—Defining Fair and Equitable Treatment in International Investment Law, JWIT 6 (2005), 297 et seq.; S. Schill, "Fair and Equitable Treatment" as an Embodiment of the Rule of Law, in: R. Hofmann & C. Tams (eds.), The International Convention on the Settlement of Investment Disputes—Taking Stock after 40 Years (2007), 31, 70–71.

[217] Article 10.4 of the Chile—US FTA reads as follows:

> 1. Each Party shall accord to covered investments treatment in accordance with customary international law, including fair and equitable treatment and full protection and security. 2. For greater certainty, paragraph 1 prescribes the Customary International Minimum Standard of Treatment of aliens as the

By and large, three conclusions may be drawn concerning the nature of the standard. Firstly, whilst this aspect in NAFTA cases is settled, the discussion in the framework of BITs remains vivid and the nature of the standard insecure. In this context, it is likely that the standard is contingent upon the specific clause's wording. Secondly, the international minimum standard in and of itself does not provide for legal certainty. By contrast, the lack of a clearly defined content is said to be one of the consistent characters of the international minimum standard.[218] In any event, since even NAFTA tribunals concede that the minimum standard has evolved and may not be regarded as frozen,[219] the magnitude of the actual differences the whole dispute is about remains somehow uncertain. Thirdly, this is underpinned by the rulings of arbitral tribunals in which they held that the distinct approaches do not necessarily lead to different results.[220]

c. *Specifications of the Content*

Inasmuch as the nature of the standard is controversial, so is its content, and thus, the protection which it provides for investors likewise is not entirely clear.[221] From the vantage point that equates fair and

Minimum Standard of Treatment to be afforded to covered investments. The concept of "fair and equitable treatment" and "full protection and security" do not require treatment in addition to or beyond that which is required by that standard, and do not create additional substantive rights. The obligation in paragraph 1 to provide: (a) "fair and equitable treatment" includes the obligation not to deny justice in criminal, civil, or administrative adjudicatory proceedings in accordance with the principle of due process embodied in the principal legal systems of the world; and (b) "full protection and security" requires each Party to provide the level of police protection required under customary international law.

[218] Cf. M. Porterfield, An International Common Law of Investor Rights?, U. Pa. J. Int'l Econ. L. 27 (2006), 79, 113.

[219] See, e.g., *Mondev v. US*, *supra* fn. 215, paras. 123, 125; *United Parcel Service v. Canada*, UNCITRAL (NAFTA), Award on Jurisdiction, 22 November 2002, paras. 84 et seq.

[220] See, e.g., *CMS Gas Transmission Co. v. The Argentine Republic*, Case No. ARB/01/8, Award, 12 May 2005, para. 284 (hereinafter, *CMS v. Argentina*): "In fact, the Treaty standard of fair and equitable treatment and its connection with the required stability and predictability of the business environment, founded on the solemn legal and contractual commitments, is not different from the international minimum law standard and its evolution under customary international law"; *Sempra v. Argentina*, *supra* fn. 156, para. 302: "On many occasions, the issue will not even be whether the fair and equitable treatment standard is different or more demanding than the customary standard, but only whether it is more specific, less generic and spelled out in a contemporary fashion so that its application is more appropriate to the case under consideration".

[221] See, e.g., *CMS v. Argentina*, id. para. 273: "The Treaty … does not define the standard of fair and equitable treatment and to this extent Argentina's

equitable treatment and the minimum standard, decisive authority is derived from a case before the US—Mexico Claims Commission. The reference to *Neer v. Mexico* where the commission asserted "that the treatment of an alien, in order to constitute an international delinquency, should amount to an outrage, to bad faith, to wilful neglect of duty, or to an insufficiency of governmental action so far short of international standards that every reasonable man and impartial man would readily recognize its insufficiency"[222] is the classic expression of the international minimum standard. However, the actual value as yardstick of such a general approach which furthermore did not concern the treatment of foreign investment as such but the physical security of the alien[223] is more than questionable even under a pure customary law approach.[224]

Other authors applied a more modern approach to grasp the concept. Muchlinski opined that the standard "offers a general point of departure in formulating an argument that the foreign investor has not been well treated by reason of discriminatory or other unfair measures that have been taken against its interest."[225] Admittedly, this is not very precise but gives an idea on the extent to which scholars are willing to evolve the standard. Schreuer's survey of the arbitral practice was intended to classify the standard's specific content. Schreuer's four categories (transparency and legitimate expectations, freedom from coercion and harassment, procedural propriety and due process, and good faith) demonstrate the breadth of conceivable state actions that may fall under the standard.[226] Further attempts by different authors did not achieve much more specified results either.[227] It is not even clear

concern about it being somewhat vague is not entirely without merit"; *PSEG v. Turkey*, *supra* fn. 210, para. 239: "Because the role of fair and equitable treatment changes from case to case, it is sometimes not as precise as would be desirable"; *Sempra v. Argentina*, *supra* fn. 156, para. 296: "The Tribunal find the Respondent to be right in arguing that fair and equitable treatment is a standard that is none too clear and precise".

[222] *Neer, LFH and Pauline E. Neer (US) v. United Mexican States* (1926) 4 RIAA 60, 61.

[223] In fact, this case concerned the Mexican authorities' lack of diligence to investigate and retaliate a "western-like" killing of an US citizen.

[224] Cf. *Mondev v. US*, *supra* fn. 215, paras. 115–116.

[225] P. Muchlinski, Multinational Enterprises and the Law (1999), 625.

[226] C. Schreuer, Fair and Equitable Treatment in Arbitral Practice, JWIT 6 (2005), 357, 374–385. On the overlap between the fair and equitable treatment standard and other standards, see C. Schreuer, Fair and Equitable Treatment (FET): Interactions with Other Standards, TDM 4 (2007), No. 05, 1 et seq.

[227] See, e.g., Vascianne, *supra* fn. 208, 162–163; M. Klein Bronfman, Fair and Equitable Treatment—An Evolving Standard, Max Planck UNYB 10 (2006), 609,

whether the standard is relative[228] or absolute,[229] i.e., whether it is contingent upon the specific circumstances in the respective host country.

A string of tribunals[230] referred to the decision in *Tecmed* where the tribunal tried to describe the essence of the standard as follows:

> The Arbitral Tribunal considers that this provision of the Agreement, in the light of the good faith principle established by international law, requires the Contracting Parties to provide to international investments treatment that does not affect the basic expectations that were taken into account by the foreign investor to make the investment. The foreign investor expects the host State to act in a consistent manner, free from ambiguity and totally transparently in its relations with the foreign investor, so that it may know beforehand any and all rules and regulations that will govern its investments, as well as the goals of the relevant policies and administrative practices or directives, to be able to plan its investment and comply with such regulations.[231]

Yet, what amounts to "basic expectations" within this sense? How far does this depend upon the precise circumstances in the host country? And to what extent do actions of a host State have to be in a "consistent manner"? Given the enormous breadth of potential factual situations which may fall under this wording, any abstract determination comes out to be worthless. Moreover, it is well established that the standard is not frozen in time but consists of a moving target which has to be adjusted to the ongoing development of investment protection.[232] In

677–680; Schill, *supra* fn. 216, 41 et seq., who enumerates the following seven principles that may be derived from the standard: (1) the requirement of stability, predictability, and consistency of the legal framework; (2) the principle of legality; (3) the protection of investor confidence or legitimate expectations; (4) procedural due process and denial of justice; (5) substantive due process or protection against discrimination and arbitrariness; (6) the requirement of transparency; and (7) the requirement of reasonableness and proportionality.

[228] S. Fietta, Expropriation and the "Fair and Equitable" Standard—The Developing Role of Investors' "Expectations" in International Investment Arbitration, J. Int'l Arb. 23 (2006), 375, 389: "That standard cannot, by the very nature of legitimate expectations, define what those expectations require in any given case".

[229] See, e.g., Görs, *supra* fn. 102, 208 et seq. In fact, it is even questionable to what extent the so-called "absolute" standards depend on the specific situation in the host country. See N. Gallus, The Influence of the Host State's Level of Development on International Investment Treaty Standards of Protection, JWIT 6 (2005), 712 et seq.

[230] See, e.g., *MTD Equity Sdn. Bhd. & MTD Chile S.A. v. Chile*, ICSID Case No. ARB/01/7, Award, 25 May 2004, para. 114 (hereinafter, *MTD v. Chile*); *CMS v. Argentina*, *supra* fn. 220, para. 279; *Sempra v. Argentina*, *supra* fn. 156, para. 298.

[231] *Tecmed v. Mexico*, *supra* fn. 176, para. 154.

[232] See, e.g., Kreindler, *supra* fn. 208, 10.

this regard, the standard's purpose is "to fill the gaps which may be left by the more specific standards, in order to obtain the level of investor protection intended by the treaties".[233] This means, however, that it remains upon the arbitral tribunals to give the standard a more precise meaning by case-to-case application. Thereby, tribunals are enjoined with a high degree of discretion which may only be restrained by more specific treaty formulations[234] and consistent case law.

2. *The Coverage of State Contracts*

The coverage of contractual contents by the fair and equitable treatment standard may chiefly be related to two overlapping concepts: on the one hand, the concept of legitimate expectations[235] which increasingly comes out to be the dominant element of the standard and, on the other hand, the provision of a stable framework for investments.

a. *Legitimate Expectations*

This relatively young standard of international law is based on the expectations which an investor may legitimately have towards the country which hosts his or her investment. The concept is regarded to be a key element[236] or a sub-category[237] of the fair and equitable treatment standard. Insofar as a host State created legitimate expectations for foreign investors through earlier policies or other behaviour, "these may not be abandoned if the result will be so unfair as to amount to an abuse of power."[238]

The legitimate expectations standard originally evolved in domestic constitutional and administrative law as a principle which requires that executive bodies fulfil legitimate expectations created by them whenever possible.[239] Nowadays, it is a principal concept in domestic

---

233 R. Dolzer, Fair and Equitable Treatment: A Key Standard in Investment Treaties, Int'l Law. 39 (2005), 87, 90.

234 See, e.g., article 15.5(2)(a) of the US—Singapore FTA (2003); article 11.5(2)(a) and annex 11-A of the US—Australia FTA (2004).

235 Schreuer, *supra* fn. 226, 379.

236 *Enron v. Argentina*, *supra* fn. 181, para. 262.

237 *Thunderbird v. Mexico*, Separate Opinion, *supra* fn. 81, 25.

238 F. Orrego Vicuña, Regulatory Authority and Legitimate Expectations: Balancing the Rights of the State and the Individual under International Law in a Global Society, Int'l L. FORUM 5 (2003), 188, 194.

239 On the recognition of the principle of legitimate expectations under domestic administrative law, see *Thunderbird v. Mexico*, Separate Opinion, *supra* fn. 81, para. 28.

constitutional and administrative law in a wide range of States.[240] Similarly, the EU has adopted the concept as a general principle of law.[241] The main tension between the principle and regulative state authority is clear: on the one hand, law must offer certainty and predictability; on the other hand, a state must maintain its capacity to adapt its legislation to changing circumstances.[242] Similarly, on the international plane, a foreign investor's decision to make an investment has to rely on an assessment which concerns the stability and predictability of its investment's protection in the host State. Under international law, the State which gave rise to an investor's legitimate and reasonable expectations can be made liable for not honouring those expectations.[243] However, it is a moot question to what extent such expectations are legitimate and thus worthy of protection under an investment treaty. In principle, the threshold for legitimate expectations varies considerably depending on the violations alleged and the circumstances of the case.[244]

Much of the debate surrounding the concept of legitimate expectations concerns the aspect of the level of protection that is granted through the standard in cases of more or less specific commitments and assurances by the host State.[245] These could be, for instance, expectations created through conduct such as "representations" (e.g., investment brochures), unilateral declarations, investment policies, or specific promises.[246] Treaty-based arbitral tribunals have upheld several times that the failure by host state authorities to meet expectations that have been specifically created by state acts may amount to a failure to accord fair and equitable treatment.[247] The benchmark generally applied

---

240 For the Member States of the EC, see J. Schwarze, European Administrative Law (2006), ch. 6.

241 See generally U. Bernitz (ed.), General Principles of European Community Law (2000), ch. 4.1.

242 *Thunderbird v. Mexico*, Separate Opinion, *supra* fn. 81, para. 27.

243 *Saluka Investments B.V. v. The Czech Republic*, UNCITRAL, Partial Award, 17 March 2006, paras. 301–302.

244 *International Thunderbird Gaming Corp. v. The United Mexican States*, Arbitral Award, 26 January 2006, para. 148; Fietta, *supra* fn. 228, 376.

245 See *Thunderbird v. Mexico*, Separate Opinion, *supra* fn. 81, 14–43; Dolzer, *supra* fn. 233, 104.

246 See, e.g., *Sempra v. Argentina*, *supra* fn. 156, para. 299: "Even if the standard were restricted to a question of reasonableness and proportionality not entailing objective liability ... there are nevertheless expectations arising from promises that must be respected when relied upon by the beneficiary".

247 Yet, such a conduct was also held to amount to an expropriation on some occasions. See, e.g., *Tecmed v. Mexico*, *supra* fn. 176, paras. 120 et seq.; *Metalclad v. Mexico*, *supra* fn. 176, paras. 102 et seq.

to such circumstances is simple: the less formal the assurance, the less likely the emergence of legitimate expectations.[248] In the present context, the existence of a very formal but maybe less specific commitment, namely, the contract is crucial. Through the conclusion of a contract, both contractual partners do not only commit to one specific legal aspect of the investment but to a wide range of determined specifications. The questions which thus arise are whether the concept of legitimate expectations may be applied to a situation where the host State's assurance is derived from or embodied in a contract and if so, which kind of contractual breaches amount to a violation of the treaty standard. In other words, what expectations of the investor towards the host State's contractual performance are legitimate under the treaty's legitimate expectation standard?

At first glance, one may be tempted to assert a wholesale protection of contractual contents. When formally given, unilateral assurances and promises may constitute the basis of legitimate expectations so why should this be different in the case of reciprocal or even synallagmatic commitments agreed upon in a formal contract?[249] A formal contract, one could argue, would even have to be conceded more protection than mere unilateral declarations. Yet, the recognition of contractual commitments as being coextensive with the investor's legitimate expectations, the breach of which by all means would entail a treaty violation, subjects the contract entirely under the treaty. It is questionable whether such far-reaching effect is intended by the standard.

Montt asserts that the existence of contractual commitments makes the idea of legitimate expectations superfluous: "Contractual rights and interests should be protected in the framework of the contract, and not pursuant to the international investment law principle of legitimate expectations".[250] Other authors see contracts as a formalisation of the investor's legitimate expectations. They leave open, however, what the

[248] Cf. *Thunderbird v. Mexico*, Separate Opinion, *supra* fn. 81, 27. See also *William Nagel v. Czech Republic*, SCC Case 49/2002, excerpts reproduced in: Stockholm Arbitration Report 1 (2004), 141, 156.

[249] A further difference between contracts and specific assurances is the scope of the undertaking. Whereas a contract concerns a wide range of subjects, an assurance is generally made for one concrete aspect of the relationship between a foreign investor and the host State.

[250] Montt, *supra* fn. 92, 363.

corollaries of such a formalisation are.[251] According to the reasoning with regard to specific assurances, a formalisation would lead to treaty protection. In the view of Schreuer, the coverage of contracts is one of the most important aspects of the legitimate expectations standard. Since contracts are the classical instrument for the creation of legal stability and predictability, the *pacta sunt servanda* principle may be seen as an obvious application of the stability requirement inherent in the fair and equitable treatment standard. He admits, however, that this result does not further the determination of when a breach of contract actually infringes the investor's legitimate expectations.[252] In a contractual relationship the contract itself is the fundamental basis for the creation and determination of the respective obligations and thus, as a reflection, of expectations. It is thus a tautology to say that the investor is entitled to expect the host country to honour its contractual obligations. In other words, not every legitimate expectation under a contract may be similarly legitimate under an investment treaty. Mere reliance on contractual terms simply does not further the pursuit of the protective level of the legitimate expectations standard.

It is thus convenient to have a closer look at the corresponding arbitral practice. Without referring specifically to the legitimate expectations standard, the tribunal in *Noble Ventures v. Romania* held that the fair and equitable treatment standard encompassed the obligation to observe contractual obligations towards the investor.[253] The tribunal, however, dismissed the claimant's allegation that a breach of contract had occurred. In *Eureko v. Poland*, the tribunal ruled that the conduct of the Polish organs had breached the claimant's basic expectations which were enshrined in the investment contract.[254] Yet, the tribunal's reasoning did not clarify whether the fact that the expectations were laid down in a contract was necessary for or at least conducive to the finding of the legitimacy of the expectations and hence of a violation of the fair and equitable treatment standard.[255] Another case concerning

---

[251] T. Wälde & A. Kolo, Environmental Regulation, Investment Protection and Regulatory Taking in International Law, Int'l & Comp. L. Q. 50 (2001), 811, 844 et seq. Accordingly, when a formalised legitimate expectation is breached, "then that breach of commitment weighs in on the side of the factors indicating expropriation" (footnote omitted).

[252] Schreuer, *supra* fn. 226, 18.

[253] *Noble Ventures, Inc. v. Romania*, ICSID Case No. ARB/01/11, Award, 12 October 2005, para. 182.

[254] *Eureko v. Poland*, *supra* fn. 29, para. 232.

[255] Cf. Fietta, *supra* fn. 228, 390.

the relationship between the creation of an investor's legitimate expectation and a contract between the host State and a foreign investor was the case of *MTD v. Chile*.[256] The claimant's project—the construction of a satellite city at a determined location—had been authorized by the Chilean authority competent for foreign investments, and several investment contracts had been signed. Subsequently, the project had to be cancelled because of its inconsistency with a sub-organ's urban development policy and the organ's consequent refusal of the pertinent authorization. The tribunal ruled that Chile had breached its obligation under the BIT to accord fair and equitable treatment by approving an investment for a project that was against the urban policy of the government.[257] Interestingly, the tribunal reached the conclusion that Chile did not breach the underlying investment contracts because they could not be regarded as a substitute for all the required permits and authorizations. Nevertheless, the contracts, conjointly with the approval of the investment, were held to contribute to the creation of the investor's legitimate expectations which, in the end, were infringed.[258] The tribunal stated:

> Even accepting the limited significance of the Foreign Investment Contracts for purposes of other permits and approvals that may [sic] required, they should be at least in themselves an indication that, from the Government's point of view, the Project is not against Government policy.[259]

The next case which raised the question of the violation of the legitimate expectations standard through contractual non-performance was the case of *Bogdanov v. Moldova*.[260] The case arose out of a privatization contract under which the foreign investor's obligation to transfer assets of the privatized company to the State should have been compensated by the exchange of state-owned shares of unspecified companies.[261] The compilation of the List of Eligible Compensation Shares by the Moldovan Government, however, constituted a remarkable restriction of the claimant's right to compensation. The tribunal stated:

---

[256] *MTD v. Chile*, *supra* fn. 230.

[257] Id., para. 166.

[258] Id., paras. 163, 166.

[259] Id., para. 189.

[260] *Iurii Bogdanov v. Republic of Moldova*, SCC, Arbitral Award, 22 September 2005 (hereinafter, *Bogdanov v. Moldova*).

[261] Id., 3.

> The Arbitral Tribunal finds that, even if the Respondent is entitled to restrict the choice of eligible Compensation Shares according to its reasonable discretion, and the Claimant must be deemed to have accepted the risk connected therewith, the Respondent was not entitled to choose the Compensation Share in such a way that the compensation was deprived of its value. By taking this measure, the Respondent has in practice avoided to pay compensation for the Transferred Assets, thus negatively affecting the Claimant's legitimate expectations of obtaining compensation.[262]

This decision is inconsistent with the conventional interpretation of the fair and equitable treatment standard. Seemingly, the tribunal did not distinguish between the government's conduct as a commercial partner and its conduct as a governmental authority. In exceedingly restricting the eligible compensation shares, the Moldovan Government made undue use of a contractual device. In any event, such an undue exertion of contractual rights could have been undertaken by any ordinary commercial partner.[263]

In the same vein, the tribunal in *PSEG v. Turkey* held that in the absence of a contract, the administration's handling of negotiations amounted to a violation of the fair and equitable treatment standard.[264] This ruling, which obligates the State to "competent" and "professional" handling of negotiations, indeed, represents a new dimension of State liability under conventional treaty standards. Since the tribunal found various other violations which included governmental conduct, it is unclear whether the improper handling of negotiations would have

---

[262] Id., 17.

[263] The decision thus discloses the problem which arises when a broad dispute resolution clause is interpreted as covering mere contractual violations. A tribunal which affirmed its jurisdiction because of such an interpretation will be tempted to misjudge the proper level of substantive treaty protection in the absence of an "umbrella clause" because the conventional protection standards do not provide a basis for the treaty's violation through commercial conduct.

[264] *PSEG v. Turkey, supra* fn. 210, para. 246:

> Short of bad faith, there is in the present case first an evident negligence on the part of the administration in the handling of the negotiations with the Claimants. The fact that key points of disagreement went unanswered and were not disclosed in a timely manner, that silence was kept when there was evidence of such persisting and aggravating disagreement, that important communications were never looked at, and that there was a systematic attitude not to address the need to put an end to negotiations that were leading nowhere, are all manifestations of serious administrative negligence and inconsistency. The Claimants were indeed entitled to expect that the negotiations would be handled competently and professionally, as they were on occasion.

sufficed exclusively to trigger liability under the fair and equitable treatment standard.

In *SGS v. Philippines*, the tribunal construed the standard on a jurisdictional basis. The dispute arose out of the non-payment of contractual debts and the tribunal clearly dismissed the existence of an expropriation. Further, it stated:

> Turning to Article IV (fair and equitable treatment), the position is less clear-cut. Whatever the scope of the Article IV may turn out to be—and that is a matter for the merits- an unjustified refusal to pay sums admittedly payable under an award or a contract at least raises arguable issues under Article IV.[265]

The tribunal thus affirmed its jurisdiction in this regard. In any event, the provisional character of the decision may partly explain this result. Presumably, the confirmation of the statement that non-payment of contractual duties amounts to a treaty violation under the fair and equitable treatment standard is rather unlikely.[266] In the view of Schreuer, the decision of the tribunal in the *Mondev* case could be regarded as a further instance of the protection of contract breaches by the fair and equitable treatment standard.[267] The tribunal stated the following:

> Indeed a governmental prerogative to violate investment contracts would appear to be inconsistent with the principles embodied in Article 1105 and with contemporary standards of national and international law concerning governmental liability for contractual performance.[268]

However, a "governmental prerogative to violate investment contracts" may barely be equated with a simple breach of contract. Therefore, the decision cannot be regarded as authority for the coverage of commercial contract breaches by the fair and equitable treatment standard.

As for the first question posed above, i.e., whether the standard of legitimate expectations refers to contractual commitments, the arbitral practice evinces a clear picture. In all the cited cases, the tribunals contend that contracts between a host State and a foreign investor may contribute principally to or may be part of an investor's legitimate expectations within the fair and equitable treatment standard

---

[265] *SGS v. Philippines*, *supra* fn. 56, para. 162.

[266] For the state of the dispute, see SGS Société Générale de Surveillance S.A. v. Republic of the Philippines, ICSID Case No. ARB/02/6, Order of the Tribunal on further Proceedings, 17 December 2007.

[267] Schreuer, *supra* fn. 226, 379–380.

[268] *Mondev v. US*, *supra* fn. 215, para. 134.

of investment treaties. As a consequence, a breach of contract may, either as one element among others or in and of itself, amount to a violation of the legitimate expectations standard and thus, may constitute a violation of an investment treaty. This leads to the second question, i.e., the threshold of the standard's protection, the answer to which remains less clear. While some tribunals tend to adhere to traditional understandings, other tribunals seem to give less dogmatic interpretations of the standard and thus appear, maybe unwittingly, to opt out of the traditional commercial—governmental dogma.

b. *Failure to Provide a Stable Framework for the Investment and Other Violations of the Standard*

The other key requirement of the fair and equitable treatment is the provision of a stable framework for the investment. The host State's failure to provide a stable framework for the undertaken investment has been repeatedly regarded as a violation of the fair and equitable treatment standard.[269] Similar to the legitimate expectations standard, it is not clear what are all the elements that comprise this "stable framework". Eventually, there may be considerable overlaps between both standards. The question which arises as far as contracts are concerned is whether contracts are encompassed by the term "framework" and if so, to what extent. Is the mere conclusion of a contract sufficient to create a *lex specialis* framework which has to be respected by the host State? In other words, is the contract between a host State and an alien part of the framework the stability of which is guaranteed?[270]

---

[269] *OEPC v. Ecuador, supra* fn. 56, paras. 190–191; *CMS v. Argentina, supra* fn. 220, paras. 274–276; *LG&E Capital Corp. v. Argentine Republic*, ICSID Case No. ARB/02/1, Decision on Liability, 3 October 2006, para. 124; *Enron v. Argentina, supra* fn. 181, para. 260.

[270] See Dolzer, *supra* fn. 233, 104, who put this question and the resulting paradox in the following terms:

> On the one hand, it is clear that contractual relations may form the framework on which the foreign investor has relied after it was negotiated and tailor-made to the needs of the specific investment, possibly quite distinct from the general regulatory framework of the host country. This nature of a contract as a kind of *lex specialis* accepted by the host state so as to attract and accommodate the foreign investor may be considered to justify special protection of the affected investor, more so than the expectation of the investor who has decided to operate under the host state's general legislation. From the opposite perspective, it may be argued that contractual arrangements deserve less protection precisely because they deviate from the general legislation which may be seen to reflect the public good more broadly than an individual contract.

It must be clear that the legal framework through which a State may perform its regulatory authority necessarily must be malleable and evolving. The regulatory power of a State can under no circumstance be restrained to an extent that the State is unable to react to changing circumstances and adapt its legal framework to its policy agenda.[271] As already stated above, such restriction cannot be the purpose of investment protection be it through investment treaty or through contract. In short, the host State's legal system must not be frozen completely. As a consequence, a contract in its totality must not be regarded as a legal framework within this sense on account of which every breach would lead to the host State's liability under the investment treaty. Nonetheless, the investment contract between a host State and a foreign investor is a constituent part of the "stable framework" the host State has to provide. In this context, the two legal concepts of "legitimate expectations" and of "stable legal framework" are not clearly severable. Conversely, both are closely related. In many instances, an investor is poised to undertake an investment in the light of a particular legal or regulatory regime. This can be specified by the host State through contract or other kinds of assurances and commitments. The alteration of this regime, however, may only be a violation of the investor's rights when his expectation of its maintenance is legitimate.[272] Hence, inasmuch as the investor may legitimately expect the perpetuation of the legal framework under the treaty, its alteration amounts to a violation of the fair and equitable standard. Accordingly, the fundamental yardstick for the determination of the core elements of the fair and equitable treatment standard—legitimate expectations and stable framework—would have to be similar. In short, the entire coverage of the contract as part of the investment's framework is not tenable.[273]

Treaty-based arbitral tribunals held that the fair and equitable treatment standard is violated by a continuous[274] or a wholesale[275] transformation of the legal environment under which the investment was

[271] Cf. *CMS v. Argentina, supra* fn. 220, para. 277; *Enron v. Argentina, supra* fn. 181, para. 261.

[272] Cf. Fietta, *supra* fn. 228, 389: "In particular, the question of whether or not there has been a violation of the standard will turn on what legitimate expectations the investor had in the light of specific assurances given by the relevant state authorities against the background of the domestic legal framework that was to govern the investment"; *Enron v. Argentina, supra* fn. 181, para. 262.

[273] Cf. Schreuer, *supra* fn. 226, 18.

[274] See, e.g., *PSEG v. Turkey, supra* fn. 210, para. 250.

[275] *CMS v. Argentina, supra* fn. 220, para. 275.

made. Such a change of legislation or policy can, of course, interfere with contractual rights. In *Bayindir v. Pakistan*, for instance, the tribunal ruled on a prima facie basis that the termination of a contract by reason of external, non-contractual provenience may amount to a violation of the fair and equitable treatment standard. In addition, the tribunal asserted that not only changes that concern the specific regulatory framework for an investment could entail such a violation but even the change of general policy towards a specific investment project subject to certain conditions.[276]

In *Siemens v. Argentina*, the tribunal took the view that contractual non-performance by the State cannot be excused by referral to the State's own structure. Argentina was under the obligation to enter into agreements with its provinces in order to implement the identification system provided by Siemens. The fact that Argentina had submitted to such an obligation towards Siemens and subsequently put forward its structure as hindrance, in the tribunal's view, ran counter to the principle of good faith and thus constituted a violation of the fair and equitable treatment standard. Moreover, the vagueness surrounding Argentina's refusal to pay compensation for the contract's termination showed lack of transparency and was likewise deemed to be a violation of the standard.[277]

In *Waste Management v. Mexico*, a more concrete contractual non-performance was examined.[278] In the claimant's view, the repeated non-payment of monthly due fees and further breaches of contract such as the inadequate implementation of the promised enforcement of an ordinance and the insufficient provision of land for waste disposal by the City of Acapulco were in breach of article 1105(1) of the NAFTA. Very interestingly, the tribunal acknowledged the breaches of contract without further contemplation and turned immediately to three aspects which it regarded as "countervailing factors" to the treaty's violation. Firstly, the city, at least, made several attempts concerning the performance of its contractual obligations. Secondly, the content of the agreement was unpopular with significant portions of the residents of the area. Finally, the Mexican financial crisis severely affected the city's capacity to perform its obligations. These factors induced the tribunal to deny the claim of arbitrary or grossly unfair conduct by the city.

---

[276] *Bayindir v. Pakistan*, *supra* fn. 28, paras. 241, 250.
[277] *Siemens v. Argentina*, *supra* fn. 26, para. 308.
[278] *Waste Management v. Mexico*, *supra* fn. 75, paras. 108–115.

Accordingly, investment treaties are no insurance policy against bad business judgments.[279] This is a clear reminder of the repeatedly stated principle that investment treaties establish no protection against commercial risks.[280] The tribunal thereby seems to have taken recourse to the traditional distinction between mere commercial and governmental conduct. The tribunal concluded:

> For the present purposes it is sufficient to say that even the persistent non-payment of debts by a municipality is not to be equated with a violation of Article 1105, provided that it does not amount to an outright and unjustified repudiation of the transaction and provided that some remedy is open to the creditor to address the problem. In the present case the failure to pay can be explained, albeit not excused, by the financial crisis which meant that at key points the City could hardly pay its own payroll. There is no evidence that this was motivated by sectoral or local prejudice.[281]

In *Impregilo v. Pakistan*, the dispute arose out of a construction contract for a hydroelectric power facility. In the decision on jurisdiction, the tribunal held that a violation of the fair and equitable treatment standard by a contractual breach would require the exertion of governmental authority.[282] Hence, the principle of separation between breaches of contract through commercial and governmental interference becomes more apparent in this section than in the framework of the determination of the investor's legitimate expectations.

3. *Conclusion*

The application of the fair and equitable treatment standard in investment treaties, in contrast to the application of the non-expropriation standard, evinces a more independent approach by arbitral tribunals.

---

[279] Id., para. 114.

[280] See, e.g., *Mr. Eudoro Armando Olguín v. Republic of Paraguay*, ICSID Case No. ARB/98/5, Award, 26 July 2001, paras. 72–75; *Emilio Agustín Maffezini v. Kingdom of Spain*, ICSID Case No. ARB/97/7, Award on the Merits, 13 November 2000, para. 64 (hereinafter, *Maffezini v. Spain*):

> In this connection, the Tribunal must emphasize that Bilateral Investment Treaties are not insurance policies against bad business judgments. While it is probably true that there were shortcoming in the policies and practices that SODIGA [a Spanish state agency] and its sister entities pursued in the here relevant period in Spain, they cannot be deemed to relieve investors of the business risk inherent in any investment.

[281] *Waste Management v. Mexico, supra* fn. 75, para. 115.

[282] *Impregilo v. Pakistan, supra* fn. 26, para. 266.

Treaty-based tribunals contributed considerably to the development of this standard, particularly as regards the legitimate expectations of the investor. On account of this, a wide range of contractual non-performances may amount to a treaty violation under this standard. However, the potentially unlimited and yet undefined scope of the standard entails the risk of an overly broad interpretation which covers commercial conduct that traditionally has not been regarded as part of it.[283]

III. *Further Standards*

International investment treaties comprise further protection standards which complement the protection provided for foreign investment. In the context of state contracts, however, they play rather an inferior role compared to the standards of fair and equitable treatment and non-expropriation.

1. *Non-Discrimination*

The host State's obligation not to discriminate the national of the other contracting party finds expression in two different clauses. On the one hand, the MFN clause prevents discrimination with regard to foreign investors from other countries. Investors rely on this provision by claiming the rights which the host State conferred upon nationals of other States in its other investment treaties. The interpretation of such clauses and their repercussion is highly controversial.[284] On the other hand, a national treatment clause usually obliges the host State to accord to the foreign investor the same kind of treatment it accords to its own nationals. Both standards may, of course, have a certain implication upon the protection of contractual contents. An example of the violation of the national treatment standard through breach of contract

[283] See, e.g., Muchlinski, *supra* fn. 194, 534:

> Not all investment risks can, or should, be protected against.... Thus, losses caused by bad management of investment risk should not, in principle, be compensable under the fair and equitable treatment standard. This may be related to the legitimate expectations element of the standard, in that it cannot be part of the investor's legitimate expectations that they should be able to avoid losses caused by poor management, by blaming them instead on poor regulation by the host country (footnote omitted).

[284] For a summary, see, e.g., H. Essig, Plama v. Bulgaria—Erster ICSID-Schiedsspruch zur Energiecharta, SchiedsVZ 2006, 311 et seq.

is the case of *Nykomb v. Latvia*.[285] The state-owned Latvian enterprise Latvenergo refused to pay a statutorily and contractually agreed double tariff for electric power to an energy firm owned by Nykomb. At the same time, Latvenergo continued to pay the double tariff to two other Latvian electric power suppliers. The tribunal could not discern a considerable difference between the latter two and Nykomb's company. It thus ruled that the non-payment of contractually due tariffs amounted to discriminatory conduct when the same tariff was continued to be paid to similar companies without legitimate reason.[286]

2. *Full Protection and Security*

The standard of full protection and security has sometimes been held to cover exclusively physical takings of tangible property.[287] Conversely, the tribunal in *Siemens v. Argentina* held that the standard likewise could cover intangible assets.[288] On account of this, the initiation of the contract's renegotiation by Argentina for the sole purpose of reducing costs and without any declaration of public interest was held to affect the legal security of Siemens' investment.[289] Although a clear separation between this standard and the fair and equitable treatment standard is not always obvious,[290] arbitral tribunals generally tend to apply the latter in the ambit of contractual conduct.

IV. *Concluding Remarks*

1. *The Dogma of the Governmental—Commercial Distinction*

In the absence of specific treaty provisions to the contrary, an investor's expectations arising out of a contract with the host State are not protected wholesale by the substantive standards of investment treaties. The investor can expect that its interests enjoy protection only insofar as such protection corresponds to the purpose of the underlying investment treaty. The general purpose of investment treaties is to protect investors against undue interference by the host

---

[285] *Nykomb Synergetics Technology Holding AB v. Latvia*, SCC-Case No. 118/2001, Award, 16 December 2003.

[286] Id., 34.

[287] See, e.g., *PSEG v. Turkey*, *supra* fn. 210, para. 258.

[288] *Siemens v. Argentina*, *supra* fn. 26, para. 303.

[289] Id., para. 308.

[290] Since both standards sometimes appear in one and the same provision, some tribunals construed them as equivalent. See, e.g., *Wena v. Egypt*, *supra* fn. 11, paras. 84–95; *OEPC v. Ecuador*, *supra* fn. 56, para. 187.

State.[291] This means that investment treaties shall provide for protection against political risks. By contrast, the commercial risks of an investment undertaking have to be borne by the investor.[292] In the words of the tribunal in *Maffezini v. Spain*:

> In this connection, the Tribunal must emphasize that Bilateral Investment Treaties are not insurance policies against bad business judgements. While it is probably true that there were shortcomings [in the State organ's behaviour] ... they cannot be deemed to relieve the investors of the business risk inherent in any investments.[293]

This commercial—governmental dogma, which is the dominant view under customary international law concerning coverage of state contracts through international law, is upheld by the majority of treaty-based arbitral tribunals. In this regard, it can thus be contended that the regime which is established by investment treaties concerning the protection of contracts against undue state interference is quite strict and does not alter the scheme envisaged by majority legal doctrine under international law. Yet, two important modifications are established: on the one hand, a higher degree of legal certainty by constituting a confirmation of the State's willingness to abide by international law rules; on the other hand, the treaties open the investor's way to direct dispute settlement with the host State and thus circumvent the traditional flaws of diplomatic protection.

Some tribunals were tempted to expand the fair and equitable treatment standard to such an extent that even ordinary commercial risks would be covered. However, on account of the foregoing reasons, it is rather difficult to contemplate such an effect if not specifically laid down in the treaty. In combination with a broad understanding of the term "investments", this stance would ultimately lead to an equation of "public" investment treaty arbitration and "private" commercial arbitration. It is nevertheless remarkable that the distinction between commercial and governmental interference with a contract, which has never been an obvious and clear-cut one, is subject to ongoing alteration and thereby, especially under a not yet precise fair and equitable treatment standard, an increasing amount of host State conduct may become scrutinized by international adjudicative bodies. In this regard,

[291] See, e.g., Dolzer & Stevens, *supra* fn. 155, 11; M. Herdegen, Internationales Wirtschaftsrecht (2007), 246.

[292] See, e.g., G. van Harten, Investment Treaty Arbitration and Public Law (2007), 28;

[293] *Maffezini v. Spain*, *supra* fn. 280, para. 64.

arbitral tribunals will face the challenge of determining more precisely which kind of conduct amount to a treaty violation. The specific conduct of a host State will have to be tested comprehensively on whether it constitutes elements of governmental authority. Thereby, criteria such as the State's intent, motivation, decision-making process and the like will become relevant. For instance, even the simple non-payment of fees due under a contract or the termination of the contract using the proper contractual devices can be deemed governmental if it was undertaken for sovereign reasons. On the other hand, the same conduct can hardly be deemed governmental if the State acted on purely commercial reasons.

From the view of the host State, this conceptual distinction entails a defence strategy which will have to rely chiefly upon the character of the claim. Consequently, the principal arguments by a State in an investment treaty proceeding based on an investment undertaken through contractual commitment will concern the contract itself. Since it is rather well established that a State may not be held responsible for reasonable decisions grounded upon commercial considerations, its government will principally allege that the investor failed to perform the contract properly or that the project's failure was due to ordinary commercial risks.[294] A further line of argumentation is to dispute the validity of the contract. Hence, a well used allegation is that the contract materialized through infringement of domestic law. By contrast, the reliance upon an argumentation that emphasizes the similarity of both claims and thereby invokes that the treaty claim is merely a contract claim in disguise which, in the past, has been put forward frequently,[295] is not recommendable given the wide recognition of the principle of coincidence of treaty claims and contract claims by arbitral tribunals.[296]

The investor, in turn, will endeavour to prove that the true reason for the State's repudiation, termination, or other kind of contractual interference was not a commercial but a political operation. That means

[294] See, e.g., *PSEG v. Turkey*, *supra* fn. 210, para. 231: "According to the Respondent, the Project implied risks which result from business decisions and for which Turkey cannot be blamed. An investor might end up disappointed, but BITs are not designed to guard against disappointment."

[295] See, e.g., *Bayindir v. Pakistan*, *supra* fn. 28, para. 139; *Impregilo v. Pakistan*, *supra* fn. 26, para. 77; *Saipem v. Bangladesh*, *supra* fn. 29, para. 139; *SGS v. Philippines*, *supra* fn. 56, para. 51; *SGS v. Pakistan*, *supra* fn. 53, para. 48.

[296] See, e.g., *Bayindir Award*, *supra* fn. 172, paras. 139 et seq.

that the investor has to provide information which evinces the government's political attitude, for instance, pronouncements by government officials or administrative organs. Further, the investor will rely on the host State's use of prerogative rights and governmental authority. In this regard, it is essential that the investor proves the involvement of activities which only the State as such is able to conduct. For example, mention can be made of obvious kinds of legislative and executive activity such as the issuance of ordinances or the amendment of legislation.[297]

2. *The Difference between the Fair and Equitable Treatment Standard and the Non-Expropriation Standard*

Arbitral tribunals under the investment treaty regime apply the non-expropriation standard which was once the main protective standard for individuals under international law only in very exceptional cases. The conditions which have to be fulfilled by an expropriation are generally regarded as more exigent than those of the fair and equitable treatment standard violation.[298] As far as contracts between a foreign investor and a host State are concerned, this holds especially true for direct expropriations, which are deemed to occur very seldom, and also for indirect expropriations for which proof of exigent requirements has to be made.[299] The fair and equitable treatment standard, in turn, seems to be applied by arbitral tribunals with much more flexibility and hence covers a much wider range of potentially impairing activities. Although the separation between an indirect expropriation

[297] But also less clear are activities such as responsibilities of a highway authority in maintaining roads. Yet, borderline cases admittedly often vary to a certain degree from one country to another. Hence, the difficulty of finding a general benchmark under international law.

[298] See, e.g., *Thunderbird v. Mexico*, Separate Opinion, *supra* fn. 81, 31; *Bogdanov v. Moldova, supra* fn. 260, 17; Schreuer, *supra* fn. 226, 25; J. Delaney, "Expropriation" and "Fair and Equitable Treatment" Standards in Recent ICSID Jurisprudence, in: R.Hofmann & C. Tams (ed.), The International Convention on the Settlement of Investment Disputes—Taking Stock after 40 Years (2007), 73, 75–77. Regularly, a violation of the fair and equitable treatment standard is merely seen as one condition among others for the determination of an expropriation.

[299] See, e.g., *Sempra v. Argentina, supra* fn. 156, para. 285:

> Many of the measures discussed in the instant case have had a very adverse effect on the conduct of the business concerned. This is, however, again a question that the Treaty addresses in the context of other safeguards for protecting the investor. A finding of indirect expropriation would require more than adverse effects. It would require that the investor no longer be in control of its business operation, or that the value of the business have been virtually annihilated.

and a failure to accord fair and equitable treatment may not be overly clear in some cases[300] and in fact, both standards may be violated cumulatively, the trend in investment arbitration goes towards a broad reliance upon the latter. Hence, the termination of a state contract or its breach may only amount to an expropriation under exceptional circumstances, for instance, when the State disregards essential contractual stipulations or terminates the contract by decree. Yet, the less impairing conduct (inasmuch as the exertion of governmental sovereignty is involved) may regularly entail a violation of the fair and equitable treatment standard. This holds especially true for any alterations of the contractual remuneration scheme.

3. *The Broad Discretion of Arbitrators*

This broad reliance upon a rather imprecise standard leads to a high degree of subjectivism as regards the arbitrators' decision.[301] The relative dearth of existing decisions, the wide variety of subject matters concerned, and the broad wording of treaty provisions are the reasons why no consistent case law has evolved yet. In order to avoid the reproach of arbitrariness, arbitrators should not make excessive use of their discretion but, at least inasmuch as traditional standards of customary international law have to be construed, adhere to traditional interpretations. Adjudicative law-making by arbitral tribunals circumvents the requirements of governmental participation in the creation of international law.[302] On account of this, an interpretation of traditional standards which would embody progressive advancements of international law without the express consent of the involved State parties has to be omitted. Therefore, the commercial—governmental dogma of contract protection cannot be deemed to have been altered under the conventional treaty standards.

---

[300] Id., para. 301.

[301] See generally H. Grigera Naón, The Evolution of International Commercial Arbitration, in: J. Bröhmer, Internationale Gemeinschaft und Menschenrechte—Festschrift für Georg Ress zum 70. Geburtstag am 21. Januar 2005 (2005), 103 et seq.

[302] For the term "adjudicative law-making", see J. Alvarez, International Organisations as Law Makers (2005), 531 et seq. On adjudicative law-making by international arbitral tribunals, see Montt, *supra* fn. 92, 134, where the author states the following:

> In fact, this particular form of adjudication derives directly from the highly open-ended character of treaties' provisions. Instead of concluding detailed treaties or 'dense' binding documents—which, together with other policy alternatives, presuppose a lesser erosion of state sovereignty—state negotiators have typically preferred to agree only on very general principles, leaving the task of concretising them to dispute settlement bodies.

4. THE UMBRELLA CLAUSE

A. General Considerations

A particularly important provision in determining the impact of international investment treaties on state contracts is the so-called "umbrella clause". In simple terms the clause is susceptible of turning breaches of contractual commitments under domestic law into violations of international law.[1] As such, the effect of the clause may have a revolutionary impact upon the resolution of contractual matters before international arbitral tribunals.

The clause goes by many names; whether "*pacta sunt servanda* clause", "sanctity of contract clause", "respect clause", "observation of undertaking clause", "mirror clause", or "umbrella clause",[2] the effect that it is contended to have remains the same. By the establishment of the host State's international obligation to "observe any obligation it has assumed" or to "constantly guarantee the observance of the commitments it has entered into", a breach of contract may entail international liability.[3] Some authors even assert that the whole content of an

---

[1] For one of the early descriptions to this effect, see F. A. Mann, British Treaties for the Promotion and Protection of Investments, BYIL 52 (1981), 241, 246. The author stated that the clause

> protects the investor against any interference with his contractual rights, whether it results from a mere breach of contract or legislative or administrative act, and independently of the question of whether or not such interference amounts to expropriation. The variation of the terms of the contract or license by legislative measures, the termination of the contract or the failure to perform any of its terms, for instance, by non-payment, the dissolution of the local company with which the investor may have contracted and the transfer of its assets (with or without liabilities)-these and similar acts the treaties render wrongful.

[2] See OECD, Interpretation of the Umbrella Clause in Investment Agreements, Working Papers on International Investment, No. 2006/3, October 2006, available at: www.oecd.org (last visited: 12 April 2010), 3. In French, the clause has been termed "traité de couverture". Cf. P. Weil, Problèmes relatifs aux contrats passés entre un état et un particulier, RdC 128 (1969-III), 95, 130 et seq. In German, the most commonly used term is the notion "Abschirmungsklausel".

[3] For a typical umbrella clause, see, e.g., article 8(2) of the German Model BIT 1992: "Each Contracting Party shall observe any obligation it has assumed with regard to investments in its territory by nationals or companies of the other Contracting Party."

eventual investment contract between a host State and an investor is elevated to the international realm in some way.[4] In any event, the unarguably fascinating impact of the clause is not at all certain.

Umbrella clauses are not of very recent appearance. In fact, the clause already emerged before the conclusion of the first BIT and became an inherent part of BITs from the very beginning of investment treaty law and onward. Nonetheless, the clause did not find any application for decades.[5] In 2003, however, the emergence of two cases, the SGS cases, abruptly altered this situation.[6] The two disputes arose out of service contracts which SGS had concluded with Pakistan and the Philippines respectively. Although the wordings of the umbrella clauses in both applicable BITs did not differ considerably,[7] the two tribunals issued contradictory judgements on the issue of the effect of the clause. Henceforth, several controversies concerning the effect and the scope of the umbrella clause became vivid.

For the present purpose, only the clause's impact upon state contracts is of interest. The questions which arise in this regard are among others whether and if so, how umbrella clauses extend the investment treaty protection to state contracts. Moreover, the question what kind of interferences a contractual relationship between foreign investor

---

[4] See, e.g., V. Zolia, Effect and Purpose of "Umbrella Clauses" in Bilateral Investment Treaties: Unresolved Issues, TDM 2 (2005), No. 5, 1, 42: "[I]f adjudicating over commitments under the original system of law where they were taken, it would make it impossible to create a uniform international standard for the protection of investors".

[5] Effectively, this holds true for the whole range of BIT provisions since virtually no use for these agreements was made before the end of the 1980s.

[6] *SGS Société Générale de Surveillance S.A. v. Islamic Republic of Pakistan*, ICSID Case No. ARB/01/13, Decision on Jurisdiction, 6 August 2003, ICSID Rev.-FILJ 18 (2003), 301; ILM 42 (2003), 1290 (hereinafter, *SGS v. Pakistan*); *SGS Société Générale de Surveillance S.A. v. Republic of the Philippines*, ICSID Case No. ARB/02/6, Decision on Jurisdiction, 29 January 2004, 8 ICSID Rep. 518 (hereinafter, *SGS v. Philippines*). In both cases, SGS had concluded contracts directly with the respective governments concerning the provision of "pre-shipment" inspection services with respect to goods to be exported from foreign countries. Whereas in *SGS v. Pakistan*, the claim was lodged due to several alleged breaches of the BIT such as the wrongful repudiation of the contract and failures to protect SGS's investment, in *SGS v. Philippines*, the dispute arose merely out of a refusal to pay open invoices.

[7] Article 11 of the Switzerland—Pakistan BIT reads as follows: "Either Contracting Party shall constantly guarantee the observance of the commitments it has entered into with respect to the investments of the investors of the other Contracting Party." Under the heading "Other Commitments", article X(2) of the Switzerland—Philippines BIT stated the following: "Each Contracting Party shall observe any obligation it has assumed with regard to specific investments in its territory by investors of the other Contracting Party."

and host State is protected from also need to be answered. As seen above, a breach of a state contract under public international law is generally not held to be per se a violation of international law.[8] This rule is based on the conceptual distinction between breach of contract under domestic law and violation of international treaties under international law.[9] In modern investment treaty law this concept is expressed in the differentiation between contract claims and treaty claims.[10] Assuming that the broad interpretation of the clause is adequate, the effect of the umbrella clause would dilute this traditional difference.[11] Not only contract violations that amount to treaty violations would be covered by the BIT but also those which remain on the level of domestic breaches. This, in fact, would be the truly iconoclastic corollary of the insertion of umbrella clauses.

B. History and Contemporary Use of the Clause

I. *Historical Analysis*

At the outset, a historical analysis of the clause and the corresponding preparatory work[12] are convenient to enhance the understanding of its effects and application in contemporary investment disputes.

1. *Anglo-Iranian Oil Company*

For the first time, mention was made of an elevation of contractual obligations into the realm of an international treaty through an "umbrella treaty" in the proposals of Elihu Lauterpacht for the

---

[8] See *supra* 25 et seq.

[9] Id.

[10] See *supra* 160 et seq.

[11] F. Orrego Vicuña, Of Contracts and Treaties in the Global Market, Max Planck UNYB 8 (2004), 341, 352–353: "'[U]mbrella clauses' or 'traités de couverture' might potentially transform a contractual obligation of a state into a treaty obligation, thus erasing the distinction between one and the other. To this extent contracts might be considered as treaties from the point of view of their legal effects".

[12] Article 32 of the Vienna Convention on the Law of Treaties states that the preparatory work of a treaty may be used as supplementary means for its interpretation. Whilst the conclusion of modern investment treaties, especially bilateral ones, is mostly carried out without the production of considerable preparatory work, the legal instruments which were created during the time of the umbrella clause's advent were constantly accompanied by a body of pertinent material. See A. Sinclair, The Origins of the Umbrella Clause in the International Law of Investment Protection, Arb. Int'l 20 (2004), 411, 413.

settlement of the Iranian oil nationalization dispute. In 1951 the Anglo-Iranian Oil Company (AIOC) held a long-term oil concession from the Iranian government. Due to political change in Iran, the existing oil industry became nationalised. The Iranian Oil Nationalisation Law of 1951 provided that all oil operations in Iran had to be undertaken by the Iranian government.[13] Subsequent to several failed attempts to gain redress, including an unsuccessful claim by the British government before the ICJ,[14] a US-sponsored coup brought pro-occidental forces back to power. In the following, a solution for the settlement of the dispute was sought that, on the one hand, enabled Iran to earn sufficient oil revenues from which it could compensate AIOC and that, on the other hand, entitled AIOC to continue its operations in a sector of the Iranian oil industry.[15]

The advice of Lauterpacht concerned the conclusion of a settlement agreement comprising of two legal instruments: (1) an investment agreement between the respective consortium of oil companies and the Iranian government and (2) an umbrella treaty concluded between Iran and the United Kingdom. The investment agreement should be incorporated or referred to in the treaty in such a way that a breach of the agreement was turned into a breach of the treaty.[16] The objectives of the "umbrella treaty" were twofold: First, any dispute related to the contractual agreement between the foreign investors and the Iranian government should be settled without the application of Iranian domestic law. Second, in case of the agreement's breach, an inter-state remedy should be created.[17]

In the view of Lauterpacht, AIOC should be entitled to choose independently whether to pursue its remedies under the dispute settlement provisions contained in the investment agreement or whether to relinquish the ultimate opportunity to claim before the ICJ to the UK Government.[18] However, the treaty procedure was supposed to be

[13] On the dispute between the AIOC and Iran, see generally A. Ford, The Anglo-Iranian Oil Dispute of 1951–1952 (1954); G. Schwarzenberger, Foreign Investments and International Law (1969), 66 et seq.

[14] *Case concerning the Anglo-Iranian Oil Co. Ltd.* (United Kingdom v. Iran) (Preliminary Objections) Judgment of 22 July 1952 [1952] ICJ Rep. 93.

[15] Sinclair, *supra* fn. 12, 414–415.

[16] E. Lauterpacht, Anglo-Iranian Oil Company Ltd Persian Settlement—Opinion, 20 January 1954, 4, cited in Sinclair, *supra* fn. 12, 415.

[17] Id., 416.

[18] E. Lauterpacht, Anglo-Iranian Oil Company Ltd Persian Settlement—Note, 12 March 1954, 9, cited in Sinclair, *supra* fn. 12, 417.

reserved for issues of a higher degree of importance or in case of an agreement's procedures failure. Further, AIOC should not be granted a direct right of recourse under the treaty and the sponsoring of minor disputes through the British government was not regarded as being probable.[19] Lauterpacht's proposals were not realized and appeared again in 1956 in the framework of an advice given by Lauterpacht to a group of oil companies that envisaged the construction of a trunk pipeline from Iraq to the Eastern Mediterranean. The purpose of creating a "parallel protection" of contractual commitments through an international treaty[20] was basically the same as in the AIOC dispute. This project, however, did not materialize either.

2. *The Abs-Shawcross Draft Convention on Investments Abroad*

From 1958 on, Dr. Herman Abs, then Chairman of Deutsche Bank, and Sir Hartley Shawcross, then a Director of the Shell-Petroleum Company, jointly developed a draft convention on the protection of foreign investments (hereafter, Abs-Shawcross Draft Convention). Before, both had published drafts on the protection of foreign investment independently. The International Convention for the Mutual Protection of Private Property Rights in Foreign Countries by Abs included two articles that contained certain elements of a modern umbrella clause. According to article IV (3), States should not act in a way that may generate "the limitation or cancellation of licences within the meaning of article III(e)."[21] Article IV(4) read as follows:

> In so far as better treatment is promised to non-nationals than to nationals either under inter-governmental or other agreements, or by administrative decrees of one of the High Contracting Parties, including most-favoured-nation clauses, such promises shall prevail.

In the Shawcross draft, one article provided for "[t]he application by States of the rule *pacta sunt servanda* to their specific engagements with aliens howsoever arising".[22]

---

[19] Id.

[20] E. Lauterpacht, Establishment and Protection of International Pipe-Lines—Opinion, 22 October 1956, 21, cited in Sinclair, *supra* fn. 12, 418.

[21] Licences are defined in article III(e) as "licenses under public law in the field of trade and industry, which confer upon the licensee a long-term title".

[22] For the cited articles of the Abs Draft and the Shawcross Draft, see the citation in Sinclair, *supra* fn. 12, 420–421.

Although these clauses are not as explicit as modern umbrella clauses, the propensity to disseminate an international protection of the host States' contractual commitments becomes clear. The progress, compared to the umbrella treaties proposed by Lauterpacht, consists in the enlargement of the obligations' coverage. The elevating effect is not limited to one particular investment agreement anymore but extends to the host State's specific engagements towards investors in general.[23]

The combined Abs-Shawcross Draft Convention, in turn, came up with the first version of an umbrella clause that is comparable to modern formulations. Article II of the Abs-Shawcross Draft Convention stated: "Each Party shall at all times ensure the observance of any undertakings which it may have given in relation to investments made by nationals of any other Party."[24]

The general opinion of the contemporaneous commentators and the intention of the authors pointed towards a coverage of contractual commitments through the clause.[25] Hence, the clause expelled existing doubts on whether the unilateral violation of an investment agreement is an internationally wrongful act,[26] and obligations under internal law were transformed into obligations under international law.[27] Moreover, the discussion extended to the question whether unilateral undertakings were covered as well. Generally, this aspect was answered in the affirmative.[28] However, this purportedly "naive internationalisation"[29] was also criticized for various reasons. The wording's impreciseness prompted commentators to doubt the States' willingness to agree to such a provision. Further, it was submitted that the one-sided extension

---

[23] Sinclair, *supra* fn. 12, 421.

[24] Article II of the Draft Convention on Investments Abroad. For the text of the convention, see UNCTAD, International Investment Instruments: A Compendium, vol. V (2000), 332. For reprints of the text and comments, see also G. Schwarzenberger, *supra* fn. 13, 109 et seq. Further, the text of the Abs-Shawcross Draft and a round table discussion involving the authors and Michael Brandon, Stanley Metzger, Georg Schwarzenberger, Arthur Larson, and Richard Gardner are reprinted in J. Pub. L. 9 (1960), 115 et seq.

[25] H. Abs & H. W. Shawcross, Comment on the Draft Convention by Its Authors, J. Pub. L. 9 (1960), 119, 120; G. Schwarzenberger, The Abs-Shawcross Draft Convention on Investments Abroad: A Critical Commentary, J. Pub. L. 9 (1960), 147, 154–155; A. Fatouros, An International Code to Protect Private Investment—Proposals and Perspectives, U. Tor. L. J. 14 (1961), 77, 88.

[26] I. Seidl-Hohenveldern, The Theory of Quasi-International and Partly International Agreements, Rev. Belg. De Droit Int'l 11 (1975), 567, 576.

[27] Schwarzenberger, *supra* fn. 25, 155.

[28] Schwarzenberger, *supra* fn. 13, 116.

[29] Sinclair, *supra* fn. 12, 425.

of investor's rights would generate a distortion of the balance of rights between a host State and a foreign investor.[30]

Opinions were completely divided with regard to the clause's relation to international customary law. Whilst some asserted that the clause is a mere reaffirmation or simple translation of the internationally accepted principle of *pacta sunt servanda* to state contracts,[31] others contemplated that the clause meant a far-reaching departure from the existing rules and principles of international customary law because it converted the nature of domestic contracts into obligations under international law.[32] In addition, the relation of the clause to the concept of *rebus sic stantibus*, a similarly recognized principle of customary international law, was unclear. According to Shawcross, the latter could only be applied in exceptional circumstances and under close judicial scrutiny.[33]

The Abs-Shawcross Draft Convention was never implemented. Its influence on further private and intergovernmental initiatives to enhance the protection of foreign investment, however, cannot be underestimated.[34] In 1959, the clause did make its way into the first BIT ever concluded between Germany and Pakistan. Article 7 of this BIT states: "Either Party shall observe any other obligation it may have entered into with regard to investments by nationals or companies of the other Party."

3. *OECD Draft Convention on the Protection of Foreign Property 1967*

After attempts to find sufficient support from Member States failed, the OECD Draft Convention on the Protection of Foreign Property (hereafter referred to as OECD Draft Convention) was published in 1967 as a mere recommendation to members serving as a model for the conclusion of BITs. The main reason for the failure was the perception of several States, especially Greece, Portugal and Turkey, that certain provisions, including article 2, created an imbalance between foreign

---

30 See Schwarzenberger, *supra* fn. 25, 155.

31 Abs & Shawcross, *supra* fn. 25, 120; E. Snyder, Foreign Investment Protection: A Reasoned Approach, Mich. L. Rev. 61 (1963), 1087, 1110.

32 Schwarzenberger, *supra* fn. 25, 155; S. Metzger, Multilateral Conventions for the Protection of Private Foreign Investment, J. Pub. L. 9 (1960), 133, 137–139.

33 W. H. Shawcross, The Problems of Foreign Investment in International Law, RdC 102 (1961-I), 335, 341.

34 Sinclair, *supra* fn. 12, 428.

investors and host States in favour of the former.[35] Article 2 of the OECD Draft Convention reads as follows: "Each Party shall at all times ensure the observance of undertakings given by it in relation to property of nationals of any other Party".[36]

According to the "Notes and Comments"[37] that accompanied the draft, "property" is to be understood in a very broad sense and thus includes but is not limited to investments.[38] The notion "undertakings" refers to "undertakings embodied in a contract or in a concession" as well as to "unilateral engagements" by the host State. A limitation of the clause's scope is introduced through the requirement that undertakings must relate to the property concerned. A mere incidental link is therefore not sufficient.[39]

Similar to the reactions delivered subsequent to the publication of the Abs-Shawcross Draft Convention, the debate on the OECD Draft Convention revolved around the question whether the clause signified the creation of new obligations or whether it was a mere confirmation of already existing customary international law.[40] However, again, none of the commentators essentially doubted the effect that such a clause, when implemented in a valid instrument of investment protection, would have on the nature of state contract violations. The assertion that the protection granted through article 2 was not absolute but subject to certain exceptions like, for example, the doctrine of *rebus sic stantibus*, did not find considerable supporters.

II. *Contemporary Occurrence and Use of the Clause*

At present, the umbrella clause is frequently included in investment treaties. However, there is no conformity in the States' practice of introducing the clause into their BITs. Nor is there uniformity in the way umbrella clauses are actually phrased and placed in the BITs.

---

35 Id., 432.

36 Article 2 of the OECD Draft Convention on the Protection of Foreign Property (1967), reprinted in: UNCTAD, International Investment Instruments: A Compendium, vol. II (1996), 113 et seq.

37 According to Sinclair, *supra* fn. 12, fn. 106, the Notes and Comments annexed to the OECD draft are partly included in the definition of "Draft Convention" as adopted by the Resolution of the OECD Council and therefore, have the authority of the OECD.

38 Article 2, para. 2 of the Notes and Comments annexed to the OECD draft.

39 Id., para. 3(a).

40 Sinclair, *supra* fn. 12, 430.

1. *Occurrence at Present*

In 2003, when approximately 2000 BITs were concluded worldwide, a scrutiny of 236 BITs showed that 94 of them about 40% contained umbrella clauses.[41] A recent OECD study[42] shows remarkable differences in the clause's use in the BITs concluded by developed States. Some States are very reluctant in using umbrella clauses in their BITs like, for example, France, Australia, Canada and Japan. Umbrella clauses can only be found in a minority of the BITs concluded by these States: Of 35 French BITs examined, only 4 contained an umbrella clause. Of the 20 Australian BITs, only 5 umbrella clauses could be found, and 2 out of the 9 Japanese BITs contained such a clause. None of the Canadian BITs examined in this study contained an umbrella clause. By contrast, Switzerland, Germany, the Netherlands, and the United Kingdom make abundant use of the clause in their BITs. For instance, an examination of 89 UK BITs showed that 87 of them contained an umbrella clause. Likewise, 68 of the 71 German BITs analysed included umbrella clauses.

The United States experienced a policy change through the proclamation of the New 2004 US Model BIT. Whilst the BITs based on the former models generally contained umbrella clauses, the new model BIT does not foresee the possibility of such a clause. This lack may be explained by the general shift in US investment policy towards more control over its sovereign abrogation[43] and a differently phrased dispute resolution clause.[44]

---

[41] J. Gill et al., Contractual Claims and Bilateral Investment Treaties—A Comparative Review of the SGS Cases, J. Int'l Arb. 21 (2004), fn. 31.

[42] For all the figures, see OECD, *supra* fn. 2, 5–6.

[43] G. Gagné & J. F. Morin, The Evolving American Policy on Investment Protection: Evidence from Recent FTAs and the 2004 Model BIT, JIEL 9 (2006), 357 et seq. The authors conclude that the change in the position of the US must be seen as a mere adjustment rather than as a complete reorientation.

[44] Through the inclusion of the term "investment agreement" in article 24 (the treaty's dispute resolution clause), the jurisdictional coverage conferred by the treaty is apparently broad. According to the definition provided for in the treaty, an "investment agreement" is

> a written agreement ... between a national authority of a Party and a covered instrument or an investor of the other Party that grants the covered investment or investor rights: (a) with respect to natural resources or other assets that a national authority controls; and (b) upon which the covered investment or the investor itself relies in establishing or acquiring a covered investment other than the written agreement itself.

2. *Multilateral Agreements*

The clause also found entry into multilateral instruments of investment protection. Whilst NAFTA does not contain an umbrella clause, the second major multilateral investment convention, the ECT, requires in the final sentence of its article 10(1) that: "Each Party shall observe any obligations it has entered into with an Investor or an Investment of an Investor of any other Contracting Party."

It is worthy to note that the derogation provision in Annex IA of the ECT permits Member States to opt out of this obligation. So far, four parties to the ECT chose not to accept this stipulation. These are Australia, Canada, Hungary and Norway.[45]

The efforts to create a worldwide multilateral agreement on investment protection, namely, the MAI negotiations, embarked as well upon the subject of contractual commitments' protection. In relation to this problem, the MAI Drafting Group considered three options: first, no special referral to contractual rights; second, the inclusion of a dispute resolution clause, i.e., a procedural solution; and finally, a substantive provision called the "respect clause". The last option was supposed to give investor—State agreements a substantive protection, establishing the application of the *pacta sunt servanda* principle for state contracts on the international plane. It was not clear, however, whether such a provision should be limited to certain contractual rights or to contracts under which the State acts as a sovereign. In the end, no provision was included,[46] and the whole MAI project did not lead to a successful end.[47]

This definition, however, signifies a considerable limitation of the jurisdictional coverage. See also UNCTAD, Bilateral Investment Treaties 1995–2006: Trends in Investment Rulemaking (2007), available at: www.unctad.org (last visited: 12 April 2010), 74.

[45] E. Paasivirta, The Energy Charter Treaty and Investment Contracts: Towards Security of Contracts, in: T. Wälde (ed.), The Energy Charter Treaty, An East-West Gateway for Investment and Trade (1996), 349, 358.

[46] The negotiating proposals in the annex foresaw following two formulations: "Respect clause-Each Contracting Party shall observe any obligation it has entered into with regard to specific investment of an investor of another Contracting Party" and "Substantive approach to the respect clause-Each Contracting Party shall observe any other obligation in writing, it has assumed with regard to investments in its territory by investors of another Contracting Party. Disputes arising from such obligations shall only be settled under the terms of the contracts underlying the obligations".

[47] OECD, *supra* fn. 2, 6.

3. *Differences in the Clauses' Wordings*

There are several formulations which are principally susceptible of embodying an umbrella clause.[48] A common feature of the wording of BIT provisions is the sparse manner in which the articles are drafted. In this regard the umbrella clause is no exception. Albeit the arbitral tribunals were not consistent about the ultimate significance of the meaning of the clauses' differences for the contrary results in interpretation, it is indispensable for the clarification of the umbrella clause's meaning to scrutinize the wording more exactly.

a. *Mandatory Language*

Nearly all clauses use mandatory language. The degree of compulsion, however, differs depending on the exact formulation used. An example for the most straightforward use of mandatory language is article 2 of the UK Model BIT: "(2)…Each Contracting Party *shall observe* any obligation it may have entered into with regard to investments in its territory by investors of the other Contracting Party" (emphasis added).[49]

The umbrella clauses of this category employ phrases like "shall observe", "shall respect", or "shall adhere to". A further, less forceful formulation of a mandatory umbrella clause is contained, for instance, in article 10 of the Australia-Poland BIT: "A Contracting Party *shall, subject to its law, do all in its power to ensure* that a written undertaking given by a competent authority to a national of the other Contracting Party with regard to investment is respected" (emphasis added).[50]

The formulation in the Swiss—Pakistan BIT that generated the famous renunciation of a broad approach by the tribunal dealing with it[51] can be regarded as being a middle approach. Admittedly, the formulation is more ambiguous than the direct "shall observe" employed in other BITs. Nevertheless, it is doubtful whether the phrase "shall constantly guarantee the observance of commitments" can be interpreted as being non-mandatory.

---

[48] Cf. J. Crawford, Treaty and Contract in Investment Arbitration, Int'l Arb. 24 (2008), 351, 355 : "There is no such a thing as *the* umbrella clause; rather, there are umbrella clauses".

[49] As cited in OECD, *supra* fn. 2, 10.

[50] Id., 9.

[51] Article 11 of the Switzerland—Pakistan BIT, *supra* fn. 7.

b. *Scope of Obligations*

Further differences can be determined as to the scope and nature of the obligations covered. Most of the clauses refer to "commitments", "any obligation", or "any other obligation". Other BITs are more specific and require the obligation to be "written"[52] or that they have to be given by "a competent authority"[53]. Further, some clauses refer to "particular" commitments.[54] Another feature is the clarification that the clause is intended to cover obligations different from those provided for in the treaty itself. For example, article 15 of the Czech Republic-Singapore BIT states: "(2) Each Contracting Party shall observe commitments, *additional to those specified in this Agreement*" (emphasis added).

Other BITs, for instance, the Austria—Chile BIT, refer explicitly to "contractual obligations". In addition, a differentiation can be made according to the degree to which the object of the obligations is specified. Whilst some clauses refer to obligations "with regard to investments", others demand "specific investments" or "investments with nationals or companies of the other Contracting Party".

Finally, differences can be observed with respect to the manner of how the host State is tied to the obligation. A widespread example is the formulation used in article 2 of the Sweden Model BIT: "(4) Each Contracting Party shall observe any obligation *it has entered into* with investors of the other Contracting Party with regard to their investment" (emphasis added).

Further formulations are "it has assumed",[55] "it may have",[56] or "given by a competent authority"[57]. The question that is generated through these different phrasings concerns the exact scope of the respective clause. One may ask whether a formulation like "entered into" is an

[52] Article 11 of the Australia—China BIT (1988), cited in OECD, *supra* fn. 2, 11.

[53] Article 11 of the Australia—Chile BIT (1996), cited in OECD, *supra* fn. 2, 11.

[54] Article 3(3) of the UK—Philippines BIT (1980), cited in OECD, *supra* fn. 2, 27. The clause reads as follows: "Each Contracting Party shall observe any obligation arising from a particular commitment it may have entered into with regard to a specific investment of nationals or companies of the other Contracting Party".

[55] See, e.g., article 10 of the Switzerland Model BIT or article 8 of the German Model BIT (No. 201), cited in OECD, *supra* fn. 2, 12–13.

[56] Article 12 of the Finland Model BIT, cited in OECD, *supra* fn. 2, 24. The clause reads as follows: "Each Contracting Party shall observe any other obligation it may have with regard to a specific investment of an investor of the other Contracting Party".

[57] Article 11 of the Australia—Chile BIT (1996), cited in OECD, *supra* fn. 2, 11.

explicit referral to contractual commitments[58] or whether unilateral obligations undertaken by the host State are covered likewise.[59]

c. *Structure*

A further feature that shows considerable variation and whose impact on the clause's effect is not completely certain is the location of the clause within the framework of the respective BIT. Plainly, there are three different variants of where an umbrella clause is placed in a BIT.[60] The first of these alternatives puts the umbrella clause among the substantive provisions provided for in the treaty. As example therefore, mention can be made of the Netherlands Model BIT. This placement of the clause argues in favour of a broad interpretation, construing the obligations introduced by the clause as a further substantive content of the BIT. A second approach is the one favoured by Swiss drafters where the umbrella clause is placed in a provision entitled "Other commitments" and is separated from the substantive provisions through the two dispute resolution clauses concerning disputes of the host State with private persons and other States. The third model positions the clause between the substantive and the procedural provisions. This structure is applied in the German Model BITs.

d. *Requisitions of the Wording*

As stated above, the wordings of umbrella clauses show certain similarities as well as some differences. At the same time, however, the evolving practice concerning the umbrella clause evinces that certain requirements must be fulfilled by the formulation so that the clause can be classified as a proper umbrella clause. In *Salini v. Jordan*, the tribunal

---

[58] See, e.g., *Noble Ventures, Inc. v. Romania*, ICSID Case No. ARB/01/11, Award, 12 October 2005, para. 51 (hereinafter, *Noble Ventures v. Romania*): "By contrast, in addition to the BIT, what are often concluded concerning investments are so-called investment contracts between investors and the host State. .... Against this background ... it is difficult not to regard this [phrase 'any obligation a party may have entered into'] as a clear reference to investment contracts".

[59] See, e.g., *LG & E Energy Corp. v. Argentine Republic*, ICSID Case No. ARB/02/1, Decision on Jurisdiction, 3 October 2006, para. 175:

> Argentina made these specific obligations to foreign investors ... by enacting the Gas Law and other regulations, and then advertising these guarantees in the Offering Memorandum to induce the entry of foreign capital .... These laws and regulations became obligations within the meaning of Article II(2)(c), by virtue of targeting foreign investors and applying specifically to their investments, that gave rise to liability under the umbrella clause.

[60] OECD, *supra* fn. 2, 9–10.

dismissed the respondent's allegations that the Italy—Jordan BIT contained an umbrella clause.[61] The article at issue stated the following: "Each Contracting Party shall create and maintain in its territory a legal framework apt to guarantee the investors the continuity of legal treatment, including the compliance, in good faith, of all undertakings assumed with regard to each specific investor."

In the tribunal's view, this formulation must be regarded as insufficient to create the effects of a proper umbrella clause. Basing its reasoning on the wording of the article 2(4) of the Italy—Jordan BIT, the tribunal stated firstly that the terms used are quite different from provisions applied in previous cases and secondly that the contracting parties to article 2(4) did not commit themselves to "observe any obligation" they had previously assumed. The only commitment established was to create and maintain a legal framework apt to guarantee the compliance of all undertakings assumed with regard to each specific investor.[62] The application of article 2(5) and article 11 of the BIT did not change this result.[63] None of these provisions was deemed to be apt to transform the content of article 2(4) in the purported manner.[64] Hence, an umbrella clause must contain explicit referral to non-treaty "obligations" or "commitments", i.e., obligations which have their origin in a legal instrument other than the treaty itself, and have to provide for their unconditional observance. Besides such general requirements, it remains questionable to what extent the different wordings of the clauses justify the different results of interpretation. It has to be emphasized that, of course, arbitral tribunals have to determine the effects of treaty stipulations on a casuistic basis. Notwithstanding the similarity of the bulk of the clauses, the exact effect of a clause depends on its specific formulation.[65] This is true for specific formulations such as

---

[61] *Salini Costruttori S.p.A. v. Hashemite Kingdom of Jordan*, ICSID Case No. ARB/02/13, Decision on Jurisdiction, 29 November 2004, para. 126 (hereinafter, *Salini v. Jordan*).

[62] Id.

[63] Article 2(5) of the Italy—Jordan BIT reads as follows: "Each Contracting Party or its designated Agency may stipulate with an investor of the other Contracting Party an investment agreement which will govern the specific legal relationship related to the investment of the investor concerned." Article 11 contained an MFN-regulation concerning treatment under legal instruments other than the BIT.

[64] *Salini v. Jordan*, *supra* fn. 61, para. 128–129.

[65] E. Gaillard, Centre international pour le Règlement des Différends relatifs aux Investissements (CIRDI)—Chronique des sentences arbitrales, JDI 129 (2002), 189,

exclusions of certain types of contracts or exclusion of unilateral commitments. However, whether the general effect of a clause is contingent upon precise formulations when acknowledged requirements of the clause's wording are met is rather doubtful.

C. The Effect of the Clause

Subsequent to the first exhaustive analysis of the clause by the ICSID tribunal in the *SGS v. Pakistan* case, the long-lasting consistency of commentators concerning the clause's effects vanished.[66] The subsequent decisions of international arbitral tribunals and opinions issued in scholarly writings disclosed the evolution of three main approaches.

I. *The Narrow Interpretation or Rejection of an Elevating Effect*

The application of a narrow interpretation approach leads to a somewhat restrained function of the umbrella clause. In order to circumvent the State's international responsibility for every single breach of contract, a few tribunals adopted such an approach. However, these decisions cannot be regarded as rejecting the broad function of the clause unanimously, but they have to be examined in the light of their specific circumstances. Among the decisions of tribunals that support a restrictive approach, the decision in the *SGS v. Pakistan* case[67] is the most important one. At the same time, it contains the clearest negation of the clause's broad interpretation. The tribunal in that case was the first international arbitral tribunal which examined the effects of an umbrella clause exhaustively[68] and against prevailing expectations, it applied a

214 et seq. An atypical and potentially controversial clause could be seen, for instance, in article 19 of the Greece—Mexico BIT. This clause states the following: "Each Contracting Party shall observe any other obligation it may have entered into in writing with regard to a specific investment of an investor of the other Contracting Party. The disputes arising from such obligations shall be settled only under the terms and conditions of the respective contract." Reprinted in UNCTAD, *supra* fn. 44, 73.

[66] See Sinclair, *supra* fn. 12, 421 et seq. Formerly, the main discussion did not concern the proper effect of the clause but whether this effect, which was held to transform municipal obligations into obligations under international law, was a departure from existing international law or not.

[67] *SGS v. Pakistan*, *supra* fn. 6.

[68] Prior to the *SGS v. Pakistan* decision, the clause was applied only once in *Fedax N.V. v. Venezuela*, ICSID Case No. ARB/96/3, Award, 9 March 1998, (1998) 37 ILM

restrictive approach.[69] Therefore, the tribunal's decision became the bone of contention of the actual debate. It has to be emphasized that with its decision, the tribunal situated itself opposite the majority doctrine. With its "outright rejection",[70] it stands aloof from the overwhelming part of traditional interpretations that have been given to the clause's effect. The tribunals that seem to follow its approach do so with regard to specific situations and not in a generally fashioned way. Admittedly, the far-reaching consequences that could be entailed by the clause's broad interpretation and the prospective impact on a State's sovereignty urged several commentators to heavily criticize the clause. After its first appearance, there were doubts whether States that may be most affected by the clause would agree to such a provision. Accordingly, the clause's unspecific, broad wording entailed an unjustified disadvantage for the capital-importing States.[71] The clause cannot be seen as a mere translation of the *pacta sunt servanda* principle into international law but rather had to be regarded as a "far-reaching departure from the law as it stands."[72] More recently, the growth of international investment disputes induced several legal scholars to admonish the devastating effect which the unlimited application of a broadly interpreted umbrella clause could generate. Dissatisfied investors can bring treaty-based claims before international arbitral tribunals although the character of the dispute was a purely commercial one.[73] Accordingly, this would constitute a dramatic alteration of the nature of international disputes.[74] The contention is made that the mere hope that investors would invoke umbrella clauses with appropriate restraint and not for "trivial disputes"[75] is insufficient to inhibit serious jeopardy to the whole system of

---

1378 (hereinafter, *Fedax v. Venezuela*). The tribunal, however, did not question the elevating effect of the clause and did not further inquire into the clause's effect.

[69] *SGS v. Pakistan*, *supra* fn. 6, para. 171: "The appropriate interpretative approach is the prudential one summed up in the literature as *in dubio pars mitior est sequenda*, or more tersely, *in dubio mitius*" (footnote omitted).

[70] T. Wälde, The "Umbrella" Clause in Investment Arbitration—A Comment on Original Intentions and Recent Cases, JWIT 6 (2005), 183, 212.

[71] Metzger, *supra* fn. 32, 134. More recently, see T. H. Cheng, Power, Authority and International Investment Law, Am. U. Int'l L. Rev. 20 (2004), 465, 473.

[72] Schwarzenberger, *supra* fn. 25, 155.

[73] D. Foster, Umbrella Clauses—A Retreat from the Philippines?, Int'l Arb. L. Rev. 100 (2006), 100, 100.

[74] See Gill et al., *supra* fn. 41, 408.

[75] C. Schreuer, Travelling the BIT Route—Of Waiting Periods, Umbrella Clauses and Forks in the Road, JWIT 5 (2004), 231, 255.

investment protection through BITs. Accordingly one has to bear in mind that the viability of international obligations depends ultimately on the States' will to abide by them. If States perceive that the balance of risk under BITs has shifted too far on the host State's side, their reluctance towards the system as a whole would increase.[76]

The narrow approach was followed by two other tribunals. The case between Joy Mining Machinery Limited and Egypt arose out of a contract concerning the provision of specialized longwall mining equipment for a phosphate mining project.[77] As the dispute did not concern an investment within the treaty's notion of investment but a purely commercial dispute, the tribunal concluded that it lacked jurisdiction.[78] Nevertheless, the tribunal addressed the meaning of the alleged umbrella clause in article 2(2) of the UK—Egypt BIT[79]:

> In this context, it could not be held that an umbrella clause inserted in the Treaty, and not very prominently, could have the effect of transforming all contract disputes into investment disputes under the Treaty, unless of course there would be a clear violation of the Treaty rights and obligations or a violation of contract rights of such a magnitude as to trigger the Treaty protection, which is not the case. The connection between the Contract and the Treaty is the missing link that prevents any such effect. This might be perfectly different in other cases where that link is found to exist, but certainly it is not the case here.[80]

In *Salini v. Jordan*, the situation was different because the clause concerned differed considerably from the formulation of standard umbrella clauses.[81] The tribunal therefore rejected a broad interpretation of the clause that would allow an elevation of contractual obligations into treaty obligations. On the other hand, the tribunal seemed to accept an elevating effect of the clause contingent upon the precise wording of

---

[76] Cf. Foster, *supra* fn. 73, 100.

[77] *Joy Mining Machinery Limited v. The Arab Republic of Egypt*, ICSID Case No. ARB/03/11, Award on Jurisdiction, 6 August 2004 (hereinafter, *Joy Mining v. Egypt*), para. 16.

[78] Id., para. 63.

[79] Article 2(2) of the BIT provides that "[e]ach Contracting Party shall observe any obligation it may have entered into with regard to investments of nationals or companies of the other Contracting Party."

[80] *Joy Mining v. Egypt*, *supra* fn. 77, para. 81.

[81] See *supra* fn. 63. The case of *Salini v. Jordan* arose out of a dispute on the amount payable under a contract for the construction of a dam. After the completion of the work, Salini submitted an invoice amounting to US$28 million. According to the evaluation by the Jordanian agency, in turn, the costs did not exceed the amount of US$49,140.

the clause.[82] Hence, the decision can hardly be regarded as an endorsement of a narrow approach.

In sum, both cases do not represent an approach as narrow as the one applied in *SGS v. Pakistan*, and both do not sustain such an approach in a general manner. In *Joy Mining v. Egypt*, the tribunal, albeit not explicitly but with regard to the context of the case, rather induces a middle approach. Accordingly, the elevating effect of the clause has to be denied in a purely commercial dispute as was the case in *Joy Mining*. However, it is not clear whether such denial is valid in the case of non-commercial disputes as well.

In the view of Gill, Gearing, and Birt, the approach taken by the *SGS v. Pakistan* tribunal has an advantage with regard to the effectiveness of dispute resolution. The non-qualification of many international arbitrators to deal adequately with the domestic law of foreign States argues in favour of the local courts' jurisdiction.[83] This argumentation ignores the fact that the evaluation of the contractual situation and thus, the application of the host State's internal law is a regular feature in nearly all investment disputes where a determination on whether the host State's conduct amounts to a breach of one of the treaty's standards has to be made.

II. *The Elevating Effect*

A broad approach to the interpretation of umbrella clauses has been sustained by an overwhelming number of legal scholars and commentators all throughout the clause's existence.[84] The same can be said of

---

[82] J. Gaffney, Case Summary: Salini Costruttori S.p.A. and Italstrade S.p.A. v. The Hashemite Kingdom of Jordan, TDM 2 (2005), No. 01, section 5(b), available at: www.transnational-dispute-management.com (last visited: 15 April 2010); G. Tawil, The Distinction between Contract Claims and Treaty Claims: An Overview, Presentation Delivered at ICCA Congress 2006 Montreal, formerly available at: www.iccamontreal2006.org. (on file with the author), 43.

[83] Gill et al., *supra* fn. 41, 408.

[84] For opinions which were issued prior to the *SGS v. Pakistan* decision, see, e.g., Schwarzenberger, *supra* fn. 13, 116–117; J. Alenfeld, Die Investitionsförderungsverträge der Bundesrepublik Deutschland (1971), 96–97; J. Karl, The Promotion and Protection of German Foreign Investment Abroad, ICSID Rev.-FILJ 11 (1996), 1, 23; K. J. Vandevelde, United States Investment Treaties: Policy and Practice (1992), 78; J. Stoll, Vereinbarungen zwischen Staat und ausländischem Investor (1982), 95: "In dogmatischer Hinsicht ist zu bemerken, daß damit die betreffende Vereinbarung zwischen Gaststaat und Investor nicht in eine völkerrechtliche verwandelt wird, sondern nur eine entsprechende Parallelverpflichtung auf völkerrechtlicher Ebene dem Heimatstaat gegenüber begründet wird".

the majority of tribunals faced with the interpretation of umbrella clauses. Subsequent to the decision in *SGS v. Pakistan* several other tribunals which dealt with the interpretation of the umbrella clause directly addressed the award to contradict its result. Their reasoning is based on ample authorities that gave the clause the effect of a substantive treaty provision which requires States to observe contractual commitments entered into with foreign investors.[85]

In his now famous Hague lecture in 1969, Prosper Weil argued in favour of the transformation of mere contractual obligations. He stated that:

> [There] is, in fact, no particular difficulty when there is an "umbrella treaty" between the contracting State and the State of the other contracting party, which turns the obligation to perform the contract into an international obligation of the contracting state *vis-à-vis* the State of the other contracting party. The intervention of the umbrella treaty transforms contractual obligations into international obligations thereby ensuring, as it has already been stated, the intangibility of contract under the threat of violating the treaty; any performance of the contract, even if it is legal under the national law of the contracting State, gives rise to the international liability of the latter *vis-à-vis* the national State of the other contracting party.[86]

In the view of Frederick A. Mann, even a variation in the terms of the State's undertakings can be tantamount to a treaty breach under an umbrella clause. He stated:

> This is a provision of particular importance in that it protects the investor against any interference with his contractual rights, whether it results

[85] In addition to the other mentioned authors, see S. Alexandrov, Breaches of Contract and Breaches of Treaty—The Jurisdiction of Treaty-Based Arbitration Tribunals to Decide Breach of Contract Claims in SGS v. Pakistan and SGS v. Philippines, JWIT 5 (2004), 555, 572; J. P. Gaffney & J. L. Loftis, The "Effective Ordinary Meaning" of BITs and the Jurisdiction of Treaty-Based Tribunals to Hear Contract Claims, JWIT 8 (2007), 5, 19; B. Kunoy, Singing in the Rain—Developments in the Interpretation of Umbrella Clauses, JWIT 7 (2006), 275, 299; D. Foster, "Internationalisation"—Contractual Claims in BIT Arbitrations, The European Arbitration Review 2007, 18, 19; H. J. Schramke, Umbrella Clauses in Bilateralen Investitionsschutzabkommen, SchiedsVZ 2006, 249, 257; A. von Walter, Die Reichweite von Schirmklauseln in Investitionsschutzabkommen nach der jüngsten ICSID-Spruchpraxis, RIW 52 (2006), 815, 823; J. Wong, Umbrella Clauses in Bilateral Investment Treaties: Of Breaches of Contract, Treaty Violations, and the Divide between Developing and Developed Countries in Foreign Investment Disputes, Geo. Mas. L. Rev. 14 (2006), 135, 163–165; Zolia, *supra* fn. 4, 22.

[86] P. Weil, *supra* fn. 2, 130.

> from a mere breach of contract or a legislative or administrative act, and independently of the question whether or no[t] such interference amounts to expropriation. The variation of the terms of a contract or license by legislative measures, the termination of the contract or the failure to perform any of its terms ... these and similar acts the treaties render wrongful.[87]

As more contemporary examples of this opinion, mention can be made of the leading work on bilateral investment treaties by Rudolph Dolzer and Margrete Stevens, the repeated allegations of Emmanuel Gaillard, as well as the comments made by Christoph Schreuer. Dolzer and Stevens assert the following:

> These provisions seek to ensure that each Party to the treaty will respect specific undertakings towards nationals of the other Party. The provision is of particular importance because it protects the investor's contractual rights against any interference which might be caused by either a simple breach of contract or by administrative or legislative acts, and because it is not entirely clear under general international law whether such measures constitute breaches of an international obligation.[88]

The opinion of Emmanuel Gaillard is that in the case of an umbrella clause, the engaged State is internationally responsible for the violation of a contract as a violation of the treaty. He calls this the "mirror effect"[89] of the clause: "You have a violation of the contract, and the Treaty says, as if you had a mirror, that this violation will also be susceptible to being characterized as a violation of the Treaty."[90]

Schreuer contends that "under the operation of an umbrella clause, the claim need not to fail if the investor is unable to demonstrate a violation of one of the BIT's substantive provisions. The often difficult proof that there has been a violation of the 'fair and equitable treatment' or 'full protection and security' standards or that there has been an 'indirect expropriation' is no longer decisive, provided a breach of

---

[87] Mann, *supra* fn. 1, 246.

[88] R. Dolzer & M. Stevens, Bilateral Investment Treaties (1995), 81–82.

[89] E. Gaillard, L'arbitrage sur le fondement des traités de protection des investissements—Les Etats dans le contentieux économique international, I. Le contentieux arbitral, Rev. Arb. 2003, 853, 868. See also E. Gaillard, Investment Treaty Arbitration and Jurisdiction over Contract Claims—The SGS Cases Considered, in: T. Weiler (ed.), International Investment Law and Arbitration: Leading Cases from the ICSID, NAFTA, Bilateral Treaties and Customary International Law (2005), 325, 344; E. Gaillard, Centre pour le Règlement des Différends relatifs aux Investissements (CIRDI)—Chronique des sentences arbitrales, JDI 133 (2006), 219, 342.

[90] See SGS's response to the objections of Pakistan in *SGS v. Pakistan*, *supra* fn. 6, para. 99.

an investment contract can be shown."[91] Hence, "under the regime of such an umbrella clause, any violation of a contract thus covered becomes a violation of the BIT".[92]

Arbitrators did not hesitate to advance this interpretation. Just a few months after the decision in *SGS v. Pakistan*, the same question was treated by another ISCSID tribunal. In *SGS v. Philippines*, the Swiss company SGS had lodged a claim for unpaid monies amounting to the sum of approximately US$140 million.[93] The factual background was reminiscent of the former case against Pakistan. SGS had concluded a contract directly with the government and the wording of the treaty's umbrella clause[94] did not seem to justify a decision distinct from the one rendered in *SGS v. Pakistan*. Based on the application of the umbrella clause and the treaty's dispute resolution clause, the tribunal affirmed its jurisdiction over the contractual claims. Throughout its reasoning, the tribunal directly addressed the argumentation put forward in the *SGS v. Pakistan* decision and contradicted it explicitly. Several tribunals[95] followed this approach relying mainly on the same reasons.

In further investment cases, the effect of the umbrella clause was not analysed thoroughly but the tribunals' statements indicated that they are in favour of a broad approach. The first ICSID tribunal that had to deal with an umbrella clause was the tribunal in *Fedax NV v. Venezuela*.[96] The tribunal did not discuss the clause's effect but applied a broad interpretation without hesitation. For this reason, Venezuela was obliged to "honour precisely the terms and conditions governing such investment, laid down mainly in article 3[97] of the Agreement (i.e., the BIT), as well as to honour the specific payments established in the promissory

---

[91] Schreuer, *supra* fn. 75, 255.

[92] Id., 251.

[93] *SGS v. Philippines*, *supra* fn. 6, para. 15.

[94] Article X(2) of the Swiss—Philippines BIT reads as follows: "Each Contracting Party shall observe any obligation it has assumed with regard to specific investments in its territory by investors of the other Contracting Party."

[95] See, e.g., *Eureko B.V. v. Republic of Poland*, Ad Hoc Arbitration under the Agreement between the Kingdom of the Netherlands and the Republic of Poland on Encouragement and Reciprocal Protection of Investment, Partial Award, 19 August 2005 (hereinafter, *Eureko v. Poland*); *Noble Ventures, Inc. v. Romania*, *supra* fn. 58; *Sempra Energy International v. Argentina*, ICSID Case No. ARB/02/16, Decision on Objections to Jurisdiction, 11 May 2005.

[96] *Fedax v. Venezuela*, *supra* fn. 68.

[97] Article 3(4) of the Netherlands—Venezuela BIT states: "Each Contracting Party shall observe any obligation it may have entered into with regard to the treatment of investments of nationals of the other Contracting Party".

notes issued".[98] In the view of most scholars, this plain application of the clause was a result of the tribunal's unawareness of the umbrella clause.[99]

Chapter 11 of the NAFTA does not contain an umbrella clause. Nevertheless, in *Waste Management v. United Mexican States*,[100] a NAFTA tribunal gave an interpretation of the umbrella clause. Accordingly, through an umbrella clause, the host State is obliged to comply with its contractual commitments.[101] Finally, the tribunal in *LESI-Dipenta v. Algeria* stated that "the effect of such clauses is to transform the violations of the State's contractual commitments into violations of the treaty umbrella clause and by this to give jurisdiction to the Tribunal over the matter" notwithstanding the fact that it denied the existence of an umbrella clause in the Italy—Algeria BIT.[102]

It is further worthy to note that up to the present the only official issuance of a State's intention to include an umbrella clause into a BIT endorsed the broad interpretation of the clause.[103] The statement was published by the Swiss authorities after the *SGS v. Pakistan* tribunal had rendered its decision. Accordingly, the Swiss authorities were "alarmed about the very narrow interpretation given to the meaning of Article 11 [i.e., the umbrella clause] by the Tribunals," which did not correspond to the intentions of Switzerland when it was concluding the treaty. In the view of the Swiss authorities umbrella clauses "are intended to cover commitments that a host State has entered into with regard to specific investments of an investor or investment of a specific investor, which played a significant role in the investor's decision to invest or to substantially change an existing investment, i.e. commitments which were of such a nature that the investor could rely on them".[104]

---

[98] *Fedax v. Venezuela*, *supra* fn. 68, para. 29.

[99] OECD, *supra* fn. 2, 15; Wälde, *supra* fn. 70, 210–211.

[100] *Waste Management Inc. v. United Mexican States*, ICSID Case No. ARB (AF)/00/3, Award, 30 April 2004.

[101] Id., para. 73.

[102] *Consorzio Groupement L.E.S.I.-Dipenta v. People's Democratic Republic of Algeria*, ICSID Case No. ARB/03/08, Award, 10 January 2005, para. 25(ii). "Ces clauses ont pour effet de transformer les violations des engagements contractuels de l'Etat en violations de cette disposition du traité et, par là même, de donner compétence au tribunal arbitral".

[103] See Sinclair, *supra* fn. 12, 413. Accordingly, these statements have to be taken "with a pinch of salt".

[104] Note on the Interpretation of Article 11 of the Bilateral Investment Treaty between Switzerland and Pakistan in the Light of the Decision of the Tribunal of Objections to Jurisdiction of ICSID in Case No. ARB/01/13 SGS Société Générale de

III. *Distinction between Commercial and Non-Commercial Conduct*

The third approach to the interpretation of umbrella clauses can be regarded as a middle way between the two other extreme positions. Interestingly, this dampened form of the umbrella clause's effect finds supporters from both opposing stances. Almost the same result is deduced from completely different points of departure. Whilst one point of view relies on the restrictive interpretation and widens the umbrella clause's scope for non-commercial behaviour of the State, the other position is based on the broad approach and tries to find a limitation through the distinction between non-commercial and commercial interference by the host State.

In *El Paso Energy International Company v. The Argentine Republic*,[105] the tribunal rejected a broad approach categorically.[106] Except for minor differences, the exact formulation is applied again in *Pan American Energy LLC and BP Argentina Exploration Company v. Argentine Republic*.[107] The tribunal in this case, consisting of two of the three arbitrators in the *El Paso* tribunal, nearly copied the *El Paso* decision concerning the interpretation of the umbrella clause. Both tribunals applied a narrow interpretation and thus followed the decision in *SGS v. Pakistan*. However, in order to grant the clause any effect at all, the tribunals, at the end of their examination of the clause, asserted that

---

Surveillance S.A. v. Islamic Republic of Pakistan, attached to the Letter of the Swiss Secretariat for Economic Affairs to the ICSID Deputy Secretary-General dated 1 October 2003, reprinted in: Mealey's Int'l Arb. Rep. E3, February 2004.

[105] *El Paso Energy Int'l Co. v. The Argentine Republic*, ICSID Case No. ARB/03/15, Decision on Jurisdiction, 27 April 2006 (hereinafter, *El Paso v. Argentina*).

[106] Id., paras. 66–88.

[107] *Pan American Energy LLC v. The Argentine Republic*, ICSID Case No. ARB/03/13 and *BP America Production Co. v. The Argentine Republic*, ICSID Case No. ARB/04/8, Decision on Preliminary Objections, 27 July 2006, paras. 96–116 (hereinafter, *Pan American v. Argentina*). Both cases, *El Paso v. Argentina* and *Pan American v. Argentina*, deal with the consequences of the measures taken by the Argentine government in response to the economic crisis 2001–2002. The respective US companies were shareholders in several Argentine power-generating companies. These companies held contracts and concessions with the Argentine government in which they were granted the right to exploit natural resources, generate and distribute power under a pre-fixed tariff scheme. The framework of this scheme was altered considerably by the enactment of the Argentine Emergency Laws. For a detailed description of the economic and financial situation in Argentina at this time see, *Gas Natural SDG S.A. v. Argentine Republic*, ICSID Case No. ARB/03/10, Decision of the Tribunal on Preliminary Questions on Jurisdiction, 17 June 2005, paras. 11–15. Both tribunals refer to this description of the circumstances.

certain breaches which are generated through governmental activity of the host State indeed may be covered by the umbrella clause.[108]

In the same vein, the tribunal in *CMS v. Argentina*[109] ruled that the pertinent umbrella clause contained in article II(2)(c) of the US—Argentina BIT was breached. It did so by reason of the non-commercial character of the measures complained of, namely, two stabilization clauses included in the contract ("the License") that obliged Argentina not to freeze the tariff regime and not to alter the basic rules governing the License.[110] Apparently, the tribunal applied the same yardstick as the tribunals in *El Paso* and *BP PanAmerican*: "Purely commercial aspects of a contract might not be protected by the treaty in some situations but the protection is likely to be available when there is significant interference by governments or public agencies with the rights of the investor."[111]

The second approach recently put forward by Wälde[112] but concerning its results originally conceived by Brower[113] has a point of departure which is diametrically opposed to the first approach. It departs by sustaining the broad interpretation of the clause but qualifies its unrestrained adoption to the contemporary BIT practice as blindfold. It argues for the clause's restrictive application based on the original intentions of the drafters and the historical circumstances of its introduction in legal instruments of investment protection. The generation of international responsibility through "governmental" breaches of contractual commitments is regarded as the general rule and not the exception. The umbrella clause in this sense becomes a provision which merely clarifies and confirms the status of customary international law.[114]

Bearing in mind that the approach departs from the acceptance of the broad interpretation and taking into account that the violation of contractual obligations through governmental conduct is already covered by customary international law and other BIT standards, it has to

---

[108] *El Paso v. Argentina*, *supra* fn. 105, para. 8; *Pan American v. Argentina*, *supra* fn. 107, para. 109.

[109] *CMS Gas Transmission Co. v. Republic of Argentina*, ICSID Case No. ARB/01/8, Award, 12 May 2005, paras. 296–303.

[110] Id. paras. 301–303.

[111] Id. para. 299.

[112] Wälde, *supra* fn. 70, 183 et seq.

[113] As cited in Sinclair, *supra* fn. 12, 428.

[114] Tawil, *supra* fn. 82, 47.

be deemed somewhat minimalist. The mere reinforcement of an existing protection barely satisfies the need for an effective interpretation.[115] Hence, when umbrella clauses are intended to provide investors with further protection,[116] they should, as a matter of logic, include something more than only non-commercial acts. Otherwise foreign investors would be left without treaty protection when the State acts in an intolerable commercial manner.[117]

D. The Central Controversial Aspects

The discussion on the effect of the umbrella clause concerns a handful of similar aspects, namely, the wording of the clause, the object and purpose of the treaty, the consequences of the respective results, the location of the clause, and alternative functions of the clause. In the following, the arguments of both stances with regard to these aspects shall be analysed and evaluated.

I. *The Wording of the Clause*

1. *Narrow Interpretation*

The tribunal in *SGS v. Pakistan* shed a closer look on the wording of the treaty's umbrella clause at the outset of its survey.[118] Accordingly, the "commitments" the observance of which a contracting party is to "constantly guarantee" could not be limited to contractual commitments. A "commitment" in this sense could come from whatever legal source, be it municipal legislative, administrative, or other unilateral measures of a contracting party. The restriction on purely contractual commitments is by no means justified and cannot be deduced from the wording of article 11. Furthermore, the term to "constantly guarantee the observance" of a statutory, administrative or contractual commitment does not signal with sufficient clarity that the contracting party is accepting a new obligation under international law. The scarce wording of the

[115] Id., 50.
[116] Cf. Alexandrov, *supra* fn. 85, 566.
[117] Zolia, *supra* fn. 4, 35.
[118] Article 11 of the BIT reads as follows: "Either Contracting Party shall constantly guarantee the observance of commitments it has entered into with respect to the investments of the investors of the other Contracting Party."

clause "appears susceptible of almost indefinite expansion" and albeit the claimant would rely on such a far-reaching interpretation, the wording of the clause does not provide for such a meaning.[119]

In *El Paso* and *BP PanAmerican*, the tribunals' analysis of the wording is even scarcer. In fact, the examination of the clause by both tribunals does not contain an exact consideration of the clauses' wording. Nevertheless, the tribunals referred to the relevance of the clause's wording several times. Firstly, the tribunals affirm that they were not convinced that the different wordings are a sufficient basis to justify the degree of distinction existing between the delivered interpretations. As a sort of confirmation, they added that the umbrella clause in the BIT between Argentina and the United States[120] is phrased very broadly. Secondly, the tribunals emphasized the soundness of the requirement that the clause's wording must be as clear and unambiguous as demanded by the tribunal in *SGS v. Pakistan* in order to establish an elevating effect. However, similar to the *SGS-Pakistan* tribunal, they dispensed with giving an example of how a clear and unambiguous umbrella clause should be drafted. Seemingly the tribunals would require the use of the words "contract" or "contractual obligation" in the clause in order to establish a clear coverage of such commitments.[121] Finally, the tribunals denote that the umbrella clause does not differentiate among obligations and thus, beside contractual obligations, all further municipal law commitments likewise would have to be elevated.[122] Apparently, this "necessary implication" entails the tribunals to deny an elevating effect of the clause. In other words, the tribunals are to deny the limitations proposed by several tribunals in order to subsequently base their own rejection of a broad interpretation on the impossibility of an unlimited application of the clause.

---

[119] *SGS v. Pakistan, supra* fn. 6, para. 167.

[120] Article II(2)(c) states: "Each Party shall observe any obligation it may have entered into with regard to investments".

[121] *El Paso v. Argentina, supra* fn. 105, para. 74; *Pan American v. Argentina, supra* fn. 107, para. 103:

> This general reasoning [of the interpretation of the wording given by the tribunal in *SGS v. Pakistan* in which the tribunal stated that the clause was not a clear and persuasive evidence of the parties' intentions to cover state contracts] is quite convincing, keeping in mind that the words "contract" or "contractual obligation" do not even appear in the so-called umbrella clause.

[122] *El Paso v. Argentina, supra* fn. 105, paras. 77, 82; *Pan American v. Argentina, supra* fn. 107, paras. 106, 111.

2. *Broad Interpretation*

The tribunals which sustain a broad approach to the interpretation of the umbrella clause unanimously begin their analysis with an examination of the wording of the clause. The tribunal in *SGS v. Philippines* asserted that "shall" is mandatory and that the expression is used similarly in the substantive articles III to VI of the treaty. Further, the term "any obligation" is capable of being applied to obligations under national law, e.g., to contractual obligations. In the tribunal's view, the interpretation's result "that each Contracting Party shall observe any legal obligation it has assumed, or will in the future assume, with regard to specific investments covered by the BIT" is stated very clearly and therefore, is not subject to doubt.[123] Although the tribunal admitted that the umbrella clause of the Swiss—Pakistan BIT[124] was formulated differently, i.e., in a less clear and categorical way than the one of the Swiss-Philippines BIT, it seems not convinced that this difference ultimately justified the "highly restrictive interpretation" given by the *SGS v. Pakistan* tribunal.[125]

The partial award in *Eureko B. V. v. Poland* even went beyond the decision of the Philippines tribunal and asserted that "any obligation" does not mean only obligations of a certain type but all obligations entered into with regard to investments. According to the tribunal, this is the "ordinary meaning" of the phrase "shall observe any obligations it may have entered into". Whilst the phrase "shall observe" is imperative and categorical, "any obligations" is capacious to include all kinds of obligations whether contractual or unilateral. The tribunal denied the existence of any uncertainty in this interpretation, because the plain meaning is not "obscure".[126]

The magnitude of the obligations encompassed was further analysed by the tribunal in *Noble Ventures, Inc. v. Romania*. The affirmation that the term "obligations" does not refer to contractual obligations was thwarted by this tribunal at least insofar as the formulation contains

---

123 *SGS v. Philippines*, *supra* fn. 6, para. 115. This interpretation has been termed "aggressive" by Cheng, *supra* fn. 71, 473.

124 See *supra* fn. 118.

125 *SGS v. Philippines*, *supra* fn. 6, paras. 119–124.

126 *Eureko v. Poland*, *supra* fn. 95, para. 246. In this case, Eureko B.V., a Dutch company, purchased 20% of the shares of a public Polish insurance group which was to be privatized. According to Eureko's allegations, several breaches of the purchase agreement occurred during the agreement's implementation period. On account of this, the governance of the insurance group was left in a state of "total disarray".

the phrase "may have entered into". The facts that States usually conclude investment contracts with the foreign investor and that they do not conclude special international agreements with reference to specific investments in addition to the BITs, entails that the notion of "obligation" can hardly be seen as one referring to other international agreements. The States' practice combined with the meaning of "entered into" indicates that a referral to specific commitments has been made. As a corollary, the tribunal excludes general commitments such as legislative acts from the BIT's coverage through the umbrella clause. Furthermore, the tribunal was convinced that through the use of the term "shall", the article's intention is to create further obligations of the host State.[127]

Whilst all the tribunals of this category, i.e., supporting the elevating function of the umbrella clause, are consistent concerning the clarity of the respective clause's wording and the non-existence of any doubts as to their purpose to protect contractual commitments internationally, they differ on the importance of the clauses' exact wording. The tribunal in *Noble Ventures, Inc. v. Romania* specifically underlined the necessity of an exact formulation:

> Indeed, it is the differences in the wording of Article II (2) (c) of the BIT and of provisions in other bilateral investment treaties that have been relied on as umbrella clauses in other ICSID cases that go far to explain the different positions taken by different ICSID tribunals that have in recent times had to consider such clauses.[128]

It then continued to analyse briefly the previous decisions and arrived at the result that the different wordings were properly interpreted by the different tribunals.[129] Plainly, in *Salini v. Jordan* and *SGS v. Pakistan*, the wording of the alleged umbrella clause was not exact enough to produce elevating effects. By contrast, in *SGS v. Philippines*, the formulation could well be understood as elevating the host State's contractual obligations to treaty obligations.[130] The formulation in the present case is "even more general and straightforward" than the one in *SGS v. Philippines*. Consequently, it "clearly falls into the category of the most general and direct formulations tending to an assimilation of

[127] *Noble Ventures v. Romania*, *supra* fn. 58, para. 51.
[128] Id., para. 56.
[129] Id., paras. 57–59.
[130] Id., para. 59.

contractual obligations to treaty ones."[131] Accordingly, the tribunal's own view of the umbrella clause's interpretation is not contradictory to any of the other decisions.

Conversely, the degree of importance granted to the formulation of the clause by the tribunal in *Noble Ventures, Inc. v. Romania* is not shared by the majority of the other tribunals. As mentioned before, the tribunal in *SGS v. Philippines* recognizes the vaguer formulation of the umbrella clause in the Switzerland—Pakistan BIT compared to the one in the Switzerland—Philippines BIT. Its pointed discussion on the arguments put forward by the *SGS v. Pakistan* tribunal indicates that it did not regard as justified a narrow interpretation. The tribunal in *Eureko B. V. v. Poland* is more straightforward, explicitly dissenting with the decision rendered in *SGS v. Pakistan* and describing it as "unconvincing".[132] The point of view that the differences in the formulations are not the reason for the distinct interpretations is issued by other tribunals and several authors as well.[133] The tribunal in *El Paso v. Argentina* explicitly rejected the assertion that the clauses' different wordings trigger the need for different interpretations.[134]

A further cleavage among the tribunals can be conceived concerning their opinion about the magnitude of the obligations covered. The tribunal in *Eureko B. V. v. Poland* simply stated that every obligation of the host State with regard to investments in case of violation is turned into a violation of the treaty.[135] Albeit the use of the formulation "may have entered into" in article 3.5 of the US—Poland BIT the tribunal declined the exclusion of non-contractual obligations.[136] This, in turn, was done by the tribunal in *Noble Ventures, Inc. v. Romania*, according to which, the formulation "entered into" argues in favour of such a restriction. The tribunal in *SGS v. Philippines* reached the same conclusion based on the formulation of "obligations…assumed with regard to specific commitments". On account of this formulation, the legal obligation has to be assumed towards a specific investment. Thus,

---

[131] Id., para. 60.

[132] *Eureko v. Poland, supra* fn. 95, para. 256.

[133] See, e.g., Y. Shany, Contract Claims vs. Treaty Claims: Mapping Conflicts between ICSID Decisions on Multisourced Investment Claims, AJIL 99 (2005), 835, 848; Crawford, *supra* fn. 48, 18; Wälde, *supra* fn. 70, 224–225; Wong, *supra* fn. 85, 163.

[134] *El Paso v. Argentina, supra* fn. 105, para. 70; *Pan American v. Argentina, supra* fn. 107, para. 99.

[135] *Eureko v. Poland, supra* fn. 95, para. 246.

[136] Id., para. 250.

municipal legislative, administrative, or other unilateral measures of the host State are excluded.[137] Both tribunals also explicitly deny a limitation to obligations under international law[138] which is an argument regularly brought forward by host States to object to the international tribunal's jurisdiction.

The interpretative stance that sustains a broad approach to the umbrella clause is in itself not consistent. Non-conformity persists over the question whether minor differences in the wordings of the clause can change its elevating impact and over the extent of the obligations covered. However, all tribunals endorse the coverage of contractual commitments in their respective cases.

3. *Conclusion*

The narrow interpretation of the clause's wording is hardly in conformity with the requirements of the Vienna Convention on the Law of Treaties (hereafter, Vienna Convention). Neither is the failure to construe the plain meaning of the clause's terms at all. According to the convention, the plain meaning of the wording is the most important element of the interpretation of treaty stipulations.[139] A tribunal's task is to read a text faithfully and only correct it if the result is manifestly absurd. A tribunal shall not supplant a clear text expressing a clear intention of the treaty drafters.[140] The formulations "shall observe", "shall respect", or "shall guarantee the observance" refer quite clearly and straightforwardly to an obligation.[141] Although the term "commitments" or "obligations" may encompass other non-contractual forms of

[137] *SGS v. Philippines*, *supra* fn. 6, para. 120.

[138] Id., para. 118; *Noble Ventures v. Romania*, *supra* fn. 58, para. 51.

[139] A. Cassese, International Law (2005), 179; G. Wetzel & D. Rauschning, The Vienna Convention on the Law of Treaties (1978), 249. See also *Aguas del Tunari, S.A. v. Republic of Bolivia*, ICSID Case No. ARB/02/3, Decision on Jurisdiction, 21 October 2005, ICSID Rev.-FILJ 20 (2005), 450, para. 91: "[T]he Vienna Convention represents a move away from the canons of interpretation previously common in treaty interpretation and which erroneously persist in various international decisions today."; Gaffney & Loftis, *supra* fn. 85, 6: "These rules [i.e., the rules set out in the Vienna Convention on the Law of Treaties], when read together, provide what is in effect a single interpretative focus: determining the ordinary meaning of the text that gives effect to that agreement and to other, related instruments of the parties concerning the meaning of the text".

[140] Wälde, *supra* fn. 70, 224–225.

[141] Id., 225. Since Wälde discusses the *SGS v. Pakistan* decision, he refers exclusively to the phrase "shall constantly guarantee the observance". This phrase is deemed to leave more room for interpretation by other commentators. See, e.g., OECD, *supra* fn. 2, 11; Crawford, *supra* fn. 48, 18; von Walter, *supra* fn. 85, 822.

obligations, an administrative assurance or an assurance provided in general legislation or other instruments of investment protection, this cannot justify the exclusion of contractual commitments from being covered. The point of view of several legal commentators is that the express circumvention of the clause's plain meaning in *SGS v. Pakistan* can solely be explained by the tribunal's policy concerns.[142] Accordingly, the will to disguise its fear of a far-reaching "internationalisation" of state contracts induced the tribunal to engage in such a creative textual analysis.[143]

The existence of more specific formulations of umbrella clauses is sometimes held to oppose a broad interpretation.[144] For instance, the term "commitments entered into"[145] is widely regarded as referring to investment-related contracts between the investor and the host State. Contracts are the most formal and explicit form of "commitments entered into".[146] In some instances, the clause's formulation refers even expressly to contracts between the host State and an investor.[147] These formulations, so the argument goes, demonstrate that treaty drafters would and need to refer explicitly to contracts when they desired their protection. However, it seems odd to assert that "all" or "any" obligations would not cover contractual commitments whereas the adjunct "entered into" would lead to their coverage. The broad scope of the clause's wording is further fostered by the interpretation given to the last sentence of article 10(1) of the ECT.[148] The ECT, being a

[142] Cf. Gill et al., *supra* fn. 41, 405; Alexandrov, *supra* fn. 85, 570; Wälde, *supra* fn. 70, 219: "The Tribunal places itself here in the shoes and minds of the most radical NIEO advocates of the 1970's".

[143] Gill et al., *supra* fn. 41, 405; Gaffney & Loftis, *supra* fn. 85, 21.

[144] This argumentation is similarly applied to broadly phrased dispute resolution clauses. The argument does not become convincing in the context of umbrella clauses either.

[145] Article 9 of the Austria Model BIT, for instance, states: "(1) Each Contracting Party shall observe any obligation it may have entered into with regard to specific investments by investors of the other Contracting Party".

[146] Schreuer, *supra* fn. 75, 253.

[147] For instance, article 2 of the Austria—Chile BIT 1997 reads as follows: "(4) Each Contracting Party shall observe any contractual obligation it may have entered into towards an investor of the other Contracting Party with regard to investments approved by it in its territory".

[148] For an interpretation of the last sentence of article 1(1) of the ECT, see Paasivirta, *supra* fn. 45, 358 et seq., who, however, proposes two alternative interpretations: on the one hand, the wholesale protection of contracts; on the other hand, a less clear-cut "special protection" of investment contracts. Yet, as far as the principal coverage of the clause is concerned, the author makes clear that the term "obligations" covers contractual obligations.

multilateral investment treaty and bringing together over 50 countries plus the EU, must be regarded as an indicator of contemporary State practice.[149]

II. *The Implications of the Purpose of Investment Treaties*

1. *In Dubio Mitius*

Investment treaties are intended to create a safe environment for the investor and by doing so, promote foreign investment fostering the host State's economic development. This objective was often held to legitimize an interpretation favouring the investor.[150] By contrast, the tribunal in *SGS v. Pakistan*, basing its reasoning on the jurisprudence of other international adjudicative bodies,[151] admonished that the appropriate interpretative approach for clauses like article 11 of the BIT involved (i.e., the umbrella clause) is a prudential one summed up in the literature as *in dubio pars mitior est sequenca*.[152] In the tribunal's view, said article 11 has to be read in a manner that enhances mutuality and balance of benefits in the inter-relation of different agreements located in different legal orders.[153]

Schreuer argues that this application of a restrictive interpretation of the tribunal's competence is at odds with the practice of previous international tribunals.[154] Whereas the argument that the State's consent shall be construed restrictively was used several times by States in a bundle of litigations, in none of these cases did the respective tribunal accept such reasoning.[155] Furthermore, this principle pertains to the realm of traditional international law. Through the entry into force of

---

[149] Wälde, *supra* fn. 70, 219–220.

[150] Nonetheless, arbitral tribunals unexceptionally held their interpretation methods to be in conformity with the requirements set out in the Vienna convention. See C. Schreuer, Diversity and Harmonization of Treaty Interpretation in Investment Arbitration, TDM 3 (2006), No. 02, 1.

[151] The tribunal referred to *The Loewen Group, Inc. v. United States of America*, ICSID Case No. ARB(AF)/98/3, 26 June 2003, 7 ICSID Rep. 421, paras. 160–164.

[152] *SGS v. Pakistan*, *supra* fn. 86, para. 171. According to this interpretative approach, ambiguous provisions should be construed in a way that is least restrictive of a party's sovereignty.

[153] Id., para. 168.

[154] Schreuer, *supra* fn. 75, 254.

[155] Schreuer refers, inter alia, to *Amco Asia Corp. v. Republic of Indonesia*, ICSID Case No. ARB/81/1, Decision on Jurisdiction, 25 September 1983, 1 ICSID Rep. 377, paras. 394, 397, 398, 400, 402; *Ceskoslovenska Obchodni Banka A.S. (CSOB) v. Slovakia*, ICSID Case No. ARB/97/4, Award on Jurisdiction, 24 May 1999, 5 ICSID Rep. 330, para. 263.

the Vienna Convention, a more flexible and less power-dependent system was envisaged.[156]

The debate between the two vantage points has also been carried out by the tribunals in *El Paso* and *BP PanAmerican*. At the outset, the tribunals identified what they call "the standards of interpretation of a BIT". Accordingly, the standards applied through arbitral tribunals until the present can be divided into two approaches. On the one hand, the tribunals refer to the position adopted by the United States in the *Methanex* case where it contented that in disputes between States and private persons involving questions relating to a State's sovereignty, ambiguities should be resolved in favour of maintaining State sovereignty.[157] This statement is a further application of the maxim *in dubio mitius*, as put forward by the *SGS v. Pakistan* tribunal. However, both tribunals avoided stigmatising the decision in *SGS v. Pakistan* which upheld the restrictive interpretation approach. Instead, they described the reasoning of the *SGS v. Pakistan* tribunal as "convincing"[158] and "more than conclusive."[159] On the other hand, the tribunals invoked the *SGS v. Philippines* case and the *Noble Ventures, Inc. v. Romania* case as examples of the application of the broad approach which favours uniquely the foreign investor's situation. In the tribunals' point of view, this approach is mainly brought forward by investors, relying on the BITs' purpose of protecting and promoting investment.[160]

The tribunals themselves contend to apply a balanced interpretation. This means that they take into account both of the conflicting interests, that is, "state sovereignty and the state's responsibility to create an adapted and evolutionary framework for the development of economic activities" on the one hand and on the other, "the necessity to protect foreign investment and its continuing flow."[161] The question which has to be answered is whether the tribunals actually do apply this balanced

---

[156] Cassese, *supra* fn. 139, 178–179; A. Verdross & B. Simma, Universelles Völkerrecht (1984), 493–496.

[157] *El Paso v. Argentina*, *supra* fn. 105, para. 68; *Pan American v. Argentina*, *supra* fn. 107, para. 97.

[158] *El Paso v. Argentina*, *supra* fn. 105, para. 74; *Pan American v. Argentina*, *supra* fn. 107, para. 103.

[159] *El Paso v. Argentina*, *supra* fn. 105, para. 71; *Pan American v. Argentina*, *supra* fn. 107, para. 100.

[160] *El Paso v. Argentina*, *supra* fn. 105, para. 69; *Pan American v. Argentina*, *supra* fn. 107, para. 98.

[161] *El Paso v. Argentina*, *supra* fn. 105, para. 70; *Pan American v. Argentina*, *supra* fn. 107, para. 99.

interpretation or whether they merely pay lip service to it. As will be shown below, the latter is more probable. Further, the tribunals state that as a rule of international law, exceptions have to be interpreted restrictively and that the umbrella clause constitutes an exception to the general rule that contract breaches are not per se breaches of treaty.[162] In this statement, one can already discern a somewhat narrow attitude of the tribunals instead of a balanced approach.

2. *Effective Interpretation*

The tribunals that endorse a broad interpretation of the umbrella clause usually emphasize that the BIT is a treaty for the promotion and reciprocal protection of investments. A similar statement can regularly be found in the preambles or the titles of investment treaties. Further, mention is made of the *effet utile* principle: an interpretation that renders the construed stipulation effective rather than one that renders it ineffective is preferred. Both approaches entail an interpretation that favours exclusively the investor.[163] As the tribunal in *Noble Ventures, Inc. v. Romania* stated: "An interpretation to the contrary would deprive the investor of any internationally secured legal remedy in respect of investment contracts that it has entered into with the host state". Moreover, the clause would be deprived of any practical applicability if it were not interpreted this way.[164] This interpretation may well be contrary to the rule of international law which establishes that under normal circumstances a breach of contract by the State does not per se give rise to its direct international responsibility. This principle, however, is not peremptory in nature. Two negotiating States are perfectly able to abrogate it through the inclusion of a clause such as the umbrella clause in a BIT. Nevertheless, according to interpretation rules of customary international law, the terms of an exception to a general rule must clearly show the parties' intention to create an exception.[165] In this

---

[162] *El Paso v. Argentina, supra* fn. 105, para. 77; *Pan American v. Argentina, supra* fn. 107, para. 106.

[163] *SGS v. Philippines, supra* fn. 6, para. 116; *Eureko v. Poland, supra* fn. 95, para. 248. This is the logical consequence of a treaty which is intended to provide protection to investments.

[164] *Noble Ventures v. Romania, supra* fn. 58, para. 52.

[165] In order to corroborate this point of view, the tribunal cited the case of *Elettronica Sicula Spa (ELSI)* (United States v. Italy) [1989] ICJ Rep. 14, 42, where the ICJ emphasized that "[a]n important principle of international law should not be held to have been tacitly dispensed with by international agreement, in the absence of words making clear intention to do so". Id., para. 55.

context, the importance of the wording, again, comes into play. The wording of article II(2)(c) in the Romania—US BIT has been formulated in such an exact manner that the existence of the intention to establish an exception can be drawn out of it. In other words, the wording of the clause is the key element which permits the assumption of the umbrella clause's broad function in the present BIT.[166]

This approach explicitly rejects the contrary position that was upheld in *SGS v. Pakistan*. The maxim *in dubio mitius* according to which sovereign rights presumably override the rights of foreign investors accordingly can be seen as "a reversion to a doctrine that has been displaced by contemporary international law".[167] Moreover, as already mentioned by Wälde, where the wording of the umbrella clause is clear (as explained above, the wording is clear in most of the cases) there is no interpretative doubt and therefore no room for the application of the *in dubio mitius* maxim. Again, the ideological clash between the two distinct views of international law's nature comes into play: One side tries to enlarge the scope of the treaty's application through the principle of effectiveness while the other side attempts to restrict it by emphasizing the State's sovereignty.

In fact, the principle of effective interpretation is a cornerstone of the argumentation that sustains a wide approach. The tribunals that reject a broad interpretation usually have difficulties in identifying another reasonable function of the clause. The impression that they deny the unlimited coverage of state contracts as a matter of principle gives their following search for a sound meaning of the clause a somewhat arbitrary element. According to Foster this is the key problem for the tribunals that contend a narrow approach.[168] The principle of effectiveness however requires that treaties and their clauses are to be interpreted so as to render them effective rather than ineffective. In other words, the umbrella clause must be interpreted to mean something itself.[169] In the point of view of the *SGS v. Philippines* tribunal, the decision in *SGS v. Pakistan* failed to give a clear meaning to the umbrella clause.[170] As will be seen below, construing the effect of the clause as "an applied affirmative commitment" lacks sense.

---

[166] Id., para. 56.
[167] *Eureko v. Poland, supra* fn. 95, para. 258.
[168] Foster, *supra* fn. 73, 100. See also Gaffney & Loftis, *supra* fn. 85, 22.
[169] *Eureko v. Poland, supra* fn. 95, para. 249.
[170] *SGS v. Philippines, supra* fn. 6, para. 125.

III. *The Consequences of a Broad Interpretation*

1. *The Narrow Approach*

The *SGS v. Pakistan* tribunal's principal concern seems to be the fear of "opening the floodgates".[171] In its view, the legal consequences of an "instant transubstantiation of contract claims into BIT claims"[172] would be "so burdensome in their potential impact upon a Contracting Party"[173] that the balance of benefits between State and investor would be broken down. In order to strengthen its argumentation, the tribunal delineated the consequences to which the claimant's interpretation of the clause would lead. These are mainly three: Firstly, any violation of an unlimited number of state contracts as well as other municipal law instruments setting out state commitments would have to be treated as a breach of the BIT. Secondly, in such a case, the articles 3 to 7[174] of the BIT, constituting its substantive obligations, would become superfluous. When every simple breach of a contractual obligation or any other kind of obligation amounts to a treaty violation, generally, there would be no need to demonstrate a violation of those substantive treaty standards. Finally, a corollary of the claimant's interpretation would be the creation of an imbalance of benefits in the investor—State relation. The investor would always be able to thwart the State's invocation of the contractually specified forum, being free to go to arbitration either under the contract or under the BIT. This could entail the serious risk of "cherry picking"[175] by the investor. Whereas an investor could "permit" the validity of some contractual clauses, others (such as a contractual dispute resolution clause) could be ignored.[176]

---

[171] For this term, see Wälde, *supra* fn. 70, 215.

[172] *SGS v. Pakistan*, *supra* fn. 6, para. 172.

[173] Id., para. 167.

[174] These articles regulate the following aspects of an investment: article 3 on promotion and admission of investments in accordance with the laws and regulations of the contracting party; article 4 on prohibition on impairment by "unreasonable or discriminating measures" and of the management, use, enjoyment of such investments and according "fair and equitable treatment" to investors of the other contracting party; article 5 on free cross-border transfer of payments relating to the protected investments; article 6 on prohibition of expropriation or other measures having the same nature or effect unless taken in the public interest on a non-discriminatory basis, under due process of law, and with provision for effective, adequate, and prompt compensation; and article 7 on most favoured investor protection.

[175] Gill et al., *supra* fn. 41, 405.

[176] *SGS v. Pakistan*, *supra* fn. 6, para. 168.

In the same vein, the tribunals in *El Paso* and *BP PanAmerican* held that the fact that a host State could be blamed for the violation of any legal obligation would not only blur the division between international law and the domestic law completely[177] but would also render the whole treaty useless. Compared to the *SGS v. Pakistan* decision, the latter concern is further corroborated. According to the tribunals, in case the broad interpretation is legitimated, a BIT could be drafted by solely including an umbrella clause and a dispute resolution clause.[178]

Besides, the tribunals criticize the inadequacy of the burden that such an interpretation would impose on the host State:

> It would be strange indeed if the acceptance of a BIT entailed an international liability of the State going far beyond the obligation to respect the standards of protection of foreign investments embodied in the Treaty and rendered it liable for any violation of any commitment in national or international law "with regard to investments".

The corollary of such liability is that the foreign investor is entitled to lodge claims even for minor disagreements on details of contractual performances.[179] This offer of "unexpected remedies" is not acceptable to those tribunals which, contrary to Schreuer, are convinced that the investors will not use appropriate restraint. On account of this, the restraint of the investors has to be provided by the arbitral tribunals themselves.[180]

The decision in *Eureko B. V. v. Poland* was accompanied by a strong dissent by Polish co-arbitrator Rajiski who argued similarly against an inclusion of commercial disputes. Among several aspects which he criticized, one was that the dispute between Eureko and the Government of Poland arose out of a commercial contract and therefore, was of a purely commercial and contractual nature.[181] For this reason, he could

[177] *El Paso v. Argentina*, *supra* fn. 105, para. 77; *Pan American v. Argentina*, *supra* fn. 107, para. 106.

[178] *El Paso v. Argentina*, *supra* fn. 105, para. 76; *Pan American v. Argentina*, *supra* fn. 107, para. 105.

[179] The tribunals cites Schreuer, *supra* fn. 75, 255, who supports a broad interpretation of the clause but hopes that "investors will invoke the umbrella clause with appropriate restraint". *El Paso v. Argentina*, *supra* fn. 105, para. 82; *Pan American v. Argentina*, *supra* fn. 107, 111.

[180] *El Paso v. Argentina*, *supra* fn. 105, id.; *Pan American v. Argentina*, *supra* fn. 107, id.

[181] *Eureko v. Poland*, *supra* fn. 95, Dissenting Opinion of Professor Jerzy Rajski, para. 1.

not find any ground which entitled Eureko to protection under the treaty.[182] Moreover, he contended that

> by opening a wide door to foreign parties to commercial contracts concluded with a State owned company to switch their contractual disputes from normal jurisdiction of international commercial arbitration tribunals or state courts to BIT Tribunals, the majority of this Tribunal has created a potentially dangerous precedent capable of producing negative effects on the further development of foreign capital participation in privatisations of State owned companies.

Further, he admonished that the decision "may lead to create a privileged class of foreign parties to commercial contracts who may easily transform their contractual disputes...into BIT disputes". Thereby, the fundamental principles upon which national and international laws on contract have been based, such as equal legal protection of all parties to commercial contracts irrespective of their nationality, will be undermined.[183]

Furthermore, the burden of proof is at stake. The far-reaching consequences of the clause's elevating effect and the "widely accepted principle" of international law that the breach of a state contract by a State is not, by itself, a violation of international law induced the *SGS v. Pakistan* tribunal to allocate the burden of proof for the effect of the clause on the claimant. It is up to him to submit clear and convincing evidence of the contracting parties' intention to introduce a clause with such far-reaching consequences in the BIT. Such evidence, according to the tribunal, was neither provided by the text of Article 11 of the BIT itself nor by the claimant's presentations before the tribunal.[184]

This argumentation is repeated in the tribunal's conclusion. Therein, the tribunal clarified that it does not generally deny the possibility of introducing in a BIT a clause the effect of which is to elevate all contractual violations to treaty violations. It rather requires that the States which conclude a treaty have to make their intention of introducing such a clause evident. Further, the claimant that relies upon such interpretation of a treaty clause has to provide the tribunal with sufficient proof of the parties' intention to do so. In the case at issue, Pakistan clearly denied that it had any such intentions. SGS, on its turn, was

---

182 Id., para. 10.
183 Id., para. 11.
184 *SGS v. Pakistan*, *supra* fn. 6, para. 167.

unable to provide the required evidence to convince the tribunal of its view.[185]

The requirement that the claimant prove the far-reaching meaning of the clause is a reversion of the normal way the burden of proof is regulated. Normally, when the plain meaning is clear, the party disagreeing with the plain meaning has the burden to persuade the tribunal that the proper meaning is different from the apparent meaning. Here, the tribunal shifted back the burden of proof onto the claimant. It required proof that the parties intended what they said in plain meaning. Further, such proof generally cannot be given. In the case of BITs, the negotiators tend to use existing models in a boilerplate fashion. It is illogical to refuse to give effect to such language by requiring in each instance and for each legal instrument using such language adopted from other models evidence that the parties have explicitly discussed the respective clause. Such requirement seems to be appropriate in modern consumer protection law where laymen have to be protected but not when highly specialized negotiators representing their States adopt the language of a well-known clause. If such requirement is made, a tribunal would have to look at the negotiation of multilateral investment treaties, like the ECT, where the process of negotiating is much more complex and usually better documented.[186] Moreover, the widespread practice of States concerning the umbrella clause can serve as proof. The existence of a frequent contemporary practice to include such clauses into BITs would have obliged a tribunal to refer to and respect the intention of hundreds of drafters and negotiators.[187]

2. *The Middle Approach*

According to Wälde, an entire elevation of contractual commitments is hardly sustainable. In his view, a limitation of the broad interpretation has to be undertaken through the adoption of the clause's effect to contemporary BIT practice. In other words, the situation of international investment protection at the time of the umbrella clause's emergence is compared to the actual state of development in order to examine whether the original purposes of the clause's enactment are still pertinent. Mainly, four aspects of international investment law would

[185] Id., para. 173.
[186] Wälde, *supra* fn. 70, 219–220.
[187] Id., 220.

indicate that the conditions of foreign investor's protection have changed fundamentally and that a prolongation of the clause's effect upon commercial transactions of the States is by no means justified. Firstly, mention has to be made of the notion of investment. Whilst in the 1950s and 1960s only the traditional foreign direct investment was deemed worthy of protection on the international plane, the constant broadening of the notion of foreign investment has led to a different situation at present. Today, "all assets" approaches are increasingly being applied in BITs,[188] and the investment protected thus moved from the mere inclusion of long and substantial commitment of capital, ownership, and control of assets in the host State's sensitive areas towards a more flexible coverage, including sales or service contracts which are merely of a commercial nature.[189] Secondly, the measures against which international investment law were intended to protect were mainly expropriations of governmental nature. The umbrella clause accordingly never focussed on commercial breaches of a contract but always on a governmental abrogation of contractual rights.[190] Thirdly, the change in the dispute settlement's nature has to be taken into account. Until the entry into force of the ICSID Convention in 1966, the resolution of international investment disputes through an adjudicative body took place exclusively on a State-to-State basis. Fourthly, for decades, the introduction of a mixed arbitration system where individuals can lodge claims directly against foreign States was inconceivable. Nowadays, by contrast, the system of mixed arbitration is a well established feature of international investment protection. However, whilst the foreign investors gained a powerful tool, at the same time, the filtering function by way of required home State sponsorship of claims disappeared.[191] Consequently, the present system offers unexpected opportunities for unsatisfied or commercially disappointed investors to obtain redress from host States.[192] Finally, majority

[188] See, e.g., N. Rubins, The Notion of Investment in International Investment Arbitration, in: N. Horn (ed.), Arbitrating Foreign Investment Disputes (2004), 283, 323 et seq.

[189] Wälde, *supra* fn. 70, 193.

[190] Id.

[191] Id., 194.

[192] For critics of this effect of chapter 11 of the NAFTA on environmental regulations, see L. Dhooge, The North American Free Trade Agreement and the Environment: The Lessons of Metalclad Corporation v. United States of Mexico, Minn. J. Glob. Trade 10 (2001), 209, 213–214.

of the contracts between investors and States are not restricted to sensitive public policy areas anymore but cover a wide range of issues, including contracts for supplies of services or loan agreements.[193]

From these developments that changed the countenance of international investment law, Wälde deduced the following with regard to the appropriate interpretation of the umbrella clause: international investment protection was never meant to address mere commercial behaviour of States. It was also not the intention of the umbrella clause to elevate pure commercial obligations into the realm of treaty protection. Therefore, a clear differentiation has to be made concerning the nature of the breach committed by the host State: when the centre of the dispute concerns merely commercial aspects, the umbrella clause has no function. By contrast, an elevation of contractual breaches through the umbrella clause takes place when the core of the dispute is about the exercise of governmental powers or reliance on governmental prerogatives.[194]

In sum, there are three requirements that restrain the clause's function: First, the contract has to be of a governmental nature.[195] Secondly, the contract must have a relevant function in the contractual regime set up for an investment, or in other words, it has to relate to an investment as defined by the BIT.[196] Finally, there is no protection of the contract against legitimate, general, and non-targeted governmental regulation which happens to affect the context of the contract.[197]

3. *The Broad Approach*

From the vantage point of the detractors of a narrow interpretation, the fear of "opening the floodgates" is not reasonable.[198] Some authors assert that neither of the parties has the interest to encroach upon the complex foreign investor—host State relationship on account of trivial contractual disputes. Given the costs and the risks of proceedings before an international arbitral tribunal[199] and given the economic

---

[193] UNCTAD, International Investment Agreements Issues Paper Series, State Contracts (2004), 10.

[194] Wälde, *supra* fn. 70, 235.

[195] Id., 224–225.

[196] See also Schreuer, *supra* fn. 75, 253.

[197] Wälde, *supra* fn. 70, 225.

[198] E.g., Schramke, *supra* fn. 85, 258; Tawil, *supra* fn. 82, 51–52; Gaffney & Loftis, *supra* fn. 85, 21.

[199] Schramke, *supra* fn. 85, 258.

interest which investors have in maintaining cordial relations with their partners,[200] one has to state that the fear that investors would lodge claims by reason of minimal contractual breaches is rather negligible. However, this school of thought is not unaware of the consequences. In its view, the broad application of the umbrella clause requires the resolution of two fundamental problems: First, the conceptual distinction between municipal and international law has to be clarified. Second, one has to examine whether all further provisions of a BIT are rendered superfluous by an all-embracing umbrella clause.

The subject matter of international investment arbitration, in the view of some authors, is supposed to be exclusively a regulatory dispute arising between the State acting in a public capacity and a private person who is subject to the exercise of public authority by the State.[201] The ICSID Convention, however, unarguably states in its article 25 that ICSID jurisdiction may extend to disputes of a purely contractual character.[202] For this reason, the tribunal in *SGS v. Philippines* seemed not concerned that the expansion of the umbrella clause is too far-reaching. The establishment of a limitation through the fact that the host State is required to assume the obligation directly towards a specific investment was sufficient for the tribunal.[203] Further, the tribunal rejected the effect of "instant transubstantiation" as brought forward by the *SGS v. Pakistan* tribunal.[204] The clause neither determines the extent of obligations nor does it change the proper law of the contract. "Article X (2) addresses not the scope of the commitments entered into with regard to specific investments but the performance of these obligations, once they are ascertained."[205] In other words, the determination of the

---

[200] On the interest structure, see generally K. Meesen, International Investment and Dispute Settlement, in: D. Friedmann & E. J. Mestmäcker (eds.), Conflict Resolution in International Trade (1993), 111, 111–113. See also E. Schanze, Investitionsverträge im Internationalen Wirtschaftsrecht (1986), 42–49.

[201] See, e.g., G. van Harten & M. Loughlin, Investment Treaty Arbitration as a Species of Global Administrative Law, EJIL 17 (2006), 121, 148 et seq.; S. Franck, The Nature and Enforcement of Investor Rights under Investment Treaties: Do Investment Treaties Have a Bright Future?, U.C. Davis J. Int'l L. & Pol'y (2005), 47, 70 et seq.

[202] C. Schreuer, The ICSID Convention—A Commentary (2001), 127–134.

[203] *SGS v. Philippines*, *supra* fn. 6, para. 121. On the specific requirements which have to be fulfilled in this regard, see also Gaffney & Loftis, *supra* fn. 85, 21. Accordingly, the requirements of "investment", "investor", and that the State must be a counter-party to the contract are sufficient restraints.

[204] *SGS v. Pakistan*, *supra* fn. 6, para. 172.

[205] *SGS v. Philippines*, *supra* fn. 6, para. 126.

obligation's extent belongs to internal law whilst only the violation of the obligation is internationalised.

On the one hand, this argumentation is accurate: the unlimited application of the clause to whatever kind of obligation is denied, and the effect of the clause is adjusted adequately in accordance with the clause's wording. On the other hand, the argumentation remains somewhat unsatisfactory as it concerns the dilution of the differences between domestic and international law. The fact that the jurisdiction under the ICSID Convention may extend to disputes of a purely commercial character is a double edged argument. Whereas it signals that ICSID tribunals are by all means capable of sitting over domestic disputes, it does not answer the question whether consent to such arbitration is given through investment treaties, namely, through an umbrella clause. In other words, the mere possibility to give consent to arbitration over commercial disputes does not substantiate that such consent actually has been given. In fact, traditionally, consent to arbitration under the ICSID Convention had been given by contract[206] and thus, logically concerned contractual disputes. However, the crucial question is whether consent regarding commercial matters has been given by the contracting parties in the respective investment treaty.

It is true that most of the authors who sustain a broad approach do not comment on the convergence between the spheres of domestic and international law which is effectuated through such an interpretation. Nonetheless, it is a fact that, as far as the effect of contracts are concerned, an umbrella clause assimilates domestic law contracts and international treaties[207] and thereby, international law and domestic law become barely distinguishable. However, several arguments can be put forward to lessen the importance which the traditional distinction between both spheres of law entails.

The relationship between municipal law and international law has never been a clear-cut one and the theoretical clash between dualism and monism was never reconciled.[208] Throughout the past decades, however, the development of international investment law tended to

[206] See, e.g., I. Shihata & A. Parra, The Experience of the International Centre for Settlement of Investment Disputes, ICSID Rev.-FILJ 14 (1999), 299, 358–359 et seq.

[207] Cf. Orrego Vicuña, *supra* fn. 11, 352–353.

[208] I. Brownlie, Principles of Public International Law (2003), 31–33; M. Shaw, International Law (2003), 121–124; P. Kunig, Völkerrecht und staatliches Recht, in: W. Graf Vitzthum (ed.), Völkerrecht, 81, 98.

erase existing distinguishing features. Based on this evolution, commentators and arbitrators apply a pragmatic approach to the coverage of domestic subject matters through treaty-based arbitration. The dogmatic differences are not to be emphasized but an integrative solution which guarantees an effective and neutral proceeding to the parties.[209] Hence, the stare tenet according to which treaty-based investment arbitration may only deal with States' actions carrying out sovereign function is contradicted. The distinction between a treaty violation under international law and a breach of contract under domestic law is not a peremptory norm of international law and may be altered through the parties' will.[210] The umbrella clause is such an alteration. It is an exceptional provision which, like other provisions of international treaties, alters the traditional rules of classic international law. This exceptional function corresponds to an effective interpretation of the clause's wording.[211] Furthermore, the umbrella clause entails no unlimited convergence between both spheres. Still, the *ratione materiae* of investment treaties is contingent upon their respective investment notion. Thereby, cases which are based on mere commercial transactions are regularly foreclosed. Finally, the boundaries between *jure imperii* acts and actions *jure gestionis* are getting increasingly vague. As Orrego Vicuña puts it:

> [A]dministrative functions of the state, earlier considered as the essence of *jure imperii* and sovereignty, if affecting the rights of individuals can be considered today to engage contractual commitments that the state is bound to observe and which largely fall within the ambit of *jure gestionis*.[212]

In fact, the true rationale underlying this reasoning is the objective to further the rule of law and the observance of legal commitments in the international community irrespective of traditional restraints concerning international law.

---

[209] For this approach, see Shany, *supra* fn. 133, 836.

[210] On peremptory norms of international law, see Shaw, *supra* fn. 208, 115 et seq.; Verdross & Simma, *supra* fn. 156, 328 et seq.; Cassese, *supra* fn. 139, 205 et seq.

[211] Crawford, *supra* fn. 48, 20; Gaffney & Lofits, *supra* fn. 85, 19 et seq.; Kunoy, *supra* fn. 85, 299; Foster, *supra* fn. 86, 19; Zolia, *supra* fn. 4, 35; *Noble Ventures v. Romania*, *supra* fn. 58, para. 55: "Thus, an umbrella clause, when included in a bilateral investment treaty, introduces an exception to the general separation of States' obligations under municipal and international law".

[212] Orrego Vicuña, *supra* fn. 11, 356–357.

The concern that the broad interpretation of the umbrella clause according to which every non-performance of a host State's legal obligation is turned into a treaty violation is one of the major arguments put forward against a broad application. Whilst the tribunal in *SGS v. Pakistan* asserted that the substantive provisions of the BIT became superfluous by reason of the umbrella clause,[213] the *El Paso* tribunal went a step further contending that this interpretation not only deprived one single provision of the BIT of its content, but rendered the whole treaty completely useless.[214] As already mentioned, this concern is rejected unanimously by legal scholars.[215] Without the BIT providing for certain standards and thereby creating legal obligations distinct from the ones under internal law and under the contract, the investor would be deprived of protection to a considerable extent. It is a fact that several substantive provisions of investment treaties create obligations for the host State which otherwise would not exist.[216] Hence, a broad interpretation of the umbrella clause does not render superfluous other substantive investment treaty provisions.[217]

IV. *The Location of the Clause*

On several occasions, the importance of the location of the clause in the treaty has been analysed. According to the tribunal in *SGS v. Pakistan*, the placement of the umbrella clause behind the provisions of the substantive obligations and its division from them through the "Principle of Subrogation" in article 8 and the two dispute settlement procedures set out in the BIT by articles 9 and 10 make it difficult to assess the clause to be a substantive obligation. Conversely, the tribunal emphasized that this location even indicated that article 11 was not meant to create a substantive obligation like those in articles 3 to 7.

---

213 *SGS v. Pakistan*, *supra* fn. 6, para. 168.

214 *El Paso v. Argentina*, *supra* fn. 105, para. 76; *Pan American v. Argentina*, *supra* fn. 107, para. 105.

215 Schreuer, *supra* fn. 75, 253; Wong, *supra* fn. 85, 164.

216 In addition to an umbrella clause, investment treaties provide for a variety of different standards such as non-discrimination, non-expropriation, and accordance of fair and equitable treatment. For the coverage of contracts by these standards, see chapter 3. Furthermore, investment treaties set out obligations such as transfer permissions; prohibition of performance requirements; and regulation of transparency, environmental, and labour issues. It is hardly tenable that the obligation to observe contractual commitment would embrace all these regulations.

217 *Eureko v. Poland*, *supra* fn. 95, para. 258.

If the parties to the BIT intended to create a "first order" standard obligation, they would have placed the umbrella clause among the substantive obligations in articles 3 to 7.[218]

By contrast, the tribunals that represent a broad approach to the interpretation of the umbrella clause do not pay too much attention to the location of the clause in the respective BIT. The *SGS v. Philippines* tribunal stated that it did not regard the location of the provision as decisive. Moreover, it would indeed be strange if the clause's legal impact were altered so drastically just because of its placement in the BIT.[219] Whilst the *Noble Ventures* tribunal did not make any reference to the clause's location in the BIT, the tribunal in *Eureko v. Poland* only noted that the clause in the Netherlands—Poland BIT is placed between the substantive obligations, adding that this is of little significance for the tribunal's view.[220]

Notwithstanding the general recognition of the validity of the structure's examination and its importance for the interpretation of a clause,[221] the conclusion drawn by the tribunal in *SGS v. Pakistan* is not very plausible when applied in a general manner. In most of the BITs, the umbrella clause is drafted among the substantive obligations of the treaty. In these cases, the tribunal's reasoning would point towards the existence of an elevating effect of the clause which was hardly the intention of the tribunal in *SGS v. Pakistan*.[222] This tribunal overestimated the value of the enumeration order. Treaty drafters tend to copy clauses from various models and subsequently put them together. Moreover, the location of the clause in the Switzerland—Pakistan BIT can well be understood as giving more importance to the clause, wanting to highlight the importance of the clause as an overarching obligation.[223] If the drafters wanted to give the clause a secondary role, they could have achieved that in a more expressive way as is done, for instance, in article 6 or 19 of the ECT.[224]

---

218 *SGS v. Pakistan*, *supra* fn. 6, para. 170.

219 *SGS v. Philippines*, *supra* fn. 6, para. 124.

220 *Eureko v.Poland*, *supra* fn. 95, para. 259.

221 Schreuer, *supra* fn. 75, 253.

222 Id.

223 In fact, it is difficult to infer any concrete significance from the clause's location in the absence of a pre-existing methodology.

224 Wälde, *supra* fn. 70, 223.

V. *Alternative Functions of the Clause*

The inability to allocate an adequate function to the clause is probably the main flaw of the narrow interpretations of the umbrella clause. In order to rebut the claimant's argument that the clause, without the function to elevate contract breaches to the international sphere, would be deprived of any normative sense, the tribunal in *SGS v. Pakistan* developed two aspects in which the clause could be of use. In the first place the clause could be regarded as a confirmation that signals an "implied affirmative commitment to enact implementing rules and regulations necessary or appropriate to give effect to a contractual or statutory undertaking in favour of investors of another Contracting Party that would otherwise be dead letter". Secondly, the tribunal admitted the possibility that contract breaches may amount to treaty violations and that in such a case, the contracting party may be regarded as having failed to observe the obligations deriving from article 11. However, it limited this possibility to the violation of contractual arbitration clauses.[225]

Both alternatives entail a high degree of uncertainty regarding their meaning and their requirements. According to Wälde, the former proposal has the potential of an enormous intrusion into domestic law, comparable with EU directives. The host State could be obliged to enact national legislation that provides sufficient protection for the investments undertaken. Whether non-implementation or insufficient implementation would enable the individual to claim for damages is not clear either. Moreover, if the establishment of such a far-reaching

---

[225] *SGS v. Pakistan*, *supra* fn. 6, para. 172:

Secondly, we do not exclude the possibility that under exceptional circumstances, a violation of certain provisions of a State contract with an investor of another State might constitute violation of a treaty provision (like Article 11 of the BIT) enjoining a Contracting Party constantly to guarantee the observance of contracts with an investor of another Contracting Party. For instance, if a Contracting Party were to take action that materially impedes the ability of an investor to prosecute its claims before an international arbitration tribunal (having previously agreed to such arbitration in a contract with the investor), or were to refuse to go to such arbitration at all and leave the investor only the option of going before the ordinary courts of the Contracting Party (which actions need not amount to "denial of justice"), that Contracting Party may arguably be regarded as having failed "constantly [to] guarantee the observance of [its] commitments" within the meaning of Article 11 of the Swiss-Pakistan BIT.

obligation was really the objective of the treaty drafters, they could have expressed it much more directly and explicitly as is done, for instance, in the OECD anti-bribery convention.[226]

Through the second proposal, the effect of the umbrella clause is reduced to certain types of clauses, namely, contractual dispute resolution clauses. The reason for such restriction remains nebulous. The wording of the clause does not point to the exclusion of other kinds of commitments by the host State. Nor do other elements of treaty interpretation. The limitation of the recognition of the clause's elevating effect solely to specific stipulations of the contract contradicts the judgment that the *SGS v. Pakistan* tribunal upheld and gives the impression of considerable arbitrariness on the part of the tribunal in selecting the clauses which ultimately may be elevated.[227]

The tribunals in *El Paso* and *BP PanAmerican* used the first part of their examination of the clause to reject its broad elevating effect, and in the second part, they ventured to determine a further meaning of the clause. Therein, they focused especially on the distinction between the State as a merchant and the State as a sovereign. This distinction, which likewise has been applied in *Joy Mining v. Egypt* and the annulment decision in the *Vivendi* case, is predicated on the reasoning that international investment protection serves to provide the investor protection from the State acting as a sovereign and not from the State acting as a merchant.[228] In order to foster this vantage point, the tribunals pointed to the dispute resolution clause of the new 2004 US Model BIT[229] which covers contracts only in the case of their conclusion directly with the State as a sovereign.[230] The necessity to undertake such

---

[226] Wälde, *supra* fn. 70, 221. Article 1 of the OECD, Convention on Combating Bribery of Foreign Public Officials in International Business Transactions (1997), available at: www.oecd.org, reads as follows: "1. Each Party shall take such measures as may be necessary to establish that it is a criminal offence under its law for any person intentionally to offer, promise or give any undue pecuniary or other advantage".

[227] Wälde, *supra* fn. 70, 221–222.

[228] *El Paso v. Argentina*, *supra* fn. 105, para. 79; *Pan American v. Argentina*, *supra* fn. 107, 108.

[229] Article 24(1)(a)(C) of the 2004 US Model BIT reads as follows: "(a) the claimant, on its own behalf, may submit to arbitration under this Section [which provides for ICSID arbitration] a claim that the respondent has breached (C) an investment agreement." A definition of "Investment agreement" can be found in article 1 where the following is stated: "'investment agreement' means a written agreement … (a) with respect to natural resources or other assets that a national authority controls; and (b) upon which the covered investment or the investor relies in establishing or acquiring a covered investment other than the written agreement itself".

[230] *El Paso v. Argentina*, *supra* fn. 105, para. 80.

distinction demands an interpretation of the umbrella clause in the light of the treaty's dispute resolution clause. In the present US—Argentina BIT,[231] the dispute resolution clause defines the notion of "investment disputes" as including disputes resulting from a violation of a commitment given by the State as a sovereign.[232]

It remains unclear whether the tribunals condone a BITs' coverage of every single provision of contracts that involve the State as a sovereign or whether only specific clauses of such a contract are protected. The failure of the *Pan American* tribunal to give clear guidelines may be an indication of the arbitrators' own uncertainty regarding the clause's effect. In any event, the lack of clear guidelines gives the impression of a certain arbitrariness in the tribunals' proposals. This impression increases when one bears in mind that the tribunals, at the end of their examinations, underlined their support for the *SGS v. Pakistan* decision which only accepted the clause's application to contractual dispute resolution clauses. The tribunals dissent with an elevation of contractual contents "unless some requirements are respected" but they neglected to provide clear standards on how to determine these requirements.

E. Resolution of Central Aspects

After having examined the jurisprudence and their respective critics and supporters, the most pertinent questions concerning the effect of the umbrella clause shall be restated and a solution, taking into account

[231] Article VII of the BIT states:

> [A]n investment dispute is a dispute between a Party and a national or a company of the other Party arising out of or relating to (a) an investment agreement between the Party and such national or company; (b) an investment authorization granted by that Party's foreign investment authority (if any such authorization exists); or, (c) an alleged breach of any right conferred and created by this Treaty with respect to an investment.

[232] It is interesting to note that one of the minor differences between the two decisions exists precisely in this regard. The tribunal in *El Paso v. Argentina*, *supra* fn. 105, para. 81, states the following:

> Interpreted in this way, the umbrella clause … will not extend the Treaty protection to breaches of an ordinary commercial contract entered into by the State or a State-owned entity, but will cover additional investment protections contractually agreed by the State as a sovereign -such as a stabilization clause- inserted in an investment agreement.

The tribunal in *Pan American v. Argentina*, *supra* fn. 107, para. 109, omits the example of the stabilization clauses.

the arguments exposed above, shall be proposed. In the author's point of view, the three most essential questions which remain unsolved with regard to the effect of the umbrella clause are (1) whether there exists a certain threshold of elevation, (2) what kind of elevation is produced, and (3) what legal character must the entity of the State which is the contractual partner have so that the investor may obtain a treaty protection of contractual violations?

I. *Threshold of Elevation*

It cannot be disputed that an umbrella clause turns certain non-treaty violations into treaty violations.[233] However, the relevant questions that remain unanswered are whether there exists a threshold above which the breach of a contractual commitment shall not be elevated and, if so, where is this boundary line located. First, this concerns the scope of obligations which the host State has to observe. The question thus becomes whether contractual commitments are part of the obligations to which the umbrella clause refers. Above all, the wording of the clause regularly does not differentiate between contractual and non-contractual commitments but refers in most of the cases to "any" or "all" obligations. Notwithstanding this broad wording, it is essential to note that the umbrella clause must not be interpreted separately but in the light of the respective investment treaty and most importantly, taking into consideration the pertinent notion of investment which determines the *ratione materiae*. A contract may be covered by an investment treaty's protection only when it falls under the notion of investment as it is laid down in the treaty.[234] In other words, the definition and limitation of foreign investment is contingent upon the definition assigned to it in the respective BIT. Given the variety of contracts that are concluded between States and foreign enterprises, it is difficult and a matter of case-to-case examination to determine which contractual contents may be included and which may not by a specific treaty formulation. A contract that concerns a single exchange of commodity and payment can rarely be seen as an investment under the majority of investment treaties and thus, will not be elevated by an umbrella clause. A breach of contractual commitments that fall within the definition of investment

[233] Even the tribunal in *SGS v. Pakistan* did not deny a certain elevating effect. Cf. *SGS v. Pakistan*, *supra* fn. 6, para. 172.

[234] See *supra* 115 et seq.

provided for in the BIT, by contrast, will be elevated through an umbrella clause. In short, the scope of obligations which the host State is obliged to observe is not determined by the umbrella clause but exclusively through the investment notion of the treaty.

Second and most importantly, there is the question whether only certain kinds of breaches of contractual obligations, namely, those where the State acts as a sovereign, are elevated through umbrella clauses. Several authors and arbitral tribunals warrant that the purpose of treaties of public international law is to exclusively restrain the State's sovereign activity.[235] Accordingly, an international treaty cannot be applied to restrict a State's purely commercial undertakings.[236] States are not subjects of international law when they act in a commercial fashion. This tenet underlines the distinction between the classic international public law of expropriation and the law of international commercial arbitration.[237] Rightly, this vantage point emphasizes that the characteristic principle of a foreign investment dispute is that it involves the use of state power and that generally, a breach of contract is not a violation of an international treaty unless the exertion of such power is involved. This rule, however, does not require absolute validity. It is not a peremptory norm of international law.[238] Hence, parties are, by all means, able to alter this rule through a special legal regime.[239]

---

[235] This reasoning is similarly brought forward in relation to expropriation and the fair and equitable treatment standard. See, e.g., *Azurix v. Argentina*, ICSID Case No. ARB/01/12, Decision on Jurisdiction, 8 December 2003, para. 315; *Salini v. Jordan*, *supra* fn. 61, para. 155; *Sempra Energy International v. Argentine Republic*, ICSID Case No. ARB/02/16, Award, 28 September 2007, para. 310.

[236] Wälde, *supra* fn. 70, 235.

[237] Von Walter, *supra* fn. 85, 823–824.

[238] Kunoy, *supra* fn. 85, 284.

[239] Even the tribunal in *SGS v. Pakistan* confirms this point of view. See *SGS v. Pakistan*, *supra* fn. 6, para. 173. See also Crawford, *supra* fn. 48, 7:

> To summarize, State responsibility for breach of international law is distinct from the liability of a State for breach of its contracts. But there may be important overlaps: for example, a State may commit by treaty to comply with a contract, in which case its failure to do so is (subject to any circumstances precluding wrongfulness) also a breach of an international obligation.

C. Amerasinghe, Local Remedies in International Law (2004), 137:

> There are special circumstances which bring about a violation of international law simultaneously with a breach of contract.... The first is where express protection is granted to contractual rights as such by international instruments.... The violation of international law is dependent on the express agreement of the states concerned, i.e. the state party to the contract and the national state of the alien.

The conclusion of an investment treaty which contains an umbrella clause constitutes the establishment of such a regime. Several arguments such as prior commentary on the clause's effects and the history of the clause which show that the founders of the clause did not differentiate between commercial and non-commercial behaviour, an effective interpretation which is consistent with the requirements of the Vienna Convention, and the general convergence between the international and domestic law sphere indicate that a broad interpretation corresponds to the intention of the parties to investment treaties. Further, the perplexity of narrow approaches endorses this point of view. Suffice it to say that all interpretations that deny an elevating effect of all contractual commitments come out to be arbitrary in their venture to find further meanings of the clause,[240] and the clause is usually rendered nugatory by these interpretations.[241] This would be a clear breach of the principle of effective treaty interpretation.[242] Mere logic sustains the inclusion of all contractual commitments. When international customary law creates the host State's international responsibility in the case of a non-commercial breach of contract, the conclusion can be deemed sound that the additional protection provided by umbrella clauses covers precisely the rights that are not covered by international customary law, that is, breaches of contract which are not based mainly on the State's exercise of its prerogatives.[243]

In sum, the umbrella clause serves to elevate all kinds of contractual breaches, be they of commercial or of non-commercial nature, into treaty violations. As a result, not only traditional international law violations of contract requiring the use of sovereign prerogatives can be claimed on the international plane but also contractual non-compliance that similarly could have been carried out by a private contractual partner such as delays in payment, non-payment,[244] or breach of duty of care. Accordingly, the tribunals in both SGS cases would have been entitled to decide whether the contractual conduct of the parties caused a breach of contract, irrespective of the question whether the same conduct amounted to a breach of a conventional treaty provision.

---

[240] Foster, *supra* fn. 73, 108.
[241] Gaillard, *supra* fn. 89. 338.
[242] Cf. Gaffney & Loftis, *supra* fn. 85, 22.
[243] Zolia, *supra* fn. 4, 35; Schreuer, *supra* fn. 75, 250–251.
[244] *SGS v. Philippines*, *supra* fn. 6, para. 159.

II. *Manner of Elevation*

A question which is easily overlooked by legal commentators concerns the exact effect of an elevation generated through umbrella clauses. Traditionally, the "internationalisation" of state contracts led to an application of international law in order to determine whether a contractual breach had been committed. The objective of this application was to avoid flaws or posterior alterations of the domestic law which regularly resulted to the prejudice of the foreign investor's rights. The question which has to be posed in this context is whether the effect of the umbrella clause generates the same kind of application of international law. In other words, does the umbrella clause change the applicable law of state contracts or is its function to elevate a mere internal breach, that is, a contractual breach according to domestic law into the realm of international responsibility? The former is contended or seems to be contended by some authors who emphasize the similarities between umbrella clauses and stabilization clauses.[245] From this vantage point, an indirect internationalisation takes place. Other commentators sustain that the question whether a breach of contract has been committed is a matter of the *lex contractus* and that the function of the umbrella clause is to elevate this breach into a breach of international law which generates the international responsibility of the host State.[246] The latter point of view is preferable since it is consistent with treaty interpretation rules and does not confound the effects of umbrella clauses and stabilization clauses.[247] Why, one has to ask, should an

---

[245] Kunoy, *supra* fn. 85, 300; Weil, *supra* fn. 2, 132 et seq.; Zolia, *supra* fn. 4, 19–22; C. McLachlan et al. (eds.), International Investment Arbitration—Substantive Principles (2007), 4.116; S. K. Gudgeon, United States Bilateral Investment Treaties: Comment on Their Origin, Purpose and General Treatment Standard, Int'l Tax & Bus. L. 4 (1986), 105, 126; T. Wälde & G. Ndi, Stabilizing International Investment Commitments: International Law versus Contract Interpretation, Tex. Int'l L. J. 31 (1996), 215, 240.

[246] *SGS v. Philippines*, *supra* fn. 6, para. 126; Schramke, *supra* fn. 85, 352; Dolzer & Stevens, *supra* fn. 88, 81; Schreuer, *supra* fn. 75, 255; Gaillard, *supra* fn. 89, 344–345; T. Wälde, Investment under the Energy Charter: An Overview of Selected Key Issues Based on Recent Litigation Experience, in: N. Horn (ed.), Arbitrating Foreign Investment Disputes, (2004), 193, 215; M. Nolan & E. Baldwin, The Treatment of Contract-Related Claims in Treaty-Based Arbitration, Mealey's Int'l Arb. Rep., vol. 21, June 2006, No. 6, 4.

[247] Cf. Crawford, *supra* fn. 48, 20: "In the absence of express stabilization, investors take the risk that the obligations of the host State under its own law may change, and the umbrella clause makes no difference to this basic proposition".

umbrella clause alter the proper law of an investment contract?[248] The proper law of the contract is determined by private international law and thus, either by the choice of law undertaken by the parties to the contract or by the closest link. It is in turn not a question that is regulated through an umbrella clause in a BIT. Although some treaties provide for the law applicable to their proper substantive standards the umbrella clause can barely be seen as a choice of law provision for covered contracts. As Schramke points out, the change of the applicable law could lead to a change of the substantial rights and obligations of the parties to a contract and thus of the contractual balance agreed upon by the parties.[249] This is not the purpose of an umbrella clause, and such a result is hardly inferable from the wording of a standard umbrella clause.[250]

Recently a proclivity towards the choice of the host State's domestic law as the proper law of investment contracts can be discerned.[251] As a consequence, domestic law regularly governs the question whether a contractual breach has occurred. Albeit the competence of international arbitral tribunals to hear mere contractual contents is not disputed, it would be wrong to assert that umbrella clauses entail the jurisdiction of treaty-based tribunals over contract claims.[252] In fact,

---

[248] The question of whether a stabilization clause in a contract alters the law applicable to the contract is not very clear either. For a detailed examination, see H. Merkt, Investitionsschutz durch Stabilisierungsklauseln (1990), 114 et seq.

[249] Schramke, *supra* fn. 85, 257.

[250] See also the recent authoritative annulment decision, *CMS Gas Transmission Company v. The Argentine Republic*, Decision on Annulment, ICSID Case No. ARB/01/8, 25 September 2007, para. 95(c), where the Committee stated the following: "The effect of the umbrella clause is not to transform the obligation which is relied on into something else; the content of the obligation is unaffected, as its proper law".

[251] See *supra* 47.

[252] However, this is done by several commentators and arbitral tribunals. See, e.g., Crawford, *supra* fn. 48, 20; Alexandrov, *supra* fn. 85, 575; *SGS v. Philippines*, *supra* fn. 6, para. 113 et seq.; *Toto Costruzioni Generali S.p.A. v. The Republic of Lebanon*, ICSID Case No. ARB/07/12, Decision on Jurisdiction, 11 September 2009, paras. 201–202. In my view, this contradicts the principal restriction of the jurisdiction of treaty-based arbitral tribunals and, as far as the effect of the umbrella clause is concerned, leads to the wrong assumption that the clause is a jurisdictional clause. The umbrella clause, however, does not contain a State's consent to submit contractual disputes to international arbitration, which would have to be inserted in the dispute resolution clause, but obligates the host State not to breach contracts entered into with investors. Cf. Gaillard, SGS Cases Considered, *supra* fn. 89, 344: "[T]he jurisdictional consequence of such an undertaking [i.e., effective umbrella clause] is that the BIT tribunal selected by an investor on the basis of the dispute resolution clause contained in the treaty may assert jurisdiction over such an undertaking, which is a treaty obligation".

the claims brought based on a violation of an umbrella clause are treaty claims which do not alter the parallel existence of the corresponding contract claims because they are based on the violation of a treaty standard.[253] According to this view, a posterior change in legislation concerning investment contracts would not be hindered by umbrella clauses. This effect, however, may be achieved through the further protective standards of investment treaties.

III. *The Contracts Covered*

In most of the cases, the investment contract is not concluded directly with the State but with an entity separate and distinct from the State or a public enterprise.[254] The question arises, which of these contracts are covered through the protection provided for by an umbrella clause. On the one hand, a State shall not be enabled to reduce the scope of its international obligations through formal spin-off of governmental functions to independent entities.[255] On the other hand, a State cannot be held liable for the actions of independent enterprises or entities over which it has no determinative influence. At the bottom, this problem concerns the attribution to the State of conduct of bodies which are not state organs.[256] Since the customary rules of international law as laid down by the ILC Articles set out a strict regime for the attribution of conduct of non-state organs, relying exclusively on the exertion of governmental authority, the question becomes whether the application of an umbrella clause alters this scheme. This would require that the umbrella clause be a provision of attributive character. Taking into consideration the present examination of the clause—its wording, history, and purpose—the existence of such an attributive function is by no means conceivable. In order to qualify an act of a State as internationally wrongful, two elements have to be met: firstly, the conduct has to be attributable to the State and secondly, the respective conduct must constitute a breach of an international obligation.[257] Within this

---

[253] Cf. Foster, *supra* fn. 85, 19; Gaillard, SGS Cases Considered, *supra* fn. 89, 344–345. Contra Crawford, *supra* fn. 48, 21: "[T]he umbrella clause is an extra mechanism for the enforcement of claims, but the basis of the transaction remains the same."

[254] See *supra* 138 et seq.

[255] Von Walter, *supra* fn. 85, 823.

[256] See *supra* 159.

[257] See article 2 of the ILC Articles on Responsibility of States for Internationally Wrongful Acts (2001).

two-step system, the function of the umbrella clause pertains to the second step. This means that when there is no conduct attributable to the State, the obligations set out by an umbrella clause cannot be breached. The effect of the umbrella clause is to widen the notion of international obligation but not to entail a more comprehensive attribution. On some occasions, this has been recognized by arbitral tribunals.[258] As a consequence, the umbrella clause exclusively covers contracts which were concluded with the host State itself, that is, with one of its organs or with a non-state organ that exerts governmental authority. As a corollary, the magnitude of the umbrella clause's effect is mitigated considerably since a contract with an agency formally distinct from the State but heavily controlled by it, for instance, a company which is enjoined with the construction of highways or power plants, is only covered as far as an exertion of governmental authority is at stake. In this case, however, and as already mentioned above, the regular substantive provisions of an investment treaty, most importantly, the fair and equitable treatment standard will usually be applicable. The effect of an umbrella clause thus comes only into play when a contract has been concluded directly with the government or with a further organ of the host State as was the case in the two SGS cases.[259]

---

[258] See, e.g., *Eureko v. Poland, supra* fn. 95, paras. 115 et seq., para. 245; *Azurix v. Argentina*, ICSID Case No. ARB/03/30, Award, 14 July 2006, para. 384; *Impregilo S.p.A. v. Islamic Republic of Pakistan*, ICSID Case No. ARB/03/3, Decision on Jurisdiction, 22 April 2005, paras. 198 et seq., para. 223. In this case, the BIT at issue did not contain an umbrella clause. The tribunal examined the question of attribution with regard to a broadly phrased dispute resolution clause. Yet, since the claimant alleged that the umbrella clause of another BIT was applicable via the MFN-clause, the tribunal extended its argumentation to umbrella clauses.

[259] By contrast, in *Noble Ventures v. Romania, supra* fn. 58, para. 85, the tribunal held that an agency which was enjoined with the task to regulate privatization was a non-state organ of the Romanian State. The exertion of governmental authority justified attribution and further, the tribunal relied on an umbrella clause to substantiate a violation of the treaty: "[w]here the acts of a governmental agency are to be attributed to the State for the purposes of applying an umbrella clause, such as Art. II (2) (c) of the BIT, breaches of a contract into which the State has entered are capable of constituting a breach of international law by virtue of the breach of the umbrella clause".

5. THE RELATIONSHIP OF PARALLEL TREATY-BASED INTERNATIONAL ARBITRAL PROCEEDINGS AND CONTRACT-BASED DOMESTIC COURT PROCEEDINGS IN INVESTMENT TREATY DISPUTES

A. Conflicting Jurisdictions under International Investment Treaties and Contracts between a Foreign Investor and a Host State

In public international law, the proliferation of disputes and dispute resolution mechanisms and their corollary, the fragmentation of international law, have led to an increased jurisdictional competition among international tribunals.[1] Whether these developments will have positive effects on the evolution of international law as a whole is subject to controversial debates.[2] The present work is not the forum to further inquire into these problems. This chapter concerns a purportedly more traditional subject matter of competing jurisdictions: the relationship between international proceedings and local court proceedings.[3]

[1] See, e.g., A. Bjorklund, Private Rights and Public International Law: Why Competition among International Economic Law Tribunals Is Not Working, Hast. L. J. 59 (2007), 101, 101, who states that: "This competition for business is not, contrary to expectation, advantageous to investors or to the world community." See generally K. Oellers-Frahm, Multiplication of International Courts and Tribunals and Conflicting Jurisdiction—Problems and Possible Solutions, Max Planck UNYB 5 (2001), 67 et seq.; Y. Shany, The Competing Jurisdictions of International Courts and Tribunals (2003). On fragmentation of international law through the example of the WTO, see J. Pauwelyn, Bridging Fragmentation and Unity: International Law as a Universe of Inter-Connected Islands, Mich. J. Int'l L. 25 (2003/2004), 903 et seq.

[2] See, e.g., ILC, Report of the International Law Commission on the Work of Its Fifty-sixth Session (2004) UN Doc. A/59/10, ch. 10; K. Nicolaidis & J. Tong, Diversity or Cacophony? The Continuing Debate over New Sources of International Law, Mich. J. Int'l L. 25 (2004), 1349 et seq.; G. Hafner, Pros and Cons Ensuing from Fragmentation of International Law, Mich. J. Int'l L. 25 (2004), 849 et seq.; B. Kingsbury, Foreword: Is the Proliferation of International Courts and Tribunals a Systemic Problem, NYU J. Int'l L. & Pol. 31 (1998/1999), 679 et seq.

[3] See, e.g., *Mexican Union Railway Ltd.* (GB v. Mexico) (1930) 5 RIAA 115; *North American Dredging Company of Texas* (US v. Mexico) (1926) 4 RIAA 26 (hereinafter, *North American Dredging Company v. Mexico*). Notwithstanding the antiqueness of such incidences, several recent developments such as the increased application of domestic law by international courts and tribunals or the increased application of international law by domestic courts, in short, the increased interaction between both spheres in general, turn this subject into a very recent problematic area.

The emergence of the investment treaty regime and its impact upon contracts concluded between a foreign investor and a host State generates the need to examine this aspect more closely with regard to investment treaty proceedings and national court proceedings. Particularly, the impact of the principle of possible coincidence of contract claims and treaty claims and the operation of umbrella clauses entail a dynamic convergence of both systems' jurisdictional competences which requires further clarification.

At the outset, this paper will explain how and what kind of jurisdictional conflicts arise between both legal systems in the framework of investment treaty arbitration. The traditional means of avoidance and resolution of jurisdictional conflicts and the treaty provisions which are aimed at the resolution of such conflicts will be examined and it will be shown that their capability to resolve emerging problems in this area of law is minimal. In the second part, the historical evolution of contractual forum selection clauses and their present impact under the investment treaty regime will be examined. Thereafter, a resolution of both kinds of conflicts between contract and treaty—asymmetrical and symmetrical conflicts—will be proposed.

I. *Jurisdictional Conflicts in Investment Treaty Law*

1. *Generation and Risks of Parallel and Multiple Proceedings*

Two of the main elements underlying the evolution of international investment law or more abstractly, the protection of the individual's rights on the international plane may be regarded in general as essential to the increase in jurisdictional conflicts in this field of law. Firstly, the multiplication of international tribunals with often vague and overlapping jurisdictions[4] entitle the investor to bring its claim before

---

Cf. Kingsbury, *supra* fn. 2, 694: "Perhaps the greatest problem associated with the growth in the jurisdiction and activities of international courts and tribunals is the connection between these bodies and national law and institutions, particularly national courts and tribunals." For a detailed analysis, see Y. Shany, Regulating Jurisdictional Relations between National and International Courts (2007). For an examination of the relationship between international courts and domestic US courts, see M. Weisburd, International Courts and American Courts, Mich. J. Int'l L. 21 (1999/2000), 877 et seq.

[4] See, e.g., Y. Shany, *supra* fn. 1; J. S. Martinez, Towards an International Judicial System, Stan. L. Rev. 56 (2003), 429, 436 et seq.; J. E. Alvarez, International Organizations as Law-Makers (2005), 401 et seq. J. I. Charney, Is International Law Threatened by Multiple International Tribunals?, RdC 271 (1998), 101, 139 et seq.

various tribunals.[5] Depending upon the nature of the alleged infringed rights, an investor may claim restitution or compensation in up to five different proceedings.[6] The remedies available may concern domestic courts and contractual arbitral tribunals on the domestic plane, investment treaty-based arbitral tribunals and human rights courts on the international plane, and finally, the ICJ in case of diplomatic protection proceedings espoused by the investor's home State. The variety of available fora not only induces but almost constrains the investor to seek for the forum which appears to be the most favourable. The resulting forum shopping has been the object of several examinations.[7] Secondly and partly as a corollary of the first aspect, the distinction between the municipal legal order and the international legal order is not as clear as positivist schools of thought tend to uphold.[8] As a consequence, an impaired investor is usually not restrained to pursue its claims in one of the two planes but on the contrary, may often have the possibility to make itself avail of both spheres' remedies. Further elements which contribute to overlapping jurisdictions pertain exclusively to the rise of the investment treaty regime. Some of them, especially those which are highly related to contractual matters, have been examined more closely in the second chapter of this work. Foremost is the independent legal value of every single investment treaty. In other words, for the State not party to it, each treaty is *res inter alios acta*, each source of law its own

[5] Of course, this proliferation of dispute settlement mechanisms has various reasons, such as growth of trade, international trade, communication, or the proliferation of international organizations. See, e.g., T. Buergenthal, The Proliferation of Disputes, Dispute Settlement Procedures and Respect for the Rule of Law, ICSID Rev.-FILJ 21 (2006), 126, 127 et seq.

[6] Z. Douglas, The Hybrid Foundations of Investment Treaty Arbitration, BYIL 74 (2003), 151, 236–237; A. Reinisch & L. Malintoppi, Methods of Dispute Resolution, in: P. Muchlinski et al. (eds.), The Oxford Handbook of International Investment Law (2008), 694 et seq.

[7] See, e.g., R. H. Kreindler, "Arbitral Forum Shopping": Some Observations on Recent Developments in International Commercial and Investment Arbitration, Am. Rev. Int'l Arb. 16 (2005), 157 et seq. For an examination of domestic "forum shopping" between different US state jurisdictions from the vantage point of game theory, see D. L. Bassett, The Forum Game, N. C. L. Rev. 84 (2005/2006), 333, who criticizes the negative stance of many authors towards "forum shopping". Cf. id., 338–339: "Forum 'shopping' suggests unfairness in choosing to litigate in a particular forum due to differences in the law and fails to acknowledge that the availability of different law is neither wrong nor unusual".

[8] The granting of enforceable rights to the investor in both spheres, in any event, allows us to speak of a certain convergence of the municipal and the international legal order.

master.[9] Thereby, the same set of facts may give rise to proceedings before different treaty tribunals based respectively on different treaties. Further, a broad interpretation of the term "investor" in investment treaties, including minority shareholders and indirect investment, broadens the scope of potential claimants.[10] Finally, as abovementioned, the broad understanding of "investment" especially makes contractual disputes susceptible of being brought before treaty-based tribunals.[11] In short, the breadth and proliferation of treaty consents increase the likelihood of initiation of different international arbitration proceedings.[12] The same holds true for international and domestic proceedings.

On the domestic plane, the existence of jurisdictional overlap and parallel proceedings is a rare occasion compared to the international arena, and in a sophisticated municipal legal system, the questions which arise from such proceedings or the circumvention of such proceedings are usually regulated by an established system of rules. Furthermore, the jurisdictional hierarchy laid down in domestic systems hinder a generation of jurisdictional conflicts and parallel proceedings comparable to international law disputes or disputes with an international law dimension.

Under international investment law, the risks which are mainly attributed to concurrent jurisdictions concern the problem of double recovery[13] and the issuance of conflicting decisions.[14] Whilst the former problem may be dealt with adequately through judicial comity,

---

[9] See, e.g., G. Sacerdoti, Case T 8735-01-77, The Czech Republic v. CME Czech Republic B.V.—Expert Opinion of Professor Sacerdoti, TDM 2 (2005), No. 05, 1, 132.

[10] On shareholder protection under investment treaties, see, e.g., S. Alexandrov, The "Baby Boom" of Treaty-Based Arbitrations and the Jurisdiction of ICSID Tribunals, JWIT 6 (2005), 387, 393 et seq.; F. Orrego Vicuña, The Protection of Shareholders under International Law, in: M. Ragazzi (ed.), International Responsibility Today (2005), 161 et seq.; C. Schreuer, Shareholder Protection in International Investment Law, in: P. M. Dupuy et al. (eds.), Common Values in International Law (2006), 601 et seq.; B. Legum, Defining Investment and Investor: Who Is Entitled to Claim?, Arb. Int'l 22 (2006), 521 et seq.

[11] See *supra* 115 et seq.

[12] A. R. Parra, Desirability and Feasibility of Consolidation: Introductory Remarks, ICSID Rev-FILJ 21 (2006), 132, 132.

[13] See *Wena Hotels Ltd. v. Arab Republic of Egypt*, ICSID Case No. ARB/98/4, Decision on Annulment, 5 February 2002, 6 ICSID Rep. 129, para. 63 (hereinafter, *Wena Annulment*).

[14] See, e.g., G. Kaufmann-Kohler, Annulment of ICSID Awards in Contract and Treaty Arbitration: Are There Differences?, in: E. Gaillard (ed.), Annulment of ICSID Awards (2004), 189, 203; Bjorklund, *supra* fn. 1, 118–119.

the latter entails more serious concerns, leading ultimately to a fragile legitimacy of the international adjudicative systems as a whole. A system, for instance, which constantly produces contrary decisions, is not reliable.[15] Furthermore, the duplication of efforts entails unavoidably a waste of resources.[16] In the case of disputes involving economically weaker States, this implication may be more of a concern. Taking into account these considerations, some authors assert that a concentration in one forum of dispute resolution regarding the same set of facts is preferable as a matter of general policy.[17] In the view of Friedman, the overarching question when dealing with the prospect of parallel proceedings relate to the balance between investor rights and efficiency. Accordingly, it is doubtful whether investors should be required to defer or abandon potentially meritorious claims to reduce the prospect of multiple proceedings.[18] Whilst this is correct, it has to be underlined that the host State's interests in the implementation of certain types of proceedings must be taken into account similarly. In addition to issues of sovereignty which may be impaired through circumvention of domestic proceedings,[19] the mere prospect of counterclaims lodged by a host State in a domestic contractual dispute shows these interests. The investor, by contrast, is interested in the availability of a favourable or at least a neutral forum rather than in the prospect of having various

---

[15] Cf. S. Franck, The Legitimacy Crisis in Investment Treaty Arbitration: Privatizing Public International Law through Inconsistent Decisions, Fordham L. Rev. 73 (2005), 1521 et seq., where the author deals with the inconsistency of the decisions of international arbitral tribunals. On inconsistency between international adjudicative bodies and domestic courts, see C. Schreuer, Concurrent Jurisdiction of National and International Tribunals, Hous. L. Rev. 13 (1975/1976), 508, 510, who merely states that different outcomes would be "undesirable and should be avoided". When international arbitral tribunals and domestic courts render inconsistent decisions, the legitimacy concern is not necessarily less urgent but is different in nature because there is not a single system but two systems. The inconsistency in such a case is especially of concern when the enforcement of the international award is not ensured. For the bulk of investment treaty awards, and especially for those rendered under the auspices of ICSID, this is momentarily not much of a concern.

[16] See, e.g., Shany, *supra* fn. 3, 17. This risk of high and superfluous expenditures may ultimately lead to a potentially restricted access to justice for some parties.

[17] See C. Schreuer, The ICSID Convention—A Commentary (2001), 359; E. Gaillard, Centre international pour le Règlement des Différends relatifs aux Investissements (CIRDI)—Chronique des sentences arbitrales, JDI 129 (2000), 189, 237.

[18] M. Friedman, Treaties as Agreements to Arbitrate—Related Dispute Resolution Regimes: Parallel Proceedings in BIT Arbitration, in: A. van den Berg (ed.), International Arbitration 2006: Back to Basics?, ICCA International Arbitration Congress, Montreal 2006 (2007), 545, 545, 567–568.

[19] Cf. M. Sornarajah, The International Law on Foreign Investment (2004), 254.

fora to select from. In essence, the question therefore is not so much how many tribunals and courts may have jurisdiction over certain claims but which tribunal's decision, the international tribunal's or the domestic court's, prevails in the end and renders an enforceable award.

As a survey of international investment treaty awards evinces, multiple proceedings in investment treaty disputes have become a common feature in the law of foreign investment protection.[20] Conceptually, different constellations of multiple and parallel proceedings on the international and domestic planes are conceivable. Yet, with regard to investment treaty arbitration and disputes arising out of the same set of facts, two different types of parallel proceedings may be discerned. The first instance concerns cases in which the same set of facts induces several investors to bring treaty claims. This can be the case when the governmental action at issue has such a wide repercussion that the rights of various investors could have been infringed without them having any relation to each other. Arbitral proceedings may then be grounded on a wide range of BITs. The wave of ICSID arbitrations commenced subsequent to Argentina's emergency legislation in 2001 is the preeminent example in this regard.[21] On the other hand, investors which pertain to the same company but on different levels may trigger BIT proceedings based on different treaties. The twin arbitrations brought by Roland Lauder[22] and CME Czech Republic BV[23] are notorious examples of such proceedings. Whereas Lauder, the controlling shareholder of CME, Ltd., lodged a claim based on the US—Czech Republic BIT, CME Czech Republic, an indirect subsidiary of CME, Ltd., commenced arbitral proceedings under the Netherlands-Czech Republic BIT.[24]

---

[20] Cf. Friedman, *supra* fn. 18, 546. The author reviewed 78 completed ICSID cases and found evidence of parallel proceedings in 41% of them.

[21] Argentina's financial crisis has generated approximately 37 ICSID arbitrations. All these proceedings, albeit having several issues in common both on the jurisdictional stage and on the merits stage, are dealt with separately. See G. Kaufmann-Kohler et al., Consolidation of Proceedings in Investment Arbitration: How Can Multiple Proceedings Arising from the Same or Related Situations Be Handled Efficiently?, Final Report on the Geneva Colloquium Held on 22 April 2006, ICSID Rev.-FILJ 21 (2006), 59, 63 et seq.

[22] *Roland S. Lauder v. The Czech Republic*, UNCITRAL, Final Award, 9 ICSID Rep. 62, 3 September 2001.

[23] *CME Czech Republic B.V. v. The Czech Republic*, UNCITRAL, Partial Award, 13 September 2001 (hereinafter, *CME v. Czech Republic*); *CME Czech Republic B.V. v. The Czech Republic*, UNCITRAL, Final Award, 14 March 2003, 9 ICSID Rep. 246.

[24] Furthermore, a local firm controlled by Lauder and CME lodged claims before the domestic courts of the Czech Republic.

Unfortunately, both tribunals reached contradictory results.[25] By and large, the solution to these types of parallel proceedings appears to be the introduction of some kind of consolidation of the numerous proceedings.[26] However, since these proceedings do not stem specifically from the involvement of contractual undertakings, their examination is not crucial for the present work.

The second type of parallel proceedings which has become paramount in investment treaty law concerns parallel domestic law and international law proceedings. This type is essentially distinct from the parallelism at the investment treaty level. Contrary to the former type, only one investment treaty and one treaty-based arbitration are involved. The parallelism in this case is generated through domestic proceedings which, at least partly, concern the same set of facts or the same governmental behaviour. Although such an occasion may arise irrespective of the existence of a contract between a foreign investor and a host State,[27] an existing contractual relation is the most likely reason for the generation of parallel domestic proceedings.[28] In the context of this work, this second type of parallelism is exclusively of interest. The impact of the international investment treaty regime upon state contracts may only be discerned properly when the jurisdictional relationship between both the municipal proceedings and the international proceedings is clarified. The underlying factual basis for this conflict is clear: on account of an unresolved dispute the local company as a subsidiary of the foreign investor or the foreign investor itself pursues contractual claims before the host State's courts. At the same time or subsequently, most presumably in the case of an unsatisfying result

---

[25] See C. N. Brower & J. K. Sharpe, Multiple and Conflicting International Arbitral Awards, JWTI 4 (2003), 211 et seq. The Counsel for the Czech Republic in the two arbitrations publicly described the situation as "absolutely ludicrous, and highly regrettable for the fact that it makes the law look so stupid". See Clifford Chance Entangled in Bitter Lauder Arbitrations, Legal Bus., October 2001, 108.

[26] See, e.g., Kaufmann-Kohler et al., *supra* fn. 21, 59 et seq.; Y. Shany, Consolidation and Tests for Application: Is International Law Relevant?, ICSID Rev.-FILJ 21 (2006), 135 et seq.

[27] Of course, an investor may pursue a claim against property infringements before municipal courts without relying on contractual provisions granting such right.

[28] This is demonstrated by the fact that a significant number of host State—investor agreements refer disputes to the host State's national adjudicative system. See also C. McLachlan et al. (eds.), International Investment Arbitration—Substantive Principles (2007), 80: "If there is a contract between State and investor, that contract will create its own justiciable rights and duties, the breach of which may give rise either to litigation before host State courts or to arbitration before a tribunal to whose jurisdiction the parties have submitted".

in the former proceedings, the foreign investor lodges a claim based upon an international investment treaty. Since the conceptual relationship between both claims has already been examined above,[29] the questions of whether and how potential jurisdictional overlaps between both claims may be resolved remain to be examined.

2. *Contract-Related Parallel Proceedings: "Asymmetrical" and "Symmetrical" Conflicts*

As already mentioned several times, a host State party to international investment treaty arbitration will regularly bring forward the argument that the contractual dispute is not covered by the respective treaty and that the treaty-based arbitral tribunal thus has no jurisdiction to sit over questions related to contractual matters. According to the point of view warranted in the present work, this is not correct insofar as the contract at issue is covered by the treaty's investment notion and the governmental action breaching the contract amounts to a violation of the substantive treaty standards.[30] In this case, arbitral tribunals are supposed to apply the above-explained mixture of international law and domestic law in order to determine whether there has been an expropriation of contractual rights or a denial of the fair and equitable treatment standard in relation to such rights. Domestic courts, on the other hand, will treat the question of the conduct of the contractual parties by applying municipal law exclusively. This type of conflict has been termed as "asymmetrical conflict" by Douglas.[31]

By contrast, a "symmetrical conflict" arises if the particular treaty contains an umbrella clause, a dispute resolution clause that explicitly refers to investment contracts, or arguably, a broadly phrased dispute resolution clause that refers to "any" or "all" disputes relating to an investment.[32] In this case, similar to a domestic court, an international

---

[29] See *supra* 160 et seq.

[30] See *supra* 65 et seq.

[31] Douglas, *supra* fn. 6, 238: "Before the municipal court or contractual arbitral tribunal, municipal law supplies the cause of action, whereas in the context of a treaty arbitration, it governs an aspect of the investment dispute where the cause of action is detached from the municipal law".

[32] It is noteworthy that several authors and arbitral tribunals endorse this effect of broadly phrased dispute resolution clauses. Douglas uses the term "symmetrical conflict" when a contractual claim is brought before a treaty-based tribunal. According to his point of view, this is not only the case when a treaty contains an umbrella clause but also when a treaty contains a broadly phrased dispute resolution clause. Accordingly,

arbitral tribunal's decision on whether a contract was breached is governed exclusively by municipal law. The distinction is thus made in recognition of the different roles played by municipal law in these *fora*. In the view of Douglas, the investor's cause of action is the decisive *criterium* to distinguish both types of conflicts. Accordingly, in the framework of asymmetrical conflicts municipal law governs the cause of action before the municipal court but merely supplies an aspect of the dispute before the treaty-based tribunal. In a symmetrical conflict, in turn, both adjudicative bodies, the treaty-based tribunal and the municipal court, are seized of the same cause of action, namely, the contractual claim based on municipal law. According to the point of view expressed in the present work, the umbrella clause turns breaches of contract into treaty violations but does not alter the law applicable to the respective contract.[33] Nonetheless, the claim brought on account of the umbrella clause is still a treaty claim. The decisive criterion for the distinction between asymmetrical and symmetrical conflicts in the case of an umbrella clause is thus the law applicable by the tribunal or court to the respective dispute. In any event, since the content between symmetrical conflicts and asymmetrical conflicts is substantially different, a proper resolution of jurisdictional overlap has to take into consideration this distinction.

3. *Traditional Means of Jurisdictional Conflict Resolution and Their Effect under the Investment Treaty Regime*

There are two mechanisms which are traditionally applied to regulate jurisdictional conflicts. Whereas the exhaustion of local remedies rule finds application in hierarchical orders, the doctrines of *lis pendens* and *res judicata* may apply in horizontal contexts among parallel courts. The applicability of both mechanisms to the relationship of international arbitral tribunals and domestic courts under the investment treaty regime is rather doubtful.

---

treaty-based tribunals have jurisdiction over mere contractual claims. See Douglas, *supra* fn. 6, 241 et seq. On the effect of broadly phrased dispute resolution clauses, see also S. Alexandrov, Breaches of Contract and Breaches of Treaty—The Jurisdiction of Treaty-Based Arbitration Tribunals to Decide Breach of Contract Claims in SGS v. Pakistan and SGS v. Philippines, JWIT 5 (2004), 555, 572 et seq.; A. Sinclair, Bridging the Contract/Treaty Divide, in: C. Binder et al. (eds.), International Investment Law for the 21st Century (2008), 92, 94 et seq. On the controversy regarding the effect of broadly phrased dispute resolution clauses, see *supra* 68 et seq.

[33] See *supra* 273 et seq.

a. *The Exhaustion of Local Remedies Rule*

Diplomatic protection is contingent upon the exhaustion of local remedies.[34] This means that private persons have to exhaust the locally available remedies prior to an espousal of their claim through their home State on the international plane. This has been regarded as one of the major flaws of diplomatic protection and thereby, of the availability of protection for foreign investment.[35] The exhaustion of local remedies rule has disadvantages for both host State and foreign investor. Whereas the flaws for the foreign investor are quite obvious, i.e., in addition to the feared lack of objectivity, the investor has to incur additional expenses and may expect delay,[36] the host State's damage is not easily discernable at first sight. Nonetheless, an exacerbation of the dispute through public attention, the difficulties in the host State's government in accepting an international tribunal's decision which is contrary to rulings of its highest courts, or a general affection of the host State's investment climate may be reasons for which a host State desires to avoid the triggering of local proceedings.[37]

In international investment arbitration, the rule of exhaustion of local remedies is generally dispensed with. This may be incurred from the standing arbitration offer[38] which is given to investors by the host State's consent to arbitration through investment treaty.[39] Moreover,

---

[34] See, e.g., M. Shaw, International Law (2003), 730; Brownlie, *supra* fn. 55, 472 et seq.

[35] See, e.g., Shany, *supra* fn. 3, 29–30; F. Orrego Vicuña, International Dispute Settlement in an Evolving Global Society (2004), 64.

[36] On the interest of an alien to conduct local proceedings, see C. Amerasinghe, Local Remedies in International Law (2004), 61.

[37] C. Schreuer, Calvo's Grandchildren: The Return of Local Remedies in Investment Arbitration, The Law and Practice of International Courts and Tribunals (2005), 1, 1. For the pros and cons of the exhaustion of local remedies, see J. Coe, The Mandate of Chapter 11 Tribunals—Jurisdiction and Related Questions, in: T. Weiler (ed.), NAFTA-Investment Law and Arbitration (2004), 215, 230–231.

[38] On this standing offer by the host State to the investor, see *supra* 57 et seq.

[39] See, e.g., *Lanco International Inc. v. The Argentine Republic*, ICSIC Case No. ARB/97/6, Decision on Jurisdiction, 8 December 1998, (2001) 40 ILM 457, 467 et seq. (hereinafter, *Lanco v. Argentina*); *Generation Ukraine Inc. v. Ukraine*, ICSID Case No. ARB/00/9, Award, 16 September 2003, paras. 13.1–13.6; *Yaung Chi Oo v. Myanmar*, Award, 31 March 2003 (2003) 42 ILM 540, 547–548. See also McLachlan et al., *supra* fn. 28, 4.27. In the context of NAFTA, this conclusion may be derived from several articles such as articles 1121, 1115, 1116(2), and 1117(2). Cf. W. Dodge, National Courts and International Arbitration: Exhaustion of Remedies and Res Judicata under Chapter Eleven of NAFTA, Hast. Int'l & Comp. L. Rev. 23 (1999/2000), 357, 370 et seq.; Coe, *supra* fn. 37, 230. On critics, see A. Bjorklund, Waiver and the Exhaustion of Local Remedies Rule in NAFTA Jurisprudence, in: T. Weiler (ed.), NAFTA-Investment Law and Arbitration (2004), 253, 284, 286.

the ICSID Convention favours such dispensation. The second sentence of article 26 of the ICSID Convention reads as follows: "A Contracting State may require the exhaustion of local administrative or judicial remedies as a condition of its consent to arbitration under this Convention."

Hence, in principle, a host State may insist on the exhaustion of local remedies. However, investment treaties which include such requirement rarely exist and those which do usually pertain to types of older vintage.[40] Only Israel gave notification to the ICSID that it will require local remedies to be exhausted.[41]

Notwithstanding the advantages which the dispensation of the principle entails, chiefly for the efficacy and reliability of the enforceability of investor's rights, at the same time, its function to resolve jurisdictional conflicts concerning the international and the municipal spheres likewise has been done away with.[42] In addition to being an impediment to investors bypassing national adjudication, the principle ensured that municipal courts were given the opportunity to rule upon municipal law issues before the dispute could be brought before an international instance which was regarded as an essential requirement of the host State's sovereignty.[43] However, it would be wrong to conclude that this flaw requires a re-introduction of the principle.[44] The displacement of the rule is an essential achievement of international investment treaties, and the resolution of jurisdictional conflicts would, by no means, outweigh its advantages for both parties to an investment dispute. Ultimately, a reintroduction would lead back to a denial of justice era the abolition of which can be regarded as one of the primary purposes of the investment treaty regime.

---

[40] Schreuer, *supra* fn. 17, 392.

[41] Israel withdrew its notification on 21 March 1991. See Schreuer, *supra* fn. 17, 391.

[42] Cf. Shany, *supra* fn. 3, 28: "The exhaustion of local remedies rule serves, in fact, as a jurisdiction-regulating rule, primarily governing the order of national and international proceedings".

[43] See, e.g., A. Bjorklund, Reconciling State Sovereignty and Investor Protection in Denial of Justice Claims, Va. J. Int'l L. 45 (2005), 809, 877 et seq.; W. Dodge, Loewen v. United States: Trials and Errors under NAFTA Chapter 11, DePaul L. Rev. 52 (2002), 563, 567 et seq. For further reasons for the domestic remedies rule, see M. Reisman, Nullity and Revision (1971), 364, who states that the rule "is founded on principles of economy, localization of delict and remedy, and good faith".

[44] Douglas, *supra* fn. 6, 241, seems to advance this opinion when he asserts that the treaty tribunal would then be in a position to survey the entire course of the dispute and test the host State's conduct against the substantive standards of the treaty.

b. *The Principles of Litis Pendens and Res Judicata*

The principles of *res judicata* and *litis pendens* are well-established under national law systems[45] and international law[46]. They even may be regarded as general principles of law within the meaning of article 38(1)(c) of the Statute of the ICJ.[47] The fundamental contents of both doctrines are the following: Pursuant to *res judicata*, an earlier and final adjudication by a court or a tribunal is conclusive in subsequent proceedings involving the same subject matter or relief, the same legal grounds, and the same parties (the so-called "triple-identity" criteria).[48] Hence, the doctrine has a positive and a negative effect. The positive effect is that the judgement is final and binding and should be implemented while the negative effect is that is serves as a bar to re-litigation, also referred to as *ne bis in idem*.[49] As a corollary to *res judicata*, the doctrine of *lis pendens* is directed against a situation in which parallel proceedings, which meet the same identity test as *res judicata*, are continuing before different adjudicative bodies at the same time. A pertinent forum may then (i) decline jurisdiction or stay its own proceedings, (ii) seek to restrain the other proceedings, (iii) make use of the rules of *res judicata*, or (iv) adopt mechanisms to encourage the parties to opt for trial in just one forum.[50] The rationales underpinning both doctrines are similar: avoidance of conflicting judgements, prevention of costly parallel litigation, and protection of parties from oppressive litigation tactics.[51]

---

[45] On res judicata, see, e.g., P. Barnett, Res Judicata, Estoppel and Foreign Jurisdiction (2001), para. 1.11 et seq.; The American Law Institute, Restatement: Second: Judgments, ch. 3, § 13–33. On *lis pendens*, see, e.g., J. Morris & D. McClean, The Conflict of Laws (1993), 97 et seq.

[46] See, e.g., B. Cheng, General Principles of Law as Applied by International Courts and Tribunals (1953), 336; S. Rosenne, The Law and Practice of the International Court—1920–1996, vol. III (1997), 1655–1661.

[47] Cf. *Waste Management, Inc. v. United Mexican States*, ICSID Case No. ARB(AF)/00/3, Mexico's Preliminary Objections concerning the Previous Proceedings, Decision of the Tribunal, 26 June 2002, 6 ICSID Rep. 538, para. 39.

[48] F. De Ly & A. Sheppard, ILA Interim Report on *Res judicata* and Arbitration, Int'l Arb. 25 (2009), 35, 36.

[49] Id.

[50] J. Fawcett (ed.), Declining Jurisdiction in Private International Law, Report to the XIVth Congress of the International Academy of Comparative Law (1995), 27–28. This broad range of options results from the differences between common law and civil law. Whereas under the former a court has discretion to rule upon the case, under the latter a court is obliged to dismiss or stay the action. See Kaufmann-Kohler et al., *supra* fn. 21, 66.

[51] F. De Ly & A. Sheppard, ILA Final Report on *Lis Pendens* and Arbitration, Int'l Arb. 25 (2009), 3,4.

The applicability of both principles to cases involving international arbitral tribunals and domestic courts, however, is more than doubtful.[52] In the framework of international commercial arbitration, in which both contractual arbitral tribunals and domestic courts are not deemed to be in a hierarchical relationship, the applicability had been endorsed on some occasions.[53] By contrast, in international investment arbitration, the situation is different when it comes to the relation between international law proceedings (that is, investment treaty proceedings) and domestic law proceedings before domestic courts or contractual arbitral tribunals. In principle, international dispute settlement organs and national courts and tribunals do not pertain to the same legal order.[54] Hence, international courts and tribunals are not bound by decisions of domestic adjudicative bodies.[55] This binding force, however, is a pre-condition for the suitability of both principles.[56] Moreover, this is not the only missing requirement for the applicability of the principles to international investment arbitration. As a corollary of the principle of possible coincidence of treaty claims and contract claims, the grounds on which both types of claims are based are not

---

[52] For general difficulties, see F. Orrego Vicuña, Lis penden arbitralis, in: B. Cremades & J. Lew (eds.), Parallel State and Arbitral Procedures in International Arbitration (2005), 207 et seq. On the applicability of the principles to proceedings of two international adjudicatory bodies, see A. Reinisch, The Use and Limits of *Res Judicata* and *Lis Pendens* as Procedural Tools to Avoid Conflicting Dispute Settlement Outcomes, The Law and Practice of International Courts and Tribunals 3 (2004), 37 et seq.

[53] On *lis pendens*, see D. D. Reichert, Problems with Parallel and Duplicate Proceedings: The Litispendence Principle and International Arbitration, Arb. Int'l 8 (1992), 237, 237–238 et seq.; G. Kaufmann-Kohler & B. Stucki, International Arbitration in Switzerland: A Handbook for Practitioners (2004), 30 et seq. However, the majority of commentators deny the existence of any question of *lis pendens* in international arbitration. Accordingly, a contractual undertaking to arbitrate is sufficient to preclude the concurrent exercise of jurisdiction by public authorities. The principle of res judicata is normally followed by international commercial arbitral tribunals. See, e.g., E. Gaillard & J. Savage (eds.), Fouchard, Gaillard, Goldman on International Commercial Arbitration (1999), para. 1419; M. Rubino-Sammartano, International Arbitration Law and Practice (2001), 787-797; B. Hanotiau, The "Res Judicata" Effect of Arbitral Awards, Complex Arbitrations: Perspectives on Their Procedural Implications, ICC Int'l C. Arb. Bul., Special Supp. 2003, 43, 43 et seq.

[54] This dualistic stance is by no means uncontroversial. For a discussion of alternative monist and pluralist theories, see Shany, *supra* fn. 3, 78–105. In any event, the assumption of a non-horizontal relationship between international and domestic courts, which would be the prerequisite for the application of the principles of res judicata and *lis pendens*, has not been upheld by monist and pluralist theories either.

[55] See, e.g., I. Brownlie, Principles of Public International Law (2003), 50; Cheng, *supra* fn. 46, 337. See also *Amco Asia Corp. v. Republic of Indonesia*, ICSID Case No. ARB/81/1, Award, 20 November 1984, 1 ICSID Rep. 413, para. 177.

[56] Conversely, the generation of binding force may also be regarded as a corollary of the principles.

similar. Finally, the proceedings before the domestic courts will often concern a local subsidiary of the foreign investor and a sub-entity of the host State.[57] The international proceedings, in contrast, confront the foreign investor itself and the host State. In sum, the fulfilment of the principles' requirements is not conceivable in investment arbitration.[58]

II. *Treaty Provisions on the Avoidance of Parallel Proceedings*

The investment treaty regime thus established a considerable burden to the avoidance of parallel proceedings without providing for the traditional ways to remedy or mitigate their effects. Nevertheless, treaty drafters were aware of the risks of those proceedings and several treaty provisions appear to be aimed at the avoidance of duplication. Of course, as it is always the case in investment treaty law, there is no uniform approach, and treaties have to be examined on a casuistic basis. Notwithstanding this, there are a handful of typical provisions which are frequently used in treaties to address problems of duplication or which, at least, appear to do so.

1. *The "Fork in the Road Clause"*

The so-called "fork in the road clause" requires the investor to make a choice: either he brings his claim before an international arbitral tribunal or before a domestic court.[59] Since the clause stipulates the irrevocability of this choice, one may suppose that the clause is a proper solution to avoid duplication of proceedings concerning the same

---

[57] In this regard, the ECJ regularly applies the so-called "single-economic entity" doctrine which, under certain circumstances, allows the attribution of a subsidiary's activity to the parent company.

[58] Contra A. Sheppard, Res Judicata and Estoppel, in: B. Cremades & D. M. Lew (eds.), Parallel State and Arbitral Procedures in International Arbitration (2005), 219, 233, who opts for a less "strict" application of the triple identity test. However, it does not become clear to what extent the requirements should be altered. For a further interesting argumentation, see Dodge, *supra* fn. 39, 382–383: "In short, Chapter Eleven tribunals should adhere to the traditional customary international law rule that the decisions of domestic courts are not binding on them as res judicata, not because the parties or the issues are different, not because of doubts about the impartiality of domestic courts or as a corollary of the local remedies rule, but rather to encourage foreign investors to pursue their remedies in domestic courts in the hopes that at least some investment disputes may be resolved at the local level".

[59] See, e.g., article 8(2) of the France—Argentina BIT:

> [Any dispute relating to investments] shall be submitted, at the request of the investor, either to the national jurisdiction of the Contracting Party involved in

dispute. However, the interpretations given by arbitral tribunals to the term "dispute" in this sense seem to turn into another direction. In concordance with the principle of possible coincidence between contract claims and treaty claims, arbitral tribunals held that both types of claims did not pertain to the same category of disputes. For example, in *CMS v. Argentina*,[60] the tribunal held the following:

> [A]s contractual claims are different from treaty claims even if there had been or there currently was a recourse to the local courts for breach of contract, this would not have prevented submission of the treaty claims to arbitration. This Tribunal is persuaded that with even more reason this view applies to the instant dispute, since no submission has been made by CMS to local courts and since, even if TGN [the Argentine company of whose shares CMS held 29.42%] had done so—which is not the case- this would not result in triggering "fork in the road" provision against CMS. Both the parties and the causes of action under separate instruments are different.

In essence, the tribunals[61] thus applied the "triple-identity" criteria which were originally conceived in the municipal law doctrines of *lis pendens* and *res judicata*.[62] Applied to investment treaty arbitration and taking into account the principle of possible coincidence of treaty claims and contract claims, the "fork in the road" provision has almost no practical effect. Often in investment treaty proceedings and local court proceedings, not only the cause of action is different but also the parties to the dispute. Whilst the claim before local courts is usually brought by a locally established subsidiary against a regional or local administrative authority, the investment treaty claim is lodged by the foreign investor itself against the host State.[63] An investor would have

---

the dispute; or to international arbitration... Once an investor has submitted the dispute either to the jurisdiction of the Contracting Party involved or to international arbitration, the choice of one or the other of these procedures shall be final.

[60] *CMS Gas Transportation Co. v. Argentine Republic*, ICSID Case No. ARB/01/8, Decision on Jurisdiction, 17 July 2003, 7 ICSID Rep. 492, para. 80 (hereinafter, *CMS v. Argentina*).

[61] See also *Azurix Corp. v. Argentine Republic*, ICSID Case No. ARB/01/12, Decision on Jurisdiction, 8 December 2003, paras. 88–89 (hereinafter, *Azurix v. Argentina*); *Occidental Exploration & Production Co. (OEPC) v. The Republic of Ecuador*, LCIA No. UN3467, Final Award, 1 July 2004, [2005] 2 Lloyd's Rep 707, paras. 48–49; *Toto Costruzioni Generali S.p.A. v. The Republic of Lebanon*, ICSID Case No. ARB/07/12, Decision on Jurisdiction, 11 September 2009 (hereinafter, Toto v. Lebanon), para. 211.

[62] Friedman, *supra* fn. 18, 552.

[63] Id., 7; C. Schreuer, Travelling the BIT Route—Of Waiting Periods, Umbrella Clauses and Forks in the Road, JWIT 5 (2004), 231, 247–248 et seq.

to bring the entire dispute, i.e., the international law claim and the domestic law claim before the same adjudicative body and against the same respondent in order to trigger the "fork in the road clause". Since this is very unlikely, it is barely tenable that an investor is banned by the existence of such a clause from pursuing in separate forums treaty and contract claims arising from the same dispute.[64] It is interesting to note that the Annulment Committee in *Vivendi v. Argentina*, i.e., the adjudicative body which authoritatively laid down the principal distinction between treaty claims and contract claims, appears to be the only instance which doubts this school of thought.[65] However, the committee's point of view may be explained by the somewhat unusual specific situation of the case at issue. In order to explain why a treaty-based tribunal should have jurisdiction despite substantial contract issues in the case, the claimants put forward the argument that they would have lost their treaty claims by submitting the dispute to local courts. Thus, they argued for a broad interpretation of the "fork in the road clause", which investors usually are not inclined to do.[66] Furthermore, the decision shows how an improperly construed broadly phrased dispute resolution clause[67] may entail unexpected corollaries.[68]

---

[64] A. Crivellaro, Consolidation of Arbitral and Court Proceedings in Investment Disputes, The Law and Practice of International Courts and Tribunals 4 (2005), 371, 396, 400 et seq. Contra McLachlan et al., *supra* fn. 28, 4.83: "In the absence as yet of direct authority, it is submitted that the fork in the road clause ought to operate should the investor choose to pursue *a claim equivalent in substance* to that created by the BIT against the host State."

[65] *Compañia de Aguas del Aconquija S.A. v. Argentine Republic*, ICSID Case No. ARB/97/3, Decision on Annulment Proceedings, 3 July 2002, para. 55 (hereinafter, *Vivendi Annulment*):

> In the Committee's view, a claim by CAA against the Province of Tucumán for breach of the Concession Contract, brought before the contentious administrative courts of Tucumán, would prima facie fall within Article 8 (2) [which is the treaty's "fork in the road" clause] and constitute a "final" choice of forum and jurisdiction, if that claim was coextensive with a dispute relating to investments made under the BIT.

However, the committee later rejected that treaty claims and contract claims are coextensive. Cf. id., para. 113.

[66] Cf. *Compañia de Aguas del Aconquija S.A. v. Argentine Republic*, ICSID Case No. ARB/97/3, Award, 21 November 2000, para. 42 (hereinafter, *Vivendi v. Argentina*).

[67] See *Vivendi Annulment*, *supra* fn. 65, para. 55. The Committee held that the treaty's dispute resolution clause did not necessitate that the claimant allege a breach of the BIT itself. For the controversy with regard to the correct interpretation of broadly phrased dispute resolution clauses, see *supra* 68 et seq.

[68] See Friedman, *supra* fn. 18, 556, who states that this would have "a perverse consequence of dramatically expanding the breadth of an otherwise innocuous fork in the road provision".

A further problem arises in relation to an improperly understood umbrella clause. As Friedman correctly points out, when an umbrella clause is interpreted as transferring contract claims directly to the international plane, the triple-identity test, at least in cases of contracts directly concluded with the host State, would be satisfied and a "fork in the road" provision would apply.[69] This would have the odd result that a clause which provides the investor with special protection could contrarily result in a restraint of the foreign investor's rights. Be that as it may, as explained above, umbrella clauses do not entail the jurisdiction of treaty-based tribunals over contract claims but transform a contractual breach into a treaty violation and thus constitute treaty claims.[70] Hence, a triggering of an eventual "fork in the road clause" is not conceivable.

2. *Prior Recourse to State Courts for a Fixed Period of Time*

A further means by which jurisdictional conflicts between international and local proceedings may be circumvented is to require the claimant to make use of the local adjudicative bodies before bringing an international suit. Such a requirement can be regarded as the "antithesis"[71] or "opposite"[72] of the "fork in the road clause". Instead of requiring the investor to choose between international and domestic proceedings, the investor is forced to use both remedies, one after the other. As mentioned above, the classic rule of exhaustion of local remedies has been dispensed with widely by the investment treaty regime.[73] By contrast, a provision which still finds entry into investment treaties from time to time is a clause that requires the investor to first have recourse to local adjudication as a sort of pre-condition to the right to refer the matter to international arbitration.[74] The domestic remedy must be utilized for a certain period of time and only after its expiration can the dispute be submitted to international dispute resolution.[75]

---

[69] Id., 16.

[70] See *supra* 273 et seq.

[71] Friedman, *supra* fn. 18, 558.

[72] Schreuer, *supra* fn. 37, 4.

[73] See *supra* 286 et seq.

[74] See R. Dolzer & M. Stevens, Bilateral Investment Treaties (1995), 149–150, who refer to the Netherlands—Jamaica BIT (1991) which contains such a provision.

[75] For instance, article 10 of the Germany—Argentina BIT states that a dispute may be submitted to international arbitration

The time periods foreseen may vary from treaty to treaty. The usual time span is between three months[76] and two years.[77] These clauses are supposed to reflect a balance between two objectives: on the one hand, the State's preference to resolve investment disputes before its own courts, and on the other hand, the protection of the investor's right to arbitrate before an international forum.[78] In principle, such a regulation may be regarded as an appropriate means to address jurisdictional conflicts between the domestic and international sphere. Similar to international adjudicative bodies under the exhaustion of local remedies rule, treaty-based tribunals would have the right to test the entire host State's conduct against the substantive standards of the treaty. However, the interpretation given to the clause by arbitral tribunals as well as by legal commentators, again, is reluctant. In *Gas Natural SDG, S.A. v. Argentina*,[79] for instance, the respondent alleged that article X(3) of the Spain—Argentina BIT constituted a requirement of exhaustion of local remedies from which no derogation is permitted. The tribunal did not accept this argumentation:

> [U]nder that provision it would be possible to have recourse to arbitration even if there were a decision in the case by the national courts, and a fortiori if no final decision had been rendered in the national courts. Accordingly, the 18-month provision does not come within the concept of prior exhaustion of local remedies as understood in international law.[80]

In *Maffezini v. Spain*[81] and in *Siemens v. Argentina*[82], the claimants were entitled to circumvent the requirement set up by the clause on account

---

> (a) at the request of one of the parties to the dispute if no decision on the merits of the claim has been rendered after the expiration of a period of eighteen months from the date on which the court proceedings referred to in paragraph 2 [which provides that the dispute shall be submitted to the competent tribunals of the Contracting Party] of this Article have been initiated, or if such decision has been rendered, but the dispute between the parties persists.

A similar provision can be found in article X(3) of the Spain—Argentina BIT.

[76] See, e.g., article 8(1) of the Egypt—United Kingdom BIT.

[77] See, e.g., article 10 of the France—Morocco BIT.

[78] *Emilio Agustín Maffezini v. The Kingdom of Spain*, ICSID Case No. ARB/97/7, Decision on Jurisdiction, 25 January 2000, 5 ICSID Rep. 387, paras. 33, 35 (hereinafter, *Maffezini v. Spain*). See also B. Cremades & D. J. A. Cairns, Contract and Treaty Claims and Choice of Forum in Foreign Investment Disputes, in: N. Horn (ed.), Arbitrating Foreign Investment Disputes (2004), 325, 345 et seq.

[79] *Gas Natural SDG, S.A. v. Argentina*, ICSID Case No. Arb/03/10, Decision on Jurisdiction, 17 June 2005.

[80] Id., para. 30.

[81] *Maffezini v. Spain*, *supra* fn. 78, para. 64.

[82] *Siemens A.G. v. Argentine Republic*, ICSID Case No. ARB/02/8, Decision on Jurisdiction, 3 August 2004, (2005) 44 ILM 138 (hereinafter, *Siemens v. Argentina*).

of the application of MFN-clauses.[83] Both tribunals held that the clause could not be compared to the exhaustion of local remedies rule because it simply required the passing of time and not the exhaustion of the possibilities offered by domestic courts.[84] In the same vein, Schreuer argues that after the expiration of the time period, the investor is free to turn to international arbitration.[85] What may be questionable is whether the investor is obliged at all to commence local proceedings or whether the requirement is met by the mere lapse of time.[86] A decision hereupon may depend upon the specific formulation utilized in the treaty at issue. In any event, the purpose of the clause is heavily criticized by commentators. Some deem it to be a mere creation of a longer reflection period rather than to truly offer the state courts an opportunity to vindicate the international obligations of the State.[87] In particular, the shorter periods, and to a certain extent the longer periods as well, do not provide enough time to expect a serious resolution of complicated investment disputes.[88] On account of this, the clause, in fact, did not entail more effects than raising the costs of dispute resolution and delaying the arbitration.[89]

It is interesting to note in this regard that the notion of "dispute" as applied in this provision is somewhat at odds with the triple-identity test set out above. According to the traditional view, the investor is obliged to lodge its treaty claims before the local court in order to meet the conditions of the clause and be entitled to submit the dispute to international arbitration. Otherwise, the dispute regarding the treaty claims might not have been exhausted.[90] In turn, this means that the arbitral tribunal seized of a cause based on a prior recourse clause after the expiration of the time limit had to accept jurisdiction over the

---

[83] On this effect of MFN-clauses, see S. Fietta, Most Favoured Nation Treatment and Dispute Resolution under Bilateral Investment Treaties: A Turning Point?, Int'l Arb. L. Rev. 8 (2005), 131, 138 et seq.; J. Kurtz, The Delicate Extension of Most-Favoured-Nation Treatment to Foreign Investors: Maffezini v. Kingdom of Spain, in: T. Weiler (ed.), International Investment Law and Arbitration (2005), 523, 537 et seq.

[84] Cf. *Siemens v. Argentina*, *supra* fn. 82, para. 104; *Maffezini v. Spain*, *supra* fn. 78, para. 28.

[85] Schreuer, *supra* fn. 37, 4.

[86] The tribunal in *Maffezini v. Spain* held that such a result would deprive the clause of any meaning and therefore, is not compatible with principles of treaty interpretation. See *Maffezini v. Spain*, *supra* fn. 78, para. 36.

[87] Crivellaro, *supra* fn. 64, 399. Crivellaro refers here to the explanations of the *Maffezini* tribunal.

[88] Id.; Schreuer, supra fn. 37, 4.

[89] Schreuer, *supra* fn. 37, 4.

[90] Cf. Friedman, *supra* fn. 18, 559.

treaty and contract claims. According to Crivellaro, this is the corollary of the whole system developed by this clause. Such a clause would only make sense if both types of claims could be pursued sequentially before the distinct fora.[91] The correctness of this assertion is doubtful. It is not clear how this clause enlarges the treaty tribunal's jurisdiction over contractual claims. Therefore, it is preferable and consistent with the principle of possible coincidence of contract claims and treaty claims to uphold the separation in the framework of the prior recourse stipulation. This means, effectively, that the investor would have to bring its treaty claims before the national court in order to meet the requirements of the clause. The consequences, however, are puzzling in both cases. Would the role played by the arbitral tribunal be limited to ensuring that the national court process did not result in a denial of justice? The international tribunal can hardly be regarded as being bound by the domestic court's judgement if a decision is rendered at all. The clause thus comes to be a mere burden for the foreign investor but does not abrogate its right to international arbitration. Ultimately, this may explain the tribunals' reluctance to give the clause a broader meaning. As an instrument for consolidation, the provision is inherent of the same stain as the exhaustion of local remedies rule.

3. *Alternative Proposals on Jurisdictional Conflict Mitigation*

a. *Article 1121 of the NAFTA*

The NAFTA system is often regarded as more sophisticated than the usual investment treaty regimes.[92] It is thus not surprising that NAFTA contains provisions which until the present have not found entry in most of the regular bilateral investment treaties. One of these provisions is article 1121 which tries to avoid the duplication of proceedings. Under this article, an investor may submit a claim to arbitration only if

> (b) the investor and…the enterprise, waive their right to initiate or to continue before any administrative tribunal or court under the law of any

[91] Crivellaro, *supra* fn. 64, 400.

[92] See, e.g., M. Hunter, Reflections on Article 1128 of the NAFTA, in: R. Briner (ed.), Law of International Business and Dispute Settlement in the 21st Century—Liber Amicorum Karl Heinz Böckstiegel (2001), 313, 313 et seq. The reasons which are cited by Hunter, namely, the broad scope of remedies, a broad range of substantive obligations, and the consent to direct investor, apply similarly to modern bilateral investment treaties. Nevertheless, the elaborated system of the NAFTA is quite unique in the area of investment protection.

> Party, or other dispute settlement procedures, any proceedings with respect *to the measure* of the disputing Party that is alleged to be a breach referred to in Article 1116" (emphasis added).

The waiver of recourse to any other forum thus becomes a condition for referring the dispute to arbitration. This provision would not entail any further achievement than a "fork in the road clause" when the pivotal link is the same, i.e., the "dispute" as understood by traditional doctrine.[93] The clause at hand, however, follows a different approach. Instead of focusing on the identity of the "dispute", the provision turns entirely on the measure being challenged.[94] Thereby, the question which legal instrument—the treaty or the contract—the claim is based on becomes irrelevant. As a corollary, the duplication of proceedings which derives from the principle of possible coincidence of treaty claims and contract claims is circumvented, and an effective consolidation of proceedings is achieved. A further element which differentiates this provision from "fork in the road clauses" is that the investor is not obliged to make an irrevocable choice. Thus, the commencement of local court action does not alter the right to later pursue a NAFTA claim.[95]

In *Waste Management v. Mexico*, the tribunal underpinned this line of thought.[96] In this case, the claimant had submitted a waiver which referred to any proceedings with respect to the measure taken by the respondent that are alleged to be a breach of chapter 11 of the NAFTA and applicable rules of international law but explicitly should not apply to the violation of duties imposed by other sources of law, including the municipal law of Mexico.[97] In the tribunal's view, this waiver did not

[93] See Crivellaro, *supra* fn. 64, 397.

[94] See Friedman, *supra* fn. 18, 561–562, who explains that this different approach stems essentially from a different understanding of res judicata under common law. While civil law and international law tradition focussed on a triple identity test in this regard, common law jurisdictions tended to rely upon a two-pronged test referring to identities of parties and subject matter.

[95] Id., 22.

[96] *Waste Management Inc. v. United Mexican States*, ICSID Case No. ARB/98/2, Award on Jurisdiction, 2 June 2000, 5 ICSID Rep. 443 (hereinafter, *Waste Management v. Mexico*). For a discussion of this award, see E. C. Schlemmer, Waiver in International Arbitration, SAYIL 26 (2001), 202 et seq.

[97] *Waste Management v. Mexico*, *supra* fn. 98, para. 4. The waiver reads as follows: "Additionally, Claimants hereby waive their right to initiate or continue before any administrative tribunal or court ... any proceedings with respect to the measures taken by Respondent that are alleged to be a breach of NAFTA Chapter Eleven and applicable rules of international law .... *This waiver does not, however, apply to any dispute*

comply with article 1121. Accordingly, "when both legal actions have a legal basis derived from the same measures, they can no longer continue simultaneously in light of the imminent risk that the Claimant may obtain the double benefit in its claim for damage. This is precisely what NAFTA Art. 1121 seeks to avoid."[98] Consequently, the tribunal dismissed the arbitration.

Contrarily to the foregoing, a waiver clause which does not refer to identical "disputes" as understood traditionally but to the measure of the host State which entailed the dispute seems to be an effective means of consolidating domestic and international proceedings. It remains questionable, however, to what extent a "measure" within this sense covers the multitude of governmental actions which normally underlie an investment dispute. Is this "measure" comprised of all actions which are supposed to have infringed claimant's rights or can the claimant base its claims on different "measures" and thereby avoid its obligation to waive further proceedings? An adequate determination in this regard has not yet occurred.

b. *Article 26 of the ICSID Convention*

In the framework of investment disputes, the ICSID is by far the most frequently used institution.[99] In order to increase consolidation of disputes which are brought to it, the ICSID secretary-general applies the so-called method of indirect consolidation.[100] This method consists merely in the recommendation for the parties to designate the same arbitrators when such choice makes sense.[101] It concerns, however, the consolidation of parallel treaty-based arbitral proceedings. The provision by which ICSID seemingly pursues to achieve a consolidation of

settlement proceedings involving allegations that Respondent has violated duties imposed by other sources of law, including the municipal law of Mexico" (emphasis added by the tribunal).

[98] Id., para. 27.

[99] See *supra* 62 et seq.

[100] On recent cases, see W. Ben Hamida, La Consolidation des Procédures Arbitrales, Gaz. du Palais 3 (2006), 30, 31 et seq.

[101] See the recommendations of the ICSID Secretary-General concerning, on the one hand, *Salini Costruttori S.p.A. v. The Kingdom of Morocco*, ICSID Case No. ARB/00/4, Decision on Jurisdiction, 23 July 2001 (hereinafter, *Salini v. Morocco*), and *Consortium R.F.C.C. v. Kingdom of Morocco*, ICSID Case No. ARB/00/6, Award on Jurisdiction, 16 July 2001, and on the other hand, *Sempra Energy International v. The Argentine Republic*, ICSID Case No. ARB/02/16, Decision on Jurisdiction, 11 May 2005 and *Camuzzi International S.A. v. The Argentine Republic*, ICSID Case No. ARB/03/2, Decision on Jurisdiction, 11 May 2005 (hereinafter, *Camuzzi v. Argentina*).

local and international proceedings, and by which the jurisdiction of local courts presumably is excluded, is article 26 of the ICSID Convention.[102] The first sentence of this article reads as follows: "Consent of the parties to arbitration under this Convention shall, unless otherwise stated, be deemed consent to such arbitration to the exclusion of any other remedy."

This article is the clearest expression of the self-contained and autonomous nature of the arbitration procedure under ICSID auspices. The main features of this provision are: Firstly, once the parties give their consent to ICSID arbitration they lose their right to seek relief from another forum, national or international, and are restricted to pursuing their claim through the ICSID. Secondly, the principle of non-interference is introduced. The independence of arbitral proceedings before the ICSID from domestic courts is thereby fostered.[103] The domestic courts may come into play only in the context of enforcement.[104]

It is questionable to what extent this provision excludes the availability of domestic proceedings pursuant to a contract. Some authors regard this provision as being similar to article 1121 of the NAFTA.[105] This conclusion, however, is more than uncertain. As Friedman points out correctly, the wording of the provision gives no clear indication of whether "remedy" is to be understood with respect to the same "measure" or with respect to the same "dispute".[106] In any event, article 26 does not refer expressly to any of both notions. The system by which the consent to arbitration in the framework of the ICSID is given favours the latter interpretation. The standing offer of the host State is

[102] Cf. K. V. S. K. Nathan, The ICSID Convention (2000), 63: "The effectiveness of ICSID arbitration is heightened by the provision in the ICSID Convention that consenting parties shall, unless they have agreed otherwise, be deemed to have excluded any other remedy such as, for example, recourse to local courts" (footnote omitted).

[103] Schreuer, *supra* fn. 17, 347: "The underlying idea of the exclusive remedy rule and of the principle of non-interference is to provide an effective forum and to dispense with other proceedings which for a variety of reasons appear unattractive to the parties".

[104] See article 54 of the ICSID Convention. Article 54(2) reads as follows:

> A party seeking recognition or enforcement in the territories of a Contracting State shall furnish to a competent court or other authority which such State shall have designated for this purpose a copy of the award certified by the Secretary-General. Each Contracting State shall notify the Secretary-General of the designation of the competent court or other authority for this purpose and of any subsequent change in such designation.

[105] See, e.g., Schreuer, *supra* fn. 17, 368; Crivellaro, *supra* fn. 64, 385.

[106] Friedman, *supra* fn. 18, 565.

accepted by the investor with regard to a specific dispute.[107] Hence, the consent to arbitration and the corresponding jurisdiction of a treaty-based tribunal exist exclusively with respect to this specific dispute. On account of this, article 26 seems to provide that only one procedure can be pending in relation to a specific dispute.[108] The same interpretation has been given to article 26 by the *Lanco* tribunal.[109] This interpretation would lead to a different result than the one reached under article 1121 of the NAFTA.[110] As mentioned above, identical "disputes" require the identity of three elements: parties, action, and subject matter. Since such identity is generally not given in local and international proceedings, the provision does not serve to consolidate both proceedings. This conclusion is underpinned by the scope of the consent given by the parties. The consent given through investment treaties covers exclusively treaty claims. The investor's acceptance of the host State's standing offer cannot alter this scope of consent.

With regard to the first sentence of article 26 it is further controversial whether the phrase "unless otherwise stated" refers to existing contractual dispute resolution clauses. This question will be dealt with below in the framework of the examination of the impact of such clauses.

c. *Transaction-Based Approaches and Dispute-Based Approaches*

As seen above, the traditional means of consolidating domestic and international proceedings do not have the desired effect as regards international investment arbitration. This conclusion is chiefly due to a

---

[107] See *supra* 61 et seq.

[108] Cf. Crivellaro, *supra* fn. 64, 385: "However, if the prior exhaustion of local remedies is not required, the State's consent makes ICSID arbitration 'exclusive of any other remedy', which excludes the parallel referral of *the dispute* to domestic courts" (emphasis added).

[109] *Lanco v. Argentina*, *supra* fn. 39, para. 36: "In other words, when the parties give their consent to ICSID arbitration, they lose their right to seek to settle the dispute in any other forum".

[110] However, both Crivellaro and the *Lanco* tribunal do not seem to endorse this result. See Crivellaro, *supra* fn. 66, 385; *Lanco v. Argentina*, *supra* fn. 41, para. 36. The referral to a specific dispute does not hinder them from asserting that disputes before domestic courts are excluded by the provision. They ought to add that this is valid only for treaty claim disputes. Cf. McLachlan et al., *supra* fn. 28, 4.61:

> The exclusivity of ICSID arbitration in the case of treaty claims will, however, only relate to the investment dispute which forms the subject of such a claim. Thus it will not operate so as to preclude pursuit of claims by the investor against the host state which are not founded upon treaty rights, and which thus only can be the subject of other forms of dispute resolution.

traditional understanding of "identical disputes" and the corollaries of the principle of the possible coincidence of treaty claims and contract claims. The only effective way to avoid the generation of parallel proceedings before local courts and treaty-based tribunals has come out to be a transaction-based approach[111] which focuses on the identity of the host State's measure instead of the identity of the dispute. Provisions which rely on such a method have recently been included in several investment treaties and investment chapters of free trade agreements. Its increasing use in investment treaties is very likely.[112] Presumably, an increased application of such provisions by arbitral tribunals will lead to a higher degree of legal certainty as regards the determination of the notion of "measure" within the sense of the investment treaty provisions. Nevertheless, in the absence of such a clause, a consolidation of local court proceedings and treaty-based arbitral proceedings is not conceivable. Up to the present, the overwhelming part of existing investment treaties does not contain such provisions, and a consolidation usually does not occur. The question which arises as a corollary of the fact that neither general principles nor treaty provisions avoid their generation, concerns the relationship and the resolution of conflicts between international and domestic proceedings.

B. The Relationship between International Treaty Proceedings and Domestic Contract Proceedings

I. *General Considerations*

As explained above, local court or domestic arbitral proceedings and treaty-based proceedings before an international arbitral tribunal may

---

[111] For the notion of "transaction-based approach", see Friedman, *supra* fn. 18, 563.

[112] In fact, these clauses appear in several new model BITs and investment chapters of FTAs. See, e.g., article 26(2) of the 2004 US Model BIT; articles 26(1)(e), 26(2)(e) of the 2004 Canada Model BIT; article 10.15(5) of the Chile—U.S. FTA; article 10.17(2) of the Morocco—U.S. FTA; article 15.17 of the Singapore—U.S. FTA. Article 26(1)(e) of the 2004 Canada Model BIT reads as follows:

> A disputing investor may submit a claim to arbitration … only if … (e) the investor and, where the claim is for loss or damage to an interest in an enterprise of the other Party that is a juridical person that the investor owns or controls directly or indirectly, the enterprise waive their right to initiate or continue before any administrative tribunal or court under the law of any Party, or other dispute settlement procedures, any proceedings *with respect to the measure* of the disputing Party that is alleged to be a breach referred to in Article 22 … except for

intersect in two distinct ways: asymmetrically or symmetrically. In the framework of an asymmetrical conflict, both adjudicative bodies sit over the same factual dispute but apply different legal norms. As for the jurisdictional conflicts which arguably[113] arise in this regard, it is still hardly tenable to obviate from a hierarchical relationship in which the international tribunals ultimately trumpet over domestic courts.[114] In turn, insofar as symmetrical conflicts are concerned, the situation becomes more complex. Both the arbitral tribunal and the local court rule upon the same factual issues and apply rules of the same legal system. On account of this, not only is the resolution of prevalence more thorny compared to asymmetrical conflicts, but a further controversial problem emerges. State contracts regularly contain dispute resolution clauses which refer the disputes arising out of contractual relationship to domestic courts or domestic arbitration. The question which therefore arises is whether these clauses, notwithstanding the impact of investment treaties, grant local courts exclusive jurisdiction over claims which are fundamentally based on a contract. The same problem stated under a different formulation is at stake in the discussion on whether a foreign investor can waive its treaty rights in an investment contract.[115]

> proceedings for injunctive, declaratory, or other extraordinary relief, not involving the payment of damages, before an administrative tribunal or court under the law of the disputing Party (emphasis added).

The formulation thus matches the formulation used in article 1116(b) of the NAFTA.

[113] See Shany, *supra* fn. 3, 2-3:

> [N]ational and international courts are often perceived as courts of a different order altogether that apply different sets of laws and fulfil different social functions. It is questionable whether claims presented in such different institutional contexts, invoking legal standards anchored in different legal systems, can ever be described as similar claims for the purpose of identifying jurisdictional overlaps. In other words, the question pertains to whether these claims possess the required degree of similarity to apply most jurisdiction-regulating rules. Hence, the existence of jurisdictional interaction between national and international courts per se and the need for regulating their jurisdictions might be disputed (footnote omitted).

[114] Contra Douglas, *supra* fn. 6, 155:

> To treat international law as a self-sufficient legal order in the sphere of foreign investment is plainly untenable. Within this domain of private or commercial interests, problems relating to overlapping adjudicative competence and the application of municipal law cannot be resolved by playing the simple "international trump card" of Article 3 [of the ILC Articles on the Responsibility of States for Internationally wrongful Acts].

[115] See O. Spiermann, Individual Rights, State Interests and the Power to Waive ICSID Jurisdiction under Bilateral Investment Treaties, Arb. Int'l 20 (2004), 179, 180.

Ultimately, the effect of these clauses on the provisions of a treaty has to be examined.

II. *Prevalence of International Tribunals in Asymmetrical Conflicts*

Since the general principles of *res judicata* and *lis pendens* do not apply to the relationship between international arbitral proceedings and local court proceedings and investment treaties seldom contain provisions which effectively avoid or resolve a conflict between both, jurisdictional conflicts have to be resolved differently. As far as the area which has been termed asymmetrical conflicts is concerned, international investment tribunals have constantly ruled that international proceedings prevail over internal proceedings. In addition to the application of a rationale which accords primacy on account of the supra-national character of treaty-based international fora, they can base their decisions on a long line of international tribunals' decisions.

1. *The Superior Status of International Tribunals*

The application of the principle that an international tribunal's jurisdiction prevails over a domestic court's jurisdiction has a long tradition in decisions of international tribunals.[116] Back in 1927, in the case of *Socaciu v. Austria*, the claimant brought a claim based on the same subject matter before the Romanian courts prior to the constitution of the international mixed tribunal. The objection by Austria according to which the international tribunal should stay its proceedings because of the *litis pendens* principle was rejected by the tribunal:

> L'exception de litispendence soulevée, en plaidant, par M. l'Agent du gouvernement autrichien, n'est pas davantage fondée, car dès le moment où le T.A.M. [Tribunal Arbitral Mixte] admet sa compétence, le procés devant la Cour d'Appel de Bucarest n'a plus d'objet, le présent jugement revêtant l'autorité de la chose jugée.[117]

The same question arose before the Iran—U.S. Claims Tribunal.[118] Whereas the Iranian Ministry of Defence had lodged a claim before a

---

[116] D. D. Reichert, *supra* fn. 53, 243.

[117] *Socaciu v. Etat Austrichien et autres*, Decision of 14 May 1927, Receuil des Décisions des Tribunaux Arbitraux Mixtes, vol. VII, 785, cited in: Crivellaro, *supra* fn. 64, 393.

[118] *E-Systems Inc. v. The Government of the Islamic Republic of Iran*, Decision of 4 February 1983, (1983) Iran-USCTR 2, 51.

local Iranian court relying on the contract, the US company E-Systems brought the same case before the claims tribunal. According to the tribunal, its decision would prevail over any decision inconsistent with it rendered by Iranian or United States courts. Seemingly, the fact that the claims tribunal was established by an inter-governmental treaty sufficed to substantiate this point of view. Moreover, the tribunal ordered the Iranian Government to request that actions in the Iranian court be stayed until the international proceedings had been completed.[119] Several further international tribunals evinced a similar school of thought as regards the primacy of international tribunals over local court proceedings.[120]

A minority of international tribunals suggested more pragmatic ways to resolve overlaps. Although the primacy of international proceedings was likewise the result obtained by the France—Mexico Mixed Claims Commission in *Estate of Jean-Baptiste Caire v. Mexico*,[121] the presiding commissioner in this case was not reluctant to clarify that under specific circumstances, the rulings of Mexican local courts with regard to civil law matters could play a decisive role. In particular, this would be the case when the commission was confronted with preliminary questions concerning rights to property under the *lex situs*.[122] In a further case[123] in which the claimant had filed a claim before the local authorities, and its home State had brought the matter before the PCIJ, the court even deferred to the pending proceedings before the Supreme Polish Administrative Tribunal:

> [I]t will certainly be an advantage to the Court, as regards the points which have to be established in the case, to be acquainted with the final decisions of the Supreme Polish Administrative Tribunal upon the appeals brought by the Prince von Pless and now pending before that Tribunal...the Court must therefore arrange its procedure so as to ensure that this will be possible.[124]

Since this is one of the few occurrences in which an international tribunal deferred to local court proceedings, one cannot but state that the

[119] Id., 51 et seq.
[120] See the references by Crivellaro, *supra* fn. 64, 393 et seq.
[121] *Estate of Jean-Baptiste Caire (France) v. United States of Mexico* (1929) 5 RIAA 516.
[122] Id., 525. Yet, prior to that, the commissioner expressly rejected any kind of obligation of the commission in this regard.
[123] *Case concerning the Administration of the Prince von Pless* (Germany v. Poland) (Preliminary Objection), PCIJ Rep. Series A/B No. 52.
[124] Id., 16.

primacy of international tribunals over local adjudication is the fundamental rule by which asymmetrical conflicts were resolved by international adjudicative bodies. According to this school of thought, local court rulings are irrelevant to the outcome of international proceedings. In fact, concurrent local proceedings usually were only taken into consideration with regard to the prohibition against double recovery for a single loss.[125]

2. *The Primacy or "Independency" of International Investment Tribunals*

In the framework of investment arbitration this rule was not subject to a lot of exception either. In the context of the ICSID Convention, a so-called "rule of abstention" was regarded to hold sway. In the words of Delaume, this rule required that:

> [D]omestic courts must abstain from taking any action that might interfere with the autonomous and exclusive character of ICSID arbitration. In other words, if a court in a contracting state becomes aware that a claim before it may call for adjudication under ICSID, the court ought to stay the proceedings pending proper determination of the issue by ICSID.[126]

Accordingly, this rule was essential to the proper implementation of the convention.[127] Early ICSID tribunals applied the rule of primacy in order to ascertain their jurisdiction. In *Holiday Inns v. Morocco*, a consent to ICSID arbitration was included only in one of the three contracts comprising the investment.[128] The other two contracts contained dispute resolution clauses which referred to local dispute resolution. In the tribunal's view, this did not impede it of having jurisdiction

---

[125] For a recent examination of this traditional hierarchical relationship with regard to the ICJ and domestic courts, see A. Nollkaemper, The Role of Domestic Courts in the Case Law of the International Court of Justice, Chin. J. Int'l L. 5 (2006), 301 et seq.

[126] G. Delaume, ICSID Arbitration and the Courts, AJIL 77 (1983), 784, 785; G. Delaume, Foreign Sovereign Immunity: Impact on Arbitration, Arb. J. 38 (1983), 34, 38 et seq.

[127] According to Delaume, the sole role assigned to domestic courts under the convention relates to the recognition and enforcement of ICSID awards. See, Delaume, ICSID Arbitration and the Courts, id., 785.

[128] See P. Lalive, The First "World Bank" Arbitration (Holiday Inns v. Morocco)—Some Legal Problems, BYIL 51 (1980), 123 et seq. In fact, the agreement which contained the consent to ICSID arbitration was the "Basic Agreement" which fundamentally regulated the whole operation. The other two agreements were lease contracts which served to implement this project.

for the entire dispute. Accordingly, the general unity of an investment operation and the principle of primacy of international proceedings over internal proceedings argued in favour of the ICSID tribunal.[129] A further case before an ICSID tribunal in which consent through investment treaty was also not involved was the case of *Amco v. Indonesia*.[130] The objection by Indonesia to ICSID jurisdiction that the investor had appeared before domestic courts and thus, had waived its rights to ICSID arbitration were rejected by the tribunal on account of the irrelevance of the domestic proceedings for the ICSID arbitration.[131]

The tribunal in *CSOB v. Slovakia*, which was the first of the hitherto mentioned cases which was based on a BIT, recommended the suspension of parallel proceedings based on the priority of ICSID arbitration.[132] The tribunal in *SGS v. Pakistan* also reacted similarly. It held that the implementation of two proceedings relating to the same or substantially the same matter would be a waste of resources.[133] Thus, the tribunal's assumption was that if it affirmed its jurisdiction, it would inevitably prevail over that of the domestic arbitrator.[134]

In the aftermath of the *SGS v. Philippines* decision, which introduced the element of admissibility and had ordered a stay of its own proceedings with regard to an existing symmetrical conflict with proceedings before local Philippine courts,[135] several tribunals turned on the

---

[129] Id., 159–160, where Lalive quotes the following statement of the tribunal on the possibility that the Moroccan courts could be referred to for the settlement of a dispute arising out of the other two contracts:

> In such a hypothetical situation the Moroccan tribunals should refrain from making decisions until the Arbitral Tribunal has decided these questions or, if the Tribunal already decided them, the Moroccan tribunals should follow its opinion. Any other solution would, or might, put in issue the responsibility of the Moroccan State and would endanger the rule that international proceedings prevail over internal proceedings.

[130] *Asia Corp. v. Republic of Indonesia*, ICSID Case No. ARB/81/1, Decision on Jurisdiction, 25 September 1984, 1 ICSID Rep. 377.

[131] Id., 382.

[132] *Ceskoslovenska Obchodni Banka, A.S. (CSOB) v. The Slovak Republic*, ICSID Case No. ARB/97/4, Decision on Objections to Jurisdiction, 24 May 1999, 5 ICSID Rep. 330, para. 9.

[133] SGS *Société Générale De Surveillance S.A. v. Islamic Republic of Pakistan*, Case No. ARB/01/13, Procedural Order of 16 October 2002, ICSID Rev.-FILJ 18 (2003), 293, 304 et seq.

[134] Crivellaro, *supra* fn. 64, 392.

[135] *SGS Société Générale De Surveillance S.A. v. Republic of Philippines*, ICSID Case No. ARB/02/6, Decision on Jurisdiction, 29 January 2004, 8 ICSID Rep. 515 (hereinafter, *SGS v. Philippines*), paras. 169 et seq.

question of whether they should stay their proper proceedings given the existence of parallel proceedings even when the jurisdictional conflict at issue was of an asymmetrical nature. In *Impregilo v. Pakistan*, for instance, the tribunal put forward mainly two reasons why a stay of proceedings would be inappropriate.[136] On the one hand, this would confuse the essential distinction between treaty claims and contract claims. On account of this difference, the two enquiries were fundamentally different and it was not obvious that the local arbitral proceedings would be undermined by the determination of separate and distinct treaty claims. The foregoing was demonstrated by the fact that unlike in the *SGS v. Philippines* case, the parties to the ICSID proceedings were different from those in the local proceedings. On the other hand, neither clear conditions for a stay and its cessation nor a determined attitude towards the local proceedings existed. The same result was reached by the tribunal in *Bayindir v. Pakistan*.[137] Accordingly, this was an "inevitable consequence of the principle of the distinct nature of treaty and contract claims". Moreover, a stay would raise practical concerns. Particularly, it was not clear which contractual issues, if any, would have to be addressed by the tribunal on the merits. The intrinsic risks of this approach of contradictory decisions or double recovery could be dealt with by numerous other mechanisms belonging to the merits of a dispute.[138]

As for the merits stage, international investment treaty tribunals declared the outcome of local proceedings as largely irrelevant for their proper inquiry.[139] Comparable to the traditional stance of international courts and arbitral tribunals under public international law, a consideration of the latter only took place in order to prevent double recovery for a single loss. For instance, in *Wena v. Egypt*, the amounts recovered

[136] *Impregilo S.p.A. v. Islamic Republic of Pakistan*, ICSID Case No. ARB/03/3, Decision on Jurisdiction, 22 April 2005, paras. 289–290.

[137] *Bayindir Insaat Turizm Ticaret Ve Sanayi S.A. v. Islamic Republic of Pakistan*, ICSID Case No. ARB/03/29, Decision on Jurisdiction, 14 November 2005, paras. 264–273 (hereinafter, *Bayindir v. Pakistan*).

[138] Id., paras. 270–272. See also *SGS Société Générale De Surveillance S.A. v. Islamic Republic of Pakistan*, Case No. ARB/01/13, Decision on Jurisdiction, 6 August 2003, 8 ICSID Rep. 383, (2003) 42 ILM 1290, paras. 185–189 (hereinafter, *SGS v. Pakistan*): "This Tribunal has jurisdiction over the Treaty claims. The right to exercise that jurisdiction does not depend upon the findings of the PSI arbitrator; that is, such findings are not a factual or legal predicate for the consideration of whether Pakistan violated the Treaty obligations to which SGS points" (footnote omitted).

[139] See, e.g., *CME v. Czech Republic*, Partial Award, *supra* fn. 23, para. 415.

by Wena in a parallel arbitral proceeding were deducted from the ICSID tribunal's award for damages.[140] In sum, for the determination of a violation of treaty rights, local court proceedings or contractual arbitral proceedings do not have any particular impact upon a treaty-based tribunal's decision.[141]

It has been argued that this stance is inappropriate given the role played by domestic law in investment treaty disputes[142] and irresponsible as a matter of general policy towards the host State's local judiciary.[143] Respondent host States repeatedly demanded that the respective arbitral tribunal should stay its proceedings in case of concurrent jurisdiction.[144] Douglas proposes a rebuttable presumption to the effect that a decision of a competent court or tribunal on questions involving subject matters of municipal law would have to be followed by treaty-based tribunals.[145] A rebuttal of the presumption could be achieved by the tendering of evidence that the judgment is defective due to a serious procedural irregularity or a serious error of law. The court of appeal role thus taken by the treaty-based tribunal towards municipal

---

[140] *Wena Hotels Limited v. Arab Republic of Egypt*, ICSID Case No. ARB/98/4, Award, 8 December 2000, 6 ICSID Rep 89, para. 127; *Wena Annulment*, *supra* fn. 13, para. 49.

[141] Exceptions to this rule are, of course, cases of an alleged denial of justice. See, e.g., *The Loewen Group, Inc. v. United States of America*, ICSID Case No. ARB(AF)/98/3, Award, 26 June 2003, (2003) 42 ILM 811, para. 153. With regard to a concession contract, see *Robert Azinian v. The United Mexican States*, ICSID Case No. ARB(AF)/97/2, Award, 1 November 1999, para. 100: "For if there is no complaint against a determination by a competent court that a contract governed by Mexican law was invalid under Mexican law, there is by definition no contract to be expropriated". Furthermore, mention can be made of cases in which arbitral tribunals stated that the non-availability of local remedies or the investor's attempt to seek redress before local courts were requirements for the violation of a substantive treaty standard. See, e.g., *Generation Ukraine, Inc. v. Ukraine*, ICSID Case No. ARB/00/9, Award, 16 September 2003, para. 20.30; *Waste Management v. United Mexican States*, ICSID Case No. ARB(AF)/00/3, Award, 30 April 2004, (2004) 43 ILM 967, para. 116. For critics of this stance, see Schreuer, *supra* fn. 37, 16: "The decision to do away with it [i.e., the local remedies rule] in investor-State investment arbitration was made consciously and for good reasons. Therefore, we should think twice before making the use of local remedies a constitutive element for substantive requirement of a violation of international law standards." In any event, these cases did not concern the concrete outcome of the respective local proceedings.

[142] See J. Crawford, Treaty and Contract in Investment Arbitration, Int'l Arb. 24 (2008), 351, 352–353. This also holds true for the reverse case, i.e., the application of international law by domestic courts. See, e.g., Nollkaemper, *supra* fn. 125, 314 et seq.

[143] Douglas, *supra* fn. 6, 273. For a criticism of hierarchy as a substitute for regulation in general, see Shany, *supra* fn. 3, 6–7.

[144] See, e.g., *Bayindir v. Pakistan*, *supra* fn. 137, para. 264.

[145] Douglas, *supra* fn. 6, 273–274.

adjudicative bodies would still be more convenient to judicial comity than to completely ignore the prior decision. A further reason for such a presumption would be the higher qualification of local judges and arbitrators to deal with often complex issues of municipal law.[146]

However, the determination of a rigid formula by which asymmetrical conflicts have to be resolved is hardly tenable. By contrast, an arbitral tribunal's tendency to defer to domestic courts could finally equal a regression to a denial of justice age the termination of which was one of the primary goals of the investment treaty regime. During the jurisdictional stage, the evidentiary situation will usually be too unclear to require a mandatory stay of proceedings. During the merits stage, a rigid introduction of a rebuttable presumption could render the proceedings overly cumbersome for the investor. In the final analysis, when the violation of international law is at stake, international tribunals must not be bound by rulings of domestic courts.[147] The fact that arbitral tribunals could use this independence from domestic courts in a much more flexible way, for instance, by taking into account the judgements where appropriate or by a concise stay of proceedings when necessary, is a different subject matter. In any event, a legal constraint upon international arbitral tribunals in this regard does not exist.

III. *The Impact of the Contractual Dispute Resolution Clause on Symmetrical Conflicts*

A different situation exists with regard to symmetrical conflicts. Since the adjudicative bodies of both legal spheres apply the same law, the superiority of international tribunals in this context is not as clear as in the case of asymmetrical conflicts. Furthermore, the claimant in such a dispute relies fundamentally on the contract to back up its claim. Over a century ago, the so-called Calvo Doctrine was introduced in order to diminish the jurisdiction of international treaty-based courts and tribunals in such situations. At present, a comparable clause has

[146] By contrast, the supposed lack of expertise on the part of national judges is sometimes put forward to underline the disadvantages of local court adjudication. See, e.g., Reinisch & Malintoppi, *supra* fn. 6, para. 21; T. Wälde, The "Umbrella" (or Sanctity of Contract/Pacta sunt Servanda) Clause in Investment Arbitration—A Comment on Original Intentions and Recent Cases, JWIT 6 (2004), 183, 189–190.

[147] This is still an unavoidable consequence of the essential principle of international law according to which the internal characterization of an act as lawful does not affect its international characterization.

increasingly found entry into investor—host State agreements.[148] The effect which is given to such clauses by treaty-based arbitral tribunals is crucial for the relationship of international and domestic proceedings.

1. *Traditional Forms—The Calvo Clause*

The Calvo Clause was the traditional means by which capital importing States emphasized the jurisdiction of their own judiciary.[149] In fact, this clause is regarded to have two principal functions: Firstly, it provides for the obligation to submit all disputes relating to the particular investment contract in which the Calvo Clause is inserted to the local courts and thereby subjects them to the national law regime of the host State. Secondly, the clause is sometimes construed as embodying the investor's waiver of its right to appeal for the diplomatic protection of its home State.[150] The clause's essential purposes are thus to preserve

---

[148] For an antique Calvo Clause, see *North American Dredging Company v. Mexico*, *supra* fn. 3, 26–27. Article 18 of the contract at issue in this case read as follows:

> The contractor and all persons who, as employees or in any other capacity, may be engaged in the execution of the work under this contract either directly or indirectly, shall be considered as Mexicans in all matters, within the Republic of Mexico, concerning the execution of such work and the fulfillment of this contract. They shall not claim, nor shall they have, with regard to the interests and the business connected with this contract, any other rights or means to enforce the same than those granted by the laws of the Republic to Mexicans, nor shall they enjoy any other rights than those established in favor of Mexicans. They are consequently deprived of any rights as aliens, and under no conditions shall the intervention of foreign diplomatic agents be permitted, in any matter related to this contract.

See also *Martini Case* (1903) 10 RIAA 644 (hereinafter, *Martini*), 663: "Las dudas ó controversias que puedan suscitarse en la inteligencia y ejecución del presente contrato, serán resueltos por los Tribunales de la República, conforme á sus leyes, y en ningún caso serán motivo de reclamaciones internacionales." On the introduction of clauses with allegedly similar effect at present, see Schreuer, *supra* fn. 37, 1 et seq.

[149] Although the creation of the doctrine is generally credited to the Argentine jurist and diplomat Carlos Calvo, it seems that the ideas of non-intervention and submission to local law by entry into the territory were first conceived by the Venezuelan jurist and founder of the Chilean Civil Code of 1855 Andrés Bello. See S. Montt, State Liability in Investment Treaty Arbitration (2009), 41 et seq.; F. Griffith Dawson, The Influence of Andres Bello on Latin-American Perceptions of the Non-Intervention and State Responsibility, BYIL 57 (1986), 253, 287 et seq. On the incorporation of this concept into the Chilean Civil Code of 1855, see A. Boggiano, Contratos Internacionales (1995), 9 et seq.

[150] See generally, e.g., L. M. Summers, The Calvo Clause, Va. L. Rev. 19 (1933), 459 et seq.; A. Hershey, The Calvo and Drago Doctrines, AJIL 1 (1907), 26 et seq.; D. Shea, The Calvo Clause—A Problem of Inter-American and International Law and Diplomacy (1955). For more recent examinations, see F. Oschmann, Calvo-Doktrin und Calvo-Klauseln (1993).

the host State's sovereignty and to uphold the idea of national treatment.[151]

Almost a century ago, international tribunals had to deal with Calvo Clauses for the first time. The decisions of the American—Mexican Claims Commission and the American—Venezuelan Claims Commission are deemed to be precedents on the clause's interpretation.[152] This may be explained by the particular impact the clause had and was intended to have on the South and Central American investment regimes.[153] In *North American Dredging Company of Texas (United States) v United Mexican States*, the claim for breach of contract was espoused by the US on behalf of the North American Dredging Company of Texas. The contract contained a dispute resolution clause which referred all disputes "concerning the execution of the work and the fulfilment of this contract" to local adjudication. In this regard, the commission stated the following:

> Where a claim is based on an alleged violation of any rule or principle of international law, the Commission will take jurisdiction notwithstanding the jurisdiction of such a clause in a contract subscribed by such claimant. But where a claimant has expressly agreed...that in all matters pertaining to the execution, fulfilment, and interpretation of the contract he will have resort to local tribunals, remedies, and authorities, and then wilfully ignores them by applying in such matters to his government, he will be bound by his contract and the Commission will not take jurisdiction of such claim.[154]

Hence, the commission applied a strict distinction between international claims and domestic contract claims. Whereas jurisdiction over the former may not be abrogated through a contract clause, the latter may be subject to contractual regulation. The commission's reasoning is based upon the *venire contra factum proprium* principle: an investor must not plead the breach of one term of the contract whilst at the same time pleading the non-applicability of another. Several other

---

[151] Shea, *supra* fn. 152, 19. D. Manning-Cabrol, The Imminent Death of the Calvo Clause and the Rebirth of the Calvo Doctrine: Equality of Foreign and National Investors, Law & Pol'y Int'l Bus. 26 (1995), 1169, 1172; G. Biggs, The Latin American Treatment of International Arbitration and Foreign Investments and the Chile—U.S. Free Trade Agreement, ICSID Rev.-FILJ 19 (2004), 61, 66.

[152] Douglas, *supra* fn. 6, 243.

[153] Cf. H. Grigera Naón, Arbitration and Latin America: Progress and Setbacks, Arb. Int'l 21 (2004), 127, 131 et seq.; Biggs, *supra* fn. 151, 66–67.

[154] *North American Dredging Company v. Mexico*, *supra* fn. 3, 33.

tribunals underlined the importance of this principle of unity of contract. Accordingly, an investor cannot rely on the breach of one term of the contract whilst at the same time alleging the invalidity of another of its provisions.[155] In other words, when the claim is based fundamentally on a contract, the same contract must likewise be taken into consideration when it provides for the withdrawal of the claim from an international tribunal's jurisdiction. This withdrawal, however, is only valid inasmuch as no international law violation has occurred.[156] In sum, the traditional interpretations of the Calvo Clause by international tribunals endorsed the point of view that the clause obligates an investor to bring its contractual claims before the respective contractually agreed forum.

As to the second function of the clause, international tribunals were much more reluctant to construe the clause as a waiver of the right to diplomatic protection. In fact, this effect of the clause has been unanimously rejected by international tribunals.[157] Since the right to diplomatic protection under classic international law did not accrue to the investor but essentially to the home State, the reasoning underlying this rejection was simple: an investor cannot waive a right which he did not possess.[158] Given the developments in the field of diplomatic protection concerning the question of who between the home State and the private person is the holder of the right,[159] one may ask to what extent this reasoning is still tenable. Be that as it may, at the time of the Calvo Clause's heydays, the doctrine that the right pertained to the State occupied a stalwart position.

---

[155] See, e.g., *Turnbull, Manoa Company (Ltd.) and Orinoco Company (Ltd.) Cases* (United States v. Venezuela), (1903–1905) 9 RIAA 261, 304; *Woodruff Case* (United States v. Venezuela), (1903–1905) 9 RIAA 213, 221.

[156] *North American Dredging Company v. Mexico*, *supra* fn. 3, 33; *Martini*, *supra* fn. 148, 663–664. Furthermore, the parties to an international treaty could agree on overriding clauses with such effect. For such a treaty provision, see, e.g., *Orinoco Steamship Company Case*, (1903–1905) 9 RIAA 180, 181 (hereinafter, *Orinoco Case*): "All claims owned by citizens of the United States of America against the Republic of Venezuela … shall be examined and decided by a Mixed Commission".

[157] See, e.g., *North American Dredging Company v. Mexico*, *supra* fn. 3, 33–34; *Martini*, *supra* fn. 150, 663; *Orinoco Case*, *supra* fn. 158, 183; *Rudloff Case* (Interlocutory), (1903–1905) 9 RIAA 244, 246.

[158] For the interests of the national State, see Amerasinghe, *supra* fn. 36, 48–49.

[159] See, e.g., Orrego Vicuña, *supra* fn. 35, 31–33. For a recent comment in favour of the traditional view, see A. Vermeer-Künzli, As If: The Legal Fiction of Diplomatic Protection, EJIL 18 (2007), 37 et seq.

2. *The Interpretation in Modern Investment Arbitration*

The relationship between a treaty's dispute resolution clause referring the dispute to international arbitration and the contractual dispute resolution clause often providing exclusively for domestic procedures is a complicated one that has not been treated with much uniformity by international investment tribunals. The situation may be sufficiently clarified in relation to treaty violations that is, to stay in the context, with regard to asymmetrical conflicts. By contrast, the major debate arises out of the treatment of purely contractual claims, i.e., claims which are based fundamentally on a breach of contract. Which of the two clauses shall prevail? Which one derogates the other by means of the *lex specialis* principle? Is it sound that an investor on the one hand argues in favour of the contract's applicability, claiming its violation before the international tribunal, and at the same time, tries to circumvent the contract's dispute resolution clause?

Regularly, the responding State in international arbitration objects to the tribunal's jurisdiction, contending that the contractual dispute resolution clause which refers the dispute to domestic courts constitutes a waiver of international arbitration.[160] Recent tribunals reacted in different ways to this contention. A direct rejection of such argumentation was sustained by the tribunals in *Lanco v. Argentina*[161] and *Salini v. Morocco*[162]. Both put forward two substantial arguments: Firstly, the dispute resolution clause in the contract, pointing to domestic administrative courts, could not be regarded as a real choice of forum. The jurisdiction of administrative tribunals under domestic law was not subject to agreement or waiver but was compelling. As a corollary, the parties' agreement upon the jurisdiction of the administrative tribunals was no more than a confirmation of existing law. Second, both tribunals relied on a certain kind of supremacy of international law over domestic law. According to the *Lanco* tribunal, there is generally a "presumption in favour of ICSID arbitration". Therefore, once a valid

---

[160] See, e.g., *SGS v. Pakistan*, *supra* fn. 138, para. 118, where Pakistan contended that SGS waived its rights by commencing local arbitration pursuant to the contract; *Aguas del Tunari S.A. v. Republic of Bolivia*, ICSID Case No. ARB/02/3, Decision on Jurisdiction, 21 October 2005, ICSID Rev.-FILJ 20 (2005), 450, paras. 94 et seq. (hereinafter, *Aguas del Tunari v. Bolivia*); *Azurix v. Argentina*, *supra* fn. 61, para. 28; *Camuzzi v. Argentina*, *supra* fn. 101, paras. 55 et seq.

[161] *Lanco v. Argentina*, *supra* fn. 39, paras. 26, 39, 40.

[162] *Salini v. Morocco*, *supra* fn. 101, paras. 24–27.

consent to ICSID arbitration is established, "any other forum called on to decide the issue should decline jurisdiction."[163] Hence, the *Lanco* tribunal did not base the prevalence of investment treaties upon the distinction between treaty claims and contract claims but on a general concept of priority of ICSID arbitration over domestic courts.[164]

The *Vivendi* Annulment Committee then introduced the general distinction between treaty and contract claims[165] which was applied by the majority of tribunals in subsequent cases.[166] As for the impact of the contractual dispute resolution clause upon the jurisdiction over treaty claims, the committee stated that:

> [W]here the fundamental basis of the claim is a treaty laying down an independent standard by which the conduct of the parties is to be judged, the existence of an exclusive jurisdiction clause in a contract between the claimant and the respondent state or one of its subdivisions cannot operate as a bar to the application of the treaty standard.[167]

Thus, the distinction between both types of claims leads to a situation in which the international tribunal's jurisdiction could not be circumvented when the violation is one of the treaty's standard. This rule applies to the abovementioned field of asymmetrical conflicts. Yet, previously, the committee had already clarified that the principle of possible coincidence similarly had to find application to the opposite case: "In a case where the essential basis of a claim brought before an international tribunal is a breach of contract, the tribunal will give effect to any valid choice of forum clause in the contract" (footnote omitted).[168]

The committee chiefly found support for this view in the jurisprudence concerning the interpretation of Calvo Clauses.[169] Subsequent to the committee's decision, a string of tribunals applied this reasoning in order to uphold their jurisdiction.[170] The underlying rationale is clear:

---

[163] *Lanco v. Argentina, supra* fn. 39, para. 40.

[164] C. Schreuer, Investment Treaty Arbitration and Jurisdiction over Contractual Claims—The Vivendi I Case Considered, in: T. Weiler (ed.), International Investment Law and Arbitration: Leading Cases from the ICSID, NAFTA, Bilateral Treaties and Customary International Law (2005), 281, 290.

[165] See *supra* 163 et seq.

[166] See only *Bayindir v. Pakistan, supra* fn. 137, para. 215.

[167] *Vivendi Annulment, supra* fn. 65, para. 101.

[168] Id., para. 98.

[169] See *supra* 310 et seq.

[170] See, e.g., *Azurix v. Argentina, supra* fn. 61, para. 79; *CMS v. Argentina, supra* fn. 60, paras. 89–94; *Siemens v. Argentina, supra* fn. 82, paras. 174–180; *Camuzzi v. Argentina, supra* fn. 101, para. 63; *Bayindir v. Pakistan, supra* fn. 137, paras. 150–151.

proceedings before a local court and proceedings before a treaty-based tribunal are based on different causes of action. Therefore, the contractual dispute settlement clause does not alter the jurisdiction for treaty claims but determines exclusively the jurisdiction over contract claims. However, in the present context, it is crucial to note that all the tribunals that upheld their jurisdiction notwithstanding the existence of a contractual dispute resolution clause were concerned with violations of contracts which, at the same time, were susceptible of amounting to a breach of the respective BIT.[171] In short, they concerned asymmetrical conflicts. In turn, this was not the case in the two SGS cases where both tribunals were confronted with purely contractual claims and thus symmetrical conflicts arose.

In *SGS v. Pakistan*, the question of whether the dispute resolution clause of the BIT covered contractual violations or prevailed over the contractual mechanism was answered in the negative by the tribunal.[172] The tribunal first addressed the coverage of the contractual dispute resolution clause. It held that it "could not seriously be contended that" breaches of contract were not covered by this clause. Article 11.1[173] of the agreement between the parties could not be construed in a way that it would not encompass contractual disputes arising out of the PSI Agreement (the contract).[174] Conversely, article 9 of the BIT[175] could not be regarded as referring to mere contractual violations. Notwithstanding the fact that both types of claims could be construed as "disputes with regard to investments", the intention of the contracting parties to cover purely contractual claims under the BIT was not

[171] Cf. *Enron Corporation y Ponderosa Assets, L.P. v. Argentina*, ICSID Case No. ARB/01/3, Decision on Jurisdiction, 2 August 2004, para. 91.

[172] *SGS v. Pakistan*, *supra* fn. 138, paras. 159–162.

[173] Article 11.1 of the PSI Agreement reads as follows:

> 11.1 Arbitration. Any dispute, controversy or claim arising out of, or relating to this Agreement, or breach, termination or invalidity thereof, shall as far as it is possible, be settled amicably. Failing such amicable settlement, any such dispute shall be settled by arbitration in accordance with the Arbitration Act of the Territory presently in force. The place of arbitration shall be Islamabad, Pakistan and the language to be used in the arbitration proceedings shall be the English language.

[174] *SGS v. Pakistan*, *supra* fn. 138, para. 160.

[175] Article 9 of the Switzerland—Pakistan BIT provides that: "1. Any disputes arising between a Contracting Party and the investors of the other, including disputes relating to compensation for expropriation, nationalization, requisition or similar measures, and disputes relating to the amount of the relevant payments ... may be submitted for settlement to ICSID arbitration".

sufficiently clear. "Disputes with regard to investment" did not relate to the legal basis of the claims; rather, this phrase was merely descriptive of the factual subject matter of the disputes.[176] Moreover, it could not be contended that the provision of the BIT would prevail over the clauses of the PSI Agreement. The BIT was concluded subsequent to the PSI Agreement. None of the BIT's provisions gave rise to the assumption that it was the intention of the Contracting Parties to entail the invalidity of all other non-ICSID forum selection clauses in earlier agreements between Swiss investors and Pakistan.[177] Therefore, article 11.1 of the PSI Agreement was valid as far as it concerned SGS's contract claims which did not also amount to BIT claims. Nonetheless, according to the tribunal, the parties are free to agree upon the submission of purely contractual claims to international investment tribunals. In the present case, however, such a choice was not undertaken.[178] Since the tribunal likewise denied an elevating effect to the treaty's umbrella clause,[179] a jurisdictional conflict between local court proceedings and international arbitral proceedings did not arise.

Such a conflict occurred in *SGS v. Philippines*.[180] In this case, the tribunal confirmed its jurisdiction based upon a broadly phrased dispute resolution clause of the treaty and an umbrella clause. However, the tribunal declared the claims as inadmissible and ordered a stay of its proceedings. In its view, the requirement of admissibility was due to the impact of a contractual forum selection clause which referred contractual disputes to local courts.[181] After a brief consideration of the clause's compelling character and the general principle according to which a binding exclusive jurisdiction clause in a contract should be respected unless overridden by another valid provision,[182] the tribunal addressed two crucial aspects: Firstly, whether the exclusive jurisdiction clause was overridden by the BIT or the ICSID Convention and secondly, what was the effect of the clause concerning the admissibility of the claim to ICSID jurisdiction.

---

[176] *SGS v. Pakistan*, *supra* fn. 138, para. 161.

[177] Id.

[178] Id.

[179] See *supra* 235 et seq.

[180] *SGS v. Philippines*, *supra* fn. 135.

[181] Article 12 of the CISS Agreement (the contract involved in this case) reads as follows: "All actions concerning disputes in connection with the obligations of either party to this Agreement shall be filed at the Regional Trial Courts of Makati or Manila".

[182] *SGS v. Philippines*, *supra* fn. 135, paras. 137–138.

Concerning the former problem, the tribunal asserted that neither article VIII(2) of the BIT[183] nor article 26 of the ICSID Convention abrogated the contractual clause. Accordingly, the intention of article VIII(2) was not to override an exclusive contractual jurisdiction clause. The provision of the BIT was a general provision which had not been concluded with any specific investment in view. As a consequence, the maxim *generalia specialibus non derogant* would argue against an abrogating character of the provision. Further, investment treaties are contended to be framework treaties. Accordingly, they should support and supplement investment arrangements. Their purpose was not to override or replace those arrangements.[184] This conclusion was not altered by the application of the maxim *lex posterior legi priori*. This principle would solely to instruments of the same legal character. Bearing in mind that the BIT was a public international law framework for investments between two States while the contract was a specific investment agreement between a private investor and a State, the application of the principle could not be sustained.[185]

According to SGS, the part of article 26 of the ICSID Convention in which is stated that the party's consent to ICSID jurisdiction was given "to the exclusion of any other remedy" must be construed as abrogating the contract's provision.[186] The tribunal rejected this argument. It ruled that article 26 was not a mandatory rule but a mere rule of interpretation.[187] In addition, the tribunal noted that article 26 contained the phrase "unless otherwise stated". The inclusion of a jurisdictional clause in an investment contract was regarded as such a statement.[188] Finally, a comparison with the UNCITRAL Rules, which do not include a similar clause, showed that the prevalence of article 26 was not intended. Otherwise, when the BIT gives the parties a choice between the ICSID

---

183 The treaty dispute resolution clause provides for international arbitration for "solving disputes with respect to investments between a Contracting Party and an investor of the other Contracting Party".

184 *SGS v. Philippines*, *supra* fn. 135, para. 141.

185 Id.

186 Id., para. 144.

187 Id., para. 146.

188 The tribunal cited Schreuer and stated: "This exclusive remedy rule of Art. 26 is subject to modification by the parties. The words 'unless otherwise stated' in the first sentence give the parties the option to deviate from it by agreement." Id., para. 147, citing Schreuer, *supra* fn. 17, 347. The tribunal furthermore stated that: "Explicit reference to domestic courts means that the exclusive remedy rule of Art. 26 does not apply since the parties have stated otherwise. Id., citing Schreuer, *supra* fn. 17, 363.

and the UNCITRAL, the choice by a party of the ICSID would mean that legal rights are affected, i.e., the contractual rights would be overridden, whilst the choice of the UNCITRAL would not.[189]

As a consequence, the tribunal introduced the element of admissibility. In the tribunal's view, the question was "whether a party should be allowed to rely on a contract as the basis of its claim when the contract itself refers that claim exclusively to another forum." The tribunal's answer was in the negative: "a party to a contract cannot claim on that contract without itself complying with it."[190] The tribunal concluded that notwithstanding the acceptance of its competence to hear purely contractual claims, the contractual claim brought by SGS was inadmissible and thus stayed its proceedings.[191] This aspect was deemed to be a matter of admissibility rather than one of jurisdiction because the treaty jurisdiction was not abrogated by the contract. Accordingly, it was up to the parties by agreement or to the Philippine courts to determine the amount payable by the Philippines.[192]

The decision is accompanied by Arbitrator Crivellaro's strong dissent concerning precisely the relationship between article VIII(2) of the BIT and Article 12 of the contract between the parties. Crivellaro's reasoning is based on the assumption that the two contradicting dispute resolution clauses, namely, the umbrella clause and the contractual dispute resolution clause, do not necessarily override or replace each other. Accordingly, co-existence between both clauses is the sounder approach. Investment treaties were intended to offer investors an additional choice, not an exclusive one. An investor who concluded a contract with a State had the right to choose between a variety of fora offered to him through treaty as well as through contract. The stipulation of the contract thus remained effective also after the entry into force of the BIT.[193] However, it ceased to be the exclusive choice of forum clause for the investor. Such an interpretation corresponded to the purpose of the BIT.[194] The innovative contribution of the investment treaty regime consisted especially in the offer of further dispute settlement fora to the investor.[195]

---

[189] Id., para. 148.
[190] Id., para. 154.
[191] Id., para. 169(4).
[192] Id., para. 174.
[193] *SGS v. Philippines*, *supra* fn. 135, Declaration by Arbitrator Crivellaro (hereinafter, *Declaration Crivellaro*), para. 4.
[194] Id., para. 10.
[195] Id., para. 6.

Further, Crivellaro brought forward a string of general arguments for the prevalence of a treaty's clause. He asserted that the use of the maxim *generalia specilibus non derogant* was not appropriate for the same reason that hindered the application of the *lex posterior deragat legi priori* maxim. This is the absence of similarity as regards the legal character of both examined legal instruments. He added, however, that in case of application, the latter maxim seemed to be more apt to the case at issue and that its application would lead to the prevalence of the later concluded treaty.[196] Moreover, the treaty claim filed by SGS was not even in the scope of article 12 of the contract. The contractual dispute resolution clause referred uniquely to disputes connected with "this Agreement". Through the application of the umbrella clause's elevating effect, the claim essentially became a claim based on the treaty. As a consequence, no claim connected with the contract had been filed.[197]

In *Salini v. Jordan*,[198] the tribunal applied a contractual forum selection clause referring all disputes to local courts. However, this result was based on a rather unusual treaty provision[199] and concerned exclusively the contract claims. The tribunal thus dismissed the claimant's argument that article 9(2) of the Italy—Jordan BIT applied solely to Article 9(1) and not to Article 9(3)[200] which paved the way for international arbitration.[201] It is interesting to note that in the tribunal's view, the obligation in article 9(2) was made to the exclusion of any other remedies. At the same time, it underpinned that this did not concern claims which are based on breaches of the BIT including breaches of those provisions of the BIT guaranteeing fulfilment of contracts signed with foreign investors.[202] Although the tribunal later dismissed the allegation that the treaty contained an umbrella clause, it had thus made clear that a contractual dispute resolution clause does not deprive a

---

[196] Id., para. 9.

[197] Id., para. 11.

[198] *Salini Costruttori S.p.A. v. The Hashemite Kingdom of Jordan*, ICSID Case No. ARB/02/13, Decision on Jurisdiction, 15 November 2004, (2005) 44 ILM 573 (hereinafter, *Salini v. Jordan*).

[199] Article 9(2) of the Italy—Jordan BIT states the following: "2. In case the investor and an entity of the Contracting Parties have stipulated an investment Agreement, the procedure foreseen in such investment Agreement shall apply".

[200] Article 9(1) obliges the parties to settle disputes amicably. Article 9(3) gives the investor the choice of submitting the dispute to local courts or international arbitration in the event that an amicable settlement is not reached within six months.

[201] *Salini v. Jordan*, *supra* fn. 198, paras. 75–79.

[202] Id., paras. 93–96.

tribunal of its jurisdiction based on such a clause even when its application is mandatory under the treaty.

3. *The Different Views and Their Resolution*

The existing jurisprudence is thus inconsistent with two jurisdictional aspects which are ultimately two sides of the same coin. Firstly, it is unclear whether an investor may intentionally abrogate from the treaty-based tribunal's jurisdiction by entering into a contract with the host State. In line with the traditional interpretation of Calvo Clauses, it has even been argued that such conduct could be regarded as a waiver of treaty protection through the investor. Secondly, it remains doubtful whether a contractual dispute resolution clause referring disputes relating to the contract to local adjudication is such a waiver and if not, what is the effect, if any, of such a clause as regards claims that fall under treaty jurisdiction but are based on breach of contract.

a. *Waiver of Right to Treaty Protection*

The question of whether an investor may waive its rights conferred under an investment treaty has not found much contemplation yet. Spiermann examined the rights involved in investment treaty disputes and came to the conclusion that investment treaties essentially create individual rights and therefore an investor may usually be entitled to waive these rights.[203] He stated that a clear and unequivocal forum selection clause in an investment contract which provides for non-treaty-based jurisdiction in an exclusive manner can be regarded as a valid waiver in this regard. He admits, however, that this effect is likely to be confined upon contract claims.[204] A further view regards contractual forum selection clauses not so much as a waiver of treaty rights but rather as an expression of their exertion.[205] Accordingly, the choice of a local court as the forum for dispute resolution is only conceivable in case the pertinent investment treaty provides for this option. If it does, the investor's choice is valid and excludes international arbitration. Moreover, this perspective seems not to distinguish between contract claims and treaty claims. On account of this, such a choice may also be

---

[203] Spiermann, *supra* fn. 115, 179 et seq.

[204] Id., 211: "Besides, a possible effect is presumably confined to contract claims, as opposed to treaty claims".

[205] J. Griebel, The Vivendi Case—Some Critical Remarks concerning the Question of Jurisdiction, Int'l Arb. L. Rev. 7 (2004), 67 et seq.

available for treaty claims.[206] The same result was apparently reached by the recent decision in *Aguas del Tunari v. Bolivia*.[207] Therein the tribunal stated that the question whether a mandatory obligation in a separate document can affect the jurisdiction of an international arbitral tribunal was one of the intent of the parties in concluding the separate document.[208] Furthermore, under article 27 of the ICSID Convention, consent by an investor to arbitration or its acceptance of the host State's standing offer has the effect of suspending the right of diplomatic protection by the home State of the foreign investor.[209] On account of this, one could presume that the home State's interests did not appear to prevent an investor from doing the opposite, i.e., waiving of the rights by accepting the host State's offer.[210] One could even argue that since the home State's right of diplomatic protection remains untouched when the investor waives its rights to arbitration, the home State's interests were protected sufficiently. Other authors argue that substantive treaty rights operate at the inter-State level and foreign investors were only holders of the procedural right to submit disputes to international arbitration. Therefore, a waiver of substantive treaty rights by the investor would not be feasible because it is the home State that possesses these rights and not the investor.[211]

However, even if one accepts the presumption that the substantive treaty rights are directly owed to the investor,[212] the point of view which accepts the availability of a waiver is more than questionable.[213]

---

[206] Id., 71–72.

[207] *Aguas del Tunari v. Bolivia*, *supra* fn. 160.

[208] Id., para. 115.

[209] A. Giardina, International Investment Arbitration: Recent Developments as to the Applicable Law and Unilateral Recourse, The Law and Practice of International Courts and Tribunals 29 (2006), 29, 32 et seq.; A. Broches, The Convention on the Settlement of Investment Disputes between States and Nationals of Other States, RdC 136 (1972-II), 331, 349–350.

[210] Cf. Spiermann, *supra* fn. 115, 205.

[211] See J. van Haersolte-van Hof & A. K. Hoffmann, The Relationship between International Tribunals and Domestic Courts, in: P. Muchlinski et al. (eds.), The Oxford Handbook of International Investment Law (2008), 962, 1002–1003; Z. Douglas, Nothing if Not Critical for Investment Treaty Arbitration: *Occidental, Eureko* and *Methanex*, Arb. Int'l 22 (2006), 27, 37–38; Z. Douglas, The International Law of Investment Claims (2009), 35.

[212] For a discussion of the debate concerning the question of whether investment treaties' substantive provisions are inter-State obligations or owed directly to foreign investors, see *supra* 81 et seq.

[213] See, e.g., *Vivendi v. Argentina*, *supra* fn. 66, para. 53; *SGS v. Philippines*, *supra* fn. 135, para. 154.

Essentially, the public character of investment treaty disputes and the requirements of a waiver under international law argue against it. First, the rights bestowed upon the investor by investment treaties are inextricably linked to the public interest.[214] On the one hand, treaties further stable investment relations and on the other hand, they provide for a neutral investor—host State dispute resolution mechanism in order to prevent the emergence of political conflicts by reason of investment disputes.[215] If the investor could be prompted in negotiations with the host State to opt out of this system, these underlying purposes could easily be rendered nugatory. Second, if the right to waive investment treaty protection is accepted, the investor's waiver of these rights would have to be made in unequivocal terms. It is correct that under a legal system in which the only subjects are States and investment treaties are regarded as merely creating a legal relationship between the host State and the home State, investors would not be vested with the right to waive international arbitration.[216] As mentioned above, this school of thought is beginning to show its age, particularly in the human rights and economic rights context.[217] Yet, it is interesting to note that the rights conferred by international human rights treaties can be waived by their beneficiaries only under exceptional circumstances.[218] Although a certain relevance of the individual's free consent as regards their application cannot be denied,[219] the European Court of Human Rights took the position that only certain rights under the European

---

[214] See *SGS v. Philippines*, *supra* fn. 135, para. 154:

> It is, to say the least, doubtful that a private party can by contract waive rights or dispense with the performance imposed on the States parties to those treaties under international law. Although under modern international law, treaties may confer rights, substantive and procedural, on individuals, they will normally do so in order to achieve some public interest. Thus the question is not whether the Tribunal has jurisdiction: unless otherwise expressly provided, treaty jurisdiction is not abrogated by contract (footnote omitted).

[215] See, e.g., P. Muchlinski, Policy Issues, in: P. Muchlinski et al. (eds), The Oxford Handbook of International Investment Law (2008), 1, 6 et seq.; P. Comeaux & S. Kinsella, Reducing Political Risk in Developing Countries: Bilateral Investment Treaties, Stabilization Clauses, and MIGA & OPIC Investment Insurance, NY L. School J. Int'l & Comp. L. 15 (1994), 1 et seq.

[216] Cf. Spiermann, *supra* fn. 115, 181.

[217] See *supra* 85 et seq.

[218] On the waiver of rights granted under the European Convention on Human Rights, see C. Grabenwarter, Europäische Menschenrechtskonvention (2008), 122–123.

[219] J. Crawford, The International Law Commission's Articles on State Responsibility: Introduction, Text and Commentaries (2002), 165.

Convention on Human Rights may be waived.[220] Such a waiver, in any event, must be established in an unequivocal manner and must not run counter to any important public interest.[221] Even if economic interests may not be comparable to human rights concerns, a modern concept of international investment protection requires similar standards for the waiver of investment treaty rights. Hence, even if one accepts the availability of a waiver, the investor would have to express this intention in clear and unequivocal terms.

b. *The Effects of a Contractual Dispute Resolution Clause*

Since the foreign investor's presumed right to waive treaty-based arbitration needs a method of enforcement to become a valid right, the effect of contract clauses in which the host State and the investor agree upon a forum for the resolution of contract-related disputes becomes paramount. Up to date, the inclusion of such a clause has been regarded as the exclusive means by which investors may use this right. In other words, the practical validity of such a theoretical right is linked inextricably to the effect of contractual dispute resolution clauses.[222] By and large, decisions of international arbitral tribunals and comments of legal scholars have evinced the emergence of two currents of thought in this regard.

On the one hand, it is argued that the choice made under a contractual forum selection clause has to be respected despite a treaty provision to the contrary. The vantage point which regards this as a waiver of treaty protection chiefly substantiates this result with the pivotal role of investors under the investment treaty regime. The argument goes as follows: If the investor is the holder of rights under an investment treaty he may be entitled to waive these rights. The waiver is effectuated through the inclusion of a forum selection clause in the investment contract which is regarded to be more specific than the general treaty

---

[220] *Albert and Le Compte v. Belgium*, Judgment of 10 February 1983, ECHR Series A No. 58, para. 35.

[221] See generally L. O. Baptista, Parallel Arbitrations—Waiver and Estoppel, in: B. Cremades & J. Lew (eds.), Parallel State and Arbitral Procedures in International Arbitration (2005), 127, 130–131. In the context of the ECHR, see *Oberschlick v. Austria*, Judgment of 23 May 1991, ECHR Series A No. 204, para. 51.

[222] See *Aguas del Tunari v. Bolivia*, *supra* fn. 160, para. 115: "[T]he Tribunal holds that the question of whether a conflicting mandatory obligation in a separate document can affect the jurisdiction of an ICSID tribunal is a question of the intent of the Parties".

provisions referring investment disputes to a different forum.[223] The same result is achieved by the school of thought that does not necessarily deem the contractual clause to be a waiver but emphasizes the principle of unity of the investment agreement.[224] The main rationale underlying this approach is that an investor must not rely on one contract provision to substantiate its claim and at the same time deny the applicability of another contract provision under which he consented to resolve the dispute before local courts.[225] Again, the contract is seen as more specific than the general treaty protection and thus according to the principle of *lex specialis non derogate*, the former prevails.

The practical consequences of both approaches are not clear. Does such a contractual choice of forum alter the jurisdiction of an arbitral tribunal? In other words, is the arbitral tribunal's jurisdiction fettered through such a clause or does the power to decide hereupon remain within the international arbitral tribunal? The answers given to these questions do not reflect a consistent approach. When the contractual clause is regarded as a waiver of treaty protection, any result other than a lack of jurisdiction of a treaty-based tribunal would appear awkward. When an investor waived its rights under a treaty, he has no standing before such treaty-based tribunal with respect to the rights subject of the waiver.[226] If the impact of a waiver is extended to all kinds of treaty claims which are related to a contract, this point of view leads directly back to an age in which denial of justice was the only grounds that enables one to bring a claim before an international tribunal. Furthermore, it is difficult to explain how a provision in a domestic law contract covers and alters the rights provided for in an international treaty. Ultimately, this point of view does not make an appropriate consideration of the differences between contract and treaty claims. Probably, that is the reason why this school of thought

---

[223] Spiermann, *supra* fn. 115, 208–210; Griebel, *supra* fn. 205, 71–72; *Aguas del Tunari v. Bolivia*, *supra* fn. 160, paras. 119 et seq. The tribunal, which generally recognised the right to waive ICSID arbitration, explained that in the case of an alleged waiver through contractual forum selection clause, "the specific intent of the parties to preclude ICSID jurisdiction will be more difficult to ascertain than in the case of explicit waiver".

[224] *SGS v. Philippines*, *supra* fn. 135, para. 134.

[225] Id., paras. 149 et seq.; Douglas, *supra* fn. 6, 260.

[226] Spiermann, *supra* fn. 115, 211, who sustains the availability of a waiver, refers exclusively in negative form to this result of his stance: "A forum clause that is not expressly to the exclusion of other forums will probably have no effect on ICSID's jurisdiction".

does not reach a consistent conclusion concerning the inclusion of treaty claims.[227]

A more subtle view is the one taken by the tribunal in *SGS v. Philippines*.[228] As explained above, the tribunal considered the existence of a contractual forum selection clause as merely triggering the inadmissibility of a claim which is primarily based on breach of contract. A treaty-based tribunal should thus stay its own proceedings pending a decision by another judicial forum.[229] The chief argument in this context is the purported unity of contract. Further, this perspective can be regarded as dismissive of the existence of an inherent hierarchy between national and international courts.[230] In this case, the burden of proving that the "fundamental basis of the claim" is a contract and that another forum for the settlement of this dispute previously had been chosen by the parties would be on the respondent. By contrast, when the claimant can prove that it is likely to encounter denial of justice before the contractually agreed upon fora, the claim would be admissible in treaty-based arbitration. However, this is only tenable if the claimant is able to demonstrate actual steps taken by the respondent State to jeopardize the local dispute resolution forum.[231]

To demonstrate the ability and flexibility of international tribunals to stay proceedings, mention is often made of the *MOX Plant* case[232]

[227] Cf. id., who admits that "a possible effect is presumably confined to contract claims, as opposed to treaty claims". By contrast, Griebel, *supra* fn. 205, 71, contents that "[c]laims concerning subject-matter which fall within the jurisdiction of for example national tribunals under a contract may not be addressed by ICSID. And this is true even for treaty claims which overlap with contract claims. Otherwise, the rights granted to investors under a BIT regarding a choice of forum would be ignored".

[228] *SGS v. Philippines*, *supra* fn. 135, para. 154.

[229] For the distinction between admissibility and jurisdiction, see J. Collier & V. Lowe, The Settlement of Disputes in International Law: Institutions and Procedures (1999), 155–156.

[230] Shany, *supra* fn. 3, 75.

[231] Douglas, *supra* fn. 6, 265.

[232] *The MOX Plant Case* (Ireland v. United Kingdom) (Order No. 3) (2003) 42 ILM 1187. In this case, Ireland lodged claims objecting to the approval and operation by the UK of a mixed oxide fuel-processing plant before a variety of tribunals such as an UNCLOS arbitral tribunal, ITLOS, ICJ, and ECJ based on several legal systems or instruments including the OSPAR (Convention for the Protection of the Marine Environment of the North-East Atlantic), the UNCLOS, European Union law and English law. The UNCLOS tribunal stayed its own proceedings pending determination of the issue by the European court due to the fact that according to article 281 of the UNCLOS, the outcome of those proceedings might influence its own jurisdiction. For a summary, see Y. Shany, The First MOX Plant Award: The Need to Harmonize Competing Environmental Regimes and Dispute Settlement Procedures, Leiden J. Int'l L. 17 (2004), 815 et seq.

before an annex VII tribunal under the UNCLOS.[233] A further case, this time in the context of international investment protection, in which an international tribunal ordered the stay of its own proceedings was the case of *SPP v. Egypt.*[234] Since the validity and the scope of an ICC arbitration clause and thus the ultimate validity of the respective ICC award concerning a contractual dispute similarly underlying the ICSID proceedings was at stake at the Court of Cassation in Paris, the tribunal, "in the interest of the judicial order", stayed its proceedings.[235] In any event, both cases did not concern a stay of proceedings due to domestic court proceedings.

Yet, whereas the general ability of international tribunals to stay their own proceedings and the convenience to do so in certain cases cannot be disputed, the obligation to order such a stay because of a contractual forum selection clause is hardly convincing. The discretion to do so ultimately remains with the arbitral tribunal which is endowed with jurisdiction.[236]

The impact given by the former stance to a contractual forum selection clause has been heavily criticized by some commentators.[237] These approaches may be divided into two different ways of thinking: whilst one stance emphasizes the prevalence of supra-national tribunals and thus regards contradictory domestic contract clauses as irrelevant,[238] a further school of thought claims the non-exclusivity of the different

---

[233] See, e.g., *SGS v. Philippines, supra* fn. 135, para. 171; Y. Shany, Contract Claims vs. Treaty Claims: Mapping Conflicts between ICSID Decisions on Multisourced Investment Claims, AJIL 99 (2005), 835, 846.

[234] *Southern Pacific Properties (Middle East) Ltd. v. Arab Republic of Egypt*, ICSID Case No. ARB/84/3, Decision on Jurisdiction, 27 November 1985, 3 ICSID Rep. 112.

[235] Id., para. 77 et seq.

[236] Cf. *Bayindir v. Pakistan, supra* fn. 137, para. 271: "In any event, accepting that it has discretion to order the stay of the present proceedings as requested by Pakistan, that discretion is only to be exercised if there are truly compelling reasons". The tribunal concerned has to consider also that a stay of the proceedings in the context of arbitration, the purpose of which is the timely resolution of disputes, could easily lead to a setting aside of the award and thus thwart the claimant's right to have its case heard. Cf. K. Hóber, Parallel Arbitration Proceedings—Duties of the Arbitrators, in: B. Cremades & J. Lew (eds.), Parallel State and Arbitral Procedures in International Arbitration (2005), 243, 256–257.

[237] See specifically for criticism on the decision in *SGS v. Philippines*, Wälde, *supra* fn. 146, 29 et seq.; E. Gaillard, Investment Treaty Arbitration and Jurisdiction over Contract Claims—The SGS Cases Considered, in: T. Weiler (ed.), International Investment Law and Arbitration: Leading Cases from the ICSID, NAFTA, Bilateral Treaties and Customary International Law (2005), 325, 334.

[238] See, e.g., Schreuer, *supra* fn. 37, 5.

fora and thus endorses the cumulative applicability of both systems of dispute resolution.[239]

Notwithstanding the differences in result, both stances have several points in common. Firstly, according to them the inclusion of a contractual forum selection clause does not alter the jurisdiction of a treaty-based tribunal. A waiver of treaty protection is thereby not effectuated. Although the tribunal in *SGS v. Philippines* pointed out that its solution would not result in such alteration either, the impact given to contractual forum selection clause by the tribunal would result in treaty-tribunals having jurisdiction over "an empty shell".[240] The *SGS v. Philippines* tribunal's attempt to reconcile the treaty and contract forum selection clauses was, in practice, impossible because it tried to render compatible two contradictory intentions: whereas the parties to a contract seek an exclusive forum, the intention of the parties to a treaty is to accord to the investors a choice of fora.[241]

Secondly, the existence of such a clause does not entail the inadmissibility of claims based fundamentally on breach of contract before treaty-based tribunals. For this reason, an international tribunal is not required to stay its own proceedings in such a case. Such a stay would have the same effect as a waiver and would ultimately result in a denial of justice. Moreover, since the conditions for an order of stay as well as for a re-initiation of proceedings before a treaty-based tribunal are highly unclear, the effect of such a stay would be an increased confusion concerning the reliability of investment treaty arbitration.[242]

Finally, the principle *generalia specialibus non derogant* is regarded as favouring investment treaty arbitration. Accordingly, a dispute settlement clause in a BIT is a mere standing offer to investors. When the investor accepts this offer, a specific arbitration agreement is created which applies solely to one specific dispute and thus, is more specific than the general contractual provisions.[243]

The differences between both lines of argumentation are mainly limited to the result. In this regard, one stance underlines the favourability of the resolution of an investment dispute in one forum and of avoiding

---

[239] *Declaration Crivellaro*, *supra* fn. 193, para. 4; McLachlan et al., *supra* fn. 28, 4.61.

[240] Gaillard, *supra* fn. 237, 334.

[241] Id.

[242] Wälde, *supra* fn. 146, 231–232.

[243] See, e.g, Schreuer, *supra* fn. 17, 294; Crivellaro, *supra* fn. 64, 385.

the risks of parallel proceedings.[244] Schreuer, for instance, argues that the conceptual separation of both claims and the following employment of parallel judicial proceedings over the same legal dispute would be uneconomical. It is preferable to refer the whole dispute to the forum with the most comprehensive jurisdiction, namely, the international tribunal.[245] The cumulative applicability of treaty and contract remedies is supported by other authors.[246] They see investment treaties essentially as a legal instrument for investment protection, among others. Thereby, the investor is offered an additional option of remedies. The purpose of investment treaties is not, by contrast, to restrain an investor's jurisdictional opportunities.

At the outset, it has to be underlined that both sides present strong arguments for their respective positions. Whereas it is reasonable to respect the unity of contract and not to allow an investor to rely on some contractual provision while rejecting others, it is likewise convincing that a State should not be enabled to circumvent its international obligations through the conclusion of domestic contracts. As Gaillard puts it, this is the impossibility of giving effect to the parties' contracts while respecting the general language of BIT dispute settlement provisions.[247] The application of the principles *generalia specialibus non derogant* and *lex posterior deragat legi priori* do not lead to a convincing result either. The former is brought forward by both stances but the question of whether the consent to international arbitration or the conclusion of a contract including a forum selection clause is more specific to the respective dispute at hand remains arbitrary. As for the latter, the tribunal in *SGS v. Philippines* discerned the problems which are entailed by its applicability. The fact that both legal instruments can be renewed after certain time periods does not enable this principle to achieve legal certainty.[248] In any event, the different legal characters of the treaty and the contract make the applicability of the principles more than doubtful.

This difference between both instruments leads us to the principle which has become paramount in investment treaty arbitration: the

---

[244] See, e.g., Kaufmann-Kohler, *supra* fn. 14, 202; Schreuer, *supra* fn. 17, 359; Gaillard, *supra* fn. 17, 237.

[245] Schreuer, *supra* fn. 37, 12.

[246] See, e.g., *Declaration Crivellaro, supra* fn. 193, para. 4; W. Kühn, Practical Problems Related to Bilateral Investment Treaties, in: G. Kaufmann-Kohler & B. Stucki, Investment Treaties and Arbitration, ASA Special Series No. 19, (2002), 43, 45.

[247] Gaillard, *supra* fn. 237, 334.

[248] *SGS v. Philippines, supra* fn. 135, para. 142.

principle of possible coincidence of treaty claims and contract claims. Its application in the present context entails a crucial corollary which may help to clarify the effect of contractual forum selection clauses with regard to claims that are fundamentally based on a contract but are covered by a treaty. The contention has been made that such contract clauses abrogate from the jurisdiction over treaty claims. Given the distinct nature of both legal instruments, it is not conceivable that a contractual provision covers claims based on a breach of treaty. In other words, contractual dispute settlement provisions can only cover claims based on a breach of contract.[249] According to the point of view warranted in the present work, such a claim can only be brought before a treaty-based tribunal on account of an umbrella clause or a precisely-phrased dispute resolution clause. As regards the latter, a contractual dispute resolution clause may indeed have the effect of depriving an arbitral tribunal of its jurisdiction.[250] In the former case, however, the claim is a treaty claim and thus not covered through a contractual dispute resolution clause.[251] Hence, the scope of a contractual forum selection clause does not extend to treaty claims. An argumentation which supports such extension does not consider the principal distinction between both types of claims appropriately. Furthermore, the unity of contract is not impaired by this claim. The investor's claim based on the violation of an umbrella clause is based on the treaty and not on the contract. Thus, the investor does not contradict its contractually agreed upon commitments. The investor is simply using a further legal instrument which has been made available by its home State and the host State.

It is clear that this interpretation generates an intrinsic risk of contradictory decisions and double recovery.[252] Nevertheless, it appears to be the exclusive way to preserve a balance between the host State's and the investor's rights by taking into due consideration the role of investment treaties. It has to be recalled that investment treaties are intended to add extra protection to the investor—host State relationship.[253] The purpose and the result of the investment treaty regime is to advance

---

[249] *Salini v. Jordan*, *supra* fn. 198, para. 96.

[250] See *Toto v. Lebanon*, *supra* fn. 61, para. 202. The tribunal in this case held that the effect of an umbrella clause was to grant jurisdiction over contract claims.

[251] Accordingly, treaty-based arbitral tribunals do not have jurisdiction to sit over contract claims.

[252] *Bayindir v. Pakistan*, *supra* fn. 137, para. 270.

[253] See, e.g., Crawford, *supra* fn. 142, 22.

from the era of traditional international law under which international tribunals only became relevant in case of exhaustion of local remedies or denial of justice. Yet, this additional protection does not replace or abrogate from the contract. As Crivellaro puts it succinctly, it is not a question of whether the treaty clause overrides or replaces the contract clause: "they both survive and coexist".[254] This result of co-existence is eminently logical when one consequently applies the principle of possible coincidence of treaty claims and contract claims.

In sum, with the exception of the rare cases in which a treaty expressly provides for a different solution, e.g., a transaction-based waiver requirement, investment treaties provide for an alternative choice for investors. In this regard, the eventual generation of parallel proceedings ensures that an investor need not sacrifice its legal right in the name of efficiency. For instance, when the revocation of a license to drill by the host State potentially infringes on an investor's rights under a treaty and under a contract, the investor, in general, may lodge claims pursuant to both legal instruments, i.e., contract claims before local court or a contractual arbitral tribunal and treaty claims before a treaty-based arbitral tribunal. It is true that there are several situations in which aspects of judicial comity and maintenance of judicial order as well as respect for domestic proceedings make a deferral to pending domestic proceedings or a consideration of the results of concurrent decisions recommendable.[255] This may be the case when, for example, the decision upon an essential aspect of the dispute, such as the amount payable under the contract, is pending before a domestic court. In such cases, international tribunals may avail themselves of several mechanisms[256] based on principles such as *abus de droit* and judicial comity which could serve to mitigate the impact of the conflicts.[257] However,

---

[254] *Declaration Crivellaro*, *supra* fn. 193, para. 4.

[255] This is even more so in the case of symmetrical proceedings since the applicable law in both cases is the same and the legal question at issue should likewise be the same. Admittedly, the eventual stay of proceedings or a rebuttal presumption appears more reasonable in this case than in the case of asymmetrical proceedings. Nonetheless, also in the case of a symmetrical conflict, the international arbitral tribunal cannot be enjoined with a legal obligation to proceed in a similar manner.

[256] See, e.g., Hóber, *supra* fn. 236, 250 et seq. In principle, the measures may range from mere consideration of domestic proceedings or awards over co-operation to consolidation or stay of proceedings.

[257] For a very detailed description of the principles of *abus de droit* and judicial comity, see Shany, *supra* fn. 3, 165 et seq. The principle of *abus de droit* requires tribunals to prevent parties from attaining advantages from overlapping jurisdictions based on

these are discretional options and no investment treaty tribunal is bound by a domestic contract to proceed similarly.

IV. *Conclusion*

It is true that the establishment of the investment treaty regime created a higher risk of jurisdictional conflicts especially in the additional presence of investment contracts. This is all the more so since the traditional ways of jurisdictional conflict resolution or mitigation are not applicable in this area of law and treaty provisions to this effect proved largely ineffective. Contingent upon the law applicable to the substance, parallel proceedings may be categorized as asymmetrical or symmetrical conflicts. Whereas the former category is generally resolved in favour of international tribunals, the latter bears more controversial aspects of overlap. This holds especially true in the case of a contractual dispute resolution clause which refers the dispute to local adjudication. Yet, the principle of possible coincidence of contract claims and treaty claims and the subsequent co-existence between both legal instruments make it very unlikely that such a clause embodies an abrogation from treaty-based jurisdiction. Although the resulting existence of two similarly applicable legal instruments of investment protection may be deplorable under jurisdictional aspects, it is an inescapable consequence of the conclusion of international investment treaties as an additional layer of investment protection.

bad faith. As an example, Shany mentions the recourse to international arbitration in breach of a contractual dispute resolution clause to the contrary. From my perspective, such behaviour will not amount to abusiveness under ordinary circumstances in the absence of an express waiver of international arbitration. According to the principle of judicial comity, international tribunals enjoy a certain discretion as to their handling of parallel proceedings. For reasons of fairness and expediency, they may opt for coordination with domestic courts or even a stay of proceedings. Yet, none of these principles enjoins international arbitral tribunals with an obligation to refrain from the exertion of its jurisdiction.

FINAL CONCLUSION

For decades, the legal problems surrounding contracts between foreign investors and host States have been the subject of much controversy. Whereas international lawyers called for an internationalisation of these contracts, the host States backed the contracts' inclusion in their domestic law systems. By offering a satisfactory solution from both the host State's and the foreign investor's perspectives, the widespread establishment of investment treaties can be held to contribute considerably to the resolution of this schism.

From the foregoing analysis, it becomes obvious that the investment treaty regime creates an additional layer of protection for contracts between host States and foreign investors. This effect of investment treaties on such contracts is contingent upon the fulfilment of two general prerequisites: First, the contract or the contractual rights have to fall within the notion of investment set out by the particular treaty. Second, the contract has to be signed with the host State or—as regards treaty claims—with an entity whose conduct is attributable to the host State. In case these conditions are met, the treaty paves the way to international dispute settlement of contractual disputes. The consent to international arbitration provided for in investment treaties operates as a standing offer of the host State to the investor to submit investment disputes to arbitration. Hence, foreign investors are directly endowed with, at the minimum, the procedural right to submit claims to international adjudicative bodies. The implication that follows is that the investment treaty system replaces the traditional rules of diplomatic protection in the field of investment protection. Insofar as this protection is based upon the reception of general international law standards, i.e., upon the standard of non-expropriation and the fair and equitable treatment standard, it is not the extension of substantive protection but the granting of direct access to dispute settlement which embodies the innovative advancement of the regime. That is so because those international law standards draw upon the traditional distinction between a host State's commercial and sovereign conduct.

The dichotomy between state responsibility for breach of state contract by commercial and sovereign conduct under general international law is only altered by the introduction of an umbrella clause. Through the States' acceptance of international responsibility for the observance of its contractual commitments, the continuity of this commercial—governmental dogma is no longer tenable. Contrarily, the international obligation to observe the sanctity of contract extends to all contents of state contracts that fall within the investment notion of the pertinent investment treaty. The conceptual separation of claims which are based on a violation of a treaty and those which are grounded on a breach of contract opens a way for neutral international dispute resolution which may be taken by the investor irrespective of contract stipulations to the contrary.

These results, however, are neither a confirmation of the reliance upon a comprehensive integrating interpretation of treaty obligations nor of its opposite, the strict disassociation of legal sources. Conversely, the system envisaged by the present work embodies a reconciliation of the contradictory philosophies and attempts to channel both approaches into a coherent system of investment treaty interpretation. The operability of a system that is built upon the States' will to consent to international arbitration and the consequent loss of state control over arbitral proceedings requires a principal limitation of applicability. This necessity is further underpinned by the breadth of the substantial standards, which are characterized by an inherent lack of normative content and density, and the exhaustive waiver of state immunity which is laid down by the system. Hence, in order to concretize the potentially unlimited scope of the system and the international responsibility of a State thereunder, the restriction of jurisdictional competence to violations of investment treaty standards appears justified in the absence of express treaty language to the contrary. This principal confinement may then be extended by the parties to the treaty through an intentional inclusion of stipulations that extend the substantial treaty protection to legal obligations grounded on other legal sources. As the foregoing examination has demonstrated conclusively, the introduction of an umbrella clause precisely effectuates such an extension as regards contracts between a host State and a foreign investor. Moreover, the protection of contracts can be fostered through dispute resolution clauses that enable the foreign investor to submit its contractual claims to international adjudicative bodies and thus, enlarge the jurisdictional competence of those bodies to contractual disputes.

This creation of an additional layer of protection by itself does not raise concerns as to the viability of the investment treaty system. In principle, the multiplicity of legal protection should further the adherence to the rule of law. From the host State's as well as from the investor's perspective, a high degree of legal protection is desirable since it contributes to the effective and risk-reducing execution of an investment. However, this presumed positive effect of multiple layers of protection may rapidly be thwarted when conflicting decisions undermine the credibility of the adjudicative findings. As for contractual disputes, the risk of conflicting decisions being rendered at the domestic and international levels has increased considerably due to the principle of possible coincidence of contract claims and treaty claims. Thus, the avoidance of conflicting decisions will become a major subject in this regard. A solution may be found either in the establishment of a strict hierarchy between international and domestic adjucative bodies or in the further development of transaction-based provisions such as article 1121 of the NAFTA.

On account of the effective provision of protection under international law, the investment treaty regime represents a transcendence of the traditional legal problems surrounding these contracts. It is therefore worthwhile for an investor to consider the questions whether the respective State in which it is about to invest concluded an investment treaty with its national State and what terms exactly have been laid down in this treaty. In the ideal case, i.e., in order to provide for the wholesale protection of contracts between foreign investor and host State, an investment treaty should contain the following provisions: (a) a broad definition of investment using terms referring to contracts such as "rights to any contractual benefit having an economic value" or "any right of an economic nature conferred by law or by contract" or even less precise terms such as "any kind of asset" or "any kind of property"; (b) an obligation to accord fair and equitable treatment to investments; (c) an umbrella clause irrespective of whether it expressly refers to contracts and contractual commitments or not; and (d) a precise dispute resolution clause that enables investors to submit mere contractual claims to international dispute resolution. Insofar as the contract at hand falls within the investment notion of the treaty, the effects of the treaty are granted independent of the contract's phrasing. In practice, this enables the investor to settle contractual disputes with the host State before international adjudicative bodies on its own account without specific agreement on this.

Hence, in the majority of cases, modern investment treaties have to be regarded as providing an effective and neutral way for resolving disputes that arise under contracts between host States and foreign investors. It is very likely that the system of the rule of law which is thereby established for thousands of existing investment contracts worldwide will enhance economic relationships and foster economic growth of all its participants.

BIBLIOGRAPHY

Aboul-Enein, M. I. M.: *Arbitration of Foreign Investment Disputes: Responses to the New Challenges and Changing Circumstances*, in: van den Berg, Albert Jan (ed.), New Horizons in International Commercial Arbitration and Beyond, ICCA International Arbitration Congress (Beijng 2004), The Hague 2005, 181–191.

Abs, Hermann & Shawcross, Hartley William: *The Proposed Convention to Protect Private Foreign Investment: A Round Table: Comment on the Draft Convention by its Authors*, J. Pub. L. 9 (1960), 119–124.

Aldrich, George H.: *What Constitutes a Compensable Taking of Property?: The Decisions of the Iran-United States Claims Tribunal*, AJIL 88 (1994), 585–610.

Alenfeld, Justus: *Die Investitionsförderungsverträge der Bundesrepublik Deutschland*, Köln 1971.

Alexandrov, Stanimir A.: *Breaches of Contract and Breaches of Treaty—The Jurisdiction of Treaty-based Arbitration Tribunals to Decide Breach of Contract Claims in SGS v. Pakistan and SGS v. Philippines*, JWIT 5 (2004), 555–577.

Alexandrov, Stanimir A.: *The "Baby Boom" of Treaty-Based Arbitrations and the Jurisdiction of ICSID Tribunals—Shareholders as "investors" under Investment Treaties*, JWIT 6 (2005), 387–441.

Alexandrov, Stanimir A.: *The Vivendi Annulment Decision and the Lessons for the Future ICSID Arbitrations—The Applicant's Perspective*, in: Gaillard, Emmanuel (ed.), Annulment of ICSID Awards, A joint IAI-ASIL conference; Washington D.C.—April 1, 2003, New York 2004, 97–121.

Alvarez, José E.: *International Organizations as Law-Makers*, Oxford 2005.

Alvarez, Aguilar Alvarez & Park, William: *The New Face of Investment Arbitration: NAFTA Chapter 11*, Yale J. Int'l L. 28 (2003), 365–407.

Amerasinghe, Chittharanjan Felix: *Local Remedies in International Law*, Cambridge 2004, 2nd edition.

Amerasinghe, Chittharanjan Felix: *State Breaches of Contracts with Aliens and International Law*, AJIL 58 (1964), 881–913.

Amerasinghe, Chittharanjan Felix: *State Responsibility for Injuries to Aliens*, Oxford 1967.

Amerasinghe, Chittharanjan Felix: *The Jurisdiction of the International Centre for the Settlement of Investment Disputes*, Indian J. Int'l L. 19 (1979), 166–227.

Amerasinghe, Chittharanjan Felix: *The Prawn Farm (AAPL) Arbitration*, Sri Lanka J. of Int'l L. 4 (1992), 155–161.

Andreeva, Yulia: *Salvaging or Sinking the Investment? MHS v. Malaysia Revisited*, The Law and Practice of International Courts and Tribunals 7 (2008), 161–175.

Asante, Samuel K. B.: *Stability of Contractual Relations in the Transnational Investment Process*, Int'l & Comp. L. Q. 28 (1979), 401–423.

Asouzu, Amazu A.: *International Commercial Arbitration and African States: Practice, Participation and Institutional Development*, Cambridge 2001.

Atsegbua, Lawrence: *International Arbitration of Oil Investment Disputes: The Severability Doctrine and Applicable Law Revisited*, African J. Int'l & Comp. Law 5 (1993), 634–660.

Audit, Bernard: *Transnational Arbitration and State Contracts: Findings and Prospects*, Centre for Studies and Research in International Law and International Relation, The Hague 1987.

Baldwin, Edward et al.: *Limits to Enforcement of ICSID Awards*, J. Int'l Arb. 23 (2006), 1–23.

Baptista, Luiz Olavo: *Parallel arbitrations—Waivers and estoppel*, in: Cremades, Bernardo & Lew, Julian D. M. (eds.), Parallel State and Arbitral Procedures in International Arbitration, Paris 2005, 127–141.

Barnett, Peter: *Res judicata, Estoppel and Foreign Jurisdiction—The Preclusive Effects of Foreign Judgments in Private International Law*, Oxford 2001.

Bassett, Debra Lyn: *The Forum Game*, N.C. L. Rev. 84 (2005/2006), 333–395.

Bederman, David J.: *Interim Report on "Lump Sum Agreements and Diplomatic Protection"*, in: ILA, Committee on Diplomatic Protection of Persons and Property, New Delhi Conference (2002), Second Report, 3–20.

Ben Hamida, Walid: *La Consolidation des Procédures Arbitrales*, Gaz. du Palais 3 (2006), 30–35.

Ben Hamida, Walid: *Two Nebulous ICSID Features: The Notion of Investment and the Scpoe of Annulment Control*, J. Int'l Arb. 24 (2007), 287–306.

Bentham, Jeremy: *An Introduction to the Principles of Morals and Legislation*, Oxford 1823.

Benton, S. Anthony: *The Protection of Property Rights in Commercial Treaties of the United States*, HJIL 25 (1965), 50–75.

Berger, Klaus Peter: *Renegotiation and Adaptation of International Investment Contracts: The Role of Contract Drafters and Arbitrators*, Vand. J. Transnat'l L. 36 (2003), 1347–1380.

Berger, Klaus Peter: *The German Arbitration Law of 1998—First Experiences*, in: Briner, Robert (ed.), Law of International Business and Dispute Settlement in the 21st Century—Liber Amicorum Karl-Heinz Böckstiegel, Köln 2001, 31–49.

Bermann, George A.: *Contracts between States and Foreign Nationals: A Reassessment*, in: Smit, Hans et al. (eds.), International Contracts, New York 1981, 183–212.

Bernadini, Piero: *Development Agreements with Host Governments*, in: Pritchard, Robert (ed.), Economic Development, Foreign Investment and the Law, London 1996, 161–174.

Bernadini, Piero: *The Law Applied by International Arbitrators to State Contracts*, in: Briner, Robert (ed.), Law of International Business and Dispute Settlement in the 21st Century—Liber Amicorum Karl-Heinz Böckstiegel; Köln 2001, 51–66.

Bernitz, Ulf (ed.): *General Principles of European Community Law*, Reports from a Conference in Malmö 27–28 August 1999 by the Swedish Network for European Legal Studies and the Faculty of Law, University of Lund, The Hague 2000.

Biggs, Gonzalo: *The Latin American Treatment of International Arbitration and Foreign Investments and the Chile—U.S. Free Trade Agreement*, ICSID Rev.-FILJ 19 (2004), 61–86.

Bishop, Raymond Doak: *International Arbitration of Petroleum Disputes: The Development of a Lex Petrolea*, in: van den Berg, Albert Jan (ed.), YB Comm. Arb'n XXIII, The Hague 1998, 1131–1207.

Bishop, Raymond Doak: *The Case for an Appellate Panel and its Scope of Review*, TDM 2 (2005), No. 02, 1–79.

Bjorklund, Andrea K.: *Private Rights and Public International Law: Why Competition among International Economic Law Tribunals is not working*, Hast. L. J. 59 (2007), 101–163.

Bjorklund, Andrea K.: *Reconciling State Sovereignty and Investor Protection in Denial of Justice Claims*, Va. J. Int'l L. 45 (2005), 809–895.

Bjorklund, Andrea K.: *Waiver and the Exhaustion of Local Remedies in NAFTA Jurisprudence*, in: Weiler, Todd (ed.), NAFTA-Investment Law and Arbitration—Investment Law and Arbitration: Past Issues, Current Practice, Future Prospects, New York 2004, 253–286.

Blackaby, Nigel: *Public Interest and Investment Treaty Arbitration*, in: Kaufmann-Kohler, Gabrielle & Stucki, Blaise (eds.), Investment Treaties and Arbitration, ASA Special Series No. 19, Basel 2002, 145–158.

Blessing, Marc: *Die LCIA Rules—aus der Sicht des Praktikers*, SchiedsVZ 2003, 198–206.

Böckstiegel, Karl-Heinz: *Der Staat als Vertragspartner ausländischer Privatunternehmen*, Frankfurt am Main 1971.

Böckstiegel, Karl-Heinz: *Die allgemeinen Grundsätze des Völkerrechts über Eigentumsentziehung—eine Untersuchung zu Art. 1 des Zusatzprotokolls zur Europäischen Menschenrechtskonvention*, Berlin 1963.

Böckstiegel, Karl-Heinz: *General Introduction to Investment Treaty Arbitration*, in: Kaufmann-Kohler, Gabriele & Stucki, Blaise (eds.), Investment Treaties and Arbitration, ASA Special Series No. 19, Basel 2002, 1–8.

Boggiano, Antonio: *Contratos Internacionales*, Buenos Aires 1955, 2nd edition.

Borchard, Edwin Montefiore: *The Diplomatic Protection of Citizens Abroad or the Law of International Claims*, New York 1916.

Borchard, Edwin Montefiore: *The "Minimum Standard" of the Treatment of Aliens*, Mich. L. Rev. 38 (1940), 445–461.

Borchers, Klaus G.: *Verträge von Staaten mit ausländischen Privatpersonen*, Göttingen 1966.

Borchers, Patrick J.: *The Internationalization of Contractual Conflicts of Law*, Vand. J. Transnat'l L. 28 (1995), 421–443.

Born, Gary B.: *International Commercial Arbitration in the United States: Commentary & Materials*, Boston 1994.

Bourquin, Maurice: *Arbitration and Economic Development Agreements*, Bus. Lawyer 15 (1959/1960), 860–872.

Bowett, Derek W.: *Claims between States and Private Entities: The Twilight Zone of International Law*, Cath. U. L. Rev. 35 (1986), 929–942.

Bowett, Derek W.: *State Contracts with Aliens: Contemporary Developments on Compensation for Termination or Breach*, BYIL 59 (1988), 49–74.

Brandon, Michael: *Recent Measures to Improve the International Investment Climate*, J. Pub. L. 9 (1960), 125–132.

Brekoulakis, Stavros: *The Notion of Superiority of Arbitration Agreements over Jurisdiction Agreements: Time to abandon it?*, J. Int'l Arb. 24 (2007), 341–364.

Brierly, James Leslie: *Le Fondement du Charactère Obligatoire du Droit International*, RdC 23 (1928), 468–552.

Broches, Aron: *Bilateral Investment Protection Treaties and Arbitration of Investment Disputes*, in: Schultsz, Jan C. (ed.), The Art of Arbitration, Essays on International Arbitration, Liber Amicorum Pieter Sanders, Deventer 1982, 63–72.

Broches, Aron: *Selected Essays: World Bank, ICSID, and other Subjects of Public and Private International Law*, Dordrecht 1995.

Broches, Aron: *The Convention on the Settlement of Investment Disputes between States and Nationals of other States*, RdC 136 (1972–II), 331–410.

Broches, Aron: *The Convention on the Settlement of Investment Disputes: Some Observations on Jurisdiction*, Colum. J. Transnat'l L 5 (1966), 263–280.

Brower, Charles N.: *The Privatization of Rules of Decision in International Commercial Arbitration*, in: Briner, Robert (ed.), Law of International Business and Dispute Settlement in the 21st Century—Liber Amicorum Karl-Heinz Böckstiegel, Köln 2001, 111–123.

Brower, Charles N. & Sharpe, Jeremy K.: *Multiple and Conflicting International Arbitral Awards*, JWTI 4 (2003), 211–222.

Brownlie, Ian: *Principles of Public International Law*, Oxford 2003, 6th edition.

Brownlie, Ian: *System of the Law of Nations: State Responsibility*, Vol. I, Oxford 1983.

Buergenthal, Thomas: *The Proliferation of Disputes, Dispute Settlement Procedures and Respect for the Rule of Law*, ICSID Rev.-FILJ 21 (2006), 126–131.

Burdeau, Geneviève: *Nouvelles perspectives pour l'arbitrage dans le contentieux économique intéressant les états*, Rev. Arb. 1995, 3–37.

Byers, Michael: *Custom, Power and the Power of Rules: International Relations and Customary International Law*, Cambridge 1999.

Canè, Giuliana: *The Enforcement of ICSID Awards: Revolutionary or Ineffective?*, Am. Rev. Int'l Arb. 15 (2004), 439–463.

Carbonneau, Thomas E. (ed.): *Lex Mercatoria and Arbitration—A discussion of the new Law Merchant*, New York 1998.

Cárdenas, Emilio J.: *The Notion of Sovereignty Confronts a New Era*, in: Pritchard, Robert (ed.), Economic Development, Foreign Investment and the Law, London 1996, 13–25.

Caron, David D.: *Reputation and Reality in the ICSID Annulment Process: Understanding the Distinction between Annulment and Appeal*, ICSID Rev.-FILJ 7 (1992), 21–56.

Caron, David D.: *The Basis of Responsibility: Attribution and other Trans-Substantive Rules of State Responsibility*, in: Lillich, Richard B. & Magraw, Daniel Barstow (ed.), The Iran-United States Claims Tribunal: Its Contribution to the Law of State Responsibility, New York 1998, 109–184.

Cassese, Antonio: *International Law*, Oxford 2005, 2nd edition.

Cattan, Henry: *The law of oil concessions in the Middle East and North Africa*, New York 1967.

Cavaré, Louis: *La Protection des Droits Contractuels Reconnus par les Etats a des Etrangers à l'Exception des Emprunts*, Valladolid 1956.

Chalmers, Jane: *Attribution Issues in State Responsibility, Remarks by Jane Chalmers, State Responsibility for Acts of Parastatals Organized in Corporate Form*, Am. Soc'y Int'l L. Proc. 84 (1990), 60–64.

Charney, Jonathan I.: *Is International Law Threatened by Multiple International Tribunals?*, RdC 271 (1998), 101–382.

Cheng, Bin: *General Principles of Law as Applied by International Courts and Tribunals*, London 1953.

Cheng, Tai-Heng: *Power, Authority and International Investment Law*, Am. U. Int'l L. Rev. 20 (2005), 465–520.

Cherian, Joy: *Investment Contracts and Arbitration—The World Bank Convention on the Settlement of Investment Disputes*, Leyden 1975.

Chiati, Ahmed Z. El: *Protection of investment in the context of petroleum agreements*, RdC 204 (1987–IV), 9–170.

Chinkin, Christine M.: *Third Parties in International Law*, Oxford 1993.

Chitos Igbokwe, Virtus: *Developing countries and the law applicable to international arbitration of oil investment disputes — has the last word been said?*, J. Int'l Arb. 14 (1997), 99–124.

Christenson, Gordon A.: *The Doctrine of Attribution in State Responsibility*, in: Lillich, Richard B. (ed.), International Law of State Responsibility for Injuries to Aliens, 1983 Charlottesville, 321–360.

Christie, George C.: *What Constitutes a Taking of Property under International Law?*, BYIL 38 (1962), 307–338.

Chukwumerije, Okezie: *International Law and Article 42 of the ICSID Convention*, J. Int'l Arb. 14 (1997), 79–101.

Coale, Margarita T. B.: *Stabilization Clauses in International Petroleum Transactions*, Denv. J. Int'l L. & Pol'y 30 (2002), 217–238.

Coe, Jack J. Jr.: *The Mandate of Chapter 11 Tribunals-Jurisdiction and Related Questions*, in: Weiler, Todd (ed.), NAFTA-Investment Law and Arbitration—Investment Law and Arbitration: Past Issues, Current Practice, Future Prospects, New York 2004, 215–252.

Coharis, Peter Charles: *U.S. Courts and the International Law of Expropriation: Toward a new Model for Breach of Contract*, S. Cal. L. Rev. 80 (2006), 1–87.

Collier, John G. & Lowe, Vaughan: *The Settlement of Disputes in International Law: Institutions and Procedures*, Oxford 1999.

Comeaux, Paul E. & Kinsella, Stephan N.: *Reducing Political Risk in Developing Countries: Bilateral Investment Treaties, Stabilization Clauses, and MIGA & OPIC Investment Insurance*, NY L. School J. Int'l & Comp. L. 15 (1994), 1–48.

Condorelli, Luigi: *L'imputation à l'Etat d'un fait internationalement illicite: solutions classique et nouvelles tendences*, RdC 189 (1984–VI), 9–221.

Crawford, James: *International Law as an Open System—Selected Essays*, London 2002.

Crawford, James: *The ILC's Articles on Responsibility of States for Internationally Wrongful Acts: A Retrospect*, AJIL 96 (2002), 874–890.

Crawford, James: *The International Law Commission's Articles on State Responsibility: Introduction, Text and Commentaries*, Cambridge 2002.

Crawford, James: *Treaty and Contract in Investment Arbitration*, Int'l Arb. 24 (2008), 351–374.

Cremades, Bernardo M.: *Clarifying the Relationship between Contract and Treaty Claims in Investor-State Arbitrations*, Bus. L. Int'l 2003, 207–211.

Cremades, Bernardo M.: *Litigating Annulment Proceedings—The Vivendi Matter: Contract and Treaty Claims*, in: Gaillard, Emmanuel (ed.), Annulment of ICSID Awards, A joint IAI-ASIL conference; Washington D.C.—April 1, 2003, New York 2004, 87–95.

Cremades, Bernardo M. & Cairns, David J. A.: *The Brave New World of Global Arbitration*, JWI 3 (2002), 173–209.

Cremades, Bernardo M. & Cairns, David J. A.: *Contract and Treaty Claims and Choice of Forum in Foreign Investment Disputes*, in: Horn, Norbert (ed.), Arbitrating Foreign Investment Disputes, The Hague 2004, 325–351.

Crivellaro, Antonio: *Consolidation of Arbitral and Court Proceedings in Investment Disputes*, The Law and Practice of International Courts and Tribunals 4 (2005), 371–420.

Croff, Carlo: *The applicable law in an International Commercial Arbitration: Is it still a conflict of laws problem?*, Int'l Law. 16 (1982), 613–646.

Daillier, Patrick & Pellet, Alain: *Droit International Public*, Paris 1994, 5th edition.

Delaney, Jo: *"Expropriation" and "Fair and Equitable Treatment" Standards in Recent ICSID Jurisprudence*, in: Hofmann, Rainer & Tams, Christian (eds.), The International Convention on the Settlement of Investment Disputes (ICSID)—Taking Stock after 40 years, Baden-Baden 2007, 73–77.

Delaume, Georges R.: *Comparative Analysis as a Basis of Law in State Contracts: The Myth of the Lex Mercatoria*, Tul. L. Rev. 63 (1989), 575–628.

Delaume, Georges R.: *Consent to ICSID Arbitration*, in: Norton, Joseph J. et al. (eds.), The Changing World of International Law in the Twenty-First Century: A Tribute to the late Kenneth R. Simmons, The Hague 1998, 155–178.

Delaume, Georges R.: *Convention on the Settlement of Investment Disputes between States and Nationals of other States*, Int'l Law. 1 (1966), 64–70.

Delaume, Georges R.: *Foreign Sovereign Immunity: Impact on Arbitration*, Arb. J. 38 (1983), 34–47.

Delaume, Georges R.: *ICSID Arbitration and the Courts*, AJIL 77 (1983), 784–803.

Delaume, Georges: *Sovereign Immunity and Transnational Arbitration*, in: Lew, Julian M. D. (ed.), Contemporary Problems of International Arbitration, London 1986, 313–322.

Delaume, Georges R.: *State Contracts and Transnational Arbitration*, AJIL 75 (1981), 784–819.

Delaume, Georges R.: *The Proper Law of State Contracts and the Lex Mercatoria: A Reappraisal*, ICSID Rev.-FILJ 3 (1988), 79–103.

Delaume, Georges R.: *The Proper Law of State Contracts revisited*, ICSID Rev.-FILJ 12 (1997), 1–28.

Destanne de Bernis, Gérard & Byé, Maurice: *Relations Économique Internationales*, Paris 1977.

Dhooge, Lucien J.: *The North American Free Trade Agreement and the Environment: The Lessons of Metalclad Corporation v. United States of Mexico*, Minn. J. Glob. Trade 10 (2001), 209–289.

Diez de Velasco Vallejo, Manuel: *Instituciones de Derecho Internacional Público*, Madrid 2005, 15th edition.

Dodge, William S.: *Loewen v. United States: Trials and Errors Under NAFTA Chapter 11*, DePaul L. Rev. 52 (2002), 563–577.

Dodge, William S.: *National Courts and International Arbitration: Exhaustion of Remedies and Res Judicata under Chapter Eleven of NAFTA*, Hast. Int'l & Comp. L. Rev. 23 (1999/2000), 357–383.

Doehring, Karl: *Völkerrecht*, Heidelberg 1999.

Dolzer, Rudolf: *Eigentum, Enteignung und Entschädigung im geltenden Völkerrecht*, 1985.

Dolzer, Rudolf: *Indirect Expropriation of Alien Property*, ICSID Rev.-FILJ 1 (1986), 41–65.

Dolzer, Rudolf: *New Foundations of the Law of Expropriation of Alien Property*, AJIL 75 (1981), 553–589.

Dolzer, Rudolf: *The Impact of International Investment Treaties on Domestic Administrative Law*, Int'l L. & Pol. 37 (2005), 953–972.

Dolzer, Rudolf & Bloch, Felix: *Indirect Expropriation: Conceptual Realignments?*, Int'l L. FORUM 5 (2003), 155–165.

Dolzer, Rudolf & Stevens, Margrete: *Bilateral Investment Treaties*, The Hague 1995.

Dominicé, Christian: *La Clause CIRDI dans les Traités Bilateraux Suisses de Protection des Investissements*, in: Haller, Walter et al. (eds), Im Dienst an der Gemeinschaft, Festschrift für Dietrich Schindler zum 65. Geburtstag, Basel 1989, 457–477.

Douglas, Zachary: *Nothing if Not Critical for Investment Treaty Arbitration: Occidental, Eureko* and *Methanex*, Arb. Int'l 22 (2006), 27–52.

Douglas, Zachary: *The Hybrid Foundations of Investment Treaty Arbitration*, BYIL 74 (2003), 151–289.

Douglas, Zarchary: *The International Law of Investment Claims*, Cambridge 2009.

Elombi, George: *ICSID Awards and the Denial of Host State Laws*, J. Int'l Arb. 11 (1994), 61–68.

Essig, Holger: *Plama v. Bulgaria—Erster ICSID-Schiedsspruch zur Energiecharta*, SchiedsVZ 2006, 311–317.

Eustathiades, Constantin Th.: *Les sujets du droit international et la responsabilité internationale*, RdC 84 (1953-III), 397–633.

Faruque, Abdullah Al: *Creating Customary International Law through Bilateral Investment Treaties: A Critical Appraisal*, 44 Ind. J.Int'l L (2004), 292–318.

Faruque, Abdullah Al: *The Rationale and Instrumentalities for Stability in Long-term State Contracts—The Context for Petroleum Contracts*, JWIT 7 (2006), 85–112.

Faruque, Abdullah Al: *Validity and Efficacy of Stabilisation Clauses—Legal Protection vs. Functional Value*, J. Int'l Arb. 23 (2006), 317–336.

Fatouros, Arghyrios A.: *An International Code to Protect Private Investment—Proposals and Perspectives*, U. Tor. L. J. 14 (1961), 77–93.

Fatouros, Argyrios A.: *Government Guarantees to Foreign Investors*, New York 1962.

Fatouros, Argyrios A.: *International Law and the Internationalized Contract*, AJIL 74 (1980), 134–141.

Fawcett, James J. (ed.): *Declining Jurisdiction in Private International Law*, Report to the XIVth Congress of the International Academy of Comparative Law—Athens August 1994, Oxford 1995.

Feuerle, Peter: *International Arbitration and the Choice of Law under Article 42 of the Convention on the Settlement of Investment Disputes*, Yale Studies in World Public Order 4 (1977/1978), 89–121.

Fietta, Stephen: *Expropriation and the "Fair and Equitable" Standard—The Developing Role of Investors' "Expectations" in International Investment Arbitration*, J. Int'l Arb. 23 (2006), 375–399.

Fietta, Stephen: *Most Favoured Nation Treatment and Dispute Resolution under Bilateral Investment Treaties: A Turning Point?*, Int'l Arb. L. Rev. 8 (2005), 131–138.

Fischer, Peter: *Die internationale Konzession*, Wien 1974.

Fischer, Peter & Wälde, Thomas: *A Collection of International Concessions and Related Instruments*, Contemporary Series 1977/1978, Volume 7, New York 1988.

Ford, Alan Wayne: *The Anglo-Iranian Oil Dispute of 1951–1952: a Study of the Role of Law in the Relations of States*, Berkeley 1954.

Foster, David: *'Internationalisation'—contractual claims in BIT Arbitrations*, The European Arbitration Review 2007, 18–21.

Foster, David: *Umbrella clauses—a retreat from the Philippines?*, Int'l Arb. L. Rev. 9 (2006), 100–108.

Franck, Susan D.: *Foreign Direct Investment, Investment Treaty Arbitration and the Rule of Law*, Global Business and Development Law Journal 19 (2007), 337–373.

Franck, Susan D.: *The Legitimacy Crisis in Investment Treaty Arbitration: Privatizing Public International Law through inconsistent Decisions*, Fordham L. Rev. 73 (2005), 1521–1625.

Franck, Susan D.: *The Nature and Enforcement of Investor Rights under Investment Treaties: Do Investment Treaties have a Bright Future?*, Symposium: Romancing the Foreign Investor: BIT by BIT, U.C. Davis J.Int'l L.& Pol'y 12 (2005), 47–99.

Franck, Thomas M.: *Delegating State Power: The Effect of Treaty Regimes on Democracy and Sovereignty*, New York 2000.

Freeman, Alwyn V.: *Recent Aspects of the Calvo Doctrine and the Challenge to International Law*, AJIL 40 (1946), 121–147.

Friedman, Mark: *Treaties as Agreements to Arbitrate—Related Dispute Resolution Regimes: Parallel Proceedings in BIT Arbitration*, in: van den Berg, Albert Jan (ed.), International Arbitration 2006: Back to Basics?, ICCA International Arbitration Congress (Montreal 2006), The Hague 2007, 545–568.

Friedman, Samy: *Expropriation in International Law*, London 1953.

Gaffney, John P.: *Case Summary: Salini Costruttori S.p.A. and Italstrade S.p.A. v. The Hashemite Kingdom of Jordan*, TDM 2 (2005), No. 01, 1–11.

Gaffney, John P. & Loftis, James L.: *The "Effective Ordinary Meaning" of BITs and the Jurisdiction of Treaty-Based Tribunals to Hear Contract Claims*, JWIT 8 (2007), 5–67.

Gagné, Gilbert & Morin, Jean-Frédéric: *The Evolving American Policy on Investment Protection: Evidence from recent FTA's and the 2004 Model BIT*, JIEL 9 (2006), 357–382.

Gaillard, Emmanuel: *A Black Year for ICSID*, TDM 4 (2007), No. 05, 1–9.

Gaillard, Emmanuel: *Centre International pour le Règlement des Différends relatifs aux Investissements (CIRDI)—Chronique des sentences arbitrales*, JDI 126 (1999), 273–297.

Gaillard, Emmanuel: *Centre International pour le Règlement des Différends relatifs aux Investissements (CIRDI)—Chroniques des sentences arbitrales*, JDI 129 (2002), 189–242.

Gaillard, Emmanuel: *Centre International pour le Réglement des Différends relatifs aux Investissements (CIRDI)—Chroniques des sentences arbitrales*, JDI 131 (2004), 213–287.

Gaillard, Emmanuel : *Centre International pour le Règlement des Différends relatifs aux Investissements (CIRDI)—Chronique des sentences arbitrales*, JDI 133 (2006), 219–367.

Gaillard, Emmanuel: *Investment Treaty Arbitration and Jurisdiction over Contract Claims—the SGS cases considered*, in: Weiler, Todd (ed.), International Investment

Law and Arbitration: Leading Cases from the ICSID, NAFTA, Bilateral Treaties and Customary International Law, London 2005, 325–346.

Gaillard, Emmanuel : *L'Arbitrage sur le Fondement des Traités de Protection des Investissements—Les Etats dans le Contentieux Économique International, I. Le Contentieux Arbitral*, Rev. Arb. (2003), 853–875.

Gaillard, Emmanuel: *Vivendi and Bilateral Investment Treaty Arbitration*, 68 NYLJ 264 (2003), 1–3.

Gaillard, Emmanuel & Savage, John (eds.): *Fouchard, Gaillard, Goldman on International Commercial Arbitration*, The Hague 1999.

Gaillard, Emmanuel & Banifatemi, Yas: *The Meaning of "and" in Article 42 (1), Second Sentence, of the Washington Convention: The Role of International Law in the ICSID Choice of Law Process*, ICSID Rev.-FILJ 18 (2003), 375–411.

Gallus, Nick: *Joy Mining v. Egypt: no joy for British mining equipment company at the ICSID*, TDM 4 (2004), No. 04, 1–9.

Gallus, Nick: *The Influence of the Host State's Level of Development on International Investment Treaty Standards of Protection*, JWIT 6 (2005), 711–730.

Gann, Pamela B.: *The US Bilateral Investment Treaty Program*, Stan. J. Int'l L. 21 (1985), 373–459.

Gao, Zhiguo: *International Petroleum Contracts—Current Trends and New Directions*, London 1994.

García-Amador, Francisco V.: *State Responsibility: Some New Problems*, RdC 94 (1958-II), 365–491.

Geibelson, Michael A. & Conn, Bernice: *Clause and Effect—Parties Agreeing to Standard Arbitration Clauses May Unwittingly Alter Their Rights*, LA Lawyer 29 (2006), 35–43.

Gentinetta, Jörg: *Befreiung der internationalen Handelsschiedsgerichtsbarkeit von der "nationalen Umklammerung"?*, AWD 1969, 46–54.

Giardina, Andrea: *International Investment Arbitration: Recent Developments as to the Applicable Law and Unilateral Recourse*, The Law and Practice of International Courts and Tribunals 5 (2006), 29–39.

Giardina, Andrea: *State contracts: national law versus international law?*, Italian YBIL (1980/1981), 147–170.

Giardina, Andrea: *The International Centre for Settlement of Investment Disputes between States and Nationals of other States (ICSID)*, in: Ŝarĉeviĉ, Petar (ed.), Essays of International Commercial Arbitration, London 1989, 214–222.

Gill, Judith et al.: *Contractual Claims and Bilateral Investment Treaties: a Comparative Review of the SGS Cases*, J. Int'l Arb. 21 (2004), 397–412.

Goldmann, Berthold: *The applicable law: general principles of law—the lex mercatoria*, in: Lew, Julian M. D. (ed.), Contemporary Problems in International Arbitration, London 1986, 113–125.

Goodman, Charity L.: *Uncharted Waters: Financial Crisis and Enforcement of ICSID Awards in Argentina*, U. Pa. J. Int'l Econ. L. 28 (2007), 449–485.

Görs, Benjamin: *Internationales Investitionsrecht—vom völkerrechtlichen Enteignungsschutz zum europäischen Binnenmarkt*, Frankfurt am Main 2005.

Grabenwarter, Christoph: *Europäische Menschenrechtskonvention*, München 2008, 3rd edition.

Grahovac, Borislav: *Privatization in Former Socalist States—Legal and Financial Aspects of the Ownership Transformation of Social Enterprises into Capital Companies*, New York 2001.

Greenwood, Christopher C.: *State Contracts in International Law*, BYIL 58 (1982), 27–81.

Griebel, Jörn: *Die Einbeziehung von "contract claims" in internationale Investitionsstreitigkeiten über Streitbeilegungsklauseln in Investitionsschutzabkommen*, SchiedsVZ 2006, 306–311.

Griebel, Jörn: *The Vivendi Case—Some Critical Remarks Concerning the Question of Jurisdiction*, Int'l Arb. L. Rev. 7 (2004), 67–72.

Griffith Dawson, Frank: *The Influence of Andres Bello on Latin-American perceptions of the non-intervention and state responsibility*, BYIL 57 (1986), 253–315.

Grigera Naón, Horacio A.: *Arbitration and Latin America: Progress and Setbacks: The Freshfields Lecture*, Arb. Int'l 21 (2004), 127–176.

Grigera Naón, Horacio A.: *Choice-of-law problems in international commercial arbitration*, Tübingen 1992.

Grigera Naón, Horacio A.: *The Evolution of International Commercial Arbitration*, in: Bröhmer, Jörg (ed.), Internationale Gemeinschaft und Menschenrechte: Festschrift für Georg Ress zum 70. Geburtstag am 21. Januar 2005, Köln 2005, 103–107.

Grigera Naón, Horacio A.: *The Settlement of Arbitral Disputes between States and Private Parties: An Overview from the Perspective of the ICC*, JWI 1 (2000), 59–103.

Gudgeon, Scott K.: *United States Bilateral Investment Treaties: Comments on their Origin, Purpose and General Treatment Standard*, Int'l Tax & Bus. Law. 4 (1986), 105–112.

Guggenheim, Paul: *Traité de Droit International Public: Avec Mention de la Pratique International et Suisse*, Geneva 1953.

Guzman, Andrew T.: *The Design of International Agreements*, EJIL 16 (2005), 579–612.

Guzman, Andrew T.: *Why LDCs sign Treaties that hurt them: Explaining the Popularity of Bilateral Investment Treaties*, Va. J. Int'l L. 38 (1997/1998), 639–688.

Haersolte van-Hof van, Jacomijn J. & Hoffmann, Anne K., *The Relationship between International Tribunals and Domestic Courts*, in: Muchlinski, Peter et al. (eds.), The Oxford Handbook of International Investment Law, Oxford 2008, 962–1007.

Hanink, Dean M.: *The International Economy: A Geographical Perspective*, New York 1994.

Hanotiau, Bernard: *The 'Res Judicata' Effect of Arbitral Awards, Complex Arbitrations: Perspectives on their Procedural Implications*, ICC Int'l C. Arb. Bul., Special Supp. 2003, 43–51.

Hafner, Gerhard: *Pros and Cons Ensuing from Fragmentation of International Law*, Mich. J. Int'l L. 25 (2004), 849–863.

Happ, Richard: *Aktuelle Rechtsprechung der ICSID-Schiedsgerichte*, SchiedsVZ 2005, 21–30.

Happ, Richard: *Dispute Settlement under the Energy Charter Treaty*, GYIL 45 (2002), 331–362.

Happ, Richard: *Rechtsprechung der ICSID-Schiedsgerichte 2005–2007*, SchiedsVZ 2008, 19–30.

Happ, Richard & Rubins, Noah: *Awards and Decisions of ICSID Tribunals in 2004*, GYIL 47 (2004), 878–921.

Happ, Richard & Rubins, Noah: *Awards and Decisions of ICSID Tribunals in 2005*, GYIL 48 (2005), 581–624.

Harten, Gus van: *Investment Treaty Arbitration and Public Law*, Oxford 2007.

Harten, Gus van: *The Public-Private Distinction in the International Arbitration of Individual Claims against the State*, Int'l & Comp. L. Q. 56 (2007), 371–393.

Harten, Gus van & Loughlin, Martin: *Investment Treaty Arbitration as a species of Global Administrative Law*, EJIL 17 (2006), 121–150.

Henkin, Louis et al.: *International Law—Cases and Materials*, Minnesota 1980, 2nd edition.

Herdegen, Matthias: *Internationales Wirtschaftsrecht*, München 2007, 6th edition.

Herdegen, Matthias: *Rechtsprobleme des internationalen Konzessionswesens: insbesondere aus völkerrechtlicher Sicht*, in: Baur, Jürgen F. & Hobe, Stephan (eds.), Rechtsprobleme von Auslandsinvestitionen — Konzessionen, Vertragsanpassung, Vergabeverfahren, Baden-Baden 2003, 1st edition, 13–35.

Herdegen, Matthias: *Völkerrecht*, München 2007, 6th edition.

Hershey, Amos S.: *The Calvo and the Drago Doctrines*, AJIL 1 (1907), 26–45.

Herz, John H.: *Expropriation of Foreign Property*, AJIL 35 (1941), 244–262.

Higgins, Rosalyn: *The Taking of Property by the State: Recent Developments in International Law*, RdC 176 (1982-III), 259–392.

Highet, Keith: *The Enigma of the Lex Mercatoria*, Tul. L. Rev. 63 (1989), 613–628.

Hiefner, Manfred: *Völkerrechtliche Grenzen hinsichtlich der Vertragsfreiheit bei Verträgen zwischen Staaten und ausländischen Privatpersonen: eine Untersuchung im Hinblick auf 'ungleiche' Verhandlungspositionen zwischen ausländischen Privatpersonen und wirtschaftlich schwächeren Staaten*, Zürich 1984.

Hindelang, Steffen: *Bilateral Investment Treaties, Custom and a Healthy Investment Climate—The Question of Whether BITs Influence Customary International Law Revisited*, JWIT 5 (2004), 189–809.

Hirsch, Moshe: *The Arbitration Mechanism of the International Centre for the Settlement of Investment Disputes*, Dordrecht 1993.

Hobér, Kaj: *Investment Arbitration in Eastern Europe: Recent Cases on Expropriation*, Am. Rev. Int'l Arb. 14 (2003), 377–444.

Hóber, Kaj: *Parallel arbitration proceedings—Duties of the arbitrators*, in: Cremades, Bernardo & Lew, Julian D. M. (eds.), Parallel State and Arbitral Procedures in International Arbitration, Paris 2005, 243–263.

Hobér, Kaj: *State Responsibility and Investment Arbitration*, in: Ribeiro, Clarisse (ed.), Investment Arbitration and the Energy Charter Treaty, New York 2006, 261–289.

Hóber, Kaj & Foerster, Alexander: *Die neue Schiedsordnung 2007 des Schiedsgerichtsinstituts der Stockholmer Handelskammer*, SchiedsVZ 2007, 207–212.

Horn, Norbert: *Arbitration and the Protection of Foreign Investment: Concept and Means*, in: Horn, Norbert (ed.), Arbitrating Foreign Investment Disputes, The Hague 2004, 3–31.

Hunter, Martin: *Reflections on Article 1128 of the NAFTA*, in: Briner, Robert (ed.), Law of International Business and Dispute Settlement in the 21st Century—Liber Amicorum Karl-Heinz Böckstiegel, Köln 2001, 313–318.

Hunter, Martin & Sinclair, Anthony: *Aminoil revisited: Reflections on a story of changing circumstances*, in: Weiler, Todd (ed.), International Investment Law and Arbitration: Leading Cases from the ICSID, NAFTA, Bilateral Treaties, and Customary International Law, London 2005, 347–381.

Igbokwe, Vitus Chitoo: *Developing Countries and the Law Applicable to International Arbitration of Oil Investment Disputes: Has the last word been said?*, J. Int'l Arb. 14 (1997), 99–124.

Jaenicke, Günther: *Consequences of a Breach of an Investment Agreement governed by International Law, by General Prinicples of Law, or by Domestic Law of the Host State*, in: Dicke, Detlef Christian (ed.), Foreign Investment in the Present and a New International Economic Order, Fribourg 1987, 177–193.

Jaenicke, Günther: *The Prospects for International Arbitration: Disputes between States and Private Enterprises: Comments on a Paper by Professor L. J. Bouchez*, in: Soons, Alfred Henry Adriaan (ed.), International Arbitration: Past and the Prospects: A Symposium to Commemorate the Centenary of the Birth of Professor J. H. W. Verijl (1888–1987), Dordrecht 1990, 155–165.

Jarvin, Sigvard: *The Sources and Limits of the Arbitrator's Powers, in: Lew, Julian D. M. (ed.): Contemporary Problems in International Arbitration*, London 1985, 50–72.

Jenks, Clarence Wilfred: *The Prospects of International Adjudication*, London 1964.

Jennings, Robert Yewdall: *State Contracts in International Law*, BYIL 37 (1961), 156–182.

Jessup, Philip C.: *Transnational Law*, New Haven 1956.

Jones, Ray C.: *NAFTA Chapter 11 Investor-to-State Dispute Resolution: A shield to be embraced or a sword to be feared?*, BYU L. Rev. (2002), 527–559.

Kahn, Philippe: *The Law applicable to Foreign Investments: The Contribution of the World Bank on the Settlement of Investment Disputes*, Indiana L. J. 44 (1968), 1–32.

Karl, Joachim: *Aktuelle Probleme des Investitions- und Enteignungsschutzes am Beispiel des Internationalen Konzessionsvertrages*, in: Baur, Jürgen F. & Hobe, Stephan (eds.), Rechtsprobleme von Auslandsinvestitionen: Konzessionen, Vertragsanpassung, Vergabeverfahren, Baden-Baden, 2003, 37–61.

Karl, Joachim: *The Promotion and Protection of German Foreign Investment Abroad*, ICSID Rev.-FILJ 11 (1996), 1–36.

Kaufmann-Kohler, Gabrielle: *Annulment of ICSID Awards in Contract and Treaty Arbitration: Are there Differences?*, in: Gaillard, Emmanuel (ed.), Annulment of ICSID Awards, New York 2004, 189–221.

Kaufmann-Kohler, Gabrielle et al.: *Consolidation of Proceedings in Investment Arbitration: How can Multiple Proceedings Arising from the Same or Related Situations Be Handled Efficiently?*, Final Report on the Geneva Colloquium held on 22 April 2006, ICSID Rev.-FILJ 21 (2006), 59–125.

Kaufmann-Kohler, Gabrielle & Stucki, Blaise: *Foreword*, in: Kaufmann-Kohler, Gabriele & Stucki, Blaise (eds.), Investment Treaties and Arbitration, ASA Special Series No. 19, Basel 2002, I.

Kaufmann-Kohler, Gabrielle & Stucki, Blaise: *International Arbitration in Switzerland: A Handbook for Practitioners*, The Hague 2004.

Kelsen, Hans: *General Theory of Law and State*, Harvard 1949, 3rd edition.

Kelsen, Hans: *Théorie Générale du Droit International Public, Problèmes Choisis*, RdC 42 (1932-IV), 117–351.

Khalaf Masa'deh, Ahmad: *International Rules for Investment and Investors: Light at the End of the Tunnel?*, European Bus. L. Rev. 11 (2000) 157–178.

Khalil, Mohamed I.: *Treatment of Foreign Investment in Bilateral Treaties*, ICSID Rev.-FILJ 7 (1992), 339–383.

Khan, Adil: Introduction: *Reinventing Public Enterprises*, in: UN, Department of Economic and Social Affairs (ed.), Public Enterprises: Unresolved Challenges and New Opportunities, Publication based on the Expert Group Meeting of Re-inventing Public Enterprise and their Management 27–28 October 2005 New York, New York 2007, 3–8.

Kingsbury, Benedict: *Foreword: Is the Proliferation of International Courts and Tribunals a Systemic Problem*, NYU J. Int'l L. & Pol. 31 (1998/1999), 679–696.

Kipp, Heinrich: *Verträge zwischen staatlichen und nichtstaatlichen Partnern*, BerDGesVölkR 5 (1964), 133–188.

Kischel, Uwe: *State Contracts*, Marburg 1992.

Kishoiyian, Bernard: *The Utility of Bilateral Investment Treaties in the Formulation of Customary International Law*, 14 Nw. J. Int'l L. & Bus. (1994), 327–375.

Klein Bronfman, Marcela: *Fair and Equitable Treatment—An Evolving Standard*, Max Planck UNYB 10 (2006), 609–680.

Kluttig, Bernhard: *Contract v. Treaty Claims : Die Entscheidung in Impregilo S.p.A. v. Pakistan*, Policy Papers on Transnational Economic Law, No. 15, June 2005, available at: www.telc.uni-halle.de (last visited: 22 September 2010), 1–8.

Kokott, Juliane: *Interim Report on "The Role of Diplomatic Protection in the Field of the Protection of Foreign Investment"*, in: ILA, Committee on Diplomatic Protection of Persons and Property, New Delhi Conference (2002), Second Report, 21–31.

Kolo, Abba & Wälde, Thomas: *Renegotiation and Contract Adaptation in International Investment Projects: Applicable legal Principles and Industry Practices*, JWI 5 (2000), 5–58.

Kosheri, Ahmed Sadek El: *Contractual claims and treaty claims within the ICSID arbitration system*, in: Cremades, Bernardo & Lew, Julian D. M. (eds.), Parallel State and Arbitral Procedures in International Arbitration, Paris 2005, 43–71.

Kosheri, Ahmed Sadek El: *ICSID Arbitration and Developing Countries*, ICSID Rev.-FILJ 8 (1993), 104–115.

Kosheri, Ahmed Sadek El: *Le régime juridique crée par les accords de participation dans le domaine pétrolier*, RdC 147 (1975-IV), 219–394.

Kosheri, Ahmed Sadek El & Riad, Tarek Fouad A.: *The Law governing a new Generation of Petroleum Agreements: Changes in the Arbitration Process*, ICSID Rev.-FILJ 3 (1988), 257–288.

Kreindler, Richard H.: *"Arbitral Forum Shopping": Some Observations on Recent Developments in International Commercial and Investment Arbitration*, Am. Rev. Int'l Arb. 16 (2005), 157–175.

Kreindler, Richard H.: *The Law Applicable to International Investment Disputes*, in: Horn, Norbert (ed.), Arbitrating Foreign Investment Disputes, The Hague 2004, 401–424.

Kriebaum, Ursula: *Local Remedies and the Standard for the Protection of Foreign Investment*, in: Binder, Christina et al. (eds.), International Investment Law for the 21st Century—Essays in Honour of Christoph Schreuer, Oxford 2009, 417–462.

Kriebaum, Ursula & Schreuer, Christoph: *The Concept of Property in Human Rights Law and International Investment Law*, in: Breitenmoser, Stephan (ed.), Human Rights, Democracy and the Rule of Law—Liber Amicorum Luzius Wildhaber, Baden-Baden 2007, 734–763.

Krisch, Nico & Kingsbury, Benedict: *Introduction: Global Governance and Global Administrative Law in the International Legal Order*, EJIL 17 (2006), 1–13.

Kropholler, Jan: *Internationales Privatrecht*, Tübingen 2001, 4th edition.

Kühn, Wolfgang: *Practical Problems Related to Bilateral Investment Treaties*, in: Kaufmann-Kohler, Gabrielle & Stucki, Blaise (eds.), Investment Treaties and Arbitration, ASA Special Series No. 19, Basel 2002, 43–66.

Kunig, Philip: *Völkerrecht und staatliches Recht*, in: Vitzthum, Wolfgang Graf (ed.), Völkerrecht, Berlin 2007, 4th edition, 81–156.

Kunoy, Bjørn: *Singing in the Rain—Developments in the Interpretation of Umbrella Clauses*, JWIT 7 (2006), 275–300.

Kurtz, Jürgen: *The Delicate Extension of Most-Favoured-Nation Treatment to Foreign Investors: Maffezini v. Kingdom of Spain*, in: Weiler, Todd (ed.), International Investment Law and Arbitration: Leading Cases from the ICSID, NAFTA, Bilateral Treaties and Customary International Law, London 2005, 523–555.

Kuusi, Juha: *The Host State and the Transnational Corporation: An Analysis of Legal Relationships*, Farnborough 1981.

Ladeur, Karl-Heinz: *Globalization and the Conversion of Democracy to Polycentric Networks: Can Democracy Survive the End of the Nation State?*, in: Ladeur, Karl-Heinz (ed.), Public Governance in the Age of Globalization, Burlington 2004, 89–118.

Lalive, Jean-Flavien: *Contrats entre États ou Entreprises Étatique et Personnes Privées: Développements Récents*, RdC 181 (1983-III), 9–283.

Lalive, Pierre: *Some Objections to Jurisdiction in Investor—State Arbitration*, in: Berg, Albert Jan van den (ed.), International Commercial Arbitration: Important Contemporary Questions, ICCA Congress Series No. 11, The Hague 2003, 376–391.

Lalive, Pierre: *The First 'World Bank' Arbitration (Holiday Inns v. Morocco)—Some Legal Problems*, BYIL 51 (1980), 123–162.

Lamm, Carolyn B. & Smutny, Abby Cohen: *The Implementation of ICSID Arbitration Agreements*, ICSID Rev.-FILJ 11 (1996), 64–85.

Lando, Ole: *The Conflict of Laws of Contracts: General Principles*, RdC 189 (1984-VI), 225–447.

Lando, Ole: *The Lex Mercatoria in International Commercial Arbitration*, Int'l & Comp. L. Q. 34 (1985), 747–768.

Larsen, Clifford: *ICSID Jurisdiction: The Relationship of Contracting States to Sub-State Entities*, in: Horn, Norbert (ed.), Arbitrating Foreign Investment Disputes, The Hague 2004, 353–386.

Lasok, Dominik & Stone, Philip A.: *Conflict of laws in the European Community*, Abdingdon 1987.
Lauterpacht, Elihu: *International Law and Private Foreign Investment*, Ind. J. Global Legal Stud. 4 (1996/1997), 259–276.
Lauterpacht, Hersch: *International Law and Human Rights*, London 1950.
Lauterpacht, Hersch: *The Subjects of the Law of Nations*, LQR 63 (1947), 438–460.
Laviec, Jean-Pierre: *Protection et Promotion des Investissements—Étude de Droit International Économique*, Paris 1985.
Leben, Charles: *La Théorie du Contrat d'État et l'Évolution du Droit International des Investissements*, RdC 302 (2003), 197–389.
Leben, Charles: *L'Évolution de la Notion de Contrat d'Etat*, Rev. Arb. (2003) 3, 629–646.
Leben, Charles: *Retour sur la Notion de Contrat d'Etat et sur le Droit Applicable à celui-ci*, in: Decaux, Emmanuel (ed.), L'Évolution du Droit International—Mélanges offerts à Hubert Thierry, Paris 1998, 247–280.
Leboulanger, Philippe: *Les Contrats entre États et Entreprises Étrangères*, Paris 1985.
Legum, Barton: *Defining Investment and Investor: Who is Entitled to Claim?*, Arb. Int'l 22 (2006), 521–526.
Lillich, Richard B.: *The current Status of the Law of State Responsibility for Injuries to Aliens*, in: Lillich, Richard B. (ed.), International Law of State Responsibility for Injuries to Aliens, Charlottesville 1983, 1–60.
Lillich, Richard B.: *The Law Governing Disputes under Economic Development Agreements: Reexamining the Concept of "Internationalization"*, in: Lillich, Richard B. & Brower, Charles N. (eds.), International Arbitration in the 21st Century—towards "judicialization" and uniformity?, 12th Sokol Colloquium on International Law, New York 1994, 61–114.
Lionnet, Klaus: *Die UNCITRAL-Schiedsgerichtsordnung aus der Sicht der Parteien*, BB 27 (1993), BB-Beilage No. 17, 9–12.
Lörcher, Torsten: *ICSID-Schiedsgerichtsbarkeit*, SchiedsVZ 2005, 11–21.
Ly, Filip de & Sheppard, Audley: *ILA Final Report on Lis Pendens and Arbitration*, Arb. Int'l 25 (2009), 3–34.
Ly, Filip de & Sheppard, Audley: *ILA Interim Report on Res judicata and Arbitration*, Arb. Int'l 25 (2009), 35–66.
MacLachlan, Campbell et al. (eds.): *International Investment Arbitration—Substantive Principles*, Oxford 2007.
Manciaux, Sébastien: *Investissements Étrangers et Arbitrage entre États et Ressortissants d'autres États—Trente Années d'Activité du CIRDI*, Paris 2004.
Maniruzzaman, *Expropriation of Alien Property and the Principle of Non-Discrimination in International Law of Foreign Investment: An Overview*, J. Transnat'l L. & Pol'y 8 (1998), 57–77.
Maniruzzaman, A. F. M.: *State Contracts and Arbitral Choice-of-Law Process and Techniques*, J. Int'l Arb. 15 (1998), 65–92.
Maniruzzaman, A. F. M.: *State Contracts in Contemporary International Law: Monist versus Dualist Controversies*, EJIL 12 (2001), 309–328.
Maniruzzaman, A. F. M.: *Choice of Law in International Contracts—Some Fundamental Conflict of Law Issues*, J. Int'l. Arb. 16 (1999), 141–172.
Mankowski, Peter: *Überlegungen zur sach- und interessengerechten Rechtswahl für Verträge des internationalen Wirtschaftsverkehrs*, RIW 2003, 2–15.
Mann, Frederick Alexander: *British Treaties for the Promotion and Protection of Investments*, BYIL 52 (1981), 241–254.
Mann, Frederick Alexander: *Die Verträge der Völkerrechtssubjekte und die Parteiautonomie*, in: Juristische Fakultät der Universität Freiburg (Schweiz) (ed.), Ius Et Lex—Festgabe zum 70. Geburtstag von Max Gutzwiller, Basel 1959, 465–487.
Mann, Frederick Alexander: *England Rejects "Delocalised" Contracts and Arbitration*, Int'l & Comp. L. Q. 33 (1984), 193–198.

Mann, Frederick Alexander: *Further Studies in International Law*, Oxford 1990.
Mann, Frederick Alexander: *State Contracts and International Arbitration*, BYIL 42 (1967), 1–37.
Mann, Frederick Alexander: *Studies in International Law*, Oxford 1973.
Manning-Cabrol, Denise: *The Imminent Death of the Calvo Clause and the Rebirth of the Calvo Doctrine: Equality of Foreign and National Investors*, Law & Pol'y Int'l Bus. 26 (1995), 1169–1200.
Martinez, Jenny S.: *Towards an International Judicial System*, Stan. L. Rev. 56 (2003), 429–529.
Martinez, Lucy & Bray, Daina: *The Interplay of Contract Claims and Treaty Claims: Bayindir v. Pakistan*, TDM 3 (2006), No. 03, 1–5.
Martiny, Dieter: *Artikel 27 EGBGB*, in: Säcker, Franz-Jürgen et al. (eds.), Münchener Kommentar zum BGB, 2006 München, 4th edition, 1674–1714.
McConnaughay, Philip J.: *Reviving the 'Public Law Taboo' in International Conflict of Laws*, Stan. J. Int'l L. 35 (1999), 255–312.
McConnaughay, Philip J.: *The Risks and Virtues of Lawlessness: A "Second Look" at International Commercial Arbitration*, Nw. U. L. Rev. 93 (1998/1999), 453–524.
McDougal, Myres Smith et al. (eds.): *Human Rights and World Public Order: the Basic Policies of an International Law of Human Dignity*, The Hague 1980.
McNair, Arnold Duncan: *The General Principles of Law recognized by civilized Nations*, BYIL 33 (1957), 1–83.
Meesen, Karl: *International Investment and Dispute Settlement*, in: Friedmann, Daniel & Mestmäcker, Ernst-Joachim (eds.), Conflict Resolution in International Trade, A Symposium, Baden-Baden 1993, 111–123.
Merkt, Hanno: *Investitionsschutz durch Stabilisierungsklauseln—Zur intertemporalen Rechtswahl in State Contracts*, Heidelberg 1990.
Metzger, Stanley D.: *Multilateral Conventions for the Protection of Private Foreign Investment*, J. Pub. L. 9 (1960), 133–146.
Montt, Santiago: *State Liability in Investment Treaty Arbitration*, Oxford 2009.
Moran, Theodore H.: *Harnessing Foreign Direct Investment for Development: Policies for Developed and Developing Countries*, Washington D.C. 2006.
Morris, John H. C. & McClean, David: *The Conflict of Laws*, London 1993, 4th edition.
Mouri, Allahyar: *The International Law of Expropriation as Reflected in the Work of the Iran-U.S. Claims Tribunal*, Dordrecht 1994.
Muchlinski, Peter: *'Caveat Investor'?—The Relevance of the Conduct of the Investor under the Fair and Equitable Treatment Standard*, Int'l & Comp. L. Q. 55 (2006), 527–558.
Muchlinski, Peter: *Policy Issues*, in: Muchlinski, Peter et al. (eds.), The Oxford Handbook of International Investment Law, Oxford 2008, 1–48.
Muchlinski, Peter: *The Rise and Fall of the Multilateral Agreement on Investment: Where now?*, Int'l Law. 34 (2000), 1033–1053
Nassar, Naglar: *Internationalization of State Contracts: ICSID, the Last Citadel*, J. Int'l Arb. 14 (1997), 185–207.
Nathan, K. V. S. K.: *Submissions to the International Centre for Settlement of Investment Disputes in Breach of the Convention*, J. Int'l Arb. 12 (1995), 27–52.
Nathan, K. V. S. K.: *The ICSID Convention—the Law of the International Centre for the Settlement of Investment Disputes*, New York 2000.
Nicolaidis, Kalypso & Tong, Joyce L.: *Diversity or Cacophony? The Continuing Debate over New Sources International Law*, Mich. J. Int'l L. 25 (2004), 1349–1376.
Nolan, Michael D. & Baldwin, Edward G.: *The Treatment of Contract-Related Claims in Treaty-Based Arbitration*, Mealey's Int'l Arb. Rep., Vol. 21, June 2006, No. 6, 1–8.
Nollkaemper, André: *The Role of Domestic Courts in the Case Law of the International Court of Justice*, Chin. J. Int'l L. 5 (2006), 301–322.

Nørgaard, Carl Aage: *The Position of the Individual in International Law*, Copenhagen 1962.

O'Connell, Daniel P.: *International Law*, London 1970, 2nd edition.

OECD: *Fair and Equitable Treatment Standard in International Investment Law*, Working Papers on International Investment, Number 2004/3, Paris 2004.

OECD: *"Indirect Expropriation" and the "Right to Regulate" in International Investment Law*, Working Papers on International Investment, Number 2004/4, Paris 2004.

OECD: *Interpretation of Umbrella Clause in Investment Agreements*, Working Papers on International Investment, Number 2006/3, Paris 2006.

OECD: *Investor-To-State Dispute Settlement in Infrastructure Projects*, Working Papers on International Investment, Number 2006/2, Paris 2006.

Oellers-Frahm, Karin: *Multiplication of International Courts and Tribunals and Conflicting Jurisdiction—Problems and Possible Solutions*, Max Planck UNYB 5 (2001), 67–104.

Oman, Charles: *Les Nouvelles Formes d'Investissement dans les Industries des Pays en Voie de Développement*, Paris 1989.

Orrego Vicuña, Francisco: *Changing Approaches to the Nationality of Claims in the Context of Diplomatic Protection and International Dispute Settlement*, ICSID Rev.-FILJ 15 (2000), 340–361.

Orrego Vicuña, Francisco: *Individuals and Non-State Entities before International Courts and Tribunals*, Max Planck UNYB 5 (2001), 53–66.

Orrego Vicuña, Francisco: *International Dispute Settlement in an Evolving Global Society—Constitutionalization, Accessibility, Privatization*, Cambridge 2004.

Orrego Vicuña, Francisco: *Lis penden arbitralis*, in: Cremades, Bernardo & Lew, Julian D. M. (eds.), Parallel State and Arbitral Procedures in International Arbitration, Paris 2005, 207–218.

Orrego Vicuña, Francisco: *Of Contracts and Treaties in the Global Market*, Max Planck UNYB 8 (2004), 341–357.

Orrego Vicuña, Francisco: *The Protection of Shareholders under International Law: Making State Responsibility more accessible*, in: Ragazzi, Maurizio (ed.), International Responsibility Today: Essays in Memory of Oscar Schachter, Leiden 2005, 161–170.

Oschmann, Friedrich: *Calvo-Doktrin und Calvo-Klauseln—wechselnde Realitäten im Internationalen Wirtschaftsrecht Lateinamerikas*, Heidelberg 1993.

Paasivirta, Esa: *Participation of States in International Contracts and Arbitral Settlement of Disputes*, Helsinki 1990.

Paasivirta, Esa: *The Energy Charter Treaty and Investment Contracts: Towards Security of Contracts*, in: Wälde, Thomas (ed.), The Energy Charter Treaty, An East-West Gateway for Investment and Trade, The Hague 1996, 349–364.

Park, William: *NAFTA Chapter 11: Capital Exporters as Host States*, in: Kaufmann-Kohler, Gabriele & Stucki, Blaise (eds.), Investment Treaties and Arbitration, ASA Special Series No. 19, Basel 2002, 9–42.

Park, William: *The Lex Loci Arbitri and International Commercial Arbitration*, Int'l & Comp. L. Q. 32 (1983), 21–52.

Parra, Antonio: *Desirability and Feasibility of Consolidation: Introductory Remarks*, ICSID Rev-FILJ 21 (2006), 132–134.

Parra, Antonio: *ICSID and New Trends in International Dispute Settlement*, Remarks Presented in a Panel Discussion of "New Trend in International Dispute Settlement" at the 87th Meeting of the American Society of International Law held in Washington on March 31-April 3, 1993, News from ICSID 10 (1993), 7–9.

Parra, Antonio: *ICSID and the Rise of Bilateral Investment Treaties: Will ICSID be the leading Arbitration Institution in the early 21st Century?*, Am. Soc'y Int'l L. Proc. 94 (2000), 41–43.

Parra, Antonio: *Provisions on the Settlement of Investment Disputes in Modern Investment Laws, Bilateral Investment Treaties and Multilateral Instruments on Investment*, ICSID Rev.-FILJ 12 (1997), 287–364.

Parra, Antonio: *The Scope of New Investment Laws and International Instruments*, in: Pritchard, Robert (ed.), Economic Development, Foreign Investment and the Law, London 1996, 27–44.

Pate, Thomas J.: *The Past, Present and Future of the Arbitral Clause in Foreign Investment Legislation: In Pursuit of "The Balance"*, available at: www.desolapate.com (last visited: 22 September 2010), 1–109.

Paterson, Robert K.: *Canadian Investment Promotion and Protection Treaties*, Can. Y.B. Int'l L. 29 (1991), 373–390.

Paulsson, Jan: *Arbitration Unbound: An Award Detached from the Law of the Country of Origin*, Int'l & Comp. L. Q. 30 (1981), 358–387.

Paulsson, Jan: *Arbitration without Privity*, ICSID Rev.-FILJ 10 (2005), 232–257.

Paulsson, Jan: *Delocalisation of International Commercial Arbitration: When and Why it Matters*, Int'l & Comp. L. Q. 32 (1983), 53–61.

Paulsson, Jan: *Denial of Justice in International Law*, Cambridge 2005.

Paulsson, Jan: *The Extent of Independence of International Arbitration from the Law of Situs*, in: Lew, Julian D. M. (ed.): Contemporary Problems in International Arbitration, London 1985, 141–148.

Paulsson, Jan & Douglas, Zachary: *Indirect Expropriation in Investment Treaty Arbitrations*, in: Horn, Norbert (ed.), Arbitrating Foreign Investment Disputes, The Hague 2004, 145–158.

Pauwelyn, Joost: *Bridging Fragmentation and Unity: International Law as a Universe of Inter-Connected Islands*, Mich. J. Int'l L. 25 (2003/2004), 903–916.

Pauwelyn, Joost: *Conflict of Norms in Public International Law: How WTO Law relates to other Rules of International Law*, Cambridge 2003.

Perera, Srilal M.: *State Responsibility—Ascertaining the Liability of States in Foreign Investment Disputes*, JWIT 6 (2005), 499–529.

Peters, Paul: *Dispute Settlement Arrangements*, NYBIL 22 (1991), 91–161.

Pfaff, Dieter: *International Licensing Contracts, Transfer of Technology and Transnational Law*, in: Horn, Norbert & Schmitthoff, Clive (eds.), The Transnational Law of International Commercial Transaction, Deventer 1982, 199–209.

Pfluger, Franz: *Die einseitigen Rechtsgeschäfte im Völkerrecht*, Zürich 1936.

Pietro, Domenico Di & Platte, Martin: *Enforcement of International Arbitration Awards—The New York Convention of 1958*, London 2001.

Porterfield, Matthew C.: *An International Common Law of Investor Rights?*, U. Pa. J. Int'l Econ. L. 27 (2006), 79–114.

Presser, Stephen B.: *The Bogalusa Explosion, 'Single Business Enterprise', 'Alter Ego', and other Errors: Academics, Economics, Democracy, and Shareholder Limited Liability: Back Towards a Unitary 'Abuse' Theory of Piercing the Corporate Veil*, Nw. U. L. Rev. 100 (2006), 405–435.

Pritchard, Robert: *The Contemporary Challenges of Economic Development*, in: Pritchard, Robert (ed.), Economic Development, Foreign Investment and the Law, London 1996, 1–11.

Pritchard, Robert & Fox, Phillip: *The Use of Joint Ventures in FDI*, in: Pritchard, Robert (ed.), Economic Development, Foreign Investment and the Law, London 1996, 175–196.

Radbruch, Gustav: *Rechtsphilosopie*, Stuttgart 1950, 4th edition.

Redfern, Alan & Hunter, Martin: *Law and Practice of International Commercial Arbitration*, London 2004, 4th edition.

Regli, Jean-Pierre: *Contrats d'État et Arbitrage entre États et Personnes Privées*, Genève 1983.

Reichert, Douglas D.: *Problems with Parallel and Duplicate Proceedings: The Litispendence Principle and International Arbitration*, Arb. Int'l 8 (1992), 237–255.

Reinisch, August: *Expropriation*, TDM 2 (2005), No. 05, 1–51.
Reinisch, August: *The Future of Investment Arbitration*, in: Binder, Christina et al. (eds), International Investment Law for the 21st Century—Essays in Honour of Christoph Schreuer, Oxford 2009, 894–916.
Reinisch, August: *The Use and Limits of Res Judicata and Lis Pendens as Procedural Tools to Avoid Conflicting Dispute Settlement Outcomes*, The Law and Practice of International Courts and Tribunals 3 (2004), 37–77.
Reinisch, August & Malintoppi, Loretta: *Methods of Dispute Resolution*, in: Muchlinski, Peter et al. (eds.), The Oxford Handbook of International Investment Law, Oxford 2008, 694–720.
Reisman, W. Michael: *Nullity and Revision*, New Haven 1971.
Reisman, W. Michael: *The Regime for Lacunae in the ICSID Choice of Law Provision and the Question of its Threshold*, ICSID Rev.-FILJ 15 (2000), 362–381.
Reisman, W. Michael & Sloane, Robert D.: *Indirect Expropriation and its Valuation in the BIT Generation*, BYIL 74 (2003), 115–150.
Rengeling, Hans Werner: *Privatvölkerrechtliche Verträge—zum Rechtscharakter eines Vertrages zwischen einem Staat und einer ausländischen Privatperson (oder einem nichtstaatlichen Verband)*, Berlin 1971.
Robbins, Joshua: *The Emergence of Positive Obligations in Bilateral Investment Treaties*, U. Miami Int'l & Comp. L. Rev. 13 (2005/2006), 403–473.
Rosenne, Shabtai: *The Law and Practice of the International Court—1920–1996*, vol. III, Procedure, Dordrecht 1997.
Roth, Andreas H.: *The Minimum Standard of International Law applied to Aliens*, Geneva 1949.
Rubino-Sammartano, Mauro: *International Arbitration Law and Practice*, The Hague 2001, 2nd edition.
Rubins, Noah: *The Notion of Investment in International Investment Arbitration*, in: Horn, Norbert (ed.), Arbitrating Foreign Investment Disputes, The Hague 2004, 283–324.
Rühl, Gisela: *Party Autonomy in the Private International Law of Contracts: Transatlantic Convergence and Economic Efficiency*, CLPE Research Paper 4/2007, Vol. 3 No. 1 (2007), available at: http://papers.ssrn.com (last visited: 22 September 2010), 1–45.
Sacerdoti, Giorgio: *Arbitration of Investment Disputes under UNCITRAL Rules and the Choice of Applicable Law*, in: Charnovitz, Steve et al. (eds.), Law in the Service of Human Dignity: Essays in Honour of Florentino Feliciano, Cambridge 2005, 276–298.
Sacerdoti, Giorgio: *Case T 8735-01-77, The Czech Republic v. CME Czech Republic B.V.—Expert Opinion of Professor Sacerdoti*, TDM 2 (2005), No. 05, 1–165.
Sacerdoti, Giorgio: *Investment Arbitration: Under ICSID and UNCITRAL Rules: Prerequisites, Applicable Law, Review of Awards*, ICSID Rev.-FILJ 19 (2004), 1–48.
Salacuse, Jeswald W.: *BIT by BIT: The Growth of Bilateral Investment Treaties and their Impact on Foreign Investment in Developing Countries*, Int'l Law. 24 (1990), 655–675.
Salacuse, Jeswald W. & Sullivan, Nicholas P.: *Do BITs really work?: An Evaluation of Bilateral Investment Treaties and Their Grand Bargain*, Harv. Int'l L. J. 46 (2005), 67–130.
Salem, Mahmoud: *Les Contrats d'Assistance Technique*, in: Judet, Pierre et al. (eds.), Transfert de Technologie et Développement, Paris 1977, 467–513.
Sauvant, Karl P.: New Sources of FDI: *The BRICS—Outward FDI from Brazil, Russia, India and China*, JWIT 6 (2005), 635–710.
Schachter, Oscar: *Compensation for Expropriation*, 78 AJIL (1984), 121–130.
Schachter, Oscar: *International Law in Theory and Practice*, RdC 178 (1982–V), 13–395.
Schanze, Erich: *Investitionsverträge im Internationalen Wirtschaftsrecht*, Frankfurt am Main 1986.

Schill, Stephan: *"Fair and Equitable Treatment" as an Embodiment of the Rule of Law*, in: Hofmann, Rainer & Tams, Christian (eds.), The International Convention on the Settlement of Investment Disputes (ICSID)—Taking Stock after 40 years, Baden-Baden 2007, 31–72.

Schlemmer, Engela C.: *Waiver in International Arbitration*, SAYIL 26 (2001), 202–211.

Schlosser, Peter: *Das Recht der Internationalen Privaten Schiedsgerichtsbarkeit*, Tübingen 1989, 2nd edition.

Schramke, Hein-Jürgen: *Umbrella Clauses in Bilateralen Investitionsschutzabkommen*, SchiedsVZ 2006, 249–258.

Schreuer, Christoph: *Calvo's Grandchildren: The Return of Local Remedies in Investment Arbitration*, The Law and Practice of Int'l Courts and Tribunals 4 (2005), 1–17.

Schreuer, Christoph: *Concurrent Jurisdiction of National and International Tribunals*, Hous. L. Rev. 13 (1975/1976), 508–526.

Schreuer, Christoph: *Consent to Arbitration*, TDM 2 (2005), No. 05, 1–42.

Schreuer, Christoph: *Diversity and Harmonization of Treaty Interpretation in Investment Arbitration*, TDM 3 (2006) No. 02, 1–25.

Schreuer, Christoph: *Failure to Apply the Governing Law in International Investment Arbitration*, Austrian Rev. Int'l & Europ. L. 7 (2002), 147–196.

Schreuer, Christoph: *Fair and Equitable Treatment (FET): Interactions with other Standards*, TDM 4 (2007), No. 05, 1–27.

Schreuer, Christoph: *International and Domestic Law in Investment Disputes—The Case of ICSID*, Austrian Rev. Int'l & Europ. L. 1 (1996), 89–120.

Schreuer, Christoph: *Investment Treaty Arbitration and Jurisdiction over Contractual Claims—The Vivendi I Case Considered*, in: Weiler, Todd (ed.), International Investment Law and Arbitration: Leading Cases from the ICSID, NAFTA, Bilateral Treaties and Customary International Law, London 2005, 281–323.

Schreuer, Christoph: *Keynote Address: The Dynamic Evolution of the ICSID System*, in: Hofmann, Rainer & Tams, Christian (eds.), The International Convention on the Settlement of Investment Disputes (ICSID)—Taking Stock after 40 years, Baden-Baden 2007, 15–30.

Schreuer, Christoph: *Shareholder Protection in International Investment Law*, in: Dupuy, Pierre-Marie et al. (eds.), Common Values in International Law: Essays in Honour of Christian Tomuschat, Kehl 2006, 601–619.

Schreuer, Christoph: *State Immunity: Some Recent Developments*, Cambridge 1988.

Schreuer, Christoph: *The Concept of Expropriation under the ECT and other Investment Protection Treaties*, in: Ribeiro, Clarisse (ed.), Investment Arbitration and the Energy Charter Treaty, New York 2006, 108–159.

Schreuer, Christoph: *The ICSID Convention—A commentary on the Convention on the Settlement of Investment Disputes between States and Nationals of other States*, Cambridge 2001.

Schreuer, Christoph: *Three Generations of ICSID Annulment Proceedings*, in: Gaillard, Emmanuel (ed.), Annulment of ICSID Awards, A joint IAI-ASIL conference; Washington D.C.—April 1, 2003, New York 2004, 17–42.

Schreuer, Christoph: *Travelling the BIT Route-Of Waiting Periods, Umbrella Clauses and Forks in the Road*, JWIT 5 (2004), 231–256.

Schwarze, Jürgen: *European Administrative Law*, London 2006, revised edition.

Schwarzenberger, Georg: *Foreign Investments and International Law*, London 1969.

Schwarzenberger, Georg: *The Abs-Shawcross Draft Convention on Investments Abroad: A Critical Commentary*, J. Pub. L. 9 (1960), 147–171.

Schwarzenberger, Georg: *The Protection of British Property Abroad*, Current Leg. Prob. 5 (1952), 295–323.

Schwebel, Steven M.: *International Arbitration: Three Salient Problems*, Cambridge 1987.

Schwebel, Steven M.: *Justice in International Law—Selected Writings*, Cambridge 1994.
Schwebel, Steven M.: *The Influence of Bilateral Investment Treaties on Customary International Law*, Am. Soc'y Int'l L. Proc. 98 (2004), 27–30.
Scott Maravilla, Christopher: *The Ability of a State-Owned Enterprise to Declare Force Majeure Based Upon Actions of the State*, The Journal of International and Comparative Law at Chicago-Kent 2 (2002), 82–90.
Sedlak, David R.: *ICSID's Resurgence in International Investment Arbitration: Can the Momentum hold?*, Penn. St. Int'l L. Rev. 23 (2004/2005), 147–171.
Seidl-Hohenveldern, Ignaz: *Corporations in and under International Law*, Cambridge 1987.
Seidl-Hohenveldern, Ignaz: *International Economic Law*, Dordrecht 1992, 2nd edition.
Seidl-Hohenveldern, Ignaz: *The Theory of Quasi-International and Partly International Agreements*, Rev. Bel. De Droit Int'l 11 (1975), 567–570.
Shany, Yuval: *Consolidation and Tests for Application: Is International Law Relevant?*, ICSID Rev.-FILJ 21 (2006), 135–149.
Shany, Yuval: *Contract Claims vs. Treaty Claims: Mapping Conflicts Between ICSID Decisions on Multisourced Investment Claims*, AJIL 99 (2005), 835–851.
Shany, Yuval: *Regulating Jurisdictional Relations between National and International Courts*, Oxford 2007.
Shany, Yuval: *The Competing Jurisdictions of International Courts and Tribunals*, Oxford 2003.
Shany, Yuval: *The first MOX Plant Award: the Need to Harmonize competing Environmental Regimes and Dispute Settlement Procedures*, Leiden J. Int'l L. 17 (2004), 815–827.
Shaw, Malcolm N.: *International Law*, Cambridge 2003, 5th edition.
Shawcross, Hartley William: *The Problems of Foreign Investment in International Law*, RdC 102 (1961-I), 335–393.
Shea, Donald R.: *The Calvo Clause—a Problem of Inter-American and International Law and Diplomacy*, Minneapolis 1955.
Shenkin, Todd: *Trade-Related Investment Measures in Bilateral Investment Treaties and the GATT: Moving Toward a Multilateral Investment Treaty*, U. Pitt. L. Rev. 55 (1994), 541–606.
Sheppard, Audley: *Res judicata and estoppel*, in: Cremades, Bernardo & Lew, Julian D. M. (eds.), Parallel State and Arbitral Procedures in International Arbitration, Paris 2005, 219–242.
Sheppard, Audley et al.: *Editorial Note—The Relationship between Local Courts and Investment Treaty Arbitration*, TDM 2 (2005), No. 04, 1–48.
Shihata, Ibrahim Fahmi Ibrahim: *Towards a greater Depoliticization of Investment Disputes: The Roles of ICSID and MIGA*, International Centre for Settlement of Investment Disputes 1992.
Shihata, Ibrahim Fahmi Ibrahim & Parra, Antonio: *The Experience of the International Centre for Settlement of Investment Disputes*, ICSID Rev.-FILJ 14 (1999), 299–361.
Shihata, Ibrahim Fahmi Ibrahim & Parra, Antonio: *Applicable Substantive Law in Disputes between States and Private Foreign Parties: the Case of Arbitration under the ICSID Convention*, ICSID Rev.-FILJ 9 (1994), 183–213.
Simma, Bruno: *Self-contained Regimes*, NYBIL 16 (1985), 112–136.
Simma, Bruno & Pulkowski, Dirk: *Of Planets and the Universe: Self-Contained Regimes in International Law*, EJIL 17 (2006), 483–529.
Sinclair, Anthony: *Bridging the Contract/Treaty Divide*, in: Binder, Christina et al. (eds), International Investment Law for the 21st Century—Essays in Honour of Christoph Schreuer, Oxford 2009, 92–104.
Sinclair, Anthony: *The Origins of the Umbrella Clause in the International Law of Investment Protection*, Arb. Int'l 20 (2004), 411–434.

Sinclair, Anthony: *The Substance of Nationality Requirements in Investment Treaty Arbitration*, ICSID Rev.-FILJ 20 (2005), 357–388.
Smit, Hans: *A-national arbitration*, Tul. L. Rev. 63 (1988/1989), 629–645.
Smith, Brian D.: *State Responsibility and the Marine Environment: The Rules of Decision*, Oxford 1988.
Smith, Ernest E.: *From Concessions to Service Contracts*, Tul. Law J. 27 (1992), 493–524.
Smith, Ernest E. & Dzienkowski, John S.: *A Fifty-Year Perspective on World Petroleum Arrangements*, Tex. Int'l L. J. 24 (1989), 13–37.
Smith, Ernest E. et al. (eds.), *Materials on International Petroleum Transactions*, Denver 1993.
Smutney, Abby Cohen: *State Responsibility and Attribution—When Is a State Responsible for the Acts of State Enterprises? Emilio Agustín Maffezini v. The Kingdom of Spain*, in: Weiler, Todd (ed.), International Investment Law and Arbitration: Leading Cases from the ICSID, NAFTA, Bilateral Treaties and Customary International Law, London 2005, 17–45.
Snyder, Earl: *Foreign Investment Protection: A Reasoned Approach*, Mich. L. Rev. 61 (1963), 1087–1124.
Sohn Louis B. & Baxter, R. R.: *Responsibility of States for Injuries to the Economic Interests of Aliens: II. Draft Convention on the International Responsibility of States for Injuries to Aliens*, AJIL 55 (1961), 548–584.
Sørensen, Max: *Principes de Droit International Public*, RdC 101 (1960–III), 1–254.
Sornarajah, Muthucumaraswamy: *International Commercial Arbitration—The Problem of State Contracts*, Singapore 1990.
Sornarajah, Muthucumaraswamy: *Power and Justice in Foreign Investment Arbitration*, J. Int'l Arb. 14 (1997), 103–140.
Sornarajah, Muthucumaraswamy: *Power and Justice: Third World Resistance in International Law*, SYBIL 10 (2006), 19–57.
Sornarajah, Muthucumaraswamy: *State Responsibility and Bilateral Investment Treaties*, JWTL 20 (1986), 79–98.
Sornarajah, Muthucumaraswamy: *Supremacy of the renegotiation clause in international contracts*, J. Int'l Arb. 5 (1988), 97–114.
Sornarajah, Muthucumaraswamy: *The Climate of International Arbitration*, J. Int'l Arb. 8 (1991), 47–86.
Sornarajah, Muthucumaraswamy: *The International Law on Foreign Investment*, Cambridge 1994, 1st edition.
Sornarajah, Muthucumaraswamy: *The International Law on Foreign Investment*, Cambridge 2004, 2nd edition.
Sornarajah, Muthucumaraswamy: *The Law of International Joint Ventures*, Longman 1992.
Sornarajah, Muthucumaraswamy: *The Myth of International Contract*, JWTL 15 (1981), 187–217.
Sornarajah, Muthucumaraswamy: *The Settlement of Foreign Investment Disputes*, The Hague 2000.
Spiermann, Ole: *Applicable Law*, in: Muchlinski, Peter et al. (eds), The Oxford Handbook of International Investment Law, Oxford 2008, 89–118.
Spiermann, Ole: *Individual Rights, State Interests and the Power to Waive ICSID Jurisdiction under Bilateral Investment Treaties*, Arb. Int'l 20 (2004), 179–211.
Spiermann, Ole: *The LaGrand Case and the Individual as a Subject of International Law*, Zeitschrift für öffentliches Recht 2003, 197–221.
Stein, Eric: *International Integration and Democracy: No Love at first Sight*, AJIL 95 (2001), 489–534.
Stevens, Margrete: *Arbitration and Investment Disputes—Are We Heading in the Right Direction?*, ICSID News, Vol. 19, No. 1, Spring, available at: http://icsid.worldbank.org (last visited: 25 March 2008), 8–9.

Stoll, Jutta: *Vereinbarungen zwischen Staat und ausländischem Investor—Rechtsnatur und Bestandsschutz*, Berlin 1982.

Subedi, Surya P.: *The Challenge of Reconciling the Competing Principles within the Law of Foreign Investment with Special Reference to the Recent Trend in the Interpretation of the Term "Expropriation"*, Int'l Law. 40 (2006), 121–141.

Suleiman, Atef: *The Oil Experience of the Middle East Emirates*, J. Energy & Nat. Resources L. 6 (1988), 1–24.

Summers, Lionel Morgan: *The Calvo Clause*, Va. L. Rev. 19 (1933), 459–484.

Szász, Ivan: *Some Disputable Issues in Investment Treaty Arbitration And in Contractual Arbitration of Foreign Investment Disputes*, in: van den Berg, Albert Jan (ed.), New Horizons in International Commercial Arbitration and Beyond, ICCA International Arbitration Congress (Beijng 2004), The Hague 2005, 192–199.

Tawil, Guido Santiago: *The Distinction between contract claims and treaty claims: an overview*, presentation delivered at ICCA Congress 2006 Montreal, formerly available at: www.iccamontreal2006.org (on file with the author), 1–54.

Turpin, Colin C.: *Government contracts*, Harmondsworth Middlesex 1972.

Toope, Stephen J.: *Mixed International Arbitration—Studies in Arbitration between States and Private Persons*, Cambridge 1990.

UNCTAD: *Bilateral Investment Treaties 1995-2006: Trends in Investment Rulemaking*, Geneva 2007.

UNCTAD: *International Investment Agreements Issues Paper Series, State Contracts*, Geneva 2004.

UNCTAD: *International Investment Agreements Issues Paper Series, Taking of Property*, Geneva 2000.

UNCTAD: *International Investment Instruments: A Compendium*, Vol. II, Geneva 1996.

UNCTAD: *International Investment Instruments: A Compendium*, Vol. V, Geneva 2000.

UNCTAD: *International Investment Instruments*: A Compendium, Vol. VII, Geneva 2000.

UNCTAD: *International Investment Instruments: A Compendium*, Vol. VIII, Geneva 2002.

UNCTAD: *International Investment Instruments: A Compendium*, Vol. IX, Geneva 2002.

UNCTAD: *International Investment Rule-Making: Stocktaking, Challenges and the Way forward*, UNCTAD Series on International Investment Policies for Development, Geneva 2008.

UNCTAD: *Recent Developments in International Investment Agreements (2008-June 2009)*, IIA Monitor No. 3 (2009) International Investment Agreements, Geneva 2009.

UNCTAD: *The Entry into Force of Bilateral Investment Treaties (BITs)*, IIA Monitor No. 3 (2006) International Investment Agreements, Geneva 2006.

Vandevelde, Kenneth J.: *Investment Liberalization and Economic Development: The Role of Bilateral Investment Treaties*, Colum. J. Transnat'l L. 36 (1998), 501–527.

Vandevelde, Kenneth J.: *The Bilateral Treaty Program of the United States*, Cornell Int'l L. J. 21 (1988), 201–276.

Vandevelde, Kenneth J.: *The Economics of Bilateral Investment Treaties*, Harv. Int'l L. J. 41 (2000), 469–502.

Vandevelde, Kenneth J.: *U.S. Bilateral Investment Treaties: The Second Wave*, Mich. J. Int'l L. 14 (1993), 621–704.

Vandevelde, Kenneth J.: *United States Investment Treaties: Policy and Practice*, Deventer 1992.

Vasciannie, Stephen: *The Fair and Equitable Treatment Standard in International Investment Law and Practice*, BYIL 70 (1999), 99–164.

Veith, Werner & Böckstiegel, Karl-Heinz: *Der Schutz von ausländischem Vermögen im Völkerrecht*, Baden-Baden 1962.

Velten, Rainer: *Die Anwendung des Völkerrechts auf State Contracts in der Internationalen Schiedsgerichtsbarkeit*, Berlin 1987.

Verdross, Alfred: *Die Sicherung von ausländischen Privatrechten aus Abkommen zur wirtschaftlichen Entwicklung mit Schiedsklauseln*, HJIL 18 (1957/1958), 635–651.

Verdross, Alfred: *Quasi-International Agreements and International Economic Transactions*, Yearbook of World Affairs 18 (1964), 230–247.

Verdross, Alfred & Simma, Bruno: *Universelles Völkerrecht—Theorie und Praxis*, Berlin 1984, 3rd edition.

Verhoeven, Joe: *Contrats entre Etats et Ressortissants d'autres Etats*, in: Centre Charles de Vischer (ed.), Le contrat économique international—Stabilité et evolution, Paris 1975, 115–150.

Verhoosel, Gaetan: *The Use of Investor-State Arbitration under Bilateral Investment Treaties to seek Relief for Breaches of WTO Law*, JIEL 6 (2003), 493–506.

Vermeer-Künzli, Annemarieke: *As If: The Legal Fiction in Diplomatic Protection*, EJIL 18 (2007), 37–68.

Vinuesa, Raúl Emilio: *Jurisdictional Objections to ICSID Arbitration under Bilateral Investment Treaties*, in: Bröhmer, Jörg (ed.), Internationale Gemeinschaft und Menschenrechte: Festschrift für Georg Ress zum 70. Geburtstag am 21. Januar 2005, Köln 2005, 331–355.

Vlad, Zolia: *Effect and Purpose of "Umbrella Clauses" in Bilateral Investment Treaties: Unresolved Issues*, TDM 2 (2005), No. 5, 1–58.

Voit, Wolfgang: *Ausländische Schiedssprüche*, in: Musielak, Hans-Joachim (ed.), Kommentar zur Zivilprozessordnung, München 2007, 5th edition, §1061.

Wälde, Thomas: *A Requiem for the "New International Economic Order"*, in: Hafner,Gerhard et al. (eds.), Liber Amicorum—Professor Ignaz Seidl-Hohenveldern in Honour of his 80th Birthday, The Hague 1998, 771–803.

Wälde, Thomas: *In the Arbitration under Art. 26 Energy Charter Treaty (ECT), Nykomb v. The Republic of Latvia—Legal Opinion*, TDM 2 (2005), No. 5, 1–107.

Wälde, Thomas: *Investment under the Energy Charter: An Overview of Selected Key Issues based on Recent Litigation Experience*, in: Horn, Norbert (ed.), Arbitrating Foreign Investment Disputes, The Hague 2004, 193–235.

Wälde, Thomas: *Multilateral Agreements (MITs) in the Year 2000*, in: Leben, Charles (ed.), Souveraineté Étatique et Marchés Internationaux à la Fin du 20ème Siècle, à propos de 30 Ans de Recherche du CREDIMI; Mélanges en l'Honneur de Philippe Kahn, Paris 2000, 389–431.

Wälde, Thomas: *The "Umbrella" Clause in Investment Arbitration—A Comment on Original Intentions and Recent Cases*, JWIT 6 (2005), 183–236.

Wälde, Thomas & Hobér, Kaj: *The First Energy Charter Treaty Arbitral Award*, J.Int'l Arb. 22 (2005), 83–104.

Wälde, Thomas & Ndi, George: *Stabilizing International Investment Commitments: International Law versus Contract Interpretation*, Tex. Int'l L. J. 31 (1996), 215–267.

Wälde, Thomas & Weiler, Todd: *Investment Arbitration under the Energy Charter Treaty in the lights of new NAFTA Precedents: Towards a Global Code of Conduct for Economic Regulation*, in: Kaufmann-Kohler, Gabriele & Stucki, Blaise (eds.), Investment Treaties and Arbitration, ASA Special Series No. 19, Basel 2002, 159–221.

Wälde, Thomas & Wouters, Patricia: *State Responsibility and the Energy Charter Treaty: The Rules Regarding State Enterprises, Entities, and Subnational Authorities*, Hofstra L. & Pol'y Symp. 2 (1997), 117–134.

Walker, Herman: *Modern Treaties of Friendship, Commerce and Navigation*, Minn. L. Rev. 42 (1958), 805–824.

Walter, André von: *Die Reichweite von Schirmklauseln in Investitionsschutzabkommen nach der jüngsten ICSID-Spruchpraxis*, RIW 52 (2006), 815–824.

Wegen, Gerhard & Raible, Martin: *Unterschätzt die deutsche Wirtschaft die Wirksamkeit des völkerrechtlichen Investitionsschutzes?*, SchiedsVZ 2006, 225–236.

Weil, Prosper: *Droit International et Contrat d'Etat*, in: Bardonnet, Daniel (ed.), Mélanges offerts à Paul Reuter—le Droit International, Unité et Diversité, Paris 1981, 549–582.

Weil, Prosper: *Problèmes relatifs aux Contrats passés entre un État et un Particulier*, RdC 128 (1969-III), 95–240.

Weil, Prosper: *The State, the Foreign Investor, and International Law: The No Longer Stormy Relationship of a Ménage À Trois*, ICSID Rev.-FILJ 15 (2000), 401–416.

Weisburd, A. Marc: *International Courts and American Courts*, Mich. J. Int'l L. 21 (1999/2000), 877–939.

Weiss, Edith Brown: *Invoking State Responsibility in the Twenty-First Century*, AJIL 96 (2002), 798–816.

Weston, Burns H.: *"Constructive Takings" under International Law: A Modest Foray into the Problem of "Creeping Expropriation"*, Va. J. Int'l L. 16 (1975/1976), 103–175.

Westring, Gösta: *Construction and Management Contracts*, in: Horn, Norbert & Schmitthoff, Clive (eds.), The Transnational Law of International Commercial Transaction, Deventer 1982, 175–189.

Wetzel, Ralf Günther & Rauschning, Dietrich (eds.), *The Vienna Convention on the Law of Treaties—Travaux préparatoires*, Frankfurt am Main 1978.

White, Gillian M.: *Nationalisation of Foreign Property*, London 1961.

Whiteman, Majorie (ed.): *Digest of International Law*, Vol. 8, Washington D. C. 1976.

Wilting, Wilhelm Heinrich: *Vertragskonkurrenz im Völkerrecht*, Münster 1996.

Winkler, Matteo M.: *Arbitration without Privity and Russian Oil: The Yukos Case before the Houston Court*, U. Pa. J. Int'l Econ. L. 27 (2006), 115–153.

Wong, Jarrod: *Umbrella Clauses in Bilateral Investment Treaties: Of Breaches of Contract, Treaty Violations, and the Divide between Developing and Developed Countries in Foreign Investment Disputes*, Geo. Mas. L. Rev. 14 (2006), 135–177.

Yala, Farouk: *The Notion of "Investment" in ICSID Case Law: A Drifting Jurisdictional Requirement?: Some Un-Conventional Thoughts on Salini, SGS and Mihaly*, J. Int'l Arb. 22 (2005), 105–126.

Yannaca-Small, Katia: *Indirect Expropriation and the Rights of the Governments to Regulate Criteria to Articulate the Difference*, in: Ribeiro, Clarisse (ed.), Investment Arbitration and the Energy Charter Treaty, New York 2006, 159–168.

Yntema, Hessel E.: *"Autonomy" in Choice of Law*, AJCL 1 (1952), 341–358.

Zeiler, Gerold: *Treaty v. Contract: Which Panel?*, TDM 4 (2007), No. 05, 1–6.

Zemanek, Karl: *Über das dualistische Denken in der Völkerrechtswissenschaft*, in: von der Heydte, Freiherr Friedrich August (ed.), Völkerrecht und rechtliches Weltbild: Festschrift für Alfred Verdross, Wien 1960, 321–337

Ziadé, Nassib G.: *Some Recent Decisions in ICSID Cases*, ICSID Rev.-FILJ 6 (1991), 514–525.

Zweigert, Konrad: *Verträge zwischen staatlichen und nichtstaatlichen Partnern*, BerDGesVölkR 5 (1964), 194–216.

INDEX

www.ingramcontent.com/pod-product-compliance
Lightning Source LLC
LaVergne TN
LVHW081514300926
849161LV00006B/1171
* 9 7 8 9 0 0 4 1 9 2 2 3 2 *